Murphy John
1997

In All

THE LIFE OF
The Legendary Tycoon

by SALLY

SIMON AND SCHUSTER

His Glory

WILLIAM S. PALEY
and His Brilliant Circle

BEDELL SMITH

New York London Toronto Sydney Tokyo Singapore

SIMON AND SCHUSTER
Simon & Schuster Building
Rockefeller Center
1230 Avenue of the Americas
New York, New York 10020

PICTURE RESEARCH BY NATALIE GOLDSTEIN

DESIGNED BY LAURIE JEWELL

Manufactured in the United States of America

1   3   5   7   9   10   8   6   4   2

Library of Congress Cataloging in Publication Data
Smith, Sally Bedell, date.
In all his glory: the life of William S. Paley, the legendary
tycoon and his brilliant circle/Sally Bedell Smith.
p.   cm.
Includes bibliographical references and index.
1. Paley, William S. (William Samuel), 1901– .   2. Broadcasting—
United States—Biography.   3. Businessmen—United States—
Biography.   4. Columbia Broadcasting System, Inc.   I. Title.
HE8689.8.P34S65   1990
384.54′092—dc20
[B]   90-42704
CIP
ISBN 0-671-61735-4

To Stephen

————

Contents

All charming people, I fancy, are spoiled.
It is the secret of their attraction.
—OSCAR WILDE

THE
Chairman

THE ONE THEY ALL wanted to see arrived late, as was his custom. To most of them he was "Mr. Paley" or "The Chairman." To a select few he was "Bill." But to everyone in the room, he was CBS, "the Tiffany Network," the tycoon who seemed to have invented the idea of style. Although the party was to honor "60 Minutes," one of television's most successful shows, center stage belonged to William Paley, now just a few months shy of his eighty-sixth birthday. On this cool spring evening in 1987, all eyes turned to the man who had led the Columbia Broadcasting System for nearly sixty years.

Over a hundred members of New York's broadcasting and corporate elite circled the ornate Louis XVI Room on the second floor of the St. Regis Hotel on Fifth Avenue that night. Executive wives, anxieties masked by smooth skins and firm chins purchased with their husbands' fortunes, sipped Moët et Chandon, and caught their reflections in the gilt mirrors on the white-paneled walls. Girlfriends and daughters, leggy and sexy in their new short dresses, made small talk, eyes constantly darting to inspect each new arrival. The men, mostly middle-aged and beyond, wore tailored dinner clothes and stood in small knots, balancing their champagne glasses, nibbling pâté, and trading gossip and opinions about their business. "I wouldn't give a nickel for Fox Broadcasting," Laurence Tisch, president of CBS, confided to RCA's former chairman Thornton Bradshaw.

Tisch was doubtless the richest man in the room; his fortune, an estimated $1 billion, was double Paley's. But Tisch lacked Paley's panache. He was a money man with a shiny bald head and deceptively amiable manner. Andy Rooney of "60 Minutes" would later tell the audience, "I went to work for CBS in 1949 and I have met William S. Paley maybe thirty times during those years and tonight was the first time I ever called him Bill. Funny thing is, I met Laurence Tisch only twice and I called him Larry both times. I don't know what the hell to make of that."

Paley, whose title was little more than an honorific now, had spent much of the day in his elegant office on the thirty-fifth floor of Black Rock, the CBS headquarters four blocks away on Sixth Avenue. In the

late afternoon he had taken a special express elevator to his waiting limousine, a maroon Cadillac Fleetwood with a television and a Sony compact
disc player, and been driven to his duplex apartment on Fifth Avenue by
Charles Noble, his chauffeur for eighteen years. After an hour with his
exercise instructor he dressed for dinner, assisted by his valet, John Dean,
once an equerry to Prince Philip. Then Paley had headed out the door,
timing his arrival to miss the cocktail hour. The pain from a lifelong back
ailment had become so persistent that he could no longer stand comfortably.

After some quick photographs with Tisch and the "60 Minutes" contingent, Paley made his way to one of the Versailles Room's round dining
tables. Standing at his dinner place, he grasped the back of his chair for
support. His thick white hair gleamed in the candlelight. (Truman Capote,
a onetime friend, said that Paley dyed his hair to brighten it, to make it
more blond than gray.) His deep tan had been a Paley signature since the
1920s, when irreverent colleagues began calling him "Pale Billy." "Purely
a trick of transposition," *Time* magazine once explained, adding, "He likes
hot countries and bright sunlight." His face was creased with age, his small
brown eyes nearly overwhelmed by pouches of skin. But the eyes still
glittered with life. His pug nose lent him an air of toughness, somewhat
softened by his smile, a slightly crooked little-boy grin that promised
mischief and mirth. He was not classically handsome, never had been, but
his face was virile and sensuous.

Age and a slight stoop had reduced his nearly six-foot stature by
several inches, but the dinner clothes (by Huntsman of Savile Row) were
impeccably tailored. The small paunch of his later years was gone. On his
surprisingly small feet, custom-made evening shoes shone like blackened
mirrors, and the air carried the scent of his musky Givenchy cologne (a
scent created for him in the 1960s). Despite his advancing years, he appeared nearly as vigorous as twenty years before, when Capote had once
murmured: "He looks like a man who has just swallowed an entire human
being."

Paley, *Mister* Paley. "He is to American broadcasting as Carnegie was
to steel, Ford to automobiles, Luce to publishing and Ruth to baseball,"
the *New York Times* had once written. The *New York Daily News* had
called him "an electronic Citizen Kane." His reign at CBS, wrote *Washington Post* television critic Tom Shales, could be summed up as more than
five decades of "brilliant brinksmanship, salesmanship, statesmanship, and
showmanship."

Once while he was touring in Los Angeles, an aide had been assigned
to follow Paley with a chair. When he paused to sit, he didn't bother to
glance back; he knew the chair would be there.

Paley had an insatiable appetite for power. But he was not outwardly dynamic in the style of Chrysler's Lee Iacocca or the late Charles Revson, the tyrannical founder of Revlon. Paley didn't stride through the corridors in a commanding way or pound tables or bark orders. He was much more subtle. His office didn't even look as if it was intended for work; it seemed organized for fun, with an antique chemin de fer card table as its centerpiece instead of a proper desk.

Like Alice's Cheshire Cat, who lingered only as a wide smile, Paley was often a shadow presence. He had the disconcerting habit of going away and letting others manage CBS for long stretches of time. But somewhat paradoxically, his absences reinforced his power. No one knew exactly when he might appear—or to what effect. He was rarely absent from programming discussions where he exercised his authority through nuance and calculated obliqueness. Since programming is an instinctive, almost mystical, process, Paley was viewed by many underlings not so much as an executive but an oracle.

The nature of his business enhanced his legend. Network television, especially in Paley's heyday, was fast-moving, highly visible, and glamorous. The industry seemed to carry limitless possibilities—and dangers. Paley's career paralleled the trajectory of broadcasting through the twentieth century. He came to symbolize its heights and, eventually, its decline.

But the Paley legend transcended broadcasting. He was a lion in high society. "Do cozy up to Bill Paley. He won't be impressed but everyone else will be," advised *Women's Wear Daily* in its tongue-in-cheek list of do's and don't's for strivers in 1987. One rarefied group of New Yorkers, including Ashton Hawkins, general counsel to the Metropolitan Museum, decorator Mark Hampton, and political consultant David Sawyer, once devoted a session of their literary discussion group to an analysis of how Paley compared with Trollope's Duke of Omnium. The participants delighted in recounting the ways each relished and used his power.

Paley's life remained the subject of intense fascination and ferocious speculation, even after his eightieth birthday. In 1987, *People* magazine listed him as one of a half dozen "sex symbols for a Corporate Age." Men were especially intrigued by tales of remedies he took to remain youthful and maintain sexual potency. "Find out about the crushed goat testicles. I hear he eats them to stay young," said Benjamin Bradlee, executive editor of the *Washington Post*. "Monkey glands, he and his friends get injections of monkey glands," said Arthur Taylor, a former president of CBS. There was never any proof, but Paley certainly was interested in such nostrums. Back in the 1960s, David Adams, then vice-chairman of NBC, sat next to Paley at a broadcasting industry dinner. "All he and the person next to him talked about was this place in Switzerland where you could get transplants of sheep glands," said Adams.

Whatever the source of his energy, Paley grabbed everything he could from life—two beautiful, trendsetting wives, a string of lovers, some exotic, an extensive collection of Impressionist and Post-Impressionist art, and exquisite homes. All the while he took pains to stay above ordinary mortals. "He kept a cocoon around himself with respect to his personal life," said Robert Wood, a former CBS-TV president. "You didn't even think to ask a personal question." Paley managed to be simultaneously visible and invisible.

He cultivated a mystique of privacy but relished his influential role. And Paley was influential. CBS shaped and reflected American society to a greater degree than its rivals. CBS told us in immediate and revealing terms about war, through the voice of newsman Edward R. Murrow in bombed-out London during World War II and later through a succession of grim images from the rice paddies of Vietnam. It instructed us about the abuse of power by Senator Joseph McCarthy and President Richard Nixon. Its newscasts showed a nightly parade of racial tension, generational rebellion, and rising feminism; advances in medicine, science, and technology; images of famine, terrorism, floods, fires, and earthquakes. If CBS News plunged viewers into the hard reality of everyday life, then CBS Entertainment let them escape, laughing with the likes of Lucy and Archie Bunker.

The flickering images on CBS represented the soul and sensibility of Bill Paley. In the early days he was practical and enlightened in his choice of CBS programs. He emphasized news shows and made sure his network served the public interest—in large part to keep his burgeoning broadcast empire out of government hands and away from strict regulation. Later, he made a calculated choice to concentrate on entertainment programs that would appeal to a mass audience. After World War II, his second in command devised a plan to transform CBS into a highbrow network aimed at a smaller but more select audience. William Paley declined. Mass audiences meant more—more viewers and more money and more power.

Despite this, Paley associated himself and his network with "a certain standard of taste." He knew how to transform prestige into profits with a legerdemain that frustrated his rivals. That was his genius. He managed to reconcile programs like "The Beverly Hillbillies" with the "Tiffany Network" image, which was sustained by a dignified, superior news organization, a sprinkling of classy entertainment programs, the most elegant headquarters building, the best graphics (what other network would have a full-time chief of design?). There were even CBS cufflinks, just a little smaller than the ones from the other networks, stamped with the familiar logo. These stylish touches helped preserve the CBS mantle of quality, and fostered the illusion that CBS radio and later, television, was better than it was.

By that spring evening in 1987, the CBS-TV network was no longer either first or best. Not only that, the medium itself was shriveling. The advent of cable television and videocassette recorders gave viewers the upper hand. They could select what they wanted to see instead of swallowing whatever the networks fed them. Paley's power diminished too. But at the St. Regis that night, Paley was still the star, though his empire—or what was left of it—now belonged to Larry Tisch, a man he did not choose.

Paley, of course, betrayed nothing of this in the St. Regis dining room as he shook hands with well-wishers. His smile widened at the approach of each woman. If she was young and attractive, his right hand glided reflexively up her forearm, while his other hand slid behind her back. Even as an octogenarian he remained the most flirtatious of men, always on the prowl, always looking for a conquest. His eyes twinkled and focused on the moment's object of his attention as if she were the only woman in the room. "He always had a roving eye and a groping hand," said Irene Selznick, a friend for more than sixty years. "Just as he is about food, money, belongings, power and glory, why couldn't he be the same about sex?"

His charm was part natural, part learned, a potent combination of power, grace, and enthusiasm. "He listens. He responds. He is affectionate. He is flattering. He laughs a great deal. He knows a great deal. It is an enormous power," said Marietta Tree, a longtime friend. "He is someone that for some reason you like to please," said Horace Kelland, a social acquaintance since the 1930s. "It is probably his delight in everything."

"You almost had the feeling the charm could go on indefinitely," remarked Charlotte Curtis, once the society columnist for the *New York Times*. "It was as though he had all the time in the world, and if you didn't end the appointment there could be dinner and dancing."

Paley had a prodigious appetite for pleasure of all kinds. Once something caught his eye, whether a painting or a woman, he pursued the quarry relentlessly. When the antique dealer Freddy Victoria insisted to Paley that a certain Venetian chandelier was not for sale, Paley, by his own account, "threw a temper tantrum" until the dealer relented and sold it to him. To capture his first wife, who was married to someone else at the time, Paley followed her and her husband across the Atlantic and through Europe.

A restless energy propelled Paley's every move. To Irene Selznick, Paley was "made of sets of super springs. He is coiled. Even at his age there is a lot of steam." John Pringle, a British friend, said, "Bill never just sat on the beach. He had a rocket up his ass. He was always doing something. At home Paley's six children routinely made wagers on how long it would take their father to walk out on one of the movies he screened for guests. Even on the golf course, he was a dervish of activity. "He would charge down the fairway like a man possessed," said William O'Shaughnessy, a radio-station owner and social friend. "He would rip off a little paper cup to get a drink, hit the ball, and go after it."

Over the years, Paley's pummeling energy proved an ordeal for his executives. One of his top programmers, B. Donald Grant, used to vomit after meetings. Paley would call his subalterns at all hours—sometimes six times a day with the same query—prompting several top executives to have phones installed in their bathrooms to ensure they picked up before he rang off. In marathon meetings, Paley would second-guess every programming proposal before settling on a prime-time schedule closely resembling the one originally put on the table. He hated agendas. Bob Wood said he had "a lovable bear way of clawing into the subject. He would shatter the orderliness of a meeting, and he was a great stimulus for a lot of discussion, maybe more than necessary." His tactics often left his executives exhausted and bewildered. So, while his energy often produced extraordinary results, it also took an extraordinary human toll.

An outward sign of Paley's internal combustion was a tic—a rapid, almost violent involuntary blinking of his eyes. Each spasm would last several seconds, accompanied by a companion tic in his lower jaw—a sort of munching motion. For Bill Paley, a man bent on total control of his person and his company, having a face that squinted, squirmed, and avoided repose must have been like a curse of the gods, a flashing neon sign of his otherwise well-concealed anxieties. The tic quickened when he was under stress, as he clasped and unclasped his hands.

Paley had chosen a business with uncommon pressures. Every day, critics and millions of Americans judged his programs at the flip of a switch. A drop of one point in the audience ratings could mean tens of millions of dollars in revenues. Paley made no secret of how keenly he felt these demands. "The nervous strain is terrible because you can never settle down to enjoy any success. It's over too quickly and forgotten," he said to one interviewer.

It was an unusually introspective observation for him, but there was another burden that far exceeded ratings points or corporate revenues: Bill Paley constantly strove to live up to his own image. A succession of public relations men had succeeded in portraying him as nearly invincible. He was the man with a magic touch, able to spot hits where others saw flops, to spot stars where others saw journeymen. Paley was determined that others believe his press clips, but it is by no means clear that he believed them himself. "He was the son of a little man, a limited man. He had to wonder, Was I lucky or brilliant?" said Richard Salant, a former president of CBS News. To smother his insecurities, Paley resorted to tranquilizers and sleeping pills, taking everything from Miltown and Seconal to Ativan and Halcion. Indeed, Paley had always been a hopeless hypochondriac and as he got older he acquired enough nurses, doctors and other attendants to staff a small hospital. Undoubtedly they earned their salaries, tending to a man accustomed to service of the highest order.

"I don't think I am a very easy person to know," Paley wrote in his memoir *As It Happened,* published in 1979. Even those closest to him—his wives, his friends, his children, a few colleagues—never knew which Bill Paley they would encounter at any given time. "Bill Paley is so contradictory you don't see the same fella twice," said Irene Selznick. "Isn't it the most baffling thing? But it makes him the most effective, functional, and maddening person I have ever met. He doesn't know himself. He is not the master of it. He is both its victim and its beneficiary."

Sometimes Paley was a model of decisiveness; at other times he was gripped by indecision, repeatedly changing his mind. Details often defeated him: he rattled program executives by losing his concentration during their presentations. Yet he could be disciplined and rigorous in prolonged briefings before annual meetings with CBS shareholders. He could spot a misplaced decimal point in a thicket of numbers on a balance sheet, and he could spend hours fiddling with the cards on a magnetic program schedule. His mind was by turns abstract and linear. He could be purely intuitive, making puzzling leaps from one thought to the next, or "he could be so logical he could make you bleed," said Kim LeMasters, a former president of CBS Entertainment.

He had a reputation for boldness, but he was neither an innovator nor a rebel. Yet he was always capable of wide-eyed optimism when it came to a program he liked or his ability to run the company while everyone else could see him slipping. In 1982—at age eighty-one—he insisted on signing a contract calling for his services to CBS through 1992.

Paley was ambivalent about his Jewishness, courting socially prominent WASPs and blending eagerly into their milieu. Many people thought he was an Episcopalian. But he did not turn his back entirely on his heritage. He was known to drag attenuated socialites into the kitchen of a Jewish delicatessen after the theater. He gave modestly to Jewish causes and prided himself on having the mayor of Jerusalem, Teddy Kolleck, as a friend. He laughed appreciatively at Jewish humor, but never used the Yiddish expressions that were so much a part of the show-biz vernacular.

He played by his own rules, which he kept changing. When CBS owned the New York Yankees baseball team, M. Donald Grant, then chairman of the New York Mets, caught Paley in a lie about Paley's role in a behind-the-scenes maneuver to deny the Mets their radio outlet. Paley replied, "That's the way business is done, isn't it?"

Within his own set, Paley was known for the thoughtful gesture— the immediate thank-you note, the unexpected phone call of reassurance. He could be generous, but on his own terms; if recipients were not suitably grateful he became petulant. The ruthless Paley and the thoughtful Paley were always at war. His warmth and charm would harden to cold anger when he didn't get his way. He was sensitive to the tiniest slight, yet was cavalier about the feelings and reactions of others, including his wives and children. "I don't think he could read character at all," said Dorothy Paley Hirshon, his first wife.

He prided himself on matters of taste and worked hard at being refined and cultivated. He assimilated the best of what he saw, aided by a sharp eye and good instincts. He developed what one of his British friends called "that lovely impeccable taste that only common people can have." A man born to wealth and cultivation might be secure enough to tolerate lapses of taste, even shabbiness, but Paley could not. Still, he had a lowbrow streak that he never tried to conceal. It was evident in his genuine enjoyment of mass programming; in the dropped "g's" of his brusque speaking style; in his equal appreciation of junk food and haute cuisine. Whatever the fare, he ate with an almost peasant gusto, draining the soup bowl in a few gulps without a hint of delicacy.

His paradoxical nature was most conspicuous in Paley's relationships with women. He was always associated publicly with elegant, high-born mannequins. But behind the scenes he savored a turn with more earthy types as well. In his living room hangs one of his favorite paintings, Toulouse-Lautrec's depiction of a Montmartre madam. She is sensuous yet disturbingly debased. "There is nothing wrong with slumming," he once said. "Going down the slope can be interesting too. I guess I am lucky. I can appreciate both."

Sitting in the candlelight at the St. Regis Hotel, Bill Paley looked as happy as anyone had seen him in a long time, leaning toward Diane Sawyer, then the ash-blond supernova of "60 Minutes." She had been seen in his company frequently, and their relationship was a cause of gossip. Cool and elegant in a peach pants suit, her hair brushing across her right eye, Sawyer whispered and smiled. Paley beamed appreciatively ("Make him laugh," she once advised. "He loves women who make him laugh.")

On this evening, Paley was surrounded by memories, good and bad. Upstairs, on the tenth floor, was the suite he had taken after leaving his wife Dorothy in 1945, ending thirteen years of marriage. As bright and opinionated as she was beautiful and stylish, she had been an important teacher. She had broadened his world and refined his tastes. But on returning from the war (and several love affairs overseas) he had wanted to change his life and his network.

Just a few years after the war, Paley's upstart network was a raging success, surpassing its rival, NBC, in profits and popularity. His St. Regis suite overlooking Fifth Avenue had been transformed into an exquisite pied-à-terre, the living room a flawless cube designed by Billy Baldwin and filled with French furniture, fine paintings, and splendid objets d'art. The most beautiful adornment of all was his second wife, Barbara Cushing Mortimer, known to everyone as Babe.

Babe had come into his life with little money but enormous social cachet. She was the daughter of a famous brain surgeon. One of her sisters had married Jock Whitney, the millionaire sportsman and publisher. Her other sister married Vincent Astor, equally rich and prominent. Paley profited not only from Babe's social connections but from her position as a fashion goddess, a stylesetter whose beauty, *Vogue* proclaimed, was characterized by "perfect bones, deep black eyes, camellia pale complexion and superb carriage." Propelled by Paley's power, Babe became a legend in her own right.

The Paleys seemed well matched. They were both perfectionists, capable of agonizing endlessly about a choice of fabric; she was so meticulous that she asked secretaries to snip off the edges of stamps when they addressed envelopes for invitations. He once sent food consultants on two separate trips to the Hotel de Paris in Monte Carlo to sample the *pommes vapeurs* so they could duplicate the dish in a restaurant he was planning.

Even more important, Bill and Babe shared a penchant for privacy and knew that it suited their purposes. From afar, they appeared larger than life. Indeed, to strangers they seemed like Nick and Nora Charles of *The Thin Man* series—witty, urbane, wonderfully romantic. Those who knew them were no less curious. They knew he was difficult and unfaithful, and they wondered how that played out behind the idealized exterior of the marriage.

As the festivities began at the St. Regis, Eric Sevareid stepped to the speaker's podium. Nearly seventy-five, his profile still handsomely craggy, Sevareid paid homage to "Chairman Bill." As one of the last of "Murrow's Boys," the legendary corps of correspondents who came to CBS during World War II, Sevareid, more than anyone in the room, reflected the good Paley, the Paley tutored by Edward R. Murrow to venerate the news division. For a time, while they were close, Murrow's idealism tempered Paley's pursuit of profits and CBS News stood at its tallest.

Don Hewitt, the exuberant, status-seeking executive producer of "60 Minutes," also traced his career back to the early postwar days when Murrow held sway. But Hewitt more closely represented the ethic that superseded the Murrow tradition; "60 Minutes" was news of a different order, designed to make waves, entertain, and score big in the ratings. Because it succeeded so well, "60 Minutes" became the yardstick for all other news programs. A news show, however worthy or well-intentioned, no longer survived unless it promised to make money. Paley knew how far CBS News had fallen as an instrument of public service. But by now he lacked the power to do anything about it. Later in the evening he would whisper to Sevareid, "I'd like to get you back on the air, Eric. But I suppose if I suggest it, they won't do it."

Of those still living, only one important figure from Paley's CBS was missing that night. Frank Stanton, for twenty-seven years president of CBS, had previously agreed to attend a conference in Aspen, Colorado. Paley and Stanton had been one of the most remarkable teams in twentieth-century business, and one of the most puzzling.

Temperamentally, the two men were opposites: Paley, the man of boundless charm, superficially warm but essentially heartless and self-absorbed; Stanton, the self-contained Swiss whose business acumen, decency, and understated humor endeared him to his colleagues. Paley had a restless, readily satisfied curiosity while Stanton probed more deeply and was interested in a broader range of subjects. Paley acted from the gut; Stanton from the brain. Paley could be disorganized and unpredictable. Stanton was disciplined and systematic. Yet their relationship worked— largely due to Stanton's forbearance and diligence. "Together and working the way Paley and Stanton did, they made an executive and they made CBS," said David Hertz, a management consultant who observed both men at close range.

Bill Paley was in peak form when he rose to salute "60 Minutes." His voice, a rich baritone, was slightly raspy but at once strong and soft. "When '60 Minutes' first went on the air in 1968, I'm sure that Don Hewitt didn't expect to be producing it nearly twenty years later," he said, reading from note cards through half-glasses. "I'm sure his first correspondents,

Harry Reasoner and Mike Wallace, didn't expect to be his correspondents nearly twenty years later. As a matter of fact the chairman of CBS in 1968" (rising laughter around the room) "didn't expect to be here" (more laughter) "as chairman nearly twenty years later." The line had been written by Paley's speechwriter, Raymond Price, formerly an aide to Richard Nixon, but Paley delivered it with the timing of Jack Benny. When he finished, the applause was loud and heartfelt. Everyone exchanged smiles and admiring glances. "Remarkable," said Eric Sevareid. "What vigor."

It was particularly remarkable under the circumstances. Only three months earlier Paley had nearly died of pneumonia. His thirty-six-year-old daughter Kate stayed at his bedside in the VIP suite at New York Hospital, with its mahogany furniture, chaise longue, console television, and a panoramic view of the city from the sixteenth floor. It was an amazing scene: Kate, the recently converted born-again Christian wearing a large cross around her neck, reading the Bible to one of the world's great hedonists. Only weeks later, Paley miraculously bounced back, drawing on his reserves of stamina. As was so often the case with Bill Paley, he had the power to surprise. Just when people began to count him out, he would gather his energies and prove them wrong.

I

———

THE

Prince

———

1

WILLIAM PALEY was born on September 28, 1901, in a dark, cramped apartment behind a small cigar shop. Glass cases displayed cigars of all shapes and sizes, and aromatic tobacco leaves hung in the storefront window where a cigarmaker sat at a table, effortlessly rolling cigars by hand. Outside, streetcars rattled and wagons clattered over cobblestones on Ogden Avenue, a wide corridor through the Jewish ghetto on Chicago's crowded West Side.

Ogden Avenue was a parade of commerce—shops of all sorts, grocery stores, saloons—where the proprietors fared slightly better than their employees. These merchants, modest immigrants only a few years removed from small towns in Russia, crowded their families into flats behind their shops. In the warrens of rooms above, on the second and third floors, lived boarders who worked for their lodging and food.

Willie Paley's parents, Sam and Goldie, were typical of these immigrant shopkeepers. Both had arrived in Chicago in the late 1880s. Sam had been born in Brovary, a small town—a shtetl—near Kiev in the Ukraine. (The family's name was actually Paley, pronounced "Paylay." Later in his life, German Jews who looked down on Paley's Russian origins used to whisper that his name had really been Palinski.) Sam Paley's early years had been more comfortable than the lives of most Jews in Russia at the time. His father, Isaac, a tall, handsome man with a Van Dyke beard, had owned a lumber business. Moreover, according to family legend, Isaac had held a special position in Brovary as the Czar's representative, making arrangements for government officials who visited the town. His post also conferred privileges such as freedom to travel that were denied to other Jews.

Life was hard for Jews in late-nineteenth-century Russia. Ninety-four percent of them lived in the Pale of Settlement, an area of twenty-nine provinces set aside by the government. In the shtetls, wooden houses were clustered around a crowded marketplace. The streets were rutted and narrow. Most residents made marginal livings as traders or artisans—tailors, cobblers, cigarmakers. There was a constant fear of persecution. Throughout the eighteenth and nineteenth centuries the Jews of Russia, depending on the whim of the Czar, were either minimally tolerated or harassed by repressive laws.

From 1855 to 1881, Russian Jews enjoyed relative calm under the generally benign policies of Czar Alexander II. But in March of 1881 he was assassinated, and his successor, Alexander III, brought on a wave of pogroms—organized mob massacres of Jews and destruction of their property—that would continue off and on for the next quarter century. The summer of 1881 marked the beginning of an exodus that would bring nearly 2 million Eastern European Jews to the United States by the outbreak of World War I.

Isaac Paley's position in Brovary grew less secure. In later years he never told his grandson whether he had actually been a victim of the pogroms. But it was clear that Isaac had been eager to escape religious persecution even if it meant leaving his business and homeland and defying the wishes of the rabbis, who feared that life in Protestant America would erode the faith. Isaac Paley used his official connections to obtain a travel permit and took one son, Sam, then nine years old, on an exploratory trip to America in 1883.

What he saw evidently pleased him, because in 1888 he took his wife, Zelda, his sons Sam, William, Jacob, and Benjamin, and his daughters Sophie, Sarah, and Celia, on the four-week transatlantic crossing. Passage cost around $25 per person, which meant an outlay of more than $200, about $3,375 in today's dollars and a substantial sum for an immigrant. That he was able to transport his entire family at once showed that he was well off—though not so prosperous as the father of Samuel Bronfman, founder of the Seagram's liquor empire, who came to Canada at about the same time with his family, a maid, a manservant, a personal rabbi, and the rabbi's family. Isaac Paley was an adventurer for someone of his means; most successful Jewish merchants postponed leaving Russia until after 1905. The immigrants of the 1880s were, according to the social historian Irving Howe, largely "the 'dissenters,' the poor and underprivileged, the unlearned and less learned, and those who were influenced by secularism."

Most of the hundreds of thousands of Jews who emigrated to the United States in the 1880s settled in the port cities of New York, Boston, and Baltimore. But Isaac Paley and his family were among those who tried their luck in Chicago. The immigrants who journeyed to the Midwestern lakeside city were drawn by its boomtown atmosphere. Chicago was a magnet for trade and an intersection of water routes and railroads; new factories and shops promised jobs and investment opportunities. In the last two decades of the nineteenth century, some fifty thousand Eastern European Jews settled there.

Isaac Paley dreamed of investing his money in stocks and living off the income. But his investments soured and he squandered his entire stake. His plight was similar to that of other immigrants who lost their status and their wealth in the New World. "A Jew who was a communal figure in a Russian town became a 'nobody' in Chicago," comments Seymour Pomrenze, a historian who studied the Chicago Jewish community. "He was forced to make a living in a factory, by peddling, or as a small store-keeper." But Isaac Paley was a proud man with aristocratic pretensions, and his reaction was extreme: he refused to work for a living as he had in Russia. (He did, however, take the time to learn how to speak English.) In Bill Paley's admiring recollection of his disoriented grandfather, Isaac spent his time sitting "next to a samovar, drinking tea and chatting with friends all day long. They did most of the talking; he did most of the listening. He had a presence that I think caused many to hold him in awe." Isaac's self-indulgence and his air of nonchalance deeply impressed young Willie, who later wondered "whether something of my grandfather's feeling for the value of leisure and luxury did not brush off on me."

It was left to Isaac's wife, Zelda, to make sure the family had food on the table and a place to live. This was a customary role for immigrant mothers when confronted with what Irving Howe calls "the dispossession and shame of many immigrant fathers." Zelda was a small, handsome woman who proved a powerful if prickly matriarch. Other women in similar circumstances cosseted their fragile husbands, maintaining their place as head of the household, however illusory. But Bill Paley recalled that Zelda frequently berated her dreamy husband. "Zelda was impossible," said Dorothy Rothe, another of her grandchildren. "She had a lot of fire and spark. I don't think she ever learned to speak English, which was part of her problem. She was a devil, a mean old lady, a troublemaker from the word go." In later life, visiting her daughter, Zelda poured a handful of salt into a pot of soup while it was cooking to ruin her efforts. Bill Paley chose to see beyond his grandmother's meanspiritedness and admired her strength. He said he believed that he had inherited her "spirit." It may be that he inherited her ruthlessness as well.

In Russia Zelda had been a milliner, but in Chicago she did not go out to work. Like other matriarchs, she supervised the household and the work of her sons, who assumed the burden of financial support. Their prospects were uncertain, to say the least. The American economy see-sawed through several depressions in the 1880s and 1890s. Many immi-grants found themselves jobless and destitute. But Sam Paley, still a teenager, moved through several jobs—selling newspapers, laboring in a piano factory—until he found a niche making cigars in a West Side factory.

He signed on as an apprentice, which meant service of at least three years. "The accurate judgment and artful manipulation required in cigar-making was not easily mastered," wrote one historian. Sam's tools were simple: a smooth, hard board about fifteen inches long; a flat blade as wide as a man's palm; a measuring device to determine the length and thickness of the cigars; and a jar of sticky gum which, diluted with water, secured the cigar head. He dipped a loosened bunch of seasoned leaves into a moisturing agent and bunched the filler tobaccos together, allowing just enough spacing to ensure the cigar would have a proper draft. Next, he rolled the filler inside a binder leaf to give the cigar its shape. Then he cut the wrapper and placed it around the cigar, pasted the head, and trimmed the cigar to its correct length.

By smoking and feeling the texture of the leaves, Sam learned the grades of tobacco and how to blend them. Different combinations of filler tobaccos—Pennsylvania seedleaf, Connecticut seedleaf or broadleaf, Ohio seedleaf, Cuban filler—could achieve varying levels of quality. He learned that the quality of a crop from the same place could change from year to year, and sought new sources or altered the conditioning to compensate for an inferior crop. He also experimented with wrappers, finally settling on leaf from Java, the best that could be obtained. Regardless of the quality of the tobacco inside, Sam learned that the consumer would judge a cigar mainly on the appearance and aroma of its wrapper. It was an epiphany akin to his son's recognition that the image of a broadcasting network could compensate for the shortcomings of its programming.

Cigar making was wet, messy, and monotonous. But if one had skill and ambition, as Sam did, it brought a decent wage. A cigarmaker was paid for piecework, often at a rate of $15 for a thousand cigars. He usually worked five and a half days a week in hot crowded sweatshops. On average, he could turn out two hundred cigars a day, bringing an income of about $20 a week. Before long, Sam Paley took a second job selling cigars from baskets, which he lugged around to cigar stores, saloons, and restaurants. He had every reason to push himself. He and the eight other members of his family were crowded into a four-room apartment in a three-story brick building at 14th and Newberry streets. They lived hard by Maxwell Street, the marketplace and hub of the Jewish ghetto, a rectangle of about forty blocks.

By the 1890s the Maxwell Street neighborhood swarmed with Eastern European immigrants. It was by any definition a slum. According to one account of the period, "The streets were mud; sidewalks were wooden slats with nails protruding. Garbage was rarely picked up. When the lungs of an overworked peddler's horse burst in the heat of summer, the beast might lie on the street for days, a feast for flies and maggots, before the fire department got around to dragging the carcass off." It was the most densely populated area of Chicago. Seventy thousand shoppers jammed the Maxwell Street market each day. One survey in 1901 found many blocks with three to four hundred people per acre—compared with the average for Chicago of around twenty people per acre.

Hard as it was, the Jewish West Side ghetto was a haven of sorts. Outside their neighborhood the Eastern European immigrants often faced discrimination and abuse. One immigrant who arrived in Chicago in 1880 wrote that "Jews were treated on the streets in the most abhorrent and shameful manner, stones being thrown at them and their beards being pulled by street thugs." But around Maxwell Street the immigrants could wear their native dress—boots and long black coats—without fear of harassment. They had synagogues and grocery stores with ample supplies of kosher food. It was a community of common customs and experiences.

In 1896, at age twenty-one, Sam Paley took his savings of "a few hundred dollars" and founded Samuel Paley & Company, cigarmakers, according to a 1926 company document. That year he also became a naturalized citizen. Two years later he married Goldie Drell, who was sixteen. She too had been born in the Ukraine. Her father, Morris, whom she described as "a very tall and handsome fellow," had eked out a living by pressing children's knee pants in Russia.

Goldie always figured that her father had taken his family to America to escape poverty. He may have been one step ahead of the law as well. Shortly before he emigrated, he hid in a neighbor's house to escape government agents who had discovered that Morris had been peddling illegal whiskey. Unlike Isaac Paley, Morris Drell had to bring his wife and four children—Goldie, her sister, and two brothers—to America in stages. Once established in Chicago, Morris peddled cigars before opening his own cigar store.

One day Sam Paley arrived at Morris's store to sell him some cigars. For whatever reason, Morris underpaid his bill, and when Sam asked him for the additional money, Morris told him to come to his house to get the payment—a maneuver that Sam later jokingly claimed was a "trick" to show off Goldie. Sam and Goldie were instantly attracted. She had a sweet smile and was spirited and plump, a "pretty juicy girl," recalled her cousin Louis Bein. Her dark eyes, with their high, arching brows, gave off a penetrating gaze. Her son considered her a "handsome, even beautiful woman," although pictures show her to be quite plain. Sam was short and stocky, with a moon face, thick features, and a heavy black mustache. His eyes, recalled his son, were "intense" and "looked out rather gaily and confidently and yet seemed somewhat startled." Goldie did not consider him good-looking, but she was drawn to his sincerity.

Neither Goldie nor Sam had much in the way of formal education. Yet they made an effective team, parlaying their small stake through diligence and cooperation. Goldie was the driving force—more energetic, outgoing, and self-assured than her husband. But Sam had a quick, native intelligence. He was also exceedingly shrewd, and a hard worker. At the shop on Ogden Avenue they took turns opening the store in the morning. Goldie worked as Sam's salesclerk and helped him strip the tobacco and roll the cigars. "I wasn't ashamed of it," she said. "I'm very proud that I helped my husband. He was a very willing man to become somebody. But he had to have help. He couldn't do it alone."

Bill Paley has never denied being the son of immigrants, but in his personal mythology his origins are more prosperous. The memoir he commissioned at age seventy-eight neglected to mention his modest birthplace on Ogden Avenue. He said that by 1896 his father was so affluent that he was "probably a millionaire." Since that very year Sam Paley staked his company with a modest several hundred dollars, his first million was still a distant goal.

The economic boom of the early twentieth century helped propel Sam Paley toward middle-class comfort. In 1904, Sam took in his brother Jacob as a partner. The following year Sam moved his family to a row house on Marshfield Avenue, a prime residential street for Jewish immigrants on the rise. The only drawback of the neighborhood was its proximity to the noisy elevated train.

With the move to 395 Marshfield Avenue, Sam left the retail business to concentrate exclusively on cigar manufacturing. He established his factory in a barn behind the house. It began as a cottage industry, with Goldie rolling cigars alongside Sam's sisters. Sam concentrated on one brand, called La Palina, a name that, depending on which version of family legend one believes, was based either on Paley or Paulina Street, a nearby thoroughfare where Sam's older brother William lived with his family. "They wanted to pass it off as a Cuban cigar, which was supposed to be the epitome of good quality," said Robert Paley, Bill's cousin. The La Palina box bore a portrait of Goldie, her hair piled high on her head. (The picture was later altered to resemble a Spanish princess wearing a mantilla.) Goldie was proud, but not surprised to be so honored by her husband. "He thought I was a good-looking woman," she said. "That's the reason."

Shortly after they began the new operation on Marshfield, when Bill Paley was only four years old, Sam and Jacob uprooted their families and transferred the business to Detroit, where they changed the name to the Congress Cigar Company. It was a puzzling move, intended to be temporary, and it had terrible consequences. At first they prospered by expanding their operation—a fairly easy accomplishment in those days, when $3,500 could obtain the necessary equipment for a complete factory unit. But a depression hit hard in 1908, and their biggest wholesaler went bankrupt, nearly forcing Congress Cigar out of business. One of Bill Paley's earliest memories was of his father's setback.

In 1909, Sam and Jacob returned to Chicago. On March 17 they incorporated Congress Cigar and started over. Sam moved to a different house on Marshfield Avenue and opened another backyard factory. The house measured about twenty feet across and had three floors and a front stoop. The Paleys rented an apartment on the second floor with three bedrooms, a sitting room, dining room, and kitchen. It was a comfortable place that Bill Paley liked to think of as his first home. Years later, in the 1970s, he even made an impulsive visit to the house, by then rundown and occupied by a new generation of immigrants, Spanish speaking. As is usually the case on such visits, he was shocked that the house was only half as large as he remembered. But seeing it brought back one vivid memory: the arguments that his parents had almost nightly about whether to buy the corner lot next door. Goldie advocated buying it, but Sam wanted to plow the money into his business instead. Given the financial pressures of the moment, Sam prevailed.

The Paleys pinched pennies, and as general economic conditions improved, so did the cigar business. The next year the brothers rented a factory on Van Buren Avenue and moved into large-scale manufacturing, employing some sixty people. Sam's smartest move was to hire a top salesman for the then exorbitant price of $7,500 a year. He knew that the salesman had good connections with jobbers and distributors, and the connections paid off. Sam was also a hard-nosed businessman who exploited his workers. "The conditions were not good," recalled one cigarmaker who worked in his factory. "It was hot and crowded and noisy."

The family lived a "modest middle-class life," by Bill Paley's recollection. He professed to have had a happy childhood, but in many ways it could not have been. At one point his family was affluent enough to have a nurse. But when he was only eight, the nurse disappeared after one of Sam's financial reversals. As an adult, Paley treated this change in circumstance with matter-of-fact hindsight. But he also spoke of the times he stood outside the ballpark where the Chicago Cubs played (his heroes were Tinker, Evers, and Chance, masters of the double play) hoping to shag a foul ball and earn the admission that his parents could not afford.

Willie was a quiet and somewhat troubled child. Physically, he resembled his father. He had a plump, round face, and he was short. (A late bloomer, he would not sprout until his senior year in high school.) For most of his childhood, he suffered from a severe inferiority complex. In part, his insecurity stemmed from being forced to sit at the back of his elementary school classroom, a Siberia for dullards. He lived up to expectations and performed badly. To avoid going to school he feigned illness, or played hookey and forged his mother's signature on excuse slips. His aversion was nearly pathological; he even inflicted what he later called "minor injury" on himself in order to stay home.

He also deeply resented his sister Blanche, who was born in 1905, the same year the family moved to Detroit. At the outset the sibling rivalry seemed rather ordinary—a three-year-old jabbing his finger in the eye of the new baby. But when Blanche was two, she fell ill with a lung infection. Goldie devoted nearly all her attention to her daughter. Even after Blanche recovered, Goldie's absorption with her daugher continued, the beginning of a lifelong pattern of indulgence. Meanwhile, Willie sat in the corner, burning with jealousy as he watched his mother plait ribbons into Blanche's braids and cater to her every need. He felt rejected and unloved.

Goldie was tough, uncompromising, and proud of her strength. She was the sort who stubbornly threw out the pills prescribed by doctors whenever she became ill. She described herself as "a tomboy" and a "tramp." "I can scrub a floor. I can drive a machine. I'm fit more for a man than a woman," she said. When Willie tried to get close to her, she reacted indifferently. In one particularly stinging indictment, he recalled how he once tried to follow her down the street. Exasperated, she took him home and whipped him. Such punishments may well have been common in those days, yet the severity of her reaction to the minor, even poignant offense revealed how callous she could be.

Paley felt that his mother not only froze him out but ran him down. Their relationship, he said, gave him "many unhappy moments." His ambivalent feelings about Goldie—love mingled with strong antagonism —he once admitted, "verged on the neurotic." Goldie constantly complained that other children were better-looking, dressed more neatly, or performed better. In later years he said he believed her "haranguing" fueled his ambition as an adult. He was determined, he often said, "to show her," to prove himself not only to her but to "anybody else who found fault with me."

Paley often said he believed his mother found him unattractive. His first wife, Dorothy Paley Hirshon, doubted that Goldie ever harbored such feeling. But Dorothy connected his feelings of insecurity about his mother directly to his lifelong compulsion to conquer women. "Each time, with each new one, he could say, 'It isn't true. I am attractive. Mommy was wrong,' " said Dorothy. Others who knew him well thought that blaming his mother was too pat. Goldie had her hands full, with an ailing daughter and demanding husband. "With Bill's appetites there could never have been enough affection or adoration. You have to take that for openers," said Irene Selznick. "Besides, she only had two children, and Bill was always so much more attractive and personable than Blanche."

Goldie also knew that Willie was adored by his father. Sam encouraged his son, praised and indulged him. One of Bill Paley's favorite stories about his father concerned the time when Willie was eleven years old and learning about sex. That summer his family went to a resort on a lake, where he and a friend became enamored of a sixteen-year-old girl. Together the two boys composed a note that said: "Dear Girl, Will you please FUCK us?" The boys stole into the girl's room when she was out and left the note on her bureau. Her father found it and in a rage showed it to Sam Paley and the father of Willie's friend, who took his son to a back room and beat him. Sam escorted Willie to a back room as well, but instead of a beating gave him a harsh lecture. Willie's friend was howling so fearfully that Sam became embarrassed. "You've got to do something," Sam said. "What?" asked Willie. "Cry," said Sam. "Scream like you are being hurt."

Willie Paley lived for his father's approval. At dinnertime he would eagerly take in every detail Sam dispensed about the tobacco and cigar business. Willie thought of his father as a "king," and he admired him unconditionally. Yet he was also intimidated by his father's fierce temper and tendency to hold his son to tough standards. As a teenager Willie got a tongue-lashing when he stayed out too late one evening. Although he later said he was "crushed," Paley allowed that the rebuke "didn't improve my character." Not long after the incident, Willie received a speeding violation while driving the family car, and he constructed an elaborate deception to avoid incurring Sam's anger again.

As a boy, Willie Paley led a sheltered existence. It was a world of his own kind—a large, extended family, along with neighborhood and school friends who were predominantly Jewish. Paley later professed not to have experienced daily prejudice while growing up, but one incident terrified him and stayed with him. He was only nine or ten at the time, and was en route to the library to borrow a book when he encountered what he later called "a Jew-hunting gang." When Willie began to run, they chased him —all the way to the library. He cowered inside while the boys waited for him to emerge. Too proud to ask for help, he lingered until after dark when the library was about to close. Then he bolted out the door and ran many blocks to his home, imagining that the gang still pursued him.

A little bit of luck helped put Willie on the right track in school. His elementary school teacher finally shifted him to the front of the classroom after she mistakenly thought he was displaying some initiative by reading during recess. (He was really dozing behind a book because he felt ill.) That encouraging move was enough to prod him to apply himself and become a star student. He especially admired the heroes of Horatio Alger and dreamed that someday he too might become rich.

As a symbol of his new status and dignity, he decided at the age of twelve to give himself a middle initial. Everyone else in his class had a middle name, and he felt self-conscious without one. So, when school officials asked the students how their name should appear on their elementary school diplomas, Willie impulsively added an "S." It stood for nothing, although everyone assumed it was for Samuel, after his father.

As a teenager, Paley worried about his appeal to the opposite sex. He continued to think his mother found him unattractive—a feeling reinforced by the nickname "Chink" bestowed by the neighborhood children because of his slightly slanting eyes. When he attended his first dance, at twelve, he cringed with anxiety. But two girls who caught his eye indicated they wanted to dance with him, and "it occurred to me for the first time that I could be attractive and that put me in a good state of mind about how girls might feel about me. There was no question how I felt about them."

With maturity, Willie Paley began feeling better about himself. On Marshfield Avenue he found a social life with a group of neighborhood children. He was gangly and not much of an athlete, but he enjoyed playing second base for a sandlot team. When Sam had the time, he took his son to the theater. Willie found that he shared his mother's interest in music, and she took him to concerts. Although he couldn't sing on key, he developed an appreciative ear. Goldie arranged piano lessons for him which he took grudgingly. He later boasted that he was good enough to contemplate a career as a concert pianist, but his friends only heard him play ten bars of one piece, "Whispering." They used to call it "Bill Paley's Unfinished Symphony."

After Bill Paley's sophomore year at Carl Schurz High School, Sam and Goldie decided to send him away for his final two years. Paley later said his parents were not so much concerned about his grades as what they saw as a pattern of unruly behavior. At age sixteen he was beginning to run wild. Several of Sam and Goldie's friends had dispatched their sons to Western Military Academy, where they had acquired discipline as well as polish; they had also gained a slight edge over students from Chicago high schools in securing admission to prestigious colleges. At the time, the elite Eastern preparatory schools seemed out of reach for a son of immigrants.

At Western Military Academy Bill Paley found himself in a non-Jewish world for the first time. But it was so regimented that there was little room for prejudice to seep through. Set among tall trees on a hill above the Mississippi River at Alton, Illinois, the Western campus, with its functional brick buildings and crenellated roofs, brought Paley a new sense of independence after an initial bout of severe homesickness. He later called his year there "a turning point in my life." He was on his own for the first time and grew so fast he went through three sets of uniforms in one year. He proudly shined the buttons on his uniform, stood at attention for inspection each morning, fought sham battles, marched in close-order drills several times a day, and endured the rigors of hazing. Twice a week he was permitted into town to buy candy bars. Once, to prove he was a big shot, he tried snuff and got sick.

Academically, he excelled and managed to compress two years' worth of high school credits into one year. At seventeen he entered the University of Chicago. During his first semester in college he applied himself. But gradually he became what one of his fraternity brothers called "a good time Charlie. He chased the girls."

Life at the university took him back into a protected world. He immediately found a welcome at the top-ranked Jewish fraternity, Zeta Beta Tau. But it was there that he had his first brush with the snobbery of fraternity brothers who looked down on him. He overcame the prejudice, as he did so often afterwards, with his charm. "One quickly warmed up to him," said a fraternity brother, "although his background was from the other side of the tracks [the West Side] and most of us came from the South Side."

Paley didn't have that much to be ashamed of. By this time his family was living in an upscale apartment building on Logan Boulevard, the scene of his first sexual encounter—with an attractive older woman he met in the lobby. Coincidentally, she turned up at a party in the building later that evening. Still only seventeen, he went home with her afterwards. Although he learned that she was married, he was undeterred—a reaction that would be repeated many times over. She was, he said later, "the most exciting person I had met."

Deeply infatuated, Paley was indefatigable in pursuit. He visited the woman every night even if it meant arriving late in the evening after a long ride on a streetcar and elevated train (he never did mention the whereabouts of her husband). They spent much of the night together, and he would return to campus only a few hours before dawn. As an elderly man he eagerly told girlfriends about this first lover, elaborating on what she had taught him.

During the affair Paley's studies suffered, and he barely squeezed by his freshman year. He had become a fairly self-possessed and appealing young man, almost six feet tall, who knew how to use his magnetic smile. "He wasn't abrasive but he was pushy, like all of us," said a fraternity brother. And another recalled, "He was a tall, slender, handsome young man with a very pleasant extrovertish personality that made him stand out. One of the striking things about him was his slick, almost coal black hair, carefully combed, which added to his handsomeness."

The inconsistencies of Bill Paley's formative years seemed to shape the polarities of his personality: charming but cold, enthusiastic but cautious, ruthless yet thoughtful, distracted as well as disciplined, sensitive and oblivious, shy but social, confident yet insecure, direct but devious. Uppermost among the contradictions of his childhood was the attitude of his parents toward their religion and culture. In such an atmosphere of what he later termed "cultural distance," Paley's ambivalence about being Jewish took root.

Like his own father, Sam was uninterested in organized religion. He accompanied Goldie to their Reform synagogue on High Holy Days, but merely for the sake of appearances. Although not devout, Goldie took religion seriously. She was influenced by her father, Morris, a student of the Torah and member of an Orthodox synagogue. Paley recalled, with considerable distaste, being dragged every Friday night of his boyhood to celebrate the eve of the Sabbath at his grandfather Morris's house. During the prayers he looked ahead to a time when he could have Friday night out on the town. He did not even bother to learn the Ten Commandments while preparing for his confirmation. When the time came to recite them in Hebrew before the congregation, he did so perfectly, but only because, in a spirit of quiet, stubborn defiance, he had memorized the phonetics. Ever the pragmatist, he later admitted that he grew impatient with religion because "I couldn't get decent answers. I said, 'My God, that's a lot of bull.' "

But whatever their differences about religion, Sam and Goldie Paley were culturally Jewish. Goldie loaded her supper table with homemade gefilte fish; *schav,* a pungent sorrel soup; *kofatellen,* fried burgers made with chopped chicken livers; and other dishes from the old country. Food was at the center of their life, much as it was for other immigrant families. As he grew older, Bill Paley would spurn virtually every aspect of Jewish culture. He did retain a love for ethnic Jewish cooking, but for that matter he had a voracious appetite for food of all sorts.

In high school Bill had begun spending his summers sweeping floors and running errands in Sam's factory. His emerging business relationship with his father fit the predominant pattern among Eastern European immigrants. It was "a culture utterly devoted to its sons," comments Irving Howe. "Onto their backs it lowered all its aspirations and delusions, expecting that the children of the New World could reach the goals their fathers could not reach themselves. . . . The fathers would work, grub and scramble as petty agents of primitive accumulation. The sons would acquire education, that New World magic." As a young boy, Paley never doubted he would follow his father into the cigar business.

Paley's desire to meet his father's expectations was touching. "I used to dream about being a salesman," he once said, "going to cigar stores and making them buy HIS cigar. I wanted everybody to own his cigar." Willie dutifully banded cigars and learned the art of blending tobacco in the factory's "kitchen." After many years of experimenting, Sam had settled on a winning blend for La Palina: Puerto Rican and Cuban tobaccos for the filler, Connecticut tobacco for the binder, and the Java wrapper that lent the cigar its distinctiveness. He went one cut above a cheap cigar, settling on the moderate price of ten cents apiece. Eventually, he offered a range of twenty shapes and sizes. He also learned tricks that he passed on to his son. During World War I, when tobacco production was curtailed, Sam had to rely on cheap tobacco from Puerto Rico. To mask its inferiority, he cured it with liquor, and no one was the wiser.

Along with other cigar manufacturers, Sam Paley introduced new machines and a division of labor into his factories to standardize and speed production. The use of molds, bunch-making machines, and other inventions could double a factory's output. But the new machines also contributed to labor unrest. The members of the Cigarmakers International Union, who considered themselves craftsmen, called strikes to protest the new machines and eventually set strict union membership rules to bar many machine workers.

The split in the cigar workers' ranks initially hampered their progress and benefited owners like Sam Paley. But in Chicago the cigarmakers union gained strength under the leadership of Samuel Gompers, president of the American Federation of Labor and himself a former cigarmaker. Gompers mounted a series of strikes against the cigar manufacturers. The final strike, in 1919, proved too much for Sam Paley and other Chicago manufacturers. Faced with a demand by workers for a 50 percent increase in wages, the manufacturers association concluded the only answer was to leave the city.

Sam Paley decided to move his operation to New York or Pennsylvania. There were numerous advantages: greater proximity to the principal tobacco production areas, a better climate, more lenient labor laws and taxes, and a plentiful supply of workers. Thirty-six years had passed since Sam had huddled against his tall, proud father to catch his first wide-eyed view of America. Now, in the summer of 1919, it was Sam's turn to take his son Bill on a shorter but equally portentous trip.

2

A BULL MARKET swept Wall Street in the summer of 1919. Businessmen had stiffened their spines against organized labor and awaited the payoff of bigger profits. Jazz bands played "I'll Say She Does" and "I'm Always Chasing Rainbows" at tea dances in Fifth Avenue hotels. The marquees of Broadway announced such hits as *Three Faces East, Friendly Enemies, Dear Brutus,* and *Up in Mabel's Room.* Women, who still lacked the right to vote, dressed decorously, their skirts only six inches above the ankle. The Eighteenth Amendment had been ratified, meaning that Prohibition was just around the corner. The New York skyline lacked the majesty it would achieve with the skyscraper boom of the coming decade. But its avenues were bigger and busier and livelier than anything a seventeen-year-old immigrant's son from the Second City had seen before.

For much of their stay in New York, young Bill Paley tagged along with his father, watching as he negotiated for factory sites. In his free time the boy prowled the streets. He also spent a lot of time fantasizing about assignations with beautiful women—or, as he later characterized it, "thinking about sin." He lingered in the lobby of a Broadway hotel and ogled the passing parade of well-heeled citizens. He longed for a life of riches and leisure. He dreamed of living in Manhattan and enjoying all its pleasures.

But Sam eventually settled on Philadelphia. Cigarmakers there had steadfastly resisted unionization despite threats and appeals by the Cigarmakers International. No sooner had Sam set up his operation than his father, Isaac, died. He returned to Chicago, leaving his son to manage the factory in his absence. During the following month Bill Paley, sometime student, frequent playboy, adored son, was forced to show his mettle as a businessman for the first time.

He had been charged with hiring workers for the factory. Most employers, intent on union busting, turned to non-union women to staff their assembly lines. Since cigars were now churned out by machines, employers no longer needed skilled craftsmen. Just as young Bill had finished hiring all his "girls," the cigar manufacturers were hit by a city-wide strike over working conditions. The girls walked out before the first La Palina rolled off the assembly line.

Bill Paley's reaction was typical. He turned on the charm. With the help of the plant foreman, Paley gathered groups of the girls in various homes where he arranged to serve them refreshments. He stood before them, making his pitch: he could offer them higher wages plus tempting bonuses; moreover, since Congress Cigar Company produced a moderately priced cigar, as opposed to a cheap variety, the factory would be a better place to work. His argument was illogical but effective. Between these parties and a free boat trip down the Delaware River that attracted several hundred girls, Paley found enough workers to fill the factory. When strike leaders threatened his girls, Paley arranged taxis to take them to and from work.

This brought Paley face to face with the president of the Cigar Manufacturers Association. The manufacturers were incensed that Sam Paley's factory was producing, offering a place for out-of-work laborers to find jobs while other factories were idle. Abandoning a pretense of solidarity with other employers, Bill Paley rebuffed the manufacturers' threats and announced that his factory would continue operating. "I knew where my loyalties belonged," he later said. His summer of power and authority changed him: "I became conscious of the fact that my boyhood had ended and that there were things in the world I could do and do well."

On his eighteenth birthday that fall, he enrolled at the University of Pennsylvania's Wharton School of Finance, which he found anticlimactic after beating back the cigar unions and manufacturers. "What a farce," he told *Time* magazine years later. He immediately hooked up with Zeta Beta Tau and plunged into campus social life. ZBT was regarded as the best Jewish fraternity at Penn, its members largely drawn from wealthy families. Sam Paley, however, kept his son on a strict allowance, distributed every three months. If young Bill ran out of money, Sam made no advance payments.

Paley considered himself "half student, half playboy," and studied only enough to get by. He knew that he was "quite bright, though I didn't shine. I was no longer a brilliant student but I felt confident enough of myself and my intellect." He later regretted not taking a full liberal arts curriculum and considered his business courses a waste.

Paley never applied himself in his liberal arts classes either, relying on charm to slide through. He struggled with Spanish, which he needed to pass in order to graduate. When he failed the final examination, Paley went to the teacher to plead for a retest. "Absolutely not," he said, citing school policy. At that moment, he took a phone call that Paley overheard: there was a funeral the next day, and the teacher had no way of getting there. Paley immediately offered to drive him. Afterwards the teacher said, "I've been thinking. I was unfair. Come in tomorrow and I'll give you another chance." Paley passed the exam and graduated. "I learned," he said later, "that I had a cunning turn of mind."

Paley was well enough liked by his fellow students to earn the nickname "Pop" for popular; his other nickname, "La," derived from La Palina. After his sophomore year he moved into one of the twenty student rooms in the spacious white-frame Victorian fraternity house at 3819 Spruce Street. Downstairs was a plainly furnished parlor and dining room, where waiters served Paley and his friends lunch and dinner. In his senior year he was voted president of the fraternity. He was chosen, friends said, because he was a natural leader.

As in Chicago, he socialized exclusively with other Jews. This didn't seem to bother him. Yet anyone in his position, the son of Russian-Jewish immigrants, had to have been offended by the overt discrimination on university campuses of the time. Of all the schools in what eventually became the Ivy League, Penn was the most open to Jewish students. Under the influence of Quaker egalitarianism, Penn began admitting Jews in the mid-1700s while Harvard did not graduate a Jew until 1870. (Harvard used an informal quota, only taking Jews it deemed could be assimilated. Yale and Princeton admitted very few Jews at all.)

But at Penn, as at most other universities, the campus was strictly divided between Jews and Gentiles. Out of a total of forty fraternities on campus, a dozen were known at the time as all-Jewish. "Penn took Jews to get their money," said sociologist and longtime Penn professor E. Digby Baltzell, "and then it segregated them. The situation could not have been worse. WASPs got scholarships while Jews paid. There were 'A' fraternities and there were 'B' fraternities. All the 'B' fraternities were Jewish." The top "A" houses, like St. Anthony Hall and St. Elmo's, clustered in the center of the campus, accepted only Gentiles. They were plush places, with wood paneling, leather armchairs, and English hunting prints on the walls. Paley's own fraternity was relegated to a building several blocks away.

The residue of his college experience must have been bitter. After his graduation in 1922, Bill Paley made only intermittent financial contributions to Penn. Several of his gifts ran into the hundreds of thousands of dollars, but Penn officials considered Paley a hard sell who never met their expectations. "He hasn't given Penn much," said Robert Levy, his nephew and a member of the Penn board of trustees. "It is not significant in relation to his wealth," said Fran Sheeley, a former development officer for Penn. "We all knew he was unhappy with his experience there."

The atmosphere at Penn during Paley's student years echoed the national mood. Since the Bolshevik Revolution a few years earlier, the country had been caught up in a Red scare, a wave of extreme nationalism with strong Anti-Semitic overtones. As part of an effort to ferret out suspected radicals, teachers and other employees were asked to sign loyalty oaths, and suspected Communists had been arrested. The hostility was directed especially at Eastern European Jewish immigrants who, because of their national origins, were suspected of divided loyalty. Henry Ford published his Anti-Semitic newspaper, the *Dearborn Independent,* with its odious suggestions of Jewish conspiracies, and the Ku Klux Klan grew rapidly, soon to reach an alarming 4.5 million members.

In Philadelphia, anti-Semitism evolved in less blatant ways. In earlier times some leading Jews had been admitted to exclusive Philadelphia clubs such as the Union League. But by the early decades of the twentieth century, the wave of Russian immigration upset the fragile social order that had accommodated a small community of assimilated Jews. The Protestant establishment quietly shut its doors. Increasingly, German as well as Russian Jews were isolated, not only from clubs but from top law firms and banks, as well as certain upper-class neighborhoods. "Philadelphia's Protestant establishment, in a cool patrician manner, built an inviolable caste-system," comments Murray Friedman, a social historian. "Upper-class and seemingly well-integrated German Jews learned the painful lesson that to their Gentile peers a Jew remained a Jew and as such an outsider."

In selecting his campus activities at Penn, Paley gravitated toward those offering experience he could apply to the practical world. He served on the business staff of the yearbook, and for a time sold button-down shirts, a new sartorial style. His sales strategy became an important element in the Paley legend: he recruited football players and other campus heroes as salesmen, figuring their popularity would generate business. His profit was a tidy $1,000. He lacked the skill to make any athletic team, but he managed both the swimming and water-polo teams. In the 1922 Penn yearbook, he is pictured standing stiffly in jacket and tie, surrounded by muscled teammates in bathing suits and sleeveless undershirts.

His friends remember him for his amiability and ease. "There was no particular spark of genius. He was a pleasant, fine guy," said Frederick Levy, a fraternity brother. "I would never have expected he would be a big tycoon," said Henry Gerstley, a friend from a leading family in the Philadelphia German-Jewish elite. "It was only after he was successful that he became dynamic." Harold Hecht, who was two years behind Paley, recalled that his fraternity brother "lived nicely but not extravagantly." Yet Hecht also observed that Paley was "ambitious in all his actions. He seemed to know what he wanted and go after it, socially and every other way. He liked to go with nice people."

One of the "nice people" Paley befriended at Penn was Ben Gimbel, of the Philadelphia department-store family. The Gimbels were among the most prominent of the city's German-Jewish families, a group that included the Lits and the Snellenburgs, the Binswangers and the Rosenwalds. None of these families, however, wanted anything to do with Russian arrivistes like Sam and Goldie Paley.

The Paleys did what they could to be accepted. It was not so much that they were ambitious for themselves, but they wanted the best for their children. For their first several years in Philadelphia they lived in the Majestic Hotel on Broad Street and Girard Avenue, a dozen blocks north of the city center. The nine-story Majestic was constructed around an Italian Renaissance mansion built late in the nineteenth century by William Elkins, a nouveau-riche WASP. By the turn of the century, when Elkins and other wealthy residents migrated to the northern suburbs, well-to-do German Jews moved in, followed by the Russian immigrants. It was a world away from the old Philadelphia society of Rittenhouse Square.

North Broad Street had once boasted block upon block of elegant brownstone mansions. But by the time Sam and Goldie arrived, the neighborhood was increasingly working class and commercial, and the Majestic was on its way downhill following a foreclosure sale a few years earlier. Still, with the Elkins mansion as its core, the Majestic was both eclectic and ostentatious; its interior architecture ranged from Roman Corinthian to German Gothic. There were marble walls from Siena, mosaic floors, murals of flirting lords and ladies, a stained-glass window from the Royal Bavarian Art Institute, and a Moorish smoking room with fireplace andirons of elephants carrying pagodas.

In 1921 the Paleys bought their first home, a plain stone dwelling with mock Tudor touches on a quarter-acre lot at the corner of Overbrook Avenue and 52nd Street. Located on the western fringe of the city, only a few blocks from the city boundary, their neighborhood was a tree-lined enclave for upwardly mobile Russian-Jewish families. The first floor had a living room, dining room, small library, and dayroom; there were five modest bedrooms on the second and third floors.

Sam and Goldie also joined the city's most prestigious Reform synagogue, Keneseth Israel, a junior version of New York's Temple Emanu-El. Founded in 1846, the synagogue was committed to Americanizing the immigrant as quickly as possible, even if it meant abandoning some Jewish traditions. Its temple at Broad and Columbia streets in North Philadelphia echoed the congregation's desire to assimilate: it included a campanile copied from St. Mark's Square in Venice and a dome modeled on the

Mosque of Omar in Jerusalem. The board of the synagogue comprised a *Who's Who* of the city's rich and powerful German Jews.

Not long after their arrival in Philadelphia, Goldie decided to give a big party and invited some members of the Jewish elite. None accepted her invitation. Bill, only nineteen, tried to soothe her feelings. "They don't really count," he said. "I'm going to New York and I'll not only make lots of money, I'll marry a Vanderbilt." Later in his life, Sam Paley told the story of Goldie's party and Bill's reaction, describing Goldie's anticipation, anxiety, and ultimate disappointment at being so roundly rejected by the leading families. Sam's account revealed not only the depth of Bill's resentment but his early equation of WASP acceptance with success.

A more profound snub occurred when Bill tried to join the Philmont Country Club, founded by the Gimbels, Snellenburgs, and Loebs after they were excluded from Gentile clubs. Philmont, located in North Philadelphia near Jenkintown, was a bastion of the German-Jewish establishment. When Paley's application was pigeon-holed for an unreasonable length of time, his proposer, a friend named Lester Hano, asked another member to find out why. He learned that while the admission board had no objection to Bill, they were afraid his father would come and play golf. "They didn't want any part of him because of his thick accent," recalled Lester Degenstein, who made the inquiry. Bill was eventually admitted; but after paying his initiation fee and first year's dues, he resigned. Sam ultimately maneuvered his way into Philmont and in an ironic twist helped keep the club afloat during the Depression through generous donations.

Assisted by Gerstley and Gimbel (who along with another friend, Nathan Hamburger, comprised the admissions committee), Paley was also admitted to "The Hundred Club," a fashionable social club for the sons of the Jewish elite. He joined the luncheon crowd nearly every day at the clubhouse at 16th and Latimer streets. He was good company and amused his new friends with his penchant for malaprops such as "I wouldn't give a red dime for that." But he was less successful with the daughters of prominent families. "While they didn't snub him they indicated they preferred others," recalled William S. Fineshriber, Jr., a former CBS executive and the son of the rabbi at Keneseth Israel. "That incensed him. He was annoyed."

Bill Paley spent his days in Philadelphia training conscientiously to take over the business. Upon his graduation from Penn he was hired by his father for a modest salary of of $1,300 a year—about $10,000 in today's dollars. He had no title and moved among various departments under the tutelage of uncles and trusted lieutenants. Jacob—everyone called him Uncle Jay—taught Bill the basics of finance. Jay was quiet and debonair, taller than Sam and more youthful-looking, perhaps because he was clean-shaven. In his later years he moved to a large home in California where he consorted with starlets and played the horses. Uncle Ben, Sam's youngest brother, was a free spirit, a prizefighter in his spare time who bet recklessly at the racetrack. Young Bill marveled at how he used his contacts to get things done.

The only non-Paley executive, Willis Andruss, instructed him in sales and marketing. Paley looked up to Andruss, who was tall, elegant, and handsome. Andruss was known in the trade as "the million-dollar cigar salesman," and he taught young Paley all his tricks. One that Paley adopted enthusiastically was to visit cigar stores that declined to carry La Palina cigars. Andruss would put a dollar on the counter, ask for a La Palina, exclaim in mock astonishment, "You don't have them," grab the dollar indignantly, and walk out.

Sam Paley of course was the master of production. Each May he took Bill to Amsterdam for the tobacco auctions, where they purchased their Java wrappers. Bill watched his father carefully analyze the color and texture of handful after handful of tobacco, then calculate the bids to be placed in sealed envelopes. He listened as Sam dissembled about the size of his bids to other buyers in an effort to bluff them into bidding lower on the next round. They spent long days together, often getting up at 5:00 A.M., working for six weeks, spending millions of dollars for a year's supply. The lesson was simple but crucial: "If you get the details right, the final work product will be correct."

Bill showed enough aptitude that eventually his father sent him alone to Puerto Rico to buy tobacco. Faced with a glut in the tobacco crop, he offered a price one third higher than the other dealers were planning to bid. Bill reasoned that if he paid the lower price, he could risk driving the farmers out of business. The other dealers were furious, but they had to match his price since he was the biggest buyer. Sam gave him a raise.

Congress Cigar was thriving. From 1921 to 1926, net earnings increased from $75,000 to $1.7 million and yearly production jumped from 55 million to 255 million cigars. The operation had grown from one eight-story fully humidified factory at Third and Spruce in Philadelphia to seven factories in four states. By 1926, Congress employed 4,635 people. In January of that year, Goldman Sachs sold 70,000 of the company's 350,000 shares to the public, netting the Paley family nearly $3 million, and Congress was listed on the New York Stock Exchange for the first time. Later in 1926 the family made its big killing, by selling 200,000 of its shares to the Porto Rican–American Tobacco Company for $13,750,000. Bill's cut was $1 million—which would be like receiving $7.3 million today. His salary jumped to $20,000 a year, and he advanced to the title of vice-president.

There were some worrisome signs, however. Cigarette smoking, by newly liberated women as well as men, was becoming the rage of the Roaring Twenties. By mid-decade, cigarette production had grown from 16 to 82 billion in only twelve years. At the same time, national cigar consumption had begun to decline. Congress Cigar jumped on the cigarette bandwagon, and Sam put his son in charge of selling and promoting a new brand. Smokers, however, hated the Palina cigarette—its taste spoiled by cheap paper. After a huge loss estimated by some at a million dollars, Sam closed down the operation. It was Bill Paley's first flat-out failure.

Afterwards, he concentrated on advertising La Palina cigars. In so doing, he joined the new vanguard of business in the twenties: the advertising men, principal agents for the prosperity heralded by Calvin Coolidge. Increasingly competitive, they developed ever more sophisticated techniques, and by 1927, $1.5 billion was devoted each year to advertising nationwide. Congress built on its pride in a cigar that was high-grade but priced moderately. As soon as sales reached a million cigars a day, its slogan announced: "America's largest selling high-grade cigar." That slogan, mingling mass marketing with aspirations to quality, became Bill Paley's talisman.

Outside the office, Paley pursued a footloose bachelor life from the Warwick Hotel on fashionable Rittenhouse Square, where he had a studio apartment with a Murphy bed and small pantry. After the family sold its holdings in 1926 and became very rich, he moved to a penthouse apartment on the twentieth floor. "I lived in the south wing and Bill lived in an identical apartment on the north wing," recalled Gerstley. "We each had an enclosed porch and two open porches, a living room, two bedrooms, two baths and a kitchen. There were other rooms on that floor but ours were the only two apartments of that kind in the building." Paley gave dinner parties and entertained his girlfriends; once, as a joke, Ben Gimbel rented the room next door and banged on the wall to interrupt Paley's lovemaking.

Paley preferred showgirls that he met at theater openings in Philadelphia. He was quite the Stage Door Johnny, using his connections with producers to send flowers and notes inviting them to late night suppers. When the shows moved to New York, he often followed the girls on the train, while his father tried vainly to locate him. He gambled and frequented speakeasies like the Beaux Arts in Atlantic City, where he watched a dancer named Ruby Stevens (later to become Barbara Stanwyck).

Several trips to Europe with his parents provided Paley with a different sort of sophistication. During one crossing in the summer of 1928 he met Hollywood mogul Samuel Goldwyn and his wife, Frances, a blue-eyed slender blonde. Frances, married only three years to Goldwyn, captured Paley's upwardly mobile fancy. "She was so crisp, so tidy, so tailored and so feminine at the same time," said Irene Selznick. "Her grooming, her posture, was perfect, but she was all natural, like a country girl."

While Sam Goldwyn gambled, Paley wooed the married woman, begging her to leave her husband as they danced. Years later, over dinner when the lights were low, Paley confided in Irene Selznick. "I was mad about Frances. I didn't give a damn," he said. "And she was crazy about me. But she wouldn't leave Sam." The mutual ardor seems believable; Paley certainly had the magnetism. But he was still only a small-time cigar man.

Paley continued his worldly education in Paris, while Sam took Goldie to Vichy. Paley stayed at the Ritz, discovered French cuisine, and frequented the legendary nightclub run by Ada Smith du Conge, a black American singer known as "Bricktop" for her orange-colored hair. He also patronized what he called the "fantastic" brothels of Montmartre. "Everyone went. It was all organized," he recalled. "They were run by very respectable people. You could dine and dance or do nothing. The brothels were a place to see." Paris gave him his first taste of decadence. Years later he would speak of the thrill of visiting the opium dens where he watched lesbians make love.

Paley enjoyed luxury but was uncertain how obvious he should be about his new wealth. His ambivalence was evident when he rashly purchased a Hispano Suiza convertible for the extraordinary price of $16,000 in 1928. After driving the car around for a while, he became embarrassed that its ostentatious novelty drew crowds. "I wanted an attention-getting object without the attention," he said in one insightful reminiscence. "It may be that I haven't changed much in that respect in the last fifty years."

After years of plowing earnings back into the business, his parents were also ready to indulge themselves. From Overbrook they had moved in 1924 to another modest home on East Sedgwick Street in Mt. Airy, an equally undistinctive middle-class neighborhood. Several years later, however, after their son and daughter had left the nest, they made the big leap to an impressive home on Hampton Road in Chestnut Hill, one of the city's most prestigious addresses.

Situated on five acres, the formal house was designed by George Howe, a local architect, in the style of a French chateau. It stood behind a large round courtyard at the end of a long driveway. The living and dining rooms were enormous. The library was oval, with an ornately carved ceiling. All the floors were black and white marble, and a marble staircase curved up to the second floor where it culminated in a balcony. Also on the second floor were Goldie and Sam's separate bedrooms, each with its own dressing room. Linking the two bedrooms was a glass-enclosed breakfast room. All the bathrooms contained intricate tiled mosaics.

Goldie filled the house with oriental rugs and antiques from England and France. She decorated her bedroom in Louis XVI style and the guest bedroom with Art Deco furniture. The living room contained two pianos, a grand and a baby grand, for decoration. Out back was a tennis court, a swimming pool lined with tiled mosaics, a bath house, greenhouse, and kennel. To help maintain their home, the Paleys hired a meticulous married couple, Helen and Edward Michiels. She served as a cook and Goldie's personal maid; he was Sam's valet and chauffeur. The staff also included a parlor maid, an upstairs maid, and a gardener. Goldie hired only Catholics as servants. "Jewish girls don't know how to work," she once said. "All they want to do is get married."

Sam and Goldie had few pretensions and led a quiet life. Goldie spoke directly and simply, sometimes ungrammatically, with an Eastern European accent that had faded only slightly with time. She loved to shop on her own in supermarkets. She would pinch the fruits and vegetables, and instruct the butcher where to cut the fat from the meat. When she finished shopping, the chauffeur would drive up and load the groceries. But Goldie was practical about what money could buy. As her son was embarking on his career, she advised him, "Never do anything for yourself that someone else could do better," and treated him to his first valet.

Goldie had more than a touch of vanity. She dressed well and was perfectly groomed. Once she had the means, she indulged in a weekly facial massage and hairstyling at Elizabeth Arden. She wore dark glasses indoors and out because she thought she looked better that way. Goldie had a sense of humor and a gift for making those around her comfortable. Her philanthropy also endeared her to others. Over the years she donated generously to organizations that helped disadvantaged children and the handicapped. The impulse behind her giving was refreshingly simple: "The old person, money cannot save 'em. They're gonna die. But if a poor child needs help, you can save him. If he has a future, I believe in helping it."

Goldie dispensed advice that reflected shrewdness as well as a deep-seated mistrust. "Never take your diamonds to the jewelry store and leave them," she told her secretary. "Don't ever leave any stones with anybody." At one point she hired someone to make certain that the bank was not cheating her, to explain her financial transactions, and keep track of dividends. When well into her nineties, with the ghetto far behind her, she insisted on visiting her "office" in the Fidelity Building in Philadelphia once a week.

She was intelligent and determined to improve herself. Having decided to lose weight, she simply did it and remained thin thereafter. She took up golf in middle age and played for many years; at age sixty she put down her clubs and began painting. She rose each morning between six and seven. She exercised vigorously, took art lessons, and went to lectures and classes. She was a learner. "I haven't allowed my system to get sluggish," she said. Yet her personal secretary suspected that Goldie remained only minimally literate because she always insisted that her mail be read aloud—"She could see well enough to sign her checks but I always had to tell her who they were made out to."

Goldie was stronger in some respects than her husband. "My husband was afraid of things," she said. "He was afraid of night. And very often we were sitting and he said, 'Goldie, do you hear the noise?' I said, 'Yes.' He said, 'Will you please go down and see who it is?' He was afraid, and I'd go down and see because I wasn't afraid." Late in life Goldie took up horseback riding over protests from Sam, who feared that horses were too high-spirited. And she loved driving her own Lincoln Continental, sometimes wildly, just to assert herself.

Still, the Paley household clearly revolved around Sam, his demands and his peculiarities. Goldie "catered to my father in every way, simply taking it for granted that her role in life was to make him happy and comfortable," her son recalled in his memoir. Goldie's attitude was typical of Jewish immigrant families of that generation. Irving Howe points out that "the patterns of the family had been firmly set, indeed, had been allowed to become rigid in the old country. The moral authority of the father, the formal submission of the wife, together with her frequent dominance in practical affairs, the obedience of children softened by parental indulgences."

Everything went according to Sam's schedule; when he took rests at odd hours, everyone else had to clear out and quiet down. He did not have much of a sense of humor. He planned every moment of his life down to the smallest detail and he was compulsively neat—too much so, his son once observed; "it was almost a mania with him." Sam always looked dapper and wore the most fashionable styles. Far from handsome, he was still vain enough to worry when his hairline began receding. In an effort to coax some hair to grow back. Sam shaved his hair down the middle of his head, leaving it black and full at the sides.

With his guttural voice, cigar perpetually clamped in his mouth, and accent as thick as a good borscht, Sam seemed hardboiled and coarse. But he was unassuming and friendly with people, whatever their station. While observers often remarked on his sweetness, he could be tough-minded and tightfisted as well; one sister-in-law called him "The Rock." Sam was frugal—when he gambled at the bridge table he played for no more than a tenth of a cent a point—and he loved making money. He always carried a little notebook in which he kept track of his investments.

Even his son had to acknowledge that his father had "strange habits." Sam was so hypochondriacal that he consulted his doctor daily and his dentist once a week. Every day he took a nap at his office. He always ate lunch at eleven-thirty because he could not wait any longer. (In later years during CBS board meetings—as an investor, Sam sat on the board from day one—he would customarily raid his son's kitchen next to the executive dining room and then eat again during the official lunch following the meeting.) Sam refused to drive a car after a first humiliating driving lesson when he crashed into a wall, having hit the accelerator instead of the brake. Nearly thirty years into his marriage, his fortune secure, Sam told Goldie, "Sometimes when men get older they get a little funny" (translation: they begin to chase other women). So in case he got "a little funny," he gave her $2 million to invest as she saw fit. Sam had peculiar superstitions as well. He was fixated on the number 13, which he considered lucky, contrary to the rest of the world. He used to go to great lengths to have addresses, names, and phone numbers add up to thirteen. The superstition was evidently contagious; once Bill Paley found himself counting the letters of his name and discovered they added up to 13 if he included the S. That sign convinced him more than ever of the rightness of his childhood decision to invent a middle initial.

Throughout Bill's youth, his sister, Blanche, remained the focus of her mother's attention, and both parents spoiled her. "No one ever said no to her," said Dorothy Paley Hirshon. "She was indulged in every way and remained a child her whole life." Blanche was quiet, shy, and nervous. After attending a girls' finishing school, she occupied herself with fashions and decorating and succumbed to hyponchondria. She was not pretty, but had a lovely figure and dressed elegantly.

As the self-appointed guardian of the Paley family's standing, Bill kept a watchful eye on Blanche's beaux. In that role he could be haughty. When a local dentist named Leon Levy came to call, Bill at first tried to prevent her from seeing him. Leon was the son of Hungarian-Jewish immigrants, and Bill thought him beneath the Paleys.

Sam and Bill continued their mutual admiration, yet Bill remained as fearful of his father's wrath as he had been in childhood. When he got in a bind with a $5,000 gambling debt, he turned to Uncle Jay to bail him out. Goldie had become quite proud of her poised and popular son. She was neither doting nor loving, but their relationship was correct, if not terribly deep. "She knew him better than he thought," Dorothy Paley Hirshon recalled. "She realized how selfish he was, and how self-centered, but she never criticized him."

Paley came to believe that he had inherited more traits from his mother than his father. Goldie Paley shared this view. "My son believes in a lot of the things I do," she said. "He is very much like myself." Above all, Paley believed he inherited his mother's determination: "She would never say no. She just went ahead and did what she wanted to do." Her knowledge of art and music was limited, but she passed these enthusiasms to her son. Like his mother, Paley was warm on the surface but could be cold and callous underneath. He also had a certain physical fearlessness that resembled Goldie's. When he was in London during World War II, for example, he seemed impervious to danger. "What's the matter?," he once said to a colleague who ducked for cover in the middle of a meeting as bombs exploded outside. "Let's get on with it."

Bill was also, of course, his father's son. "Sam was very much like his son in many ways. He was pretty egocentric and dominating," said Dorothy Paley Hirshon. Like his father, Bill Paley would demand a great deal from others—wives as well as minions. Unlike his father, however, he needed their help to organize his life. He lacked his father's innate neatness. Much to his embarrassment, though, he shared his father's hypochrondria, a trait he tried to deny in later life. Friends and colleagues alike attested that Bill Paley was obsessed with his health from an early age.

After the Paleys sold their stock in Congress Cigar, Bill Paley became noticeably restless. "He was always more ambitious than the rest of us put together," said Gerstley. His social aspirations drove him hardest. He pined for the high life in New York City. He used to leaf through the pages of *Vogue* and *Harper's Bazaar* and admire the delicate, ivory-skinned beauties in the photographs. At bottom, he felt uncomfortable in Philadelphia, never quite at ease with the Jewish elite and shut out by the old society establishment. "I don't think he ever felt secure," said Gerstley.

Outside Philadelphia, the mood seemed to be turning more tolerant. By the latter years of the 1920s the Red scare had abated and a new spirit of openness had taken hold. No place symbolized this new freedom more than New York City, with its cosmopolitan air and promise of social mobility. In Manhattan, it seemed that anyone with style and ambition could win acceptance. But Paley felt that manufacturing cigars was not an impressive enough career for a rising Manhattanite. "He made it clear he didn't want to be in the cigar business," said Gerstley. What Bill Paley needed was a business that was lucrative, glamorous, and, above all, respectable.

3

—————

H E HEARD THE FIRST SOUNDS of radio—surprisingly loud, amazingly clear—through earphones attached to a primitive crystal set at a friend's apartment in Philadelphia. The year was 1925, and at first Paley couldn't believe that music was actually coming through the air, without benefit of wires. "I was very dubious," he said. "I thought my friend was playing a trick on me." Paley immediately had a set made for the extravagant sum of $100. Night after night, until three or four in the morning, the twenty-four-year-old Paley sat transfixed, trying to pick up signals from points as distant as Pittsburgh or even Kansas City.

William Paley's discovery of radio is a story he recounted often over the decades. To society matrons and junior executives, he enthusiastically described it as a singular revelation, as if he alone had become mesmerized by the medium. In fact, the experience was common for young people of the day, and he came to it several years later than most. Since the winter of 1921–22, the country had been buzzing about the amazing wireless; 2.5 million radios had been sold by 1923. One San Francisco paper reported as early as 1921, "There is radio music in the air, every night, everywhere." The first commercial radio station, Westinghouse Corporation's KDKA in Pittsburgh, had gone on the air in 1920 with the simple goal of provoking listeners to buy Westinghouse receivers. As radio's popularity spread, the number of stations grew. By 1924—a full year before Paley caught up with the fad—1,400 broadcasting licenses had been issued by the Department of Commerce, which was charged with regulating the infant industry, a task taken over by the Federal Radio Commission in 1927.

Stations popped up in all sorts of unlikely places. To entice customers, Wanamakers, Gimbels, and a score of other department stores set up transmitting studios on their sales floors. Hotels did the same to attract guests, and newspapers to advertise themselves. There were stations at universities, some of which allowed students to listen to lectures as part of their coursework. Stations even beamed from laundries, stockyards, and poultry farms. The programming was often amateurish and gimmicky. KDKA, whose first programs originated in a cloakroom at the Westinghouse meter factory, broadcast concerts by the Westinghouse employee band, poetry readings by employees, and arias by a soprano snatched from the assembly line. When a makeshift studio couldn't contain the echoing of the employee band, music was transmitted from underneath a tent on the roof, which offered fine acoustics until the canvas blew down in a rainstorm.

At first, no one envisioned using this new medium for advertising; it was designed to sell radios and reap various indirect public relations benefits. But the American Telephone & Telegraph Company, then in the business of selling radio transmitters, had another idea. In August 1922, AT&T had launched WEAF (for Wind, Earth, Air, and Fire), an experimental station in New York, and offered advertisers the opportunity to buy time on the station. AT&T called its approach "toll broadcasting." More broadcasters adopted AT&T's "toll" approach. AT&T meanwhile put together the first rudimentary network, using long-distance phone lines to connect stations around the country to remote broadcast locations like football stadiums. The phone company even made a $150,000 profit from its baby network in 1925. Soon it became clear to government officials and broadcasters that advertising could provide revenue to pay top performers and make the medium more professional.

Something needed to be done: apart from the success of one incipient network, the radio craze showed signs of fading. The novelty was wearing off by 1926. Listeners were tiring of two-bit programs. Although plenty of performers worked without pay, many stations couldn't keep up with costs. Between 1924 and 1926, the number of stations shrank by more than half, to 620. Set manufacturers became alarmed. They saw their market drying up.

As the year continued, the principal broadcasting and radio manufacturing companies squabbled about who had which rights to profits from the sale of radios. At the same time, the federal government accused these companies of anti-trust activities. A settlement was finally fashioned by David Sarnoff, a hard-driving executive at the Radio Corporation of America. RCA was then the largest distributor of radios, which were manufactured by General Electric and Westinghouse but sold under the RCA name. Sarnoff's plan called for creation of a new entity, the National Broadcasting Company, that would link stations around the country to present programs simultaneously to a national audience.

The new "chain" would be owned by RCA, General Electric, and Westinghouse. AT&T would sell its network to NBC for $1 million and withdraw from broadcasting. The phone company would make its money by leasing telephone lines to NBC to connect its affiliated stations. The new network would not aim to make money through its broadcasts but rather by stimulating radio sales. The NBC founders assured wary government officials that whatever advertising revenue its broadcasts generated would be channeled into improved programs. NBC's stated purpose sounded almost philanthropic: an "investment in the youth of America," an effort to serve and uplift the public with "better programs permanently assured."

It was a brilliant stroke for the man with whom Bill Paley would match wits. Ten years older than Paley, Sarnoff had also come from a Russian-Jewish background. But unlike Paley, he was born in the mother country, in a grim shtetl near Minsk. As a child he had suffered through the raids of Cossacks, the ordeal of traveling by steerage to the United States, and grinding poverty on arrival in the Lower East Side ghetto in Manhattan. He never had the luxury of a childhood. From the age of four he was drilled in the Old Testament and the Talmud by his rabbinical elders, from dawn to dusk, six days a week. He later said that after four years of having to memorize two thousand words a day, he could not bring himself to become the rabbi his family wanted him to be.

On the Lower East Side, Sarnoff found work selling Yiddish newspapers, ran his own newsstand, and dashed through the streets as a telegraph messenger. He studied English by reading New York newspapers picked out of garbage bins. Soon he was speaking without a trace of an accent. By 1906 he joined the Marconi Wireless Telegraph Company, where he started as an office boy and worked his way up to telegraph operator. He achieved his first fame at age twenty-one on the night of April 14, 1912. As manager of the wireless station in the Wanamaker department store, he was one of several people along the East Coast in touch with the sinking luxury liner *Titanic*. It was the beginning of a legend—embellished and repeated by Sarnoff himself—that cast him as the sole link to the disaster for seventy-two hours. His coolness under pressure impressed Marconi executives, and his responsibilities grew accordingly.

But Sarnoff was more than a young employee on the rise. In a 1916 memorandum to his superior at Marconi, the twenty-five-year-old visionary described how the wireless could become "a 'household utility' . . . a 'radio music box' . . . which can be placed in the parlor or living room . . . to enjoy concerts, lectures, music, recitals, etc., which may be going on in the nearest city within their radius." Although he calculated that radio sales could yield $75 million a year, his superior rejected the idea as "harebrained."

Three years later, Marconi was swallowed by the Radio Corporation of America, which had been created by a powerful cartel of four companies with interests in wireless communication—General Electric, Westinghouse, AT&T, and United Fruit Company. Junior executive Sarnoff wasted no time dusting off his "radio music box" memo and getting it into the hands of the new RCA chairman, Owen D. Young. He succeeded not only in pushing RCA into selling radios but into radio broadcasting as well, and Young made him the company's general manager. By the mid-1920s, the burly and balding immigrant with piercing blue eyes was being hailed as a prophet of the radio age.

Sarnoff's radio brainchild, NBC, burst on the air on November 15, 1926. The inaugural program was a four-hour extravaganza transmitted live from the Grand Ballroom of the Waldorf-Astoria Hotel in Manhattan. Walter Damrosch conducted the New York Symphony Orchestra, the Metropolitan Opera's Tito Ruffo sang arias, Will Rogers impersonated Calvin Coolidge, and soprano Mary Garden trilled "Annie Laurie" from her apartment in Chicago. It was an unqualified success. By the turn of the year NBC had two networks, the Red and the Blue, comprising twenty-five stations. RCA's tightly controlled monopoly on broadcasting was on its way.

NBC had first call on the strongest stations. Newcomer stations in cities already covered by NBC had no prospect for a network affiliation. One of those left out of the new network was a shoestring station in Philadelphia called WCAU. Located in one room on an alley next to the boiler room for the Philadelphia Hotel at 39th and Chestnut streets in West Philadelphia, it was owned by a couple of enterprising brothers, Isaac and Leon Levy, who had bought it in 1924 for $25,000. Isaac, known as "Ike," was a tough and aggressive young lawyer with a weakness for high-stakes poker. Leon was a dentist, soft-spoken and reserved. With his knack for persuasive and canny negotiating, Ike handled most of the business deals. Leon divided his time between filling teeth in the mornings and programming the station in the afternoons.

The station was making little headway selling advertising against its two entrenched competitors, stations owned by the Wanamaker and Lit department stores and affiliated with the NBC Red and Blue networks. Ike and Leon needed the prestige and professionalism of a network. So when a fast-talking promotor named George Coats came to call one day in the spring of 1927, Leon listened eagerly. Coats was part of an unlikely trio. The others were Arthur Judson, a cultivated but forceful manager of performing artists and orchestras, and Major Andrew White, a well-known radio announcer who wore a pince-nez on a black ribbon and a white carnation in his lapel. All three itched to challenge the NBC monopoly.

Coats and Judson had hooked up in the fall of 1926. Judson had recently organized a bureau to represent concert artists who wished to perform on radio and had been counting on an exclusive arrangement to supply programs and talent to NBC. When the two entrepreneurs visited Sarnoff in January 1927 to iron out what they hoped were the details of Judson's proposed agreement, Sarnoff showed them the door. It turned out that Sarnoff had already formed his own artists' bureau within NBC. Furious at Sarnoff's rejection, Judson threatened to start a rival network. Sarnoff leaned back in his swivel chair and guffawed. "You can't do it," he said. At minimum, he told them, they needed a million dollars, the amount he had just paid for the phone lines connecting NBC.

Within weeks of that humiliating meeting, Coats and Judson organized United Independent Broadcasters with $6,000 from an heiress, Betty Fleischmann Holmes. They brought in Major White to give the new enterprise a bit of prestige. White joined them because he thought their network could have greater freedom than one beholden to the corporate parents of NBC. But the prospects for the United Independent network were bleak. AT&T told Coats it would take at least three years before enough phone lines would be free to serve a competing network.

There matters stood in the spring of 1927 when Coats sat across the desk from Leon Levy, a friend of Judson's through the Philadelphia Orchestra, which Judson managed. Levy had nothing to lose, so he named his terms. United Independent had to pay his station $500 a week—$50 an hour—to carry a guaranteed ten hours of professional network programming. During those ten hours, the network was free to sell advertising and pocket the proceeds. The rest of the time, the station would make money by selling advertising locally. They had an agreement.

Leon was so taken with the new network that he hit the road with Coats and signed fifteen additional stations to United Independent on similar terms. A guaranteed weekly income was irresistible to stations when advertising revenue was scarce. But that arrangement proved a crushing burden to the fledgling network. Coats could not find sponsors to cover the $8,000 in weekly compensation to sixteen stations, much less overhead for programming and telephone lines, should they become available.

In April 1927 an angel materialized. The Columbia Phonograph Company was alarmed that a rival manufacturer of record players, the Victor Company, was poised to merge with RCA. Coats persuaded Columbia executives that an investment in United Independent could be used to promote Columbia records and players on the new network. The investment came to $163,000, enough to cover United Independent's debts. Columbia stipulated that the network be called the Columbia Phonograph Broadcasting System. In return, Columbia had to pay the stations and performers, and to find advertisers to buy time during the ten weekly hours of network programming. As *Fortune* magazine pointed out a few years later, Columbia "bought the operating rights of United Independent, which wasn't even operating."

Fortified by its new backer, United Independent coaxed the phone company into making lines available by the autumn. Arthur Judson organized a program schedule populated with his artists. Of the ten weekly hours, five would be filled by Howard Barlow conducting a new twenty-three-piece orchestra, the other five by a dance band led by Donald Voorhees. The Columbia network made its debut on September 18, 1927. The afternoon began with Barlow's orchestra in a program concluding with "Tales from the Vienna Woods," a sly tribute to the intended sponsor, a furniture-manufacturing company. In the evening, the Metropolitan Opera performed *The King's Henchman,* by Deems Taylor and Edna St. Vincent Millay. Not only was the evening performance delayed, but stations west of the Alleghenies heard nothing for the first fifteen minutes because of thunderstorms. The program was nearly drowned out by dreadful static and ran more than an hour long. It was remarkable that anything got transmitted at all; a men's lavatory served as the makeshift control center. It was the only soundproof room at WOR, the flagship station for the Columbia network in New York.

Columbia Phonograph lost $100,000 in the first month and decided to bow out. Once again, United Independent turned to the Levys. At this point, anyone with any sense might have seen the United Independent trio for the overreaching amateurs that they were. But Judson prevailed on Leon Levy's friendship and appealed to Ike Levy's ego. Ike was proud of his affiliation with a new network. He had used it to build up his station. He couldn't bear that Columbia was about to go under so quickly. But he did not have enough money to help on his own.

He knew, however, that the newly prosperous Sam Paley had plenty of spare capital. Sam's daughter, Blanche, had married Leon Levy only weeks earlier. Sam was now family, so in October 1927, Ike approached him with his proposal: Ike would put up $50,000 if Sam would contribute another $50,000 to rescue the ailing Columbia network. Sam agreed.

That evening, Ike went to the Locust Club, a downtown gathering place for Philadelphia's Jewish elite, for his regular poker game. But he appeared preoccupied, not his usual self. Walking home afterwards, Ike confided his troubles to his friend Jerome Louchheim, a millionaire sportsman and builder of bridges and subways. "Jerry, I'm worried," he said. "I'm very anxious to see happiness in our family and I'm concerned whether I made a wise move in asking Sam Paley to come along with me. Should this venture fail, it might be embarrassing to Leon." Louchheim replied, "You've got a nerve asking him to come in and not inviting me. We are such close friends." Ike was surprised by his friend's eagerness.

The next day he told Sam he would like Louchheim to assume Sam's stake. "Anything you do suits me," said Sam, who wanted to keep relations with his new in-laws harmonious.

Why had Sam Paley, notoriously tight with his money, so readily agreed in the first place to part with $50,000 for a shaky enterprise like the Columbia network? He knew the power of radio. Several months earlier, in the summer of 1927, he and his brother Jay had signed a contract with the Levy station, WCAU, to advertise La Palina cigars. At the time Leon Levy was courting Blanche, and Bill Paley, the vice-president of advertising for Congress Cigar, was on vacation in Europe. The hour-long program, for which Sam and Jay paid WCAU $50 a week, starred Harry Link, the composer of "I've Got a Feelin' I'm Fallin'," as the "La Palina Boy." He thumped the piano, sang songs, introduced the occasional guest solist, and plugged La Palina cigars. After a few weeks, young Bill returned from vacation. He was incensed when he learned that his father had bought a radio program behind his back. In the face of his son's disapproval, Sam had second thoughts about the radio contract. But within a few weeks it became clear that the radio exposure was boosting sales of La Palina cigars. Congress Cigar quickly signed on to sponsor a second show on WCAU, "Rolla and Dad," an early soap opera.

Sam Paley bowed out gracefully when Ike Levy turned to Louchheim to finance the Columbia network. But, still keen on the potential of radio, he agreed to spend $6,500 a week to mount a network program advertising La Palina cigars. He was also receptive when Louchheim proposed that Bill, then twenty-six years old, be tapped to run Columbia in the fall of 1927. Louchheim was only fifty-five at the time, but he had retired from the construction business and preferred overseeing his stable of horses to running a new radio network. The Levy brothers agreed with Louchheim and Sam Paley that Bill was the ideal candidate for the job. He was energetic. He was restless. He knew advertising. But they caught him at a moment when his pride temporarily overrode his ambition. Still simmering over the way his father and uncle had bought a radio program without consulting him, he refused. "I don't want anything to do with this pipsqueak radio network, this phony chain," Bill said. Reluctantly, Louchheim determined to take on the job himself.

At his father's insistence, however, Bill agreed to supervise the half-hour program that Sam had bought on the Columbia network. Called "The La Palina Smoker," it was once described as "a kind of parlor car *Arabian Nights.*" Bill Paley felt that the La Palina Boy lacked pizzazz, so he concocted "Miss La Palina." Glamorous and sultry-voiced, she was the sole female guest at a "smoker," an all-male gathering fashionable at the time. Surrounded each week by her pack of wise-cracking admirers, Miss

La Palina sang, accompanied by an orchestra, and a comedian served as master of ceremonies. Four months after "The La Palina Smoker" began on Columbia, Congress cigar sales—which had dipped to 400,000 a day from 600,000 with the advent of cigarettes—jumped to one million a day. "It was one of radio's earliest spectacular achievements," *Fortune* magazine reported.

In what would become a lifelong pattern, Bill Paley gives a contradictory—and self-aggrandizing—version of these events. By his account, it was his father and Uncle Jay who went on vacation during the summer of 1927, leaving Bill in charge. And it was he who signed with WCAU for $50 a week. But here the story begins to crumble. In a 1958 speech to a group of broadcasters, he said his show featured a male vocalist, a female vocalist, a small chorus, an "outstanding guest," and a twenty-piece orchestra—which would have cost ten times his programming budget. Nowhere does Paley mention the "La Palina Boy" and his piano, whose talents would more logically be included in a $50 fee.

Paley's tale becomes even more self-serving. Instead of proudly telling his father and uncle about the surge in cigar sales when the two men supposedly returned from Europe a month later, he claimed that they had not even heard of the show. "Their first knowledge of 'The La Palina Hour' came when my uncle, who was in charge of finances, came across the $50 charge for the first broadcast and called me onto the carpet," Paley recalled in 1958. "He not only objected to the $50; he was also fearful that radio advertising might damage the prestige of our high-caliber cigar." Over Paley's protests, Uncle Jay forced him to cancel the contract. The objections of Uncle Jay, a gambler by nature, to a mere $50 a week seem odd indeed, especially since Congress Cigar was spending a half million dollars a year on advertising in newspapers and magazines and showing profits of $1.3 million.

The denouement of this chapter in the Paley mythology occurred about three weeks after the contract had supposedly been canceled. Bill, his father, and Uncle Jay were having lunch. According to Paley, neither he nor his uncle had by then told Sam about the radio program and its subsequent cancellation—a silence that remains mystifying. During the lunch, Sam finally asked his son and brother why so many people had approached him to ask what happened to something called the La Palina radio program. Sam marveled that he was hearing so much more about these radio advertisements than he ever heard about the company's advertising in newspapers around the country. Sheepishly, according to Paley, his uncle admitted he had experienced the same reaction. "You know, there must be something to this," said Jay. It was a moment, Paley recalled, when "vindication rose within me" because father and uncle decided to resume radio advertising.

The earliest detailed account of the Paleys' involvement in radio was published in *Fortune* magazine in June 1935. It clearly credited the senior Paleys, not Bill, with taking La Palina into radio advertising. *Fortune* cited Bill's initial resistance, followed by his conversion to the merits of radio, to illustrate "an objectivity of mind." *Fortune* concluded: "What really caught Bill Paley's mind was the commercial success of the La Palina program. Which led him, by an inevitable logic, to a consideration of the commercial possibilities in radio broadcasting itself." By the 1940s, Bill Paley's version had supplanted the account crediting his father and uncle, and before long it became the official story.

"It is a lie," said Jerome Louchheim's son William, still irked nearly sixty years later. "If Bill Paley told the truth he would be a bigger man, because when he saw that sales went up, as much as he had downgraded radio at first, he wanted in. His turnaround made such a man of him. For him to say his father was against and he was for it seems like a guy who always wanted to be right."

There is no dispute that once "The La Palina Smoker" took off, Paley was hooked on radio. Producing the show took him to New York City once a week, where he fell in love with programming and made connections in the show-business world. For the next ten months he watched intently as United Independent struggled to keep the Columbia network afloat. Louchheim and the Levys had paid $235,000 initially to buy control of Columbia, with Louchheim supplying the bulk of the money. At the time, Louchheim's lawyer, Ralph Colin, had warned him that the investment would be a bottomless pit.

Colin's prophecy seemed to come true as the investors poured more money into the enterprise: $50,000 from Louchheim and $14,000 from Ike Levy in December 1927; $15,000 from Louchheim in mid-January 1928; $100,000 from Louchheim the following June; $10,000 from Louchheim and $10,000 from Ike Levy in July; $40,000 from Louchheim and $7,500 from Ike Levy the following September. All told, Jerome Louchheim injected nearly a half million dollars into the network. He tapped other relatives and friends in the Philadelphia Russian-Jewish community along the way as well: his brother Harry, Arthur Lipper, and David Bortin, who among them contributed tens of thousands of dollars.

Throughout that year Louchheim and Ike Levy would meet two or three times a week at 6:30 A.M. in Louchheim's Philadelphia apartment. Ike would watch Louchheim eat fricassée of chicken and frogs' legs for his breakfast, then the two men took the train to New York to try to sell advertising time. Congress Cigar led the way, followed by Bromo-Seltzer, Chrysler, *True Story* magazine, the Kolster Radio Company, and Dodge motorcars. But the accounts came in slowly. The new owners did achieve an early breakthrough in November 1927 when Major White and Leon Levy persuaded all of Columbia's affiliated stations to accept new contracts that cut network costs. Instead of paying each station $500 a week to carry ten hours of network programs, whether Columbia had found sponsors or not, Columbia would only pay the affiliated stations for sponsored shows that they broadcast. Since just two hours out of the ten distributed by Columbia were sponsored, the network was able to reduce its weekly station payment to $100. On the strength of this new arrangement, *Fortune* pointed out in 1935, "United's affairs and those of its operating company (which had dropped the 'phonograph' from its name and had become Columbia Broadcasting System) began to get straightened out."

Still, losses mounted at a rate of $20,000 a week. By August 1928 the Columbia network had devoured nearly $1 million. Louchheim and Ike Levy were in Atlantic City that month, walking along the boardwalk. Suddenly, Louchheim turned to Levy and said, "How far do you think we ought to go?" Replied Levy: "Let's give it ten more days and if nothing happens, we'll forget it and fold." A week later Louchheim and Levy got word that Major White had just signed a $750,000 advertising contract with Vitaphone, a subsidiary of Warner Brothers. Vitaphone was a new system for joining sound to motion pictures that had revolutionized the movie industry since its use in the first "talkie" the previous year, *The Jazz Singer,* starring Al Jolson. To the Warners, radio seemed the perfect way to alert people to what movie stars sounded like. On August 18, 1928, Ike Levy sent a telegram to Columbia investor David Bortin: "Vitaphone signed Columbia contract today. Over the top."

Shortly after the Columbia network broke into the black, Louchheim fractured his hip. Unable to travel to New York to supervise the network, he asked Leon Levy to assume the presidency. Leon preferred to remain in Philadelphia and gently declined. At that point Louchheim wanted out. Once again, Ike Levy approached Sam Paley, this time with Louchheim at his side. Levy and Louchheim knew that Bill Paley was captivated with radio, so they suggested that Sam buy the network for his son. "You at least have a cigar to advertise and you can make some use out of it," said Louchheim. While Sam would not agree to buy Columbia for Bill, he did tell his son that the network was for sale.

Bill Paley leaped at the bait. He had a million-dollar patrimony from the sale of Congress Cigar to Porto Rican–American Tobacco two years earlier, and Columbia seemed the ideal place to invest. He went to Louchheim and asked for a ten-day option to buy his stock. Louchheim agreed to the option only if Paley paid him $45,000. If Paley ultimately bought Louchheim's shares, the option price would be applied to the total; if not, Paley would forfeit his money. Louchheim's non-negotiable price for the stock was $200 a share—a total of $503,000 for the 50.3 percent of the company Paley needed to assume control.

Louchheim and Paley signed the option agreement on September 19. Paley immediately hopped a train to New York to make the rounds of advertising agencies with one question: "Is there any future for radio as an advertising medium?" Over the next five days he received one discouraging reply after another, until he met with John Orr Young and Raymond Rubicam. He had known both men when they worked on the Congress Cigar account in Philadelphia, and now they had come to New York to start their own agency. They introduced him to Tony Geohagan, their expert on radio. Geohagan told Paley that while it was still early, the future of radio looked very good. These soundings on Madison Avenue showed how cautious Paley could be when it came to business. But equally characteristic was his dismissal of the nay-sayers once he received encouragement from a source he knew and trusted.

Back in Philadelphia, he faced one final hurdle. Since he was using half of his million-dollar fortune, he felt obligated to secure his father's approval. He addressed Sam politely and formally, as was their custom. "Ours was an old-fashioned relationship in which he was the authority figure," Paley recalled. "I was troubled even then by the thought of possibly disturbing him. Our relationship was then a crucial thing in my life. . . . I was very conscious as a young man of my father's confidence in me. It was not an uncomplicated confidence. We had our differences in philosophic outlook. My father . . . was far more cautious than I and, despite his confidence in me, he thought me rather rash."

Sam not only gave his blessing but offered to kick in some of his own money. On September 25, 1928, the Paleys assumed control of United Independent and its Columbia network. William Paley was elected president on the 26th, just two days shy of his twenty-seventh birthday. He put up $417,000, which gave him 41 percent of the company. The remaining 9.3 percent of the Paley holdings was controlled by Sam, Uncle Ben, Uncle Jay, and Jay's wife, Lillian. Ike retained a 20 percent stake and Louchheim held 7 percent. At the same time, Sam, Jay, and Bill Paley bought a one-third interest in WCAU for $150,000.

It was a heady moment. But while Paley was eager to plunge into New York life, he was nervous about his prospects for success. He hedged his bet, promising his father that he would only take a three-month leave of absence to reorganize United Independent, install a new management team, and bolster the Columbia network. Afterwards, he told his father, he would watch Columbia from afar as an investor. Although Sam did not tell his son at the time, he reasoned that if Bill succeeded, he would build a bigger and more important business than the cigar trade. If he failed, he would return to Congress Cigar with broadened experience. The Paleys would win whatever the outcome, and Sam took pride in giving his son an opportunity. "I just bought the Columbia Broadcasting System for my son," Sam boasted to a fellow passenger on an ocean liner en route to Europe that fall.

Investing in Columbia was a bold move for the Paleys. Still, it was not as risky as it would have been a year earlier. Thanks to the persistence of Ike Levy and Jerome Louchheim, the network had a good chance of surviving. Yet in building his legend, Paley chose to ignore that Columbia was gaining ground when he bought it. He loved to describe how Louchheim thought he had a "lemon" and a "pig in a poke." "Louchheim had failed in all his efforts to turn the company around," Paley declared in his memoir.

Paley's portrayal of himself as Columbia's savior rankled the Louchheims, the Levys, and other original investors. So did his later efforts to describe himself as the "founder" of CBS, and to christen himself "Founding Chairman" during his second phantom retirement in the 1980s. "William Paley had an inordinate need for publicity," said Richard Levy, Ike's son. "My father and my uncle Leon were pretty much written out of the history. Bill Paley didn't found the company. He built it."

4

IT IS SAID THAT ANYONE can invent himself in America. In the case of Bill Paley, the process began on October 1, 1928, the day he walked into his paneled office at United Independent Broadcasters in Manhattan. An ambitious but inexperienced twenty-seven-year-old, he was determined to make his mark on the world. The next two years, crucial to the development of CBS, would also set patterns of behavior that would be evident throughout his life. Paley had the ability to absorb the best of what he saw around him—whether it was management techniques, bargaining tricks, elegant tailoring, taste in art, ways to charm a woman, the manners of high society. As he watched and absorbed, the

Paley of legend began to take shape. Like many people who invent themselves, he came to venerate the invention.

The headquarters of United Independent Broadcasters occupied a four-room suite near the top of the Paramount Building on the west side of Times Square. From there Paley could take in the glittering sweep of Broadway, bathed in the glow of one million electric lights. Enormous signs blazed their white letters: advertisements for Lucky Strike, Squibb's Dental Cream, Maxwell House Coffee, Chevrolet. An elaborate display for Wrigley's gum sparkled with curlicues, leaves, and flowers. Everywhere he looked he saw reminders of the commerce he sought to exploit with his tiny network. The people were out there, ready to listen; NBC was proving that every day by attracting audiences as large as 15 million.

The Paramount Building was appropriately flashy. Its twenty-nine stories rose theatrically with eight setbacks illuminated by floodlights. Adorning its pinnacle were four lighted clocks and a glowing glass sphere symbolizing Paramount's worldwide movie-making activities. On the ground floor was the Paramount film palace, where ushers dripping gold braid marched with the precision of the guards at Buckingham Palace. Lewis Mumford said the interior of the theater was so ornate that it was "reminiscent of a grandiose nightmare that might follow a rather arduous day of sightseeing in Paris." On the theater's opening night Harry K. Thaw was heard to say, "I shot the wrong architect."

Paley's office, the most spacious room in his company's suite, had been extravagantly outfitted by his predecessors. It had dark wood paneling, fluted pilasters, and a fireplace. Above the mantel was a cabinet and decorative grill concealing—naturally—a radio. By one estimate, the cost of the furnishings ran to $40,000. Paley initially dismissed his new quarters. His predecessors had erected a false front, he thought, a luxury they obviously could not afford. They had designed it, he said, merely "to impress advertisers and prospective investors in the network." It only took the young president a short while to understand the value of such image making and to incorporate it into his business philosophy. He came to cherish that office so much that he transported it intact when his company changed headquarters.

United Independent's dozen employees were hardly impressed by the sight of their new boss: a full six feet but a bit hefty, with a slight "cocktail slouch." His smooth, round face and shy air made him seem immature. It was easy to sell him short. On his first day at the office, he was barred by an overly efficient office boy who demanded proper identification. "Bill Paley was like a polite Fuller Brush salesman," recalled Edward Bernays, who became his public relations adviser in 1929. "He was actually bashful meeting people of intellectual prominence. He didn't know much more than he had learned in school. He was reticent. In a roomful of people he would appear to be an inarticulate young man."

Paley was, in fact, scared. "There was a very dramatic change in my life," he told an interviewer years later. "From a young kid working for his father to becoming the head of a company where I had to deal almost immediately with very important people. It was frightening, terrifying. It took me a long time to get over it." Paley was self-conscious about his youthful appearance—David Sarnoff called him "the Kid"—and tried to rectify it. He ordered a custom-made wardrobe of high-collared shirts and dark suits to project a more worldly image. He succeeded in looking old-fashioned and a bit fussy, like a youngster impersonating J. P. Morgan, but his reputation as a playboy didn't help his cause. The men at United Independent viewed him, in the words of one observer at the time, as "just a rich man's son, another angel with money to burn and ten fingers to singe." He was so poorly regarded at the law firm retained by his father that when Bill showed up with some papers to sign he was passed down to the most junior associate, Ralph Colin. As it happened, Colin had done work both for Louchheim and Sam Paley and could therefore be trusted to keep a watchful eye on the young man.

Paley quickly impressed skeptical underlings by immersing himself in every aspect of the business. "There was nothing remarkable about Paley when he took over the company, nothing in his past career that might throw a light on this remarkable ability in the broadcasting world. His grasp of the new picture was amazing," Colin said several years later. Only three weeks after he arrived, Paley told his father and uncle that he would not return to Congress Cigar. "My imagination went wild," he would say over and over again, recalling his feelings at the time. How could it have been otherwise? There he sat above the Great White Way, a young man in a hurry, floating on the ether.

He took in everything. He directed one executive, Julius Seebach, to sit at his elbow and coach him on what to say about broadcast problems and policies when station owners called him on the phone. An engineer named Paul Green tutored him in the fine points of radio engineering. Major White, then the nominal head of the Columbia network, taught him how to deal with affiliates. In fact, when Paley arrived, White was in the midst of negotiating with several dozen stations to expand the network.

It was in this negotiation that Paley first displayed his genius for broadcasting, pulling off a maneuver that would invest CBS with new strength and forever change the balance of power between network and station. He conceived it when he was in bed with a cold—doubtless the first of many anxiety-induced illnesses that would mark his professional life. Under his new formula, the network would continue to pay a station $50 an hour for sponsored shows that were broadcast by the station. But he gave the station a new incentive by offering twenty hours of network programs each week instead of ten. In exchange for this increase in much-needed national programming, Paley extracted a concession: the Columbia network would pay a station nothing for carrying the first five hours of sponsored network programs each week. Compensation of $50 an hour would begin only with the sixth hour of programs.

At the outset, the stations received no money from this arrangement. Only one fifth of Columbia's schedule was sponsored—roughly four or five hours of the total of twenty produced by the network. Consequently, there were no sponsored programs in excess of the five hours that the stations had agreed to run for free. Columbia benefited initially from not having to compensate affiliates at all. At the same time, the network helped its stations by supplying them with fifteen hours of free non-sponsored programs to fill their schedules. These non-sponsored programs were called "sustaining" because the network, and not a sponsor, sustained their costs. Paley claimed to be the first to offer free sustaining programs to the Columbia stations, although independent accounts say that Columbia had begun doing so under Major White.

The notion of free sustaining programs was an inspired tactic. It was aimed at NBC, far and away the dominant network. NBC forced its stations to *buy* unsponsored programs for a hefty price—$90 for each hour in the evening. The stations bridled at the fee, but NBC argued that it was necessary if the network was to keep airing programs free of advertising. Corny as it sounds today, NBC felt strongly that this was in the public's interest. Paley, however, had no comparable theories of public service. He wanted to make money; to do so he had to earn the loyalty of his stations and simultaneously increase his control over them.

The most significant element of that control was the so-called option clause that Columbia persuaded the stations to accept. It gave Columbia the power to take any part of a local station's schedule for a sponsored network program. No longer did the network have to ask the station's permission to run a sponsored program in a given time slot. For the first time, Paley could sell a program to an advertiser—say at 8:00 P.M. on Fridays—and guarantee it would appear throughout the network at that time. NBC still had to struggle with station owners who considered the network's compensation inadequate and periodically substituted their own locally sponsored shows for NBC programs in the prime evening hours. Not only did Columbia's option impress advertisers, it forced the network's affiliates to take Columbia's program schedule intact.

The stations did not seem to regard the option clause as onerous. Compared with the payment NBC compelled them to make for sustaining programs, Columbia's promise of twenty hours of programs a week looked like a good deal. Previously unaffiliated stations flocked to CBS in the months after Paley took over. During one weekend in November 1928, he invited twelve key station owners from the South to meet at New York's Ambassador Hotel and signed all of them to the Columbia network. The following month the network released the names of the new stations, which prompted a deluge of phone calls to Major White's office. As *Fortune* magazine reported several years later, "The Major closed deals right and left. It was dramatic action of a sort entirely irresistible to the number one stockholder, who was to be found in the Major's office helping with the phones and stirred to typical Paley enthusiasm." In his own accounts, Paley never mentioned White's role in securing affiliates.

Paley took enormous pride in winning the affiliation of a group of West Coast stations run by a wealthy Cadillac dealer named Don Lee. His accomplishment revealed no particular business savvy, but it did show what he was willing to do to succeed. Lee ordered him to California and forced him to waste nearly a week on his yacht, just so Lee could take the young man's measure. When they finally met in Lee's office, Lee refused to negotiate. "Mr. Paley," Lee announced to his secretary, "is now going to dictate the terms and conditions of this contract that will exist between us." Paley did so, and admitted later that his terms were probably overly generous to Lee.

Paley correctly calculated that Columbia had to own its flagship station—the facility where it produced programs for distribution to the network—if it were going to expand significantly. Before Paley's arrival the network leased time from two stations, WOR and WABC, to originate programming. Paley made overtures to both stations, and in December 1928 bought WABC because its price, $390,000, was lower. Paley now had a transmitter, a license, and an outmoded production studio in the penthouse of Steinway Hall on 57th Street. With them came an odd assortment of pots and pans, jewelry, and even a few live chickens that advertisers had given the station in lieu of cash.

For correct soundproofing, a studio needed ceilings reaching as high as two stories. On the advice of a real estate agent named Jim Landauer, Paley looked at a building under construction at the southeast corner of Madison Avenue and 52nd Street. He liked its location on the street synonymous with advertising; the architect agreed to modify his plans to construct two floors of windowless studios. At four o'clock on the day on which the last structural change could be made, Paley signed a lease for the twentieth through twenty-fourth floors. "If Paley had not done this, the new company never could have clicked," Ralph Colin told a *Time* magazine reporter in 1935.

Paley was justifiably proud of his boldness. It was, of course, a necessity. But in recounting his accomplishment, Paley has emphasized the risks of committing to a $1.5 million lease. "That was one of the most dramatic moments of my life, when I had to sign my name to, my God, a contract for ten years and for an amount of money that seemed exorbitant," he told one interviewer. "I didn't sleep nights." Trouble was, in constructing his legend, Paley significantly inflated the amount he had agreed to pay. A document signed by Paley in 1929 states that the rent for the new Columbia headquarters at 485 Madison was $63,800 a year—or $638,000 for ten years.

Luck was crucial in Paley's early days. He could concentrate on building his network because advertising revenue was taking care of itself. He was fortunate to take over during a presidential election contest between Herbert Hoover and Alfred E. Smith, Democratic governor of New York —the first national election in which radio had a critical role. To advertise their candidates, both political parties poured money into radio—nearly $600,000 in October and November 1928 alone. NBC received the bulk of that money, but CBS received an infusion of nearly $200,000.

Columbia got another break by being able to rely on radio manufacturers competing with RCA, the parent of NBC, to sell their wares on the Columbia network. Columbia already had Kolster Radio sewn up as a sponsor. Paley hardly had to lift a finger to convince the Grigsby-Grunow Company—the largest radio set manufacturer—to buy programs to advertise its Majestic model.

Paley made one key change in those first months to streamline advertising sales. It was customary for sponsors to buy time on a basic network of twenty stations in the East and Midwest. If they wanted additional coverage they would buy "legs," or small groups of stations in the South, Midwest, and West. But this approach created uncertainty; stations were never sure when they were part of a large or a limited network. Paley figured he could increase Columbia's listeners and simplify the process if he could encourage sponsors to buy the entire network. He came up with a formula (typically, while he was in bed—this time with a bad back) that in retrospect seems stunningly obvious: he gave sponsors discounts for buying the whole network. Audiences grew, and so did Columbia's revenues.

Paley often recalled his early days as if he were a solo player. "In those days of course I was everything. I swept out the office . . . and did the selling and the programming and almost kept the books too," he told *Broadcasting* magazine years later. "There's no question that it was a sort of a one-man show," he boasted to *Fortune*. Of course he made the ultimate decisions, and he did have his hand in everything. He worked hard. He was shrewd. But he also drew heavily on the ideas of others. As he has often pointed out, building an organization was one of his first priorities in those early days. Bill Paley relied on a handful of key people to build up the network—and to build up Bill Paley.

Early in 1929, Paley hired Edward L. Bernays, the nation's foremost public relations man. Paley had already shown a crude grasp of image making late in 1928 when he announced that Columbia had become the largest network, with a total of forty-nine stations. As he later admitted, "It was literally true, but only literally." NBC was in fact larger, with fifty-eight stations, but they were divided between two separate networks. The lesson was clear: if you say something long enough and loudly enough, people will believe you. Paley had stretched the truth and it had worked.

In hiring Bernays, Paley revealed his personal priorities as well. "I thought, my God, to be important enough to have a public relations man," he said years later with inadvertent candor. "Somebody who could tell you what to do and what not to do." He had extracted as much as he could from the executives he inherited. Now it was time for the advice of a professional. Bernays was the best. The nephew of Sigmund Freud, he was regarded as the father of public relations. He had been in business since the end of World War I, with such prestigious clients as the U.S. War Department, Procter & Gamble, and an array of theatrical producers and performers that included Enrico Caruso. He had already set down his principles in a landmark book published in 1923, *Crystallizing Public Opinion*.

Bernays gave Paley ideas not only about publicity, but about organizational structure, sales techniques, and scouting talent. He told Paley that the company was disorganized because of overlapping departments. He improved efficiency by coordinating the schedules of receptionists and secretaries. In the publicity department, Bernays set standards for headlines and brevity. He established a procedure to ensure that newspapers printed correct radio listings. He gave Paley a long list of possible humor writers for the network, including Ring Lardner, P. G. Wodehouse, and Don Marquis. He urged that prospective performers be considered not only for their talent but for their potential public relations value. He recruited Paley's first publicity director, Jessie Butcher, from the *New York Times*. "The first period of his tenure was difficult for him, so disorganized was the department. But our constant letters to Paley to tighten and improve its efficiency increased the efficiency," commented Bernays.

Bernays guided Paley in refining Columbia's approach to advertising agencies. "I urged him to ferret out by research the name of every agency that bought radio time," he wrote later. "There were no directories with this data. I urged that visual presentations of CBS coverage be prepared and presented to agencies by a pleasant person. I urged publicity aimed at advertising journals. Columbia should offer its services to agencies to solve problems of radio research. I urged Columbia to advertise in leading advertising journals and independent researchers be induced to survey the listening audience. Columbia should look for encomiums of past results in its files and publish pamphlets about them for agencies and advertisers."

Nor was Bernays afraid to knock down Paley's ideas. When Paley wanted to protest the *New York Times* policy of devoting more space to programs on NBC than on Columbia, Bernays pointed out that NBC, with its two networks, was entitled to greater coverage. Besides, if Paley "wasn't satisfied with the number of mentions, he would also discover that CBS offered fewer outstanding programs." But Bernays later regretted having rebuffed Paley's inspired suggestion that Columbia publish a monthly magazine about radio performers. Bernays consulted with an expert who advised him that listeners wouldn't be interested in reading about radio personalities. "Paley was right," Bernays wrote. "He did not go ahead with the venture. There was no magazine about radio, but *TV Guide,* started later by a fellow Philadelphian, made a mint."

Around the time he hired Bernays, Paley also brought in Sam Pickard, the brightest man on the Federal Radio Commission in Washington, as vice-president of station relations for Columbia. "If Major White's knowledge of the radio map had been competent, Mr. Pickard's was minute," said *Fortune*. Working the telephones in tandem, Pickard and Paley expanded Columbia to seventy-six stations by the end of 1929. It was Pickard who had come up with the option clause.

Paley was following his father's advice to "hire smart people and then have the good sense to listen to them." He showed confidence in his employees. He was proving himself to be a talented leader and a wise manager. Only in later years would his contradictory impulse to appropriate the good ideas of his subordinates—taking credit for the option clause, for example—cost him the respect of his executives.

Even in the early days, Paley relished—and fiercely protected—his power. His actions began to betray his ruthlessness. Howard Barlow, then Columbia's resident orchestra conductor, caught a glimpse of the hardness beneath Paley's exterior one day when he and Paley were entering the elevator in the Steinway Building. Barlow happened to make an offhand remark at the expense of a CBS program. Paley "proceeded to refute my joking statement and get right down to hard tacks immediately. I was put on the defensive before we got from the sixteenth floor down to the main floor." No one spoke lightly about business in Bill Paley's presence.

For whatever reason, some of the original Columbia executives became disenchanted with Paley's leadership early in his tenure. Julius Seebach and Paul Green, the two men who tutored Paley in his first months, joined forces with a third unnamed executive. Their purpose, according to rumors swirling around the company, was to seize control. When Paley heard of it, he demoted Seebach and fired Green and the other executive. Needless to say, the swiftness and severity of Paley's response impressed the survivors.

When Paley merged United Independent and the Columbia network at the end of 1928 and renamed the company Columbia Broadcasting System, Inc., he made himself president and appointed Major White managing director. No longer would White oversee station relations; instead, he would concentrate on putting programs together. Even though White had made crucial advertising sales such as the Vitaphone account and originated the basic formula for Columbia's affiliation agreements, Paley later asserted, "The business of radio or radio operations were [sic] not his talent or even within his knowledge." White did not object to losing some of his responsibilities. He continued as the network's public spokesman while Paley served his apprenticeship. White also exploited his contacts with Broadway celebrities to help Paley sign famous performers for Columbia. But by mid-1930 White's usefulness would be over and Paley would fire him.

Paley would also ease out Arthur Judson, while reshaping Columbia's programming philosophy along more practical and lowbrow lines. Under Judson, the emphasis at Columbia was on classical music. He brought prestige to the network by booking great opera stars and symphonies. "It is perhaps not too much to say that the immediate success of the youthful network in winning public favor was due in large measure to Arthur Judson's ability to stage programs of outstanding excellence," wrote Gleason Archer, an early radio historian. At first, Paley was pleased with the Judson approach and used the cachet of Judson's programs to attract advertisers.

A more lofty philosophy of broadcasting held sway at rival NBC at this time. Led by Owen Young and David Sarnoff, NBC emphasized its role as a guardian of the public trust. Young formed an advisory council of sixteen prominent men and one woman (the president of the General Federation of Women's Clubs of America) early in 1927. For several years the group shaped NBC's schedule of cultural, educational, and public service programs. These included lessons in music appreciation, concerts, productions of Shakespeare, political debates, sermons, and lectures on the workings of government by such speakers as Walter Lippmann. Millions of listeners tuned in, and advertisers eagerly bought time. On the strength of this approach, NBC made its first profit in 1928.

But forces began working against NBC's high purpose. The most important was the impact of "Amos 'n' Andy," a comedy series about a pair of black buffoons. It was performed by Freeman Gosden and Charles Correll, two white comedians in blackface who used heavy Negro dialect and shameless stereotyping ("I's regusted"). The show began in Chicago in 1928. It was distributed to thirty other stations, not by one of the existing networks but by recordings sent out for later play. "Amos 'n' Andy" was radio's first light entertainment, and it was a huge hit, attracting an audience far larger than that for cultural fare. NBC finally capitulated in 1929 and signed Gosden and Correll for the exorbitant price of $100,000 a year. Soon 40 million listeners were tuning in. Advertisers clamored for more shows like it.

The trend was not lost on Bill Paley. The high-minded Judson, who had been so instrumental in establishing Columbia, had become "a problem." At the end of 1928, Paley told Judson his style of programming was out of date because he was unable to produce vaudeville or comedy. After coaxing him into relinquishing his contract, Paley skimmed the most popular talent from the Judson Radio Program Corporation and signed those artists to contracts with Columbia. Eventually Paley would give Judson a job managing classical artists in a new Columbia subsidiary, but by early 1929, Judson had vanished from the mainstream of the network. Fifty-six years later, on his ninetieth birthday, Judson had this to say about Paley: "He would never have had the courage to found the network; I would never have had the means to build it."

With Judson out of the way, Paley began the drive toward more popular entertainment. He had decided that the quickest route to making the biggest profits was by appealing to the largest possible audience, which in turn would attract more advertisers. His first big coup was signing up Paul Whiteman, the musician who had built a sizable following by creating the first symphonic jazz band. Paley tracked down Whiteman at the Drake Hotel in Chicago. He pestered Whiteman between sets and then sat talking with him well past midnight until he had won him over. Paley paid a weekly wage of $30,000 to the band and $5,000 to Whiteman. "The Old Gold Program" used as its signature theme Gershwin's "Rhapsody in Blue."

Increasingly, Paley filled his airwaves with popular musicians, comedians, and soap operas. Columbia's "True Story" program, based on the eponymous pulp magazine, was, in the view of broadcast historian Erik

Barnouw, "both lurid and respectable enough to be a smashing 1928–29 success." Paley did not ignore cultural and educational programs, but clearly he was changing the emphasis of network broadcasting.

5

FOR BILL PALEY it was all coming together. He was making headlines—and waves. Only twenty-eight, he had become someone to be reckoned with. This was a time of peak creativity, of enormous energy. He was working overtime to shape a new network, but he was also playing hard, dating exotic film stars and socialites featured in the pages of *Vogue*. It was a sybaritic time of nightclub hopping and theatergoing. He seemed to be testing his limits, personally as well as professionally.

Nothing symbolized his dual preoccupations—his devotion to Columbia Broadcasting and to high living—so clearly as the apartment he moved to in January 1930. The first in a series of Paley pleasure palaces, it was also a study in contradictions. The apartment was remarkable in several ways, not least the ubiquity of radios (eight in all) that he listened to for hours. "He was like a little child with teddy bears, indulging himself with a radio in every room," recalled Bernays.

The apartment occupied the top three floors of a newly completed apartment house at 480 Park Avenue, on the corner of 58th Street. Its six rooms were decorated for the then-astonishing cost of $10,000 a room—much to the dismay of his public relations adviser: "It seemed a Croesus-like extravagance in a growing Depression and entirely out of keeping with the times."

Yielding to his impulse for flash and sensation, Paley hired Lee Simonson, Broadway's best scenic designer, who combined the futuristic with the theatrical. He turned three of the apartment's rooms into a grown man's playpen where the push of a button could produce any number of diversions.

The master bedroom, on the first floor, was sleek, austere, and dark. Its centerpiece was a customized bed, set at an angle as in a stage set. The bed was equipped with remote controls that switched on a radio and various combinations of lights. Behind the bed were built-in shelves with space for several hundred books—few of which Paley had time to open. Next door was a dressing room furnished with its own desk and sofa. It was lined with closets and drawers and a massage table that folded into the back of the door. When all the closets were shut, the room was a shiny, seamless cubicle of African walnut broken only by broad aluminum molding and a screened loudspeaker set into the wall. One huge closet could accommodate three hundred suits, with racks for one hundred shirts and one hundred neckties. Wealthy as he was, Paley didn't come close to filling all that space with his wardrobe.

The high-ceilinged third-floor barroom was even more urgently modernistic. Its paneled walls were painted silver, with red and blue stripes running diagonally across. It had built-in seats and lounges surrounding a semicircular bar. One wall concealed an upright piano with only the keyboard showing. A winding aluminum staircase rose to a silver-painted balcony. Behind a pair of French doors was a terrace and roof garden.

The apartment's remaining three rooms represented a decorous pass at old-money blandness. On second thought, Paley evidently concluded that understatement might be more appropriate than nouveau-riche flamboyance. A guest bedroom on the first floor was decorated with traditional furniture. On the second floor were the living and dining rooms, richly paneled in oak. The decor was beige and brown, with proper English furnishings and Paley's humdrum collection of sporting prints of herrings, pelicans, and other unremarkable fauna.

It took many months to prepare the apartment properly. In the meantime Paley lived at the Elysée, a small hotel on 54th Street between Madison and Park where he rented a suite decorated in the French style for $15 a day. When he finally moved into his new home, he felt uncomfortable sleeping on his stage set. Two days later he moved into the conventionally decorated guest room; he never spent another night in the opulent master bedroom.

Paley's social life was as improvisational as his evolving executive style. Some of his early social maneuvers were, like his Simonson interiors, embarrassingly gauche. A year after arriving in New York he sent out ten-foot banners, wound around sticks, as Christmas cards. In large black letters the banners said: "A Very Merry Christmas from Bill Paley." His inexperience announced itself again shortly after he moved to his new apartment when he decided to show it off with a housewarming for one hundred guests, including members of the press. Called to Chicago suddenly on business, Paley never appeared, leaving Simonson in charge.

As it turned out, the absentee host nearly got into trouble with the law when his guests drank liquor from the silver bar at the height of Prohibition. Bernays heard that the *Chicago Tribune* was running a story that Paley stocked bootleg alcohol; he managed to suppress it by convincing the editors that the peccadillo would ruin the young executive's career

—the first of many interventions on Paley's behalf by adept public relations functionaries. Other accounts of the party did appear, rhapsodizing Paley's lavish style.

Bernays later wrote that in arranging the elaborate party, Paley was acting as "the self-indulgent son of the big Philadelphia cigar tycoon." However, when asked about the incident in 1979 by a reporter, Paley professed to have had no involvement in the well-orchestrated affair. Simonson, he said, had "asked me if he could bring a few of his friends" to see the new apartment. "I was going out of town, and lo and behold the next day—I was in Chicago—I read that he had given a big party of press people there and it became a story, this apartment of mine. I wasn't there . . . had nothing to do with it." Paley claimed that the press exaggerated the details of the apartment. Furthermore, Paley added, "I have never had anybody to any of my houses for the purpose of writing about what they saw, or reporting it." (He must have forgotten having invited reporters from *Time* to write about Kiluna Farm, his country estate, and from *Holiday* to photograph and describe his resort home at Round Hill, Jamaica, not to mention the reports in *Vogue* over the years offering details about various rooms in his homes.) Paley's first brush with the press over his private life clearly unnerved him. From that time on, he only dealt with reporters under the most controlled circumstances, and he took great pains to project a dignified public image.

In truth, Paley's private life was that of a full-fledged, free-swinging, extravagant tycoon. He threw numerous parties. He hired a chef who had once worked for Caruso and was regarded as the best in New York. His butler/valet, an Englishman named Watts, arranged elaborate dinners on a few hours' notice. Another servant was hired to drag Paley out of bed each morning, lead him through calisthenics, and give him a massage. In a scene reminiscent of *My Man Godfrey,* Paley—who often stayed out until three or four in the morning—would fire his man each day on awakening and then rehire him after his morning shower.

Compared to the tightly stratified society of Philadelphia, New York was refreshingly open. Paley arrived during the heyday of Café Society, the elite cross-section of socialites, financiers, actors, showgirls, singers, writers, sportsmen, and tycoons united in pursuit of pleasure. Café Society had been officially christened in 1919 by the columnist Maury Paul, who wrote for the Hearst newspapers as Cholly Knickerbocker, although its origins extend back earlier in the century. In the late 1800s, New York's elite was a closely knit group of four hundred citizens whose pedigree entitled them to be entertained at the annual ball given by Mrs. William Astor. Some say that Café Society began one evening in the late 1890s when Mrs. Astor dined in Sherry's elegant restaurant on 44th Street and

Fifth Avenue—the first time the great lady deigned to appear in the company of those not included in her pantheon of four hundred. Other socialites followed her lead, and in subsequent years drank in the nightlife of jazz music and cabarets, where couples danced in sinuous embrace.

By the twenties, many of the distinctions between old and new money had vanished. It was a giddy, hedonistic time, abetted by the mood of prosperity fueled by a runaway bull market on Wall Street. Parties began in the early evening and ended after dawn. Café Society was gaudy, glamorous, and slightly sinister. But above all it was not governed by bloodlines. Membership was open to anyone with money, power, charm, or celebrity.

After a year in New York, Bill Paley had plenty of each. He had become a certified member of the smart set. He dined at speakeasies, hidden in sedate brownstones with darkened windows on the side streets off the Great White Way. The most exclusive of these was the "21" Club, then as now located in an ornate mansion on West 52nd Street. Beside two bars and restaurants, "21" had a dance floor and orchestra, lounges and rooms for Ping-Pong, backgammon, and mah-jongg. Food was exorbitantly priced. Bootleg cocktails cost a dollar and illicit champagne twenty-five dollars a quart.

Paley also frequented the city's nightclubs (there were more than seventy of them), seeking diversion and scouting talent for his network. His favorite was the Casino, overlooking the mall in Central Park. (Decades later it was razed by New York's Parks Commissioner, Robert Moses, and replaced by a playground.) With its silver and maroon dining room and ballroom of golden murals and black glass walls, the Casino was the most lavish restaurant in town, decorated at a cost of $400,000. It was presided over by New York's exuberant bantam of a mayor, Jimmy Walker, and his mistress, Betty Compton, a musical comedy actress. Paley savored the Casino's glittering array of men in white tie and tails, and beautiful women in expensive dresses.

Even more important, he gained membership to the Mayfair Club Dance, a vestige of Mrs. Astor's day. Held each Saturday night in the Crystal Room of the Ritz Carlton Hotel, the Mayfair Club was designed to introduce debutantes to eligible young bachelors. Its elderly and well-born gatekeeper was Juliana Cutting, who compiled meticulously graded lists of those worthy to attend. Increasingly, she found it difficult to keep the social climbers at bay. By the late twenties, wrote one participant in the scene, "theatre, Hollywood, and society mingled in the Mayfair dances at the Ritz, where society women could monitor their theatrical enemies and snub them publicly."

By jumping so enthusiastically into Café Society, Paley vaulted over

Our Crowd, the German-Jewish elite of New York. These families were not impressed by the likes of Bill Paley. To them, show business was a bit vulgar, barely more respectable than cigar making. Paley would have liked to have been accepted by Our Crowd, but when he was not, his resolve to move in WASP circles intensified. This was a completely new experience, because in Philadelphia his circle had been entirely Jewish. His friend Henry Gerstley was not the least surprised at Paley's choice of new friends. "He was always socially conscious," said Gerstley.

Paley's first link to WASP society, ironically enough, was through his friend Lawrence Lowman, who came from a socially prominent German-Jewish family in Philadelphia. When Paley said goodbye to Philadelphia, he also said goodbye to all his friends with the exception of Lowman, who joined him at CBS. Lowman occupied the office next to Paley's and was known at the beginning as "the vice-president in charge of everything." One of Lowman's first jobs was to set up the company's accounting system. He had to spend hours interviewing the company's treasurer, Ted Husing—later a successful sports announcer—who kept all the records in his head.

Not only was Lowman Paley's confidante and right-hand man; outside the office, he and Paley were inseparable playmates. Lowman was smart and cultivated, with a keen sense of humor and a graceful manner—the sort of amusing man Paley was drawn to throughout his life. Lowman instructed Paley in such gentlemanly arts as finding the right tailor. It was Lowman who arranged Paley's entrée to the Mayfair Club Dance. Significantly, at the time Paley hired him, Lowman was courting Cathleen Vanderbilt Cushing, the daughter of Reggie Vanderbilt and half sister to Gloria Vanderbilt. With that sort of connection. Paley's social contacts quickly multiplied.

Still, Paley never really penetrated the WASP establishment. He was not welcomed as a member by the Brook, Union, Racquet and Tennis, and other old-line clubs exclusive to WASPs at that time where his friends from St. Paul's and Groton, Skull and Bones and Porcellian, retreated from the world. The Whitneys and Vanderbilts would slum in Café Society for thrills and diversion, but in the end they withdrew behind their exclusive heritage. In later years Paley would achieve tokens of WASP recognition—membership in the fashionable National golf club in Southampton, for example—but all his life he would remain caught between two worlds, WASP and Jewish, firmly rooted in neither.

Paley chased women with the same ardor that he chased success. Both pursuits involved conquest and drew on his legendary persistence. He was usually seen with stunning women, from showgirls to socialites. They were of a type—fine-featured, fashionable, and WASP from head to manicured toe. Sometimes friends and colleagues acted as administrative assistants in his romantic endeavors. Ralph Colin once recalled, "I used to wet nurse him, keep a girl on the backburner if he had two dates."

One of Paley's first infatuations was Dorothy Hurt Meacham, the sister of an early New York friend, a stockbroker named Harry Hurt. Paley had spotted her several years earlier in the pages of *Vogue, Vanity Fair,* and *Harper's Bazaar,* and was thoroughly smitten. She came from Dallas, where her father owned a prosperous lumber company. She had been brought to New York with her identical twin sister by their mother, who was determined that they get a proper finishing school education at Miss Spence's. Dorothy was willowy, with blue eyes and brown hair cut in a fashionable short bob. Paley called her "the woman of my dreams," and even more revealingly, "a myth personified in a photograph." When he first saw her face to face, he later recounted, "my knees almost buckled."

She was married when they met. Her husband, Malcolm Meacham, was a real estate developer who owned half of Hobe Sound and Key West. With his partner, Angier Biddle Duke, he had made a fortune in the fevered Florida real estate boom of the 1920s. Several weeks after Paley met Dorothy in passing, her husband had, as Paley delicately put it, "died in a fall from his apartment." Following a suitable interval Paley began his pursuit by arranging to accompany Harry Hurt to dinner at Dorothy's apartment on Park Avenue. She found Paley rather introverted, but was flattered by his attentions. He showered her with invitations to dinner and the theater. "He always had the best seats in front," she said years later. "He knew everyone in the theatrical world. He was charming and bright and always the perfect gentleman. There was never any romance on my side, but he was devoted to me."

When she gave a dinner party, he supplied the flowers. He was always sending her small gifts, invariably tasteful and imaginative—a rare orchid in a beautiful box was typical. He called her every day on the telephone. He entertained her at his apartment, sparing no expense. He took her dancing and dazzled her with his footwork. He had impeccable manners and catered to her every need. He introduced her to the most famous names in show business. "I loved going out with him," she said. "I saw a new world I never would have seen. It was never my world. He didn't leave a stone unturned.

"He was a little shy at first," she added, "but he got over that very fast. When you are in demand everywhere, you lose your shyness." She was impressed by his probing mind, especially when it came to art, an emerging passion. "He was very much interested in art, although he didn't know much. He talked about seeing things at exhibitions, and when we would go to a party and he would see a beautiful picture, he wouldn't know much about it but would want to know. He always wanted the best, the biggest and best business, the best apartment, the best art, the best food." Besides art, Paley most liked to talk about people he had met and sights he had seen, "the things he had never had, I suppose," Dorothy said. "His mind was opening to all new things. He was learning. He was interested in everything. He liked everything and was very broadminded."

Still, Dorothy Meacham knew from the outset that Paley was not the man of *her* dreams. For all his popularity, gregariousness, and eligibility, for all the fun they had together, she felt a vague unease. It was clear to her that "his real love was his company." She also thought his hypochondria a bit odd; when someone had a cold, for instance, Paley conspicuously avoided getting too close. And she saw the possibility of trouble: "He was very brilliant in his field, but he was complicated, due to his inheritance." By that she meant the submerged conflicts in his background and parental relationships. In the end, his world and hers were too different. After going out with him for more than a year, she gently said goodbye.

Doubtless it did not come as a surprise. During the year they were together, she had frequently been in the company of other beaux, just as he pursued a parade of chorus girls. If he was jealous, he kept his feelings in check. He was always calm and contained, never excitable. When they parted company, she explained that she was not ready to remarry but wished him well. "He took it like a good sport," she recalled. He remained friendly with Dorothy and her brother Harry for years afterwards. Although Dorothy Meacham never loved him, she always respected him. "He was proud and ambitious. And he fought every inch of the way to make himself what he became."

Paley rebounded quickly. Toward the end of 1929 he developed a passion for a woman considerably more unconventional than Dorothy Meacham. Louise Brooks, a former Ziegfeld girl, had just finished making a scandalous film in Germany called *Pandora's Box*. Brooks had a breathtaking beauty that rivaled Garbo's. Her face was a porcelain oval, with an exquisitely sculpted nose, perfect bow lips, and enormous dark eyes. She was known as the girl in the black helmet, after her sleek jet black bob with long straight bangs. She was overwhelmingly erotic, and the role she played in *Pandora's Box,* directed by G. W. Pabst, exploited her sexiness to the utmost. The film tells the story of a prostitute named Lulu, an unrepentant hedonist, who destroys her lovers and is ultimately killed herself. Lulu is seen embracing women as well as men. Although she made other films in Hollywood before and after, Louise Brooks became identified in the public mind with the kinky Lulu.

Kenneth Tynan, the British theater and film critic who wrote a profile of her many years later, saw Brooks as a "shameless urchin tomboy . . . a creature of impulse, a temptress with no pretensions, capable of dissolving into a giggling fit at a peak of erotic ecstasy; amoral but totally selfless . . . lesbian and hetero." Kansas-born, Brooks came to New York and, like Paley, reinvented herself, but with a higher degree of self-awareness. She was a free-thinking rebel, an avid learner, a withering observer and, it later turned out, a skilled storyteller.

Paley was bowled over by Louise's independent spirit, and found her as amusing as she was seductive. For her part, she appreciated his "screwy sense of humor." Almost at once they plunged into an affair. She was twenty-two years old and living in an apartment two blocks away from Paley, at Park Avenue and 56th Street. She was also engaged to marry a man named George Marshall, a Washington businessman who had made a fortune with a chain of laundries. When Marshall heard Louise was two-timing him, he shot off a telegram: "Next time bring your little Paley and shovel." Marshall's anger subsided, and he took her back, but only temporarily. "He had given up all thoughts of marrying me," Brooks later wrote. "He had repossessed me for reasons of pride and jealousy, but now, viewed in a sensible light, I threatened to become an expensive burden."

Paley was exceedingly proud of his fling with Louise Brooks. Not only did he boast about it later in life, he expressed a touching gratitude to her privately. Perhaps he had a lingering sense of guilt, since he had ruined her prospective marriage. Twenty-five years later, according to Brooks, after hearing that she was living in poverty, he arranged for the Paley Foundation, which he set up in 1936, to provide her with $400 a month for life, thus ensuring her some degree of comfort and security. The foundation shows no record of this expenditure, and such a stipend would seem to violate its purpose, which is to aid organizations involved in education, cultural programs, and health. Whether from his own pocket or through his official philanthropy, Paley managed to get the funds to her.

The late 1920s and early 1930s were the pivotal years of Paley's life. With every success, his confidence grew. At work, the admiration of his subordinates became tinged with awe. They were impressed by his brain-power, dynamism, and winning way with people. "He was very energetic, a brilliant mind, a quick thinker," said Howard Barlow. Paley's charm was apparent throughout the ranks. "He was always glad to see you. He would look at you in a frank, happy way," said Helen Sioussat, an early recruit for the public affairs department. "He was accessible and understanding. He knew every employee by first name," said John "Jap" Gude, who worked in the publicity department. At one point in those early days Paley distributed vitamins to the entire staff so they could take one every day. But "he was in no sense bossy," said Gude. His enthusiasm infected everybody, and they worked hard to please him.

Edward Bernays offered the most insightful assessment of the Columbia's president's emerging executive persona:

A poker face is often a sign of insecurity, usually covering unwillingness to face unpleasant situations. Paley appeared to retreat before matters needing pat decisions. After a year's experience with him I never knew how his decisions were arrived at—whether he communed with nature, whether earthly advisers directed him, whether he flipped a coin or whether he was possessed of innate wisdom and intuitive judgment. Whatever his methods, they led to success. His closer colleagues confided to me that they never felt he exerted authority in their presence. Paley never threw his weight around in public. Like other men with his personality traits, he used a "trigger man" when he wanted to exercise decision. I felt that native shrewdness made up for a lack of intellectual grasp of the realities he was dealing with. And that practical considerations played a more important role than ideological ones.

These were all essential Paley traits—the insecurity, the deliberative and somewhat secretive decision making, the reluctance to display his power overtly, the overriding pragmatism—that would define his style at CBS over the decades.

Not a day seemed to pass at CBS without Paley making some sort of deal with a performer or affiliate or advertiser. These were the building years, the happiest of his life, he often said. "They gave me more day by day pleasure than I've ever had. It was easy because we had a very small organization and I had to make almost all the decisions, and that was very easy and very quick and it wasn't very complicated." Even though he worked anywhere from twelve to sixteen hours most days, he was continuously invigorated. "Sleep didn't mean anything to me," he said. "There was a drive, a kind of aspiration to succeed. It never has been the same. You undertook the impossible and found that it worked." He also reveled in being on his own for the first time. "I developed a high sense of responsibility for the success of CBS that I had seldom been called upon to have when working for my father . . . I no longer had my father or Uncle Jay looking over my shoulder."

From July 1928 to December, Columbia's revenues had tripled, and the total for the year was $1.6 million. However, revenues could not possibly keep pace with Paley's rapid expansion. Although Columbia had broken into the black in August, it ended the year with a deficit of $172,655. Paley knew he needed additional funds to keep his dream going.

Initially he drew from his family and friends as well as his own fortune. At the end of 1928 he bought an additional thousand shares of Columbia stock for $200,000, bringing his personal investment to around
$600,000 and his ownership to 61 percent. With another $300,000 from
the Paleys and Levys, he bought WABC and financed his expanded program schedule. Six months later he took out two loans—totaling $125,000
—from the Chemical Bank & Trust Company. Still, it was not enough.

Strapped for cash, and with the opening of Columbia's fancy new
headquarters scheduled for July, Paley was receptive when the head of
Paramount-Famous-Lasky Corporation, Adolph Zukor, sent an emissary
in the late spring of 1929 to talk about a partnership. For several years the
big Hollywood studios had been simultaneously intrigued by and apprehensive about radio. As its popularity grew, movie moguls worried that
prospective moviegoers might prefer listening to the box in their living
rooms. It seemed sensible to try to control this potential competitor.

Zukor and other studio executives were also becoming concerned
about the potential of television, still in its technological infancy. General
Electric, RCA, AT&T, and Westinghouse were experimenting with the
new medium, and its arrival seemed imminent. The movie companies,
which only recently had introduced sound to the movie screen, saw television as an opportunity as well as a threat. They were especially wary of
RCA, which not only owned the NBC networks but had invested in the
RKO movie studio. If only in self-defense, Zukor and other moguls were
eager to have an alliance with radio.

William Fox, who had a controlling stake in MGM, actually beat
Zukor to Paley's door early in 1929. Fox lorded over Paley at dinner and
in a meeting in Fox's office. "We'll make you into something," he told
him. Suitably intimidated, Paley handed over all of Columbia's books to
Fox's financial men. After several weeks, Fox offered to buy a half-interest
in Columbia for $503,000, precisely the amount Paley had paid six months
earlier. Infuriated, Paley stalked out of Fox's office. Fox had pegged him a
fool, and Paley resolved to have no further dealings with him.

There is no doubt the encounter with Fox stiffened Paley's spine. In
his subsequent dealings with Zukor, he showed not only an aptitude for
high finance but a relentless and fearless negotiating style. Paley was so
adamant, in fact, that he risked a rupture with his father and Uncle Jay.

Paley's account of his negotiations with Paramount bristles with boldness. He told it many times at fashionable dinner parties and described it
in self-congratulatory detail in his memoir. His gambit was demanding $5
million for a half-interest in Columbia and then refusing to negotiate. In
separate conversations, his Uncle Jay and his father called him stubborn
and arrogant for rebuffing a Paramount offer of $4.5 million. The same

Bill Paley who had meekly sought his father's approval to buy the Columbia network less than a year earlier had become defiant. Although still beholden to his father financially, Paley had been infected by the power of ownership. No longer was he adhering to the "family tradition" that "prevented either of us from knowingly giving offense to the other." Faced with his father's objections, Paley said, "You can think I'm stubborn and arrogant if you want to, but I have figured out what I want to do. I have the right to say yes or no to Paramount, and my answer is no."

Finally, Zukor agreed to try negotiating with Paley himself. Zukor was twice Paley's age and the most powerful of the Hollywood moguls. Paramount controlled such stars as Mary Pickford, Douglas Fairbanks, and Rudolph Valentino, as well as a chain of a thousand theaters—which Paley once said were "spread like a monster blanket over the country." Zukor brought a dozen staff members to his meeting with Paley. The Columbia president came alone. Paley delighted in recalling his surprise to see that his adversary was no more than five feet tall and "walked with his feet turned in." Zukor tried flattery and cajolery, but Paley stuck with his price. "Don't call it stubborn. Call it conviction," he recalled having said shortly before Zukor agreed to the price of $5 million.

By Paley's account, he triumphed over Zukor in every way. In fact their agreement, signed in June 1929, was evenly balanced. Since Columbia stock was privately held—it would not be listed on the New York Stock Exchange until 1937—Paley deserves credit for forcing Paramount to place a value on the company far greater than he had paid the previous year. But Paley was thwarted in his effort to have Paramount pay cash for its half of Columbia. Zukor prevailed with his insistence on paying with Paramount stock. Paramount gave Columbia 58,823 shares of Paramount stock—then valued at $65 a share, or $3.8 million. On March 1, 1932, Zukor would pay CBS $85 a share—or $5 million—to buy back the Paramount stock given to Columbia in 1929. The deal in effect permitted Paramount to delay paying for its half of CBS for nearly three years.

There was one additional condition that Paley said he devised, although other accounts said it was imposed by Zukor. During the period from September 8, 1929, through September 6, 1931, Columbia had to earn a net profit of at least $2 million. If Columbia fell short of the goal, Paramount would not have to buy back its stock; Columbia could keep the Paramount stock and sell it for whatever price it could fetch on the open market. Whether Paramount paid the deferred $5 million to Columbia or not, Paramount would still control half of Columbia's 150,000 shares of stock.

Paley never disclosed the other features of the agreement. It required Columbia to give Paramount one free hour of broadcast time on any weeknight except Saturday for five years. And it compelled Paley to sign a five-year employment contract for his services as Columbia's president at $40,000 a year, plus a bonus of 2.5 percent of Columbia's net profits (after taxes) up to $600,000, and 5 percent of any net profits over $600,000. Thus, if Columbia were to make $1 million in annual net profits, Paley stood to make $95,000 in that year.

In light of this contract, it seems somewhat peculiar that Zukor would have made a subsequent approach that looms large in the Paley legend. According to Paley, Zukor offered him a job as his assistant at Paramount for $450,000 a year plus a bonus of $150,000. Although Paley was fond of Zukor—and mightily impressed that he was "not the least bit self-conscious about the extraordinary luxuries with which he surrounded himself"—he said he turned down the extravagant offer because his ambitions were in broadcasting.

Yet the very partnership he struck with Paramount carried the risk of extinguishing his broadcasting dreams. Given the amount of money he had already spent, selling half of the company had become essential for Columbia's survival. All his justifications at the time made sense. It was better, he said in the fall of 1929, for the two entertainment titans to avoid competition by joining together "in a master combination of direction, facilities, talent and resources." In television, Paley said, "Columbia can lean on Paramount for the new problems entailing actual stage presentations in full costume to be broadcast, and Paramount knows it has an outlet in presenting its television features to the public."

Although he didn't say so at the time, Paley was nervous enough about having "all our eggs in one basket, if something went wrong with radio," to welcome the security of associating with a larger, more successful company. That Paley would have agreed to sell half of Columbia a mere nine months after buying it shows he was unwilling to chance much in those days. The fact remains that on a crucial day in June 1929, Paley ceded considerable power and risked losing control of his fledgling network.

6

THE STOCK MARKET crash four months later intensified the pressure on Paley to earn $2 million in profits by his deadline in 1931. The market value of Paramount stock had plummeted to $10 a share. If CBS had to sell that stock on the open market, it would realize only about $600,000 instead of the $5 million the company stood to make under the agreement with Paramount. Moreover, Paley's own bonuses were linked to CBS profits. The clock was ticking. Paley's overriding goal was to make as much money as he could, as fast as possible. He pandered to listeners with more and more mindless programs, from fortune-tellers to gory thrillers, and he permitted commercial messages on CBS to become louder, more insistent, and more numerous.

These were desperate times of rising unemployment and plummeting wages. Yet radio was proving itself one of the few Depression-proof businesses. Listeners flocked to escapist entertainment, and advertisers saw in the radio audience an opportunity to build demand for their products and prop up sagging profits. By 1932 there were 12,546 commercial interruptions in 2,365 hours of programming on NBC and CBS. More time was filled by advertisements that year than was devoted to news, education, lectures, and religion.

Leading this eager exploitation of the airwaves was George Washington Hill, president of American Tobacco. The flamboyant Hill always appeared in his office wearing a hat from an eclectic collection that included a sombrero festooned with fishhooks, a knox crusher covered with trout flies, and a jaunty tyrolean. Each morning he rode to work down Fifth Avenue with a bodyguard in a Cadillac convertible decorated with packages of Lucky Strike cigarettes. Hill believed passionately in the power of advertising, the more irritating and repetitive the better. He was tyrannical, domineering, and crude, and Paley desperately wanted his business for CBS.

American Tobacco was NBC's biggest advertiser. But Paley's decorous rival wouldn't allow Hill to use his most obnoxious sales pitches. Seeing an opening, Paley asked Edward Bernays to arrange a meeting with Hill. The thought of facing this formidable man terrified Paley. After a sleepless night, he arrived wearing his darkest, most conservative suit. Hill sat at his desk with a cowboy hat pulled low over his eyes and initially ignored Paley, who later admitted to feeling like "an ill-clothed scarecrow." Paley finally screwed up the courage to urge Hill to advertise American Tobacco's Cremo cigars on CBS. The young network president offered an array of program ideas; Hill shot each of them down.

It took Paley several days to figure out the key to his eccentric adversary: Hill only took to an idea if he thought it was his own. When Paley called again, he had devised a cunning ruse to win Hill over. He requested a meeting, ostensibly to discuss a charitable cause. After the two men had covered Paley's bogus agenda, Hill asked Paley if he had any more ideas. Offhandedly, Paley said that he had conceived a program of military music that would appeal to men—cigar-smoking men. But he had decided that the idea wasn't right for Cremo. Faced with Paley's seeming indifference, Hill seized on the notion, summoned his minions, and marched around the office to show his enthusiasm. In a matter of months Arthur Pryor's band was playing six nights a week on CBS under the banner of Cremo.

Whatever Hill wanted, Paley gave him, no matter how brassy or crude the message. "There is no spit in Cremo," blared the announcement on CBS. In 1932, Paley capitulated to Hill completely. Breaking the self-imposed network prohibition on mentioning prices on the air, Paley allowed Cremo to declare that its cigars cost only five cents. Characteristically, Paley tried to mute this cheapening of the medium by announcing at the same time a reduction in the length of advertising messages. NBC initially opposed the move, but soon permitted prices on its airwaves as well.

Regardless of what Paley or his counterparts at NBC said about the impact of radio, the country's producers of goods and services—the George Washington Hills of the world—wanted to know more precisely the size and composition of the radio audience. They needed proof that radio advertising was persuasive. Back in 1930 the Association of National Advertisers had devised the first audience rating system, a survey called the Crossley Report. It was based on telephone polls of several thousand people who were asked to recall the programs they had listened to.

The results devastated CBS. NBC could claim nearly all of the most popular shows. "Amos 'n' Andy" had 53 percent of the listening audience. The second most popular show was NBC's "Rudy Vallee Varieties," with 36.5 percent. Only two CBS shows registered ratings higher than 3.3. As Paley later recalled, "When it had been impossible to say with authority how many people were listening to any program, CBS had been doing quite well competitively against NBC. Now sponsors could think that their programs on CBS were simply wafting off into the air." The Crossley numbers "threatened, if not to put us out of business, then to deprive us of success as defined in the Paramount contract." Paley fought back in the manner he knew best, by rewriting the rules of the game with his own rating system.

It was actually the invention of Paul Kesten, Paley's man in charge of promotion, who designed what he called an "audit" of the Crossley survey. He hired the accounting firm of Price Waterhouse to send out 240,000 postcards to radio owners in 67 cities asking which radio station they listened to most. CBS received 40,000 replies, and not surprisingly reported that CBS affiliates were listened to more frequently than other stations. Kesten's slick presentation of these results impressed advertisers enough to cast doubt on Crossley as the final word.

NBC executives cried foul, with some validity. They pointed out numerous inaccuracies. They emphasized that Crossley was conducted independently of the networks while the Price Waterhouse survey was paid for by CBS. The CBS survey was in fact slanted. It covered only cities with CBS stations and ignored cities such as Springfield, Massachusetts, and Schenectady, New York, in which NBC had powerful stations and CBS had no affiliates. But NBC's objections came too late to counter the ingenious stroke. CBS did not need to supplant Crossley. All that was necessary to restore the network's credibility was a draw. Out of this popularity contest grew a mania for ratings that would eventually dominate radio and television broadcasting.

The Price Waterhouse results helped push advertising sales for the CBS network in 1931 to $14.5 million. By the autumn of that year, it was clear that Paley would meet the terms of the $2 million "success clause" in the contract with Paramount. CBS profits from August 1929 to September 1931 amounted to $2.9 million—a sum that incidentally gave Paley a tidy bonus of $101,000 on top of his $40,000 annual salary and $107,082 in stock dividends. Paley knew that Paramount, after its terrible dive in the Depression, could not possibly afford to pay $85 a share to buy back its stock. He had earlier sold off $1 million worth of the Paramount stock to raise capital, so Paramount now had to come up with $4 million for the remaining 48,000 shares held by CBS—the price set by the agreement between CBS and Paramount in 1929.

At first Paramount asked for a three-year extension and Paley nearly buckled under Adolph Zukor's insistence. Then Zukor made an offer Paley could not refuse. CBS could buy back the 63,250 shares of CBS stock owned by Paramount for $5.2 million. Paramount would thereby have the $4 million necessary to buy its own stock back from CBS, with a tidy $1.2 million profit besides. Most important for Bill Paley, he would regain operating control of CBS.

But there was one small problem: CBS did not have the cash to pull off the deal. Enter Paley's well-connected friend, Herbert Bayard Swope, former editor of the *New York World*. In January 1932, Swope brought Paley into the ornate, wood-paneled offices of Brown Brothers Harriman at 59 Wall Street to meet with two of the investment company's partners, Prescott Bush (later U.S. Senator from Connecticut and father of George Bush) and Averell Harriman. Paley explained to them that he and his associates could only raise half of the $5.2 million needed to buy back the CBS stock. With Harriman's encouragement, Bush agreed to round up the remaining $2.5 million. Lehman Brothers and Brown Brothers each agreed to put up half a million, Field Glore & Co. chipped in a quarter million, and the rest came from various private investors. Swope, who brokered the deal, was hoping for a financial cut. Instead, Paley gave him a seat on the CBS board and some stock options. Prescott Bush secured a CBS directorship as well.

Paley's version of these events is distorted in his usual way. By his account, he offered to buy the CBS stock from Paramount for "the same amount that Paramount owed us, namely $4 million." When Paramount insisted on more, Paley claimed to have stood firm, not only against John D. Hertz, chairman of Paramount's finance committee, but Paramount's investment banker, Otto Kahn. There is no question, however, that even by paying $5.2 million Paley profited handsomely from the deal. He now personally owned 40 percent of CBS's stock—itself worth $4 million.

Throughout this period, Paley's counterparts at NBC were learning how slippery an opponent he could be. In 1935 he plucked off some choice NBC affiliated stations, violating an understanding between the networks not to raid each other's stations. This gentleman's agreement between Paley and David Sarnoff had been advantageous to NBC, which as the older of the networks had the more powerful string of stations. The raid, in Paley's view, was a necessity.

Paley's executive in charge of station affiliation since 1929, Sam Pickard, had proved to be a slick wheeler dealer. Paley saw him as "a dapper fellow, usually soft and quiet, but also shrewd." As a former Federal Radio commissioner, Pickard had persuaded his old colleagues to permit more powerful transmitters for a number of CBS affiliates, giving them greater reach. He also engaged in some shady dealings by becoming a part owner of several CBS-affiliated stations. For a time, Paley tolerated these conflicts of interest but then thought better of it and asked Pickard to leave his job. Paley did permit the well-connected Pickard to stay at the network, however, in another capacity. When Pickard's part ownership of WOKO, CBS's Albany, New York, affiliate, later came to light, WOKO lost its license to operate.

In April 1935, Paley summoned Pickard's replacement, Herbert Ackerberg, to his office. The dour, chain-smoking Ackerberg specialized in the sort of high-pressure salesmanship needed for the campaign Paley was planning. Ackerberg's mission was to go to Detroit and meet with George Richards, the owner of WJR, a strong station affiliated with NBC. Richards was an unsavory character, an overt anti-Semite who said Jews were Communists and ordered his newscasters not to read items favorable to Roosevelt. Some years earlier, Richards had given Father Charles E. Coughlin, the Anti-Semitic priest, his first radio pulpit. Paley, pragmatic as ever, was prepared to ignore these unpleasantries. He needed WJR to strengthen the CBS lineup. Ackerberg was to offer Richards $1.5 million to buy WJR; failing that, he was empowered to give higher compensation —the money CBS paid its stations for carrying sponsored network programs—as an inducement to switch affiliation from NBC to CBS.

Richards agreed to the affiliation switch without even giving NBC the chance to make a counteroffer. Sarnoff and his subordinates were infuriated by this breach of network protocol. In a conversation with Richard Patterson, a vice-president of NBC, Paley by turns feigned indignation that he would be accused of breaking the rules and then tried to turn the tables on his accusers. He claimed that NBC had voided the protocol by stealing CBS's affiliate in Norfolk, Virginia. When Patterson assured Paley that Norfolk had approached NBC, Paley replied, "It's just a case of technicalities. You have broken the agreement, and I won't be satisfied until I am even." Paley then claimed it had been Richards's idea to bolt NBC. "If you have gotten even, are you going to continue to raid our stations?" Patterson asked. Paley adroitly ignored the question and asked Patterson what NBC's position was. When Patterson said NBC had no plans to raid CBS stations, Paley growled, "This is the first I have heard of it." Patterson was flummoxed.

In subsequent months, the dimensions of Paley's campaign unfolded. Ackerberg signed up George Richards's other station, WGAR in Cleveland. He approached Powel Crosley, Jr., owner of WLW in Cincinnati, the most influential station in the Midwest, with a stunning offer: membership on the CBS board of directors, CBS stock, and generous payments for carrying sponsored CBS programs. Other key NBC stations, including WSB in Atlanta and WSM in Nashville, were subject to frequent entreaties from Ackerberg, always with promises of more money than NBC paid. NBC ultimately headed off most of the defections by raising its payments to stations. When Sarnoff eventually complained to Paley about CBS's conduct, Paley could only say, "Mr. Sarnoff, radio broadcasting is a highly competitive business."

When Paley wasn't wooing advertisers and NBC stations, he prowled the nightclubs and Broadway theaters for performers to put on his network. Although relatively inexperienced, he had good instincts about what made a program work and who could draw a large radio audience. His programming sense may well have originated in his early teens when he had a summer job selling candy at a Chicago theater. Week after week he saw hits and flops, and he could ponder what made the difference. For all his new sophisticated airs and quest for quality in his personal life, Paley retained some common tastes. "I am not a highbrow," he once said. "I do not look down on popular taste. Oftentimes popular taste is my taste."

He best described his approach to CBS programming in a 1934 interview. A radio program, he said, "must appeal to either the emotions or the self-interest" of the listener, "not merely to his intellect." Radio broadcasters "cannot calmly broadcast programs we think people ought to listen to if they know what is good for them."

Paley first spotted Morton Downey at Delmonico's club on Park Avenue. Downey was already well known on the nightclub circuit, and Paley figured his soft tenor would work well on CBS. Downey drew more fan mail than any other performer on CBS at the time. (Fifty years later, Morton Downey, Jr., would become one of television's most controversial talk show hosts.) And at a party at the home of Mona Williams, a beautiful New York socialite, Paley was captivated by Fats Waller, who played the piano and sang. Paley's program executives worried that Waller's music sounded like a "whorehouse piano," but Paley signed him up anyway and he was a hit. Often over the objections of other more experienced colleagues, Paley brought other little-known vocalists—the Mills Brothers, the Boswell Sisters, Kate Smith—to national radio.

Paley's prize catch was Bing Crosby. Although the baritone crooner was a star on Decca Records at the time, Paley had not heard him until June 1931, when he was traveling to Europe on the S.S. *Europa*. Restless as always, Paley had a habit of pacing the deck each morning. On one of his rounds he heard Crosby's voice on a portable phonograph. He sent a wire to CBS with orders to sign up Crosby. Edward Klauber, Paley's second-in-command, wired back that he was working on it and noted encouragingly that Crosby was a "Pacific coast ballad sensation and appeals [to] both sexes." But when Paley returned to New York later that summer his program executives had failed to act. Crosby had a drinking problem, they explained, and was considered unreliable. Paley overrode them all, hired Crosby to do six fifteen-minute broadcasts a week at 11:00 P.M., and agreed to pay him an extravagant $1,500 a week when $100 was customary.

True to predictions, Crosby failed to appear for his first broadcast. At Paley's insistence, CBS nervously rescheduled Crosby a few days later.

That evening, Paley was on Long Island in a rented home without a radio. Out in the garage, he tuned in from his car. "Crosby was awful," he recalled. Paley dashed back to the house and called the studio. Crosby was drunk, as Paley suspected, and two men were holding him up as he tried pathetically to sing. "Change the program, get him off," Paley shouted. The power he felt at this moment made him giddy; years later he would say, "Think of it. I could even change a program while it was on the air!" But Paley stubbornly refused to let Crosby go. He assigned the singer a round-the-clock guard to prevent him from drinking. "It worked," said Paley. "He knew his job was at stake."

The most popular programs at the time were still those featuring comedians, and CBS introduced many of the best: George Burns and Gracie Allen, Goodman and Jane Ace, Jack Benny, Fred Allen. More often than not, once a comedian established himself on CBS, the advertiser would take him over to the larger and more powerful NBC networks. But Paley kept bringing comic performers to CBS. He traveled across country to entice Will Rogers to join the network. Rogers had no use for radio; he thought it cold and impersonal. Paley coaxed and cajoled, and finally won Rogers over by promising a studio audience to help create the warmth and intimacy he needed for his shows.

For all of Paley's efforts, NBC still had the five most popular shows in the 1934–35 season. In 1936, Paley opened the CBS purse strings and staged his first talent raid. He captured Al Jolson, Nelson Eddy, and Major Edward Bowes, three of NBC's top performers. While it was considered fair play when an advertiser took its star to a better position on NBC, Paley's raids violated an understanding between CBS and NBC not to make direct approaches to each other's personnel.

Paley's scheme to capture Bowes was typical. Bowes ran an amateur hour that had become a national sensation. The Major was an avuncular sort who touched his audience with the warm questions he asked of contestants preparing to yodel or sing or play the harmonica. Then he would tickle listeners by gleefully ringing a gong that signaled failure for the hapless performers. Although Paley thought the program "cruel," he wanted it on his network.

To cultivate the Major, the CBS president became a regular at the NBC studio where Bowes broadcast his show. While NBC executives could guess his intention, they could hardly eject him from the premises. Whenever Bowes threw a party after the program, Paley was there. Before long, Paley's persistence paid off and he persuaded Bowes that he could do better on CBS. Paley knew Bowes was about to switch his sponsorship to the Chrysler Corporation, and he began dropping in on Walter Chrysler as well. Gently but insistently Paley convinced Chrysler that Bowes belonged on CBS, which was more energetic, ambitious, and fast-moving than NBC.

Paley had become a bona fide impresario. He lavished attention on his performers and entertained them at elaborate dinner parties. He greatly preferred the company of those on the "creative" side to that of his executives. But his attentiveness was also calculated: keep them happy and keep them on CBS.

Paley became an expert in the art of seduction. His courtship of Frank Hummert, the decade's most prolific and influential producer of daytime soap operas, was a case in point. In the early 1930s, Hummert and his wife, Anne, churned out serial melodramas that ran during the daytime hours and caught fire with a huge audience of housewives. These dramas, the models for today's television soap operas, portrayed the domestic crises of ordinary people. During the 1930s the Hummerts produced half of the serials on network radio. "It was very important to have Frank Hummert on your side," said Paley. "He was so powerful. If he said he wanted a program to go on NBC or on CBS, that was it. We fought to get him."

Twice a month, Paley dutifully met for lunch with Hummert and his wife at the Park Lane Hotel. For all his understanding of the mind of the housewife, Hummert was something of a misanthrope. He always insisted that they be shielded from the other diners by potted ferns. While Hummert picked at a plate of raw vegetables, Paley turned on his famous soft sell, plying him with questions about his programs. Paley managed to flatter Hummert and simultaneously learn a great deal about which programming formulas worked and which did not.

"I think he liked my style," Paley said later. "I never pressed him hard for anything. In a paternal sort of way he would tell me what I wanted to know. I hardly ever talked business directly with him. He just placed his productions where he wanted to, and from what I got from him, I think he favored me."

7

S HE HAD A DAZZLING, dimpled smile. Her wide brown eyes, fringed with long black lashes, sparkled with intelligence and spirit. Her brown wavy hair brushed the nape of her neck. She had a perfectly proportioned figure, with a tiny waist and narrow hips. Her legs curved elegantly down to slender ankles and size five feet. Not only was Dorothy Hart Hearst ravishing, she was breathtakingly chic. On a summer day at New York's fashionable Colony Restaurant on 61st and Madison, she turned heads when she arrived wearing a closely tailored black dress and a large black straw hat adorned with a white flower.

Throughout his life, Bill Paley was a man of instant infatuations. When he first saw Dorothy across a luncheon table one Sunday afternoon in 1931, he fell hopelessly in love. It was a suitably romantic setting—a tiny house called Alley Pond in the woods on Long Island's north shore. He was twenty-nine and only tenuously attached to a rather ordinary young woman he was keeping in a New York apartment. Dorothy, just twenty-three, had been married for three years to John Randolph Hearst, the third son of the publisher William Randolph Hearst. Typically, Paley viewed her marriage as a trifling impediment once he determined he would have her.

Dorothy was born on February 25, 1908, in Los Angeles, the only child of Seth and Dorothy Jones Hart. Hers was an all-American heritage, and on the surface Seth and Dorothy brought up their daughter in predictable upper-middle-class comfort. The Harts had a maid and two cars, and summered at a house in Hermosa Beach. But neither of Dorothy's parents was entirely standard. Both had forceful personalities and fostered strong ideas that they impressed upon their daughter.

Dorothy Jones Hart was a lively and independent character, a marvelous storyteller and a voracious reader. She had an ebullient sense of humor and intense curiosity. A devoted wife and homemaker, she nevertheless believed women should have a more important place in the world, and Seth deferred to her on nearly every important decision about their life together. She selected her daughter's school and closely supervised her upbringing, with an eye to teaching her how to capture and please a man. She also introduced Dorothy to a variety of Protestant denominations, including Christian Science and New Thought. "Nothing took," Dorothy recalled. "I ended up having no religion at all."

Although he could not be called weak, Seth Hart was easygoing enough to give his wife the independence she needed. He was something of a free spirit, neither as socially ambitious nor as acquisitive as his wife. He was a quiet man who ran his own insurance business in Los Angeles and read all he could on the issues of the day. His daughter adored him, and thought him the "best-informed man I have ever known." He called her "Pete" to compensate for not having had a son. He brought her around to automobile factories, taught her about mechanics, discussed politics with her. When he voted—always straight-line Republican—he took her along.

Dorothy looked back on her childhood as pleasant and stimulating, but in many respects, her parents never treated her like a child. Nothing was considered over her head. From the time she was five years old, she joined the adult world.

When Dorothy was in elementary school, her family moved to Dayton, Ohio, for three years while her father tried to start a new business selling equipment to the Army. Dorothy loved living in a small town where life was simple and easy, but her mother found the atmosphere confining. At every opportunity she took her daughter to Chicago to shop and go to the theater. Her mother had been dragging her to amateur theatricals from the time she was a toddler. At age eleven, Dorothy visited New York with her mother for the first time, and they went to the theater day and night.

When the family returned to Los Angeles, Dorothy attended Marlboro, at that time the city's most exclusive girls' school. "Dorothy's parents knew what they had on their hands. Her father adored her. He took all his dough and invested it in this girl. It was a practical decision," said Irene Selznick, who as a rather sheltered girl used to watch Dorothy from afar. Marlboro encouraged its students to perform community service once a month at a children's hospital. There Dorothy developed an activism that she would carry through her life. While she loved her time at Marlboro, she was something of a loner because her interests in politics and world affairs were so much more sophisticated than those of her peers. At her father's urging, she read the five-year plan for the Soviet Union when she was sixteen years old—an achievement no other Marlboro girl could match.

Still, Dorothy was molded more by her mother's social aspirations than her father's academic ambitions. After Marlboro she spent only one year at Bennett College, a fancy Eastern finishing school. "One didn't think of a career," she noted. "What the hell, women didn't have careers then." Her one passion was art. She had always loved to draw, and she took as many art history courses as she could.

Back in Los Angeles, Dorothy Hart became the belle of her social set. "She was one of the most beautiful girls in Southern California," Irene Selznick recalled. "She could stop traffic. Every Friday night at the Coconut Grove, all eyes were on her." The summer after her eighteenth birthday Dorothy was sailing off Santa Barbara on *The Invader,* a yacht owned by Don Lee—the Cadillac dealer who would give Bill Paley such a hard time—when she met Jack Hearst. He was as slender and handsome as she was beautiful. He captivated her with his shy charm, and they began seeing each other. Jack's brainpower was substantially less than Dorothy's. At a time when a fortune of Hearst magnitude could easily secure a spot in an Ivy League college for an underachieving son, the best W.R. could do for Jack was Oglethorpe University in Atlanta. Before he left for his freshman year, Jack proposed and Dorothy accepted. Her parents were opposed at first. William Randolph Hearst, for all his riches, was socially unacceptable. Not only did he have a mistress, the actress Marion Davies, but he flaunted the liaison. W.R. was quite taken with Dorothy and did not oppose the match. His wife, however, thought Dorothy and Jack were too young.

The young couple ultimately secured their parents' permission—which they needed as both were underage—and were married in New York in December 1927. Instead of their planned European honeymoon, they joined the holiday whirl in New York, spending every evening at the theater and nightclubs. Life in Atlanta was dull by comparison, and at the end of the school year Jack dropped out of college. Back in New York after a trip to Europe, they settled into the Lombardy Hotel while Jack joined the Hearst Corporation to learn about magazines. Dorothy and Jack were regulars at "21" and other speakeasies. They were out on the town virtually every night.

Jack, however, was sinking at his father's company. He knew he had entered the ranks at too high a level and felt uncomfortable. He began to drink heavily. Dorothy went to his father and begged for a transfer to a small Hearst paper, away from New York, where Jack could learn the business from the ground up. W.R. refused. Jack's drinking worsened, and he worked less and less.

In an effort to shame him into applying himself, Dorothy found a job at *Harper's Bazaar,* first in the fashion section, then as the head of the cosmetics department. She was in her element. She had her own office and an assistant, and she wrote a monthly column. But her success only made Jack's condition worse. From the time she began working, he rarely got up in the morning, and when he did he was hung over.

Dorothy's marriage was shaky, to say the least, when she met Bill Paley. While he didn't sweep her off her feet, she was struck by his curiosity, enthusiasm, and attentiveness. Here, she thought, was a man with enormous sex appeal. His only problem was he needed a new tailor—"I thought he dressed like a 105-year-old man." His sartorial idol—it stood to reason that he would have one—was Anthony Drexel Biddle, a middle-aged sportsman.

In June 1931, Dorothy and Jack sailed for a European vacation on the S.S. *Europa*. Joining them on board were Dorothy's close friend Marjorie Oelrichs (a New York beauty said by *Vogue* to have "waxen skin and eyebrows like butterflies' antennae," who would later marry the pianist Eddy Duchin), Larry Lowman—and Bill Paley. "He got on that boat and didn't get off," said Irene Selznick. "I don't even know if he had any luggage. He was that determined to marry her."

In London they all stayed at the Savoy. Dorothy arranged for Bill to visit a new tailor on Savile Row, Kilgore & French. Once suitably outfitted, "he looked divine." The Hearsts took an impressive detour by visiting the Churchill family at Chartwell, their country home. Dorothy had met Winston and his son Randolph on a trip to New York, and she and Randolph had become good friends. At the time, young Churchill was a promising newspaper journalist. But like Jack Hearst he was a hard-drinking college dropout struggling to live in the shadow of a famous father. Arrogant and somewhat feckless, Randolph was nicknamed "Britain's ambassador of ill-will" by some American acquaintances.

From England the Hearsts journeyed to Berlin, where they rejoined Paley and his friends. Ronald Tree, a friend from England, watched Dorothy and Bill dancing one evening in a Berlin nightclub and later recalled that he had never seen anyone as beautiful as Dorothy was that night.

The five travelers drove through Germany to Salzburg where they stayed with the theater director Max Reinhardt, another friend of Dorothy's. There, in Reinhardt's Baroque castle on a lake, with its dark halls illuminated only by candles, things began coming apart. It was obvious to everyone, including Jack, that Dorothy and Bill were crazy about each other. Paley was constantly attentive to Dorothy. Jack turned to the bottle. Dorothy felt simultaneously drawn to Paley and guilt-stricken about Jack. Her nerves stretched to the breaking point, she collapsed and entered a Salzburg hospital.

When Dorothy and Jack returned to New York, she began sleeping with Paley. He was, she later said, "a perfectly good lover." Though not extraordinary, he had "maleness, an animal component, a sexual vitality." On any number of occasions she and Paley could be seen dancing to Eddy Duchin's music at the Central Park Casino. Jack didn't protest, but he insisted that she stay married to him. He was drunk constantly, which in turn drained her emotionally. "You have to get out of this," her doctor finally advised her. Dorothy took the train to Las Vegas to begin divorce proceedings. Just as she had finished her residency in Nevada, Jack arrived and pleaded with her not to file for divorce. Overcome by guilt, she returned to New York to give their marriage another try. It was a disaster. Five months later she was back in Las Vegas for the divorce.

On May 12, 1932, Dorothy and Bill Paley flew to Kingman, Arizona, where one could obtain a license—and marry on the spot—away from the glare of publicity. They stood before a judge and said their vows. Paley wore his usual navy blue suit. She was dressed in navy as well, a Hattie Carnegie wool suit with a short close-fitting jacket and A-line skirt. On her head was a jaunty navy blue straw beret. Her parents were displeased, in part because he was Jewish. "I don't think my father ever knew any Jews," she said. "He didn't welcome the idea of a Jew, but he also saw Bill as a grownup." Dorothy's mother objected less to Paley being Jewish. She was upset primarily because she had grown fond of Jack Hearst and found the stigma of divorce distasteful. Paley chose to ignore the nature of Seth Hart's initial displeasure and came to like his father-in-law. He never warmed to Dorothy's mother, however.

After a brief stop at the Santa Barbara Biltmore, the couple sailed for Hawaii, where Dorothy wept through the first few days of their honeymoon. She was still torn apart by the break-up with Jack. She knew Jack's alcoholism was serious—although his family refused to acknowledge it—and she felt she had deserted him. She had genuinely loved him and now, as she and Bill began their life together, she could not dismiss her distress. "It was not terribly easy for the new bridegroom," she said bluntly.

Paley tried to make the best of it, offering sympathy and understanding. After the initial anguish, they settled into a routine at the Royal Hawaiian Hotel. Paley threw himself into surfing lessons with such brio that he managed to bruise several ribs. When their two weeks were nearly over, they agreed that neither was ready to face the world and extended their stay for another week.

There had been many beautiful women in Bill Paley's life by the time he settled down with Dorothy at age thirty. He was known to cool on his women as quickly as he was inflamed by their first glance. What was it about Dorothy that broke this sybaritic spell and carried him to the altar? Part of the attraction was her connections. (Indeed, in his memoir, Paley identifies Dorothy only as the daughter-in-law of the man who owned the "famous newspaper chain.") Another factor was Paley's increasing frustration with bachelorhood. He felt it was time to settle down. Dorothy had self-confidence, a strong sense of likes and dislikes, and a clear and enviable style.

Although seven years his junior, Dorothy was more worldly than he. She knew her way around in sophisticated circles; friendships with men like Randolph Churchill counted a great deal to the ambitious Paley. In New York she joined the Algonquin set—the playwrights, journalists, and other intellectuals whose luncheon ripostes during the 1920s became a literary legend. She was brainy, and Paley—still diffident when expressing himself on weighty topics—admired her inquiring mind and strong opinions. And, like Paley, she was an outsider, just as intent as he on finding a comfortable niche within New York society.

Over the years Dorothy would have a significant impact on her husband—her political leanings, appetite for news, taste in art, and sense of style. She supported Franklin D. Roosevelt and embraced his proposals for social welfare. Both Dorothy and Bill had been raised Republican. His father had been conservative politically, with little tolerance for organized labor or governmental intervention. But Paley's political preferences became situational. He drifted toward what was convenient. When confronted with Dorothy's views, he quickly fell into line. "I can't imagine he would have voted Democrat without me," she said. As a wealthy entrepreneur, Paley believed in big business as unencumbered by regulation as possible. But he could feel comfortable with the Democratic Party in the early 1930s. The stock market crash of 1929 and ensuing Depression had discredited the Republicans. All his friends in the theater world, and others he admired like Averell Harriman, the aristocratic banker, and Herbert Bayard Swope, were die-hard Roosevelt supporters.

Dorothy introduced her husband to many Roosevelt liberals. She encouraged him to befriend people he would not ordinarily have cottoned to. "She would say, stick with him, you goddamned snob, you need him," recalled Selznick. Dorothy's social concerns embraced progressive education; assistance for the poor, the needy, and the sick; and equal rights for blacks. She brought to Paley's attention many political issues he might otherwise have missed.

Dorothy also led her husband into psychoanalysis, which had emerged as a new religion in the 1920s. Freud's theories had animated much of the libertinism of the decade and captured the fancy of intellectuals. In those circles, it was fashionable to undergo analysis. Dorothy was drawn to psychoanalysis both intellectually and personally. When she first came to New York, she had been almost as shy as Bill Paley. Although she never betrayed her feelings, she lacked self-confidence. She dove into analysis devoting fifty minutes each day to it, and found it liberating. It removed certain inhibitions and built up her self-esteem. Now she convinced Paley to try analysis as well. Although he did the standard daily session, he was never as interested as she was—probably because of his tendency to avoid introspection.

Dorothy's most enduring impact was on Paley's taste. When she first saw Bill Paley's glossy apartment, with its insipid collection of sporting prints, she was appalled. She could not believe how little cultural education he had: "He had no idea about Matisse before we met. He knew nothing." With her passion for art history, Dorothy set to work to help fill in the gaps, guiding him in a crucial way. "They were both eager, they had an appetite, they concentrated so," said Irene Selznick. "I got my first knowledge of art from them, from their walls, what they said together. Dorothy loved to teach, but she was learning too. She was avid for knowledge."

Like other business tycoons before him, Paley wanted to use some of his fortune to collect paintings; it was the most respected and socially prestigious hobby one could have. But unlike the financier J. P. Morgan, who was mocked for his ignorance of art when he began buying on his own, Paley sensibly recognized his limits. In the beginning, he relied on those more knowledgeable—professional art buyers as well as his own wife—to direct him. But, just as in business, Paley was reluctant to credit those who helped mold his taste, and has never acknowledged Dorothy's role.

Dorothy recalled taking him to Valentine Dudensing, a respected New York dealer, who sold Paley his first four paintings for around $2,000 apiece. They were by John Kane, a primitive artist who had been a coal miner and steelworker. Kane painted urban scenes as well as landscapes of great strength, and Bill was as captivated with his style as Dorothy was. The purchase whetted Paley's appetite. Thereafter he and Dorothy spent every Saturday visiting galleries. "He was a willing subject," said Dorothy. "He was a quick learner. Exposure was very important for him. It doesn't work with everyone but it worked with him. He learned by osmosis. He wouldn't make a study of anything, but he picked it up by exposure."

On a trip to Europe in the summer of 1935, Dudensing took Bill and Dorothy to several choice collections in Paris, including the Bernheim Gallery and the huge apartment of the dealer Paul Guillaume. They saw works by Cézanne, Derain, Picasso, Renoir, and Gauguin. Paley took a plunge by arranging with Dudensing to buy his first Cézanne, entitled *L'Estaque,* for $25,000. These Impressionist and Post-Impressionist artists were no longer avant-garde, nor were they yet popular. Astute American collectors had been buying their paintings for several decades. Among the wealthy buyers was the Harriman family of New York. Averell Harriman and his wife, Marie, were the Paleys' traveling companions that summer. Marie ran a gallery in New York, although Averell was the more serious collector. On a visit to the studio of André Derain, who was working on a portrait of Marie, the Paleys purchased two paintings. Dorothy bought one on the sly, a small study of a boy's head, that she later gave to her husband for his birthday. The other, of two Italian actors, entitled *The Rehearsal,* was unfinished when Paley spotted it. He insisted that Derain complete it and then bought it.

That, at least, is how Dorothy remembered events. In his memoir, Paley vividly described what he characterized as an "art hunt" that summer led by Averell Harriman—no mention of Dudensing or Dorothy or Marie. He recounted how he had found Derain's painting of the boy's head covered with grime, had urged Derain to clean it, and had then received it as a gift of friendship from the artist. Derain, according to Paley, had also finished *The Rehearsal* in his presence. The grimy-painting story is "just not true," according to Dorothy. "I gave him that painting." She agreed that Derain had to finish *The Rehearsal,* but "I can tell you it was not completed while Bill stood there." As to Paley's claim that "in the mid-thirties I would often visit the studio of André Derain," Dorothy could only recall their having been there once—and when it came to art buying, they were definitely a team in those days.

Paley's tales about his friendship with the brilliant Post-Impressionist Henri Matisse were similarly embroidered. His first Matisse purchase was in 1936, when he bought a marvelous *Odalisque* from the artist's son, Pierre, who had a gallery in Manhattan. During a subsequent visit to Paris, according to one dramatic Paley recollection, he was visiting the artist's apartment when he fell in love with a painting called *La Voilette (Woman with a Veil).* "Everybody in the world has been trying to buy this painting for years," said Matisse, according to Paley. To which Paley recalled replying, "There must come a time when you will want to sell and here I am and I want to buy it." Naturally, Matisse capitulated on the spot and sold the painting to Paley.

But Paley did not pluck *La Voilette* off Henri Matisse's wall. He bought it from Pierre Matisse at a Paris art exhibition in the summer of 1937. "I remember quite well that it was hanging at the exhibit in a sort of three-sided partition," said Dorothy. The conversation that Paley remembered could not have possibly occurred, according to Dorothy; Henri Matisse knew no English, and Paley spoke no French.

Dorothy was in a position to know such things, because that same summer Paley arranged with Pierre to have Matisse paint a portrait of her. For three weeks she spent every morning at the artist's apartment in Montparnasse while he did hundreds of charcoal sketches, each drawn in one continuous line. She spoke passable schoolgirl French, so they became pleasantly acquainted. At the end of the sessions, he gave her one of the drawings, dedicated (in French): "To Madam Dorothy Paley, your respectful servant, Henri Matisse 1937."

Paley claimed to have accompanied Dorothy each morning to the studio (no matter that Matisse did not have a studio per se, but painted in his living room). The artist was unable to paint Dorothy's portrait in oils, said Paley, because "he fell ill," and although Matisse promised to paint it the following year, "he never did do the painting." "That is all an absolute lie," countered Dorothy. "Bill never went with me to Matisse's apartment. He had no personal contact with Matisse whatsoever. All his arrangements were through Pierre. And Matisse didn't fall ill. We left Paris, and that's why he didn't do it. But the next summer we went back to Paris and Matisse spent a week trying to paint my portrait. He seated me on a sofa upholstered in cow-yellow and brown. It was awful. He kept moving me up and down the sofa. He finally gave up."

With each purchase, Paley's taste became more refined, although he was never a dedicated student along the lines of collectors such as Norton Simon. "He didn't always make the easiest selections, but I don't think he was adventurous," said Dorothy. He lacked the daring to find a brilliant unknown. Clearly he loved the range of Impressionists and Post-Impressionists; years later he said that he felt a sensuous connection to them. It obviously did not hurt that Averell Harriman and other role models had also placed their imprimatur on the Impressionists.

There is no doubt that Dorothy brought order and direction to the life of her husband. When she met him, he was incapable of coping with the details of living. As a bachelor, he only managed to speak with his cook once. He smoked four packs of Chesterfields a day, but he was always running out of cigarettes and constantly borrowing from friends. He frequently ran short of money and was forever putting the touch on his cronies for small amounts. He was oblivious to such matters as picking up the check in restaurants; he simply assumed it was somehow taken care of.

"There were lots of things he didn't know," said Dorothy. "Social things, for example. He learned that from me." She threw herself into her role as wife and hostess and was appropriately attentive. "It is not necessary for a man to bring his business home with him," she once told a newspaper interviewer. "An intelligent wife, if she helps her husband to relax and enjoy his free time, does him a great deal more good than she would by helping him worry about business." Irene Selznick noted that both Dorothy and her successor had one thing in common, "the monumental task of pleasing Bill."

Dorothy elevated and rarefied Paley's style of living. She got him out of his triplex apartment at the end of 1932, when they rented a five-story townhouse at 35 Beekman Place, a quiet enclave in the East Fifties that had recently become a fashionable colony for millionaires as well as artists and writers. The Paleys were so fond of Beekman Place that in 1934 they tore down another townhouse, number 29, and erected a six-story home in its place. Paley supervised the architecture—he later said he put his "heart and soul" into it—and Dorothy oversaw the interior design.

In 1937 they moved into what Irene Selznick called "that crazy narrow crystal house," a lavish, eclectic, and thoroughly modern home. One side of the small entrance hall was mirrored, as was one wall along the second-floor landing, to create an illusion of spaciousness. The gracefully curving staircase was covered with carpet made of zebra skins, an echo of the fashionable nightclub El Morocco. The drawing room had a maple floor stained black and defined by thin lines of brass inlay. The room was decorated entirely in a pale gray-blue and was filled with eighteenth-century English furniture. The Paleys' newly acquired paintings were illuminated by the latest Wendel lighting system—small spotlights concealed in moldings and end tables and operated by switches on a control panel. Propped on one table was Matisse's droll sketch of Dorothy Paley, chin resting on hand. Nearby were photographs of her by Cecil Beaton that he had signed in red ink. The library, with its sweeping river view from large windows, was painted a rich dark green. "It was all quite unique, and quite dazzling," said Irene Selznick.

In the European style, the Paleys kept separate bedrooms. The singular characteristic of his understated beige decor was a bedside table equipped with three telephones. Dorothy's room was dominated by a custom-designed four-poster bed with antique mirrors on the foot posts and on the exterior of the canopy. E. J. Kahn, in an article for the *New Yorker* in 1939, said the bed looked "as if a queen might have died in it." All the fabric in the room, including the bed and window draperies, was a pale, flesh-colored Scalamandre satin damask. Camellias grew in pots embedded in tables scattered about her room. Dorothy's dressing room and bathroom were mirrored from floor to ceiling, with pale pink marble to match the porcelain basins and bathtub.

Dorothy took her decorating seriously, but she was no Syrie Maugham. Her taste ran to the avant-garde, with occasional showy touches. To Bill, a man who had once had a silver barroom, Dorothy seemed to know what she was doing, and he went along with her schemes. But after only three years at 29 Beekman, Paley grew tired of the place. The reason, he later claimed, was that "it had no charm or warmth . . . it was antiseptic." More to the point, it may have seemed too nouveau riche for his aspirations. E. J. Kahn's description of the interior was filled with catty digs. Paley was furious with Kahn—who had drawn his impressions during a house tour for a charity when the Paleys were away—for violating his privacy, and refused to speak to the writer for years. Dorothy was crushed by Paley's decision to leave Beekman Place; she considered the house "my baby." But he was unyielding. In 1940 they moved to the Waldorf until they could find a home more to his liking.

Despite his reservations about the house on Beekman Place, Paley asked his wife to bring her rather exotic taste to the new CBS headquarters at 485 Madison Avenue. She gave the boardroom a fresh, sophisticated look with blue walls, black door frames, and English antique chairs upholstered in a soft floral pattern. The room doubled as a studio for talk shows when a panel at one end would slide open to reveal a control room behind a glass wall. In an atmosphere that seemed more like the living room of a country house than a recording studio, Dorothy reasoned, guests would be calmer and more effective. Paley's office showed her touches as well. She bought all the antique furniture, including a handsome desk chair covered in dark red leather. To some, her efforts seemed precious. Wrote Alice-Leone Moats, a writer who belonged to the Paley social set, "She has great roughnecks using little Louis XV desks that they can't get their legs under."

Of great importance to Paley's reputation was Dorothy's image as a trendsetter. "She was always ahead in color, style, clothes, food and decor. She was so expert in so many fields," said Irene Selznick. Dorothy headed the list of the world's ten best-dressed women, and her photograph appeared in Paley's favorite magazines, *Vogue* and *Harper's Bazaar*.

Bill Paley doted on his wife and thrilled to her confident spirit. "He was always very sweet and gentle to her and would give way to her," one of his colleagues said at the time. He was reasonably generous, selecting gifts he felt she would like. He bought her jewelry, but oddly, none of it had great intrinsic value. He did, however, give her two of her most treasured paintings—at her behest. On a visit to Paris she found a delicate pastel by Degas of three girls sitting on the grass, and he agreed to buy it for $10,000 sight unseen. Another time Bill and Dorothy saw two works by Rousseau at an exhibit. He liked one and she liked the other. He bought both and gave Dorothy the one she preferred.

Dorothy's friends were devoted to her and marveled at her cleverness. Dorothy became a mentor to Marietta Tree, granddaughter of the Brahmin rector of Groton School, Endicott Peabody, and to Irene Mayer, who had recently married Hollywood producer David O. Selznick. "She lavished knowledge and affection on me," said Irene Selznick, who was insecure about her lack of worldliness. "She let me feel that her time was at my disposal and raised my self-esteem a hundred points. She put me down a few pegs and enlightened me at the same time."

That method applied to Bill as well. Dorothy always appeared slightly superior in her attitude toward him. Her assertiveness seemed masculine at times. "There were warning signs from year one," Irene Selznick recalled. "I used to say to Dorothy, 'If I were Bill Paley I would kick you in the balls.' She could be charming and say 'darling' and do everything superbly, but she was also domineering and opinionated." To Diana Vreeland, then fashion editor of *Harper's Bazaar,* Dorothy was "a very cute nippy girl, and very smart. She never had two decisions on anything. She didn't give a damn about men. She was always surrounded by men though." If Paley was troubled by Dorothy's tendency toward high-handedness, he showed no sign of it. He was so keen to learn and so enchanted with her that he scarcely seemed to notice that she patronized him.

8

TO ALL OUTWARD APPEARANCES, Dorothy and Bill Paley were a dream couple—bright, handsome, young, eager, and very much in love. "There is no question in my mind that he was the love of my life," said Dorothy many years later. They shared boundless energy and restlessness; both rejected anything quiet or introspective. There were some glimmers of incompatibility, but by and large, their personalities appeared complementary. She was more interested in intellectual matters than he and enjoyed giving her views on a range of subjects. Bill was never a brilliant conversationalist, but he was a good listener. He had an appreciative sense of humor, while Dorothy could be witty in an offhand, sardonic fashion. After the Hollywood producer Walter Wanger lost his home in a fire, she wrote to him, "At the first blush it seems a major catastrophe, but if servants in California are what they are in New York and I understand that they are, then maybe the Lord did you a good turn and you can live in a hotel for the duration."

They seemed to be in a race with life—virtually every night of the week they were at Broadway openings, nightclubs, and dinner parties at the Central Park Casino. At El Morocco they came to see and be seen amid the white palms and zebra-striped banquettes; Marietta Tree recalled that the first evening she saw Paley at El Morocco, "he couldn't stop smiling. He was surrounded by beautiful women. He danced with all the women there. I remember him absolutely flying around the room as he danced." Dorothy and Bill loved Edith Piaf and went to hear her sing at every opportunity. They frequented the Versailles nightclub in midtown so Bill could watch Zero Mostel. They drove by limousine up to the Cotton Club in Harlem to hear Duke Ellington because Dorothy was mad about his music. Their energy charged the atmosphere around them. "You could see them floating up and up. They were gobbling everyone right and left," said Irene Selznick.

The couple stormed Hollywood, too. Paley had been a frequent visitor since he first arrived with Adolph Zukor in 1929. At a party given at a beach house in Santa Monica by Paramount's head of production, Jesse Lasky, Irene Selznick, then only nineteen years old, witnessed Paley's Hollywood debut. "He was eager, full of beans, healthy, poised and enthusiastic. He made a good impression." Paley was agog to find himself in the company of those he had only seen on the shiny pages of magazines. "For a kid who loved motion picture actresses, and who hadn't been around anyplace," he said, "to suddenly have a party given for HIM, with every great star in the country there, sort of honoring him and being nice to him, was more than I could stand! Fantastic!"

Paley established a friendship with Sam Goldwyn and his wife, Frances, who entertained Dorothy and Bill at lavish dinner parties. But of all the movie producers Paley met, he had the most rapport with David O. Selznick. Like Paley, Selznick was a son of Russian-Jewish immigrants; his father had been a jeweler in Pittsburgh. Selznick was bespectacled, curly-headed, earthy, impulsive, and every bit as zestful as Paley. A nonstop talker who spouted ideas, Selznick routinely convulsed Paley with laughter. "They had a lot in common," said Irene Selznick. "They were two Jewish fellows with big success, great talent and energy, great appetites. They traded information and stimulated one another. They were fast thinkers. They were competitors, always outsmarting and topping each other."

Selznick's puckish view of Paley—affectionate yet clear about his foibles—was evident in a poem he composed one evening in 1937 at Fefe's Monte Carlo, a popular New York nightclub. It was titled "BILL As Seen by David O.," and it read:

> The American way . . .
> Hypochondriac's holiday . . .
> Tycoon—absent without leave . . .
> Horatio Alger in Tel Aviv . . .
> Action . . .

Distraction . . .

New Wine . . .

Life begins at thirty-nine . . .

Ambition's zipper . . .

Jay Gould on Yom Kippur . . .

Fortune's feel . . .

Friendship: a portrait in steel . . .

Sears, Roebuck tries modern art . . .

The Streamlined Heart . . .

Weizman in a white tie . . .

New Dealer's sigh . . .

Hearst and Sarnoff frown . . .

Insomnia in eiderdown . . .

Sentiment in a top hat . . .

Tom Sawyer on a bat . . .

The Paleys widened their circle of friends through frequent vacations abroad. In the wintertime, Bill and Dorothy went south to Florida, Cuba (where he had many acquaintances from his cigar days), Nassau, or Bermuda, whose governor was a friend. During the summer they spent anywhere from two to three months in England and on the Continent, always surrounded by friends. One summer they stayed six weeks in London before moving on to Austria and France. They also visited Germany, Switzerland, and Monte Carlo.

In England their friends were from the highest rungs of British society: the Duke of Sutherland and his wife, Elaine; Alfred Duff Cooper, Viscount Norwich and First Lord of the Admiralty, and his wife, Lady Diana, a legendary beauty; and Olive, Lady Baillie, who entertained Bill and Dorothy at Leeds Castle, where Henry VIII had kept Anne Boleyn. In the summer of 1936 the Paleys and their friends Dolly and Jay O'Brien, a society couple in their early sixties who lived in New York and Paris, spent two weeks during stag-hunting season at Dunrobin, the Sutherlands' enormous country estate on the northeastern coast of Scotland. Bill went clambering over rocky hills stalking stag by day. At dinner each evening, bagpipers in kilts surrounded the table for a serenade. Afterwards there were long games of poker for the men while the women demurely did needlework in another room. Dorothy quickly tired of such segregation —she never did finish her needlepoint—and complained so much that the men admitted her into their game. Other evenings they would go to the village hall where they danced Scottish reels with the villagers, Dorothy so vigorously that she knocked a heel off Jay O'Brien's shoe. One day they were joined for lunch by the Coopers, who were cruising on the Admiralty's yacht with their eight-year-old son, John Julius, all three dressed in sailor suits of white trousers, blue blazers, and peaked caps. John Julius remembered that Dorothy had the longest fingernails he had ever seen.

The Paleys met a number of distinguished friends in Austria through Dorothy's friend Max Reinhardt and his rather mysterious aide-de-camp, Rudolph Kommer. Rotund and bald, Kommer lived lavishly as what would later be called a "walker," a man of indeterminate sexual preference who allied himself with beautiful women and escorted them when the need arose. His nickname was "Kaetchen," after the kitten owned by the proprietor of a famous Viennese café. Kommer's first object of devotion was Lady Diana Cooper—as an actress in the 1920s she had appeared in Reinhardt's extravagant production of *The Miracle* in New York. Second came Dorothy Paley.

It was through Kommer that the Paleys had come to know the Coopers and many other eminent Europeans. By the late 1930s, Kommer was living at the Ambassador Hotel in New York and visiting the Paleys frequently. He introduced Dorothy to Raimund von Hofmannsthal, son of the famed Austrian poet and librettist; the author Thomas Mann; Niels Bohr, the Danish physicist and Nobel laureate; and the Austrian actress Eleanora von Mendelssohn. Kommer, more than any other, contributed to the air of sophistication and diversity that surrounded the Paleys when they entertained.

Bill Paley liked to be around creative people so he could pick their brains. He was drawn to style, accomplishment, glamour, power, and money—all of which he found in abundance at the home of Herbert Bayard Swope, an acknowledged leader of Café Society. In the late twenties when Swope quit as editor of the *New York World* in a dispute with the publisher, a series of shrewd stock market plays had already made him a millionaire. His thirty-room duplex apartment on West 58th Street in Manhattan was open house to a diverse group that included theatrical and literary figures as well as wealthy socialites eager to keep company with celebrated intellectuals. The Paleys and other guests routinely dropped in after the theater for an impromptu party. They attended non-stop house parties nearly every weekend at the Swopes' sprawling home in Sands Point on Long Island's north shore. Sometimes referred to as the "Gold Coast," the north shore was the most fashionable retreat for the city's wealthy elite. It began about a half-dozen miles outside the city limits, extended along the coast between Manhasset Bay and Hempstead Harbor, and stretched inland for many miles, encompassing thousands of acres of country estates.

A large, red-haired man who talked all the time, Swope was once described by Westbrook Pegler as "all gall, divided into three parts—Herbert, Bayard, and Swope." He fostered a kind of manic congeniality among his guests. A typical weekend roster might include playwrights George S. Kaufman and Robert Sherwood; Alexander Woollcott, the drama critic turned CBS radio personality; and newspaper columnist Heywood Broun—all veterans of the Algonquin Round Table, which had broken up in the late 1920s. FDR's aide Harry Hopkins might drop by, as well as comedian Harpo Marx, columnist Walter Lippmann, pianist Oscar Levant, playboy Alfred Vanderbilt, composer Howard Dietz, and publishers such as Dolly Schiff Backer and Condé Nast. Errol Flynn and Jimmy Stewart made cameo appearances. The elusive Howard Hughes showed up once, remaining solitary and silent the whole day. "Age or social standing meant little at the Swopes'," wrote E. J. Kahn, Swope's biographer.

The Swope weekends were said to have been the model for F. Scott Fitzgerald's party scenes in *The Great Gatsby*. Guests drifted in and out, the uninvited as well as the invited. Some stayed for weeks at a time. Herbert Swope and his wife, Maggie, entertained on a scale that made a mockery of the Depression. "I learned quickly that the rich are never affected," said Dorothy. Everyone played games incessantly. Walking through the Swope house, one could find any number of small clusters of guests playing poker, mah-jongg, dominoes, backgammon, hearts, gin rummy, and bridge. Outdoors, Swope and his guests took up croquet with ferocious intensity. Called loose or open croquet, it was played with no boundaries, which raised the competitive stakes considerably. After his guests insisted on using their automobiles to illuminate the field at night, Swope installed lights so that games could begin at any time. Averell Harriman, a dedicated player, always brought a mallet custom-designed in England. Paley was an enthusiastic regular. Croquet not only appealed to his competitive instincts, it enabled him to get to know an assortment of new friends. His favorite partner was Neysa McMein, a faded but still engaging beauty who had achieved celebrity as a magazine illustrator and charter member of the Algonquin set.

There was always a dizzying array of parlor games: charades, twenty questions, the picture game, the psychology game, anagrams, the number game, the alphabet game, the drawing game, murder, and The Game, a variant on charades which combined pantomime and drawing. Always boisterous, often frantic, these contests attracted large crowds. In the typical game of charades, Neysa McMein's husband, a handsome and rather vulgar mining engineer named Jack Baragwanath, "could be counted on to take off his trousers at least once." During a Swope New Year's Eve party, one charade ran from two until seven in the morning. The best players had to be clever, agile, and well informed, while the inhibited and unimaginative played at their peril. Dorothy excelled, and Bill struggled through bit parts with obvious discomfort. He preferred to laugh heartily at the antics of others. "I was just happy to be in their company," he wrote later.

Sometimes the Swopes brought in a five-piece orchestra and cleared the drawing room of all furniture but the sofas so their guests could do the Charleston and play musical chairs. On Saturday nights, the crowd would troop over to the palatial home—everyone called it the chateau—owned by W. R. Hearst's estranged wife Millicent—Dorothy Paley's former mother-in-law—to watch a movie. When Millicent closed the chateau, the Swopes rented the local movie theater for special midnight screenings of new films. Meals were served around the clock. It was not unusual to have breakfast of hamburgers and hot dogs before the last partygoers left at seven in the morning.

Swope was already fifty years old and Paley only thirty-one when they first met. Yet the two men developed a lively friendship that deepened when Paley invited Swope to join the CBS board of directors in the mid-thirties. Paley was stimulated by Swope, who had a talent for bringing out the best in his friends. "Swope had a curiously humanizing effect on people," said Dorothy.

Paley had also cultivated Averell Harriman as a friend. A decade older, Harriman was not only important to Paley as an entrée into the art world but for his social connections. A founder, with his brother, of the W. A. Harriman (later Brown Brothers Harriman) investment banking house, Averell was the son of a railroad baron, heir to a $70 million fortune, and a polo-playing sportsman. Although he was rather dull and humorless, Harriman's looks—tall, somewhat haggard, with a long nose and strong chin—struck Paley as quintessentially aristocratic. He was just the sort of man Bill had dreamed of knowing only a few years earlier. Paley said he admired him as a "natural patrician" who would "have an influence upon my life and my own sense of values."

They had first become acquainted when the W. A. Harriman Company represented CBS in the Paramount merger in 1929, and had seen each other frequently around town and at Sands Point, where the penny-pinching Harriman bought a two-bedroom Hodgson house, one of America's first prefabricated models. During their trip to Europe with their wives in the summer of 1935, Harriman introduced Paley to hunting at an estate in Hungary. The night before the hunt, Harriman coached as Paley shot blanks at the flame of a candle until dawn. At Harriman's suggestion, Paley equipped himself with customized shotguns at Purdeys, the famous London gunmaker. Not surprisingly, Paley came to like hunting for its "sensation."

Still, their friendship was not particularly easy or close. Paley envied Harriman for being born to so much wealth and opportunity. He failed to recognize how much of a plodder Harriman was, and how hard he worked.

Once a year, over the five-day Thanksgiving weekend, the Harrimans hosted an enormous house party that the Paleys faithfully attended. It was held at Arden, the hundred-room mansion built by Harriman's father on Mount Orama in upstate New York. Surrounded by 20,000 wooded acres, the three-story house had forty bedrooms, a tennis court, a lawn for croquet, a polo ground, and bowling alleys. A crowd of at least forty usually showed up from a guest list carefully drawn up by Marie Harriman and Alexander Woollcott. Most of them were Swope habitués. The festivities began on Wednesday and ended in exhaustion the following Monday.

"The house was so immense that it was difficult to keep track of people," wrote one participant, Alice-Leone Moats, of a Thanksgiving in the mid-thirties.

> The first night we had dinner in a small dining room but after that we ate in a huge marble hall. Thursday there was a shoot of driven wild duck. . . . Every night we bowled and the rest of the time there were games of various kinds. Some of them played badminton on a court that had been marked out on the marble floor of the old chapel. . . . The house . . . is hideous, all excepting the big drawing room that Marie has built on. We drank champagne every night which was delicious but the food was practically inedible. At one moment, I had a terrible time restraining Maggie Swope who wanted me to go out in the kitchen and make some Mexican rice. She said she didn't think she could stand it if she didn't get something to eat with some flavor.

For all the grandeur of the house, Thanksgiving weekend reflected Averell's well-known parsimony and Marie's haphazard approach to entertaining. Averell employed only one full-time manservant at Arden, whom everyone called "Woods, the poor slave" because he was unable to keep up with the demands of the guests. Not only was the food dreadful, but there was never enough of it. Little bands of guests used to forage the kitchen in vain for leftovers. Dorothy Paley always brought several large boxes of candy to satisfy her ravenous husband.

But the entertainment was lively. Besides the games—including some frosty croquet played amid the snow on a freshly shoveled lawn—various members serenaded each other with outrageous songs. Heywood Broun, large and disheveled, did a wicked imitation of the French musical comedy singer Anna Held's "Who Was You Wiz Tonight Tonight?" And Robert Sherwood, a droll beanpole at six feet seven, sang and danced what one guest called a "gravely ludicrous" rendition of "When the Red Red Robin Goes Bob Bob Bobbin' Along" until the other guests doubled over with laughter. Everyone drank far too much. One year the playwright Charles MacArthur passed out in the pantry on three consecutive nights.

Not all the guests were amused by the antics. On a visit in 1939, Duff and Diana Cooper had what Lady Diana's biographer Philip Ziegler called a "nightmare weekend." The guests were "mostly writers of one kind or another . . . but they might as well have been the most illiterate philistines. Any conversation was drowned by the thunder from the bowling-alley. . . . Diana was forced to creep into the kitchen and beg for a piece of cake. . . . She spent most of the weekend in her room trying unavailingly to sleep." Marie Harriman took an equally dim view of the Coopers, apologizing to her other guests and imploring, "What shall I do with them?" Maggie Swope dubbed them the "dull Coopers."

In 1938 the Paleys paid less than $200,000 for their own country estate in Manhasset, down the road from Sands Point. Called Kiluna Farm, it was set on 85 acres that included a saltwater pool, indoor tennis court with a glass roof, barns, greenhouses, and gardens. Paley had coveted the house, which was owned by Ralph Pulitzer, son of the publisher of the *New York World,* since his first visit back in 1929. Built of white clapboard in the late nineteenth century, Kiluna was a rambling assemblage of more than twenty rooms, including servants' quarters. It looked, *Time* magazine once observed, "like ten shingle farmhouses delivered all at once by airdrop." Connected to the main house by a large game room was a smaller cottage. Set on a rise, Kiluna offered a fine view of the distant Sound.

Although Paley always said he was drawn to Kiluna's simplicity, he and Dorothy added a columned portico that made the house look more grand. They bought two full-grown linden trees to flank the brick terrace they built out back. Dorothy redid every room in the house. The white sitting room overflowed with cheerful red and green English chintz. On the walls were a Lautrec, a Gauguin, and a Cézanne. Dorothy used green faille swags in the dining room and covered the walls above the dado with paper of a delicate green stripe intertwined with flowers. Her pale yellow bedroom was feminine and romantic—with a canopy bed of white tambour trimmed with red satin ribbon.

Paley's bedroom overlooked the garden. The walls were painted écru, as was the plain wooden fireplace. The single bed in one corner was covered in a masculine chintz of green leaves, with matching draperies. A Dufy watercolor hung over the fireplace; on an adjacent wall was a scene of a burning ship. Both paintings were gifts from Dorothy. Paley had a kitchenette built into a closet just inside the door, where he often cooked scrambled eggs after midnight. He kept an assortment of caviar, foie gras, and dried biscuits in the cabinet. "I suffer from night hunger," he explained to friends as he flung open the cabinet.

In the north shore social set, the Paleys became renowned for their style of entertaining. Less hectic than the Harrimans, less freewheeling than the Swopes, house parties at Kiluna set new standards of elegance and luxury. Kiluna, said Horace Kelland, a visitor in the thirties, "was polite and pretty, rather like a nice stylish country club."

At Paley's insistence, Dorothy filled Kiluna's five guest bedrooms every weekend. He could not bear it unless something was happening all the time. As a result, Dorothy and Bill had little time alone—time that might have helped nurture their marriage. In addition to the north shore regulars, the Paleys included numerous guests from the motion picture world; artistic and literary types such as Samuel Chotzinoff, a pianist and musical scholar; and titled Europeans. "My eyes were in my cheeks the whole time," said the young Marietta Tree of her first visit fresh out of the rectory. "I was overcome by the brilliance and charm and beauty and style of life at the Paleys'." One trait united everyone who visited the Paleys: they were all famous.

The Kiluna routine mimicked the Swope weekends, with endless games indoors and out, drinks by the swimming pool—Dorothy's mysteriously flavored iced tea was a famous concoction—and strolls through the garden with its abundant flower beds and reflecting pool, hedges, and arbors. After dinner on Saturday evenings, Gauguin's *Queen of the Areois* would swing away from one wall in the living room to reveal a projector, and a new movie would be shown. Twenty-two servants, including a platoon of gardeners, were on hand to keep everything in a state of perfection. One maid was kept working full time in a room on the third floor just pressing freshly laundered curtains.

The food at the Paleys' was exquisite. In the afternoon there would be tea, with delicate pastries, cinnamon toast, and tiny sandwiches. Partly to cater to Bill's constant craving for food, orange juice and sandwiches were often served at ten-thirty in the evening, only an hour or so after the formal dinner had concluded. Occasionally there was a complaint. "The food wasn't very good," wrote Alice-Leone Moats in 1939. "For some reason Dorothy always serves pork—maybe just to show they aren't orthodox."

Lady Diana Cooper, who had complained about the noise and food at the Harrimans', was amazed at the lengths to which Dorothy went as a hostess. When she inspected her bathroom cupboard, she found "aspirin, witch-hazel, peroxide, a bottle of 'Soporific' bathpowder, one of 'Soporific' rub and another labelled 'Soporific nightcap,' some earplugs and an eye-bandage. . . . There are radio sets, television, and thank God, plenty of pianos . . . [but] no incentive to read a book." In her mildly disdainful view, the Paleys seemed to try just too hard. "This luxury taste slightly depresses me," she complained.

> The standard is unattainable to us tradition-ridden tired Europeans. There was nothing ugly, worn or makeshift; brief and exquisite meals, a little first-class wine, one snorting cocktail. Servants were invisible, yet one was always tended. Conversation was amusing, wise-cracked, light and serious. A little table in your bedroom was laid, as for a nuptial night, with fine lawn, plates, forks and a pyramid of choice-bloomed peaches, figs and grapes. . . . In the morning a young, silent girl, more lovely than the sun that blazed through the hangings, smoothed all and was never seen again.

Years later Dorothy ascribed Lady Diana's "bitchery" to jealousy, specifically over Rudolph Kommer's devotion to Dorothy in the last years of his life when he was a constant visitor at Kiluna.

The Sands Point and Manhasset social whirl was an essential part of Bill Paley's existence. It established him as a formidable social presence, exposing him to a wide array of talented and provocative people. It provided diversionary relief from the enormous tension he felt in his job. Indeed, with the exception of Larry Lowman, who had married a Vanderbilt, no executives at CBS ever appeared. For all its talent and intelligence, Bill Paley's crowd in the thirties spent much of their free time frivolously —playing games, visiting nightclubs, drinking until they dropped. In many respects it was an era of blinding superficiality, where everyone concentrated on striking attitudes and tossing off clever quips. Yet it was not entirely empty-headed. "There was a lot of talk of politics, especially what was happening in Germany. There was a lot of talk about the theater," said Dorothy. "People like Herbert Swope loved serious talk. You were aware you were with serious people, not fools. They were serious people who knew how to have a good time. It was lively and fun and interesting." The more Paley listened, the more he learned, and the more he participated when the conversation turned to world affairs. "He had ideas," said Dorothy. "He enjoyed all the levels. He held his own."

Bill Paley's social life was significant in one other way as well. It was elitist but not exclusive. Jews such as the Swopes and Kaufmans mixed

comfortably with Vanderbilts and other super-WASPs. People were valued for their talent, their liveliness, their accomplishment, not their ethnic
origin. Yet overt displays of ethnicity were unwelcome. Bill Paley and
other prominent Jews subtly adopted WASP ways. He never actually tried
to hide his Jewishness. But he never flaunted it and in large measure
withdrew from it.

Hints of anti-Semitism lingered beneath the surface in those days.
Otto Kahn, the investment banker and patron of the arts, sometimes reminded friends of Disraeli's definition of a "kike" as "a Jewish gentleman
who has just left the room." The crack made about the Paleys' serving
pork seemed to bear out such suspicions. So did Diana Cooper's description of Bill Paley as "physically a little oriental . . . 100 percent Jew but
looking more like good news from Tartary." Madeline Sherwood once
recounted to Alice-Leone Moats how before spending a weekend at playwright Moss Hart's with the Paleys and the Kaufmans in early 1938, she
had her maid spend an entire night scraping German steamship labels off
her luggage, even if it meant taking off chunks of the Vuitton design as
well.

For all of Paley's social accomplishments, one pinnacle remained.
Living next door to the Paleys in Manhasset was John Hay "Jock" Whitney, heir to one of the biggest fortunes in America. Jock was a true American prince who stood at the apex of social position, and Paley could not
get to first base with him—even though Paley and Whitney shared a friend
in David Selznick. Whitney had invested in Selznick International Pictures
back in 1935 and served not only as chairman of the board but East Coast
manager as well. While Paley and Selznick had much in common, Whitney
and Selznick seemed barely compatible on the surface. But the patrician
Whitney, handsome and strong despite his perpetual stutter and what one
friend called "elegant shyness," thrived on Selznick's vibrancy and the
electricity of the theatrical and film world.

Primarily through Selznick, Paley and Whitney would periodically
cross paths in those days. They ended up at the same dinners at "21" and
occasional parties on the north shore. In 1939, the Paleys and the Whitneys
were among the guests who traveled to Atlanta for the world premiere of
the epic film *Gone With the Wind* that Selznick produced and Whitney
financed. But Jock and Bill never became intimate, despite the tantalizing
proximity. When the Selznicks came east, they visited the Paleys and the
Whitneys separately. "They were poles apart, so we never proposed joining up," said Irene Selznick. Dorothy had little in common with Jock's
wife, Liz, a socialite horsewoman uninterested in the world of books and
ideas. Nor did she have much use for Jock, whom she considered a stuffed
shirt. But Jock in those days showed little affinity for Bill Paley either.

"They were apples and oranges," said Irene Selznick. "They were never ardent from the start as David and Jock were." With time, this situation would become more aggravating for Paley—a nagging symbol that until he was embraced by the consummate American gentleman, he still had not quite arrived.

9

BILL PALEY'S BIRTHDAY in the autumn of 1936 occupies a cherished place in the Paley mythology. He called it "one of the most dreadful dilemmas of my life" because of a solemn vow he claimed he had made eighteen years earlier to retire when he reached thirty-five. As he later recounted, he approached the day with agonized deliberation. Should he or shouldn't he? His talent for salesmanship had paid off handsomely. From 1929—the year Paramount bought half of the company—through 1936, CBS advertising revenues increased from $4.8 to $18 million. During the same years its net profit rose from $480,000 to $3.9 million. From 1929 to 1936 NBC advertising revenues grew from $15.5 to $26 million, and its profits from $713,000 to $3.5 million. Yet despite CBS's success, Paley was superstitious enough to profess worry that if he defied his oath he might be punished by a reversal of his fortunes.

The retirement fantasy came from his father, who in Chicago days often spoke of buying an orange grove and living a leisurely life once he earned his first $25,000. From time to time young Willie, who imagined himself as a beachcomber in his father's idyll, would inquire whether the time had come. Finally his father conceded that he had the $25,000 but he could not bring himself to retire. "I thought he had double-crossed me," Paley said years later.

Willie was unable to shake the fantasy so easily. In his early hard-driving days at CBS, Paley periodically spoke of his vow to retire at thirty-five in conversations with friends, even to a reporter for the London *Daily Mirror*. He mentioned it to Dorothy not long after they met, and she was mildly amused. "When he made that decision, thirty-five seemed ancient, as if he would be in a wheelchair," she recalled.

Needless to say, Bill Paley stayed with the job that made him rich and powerful. Suddenly beachcombing had lost its appeal. "Life was not meant to be devoted to the acquisition of money, followed by a lazy life of leisure," he wrote later. "I knew that life was meant to be lived to the fullest, day by day, to the very last one." Many years afterwards, when the time came to step down, Bill Paley would be unable to let go.

In retrospect, the notion that Paley would leave CBS at thirty-five was ludicrous. If he agonized about his vow, he never gave any indication at the time. "I don't remember when he gave it up," said Dorothy. "It had disappeared long before he reached thirty-five. It just vanished. It was never mentioned. He never said, 'Say, can you imagine I ever said that about retiring?' "

Paley also found the burden of leading CBS was lightened by two key executives who came to CBS in 1930—a yin and yang pair who embodied the poles of Paley's contradictory nature. They were Edward Klauber and Paul Kesten, each enormously talented but obviously flawed. Klauber was the unimaginative straight arrow who put CBS News on the map. Kesten was the brilliant imagemaker, an aesthete who helped refine Paley's taste. Each man resented the other and vied for Paley's attention.

Bill Paley's first reaction to Ed Klauber was thorough dislike. A burly and dyspeptic man, Klauber was preceded by his reputation as a tough, cold, and sometimes cruel taskmaster. When he met Paley in 1929, the misanthropic Klauber had an unlikely job in public relations at a New York advertising agency, Lennen & Mitchell. Charmless and utterly lacking in humor, Klauber seemed the antithesis of everything Paley valued in a man.

Klauber had drifted into public relations from journalism for the usual reasons: more money and better hours. A two-time college dropout (from the Universities of Louisville and Pennsylvania), he used the connections of his uncle Adolph, drama critic for the *New York Times,* to land a job first as a reporter for the *New York World,* then as a rewriteman and editor at the *New York Times*.

As night city editor at the *Times,* Klauber proved a rigid enforcer of objectivity and fairness. He insisted on the highest ethical standards. He was by one account "a perfectionist who took infinite pains with his copy." Reporters feared and loathed him, not so much for his journalistic demands but for an apparent lack of compassion. Newsroom legend had it that Klauber took sadistic pleasure in giving assignments to reporters who desperately wanted to be with their families on holidays.

The late hours of newspapering finally took their toll, and Klauber asked CBS's public relations man Edward Bernays, a social friend, where he might find a more congenial position. Bernays steered him to Lennen & Mitchell and ultimately took him at his own firm. When it became clear that Klauber's abrasiveness was too overpowering for a small shop, Bernays recommended him to Paley. Klauber's blend of experience in journalism, advertising, and public relations, Bernays told Paley, could help

CBS enormously. Bernays was certain Klauber's difficult personality would be less of a problem in a large organization.

Only after Bernays praised Klauber's superior executive ability and sound judgment did Paley overcome his initial aversion and hire him as his administrative assistant. But at forty-three, the ungainly and formal Klauber never fit into Paley's youthful executive cadre, where the average age was twenty-seven. Klauber was widely disliked; Paley's legal adviser Ralph Colin turned against him after watching Klauber humiliate one staff member after another in meetings. Klauber grew increasingly tyrannical as he assumed greater day-to-day responsibilities. By 1936, he was being paid more than $71,000 a year—the equivalent of around $700,000 today —second only to Paley's salary and bonus of $140,000. Klauber was proud of the salary he received at CBS, and referred to it as his "loot."

Executives dreaded the summons to Klauber's forbidding office. He decorated it entirely in dark brown—rugs, upholstery, and draperies— and always kept the venetian blinds nearly closed. Wearing double-breasted suits that accentuated his stockiness, he sat stiffly behind a massive desk, peering over his pince-nez and smoking a cigarette in a long holder. Periodically he dropped the ash over his shoulder onto the carpet as he growled his commands.

He installed direct telephone lines to the offices of all his subordinates; secretaries were never permitted to lift the receiver even if it rang off the hook. Whenever the ringing began, executives would tremble so badly that the instruments quickly became known as the "shaky phones." Klauber never even said good morning or hello. His conversations began with a gruff complaint or a tough question. Although every executive in those days called Paley "Bill" to his face, Klauber decreed that they refer to him only as "Mr. Paley" when they discussed him out of his presence. Paley found that he liked this formal gesture of respect.

Klauber's few defenders insisted that his autocratic demeanor compensated for an almost pathological shyness. They also attributed some of his ill-humor to constant stomach problems that kept him in frequent pain. "He was a just man, and very sensitive," said Lyman Bryson, a Columbia professor who advised CBS on educational programming in those days.

As Dorothy did in his personal life, Klauber imposed discipline and organization on Paley at work. He insisted that Paley have only male secretaries and hired Franz Kizis, a stern gentleman who habitually dressed in a black suit, black tie, and stiff collar. Klauber streamlined CBS operations, which had been too loose and informal.

Klauber's arrival marked a change in Paley's relationship with other executives at CBS. An extra door connected Paley's corner office to Klauber's adjacent office, allowing Klauber unlimited access to his boss.

Moreover, the main entrance to Paley's office was always within range of Klauber's two receptionists. Klauber became Paley's gatekeeper, much to the dismay of Ralph Colin and others whose access Klauber now controlled. Paley chose to ignore Klauber's cruelty because of his usefulness. Paley preferred to avoid confrontations, and Klauber eagerly took them on, allowing the boss to remain comfortably above it all. Thus, late in 1930, Klauber summarily fired Bernays, his own sponsor, over lunch. Despite the fact that Bernays was a man who had done much for CBS, Paley looked the other way. Klauber said it cost too much to retain an outside public relations firm. But soon afterwards, he hired a publicist from the Ivy Lee Company, which was better connected than Bernays to the WASP establishment to which Paley aspired. "Ed was Paley's first hatchet man," said Klauber's widow, Doris Wechsler, "the first in a series of people who tried to do the dirty work and ended up somewhat victimized."

In those early days Klauber acted as the father figure to a boss thirteen years his junior. He checked Paley's recklessness and channeled his enthusiasm into action. Paley had great confidence in Klauber's judgment. "He was a stickler," Paley said years later. "He had the highest standards of any man I've ever met. He'd drive you crazy but he was right." Even when Paley's power grew, Klauber had the temerity to stand up to him. "He had a Rock of Gibraltar quality," recalled Dorothy. "Bill knew he would always get an honest answer. Ed would support him if he thought something was right and tell him otherwise if he didn't. In that way he was the opposite of Paul Kesten. Kesten would never say if he thought Bill was wrong."

It was Klauber, not Paley, who hired Kesten from Lennen & Mitchell toward the end of 1930 to direct CBS's promotion. Kesten was as clever and affable as Klauber was earnest and dour. Thin to the point of frailty, Kesten was already so plagued by arthritis at thirty-one that he had difficulty turning a doorknob. He wore his dark blond hair neatly slicked back from a high, intelligent forehead. Kesten dressed stylishly in fashionable, closely fitting suits nipped at the waist. His most famous display of fastidiousness was a pair of shoes with polished black soles. He wore them only in the office because he had a habit of sitting with his feet propped on his desk. His apartment in the Lombardy Hotel on East 56th Street was designed by his close friend William Lescaze, a prominent architect schooled in contemporary European design. Kesten's suite was elegant, tasteful, and spare.

Born in Milwaukee, Kesten first displayed a knack for clever self-expression as a caricaturist and writer for his high school newspaper. But he dropped out of the University of Wisconsin after only a few months and signed on with the Gimbels department store in Milwaukee, rising to advertising manager by age twenty-one. From the retail trade, Kesten moved to Madison Avenue. At Lennen & Mitchell, Klauber first witnessed Kesten's brilliance as a copywriter.

When Kesten dictated copy to his secretary, he specified typesizes. "Elsie, set the head in 72-point italic," he would say, "and set the text flush in 14 point." If he was interrupted by a phone call, he would pick up precisely where he left off. Kesten hated it when the last line of a paragraph was a widow—a single word. Whenever that happened he would instruct his secretary to go back a few lines—he always knew precisely where— and insert some additional words to fill out the last line. "His big asset is a brain that delights in the subtle inferences, the plausible turning of arguments, and the rarefied logic on which promotion must subsist," wrote *Fortune* in 1935.

Paley loved Kesten's cleverness and charm. Both men brimmed with ideas and were adept at figures. In meetings they were so in sync that they finished each other's sentences. Kesten's interest in design fueled Paley's growing fascination with the symbols of quality—the best typeface, the best paper, the best graphics. "Kesten had a feeling for elegance and taste along with a touch of majesty," said Paley.

Still, the two men never socialized. Kesten certainly had the requisite polish and skills; he was legendary for his scintillating conversation. "He may just as readily dwell on Italian morphology, the toxic effect of a Manhattan as opposed to a Martini, and the merits of T. S. Eliot," wrote Jack Gould in the *New York Times*. But Kesten was a rather eccentric bachelor, a loner who lived mysteriously outside the office. "He was a strange man with a strange temperament. He was not terribly warm. He never seemed at ease," said Dorothy.

Kesten had a proclivity for the supernatural and mystic, and he gravitated to odd cures for his arthritis such as experimental gold treatments and mud baths in Mexico. He collected watches, cigarette lighters, and other gadgets. And he was known to drive after midnight to Jones Beach in one of his souped-up cars. There he would spend hours racing up and down the deserted beach road at over 100 mph.

For all his peculiarity, Kesten was a popular and amiable executive— perhaps too much so. He was sensitive and solicitous, and could not bring himself to fire anyone. If he wanted something done, he rarely gave an order. Rather, he would politely note, "I am turning this over to you." With Paley, he was often obsequious.

Between the iron fist of Klauber and the delicate felicity of Kesten, Paley's executive style took shape. He dressed conservatively in the bespoke blue serge suits that Dorothy had helped him select in London. He continued to drive himself hard. He was always nervous and tense; his tic was already in evidence. "Momentarily he can become so emphatic that his powers of speech desert him," wrote one observer in 1932. He still smoked four packs of Chesterfields a day. He invariably had at least two cigarette packs in his pockets, and they were usually empty. Yet in a crucial negotiation he could appear cool and relaxed—the result, apparently, of his powers of intense concentration.

His days were so crowded that he often held meetings while he ate breakfast—long before the power breakfast came into fashion. He wrote few memos. A man of action rather than ideas, he preferred to conduct business face to face or on the telephone. He kept a radio going continuously from seven-thirty in the morning until midnight. He rarely left the office before 7:00 P.M.

In these years Paley began a lifelong habit of treating executives like servants, with little regard for their personal lives. His demands on their time outside the office started to escalate. Paley insisted that Klauber, Kesten, Colin, or Lowman always accompany him home to Beekman Place after work. Most nights Klauber performed this service. He would keep his office door open until Paley was ready to leave, and the two men would walk across town together. They always parted at Paley's door, and Klauber then hailed a cab to his home on East 67th Street. Once Paley pressed Colin to accompany him to Pennsylvania Station to finish a discussion. Paley was dissatisfied with the outcome, and Colin found himself continuing the meeting on a two-hour train ride to Philadelphia.

The patterns and quirks of Paley's decision making grew more familiar if no less baffling. "He has a peculiar manner of listening in a way that suggests he is turning over one side of your argument to get the right slant on the topic," a newspaper reporter wrote late in 1930. Paley could show great patience in the face of arguments from subordinates. "He listened, as he would all his life, to people he thought mattered," said Lyman Bryson. "He is one of the very few really powerful executives I've ever known who really listens to an opinion when it is contrary to his own. I've never seen anybody hesitate to say what he thought in Paley's presence"—a boldness, it should be noted, that diminished over time as Paley grew more intimidating.

Yet some felt that even in those early days Paley merely gave the appearance of being open-minded. From the way he asked questions it was clear that he had a desired answer in mind. "He never raised his voice, but what he wanted to do was done," said Joseph Ream, an attorney who joined CBS in the 1930s. And even when Paley finally steered everyone to a decision, he often reversed it the next day. His executives began to avoid acting on his first decision—a practice that would grow increasingly disruptive over the years as Paley's vacillation intensified.

Left to his own devices, Paley showed little regard for lines of command. If he came across a matter that intrigued him, he would handle it himself instead of delegating it. He cared little if his actions caused confusion among his troops. "In that way he is a bad organization man," Ralph Colin told a reporter in 1935. Paley also tended to personalize management problems. Once when a CBS executive, Paul White, had an accident and was out of the office for a few months, Paley hired a man named Quincy Howe in his place. When White returned, Howe felt uncomfortable and asked Paley if he could resign. Paley simply went to White and asked: "What's the matter up there? Why don't you get along with Howe? He's an easy man to get along with."

Paley's analytical skills were becoming legendary. "When someone has prepared a lengthy and complicated report for him, he will glance down the page and be certain to ask just one question the man hoped he wouldn't," Ralph Colin said in 1935. If Paley was given an audience rating for a show, he could be counted on to remember it to the decimal point six months later—and to crisply correct any subordinate who tried to tell him otherwise. He blazed through balance sheets and profit-and-loss statements. He spent hours figuring the CBS accounts, going over the books as he had in the old days at Congress Cigar.

The occupants of the executive suites on the twentieth floor of 485 Madison were fascinated by Paley's fickle enthusiasms. One month he would take up watercolor painting, the next it would be oil painting, then motorboating, then flying airplanes, then photography. He became so enamored of broadcasting to Latin America that he arranged for a teacher to visit CBS once a week to give Spanish and Portuguese lessons to employees. He was equally absorbed with his own aches and pains. "He has tremendous faith in medicine," wrote a reporter in 1932. "No matter what he takes it always makes him feel 'one hundred percent better.' A pill, a nostrum, a week on a yacht or a bit of sugar dissolved in water always sets him up at once."

Paley was steadily moving away from the informality that characterized his earliest days at CBS. No longer the easygoing stripling from Chicago, he had presence and a quiet confidence that grew from his achievements. He acquired imperial trappings, such as the dining room he opened near his office, complete with private chef and waiters. When Paley wanted to change for the evening, his valet would arrive at the office with fresh clothing. And with Klauber firmly in charge, Paley grew more aloof. "He never would walk around the office," said H. V. Kaltenborn, a former reporter for the *Brooklyn Eagle* and a pioneer of radio news. "You'd never see him. He'd pop into his office in a remote corner and stay there. He did attend certain functions, and sometimes I saw him at official lunches or dinners. He kept pretty much to himself and dealt only with the top executives."

Subordinates began to take note of Paley's absences from the office. "He was away quite frequently," said Kaltenborn. "He got a great deal of pleasure out of outside things." Paley was making good on his goal of savoring the pleasures of life and work simultaneously.

But he never totally disengaged from the office, even when he was frolicking through Europe for months at a time. Klauber assiduously kept him informed by telephone and by what Paley referred to as "yard-long telegrams" sent every few days. "There was never business per se on those trips," recalled Dorothy. "But it was with him. He was thinking about it and referred to it often. There was no question that CBS was always on his mind."

10

NEW SKYSCRAPER SPIRES glistened against the clear sky when Frank Nicholas Stanton turned his black Model A Ford toward the Holland Tunnel into Manhattan. It was a crisp Saturday afternoon in early October 1935. Twenty-seven years old, with a newly minted Ph.D. from Ohio State University, he had spent the previous seventeen hours driving 560 miles from Columbus, Ohio. He had stopped only once—to have lunch with an aunt in Newburgh, New York, and to leave his wire-haired fox terrier, Skipper, in a kennel for safekeeping.

Frank Stanton was every city slicker's dream of a corn-fed Midwestern lad. Compact and muscular, he stood five feet eleven inches. His straight flaxen hair was neatly parted and perfectly combed. He had a strong jaw, straight nose, and intense blue eyes. At his side was Ruth, his wife of four years. She had a pretty, open face, with flashing dark eyes and brunette hair styled in a long bob.

The Stantons had left all their furniture—barely enough, he once said, to fill a phone booth—back in Columbus, packed for shipping. They brought with them a list of modestly priced hotels and a black aluminum box that was Frank Stanton's ticket to the world of network radio broadcasting. They settled into the Pickwick Arms Hotel on 51st Street between

Second and Third avenues. Flushed with excitement, they wandered Manhattan's streets, gazed at the shop windows along Fifth Avenue, and sampled their first toasted English muffins. On Monday morning Frank Stanton smoothed out his favorite suit, a salt and pepper tweed, and walked the four blocks to CBS headquarters on 52nd Street and Madison Avenue.

Understanding the role of Frank Stanton at CBS is crucial to understanding William Paley and the success of the network. Stanton was everything Paley was not. Like many great entrepreneurs, Paley was long on creative spark but short on follow-through. Paley, in effect, provided the architectural drawings; Stanton turned them into steel and concrete. It would be Paley's good fortune that Stanton was one of the great corporate builders of the era. The young midwesterner combined Klauber's discipline, executive ability, and high principles with Kesten's taste and instinct for promotion. Stanton was to prove the perfect man at the perfect place at the perfect time.

He was born on March 20, 1908, in Muskegon, Michigan. His grandfather, Curtis Stanton, had been a Navy engineer in Newburgh, the product of a family of English sea captains and shipbuilders. Curtis's son, Frank Cooper Stanton, moved to Dayton, Ohio, where he taught woodworking and mechanics in the city high schools. There he married Helen Josephine Schmidt, the daughter of the treasurer for the Dayton public school system whose Swiss forebears had been silk weavers. After the wedding he took her to live in Michigan.

When their firstborn son, Frank, was three months old, the Stantons moved from Muskegon back to Dayton, where Frank Senior accepted a job supervising the industrial arts instruction in Dayton's schools. Tools and machinery filled the basement of the Stanton's modest frame bungalow. Frank Senior built most of the family's furniture, and Helen was a weaver and a potter.

In this atmosphere, the work ethic became embedded in young Frank at an early age. "It was all I knew as a child," he said. "They were always working. I was always helping." By age five, he was carrying plaster chips and wood shavings from his father's workbench and his mother's kiln. The only trouble his mother remembered was his habit of "banging his head on the floor when he didn't like something to eat. He outgrew that, though."

At seven, Frank was photographed amid his father's paint cans, drills, hammers, saws, lumber, lathes, and wires. A profile in *The New Yorker* said he looked "remarkably like Mickey Rooney in 'Young Tom Edison' —in the basement, on the threshold of an experiment; he is wearing a long white apron, his yellow hair is wildly tumbled, and his solemn, purposeful expression clearly reveals intimations of immortality." Frank, along with his younger brother John, who would become an electronics engineer, spent hours in that basement and learned their father's exacting craftsmanship. Frank's hands grew rough calluses that remained throughout his life, a reminder of his humble beginnings.

While still in the primary grades at the Ruskin Public School, Frank showed a flair for art and graphics. He drew posters for the local YMCA and took a correspondence course in cartooning with his friend Milton Caniff—who would later achieve fame as creator of the "Terry and the Pirates" and "Steve Canyon" comic strips. At Steele High School, Frank put his talent to work as cartoonist and photographer for the school's daily newspaper.

He maintained an A− average even as he sought every leadership post he could find. This future trustee of the RAND Corporation, the Stanford Research Institute, the Rockefeller Foundation, and Lincoln Center for the Performing Arts, served on as many committees in high school as possible. Naturally he was president of the senior class and editor of the yearbook as well as a member of the debating society and the glee club. "Frank always had to be president of everything," said Caniff. In a town of 250,000, Stanton and Caniff were well known for their achievements. "It is surprising that they were so outstanding in a city of that size when they were still in high school," said *New York Times* columnist James Reston, who was two years behind them at their high school.

Despite his solid build, Frank never took to sports. As a neophyte member of the high school track team his name was mistakenly entered twice in the same race; he managed to tie himself for last place. Once years later he was coaxed into a softball game by some friends. To his teammates' dismay, he couldn't throw a ball from shortstop to first, and he struck out three times.

Frank Stanton had always been too busy for play, even in his youth. His industriousness took him out into the world at age twelve when he began delivering newspapers. He built his business by trading customers with other newsboys to ensure the most deliveries in the smallest geographic area. When he had reached a hundred customers, he sold the route for a small profit.

His shaping experience was a part-time job he took at thirteen at the Metropolitan, Dayton's largest men's clothing store. Each day at 2:00 P.M. —his high grades earned him early dismissal—he would ride his hand-built bicycle downtown to what he came to call "the Store." Most evenings he did not come home until seven. He often worked far into the night, squeezing in his homework during breaks. Before long he graduated from wrapping packages and running errands to tallying inventories, redesigning advertising, and redoing the store's twenty-three window displays. Through his display work, he learned techniques of lighting and set design that years later he would apply to television studios and news sets.

For nine years Frank worked everywhere at the Store, from the stockrooms to the boardroom. It was the beginning of what *The New Yorker* called his penchant for making himself indispensable: "A few people are born to indispensability. They serve on committees, spring to the fore in emergencies, establish liaisons, and act as catalysts whenever catalysis is in order. Stanton is one of these." By the end of his senior year in high school in 1926, the Metropolitan was paying him $50 a week, and his tutorial in the fundamentals of business administration was advancing smartly.

There are some parallels in the childhood experiences of Frank Stanton and Bill Paley, despite the basic dissimilarities of their backgrounds. Each had a father whose work often kept him away from the family. Each had a sibling whose illness frequently drew all their mothers' attention. The reactions of Stanton and Paley to these circumstances reflected their temperamental differences and foreshadowed the nature of their relationship years later.

For all practical purposes, Frank Stanton left his parents' orbit at age twelve. He sometimes said his mother was the more influential parent, but only because he so strongly defied her ambitions for him. She was a strict Methodist, a faithful member of the Women's Christian Temperance Union who banned all alcoholic beverages from her home. Her vision for young Frank began with Sunday school and ended with his living unmarried at home as a teacher or doctor. He was a dutiful and thoughtful son. Helen Stanton once remembered tearfully the time he came home from his paper route carrying an Easter lily for her.

But she was diverted from her plan when her second son, John, developed diabetes. Few children survived diabetes in those days. Insulin had not yet been invented, and the only way to control the illness was through diet. Helen Stanton threw herself into saving John, weighing every ounce of his food. Sad as the situation was, Frank saw his opportunity: "My mother and father were concerned about his health and I got out from under the net."

Although when Frank was small his father had read to him and taught him his trade, they drifted apart as Frank edged toward adolescence. "My father was so busy with his own life he didn't pay much attention to me," Stanton said many years later. "I didn't understand when other boys would have close relations with their fathers. They would hunt and fish together, and I just took note that it was a different way of living."

Paley transformed resentment of his father's frequent absences into worship of him; Stanton retreated into a fierce independence. Paley strove to match his father's achievements and take his help whenever he could; Stanton was determined to find success in his own way. Years later, on becoming Bill Paley's second-in-command, Frank Stanton would once again follow a separate track. It was the only way to survive with a man as self-involved as his father had been.

Stanton's independent spirit was fueled by the idea of New York City. By his senior year in high school he had traveled there three times, once alone and twice with friends. He would drive straight through in thirteen hours on a Thursday night and stay for a pittance at a YMCA or a Columbia University dormitory. On Monday he returned to Dayton after a non-stop round of art museums, theater, gawking at the stores, and feeling the vicarious thrill of the Jazz Age. By the time he was seventeen he knew that he would never be satisfied until he lived in New York.

Unlike Paley, a precocious playboy, Stanton followed the strait and narrow, not out of any sense of rectitude but because those were the lines of his character. At fourteen he lost his heart to Ruth Stephenson at Sunday school at the Methodist church they both attended in Dayton. He was the president of the youth fellowship, and she was the vice-president. They were the same age and saw each other steadily through high school and college.

He was also active in the Dayton Young Men's Christian Association, whose members routinely heard lectures about such sinful practices as sex, gambling, smoking, and drinking. Frank attended YMCA camp for four summers, and served as Dayton's delegate to statewide YMCA conferences. In his senior year in high school he was chosen to represent Ohio at an international meeting in Helsinki. The agenda was an extended discussion on sin, but after ten days he returned with more broadened horizons than were intended. He heard his roommates from Ceylon and Germany talk into the night about the possibility of another world war. He visited Finnish baths. He even tried to visit Leningrad but was turned back by Soviet authorities for lack of a visa.

As a boy, Stanton was fascinated by architecture. His parents were forever remodeling the house, and he would spend hours studying the blueprints. He read books about the subject and idolized Hugh Ferriss, a pioneer in skyscraper design. One year in high school he took a break from the Store to parlay his skill at drawing and lettering into a job with a Dayton architectural firm; at the end of the school year he regretfully concluded that he could make more money at the Store. Still, his experience led to an offer of a scholarship in architecture at Cornell University. Lacking encouragement from his parents, he did not pursue it. "It was a fork in the road," he said years later. "I might have taken the wrong turn."

He ended up at Ohio Wesleyan, a small Methodist university 90 miles outside of Dayton, because his best friend was there and it was close to Ruth, who was attending Western College for Women. He accelerated the pace of his life during his four college years, sometimes to frightening speed. Every weekend and on free days he commuted back to the Store to earn the $90 a week that helped pay his tuition. As editor of *Le Bijou,* the college yearbook, he applied strict cost controls, set new standards of design, and enlisted his friend Milton Caniff to create the illustrations. The yearbook made a profit of $200, which Stanton split with the business manager.

He produced dances for fraternities and sororities, hiring the orchestra and the hall, designing the programs and decorations, nearly always breaking even and sometimes making a $25 profit. He pioneered the use of 16mm movies to scout opposing football teams, and honed his skills as a photographer by selling exclusive pictures of school football games. Throughout he maintained a three-point grade average. He was, as he always would be, amazingly productive. By his own admission he was "a pretty dull guy."

But it was the twenties, after all. Stanton took up smoking a pipe and danced the Charleston. The Methodist Church had no hold on him; like Paley, he spurned organized religion after graduating from college. In his senior year, as a member of the honors fraternity, he produced the homecoming play, a revue called *1984*—a lighthearted frolic with a handful of risqué jokes. When a faculty committee reviewed the dress rehearsal, it ordered the bawdy jokes out. Stanton made it his business to spread the word that he had been censored. He also hinted to fraternity brothers that some of the censored material might remain. Shortly afterwards the show was sold out.

On the final night, Stanton permitted one of the banned jokes (about a nude photograph of a co-ed) to be reinstated. The administration immediately placed Stanton on probation and ordered him to leave campus. On his way home he stopped to visit Milt Caniff, by then a cartoonist for the *Columbus Dispatch.* Caniff immediately summoned a reporter from the Associated Press, and Stanton told him that he was puzzled why he had been kicked out, since the university had kept the profits from the show. By the time Stanton got to Dayton, the phone was ringing with inquiries from newspaper reporters and entreaties from Ohio Wesleyan officials to return fast.

Stanton had begun his studies at college halfheartedly intending to be a doctor, primarily because all his friends were in pre-med. He concentrated in zoology and psychology, and completed his requirements for a zoology major by the end of his junior year when he was admitted to medical school at the University of Michigan. (In those days medical students left normal undergraduate coursework after their third year in college.) After a visit to the campus, Stanton concluded that he would be unable to pay his bills with part-time work and manage his studies.

At that point he got a job offer from N. W. Ayer, a prestigious Philadelphia advertising agency. Executives there had been impressed by the yearbook Stanton produced and asked him to join their training program as a junior art director. He leaped at the chance, even if it meant foregoing his college degree. During the summer of 1929 the company sent him to a two-month course at the Bauhaus in Germany, where he was dazzled by the world of design. But when he reported for work that fall, the stock market crash had Madison Avenue reeling, and Ayer advised him to return to Ohio and complete his degree.

Frank Stanton was drawn into studying radio through psychology. In his junior year, he spent a semester exploring a topic on his own and writing a paper. He decided to survey the development of radio as an advertising medium—a choice akin to studying computers in the early 1970s. The library had no information on commercial radio, so Stanton wrote to scores of advertisers inquiring how programs were chosen for sponsorship and how the effectiveness of commercials was tested. He spent months cataloguing the number of sets and stations in use. The outcome was what he later called a "gaudy paper," superficial but chockablock with statistics, charts, and graphs. It earned him an A.

Although he became known as the resident expert on radio in the psychology department, he still had not set himself on a broadcasting career. He had no job prospects at all, in fact, when he graduated in 1930. To pay bills, he worked for the next year teaching typography and advanced typesetting at Roosevelt High School in Dayton. He and Ruth were engaged by then. Shortly before their wedding day the bank in which they had deposited their combined savings of $3,000 failed, and they lost everything. They were married as planned, on New Year's Eve, 1930, the only time he could break away from his work.

In the meantime, Stanton blanketed graduate schools with applications for fellowships in psychology. Ohio State finally offered him a post as teaching assistant for $83 a month—$750 a year—in the Industrial Psychology Laboratory where he planned to earn an advanced degree. Frank Stanton would always regret not having attended an Ivy League school. Attaching a doctorate to his name partly compensated, yet he would forever feel the outsider in the world of East Coast powerbrokers. In his seventies he would be invited to join the Harvard Board of Overseers— the first non-Harvard graduate to be so honored. Afterwards he could be seen dining in the New York Harvard Club—often with a guest, but just as frequently alone—savoring the richly paneled ambiance he missed in his youth.

Stanton grew more intrigued by the psychology of mass communications, specifically why and how people react to the information they receive. He tried to assess how the format and design of magazines and newspapers influence readers. For his master's thesis, completed in 1932, he concluded that print on dull paper was easier to read than that on slick paper ("The Influence of Surface and Tint of Paper on the Speed of Reading").

The studies leading to Stanton's doctoral dissertation firmly planted him in radio at last. He believed the impact of radio was more profound than print, yet few people had bothered to analyze why. He wrote to NBC and CBS, describing his views not only on how audiences were measured, but how radio affected attitudes toward purchasing and politics. NBC sent a polite, perfunctory reply; but Paul Kesten at CBS weighed in with a three-page letter he had obviously typed himself. He said that CBS was keenly interested in many of the same questions, and he would be eager to see any information Stanton could produce. He tried to steer Stanton away from fruitless research while nudging him toward those areas CBS would find most useful. Stanton responded "like a puppy who finally got attention," he recalled later. "I reoriented my problems and went to work on my thesis."

Stanton focused on the way networks measured the size of the audience by use of postcards and telephone calls. He studied and catalogued the advantages and disadvantages of each approach. Something was needed, he reasoned, a mechanism to measure viewing patterns without bias or reliance on memory. So Stanton the lifelong tinkerer invented a device, a black box that he could plug into a radio—a crude antecedent of the Nielsen audimeter that would become the primary measurement of broadcast audiences for more than four decades. Inside the box was a small motor that he built himself. Connected to the motor was a moving waxed paper tape and a stylus that would scratch across the tape to show which station was tuned in during given time periods.

He built fifty of the boxes, casting the aluminum casings himself. He went door to door and persuaded families to plug in the device for several weeks. His cover story was a sly fabrication that would have made Paley proud: Stanton passed himself off as an engineering student interested in using the devices to measure electrical current.

He visited the families every few days and quizzed them on what they had heard the previous evening; then he unspooled the rolls and studied the tapes. He discovered that the memories of listeners were often faulty.

After two years of this research, Stanton wrote to Kesten, describing his results. Kesten was intrigued by the recording device and wanted to see it. He offered to pay Stanton's railway ticket if he would come to New York for a meeting; instead, Stanton bundled Ruth into the Model A and headed for New York on an icy day in February 1933. As he drove her down Fifth Avenue for the first time, she gasped at the fancy shops. They stayed for two nights at the New Yorker Hotel, where they drank sloe gin fizzes—all on a CBS expense account.

Stanton took his black box to CBS for a meeting with Kesten and two other executives to present his preliminary evidence on network listening habits. The chief engineer for CBS, Ed Cohan, was openly contemptuous. He considered it an amateur contraption, and as Stanton winced he banged it down on the table to show his disgust. Kesten, however, was enthusiastic. CBS was in the throes of its fight with NBC over the Crossley ratings. He knew that because NBC was better established than CBS, with stronger stations and bigger shows, a listener's memory would probably favor the more prominent network. An impartial device might help buttress CBS's claims to popularity. He told Stanton to return to Columbus, conduct further experiments, and send in all his studies.

The two men kept in close contact. Stanton sent Kesten a pamphlet called "Checking the Checkers" that showed the inadequacy of the Crossley system of recall against the recording device. Later Stanton told Kesten that he wanted to compare the effectiveness of advertisements heard on the radio with those read on the page. CBS sent Stanton $100, and he produced "Memory for Advertising Copy Presented Visually vs. Orally," which gave the edge to the spoken over the printed word.

Kesten found this study useful in CBS's campaign to persuade advertisers that the ear was more receptive than the eye. CBS had been publishing similar studies on its own. Here, at last, was research conducted outside the network—albeit with quiet underwriting—that came to the same conclusion. When Stanton sent Kesten his dissertation, an exhaustive analysis of his work with the recording devices entitled "A Critique of Present Methods and a New Plan for Studying Radio Listening Behavior," Kesten knew he must have the young man on his staff. Without hesitation, Stanton accepted an offer of $55 a week, and in October 1935 he joined CBS's two-man research department.

Frank Stanton never pursued a grand design, yet somehow all the pieces of his background had fallen into place as he entered the elevator at 485 Madison Avenue: his experience in marketing, advertising, and design at the Store; his architectural avocation; his knowledge of typography and layouts, photography and film; his research in psychology; and his extensive study of radio broadcasting and its effects on listeners.

The young Ohio State graduate brought a prestigious credential to CBS: the world of business, particularly show business, could boast few doctors of philosophy. "The Sales Department used my degree for all it was worth, to my embarrassment," Stanton said years later. Midway through the 1930s, when CBS was avidly upgrading its image, it was very useful to have a doctor in the house.

11

IN LATER YEARS CBS would glory in its reputation as the "Tiffany Network." The public perceived CBS as an organization seeking excellence in every facet of its operation—from its programming to the decor of its offices. CBS's image was no accident. It was spurred by the federal government's efforts in the 1930s to tighten regulations on radio. Bill Paley and his key executives recognized that unless they created a medium that seemed above reproach, they faced strict regulations, restricted operations, and diminished profits.

Guided first by Edward Bernays, then by Klauber and Kesten, Paley carefully decorated the CBS schedule with superior educational, cultural, and news programs. Although these offerings constituted a tiny portion of CBS programming, the network publicized them aggressively—even deceptively—so that in the public's mind they overshadowed the endless hours of middlebrow and lowbrow entertainment.

Despite his emphasis on public relations, Paley was largely to blame for radio's troubles with the regulators. While NBC had opened the door to light entertainment by signing "Amos 'n' Andy" in 1929, it was Paley who flooded his network with escapist fare and strident commercials. NBC had little choice but to follow suit.

The excesses of network radio in the late 1920s and early 1930s—even broadcasters at the time admitted that radio was "nothing but a huge three ring vaudeville and circus"—inevitably drew the attention of Washington politicians. A new group called the National Committee on Education by Radio prodded Congress to consider legislation to regulate broadcasting more closely than the Radio Act of 1927. Among the provisions of the proposed bill was a requirement that 15 percent of all channels be reserved for educational use.

On Friday, January 17, 1930, Paley appeared before the Senate Committee on Interstate Commerce. It was the first of ten days of scheduled hearings, and Paley knew that his network's future prosperity depended on defeating the 15 percent provision. For slightly more than an hour, Paley patiently explained the structure and finances of CBS, and fielded questions from seven inquisitive but polite senators who were largely ignorant about network radio.

Paley's presentation was entirely scripted by Edward Bernays. It must have been difficult for Paley, who suffered from a lifelong fear of speaking from a prepared text. The thought of uttering even one inappropriate word filled him with dread; in later years he would make his speechwriters go through as many as twenty-five drafts. He had made no revisions in the Bernays text, but had drilled himself hard in his room at the Carlton Hotel in Washington, D.C., reading the statement over and over.

Paley gave an effective performance, a cunning blend of apparent candor and high ideals. He described CBS's success as an advertising medium, displaying a chart entitled "The Phenomenal Growth of Broadcast Advertising . . . The Greatest Media Development in the History of Advertising." But Bernays had also cast him as a concerned businessman. "I do not wish to lead you into believing that I regard radio as other than a business," said Paley. "It is the function of enlightened business, however, to serve the public, and in doing that, we are following in the footsteps of the greatest and most successful industries in America. Happily in the case of our own industry, there are larger opportunities to be of such service than may be found perhaps in any other line of activity, with the possible exception of the public press."

CBS had been able to serve the public well, Paley insisted, because it was independent—free of "special interests" and "entangling alliances." He conveniently ignored the ways advertisers dictated the content of programs and compromised radio's so-called independence. Radio's only legitimate regulators were the listeners, he said, who could register their disapproval by turning off their sets. The competition for listeners and advertisers between CBS and NBC had been "of almost inestimable benefit." If this competition was permitted to continue unimpeded, he promised, even better radio programs would result. Competition, after all, was "the winning principle of American business."

Bernays had directed Paley to avoid saying much about the mass appeal programs that enabled CBS to profit handsomely—programs like the "Street and Smith" detective magazine stories that included what one complaint to the Federal Radio Commission called "dramatic and bloody murder" scenes. Instead, Paley kept repeating that just 22 percent of CBS's schedule was taken up by sponsored programs; only when pressed by one senator did he acknowledge that the sponsored shows were broadcast during the most desirable evening hours of the CBS schedule.

It was the other 78 percent, the unsponsored programs, that Paley wished to impress on the senators. He didn't seem the least self-conscious that many of these shows stretched the notion of public service with such offerings as "Nit-Wit Hour," "Hank Simmons' Show Boat," and fifteen minutes of "Fashion Talk" by Dorothy Paley's friend Marjorie Oelrichs. The biggest unsponsored category was popular music, the sort usually played among the potted palms at tea dances, and it accounted for nearly 32 out of the previous week's 86½ unsponsored hours. There were still 28 unsponsored hours of symphonic music a week as well. Not that Paley had any commitment to high culture. Music filled the airwaves in those days, he later admitted, because "it was the cheapest and easiest thing to do."

Paley also catered to the self-interest of his interlocutors by mentioning no less than three times the CBS shows that featured the views of senators and congressmen—although such programs comprised a two-hour sliver of the weekly schedule. Foremost among these fledgling news programs were regular Washington political analyses from Frederic William Wile in "The Political Situation in Washington Tonight"; a weekly commentary by H. V. Kaltenborn; and the National Radio Forum from Washington. Paley was gratified to find the senators "very interested and I must say not hostile at all. I think they were beginning to see the magic of radio"—not to mention radio's political uses.

News and public affairs programs formed the cornerstone of the image-building strategy Bernays and Paley had launched the previous year. Initially neither CBS nor NBC had done much in news broadcasting. NBC saw itself performing a noble mission in creating the first national network, but at the same time it was reluctant to appear too powerful or influential. The passage of the Radio Act of 1927 had come amid congressional concern that a single corporation—namely, RCA—might dominate the flow of information on the airwaves. Thus the emphasis of the Radio Act was on the responsibility of local station owners to serve their communities; there was no mention of networks and their duties. In keeping with its low profile, NBC did not set up a service to regularly report and comment on national news. It merely broadcast important public events, such as political conventions, Independence Day ceremonies, and speeches.

At first Paley followed NBC's lead. CBS covered official functions to fill time while trying to seem public-spirited and responsible. Like NBC, it broadcast countless campaign speeches as well as the presidential election returns in 1928. But on Inauguration Day in March 1929, Paley began to appreciate the public appetite for news programs. CBS and NBC devoted the entire day to Herbert Hoover's White House reception, motorcade, swearing in, and inaugural ball. The two networks were rewarded with the biggest combined audience up to that time, 63 million listeners.

Bernays, meanwhile, was prodding Paley to create an identity distinct from NBC. His prescription for CBS was to emphasize information and communication. "I recognized the importance of freedom of speech and freedom of the press, so I told him to keep stressing these elements, which he did," said Bernays. Paley saw that news programs could attract listeners. But he also recognized that CBS's prestige "would depend to a considerable extent upon how well we could provide" radio news.

Paley's appearance on Capitol Hill in 1930 helped create the impression that CBS was the leader in public affairs and news programs. Ironically, Paley made his pronouncements just as he was poised to unleash a tide of mindless programs and tasteless commercials—all in the interests of meeting the profit goals imposed by Paramount. But, for the moment, his soothing words kept the legislators at bay. They believed his assurances that CBS would continue to uphold the public interest even as it competed against NBC. The legislation calling for the 15 percent quota disappeared.

Bernays later called his and Paley's words an "empty promise." "The public interest programming the statement bragged about was the result of Columbia's inability to get sponsored programs," said Bernays. "Compared to its older competitor, NBC, Columbia had hours of time unsold. If Columbia's policy, enforced by its lack of business, could have been carried forward it would have been a great boon to the public. Regrettably, the implied promise was never maintained."

Paley had learned his lessons from Bernays well. He knew how to maintain a facade of quality by announcing highbrow programs with great fanfare. While NBC spent far more money to develop its cultural programs—$2 million in 1932 versus CBS's $827,000—CBS was widely thought to be the leader. In the autumn of 1930 Paley signed the New York Philharmonic, then conducted by Arturo Toscanini, for a series of unsponsored broadcasts on Sunday afternoons. Although advertisers had no interest in that time period, Paley hoped that the Philharmonic would draw more upper-class listeners to radio. "Radio had so little appeal to top people," recalled Bernays, "that neither Clarence Mackay . . . who headed the orchestra's board, nor Arthur Judson, the manager, were willing to lend themselves to personal publicity in connection with the orchestra's engagement. We sent a telegram to 50 leaders in the music field all over the country telling them of the contract with the orchestra and asking their opinion."

Around the same time, Paley sensed another public relations payoff when he organized Columbia Concerts Corporation, which merged the seven leading concert bureaus in the country, all of which were on the verge of going under in the Depression. Paley worked hard to pull these bitter rivals together. He conducted most of the negotiations by long-distance telephone from Havana, where he was vacationing. One night he was on the phone from midnight to three in the morning.

The new bureau was intended to keep struggling performing artists employed by booking them in concert halls around the country, and even on rival NBC. But Paley also found the bureau useful in other ways. He earned congratulations for his heroic rescue, and he mollified Judson, who had been hurt when Paley bounced him from the network in 1928, by making him president of the bureau. The enterprise also would provide a cheap training ground for singers and other musicians, giving CBS an endless supply of new talent. "Out of this liaison has grown the CBS reputation among musicians as a medium of first-class musical programs," wrote *Fortune* in 1935. "Mr. Paley made a shrewd move in the direction of network prestige when he put Columbia's name on it."

In reality, neither network had a clear edge in quality musical programs during the thirties. NBC had its acclaimed "Music Appreciation Hour" with Walter Damrosch, NBC's resident conductor. Paley countered with "Piano Pointers," a series of Saturday afternoon recitals and discussions of piano techniques by Abram Chasins, a prominent pianist. Paley had met Chasins at the summer home of his friend Adam Gimbel; when Chasins described his proposed program, Paley recognized its value in appealing to an elite audience at little cost.

After CBS scored its coup with the Philharmonic, Paley tried in 1930 to lure the Metropolitan Opera for a series of Sunday concerts. But NBC executives convinced Met officials that their productions would be better served on their network. The maneuver infuriated Paley: "It was a bitter blow and one that I resented for a long time." He could console himself, however, that his Philharmonic broadcasts cost him only $35,000 a year, while the Met cost NBC $191,000.

Paley's motivation for his cultural venture was not only to build CBS but to enhance William Paley. "There was a twofold impetus on Bill Paley for cultural programs," said William Fineshriber, who joined CBS's publicity department in the 1930s. "He had to show Washington a record for public service. But he also had a genuine desire not to be a cigar salesman. He wanted to do something with meaning."

Despite such high-profile ornaments as the Philharmonic and the Columbia Concerts Corporation, Paley was steadily reducing the number of classical music programs on CBS. By the mid-thirties they comprised only 10 percent of the unsponsored schedule, compared with 26 percent in 1930. Clearly, he was walking an indistinct line when it came to stating what precisely CBS stood for.

Paley followed twin tracks in the early 1930s—garnering prestige through his unsponsored programs while also pandering to men like George Washington Hill, president of American Tobacco. Not only were advertisers buying commercial time, they were creating and shaping an increasing number of programs. Commercials and programs were often indistinguishable as stars routinely plugged products in their shows. By the mid-thirties, a handful of advertising agencies held enormous power over more than one third of the CBS and NBC schedules—and nearly all the network time in the prime evening hours.

As network commercialism increased, Senator Burton K. Wheeler, one of Paley's questioners in 1930, announced that the airwaves had become a "pawnshop." In January 1932, Senator James Couzens, chairman of the Interstate Commerce Committee, introduced a resolution noting "the growing dissatisfaction with the present use of radio facilities." Among other questions, Couzens asked the Federal Radio Commission about the feasibility of limiting advertising or converting the system to government ownership.

The election of Franklin D. Roosevelt in November 1932 intensified the impulse to reform radio. The nation's economy was in such a shambles that even conservative bankers on Wall Street agreed with FDR's calls to regulate certain industries. As the political climate shifted leftward, critics of the commercial system of broadcasting—an assortment of scholars and educators—grew more influential. James Rorty, a socialist writing in *Harper's, The New Republic, The Nation,* and *The New Masses,* eloquently attacked advertising as a corruption of radio's potential. The National Committee on Education by Radio renewed its lobbying in Congress, contending correctly that the educational function of radio had been subverted by businessmen. At the networks, the educators said, public service meant little more than service to the advertisers.

In 1933 the advocates of reform attracted two strong Washington allies, Senator Robert F. Wagner of New York and Senator Henry D. Hatfield of West Virginia, who co-sponsored a tough amendment to the proposed new communications act. The Wagner-Hatfield Amendment would cancel all broadcast licenses and redistribute them among commercial as well as non-profit broadcasters. Twenty-five percent of the nation's radio stations would be assigned to educational operators, an even larger proportion than was envisioned in 1930.

The elimination of one fourth of the radio stations would have been devastating to commercial broadcasters. Station owners and network officials united in a strong lobby to fight the proposed amendment. Paley appeared before congressional committees to argue for the status quo, as he had in 1930. This time he pleaded not only for CBS but for the entire radio industry—a strategy designed by Kesten to put the second-ranked network in the forefront of the fight. Working from speeches and testimony written by Ed Klauber, Paley served as the broadcast industry's most eloquent spokesman.

CBS was in a better position to meet the reformers' challenge than it had been in 1930. Having bought back CBS's stock from Paramount and regained control of his network, Paley could more readily counter his critics with classy new programs—and ever more sophisticated promotional strategies.

Today corporations routinely make statements about themselves through such devices as post-modern buildings or art galleries in their lobbies. But in the 1930s, striking a corporate attitude was still a novelty. Paul Kesten had a genius for devising a classy CBS "look" that would impress advertisers, government officials, and those who wrote about the radio business. He enlisted his friend, the designer William Lescaze, to carry this CBS style through offices and studios, reception areas, clock faces, signs, microphones, even lighting fixtures. The style was sleek and spare, with hints of Art Deco. It included "smooth surfaces, fluid forms, and unadorned wall planes," wrote one architectural critic. Kesten insisted on such consistency that the curve of a stairwell in CBS's Los Angeles studios was patterned after the arm of the microphone Lescaze designed for CBS. The idea behind these images was to portray CBS as a vital new industry that had its eye on the future.

Paley has always received credit for creating the CBS look. Paradoxically, one of his favorite stories about the earliest days at CBS was a resolution he made to ignore trappings like handsome studios and offices. It happened, he said, when he was walking by the Capitol Theater, Manhattan's fanciest movie house, which was showing an inferior motion picture. He glanced across the street where he saw a rundown theater that was offering a high-quality movie. He found himself spurning the Capitol's film, despite its elaborate surroundings, and choosing to see the better movie, despite the shabbiness of the theater. "I realized that it was because the quality of the picture and what I had heard about it were more important than the trimmings," he later recalled. "We were competing very strongly against NBC, and they were very rich, with palatial headquarters. . . . We decided to put every nickel we had into the programming and the quality of our shows. We didn't care about the fancy stuff that the people at home never saw anyway."

Only at Kesten's urging did Paley eventually succumb to spending money on the trimmings as well as the programs. Paley was smart enough to see that creating a visual identity for CBS could not only enhance the network's best programs, but image making could help override deficiencies in quality on the air.

This was as true of CBS's written promotions as it was of its lobbies and neon signs. Kesten produced a stream of eye-catching booklets, pamphlets, and magazine advertisements with snappy titles like "The Flood Hits the Valleys" and "The Added Increment." In one slick handout called "The Air Bites Shrewdly," Kesten described CBS as "a concert hall, a herald of news, a public forum, a field of sport, a hall of learning, a carnival of music, of laughter. All the world's its stage, and all the nation its audience. Today's air is bright with magic Shakespeare never dreamed of, summoned at the touch of a dial."

CBS's maneuvering in Washington complemented its public pronouncements. In 1933, Paley hired Henry Adams Bellows, a Federal Radio Commissioner and Harvard man who was close to Roosevelt. Bellows led CBS's lobbying effort along with Harry Butcher, another Roosevelt intimate. Throughout the early months of 1934 they met with key players on Capitol Hill and in the White House. In a message that May to Stephen Early, Roosevelt's press secretary, Bellows asked that the president be told "exactly what this amendment [the Wagner-Hatfield] means, because in the whole industry of broadcasting in this country, nothing has been suggested which has the destructive possibilities of this proposal." By then Roosevelt grasped for himself the power of radio; the previous year he had given his first four "Fireside Chats" to a rapt public. The Roosevelt White House was keenly aware of the need for good relations with the nation's broadcasters. Roosevelt did not press for passage of Wagner-Hatfield.

The amendment was defeated, and the Communications Act of 1934 was signed into law in June. Other than substituting a Federal Communications Commission for the old Federal Radio Commission, it perpetuated the laissez-faire approach of the 1927 radio law. The federal government could only regulate stations, not the influential networks and their partners, the advertisers. The commission could strip stations of their licenses if they failed to operate according to the "public interest, convenience, and necessity"—a phrase borrowed from railroad regulation that was sufficiently vague to cripple the commission's ability to do much of anything except correct the most egregious abuses. As the broadcasting historian Erik Barnouw has noted, "The FCC's licensing power was essentially a life-or-death authority. Its grimness was its main difficulty. A weapon so total was hard to use."

Congress referred the question of educational broadcasting to the new FCC. The commission held pro forma hearings in October and November of 1934 with ample testimony from both sides. M. H. Aylesworth, president of NBC, proclaimed the programs of Amos and Andy to be one of the greatest educational forces on the air; Paley reiterated his pledges of devotion to cultural and public affairs programs; and the commissioners reported to Congress that broadcasters were devoting sufficient time to educational programs. The reformers had lost their battle to change the course of American radio.

Had the outcome been different, with one quarter of all stations devoted to educational programs and with tighter regulations on commercial operators, broadcasting might have been a tool for greater enlightenment throughout its history; the troughs of lowest-common-denominator sameness that dominated radio and television for several decades might have averted. Entrepreneurs like Paley would have been given enough leeway to thrive, although their enormous profits would have been smaller. And they would have been forced to maintain their commitment to public service and diversified programming.

As it happened, it was only technological innovations—FM radio, cable television, videocassette recorders—that gave radio and television the range of choices available today. The principal reason these technologies eventually prevailed was that the traditional networks had become so profoundly unsatisfying. And it was radio's pioneers, Paley chief among them, who worked hardest—by encouraging restrictive regulation—to hold back the very technologies that have helped broadcasting fulfill its potential.

12

B ILL PALEY emerged from the battle over the Communications Act of 1934 the proud victor. Broadcasting would continue as a paradoxical hybrid: a competitive, private, profit-making enterprise supported by advertising, and a public trust obliged to serve a vague public interest. "What I would like to know is how you Americans can successfully worship God and Mammon at the same time," Lord Reith, the founder of the British Broadcasting Corporation, once asked a pair of CBS executives in the early thirties. In the long run, they could not. To build advertising revenues, radio broadcasters put on more programs aimed at a mass audience, squeezing out programs for a smaller, selective audience. The FCC turned out to be a paper tiger, and Paley saw that he could get away with steadily diminishing the public service programming that he had proclaimed on Capitol Hill.

At first, though, Paley and his counterparts at NBC had to deliver on their promises to Congress. The late 1930s brought a flowering of cultural and public affairs programs that has never been equaled. Not only did CBS underwrite bold new programs, it deftly exploited them to further enhance its prestigious image—usually at NBC's expense.

Paley hired his first full-time programming chief in 1936, a failed advertising executive and college dropout named William B. Lewis. Paley had placed an ad in broadcasting journals headlined: WANTED: A BIG MAN. But Lewis was not even among the six hundred applicants who responded. He had read about Paley in *Fortune* magazine and sent a letter to the CBS president at home. Paley mistakenly dropped the letter onto Klauber's file of a half-dozen finalists for the job. Klauber hired Lewis after one interview.

Recognizing that most of CBS's unsponsored programs were simply filling time, Lewis transformed them into a testing ground. His first venture was the Columbia Workshop for experimental drama. He hired talented directors like William N. Robson and Orson Welles and produced acclaimed verse plays by Archibald MacLeish, Stephen Vincent Benét, W. H. Auden, and a young journalist named Norman Corwin. CBS's Mercury Theater on the Air, run by Orson Welles and John Houseman, also offered bold new productions.

These dramas were rather highbrow for Paley; he wisely let Lewis select and shape them. But he appreciated their quality, and he got the most out of them. He placed the Workshop opposite NBC's top-rated Jack Benny program in prime time and the Mercury Theater opposite the Edgar Bergen–Charlie McCarthy program on Sundays at 8:00 P.M. These were throwaway positions, because no advertiser would bother going up against either NBC powerhouse, yet they served to further the image of CBS as the more enlightened network.

To reinforce this impression, CBS ran publicity campaigns—designed by Kesten and approved by Paley—that were replete with misstatements. Initially the competition declined to retaliate. NBC officials assumed that the public would recognize CBS's deceptions. "In the past, Columbia has issued several promotion pieces which might have goaded us to a rebuttal. But it has always been our policy to avoid this type of fight," an NBC official wrote in November 1934. "This is the stronger attitude to take, even though many of the Columbia pieces have been full of loopholes which we could easily have turned to our advantage."

Time after time NBC underestimated CBS's promotional skills. Pal-

ey's biggest coup was a grand announcement on May 15, 1935, timed to
coincide with the opening of a FCC conference on ways to increase educational programs on the networks. CBS and NBC had previously agreed
to issue a joint statement of principles. As late as May 13, Fred Willis,
Paley's special assistant, wrote a letter to NBC president M. H. Aylesworth urging that the broadcasters should "not represent ourselves individually, but solely as an industry."

NBC officials were consequently stunned when Paley announced, in
a handsomely bound booklet, three sweeping policies. There would be
new time limits on commercial announcements. They would be restricted
to a maximum of 10 percent of the time allotted to programs after 6:00
P.M. and 15 percent of daytime broadcasts. Children's programs would
have to conform to new standards that eliminated eight themes, such as
exalting gangsters, fostering disrespect for parents, and glorifying "con-
ceit, smugness or an unwarranted superiority over others." And CBS
would ban all advertising for products such as laxatives, deodorants, de-
pilatories, and other products having to do with "internal bodily functions
or the symptomatic results of internal disturbances" that violated standards
of good taste.

The announcement was viewed at NBC headquarters as classic Paley
grandstanding. "No one in NBC should become particularly excited about
this bit of publicity," wrote an executive named M. C. Witmer to Richard
Patterson, a vice-president of NBC, the next day. "It is one of those things
that creates quite a stir at first, but re-acts very negatively indeed a little
later on." NBC had already studied similar restrictions on commercial
time but had been unable to devise a workable formula. "Some ten-word
commercials are too long," wrote Edgar Kobak, an NBC executive, to
Patterson. "Copy length cannot be measured in minutes—but in interest."

Kobak was dead wrong, as the adoption of industrywide standards
on commercial length later showed. Characteristically, Paley had found
the simplest solution, a numerical formula in this case. He was also canny
in singling out the murder and mayhem on children's programs before
educators had a chance to pounce. NBC, by contrast, was astonishingly
shortsighted. "Let's not go 'sissy' with the kids or they won't listen now
—or when they grow up," Kobak wrote. "We still want to raise kids with
some adventure and fight and imagination. The best way to plan programs
for youngsters is to let them judge."

As a result of the new policy, CBS lost all its children's adventure
programming to NBC. And when CBS's uplifting substitutes failed to
attract enough viewers, the network gradually permitted the old "blood
and thunder" forms to creep back. But by then no one was paying much
attention. Paley had established himself as a public-spirited broadcaster.

Paley's gamesmanship was more egregious when it came to "bodily function" advertising. NBC had decided to ban commercials for laxatives, deodorants, and similar products back in November 1933—eighteen months before CBS's announcement. Instead of making a public proclamation, NBC chose to work quietly with advertisers to eliminate abuses. When all the offending commercials had been eliminated, NBC planned to announce the results. NBC asked CBS to institute a similar policy, but CBS declined. Instead, CBS picked up countless laxative and deodorant commercials turned down by NBC. "They got so many and they were so bad that they were forced to clean house and do it in a hurry," wrote Kobak to an RCA official in June 1935. "Columbia told the world about their rules before they set up a department to clean up the bad things."

In fact, CBS's policy was even more devious than that. It was set up so that the network would accept no new contracts for the taboo products. However, it would honor renewals of existing contracts. In those days sponsors routinely deserted the networks during the slow summer months. But in the summer of 1935, the laxative manufacturers would have lost their spots on CBS had they taken their usual hiatus. So they stayed on and were permitted to renew in the fall. Ethical or not, Paley had pulled off a business coup: in the year he banned laxative advertisements, he reaped more revenue from those commercials than ever before. It was only a matter of time before the ban was quietly phased out.

Meanwhile, Senator Burton Wheeler read the CBS policies into the *Congressional Record* with accompanying encomiums. Newspapers and magazines ran laudatory articles. As the weeks went by, even NBC executives grudgingly acknowledged that Paley had reaped a publicity bonanza. But NBC's Aylesworth deluded himself into believing that "it is apparent to the press . . . that we acted before Columbia did, but in a different manner. . . . I think our method was much more dignified and will have a lasting effect in the history of broadcasting." How wrong he was. In one history book after another, Paley's announcements in 1935 mark his emergence as the industry leader.

CBS's tactics wore NBC down. By 1938 John Royal, the vice-president for programs hired by Sarnoff to counter Lewis's innovations over at CBS, was complaining in a letter: "I cannot impress upon you how much they are doing to try to take first place in prestige, and they will not stop at anything." NBC's new president, Niles Trammell, wrote less than a year later: "I am certain that we do a much better job than Columbia in every part of educational and cultural programs. The thing that I think probably irks us all is the fact that Columbia with an inferior schedule gets a break on publicity."

Throughout the late thirties, David Sarnoff continually harangued his executives to match CBS's tactics. "We simply cannot ignore Columbia's consistent and persistent claims to leadership in network broadcasting," he complained to Lenox Lohr, another NBC official, in August 1939. "We must meet it with facts and with skill."

CBS's aggressiveness eventually forced NBC to play by CBS rules. Just as in the early wars for affiliated stations and ratings, NBC joined CBS in hand-to-hand combat over programs and promotions. In 1937, NBC launched a campaign to sign Toscanini—who had left the New York Philharmonic in a dispute the year before—as conductor of a new NBC Symphony; it would give weekly broadcasts with no commercial interruptions. Sarnoff was every bit as relentless in his pursuit of the maestro as Paley had been in courting such middlebrows as Will Rogers and Major Bowes.

Sarnoff's success brought NBC wide acclaim. That summer the two networks found themselves in a pointless competition dubbed the "Shakespeare War." CBS announced a series of Shakespeare plays starring Burgess Meredith, Walter Huston, and Edward G. Robinson; Sarnoff countered with a similar series showcasing John Barrymore. NBC's Royal admitted at the time, "We didn't put it on because we were great enthusiasts for Shakespeare; to be strictly honest we put it on for Exhibit A, to show educators . . . that we were adding something to culture."

With these highly publicized contests, a personal rivalry between Paley and Sarnoff burst into public view. In large measure, NBC's original indifference to CBS's promotional tactics had arisen from Sarnoff's hostility to Paley and CBS. In Paley's early years at the network, NBC executives declined even to meet with the upstart broadcaster for fear of dignifying his enterprise. But with every Paley success, Sarnoff grew more jealous, not only of Paley's professional achievements but his social advancement. Sarnoff had a bright and fashionable French wife, Lizette, yet he was uncomfortable in the world of high society where Paley now moved so easily.

"He couldn't understand why women were so attracted to Bill," Frank Stanton said. "He couldn't understand why Bill spent so much time on social events. He didn't think Bill worked very hard, and he really resented the attention Bill got."

Sarnoff became obsessed with learning about Paley's operations and techniques. He regularly pestered his executives for figures on CBS's profitability. In 1937, for example, NBC earned only $3.7 million on revenues of $41.3 million, compared to CBS's $4.2 million on revenues of $28 million. Sarnoff demanded an explanation. The main reason, NBC executives concluded, was that CBS did not spend as much on unsponsored programs.

During the Depression, Sarnoff was making $100,000 a year, the equivalent, in today's dollars, of nearly $1 million, but only about half what Paley earned in salary and bonus. Both men had majestic offices. Sarnoff's, paneled in white oak, occupied a spacious corner of the fifty-third floor of the RCA Building in Rockefeller Center. Adjoining the office was a private barbershop, lavatory, and dressing room. From his desk he could see across Manhattan and up the Hudson River. He had bought a thirty-room town house, complete with an elevator, on East 71st Street, that was larger than Paley's on Beekman Place.

Although Sarnoff had the superior intellect, he was deliberate and methodical and in his eyes, everything Paley achieved came too easily. To Sarnoff, Paley was a child of privilege. He also envied Paley's operation. "He could not understand how Bill got so many good people," Stanton said. Once, in the 1930s, Sarnoff even tried to lure Paley to run NBC—a tacit recognition of Paley's superiority in programming. But Paley spurned the offer quickly. Not only was it patronizing, it confirmed to Paley that he had the upper hand.

Sarnoff never appreciated that Paley was a creative and shrewd entrepreneur who leaned on and learned from his top administrators, Klauber and Kesten. Paley was not in charge all the time as Sarnoff was. Although Paley might reverse himself several times, he at least could be reached directly and quickly by subordinates for crucial decisions.

A starched shirt who remained aloof from NBC executives, Sarnoff surrounded himself with a tight circle of loyal RCA yes-men. He was a visionary, and did not absorb ideas from others as Paley did. Sarnoff kept his desk spotless, permitting only one memo to cross it at a time. He worked long hours and frequently went home later than his staff. Many of those evenings he spent alone at his desk, pondering strategies to solidify RCA's leadership in communications and electronics. When a problem arose, a stream of memos had to wend its way through layers of executives. Sarnoff would express his displeasure with rough marginal notes in a dark, heavy scrawl. The thin precise lines of Paley's handwriting, by contrast, were studied and refined, conveying the image of a cultured man.

Paley shared some of Sarnoff's traits—an enormous ego, a hunger for publicity, a growing contempt for underlings. Yet Paley's strivings were nearly invisible, his actions always veiled in gentility. Sarnoff was harshly despotic, and fairly bristled with cockiness and authority. "There was no mistaking what David Sarnoff wanted. He was very lucid and direct. There was no bullshit," said David Adams, a longtime NBC executive and Sarnoff intimate.

Sarnoff lacked Paley's feel for popular culture. He adored classical music; his idea of relaxation was to sneak down to Studio 8-H in Rockefeller Center and listen to the rehearsals of the NBC Symphony. When his wife tuned into "Amos 'n' Andy," Sarnoff left the room. He had nothing but contempt for comedians. "If comedy is the center of NBC's activities, then maybe I had better quit," he once confided to one of his executives. Given a preference, he would have aired only symphonies and classical dramas on NBC. As one of his former executives said, "His outlook on life was simply too serious to accommodate to popular taste. . . . He did not understand the hunger for easy entertainment. . . . He saw broadcasting as a means of bridging cultural differences, bringing people together in greater understanding of one another."

Paley, on the other hand, had a genius for mass programming, mainly because it mirrored his own taste. He also understood that it was the path to big money. Paley liked popular entertainers and wooed them with his customary energy. When the actress Alice Faye came to New York, he filled her hotel room with flowers; Sarnoff never sent her a posy. Paley had a good ear for musical talent. He knew enough about dramatic structure to criticize a program intelligently. To Paley, Sarnoff was a hardware man in a software business.

Publicly, Paley liked to portray their relationship as cordial and avuncular. "He liked me very much. I liked him very much," said Paley. "We would have weeks or months of battle and then suddenly there would be calm again." Their relationship, he maintained, was "sort of intimate. He was a man with an exaggerated ego, a little jealous of a young snip who had come along and made progress at a pace which was greater than his."

Paley was put off by Sarnoff's more obvious identification as a Jew, and Sarnoff was irritated by Paley's WASP pretensions. Unlike Paley, Sarnoff talked and wrote from time to time about the meaning of being a Jew. "To Sarnoff, Paley wanted to operate in a gentile fast-paced high society world. He basically gave up being Jewish," said David Adams. "Sarnoff wasn't much of a Jew either, but he was a member of Temple Emanu-El."

More than anything, it galled Sarnoff—the broadcasting pioneer, the medium's idealist—that Paley was referred to as "radio's restless conscience." When *Time* magazine ran a cover story on the radio boom in the late thirties, a broadly grinning Paley wearing a snappy glen plaid suit was the cover boy. In Sarnoff's view, Paley was an opportunist who lacked any long-range vision for the industry. Paley did indeed lack the capacity for pure ideas, the defining characteristic of a visionary. Unlike Sarnoff, Paley needed to see how something worked before he could embrace it. Paley reaped where Sarnoff sowed—which rankled Sarnoff no end. "He thought Paley had no concern with advancing broadcasting," said David

Adams. "Sarnoff was his own hero, and Paley wanted to make a name and money for himself."

To that end, Paley sanctioned two maneuvers in the late 1930s that brought CBS into the big-time corporate world: the company went public, and it made its first acquisition. The first move was motivated by Paley's financial ambition, the second by his sense of competition. Both accelerated CBS's growth and raised the company's visibility.

A limited number of CBS shares began trading publicly in 1935. A brisk market for CBS stock quickly developed on the strength of the network's impressive revenues and profits. For the first time Paley could watch the value of his holdings fluctuate with the demand of investors. He liked what he saw. By 1935 his share of the company had dropped to 33.7 percent from a high of 61 percent at the end of 1928. Yet his holdings were worth as much as $13.8 million—approximately $131 million in 1990 dollars—compared with $4 million following the 1932 Paramount buyback. In 1936, investors drove the market value of CBS even higher. At one point that year Paley's stake was worth $17.3 million, based on bids of $60 for each scarce share of stock.

Top CBS executives disagreed about the wisdom of opening CBS to extensive public trading. In 1937, Paley held a meeting in his office to discuss the pros and cons of listing the company on the New York Stock Exchange. As was his custom, he went around the room seeking opinions. Klauber was against it, along with Joseph Ream, the corporate lawyer. They argued that CBS should remain a small organization; staying private would allow the company greater flexibility. "The stock had already gotten a little public," recalled Ream. "It was already making us more bottom-line conscious."

Everyone else favored the move. Kesten endorsed it, as did CBS's chief counsel, Ralph Colin. "You're out of step," they told Klauber and Ream. "It's a great deal." Paley remained impassive, but his views came clear on June 7, when CBS common stock was listed for the first time on the Exchange.

Before that date, Paley sold off 7 percent for an estimated $1.3 million—some $11.1 million in 1990 dollars. That left him with 26.3 percent of the stock, which was worth $7.6 million by year's end when the price was $17 per share—nearly $80 million in today's dollars. In 1940 he cashed in again, selling 100,000 of his shares to the public. He netted $2.4 million (approximately $22 million in 1990 dollars) and retained 20 percent of the company—half of his original stake of 41 percent.

This began a steady erosion in Paley's share of CBS—a course that would continue and that reflected Paley's anxieties about putting all his eggs in his own company's basket. Despite his confidence in CBS, he always had an underlying fear, perhaps even a superstition, that the network's prosperity could not last. He would willingly pare down his holdings gradually so that he could invest in other moneymaking schemes—real estate, oil wells—unencumbered by the public interest and other restraints.

The decline in his stake had no effect on Paley's proprietary view of CBS. He continued to run the company as if he owned it entirely. During the Depression years he took a salary of $40,000 ($400,000 in 1990 dollars) and bonuses averaging $150,000 ($1.5 million in 1990 dollars). But his big score came in his yearly stock dividends, particularly before CBS went public. Through the thirties they rose to a peak of $1.1 million in 1936 ($11 million in 1990 dollars). In subsequent prewar years his annual dividend never dropped below $778,000.

Paley frequently lamented taking the company public. He would say to friends and colleagues that CBS could have taken risks and better served the public without accountability to shareholders and the constant pressure from Wall Street to increase profits. Yet he had ample resources to buy more stock and run the company privately. He chose not to. The fact was that Paley savored the barometer of Wall Street as a measure of his success. And even without shareholders he would doubtless have made the same bottom-line demands. "His desire for more profits was insatiable," said John A. Schneider, a longtime top CBS executive. "He had a rapacious attitude about money and profit that was second to none in his time," said a former high-level CBS executive.

Another way Paley sought to cushion himself from the vicissitudes of a regulated business was by diversifying CBS. He took his first step by happenstance, however. Once again, his in-law Isaac Levy played a pivotal role.

Edward (Ted) Wallerstein, the head of RCA's records division, RCA Victor, was a neighbor of Ike Levy's. One day in December 1938, Levy complained to Wallerstein that Victor Records had not given the Philadelphia Orchestra adequate opportunity to record a prestigious repertoire. Wallerstein countered that if Levy wanted to do something about it he could buy another record company and sign the Philadelphia Orchestra himself. Wallerstein even knew of a candidate, the American Record Company, which owned the old Columbia Phonograph Company—the same Columbia that had briefly owned United Independent Broadcasters in 1927.

Since bailing out of the radio business, Columbia Phonograph had nearly gone broke as a result of competition from newcomers to the recorded music field. It had become a minor player, the victim of mismanagement and inferior disks. In 1934, American Record bought Columbia for $250,000. The president of American Record was Herbert Yates, who also owned Republic Pictures in Hollywood. Yates had moved into recorded music because he believed that movie sound would be on disks and not film. When that bet proved wrong, he was eager to unload the record division.

Levy got wind that American Record could be bought for $800,000 —more than three times what Yates had paid four years earlier. Levy did not even flinch at the price; he was convinced the record business had a great future. He first approached his cohorts in the high-stakes poker game he played each week at the Manhattan Club in New York City. The crowd there included Jerry Louchheim, Herbert Swope, and Jock Whitney, who agreed to join him in the purchase. The next day Levy mentioned his plans to Paley. When Paley heard the lineup of investors, his competitive instincts flared. Although he knew little about the record business, he pressed Levy to let CBS buy the company instead.

As in the original purchase of CBS, nowhere did Paley credit Levy for spotting the record company. "I did the whole thing," Paley once boasted to two reporters from *Fortune* magazine. Indeed, as the decades rolled by, Paley's accounts of his prescience grew. He said that he had watched the record business fall apart during the 1930s as people turned to radio for music. But he knew that with the advent of drama, variety, comedy, and news on the radio there would be less room for music. Paley said he felt that the record business would boom as a result. All of that was true—with the benefit of hindsight.

"I wanted to expand," he maintained to one writer, "and there was a natural affinity, I thought, between records and broadcasting. Besides, the thing was so cheap." Here Paley got confused, because the eventual price tag of $700,000—nearly $6.5 million in 1990 dollars—was regarded at the time as excessive, a criticism Paley even acknowledged in his own memoir. Nor, for that matter, was there ever a particularly "natural" affinity between records and broadcasting, despite the obvious temptation to promote CBS records on the CBS airwaves. "I devoted my life to keeping that from happening," said Frank Stanton, "because it would have given us problems with the license renewals for our stations. CBS Broadcasting and CBS Records were run just as far apart as if CBS Records were another company."

At Levy's suggestion, Paley hired Wallerstein to run the renamed Columbia Recording Corporation. At one stroke, CBS robbed RCA of a top executive and enlisted an experienced hand in the record business. Wallerstein saw that Paley would give him leeway in running the company. "He felt that Paley didn't really want to run CBS Records," said

John Hammond, the first executive hired at CBS by Wallerstein in January 1939. "Ted said the Levys felt there was a real future for records but Paley wasn't a record man. He was a radio man." Paley's hands-off approach toward CBS Records would apply to other CBS subsidiaries. If he had an instinct or special interest in a business, he would get deeply involved; otherwise he was content to approve the decisions made by others.

Such was the case with Wallerstein's first major move. As John Hammond recounts in his memoir, "In August 1939 Wallerstein revolutionized the record business. Victor classical records had been selling for from $1.50 to $3 . . . Victor and Brunswick popular records sold for seventy-five cents. Wallerstein believed these prices were too high for the market. He reduced Columbia Masterworks . . . to $1. Columbia popular records . . . were reduced to fifty cents." By Hammond's recollection, Paley simply gave the rubber stamp to Wallerstein's plan. Record sales skyrocketed and RCA eventually dropped its prices as well. After losses of $73,000 in its first year, CBS Records moved into burgeoning profitability, while Paley watched approvingly from the sidelines.

He did manage, however, to claim Wallerstein's idea about price reduction along the way. "I asked him to do it—put out classical records at a dollar each," Paley wrote in his memoir. "The price cut was Wallerstein entirely," insisted Hammond. "I remember his talking about it. He was operating head. I can't conceive of Paley thinking of that."

13

ALTHOUGH FRANK STANTON and William Paley had only glancing contact during the thirties and early forties, Stanton was making his mark and moving up fast. Since his arrival in the autumn of 1935, the self-effacing midwesterner had been building a power base.

He impressed his colleagues as a diligent, energetic worker and a stickler for detail. "I was a bore," he admitted. "I worked around the clock. I wasn't much fun to be with. I didn't do a lot of drinking. I wasn't out on the town." There were 24 million radios in American homes, 3 million more in automobiles, and Stanton was determined to find out everything he could about who was listening, where or when they listened, and why they listened. In a paper presented at a radio industry meeting in January 1936, Stanton displayed the sophistication of his analyses. He said that 78 percent of the nation's radios were turned on some time during the day; the average radio was in use four and a half hours daily. After analyzing the top twenty programs, he concluded that variety formats were the most popular, followed by comedy, then popular music, classical music, and drama. While listening to radio, men tended to eat, read, or rest, while women—who listened twice as much as men—usually sewed, ironed, ate, rested, cooked, or did housework. In general, listeners tuned in to follow favorite entertainment programs or be informed. Listeners were most attentive when programs were simple yet meaningful. They listened closely to factual material if it was presented in short, simple sentences; longer sentences could be used if the material was especially interesting. News was broadcast most effectively at 120 words per minute; more difficult material had to be read more slowly.

Decades later, most of these conclusions seem like common sense. At the time, they were a revelation. One participant from NBC at the conference concluded, "Dr. Stanton has developed an excellent technique in the discovery of listener attention and habits."

Stanton was restless his first year. He felt underused and thought his superiors were treating him like a statistical clerk. He kept one foot in academia with a busy schedule of professional meetings—"There was a period of nine months when if a decent university had said 'come join us,' I would have packed up and left," he said. MIT offered Stanton a job as an assistant professor for $3,000 a year. If it had been an associate professorship, he would have moved to Cambridge.

But in 1936 Stanton got his big break. The FCC had done a survey to determine who was listening to powerful stations across the country. The results were particularly unfavorable for CBS, so Kesten asked Stanton to conduct an analysis.

Stanton visited the FCC offices in Washington on a Saturday morning, and he and Ruth spent the day picking through bins filled with thousands of questionnaires to find the responses from Pennsylvania as a sample. After retabulating the results, Stanton told Kesten that the FCC had asked the wrong questions and had gotten too small a return—7 percent of the respondents—to draw conclusions. For $125, Stanton said he would go to Pennsylvania and conduct his own research face to face instead of by mail as the FCC had done.

He crisscrossed two counties, ringing doorbells. At each home he asked to see the radio set. If it was turned on, he noted the station; if not, he checked where the dial had been left. He than asked questions about which stations had interference and which did not. He emerged with a set of statistics at odds with the FCC results. CBS lodged a formal protest, and the FCC called a hearing. Stanton appeared as CBS's star witness, armed with colorful charts, graphs, maps, diagrams, and tables. However, the FCC barred him from speaking on the grounds that he was not an engineer. CBS milked the brouhaha for the maximum publicity, and the network management finally took notice of its new whiz kid. "By that time I had no interest in MIT or anybody else," said Stanton.

Increasingly Stanton was called on to buttress what one CBS executive called Paul Kesten's "lightning intuitions." Stanton had his tiny research department churning out facts and figures to salesmen trying to lure advertisers and choice affiliates from NBC. He was establishing himself as an executive with precise methods. Stanton "brought respect to the flashy side of show business," said Peter Goldmark, an inventor who joined the company in 1935. Everyone called Stanton "Doc." Advertisers were bemused by his elaborate stratifications of the audience according to age, sex, and education, but Stanton showed them more effectively than anyone else how radio was reaching the groups that sponsors wanted to buy their products. No longer was he being called on simply to brief other executives before conferences or meetings with sponsors. Now he made the presentations himself. Before long, his research was used in almost every facet of CBS's business—to help attract advertisers and audiences, to select and build programs, and to help coax affiliates to switch from NBC to CBS. By 1938 he was research director with a staff of one hundred.

Stanton was not content to remain pigeon-holed in the research department, however. He was terrifically ambitious. Working eighty hours a week, he made himself indispensable throughout the company. "Most researchers," Paul Kesten once remarked, "face the problem of stuffing their reports down the throats of the people who have ordered the studies. Stanton had a way of making his facts so useful that he soon had all the executives calling on him for help." To ingratiate himself with Kesten, Stanton concocted a formula that could estimate advertising sales and profits a month before the accounting department tallied them. The first time Kesten took these projections to the CBS board of directors, he called Stanton later and said, "Are you sure?" "If you are right in that kind of circumstance," Stanton recalled, "people sort of lean on you."

Artifice played a part in Stanton's dealings with his superiors as well. "Every time management would ask me a question, if I didn't know it, I would fake it to a certain extent, and then run like hell down the back stairs and get the *World Almanac*," Stanton said. "At that time I had more information than I think most agencies had on Madison Avenue, because I kept this thing on my desk. I'd get a lot of curious calls. And I'd look through the *Almanac* very quickly and I'd say, 'Oh, you mean that place in DeKalb County, Georgia? That's it.' It was all in the *World Almanac*, which cost thirty-five cents. It was there for anybody that wanted to find it."

Stanton's bywords around CBS became "Let's find out." Wherever there was a vacuum, Stanton would fill it with enthusiasm and dedication. "The question might have arisen whether to expand the facilities of station KMOX in St. Louis," wrote *The New Yorker*. "The CBS executives would have begun their meeting on the subject by agreeing that there were several points to be borne in mind. 'Indeed there are, gentlemen!' Stanton would cry, coming in through a side door without an invitation. 'We have only six floors there—twenty-three rooms—with an overall space of 132,000 cubic feet. The adjacent buildings, erected in 1904 and 1926 respectively, are owned by the Hokenson Brass Works and Abrams & Sons, Pants. Abrams won't sell, but Hokenson would like to move over to Market Street and wants $185,000 for his five-story building and ninety-two-foot lot. I have private information, however, that he would sell for $73,400.' The executives' reply to an outburst of this kind was generally, 'O.K. Stanton, you handle it.' "

When Stanton needed something and couldn't get it, he organized it himself. In trying to compile a study of advertising trends, he was amazed to learn that no one had kept a record of CBS's advertising rates. That prompted him to bring in a friend, who set up a CBS library that became the model for the industry.

Stanton also developed, along with Paul Lazarsfeld, a social scientist from Vienna, a mechanism called the program analyzer, which measured listener responses to radio programs. It was a simple device with two buttons, red and green. If the listener heard something pleasing, he pushed the green button. If dissatisfied, he pushed red. The responses were charted on a graph inside the analyzer; as many as one hundred listeners could be tracked simultaneously. After the program had ended, a team of psychologists would use the graph to probe the listeners. Why, the listeners were asked, did a given character or joke or plot turn or phrase of music elicit the various responses?

CBS had nothing to do with Stanton's work on the analyzer; he did it with a $75,000 grant from the Rockefeller Foundation. But when the mechanism was perfected in 1940, Stanton took it to CBS, where it became an integral part of selecting programs for the network for the next five decades. In a research center at the CBS Building that was eventually dubbed "Black Rock Bijou," volunteers were brought in groups of twenty to listen to a variety of shows and record their reaction on the analyzer, nicknamed "Little Annie." "We used it and made a lot of hay with it because it was a razzle-dazzle thing to give to Hollywood and the advertisers," said Stanton.

Stanton always maintained that the interviews by trained psychologists were crucial to evaluating a show. They could, for example, screen out irrelevant reactions, such as the woman who preferred a soap opera villain to the hero simply because she liked the way the villain closed doors. But if listeners uniformly disliked an announcer's voice or a loud burst of music, the sponsor would probably ask that the program be changed. Indeed, CBS found that its analyzer results were 85 percent accurate; poor test results turned back many programs in the early stages.

Critics of the analyzer have argued that it helped homogenize first radio and later television programs. Its inherent bias toward the familiar, the argument goes, deflected anything innovative. Over the years, in fact, groundbreaking shows have often tested poorly, only to be saved by the instincts of various network executives. "I guess I could have been accused of cutting the highs off some of the programs," Stanton conceded, "but I certainly eliminated many of the lows."

Partly because of his invention of the analyzer, Stanton earned a reputation as a man who did it by the numbers. But the prevailing portrait of Stanton as a cold, narrow, and somewhat forbidding technocrat emerged largely from Victor Ratner, Kesten's garrulous assistant, who over the years spoke harshly of Stanton to authors writing about CBS. He told Robert Metz, the author of *CBS: Reflections in a Bloodshot Eye,* that Stanton had a mind like a "Swiss hotel clerk" and that he was a "frightened man," wary of being surrounded by smart people. To David Halberstam, author of *The Powers That Be,* Ratner was even more scathing. Stanton, he said, was a "very neurotic, insecure man." These judgments took hold and became part of the CBS mythology. In fact, Ratner's reaction to Stanton was deeply colored by jealousy. Although Ratner was initially Stanton's superior, Kesten usually bypassed him for Stanton's opinions, often calling on Stanton to correct advertising copy written by Ratner. And as Stanton vaulted up the ladder, Ratner remained in place, fuming with resentment.

Stanton could keep an icy reserve, and he was always in control. Yet those who knew him found warmth and decency. His demands sometimes engendered fear, but he inspired respect and strong personal loyalty. "He had a real, good solid business head," said Helen Sioussat, who served as CBS's Director of Talks in the 1930s and 1940s. "He was very strong. But he had a polite way about him. He wasn't a smoothie but he was nice and direct. He was so efficient, and he had no patience with people who were not efficient. People were afraid of upsetting him, of going down in his estimation."

Stanton was anything but the man in the empty suit. In some respects, he was even more versatile than Paley. Outside CBS, Stanton pursued an array of activities in the worlds of architecture, modern art, graphics, and design. He was endlessly curious; when he delved into a topic, he mastered it. "No living man has ever caught Frank Stanton at a loss for the precise answer to a question even remotely within his competence, which ranges from the sculptures of Henry Moore to the number of women watching a soap opera," wrote *Business Week* magazine.

In his love for statistics, Stanton could be termed a technician. But he was imaginative in applying the numbers as well. In the network's earliest days, for example, its programming schedule was a hodgepodge. A quarter hour of poetry reading would be followed by organ music, fifteen minutes of vespers, a fifteen-minute soap opera, a talk broadcast, and a little dramatic sketch. The cycle would be repeated throughout the day. Not long after his arrival, Stanton noticed that CBS's ratings were higher in one city than in all the others.

The station in that city (though the network did not know it) had taken similar shows and grouped them back to back. Stanton thought the idea ingenious and proposed that the network try the same tactic. The sales department was offended, the program department outraged. So Stanton did what he called some "missionary work." He told advertisers of soap operas that if they asked CBS to cluster their programs together, higher ratings would result. They followed his suggestion, and block programming, one of the most sacred scheduling techniques, was born.

Bolstered by that success, Stanton urged that news programs be similarly grouped. The idea outraged Klauber. "He thought I was an idiot," Stanton recalled. "People had to have their news separated. You couldn't put [H. V.] Kaltenborn back to back with [Edwin C.] Hill. It was a crime you shouldn't commit." Stanton went to Kesten, who persuaded Paley it was worth trying. It worked. Henceforth, the hour from 6:00 P.M. to 7:00 P.M. was given over to news and analysis.

From the standpoint of the network's prosperity, Stanton's biggest contribution was in the service he gave to advertisers. NBC had a great advantage in its stronger stations, better positions on the radio dial, and more popular programs. To attract advertisers, CBS had to overcome this edge. One way was to generate goodwill by providing advertising agencies and clients with information they could not obtain elsewhere.

"NBC was a sleepy organization," said Stanton. "If we wanted business we had to give our all. In research I wouldn't let our people leave until the traffic died down. NBC closed at four-thirty every day. It paid off when an agency guy would call me on a Friday wanting information. I would bring people in on Saturday. We would work our hearts out and get him the information on Monday. We got business that way, not because of our facilities but because we helped the agencies get the business."

By the late 1930s, Stanton had developed a high profile outside the organization. Elmo Roper, a pioneer in public opinion polling, asked him to be his partner, and A. C. Nielsen offered him the vice-presidency of his radio research organization. But Stanton knew that his lot was cast with CBS. "I was enjoying myself, no question about it. The fun was building a new profession, and building a new industry."

At network meetings, Stanton, standing by with all the salient information on three-by-five cards, occasionally caught a glimpse of Bill Paley. Based on those few sightings, he came to a perceptive conclusion about the CBS president: "He was very skeptical. I don't recall that he ever said yes once."

Stanton sensed that it was wise not to get too close to Paley. He was content to work for Kesten, to learn what he could, to meet new challenges. In 1942, Stanton was named a vice-president, in charge not only of research but advertising, sales promotion, public relations, building construction, operations and maintenance, and supervising the seven radio stations owned and run by CBS. In seven years he had become one of CBS's handful of top executives, with broad-ranging responsibilities for network policy. Still, he never had a single one-on-one meeting with Paley. If he advanced farther at CBS, Stanton knew that would change. But he was in no hurry.

2

THE

Alchemist

14

CBS NEWS WAS ORGANIZED more by fluke than design. Back in 1931, CBS press releases had been emblazoned with the slogan "Columbia—The News Network." Yet at that time CBS News had neither editors nor correspondents. Instead, a half-dozen public relations men rewrote wire copy for announcers who had been selected for the quality of their voices. News programs consisted of bulletins, public ceremonies, talks by prominent citizens, and only intermittent analysis by legitimate journalists such as H. V. Kaltenborn.

Behind the promotional facade, however, CBS was steadily increasing its commitment to news. An attentive listener could detect the shift: CBS began to interrupt its programs more often for news bulletins than did NBC. In 1931, CBS broadcast 415 special events as compared to 256 on NBC's two networks. These stirrings were the first evidence of Ed Klauber's most important role at CBS.

After Edward Bernays had persuaded Paley to stake out radio as something more than a medium for entertainment, Klauber gave Paley an extended tutorial in the fundamentals of journalism. "Ed Klauber was an intolerant man," said Edward R. Murrow many years later, "intolerant of deceit, deception, distortion, and double talk. . . . If there be standards of integrity, responsibility and restraint in American radio news, Ed Klauber, more than any other man, is responsible for them." Klauber's presence at CBS doubtless prevented the network from following the banal model of the movie newsreels, filled with puffery and self-promotion, that Paley's friends in Hollywood were churning out.

The guidelines developed by Klauber largely covered questions of fairness and balance. Paley frequently claimed to have "invented" a fairness policy for broadcasting that was eventually codified by the Federal Communications Commission in 1949. Over the years this Fairness Doctrine required broadcasters not only to devote a reasonable amount of time to coverage of controversial public issues but to provide contrasting points of view.

By Paley's account, he initiated rules for fairness in the early 1930s because he was worried that broadcasters would use their power to promote their own views on the air, or that government might step in and take over broadcasting. "These guidelines were not imposed on us by government," he said in one interview. "They were imposed on us by our own volition."

In fact, CBS was responding to clear government signals. As early as the mid-1920s, Herbert Hoover, then secretary of commerce, had noted the duty of broadcasters to give listeners a range of viewpoints. The nascent Federal Radio Commission went even further in a 1929 decision affirming the need for "ample play for free and fair competition of opposing views" when it came to "all discussions of issues of importance to the public."

Lacking any background in news, Paley took many wrong turns in the early days. Fortunately, Klauber was usually there to point his young chief in the right direction. Early in Klauber's tenure, Paley blundered by providing a weekly slot for Father Charles E. Coughlin, the demagogic Roman Catholic priest. It was not an altruistic gesture on Paley's part. Coughlin had been broadcasting his unsavory views since 1926 on WJR, NBC's Detroit affiliate, which was owned by the right-wing extremist George Richards. In 1930, Coughlin wanted to extend his reach and contacted WMAQ, CBS's station in Chicago. Paley, who was eager to snare WJR as a CBS affiliate, agreed to put Coughlin on the CBS network to please George Richards. Moreover, Coughlin bought the time and thus provided CBS with a tidy annual revenue.

But the radio priest grew increasingly inflammatory; his railing against "international bankers" carried the ugly whiff of anti-Semitism. Klauber became alarmed and asked Coughlin to submit all his scripts in advance. When Coughlin denounced CBS as a censor, some 400,000 of his supporters flooded the network with threatening letters. In April 1931, Paley had no choice but to cancel the arrangement with Coughlin.

In the aftermath, Paley announced a policy designed to ensure free speech yet maintain balance. As devised by Klauber, CBS's new "Church of the Air" would feature rotating speakers from the Catholic, Protestant, and Jewish faiths. No longer would CBS pay for religious broadcasts because, Paley said, "so long as we view this question solely in the light of business practice, we are likely to fail to give to the radio audience the balanced religious broadcasting it is entitled to." As usual, Paley was hailed for his enlightenment, although NBC had since its earliest days rejected paid religious broadcasts and offered a balanced schedule of interfaith programs.

Paley's appetite for commercial success in the early 1930s also skirted fairness by giving corporate sponsors unusual latitude to air their political opinions. After a brief honeymoon, American businessmen had lined up staunchly against the Roosevelt program by the mid-1930s. They thought the 1935 Social Security Act and other New Deal programs were government boondoggles, and deeply resented Roosevelt's higher taxes on wealthy individuals and corporations. "The gentlemen sitting in big easy chairs at wide-windowed clubs," wrote the social historian Frederick Lewis Allen, "agreed vehemently that Roosevelt was not only a demagogue but a Communist . . . a traitor to his class."

"Voice of the Crusaders," organized in 1934 by a group of advertising agencies and corporations, featured weekly harangues on CBS against the New Deal. In 1935 the "Ford Sunday Evening Hour," ostensibly a program of classical music, offered an intermission in which Ford executive William J. Cameron attacked the New Deal and praised Henry Ford, who had been fomenting anti-Semitism since the 1920s with his newspaper, the *Dearborn Independent*.

As so often, Paley was trying to have it both ways. Away from the office he mingled with Café Society liberals and was identifiably a New Dealer. But as a practical businessman he catered to advertisers who opposed Roosevelt. Eventually the propaganda became too blatant. One by one, at Klauber's urging, CBS eliminated the offending programs. When CBS asked the Ford Motor Company to remove Cameron's intermission diatribes, Henry Ford replied, "Send that Jew to me." Soon afterward CBS dropped the entire program.

Although Paley never again gave his sponsors such editorial leeway, he let them have significant control over news by allowing single-advertiser sponsorship of certain programs. In the mid-1930s this control did not loom as a major problem because, as Erik Barnouw points out, "most sponsors did not want news programming. Those that did were inclined to expect veto rights over it." By being able to buy entire programs instead of time slots of sixty seconds or less—which did not become customary until about 1960—advertisers on CBS could choose which journalists they would sponsor. (NBC's policy was even worse. Its roundup of world news in the 1930s was produced at the Sun Oil offices in Philadelphia by the company's public relations department.) If an advertiser did not like what was said on its news program, the journalist in residence lost his sponsorship—and often his slot on the network as well. It was, recalled Blair Clark, a former CBS News executive, "a practice Murrow strongly objected to even in the early days of his brilliant career as a war correspondent in London."

At the same time, Paley risked offending his conservative advertisers by pursuing policies favoring the Democratic Party. Paley was well aware that the Roosevelt administration held regulatory power over CBS, so he made sure his network quietly curried favor with the White House through his Washington aide and lobbyist Harry Butcher. When Paley sought an audience with Roosevelt late in 1935, Stephen Early, the presidential press secretary, wrote in a White House memo: "I urge that the president see him. He is friendly. So is Columbia. Confidentially, I understand that he desires to tell the president something of Columbia's political policy, plus a willingness to be of service during the campaign."

The "service" performed by CBS during the 1936 presidential campaign stopped short of blatant partisanship, but it certainly helped. In January 1936, Roosevelt unveiled his political platform for the campaign with his State of the Union Address. Because the address was openly political, Henry P. Fletcher, the Republican national chairman, asked for time to reply. NBC agreed but CBS refused. In this stance Klauber slipped from his pinnacle of journalistic ethics and let his ardent support for Roosevelt cloud his judgment. He claimed that the address was an official presidential act and had not been labeled a political message. In a statement, Paley insisted that CBS wished to avoid a "mathematical formula of fairness." Fletcher countered that CBS, fearful of punitive action by the FCC, was beholden to the "party in power," a charge Paley denied.

Later that year, on the eve of the election, the Republicans placed a mock debate on CBS in which statements from Republican senator Arthur Vandenberg were juxtaposed with selections from a phonograph record of Roosevelt's speeches. CBS permitted the debate to run for several minutes, then pulled the plug, claiming disingenuously that it violated the network's prohibition against recordings on the air—a rule designed for entertainment programs, not public affairs broadcasts. When CBS denied the Republicans' request for a rebroadcast of the "debate" in its entirety, John Hamilton, the new Republican national chairman, charged "intimidation" of CBS by the administration. Hill Blackett, the radio adviser for the Republicans, added: "Now the public can see how a party in power can cut free speech . . . a perfect example of the precarious position of radio in America."

CBS's partisanship was evident in a letter from Harry Butcher to presidential aide Marvin Macintyre after Roosevelt's landslide victory over Alfred Landon. "We had a big election party at our house last night and needless to say they were all for the President before and after," wrote Butcher. "To me, the greatest gratification in the tremendous victory of the President is that it is quite largely a personal victory for him and he is not obligated to any special interest. Also the fact that while 80–85 percent of the newspapers were against the President, and vitriolically so, radio short-cut the press and enabled the President to get his message direct to the people. And how they did respond!" Butcher then reminded Macintyre that "two of our news commentators, H. V. Kaltenborn and Boake Carter, both predicted and advocated the reelection of the President."

Klauber and Paley gave commentators in those early days considerable leeway in expressing their opinions, which were usually liberal. CBS commentators derived their freedom from being independent operators. There were no news editors at the network to supervise them. Boake Carter, for example, broadcast from Philadelphia under the sponsorship of Philco, which presumably knew more about what he planned to say than did CBS in New York. Given Carter's liberal political slant, one can only assume that Philco had a different view of the world from most businesses.

Except for a brief three months when the Cunard Line sponsored his program, Kaltenborn had appeared on CBS since 1930 only in unsponsored time. In 1936, at the age of fifty-eight, he was still being paid the standard fee of $50 per broadcast, $100 a week. Despite his network fees, Kaltenborn was allowed to endorse Roosevelt. In 1936 and 1937 he broadcast reports on the Spanish Civil War that pointedly reflected his loyalist sympathies—at a time when the United States stood aside while the Germans and Italians helped Franco in his revolt against Spain's elected government. Because the government was Socialist, many American newspapers decried it as the "Red" faction while terming the insurgents "the Franco regime." Kaltenborn called the government "loyalists" and the Franco forces "Fascists" and "rebels."

Paley's initial tolerance of partisanship on the air can be traced partly to the influence of Dorothy Paley, who frequently urged him to permit bolder news broadcasts. Like many liberals, she enthusiastically supported the republican loyalists, and Paley respected her position. Moreover, the CBS commentators were useful adornments, rivaling the clout and prestige of their counterparts in the press.

But both Paley and Klauber were growing more uncomfortable with editorializing on the CBS airwaves. In 1936 the American public was overwhelmingly isolationist—from Midwestern conservatives who recoiled at involvement with Europe to liberals who believed that rearming would cut into the money available for the liberal reforms of the New Deal. The U.S. policy toward Spain was the first test of the Neutrality Act passed in 1935; it stipulated that if a war broke out, Americans would not sell arms to either side.

Under the circumstances, it seemed best for CBS to limit opinions to round-table discussions where differing viewpoints could be carefully balanced. Paley had been burned by broadcasting agitprop from the left as well as the right. He had learned that too much controversy upset advertisers and affiliates, and created an overheated environment that weakened or obscured the commercials on which CBS depended. Objectivity and neutrality became the network's goals.

In December 1937, a full year after CBS commentators had openly endorsed a candidate for the presidency, the network unveiled Klauber's code of ethics. In a speech to a conference on educational broadcasting, Paley declared that CBS would be "wholly, honestly and militantly non-partisan. . . . We must never have an editorial page. We must never seek to maintain views of our own . . . and discussion must never be one-sided so long as there can be found anyone to take the other side." Nor would sponsors be allowed to buy time for propaganda again—except during election campaigns, when politicians could pay for time to present their views.

For all of Klauber's influence in developing editorial policies for CBS, it took a threat from the outside to push Paley into developing a full-scale news organization, and even then the young CBS president suffered a failure of nerve. As network news bulletins increased in the early 1930s, newspaper owners had grown nervous. They felt that by broadcasting news before it hit the streets in the newspapers, radio cut into newspaper circulation and advertising revenues.

A series of events heightened this anxiety. The first was a fire at the Ohio State Penitentiary in 1930 that took 320 lives. In the middle of the tragedy, a convict grabbed a microphone linked to a CBS affiliate for broadcasts by the prison band. For several hours he relayed a graphic account to the CBS network, complete with the screams of prisoners burning to death. Paley later expressed misgivings about CBS's scoop to Bernays. "Paley feared that Columbia's news policies might be too aggressive," Bernays wrote. " 'We are competing with NBC,' I told him. 'We must take the lead, not draw back. . . . If Columbia and NBC withdraw from this field, the public's appetite will be satisfied by someone.' "

In March 1932, events propelled CBS into the lead again when the Lindbergh baby was kidnapped. Both CBS and NBC heard the news from a tipster; NBC held back until the newspapers hit the stands while CBS broadcast the news immediately. Throughout the weeks of the drama, live radio bulletins beat the newspapers day after day.

Afterwards, newspaper publishers began urging the wire services—AP, UP, and INS—to stop supplying news reports to radio broadcasters. In April 1933, the services succumbed to the pressure and boycotted the networks. CBS had an opportunity to fulfill its frequent claim of being the number-one news network by organizing its own news-gathering service. Yet it wasn't until General Mills offered to help underwrite the service that Paley gave the go-ahead. The terms set by General Mills were enticing: if

CBS kept the costs to $3,000 a week or less, the cereal company would pay half and be sole sponsor.

Klauber assigned the task to Paul White, a star reporter at United Press who had joined the public relations staff at CBS. White was a prototypical newspaperman of the era—large and boisterous, a prankster who drank too much yet had a nose for the big story. Paley must not have had occasion to see the real Paul White; he once described him as "a rather quiet person." But White had a sharp organizational mind and a set of journalistic principles as uncompromising as Klauber's. He "sensed radio's great opportunity of reaching more people more directly than through the press," said Kaltenborn. "He was always eager for new adventures in radio broadcasting. He had a great sense of competition." Klauber trusted White and recognized his capacity for innovation.

Within a few months White assembled a corps of some six hundred reporters, most of them part-timers, in major cities around the world. As the teletypes clattered with reports from the new service in the autumn of 1933, CBS broadcast three news programs every day and scored some respectable scoops. It was a classy operation befitting Paley's command to be first and best. NBC, on the other hand, gathered its news on the cheap, hiring one harried public relations man to work the phones overtime and feed news bulletins to newscaster Lowell Thomas, as well as to Walter Winchell, who broadcast gossip and crime tidbits every Sunday night.

The newspapers responded to CBS by threatening to drop radio listings from their pages, although few actually did so. Far more ominous was the publishers' retaliatory lobbying in Washington for more stringent government control of radio in the new Communications Act. That threat struck at the networks' ability to survive, and Sarnoff pressed Paley to seek peace.

In December 1933, after a series of meetings among the networks, wire services, and newspaper publishers at New York's Biltmore Hotel, the so-called Biltmore Agreement was announced. CBS would disband its fledgling news organization, and the networks would pay for a Press-Radio Bureau as a subsidiary of the wire services. No item released to the networks by the bureau could exceed thirty words, and the networks were permitted to broadcast only two five-minute newscasts daily, one after nine-thirty in the morning, the other after nine at night. The bureau could allow the networks to offer news bulletins only if they were of "transcendent" importance, and the bulletins had to direct listeners to newspapers for more comprehensive coverage. *Newsweek* characterized Paley at the time as "the man who had made the most concessions." Not only did he abandon White's best efforts, he agreed to restrictions that in the view of Eric Barnouw "virtually sabotaged—or tried to—the possibilities of broadcast news." Paley later rationalized his actions by asserting that there wasn't sufficient demand for a CBS News service at the time. Typically, he also insisted that he had been the victor, indeed, that the newspapers had capitulated. "We held out for unrestricted service and finally won the day," he said in a 1958 speech. Any restrictions were "insignificant."

The Biltmore Agreement fell apart within a year, but not because of CBS. A group of renegade stations, among them WOR in New York, refused to knuckle under and aired newscasts forbidden by the agreement. Moreover, the wire services eventually got greedy and sold their material directly to the radio networks, bypassing the Press-Radio Bureau.

From the earliest days, Paley knew how to use principles for profit at CBS. But if principles collided with profits or ran afoul of one of his friends, Paley made exceptions to the rules. "It all depended whose ox was being gored," said one longtime associate. That was probably to be expected from a man governed by pragmatism and profits. Paley created a news organization not out of idealism but as a response to circumstances. In the end, he would be virtuous about CBS News when it suited him.

15

ONE OF THE GREAT IRONIES of CBS is that what started as a public relations ploy by Paley and his aides eventually became one of the most prestigious news organizations in the world. The turning point came when Edward R. Murrow's broadcasts from Blitz-ravaged London filled America's living rooms and helped bring the nation out of its isolationist mood. Murrow not only reinforced the journalistic principles that had been laid down in fits and starts at CBS since the early 1930s, he came to symbolize the integrity and independence of the news division.

To Bill Paley, Murrow was a magical combination of star quality and unquestioned integrity. His high principles tempered Paley's hard pragmatism. A lean six-footer, Murrow was as handsome as a matinée idol. He was also a heavy-smoking brooder who periodically plunged into dark moods. Paley didn't like gloomy types, but Murrow was an exception. The eloquence of his voice, the glints of wit, his swashbuckling love of adventure, and his Savile Row style were irresistible to Paley. Murrow had enormous dramatic flair, a quality Paley valued highly. "Even when

Ed was telling a story, it was a performance," Eric Sevareid said. Paley thought of Murrow as a friend.

Like Paley, Murrow had meticulously fashioned an image for himself. A small-town North Carolinian by birth, he had grown up in Washington State, surrounded by rough-hewn loggers, railroad engineers, and farmers. The women in his life—his Quaker mother and his teachers—were prim moralists who filled him with ideals and gave him a feel for words and cadence. His family was poor, and his childhood strict and ascetic. There was little room for gaiety or fun; in that respect he had a lot in common with Frank Stanton.

Like Stanton, Murrow was an ambitious overachiever who held leadership positions in high school and college, participating in extracurricular activities ranging from debating to cheerleading to basketball, and always working part time. He took up debating when he got to high school. "Neighbors remember when he was a little boy that he had that big voice," said his widow, Janet Murrow. "The voice was always special."

After graduating from Washington State University, Murrow worked in New York for what was grandly called the Foreign Relations Office of the National Student Federation, which represented the student governments of more than three hundred colleges around the country. In 1929 he helped organize a Student Federation program on CBS. The students were assigned a weekly slot in the afternoon, when airtime was plentiful, and they filled it with guest speakers. It was as a host of this program that Murrow first appeared on CBS in September 1930, although his resonant voice didn't catch anyone's ear.

In 1931, Murrow moved on to the Institute of International Education, a group that arranged student exchanges, as assistant to the director, Stephen Duggan. At age sixty-seven, Duggan was a man of the world, a compelling speaker with friends in high places. Murrow viewed the high-minded Duggan as his mentor. He embraced Duggan's liberal causes and eagerly mingled with Duggan's friends in politics, finance, and academia. Murrow fit in anywhere; though still in his early twenties he had what one longtime observer called "intuitive poise." When CBS invited Duggan in 1934 to appear as a weekly lecturer on its "American School of the Air," Murrow was charged with developing the series. There he caught the eye of Fred Willis, Paley's personal assistant, who also oversaw educational programs on CBS.

Willis was a foppish Anglo-American who always kept a handkerchief tucked into his sleeve and spoke with a pronounced British accent. His colleagues thought he was a homosexual; his estranged wife, Helen, a fashion designer, committed suicide in the mid-1930s dressed in a black negligée after smoking thirteen cigarettes and turning on the gas in her Park Avenue apartment. Around CBS, Willis was known for his effectiveness in working with Paley and in getting good people on the air.

Murrow's sophistication and executive ability impressed Willis, who urged Klauber to make him CBS's new director of talks, the executive responsible for lining up prominent speakers to appear on the network. Murrow signed on in September 1935, arriving at CBS only weeks before Frank Stanton, who would be his chief rival for Paley's favor.

Since the infant CBS News Service had folded in 1933, the network had reverted to its skeleton staff of publicity men funneling news copy to announcers. Paul White took charge of covering special events, while Murrow threw himself into scheduling talks. CBS always guaranteed his speakers time on its own station in New York, but otherwise Murrow and his assistant spent their time convincing stations to carry the talks.

Paley admired CBS's new recruit, particularly for his knowledge of international affairs picked up at the Institute and the Federation. He even recommended that Murrow be in the running if the network needed someone to head its international broadcasting efforts. Dorothy Paley too was delighted by the new director of talks. She was challenged by his ideas and loved to engage him in conversation. "She was very influential with Murrow," recalled Irene Selznick. "She guided his interests. She thought Ed was a great asset and she pushed on his behalf with Bill."

Dorothy invited Murrow out to Kiluna for a number of Sunday gatherings so her husband could get to know him better. Murrow, somewhat shy in those days, sat apart, taking everything in. When he spoke, he was concise and provocative. Irene Selznick recalled that he was "very observant. His eyes would dart around. But after a while he was looking to catch [his wife]'s eye so they could leave. He wasn't a great social creature then."

Murrow soon found himself interpreting CBS's new rules on fairness and balance. During the 1936 presidential campaign, for example, CBS announced a policy of giving free time to all the candidates—with the exception of Communist Earl Browder. At Murrow's urging, Browder was given fifteen minutes. The next day the *New York Journal-American,* one of William Randolph Hearst's conservative papers, castigated CBS in an editorial and published a color cartoon that showed Paley on a soapbox waving a red flag.

When he encountered Murrow that afternoon, Paley said sternly, "What are you trying to do to me?" Then he smiled his most charming smile, clapped Murrow on the back, and said, "Thanks, pal. You're the only guy around here who could get me into a color cartoon in a Hearst paper." Paley may well have sensed that there was more than politics behind an attack by his wife's former father-in-law. Indeed, when Frank Stanton went over to the Hearst offices to make an inquiry, Bill Hearst, Jack's brother, unloaded the entire story of Dorothy's adultery on the unsuspecting CBS executive.

Demand for radio news was increasing as America nervously watched the Fascist dictators in Europe consolidate their power. Hitler had attained absolute dominance in Germany in 1933 and was rearming. In 1936, as Mussolini completed his invasion of Ethiopia, Hitler marched into the Rhineland and Franco launched his uprising in Spain. Observing the coming crisis in Europe, Klauber decided CBS needed someone in charge who would know the territory and understand the significance of what was to come.

CBS's man in Europe at the time was forty-eight-year-old Cesar Saerchinger. A former newspaper reporter, Saerchinger had been with the network since 1930, booking dignitaries for broadcasts to America. Every Sunday at noon he came on the air to say "Hello America" and broadcast a quaint feature from London. At the end of 1936, CBS and NBC had gone head to head covering the dramatic love affair of England's King Edward VIII and Wallis Simpson, an American divorcée. Murrow, coordinating in New York, helped Saerchinger break into the network and scoop his rivals by announcing the king's abdication. But in this first competitive test from Europe, NBC overall provided faster, more expert coverage than CBS. "Saerchinger was a dear man, but he wasn't right for what Klauber anticipated," said John "Jap" Gude, one of CBS's publicity men.

The head of programming, William Lewis, suggested Murrow take his place. Klauber at first rejected the idea. Murrow, he said, was too important in his job in New York. But he reconsidered, and in late February 1937, he called Murrow at a conference in New Orleans to offer him the job. Klauber insisted Murrow give him an answer that day, and after a quick consultation with his wife, Murrow said yes. Three months later, Murrow was in London. He had just turned twenty-nine.

Paley did not at the time conceive of Murrow as a star broadcaster. The post in London was purely administrative. Murrow would continue to find politicians and other guests and organize broadcasts, using newspaper reporters as hosts on the air. Murrow hired William Shirer, a reporter for International News Service, to help him make the arrangements. Shirer was dismayed when he learned that his first assignment, on direct orders from Paley in the early autumn of 1937, was to follow the Duke and Duchess of Windsor to Munich and persuade the duke to broadcast for CBS when he visited New York afterwards.

The duke was a friend of the Paleys; the assignment, said Shirer, was "dear to Paley's heart." Shirer thought the mission "quite foolish" because the purpose of the duke's Munich visit was to survey German "labor conditions"—a preposterous notion since Hitler had smashed the labor unions and replaced them with his own bogus organization, the German Labor Front. Clearly the Nazis were crudely using the celebrated royal couple for propaganda. The duke, "a very stupid man" in Shirer's estimation, unwittingly had got trapped. Paley was spared the embarrassment of having him on CBS only because, said Shirer, "there was such an outcry at home about the duke and duchess visiting America to study the labor situation after first going to Nazi Germany for the same purpose that the trip [to New York] was called off."

As Hitler tightened his grip in the autumn of 1937, Murrow and Shirer became increasingly frustrated that they were unable to broadcast on CBS themselves. Shirer later wrote that Paley believed "for us to do the reporting ourselves would be to commit CBS editorially. . . . Paley and the rest of the brass in New York simply would not listen to the pleas of Ed Murrow and me to broadcast the news ourselves. The idiocy of it staggered me." Paley's refusal, in the face of compelling events, to allow Shirer and Murrow on the air resulted from his literal interpretation of the policies he and Klauber were preparing to unveil in Paley's December speech. They were sensitive to any appearance of an editorial position.

Once again events forced CBS into making a commitment to full-fledged news broadcasting. Throughout the early months of 1938, Hitler brought increasing pressure on the leaders of Austria to submit to Germany. Shirer correctly saw that if Hitler achieved annexation of his native land it would be the end of Austria for the duration of the Third Reich. By now stationed in Vienna, Shirer had inside information on Hitler's machinations that he tried repeatedly to get on the air. Each time he was rebuffed. Instead, the brass in New York instructed him to line up children's choirs for "American School of the Air."

On March 11, 1938, the German Army marched into Austria. Shirer called Murrow from Vienna to tell him that "the opposing team has just crossed the goal line." Max Jordan, NBC's man in Vienna, was out of the country, so Shirer knew he had a shot at the only eyewitness report of the event. He raced to London while Murrow flew to Vienna. This time, CBS agreed to give Shirer some time. His account, broadcast from London late on Saturday night, March 12, marked the first time a CBS news staff member was allowed on the air with a report from the field.

In the following hours, Paul White and his small staff improvised wildly to cover the story. There was no studio for news broadcasting at CBS, only a suite of offices on the seventeenth floor for the Special Events and Talks staff. White ordered a makeshift studio in the office next door by having blankets tacked to the walls for soundproofing. Newspaper reporters contacted by CBS in various European cities offered periodic updates.

NBC's Jordan meanwhile had rushed back to Vienna, where he was scooping CBS with on-the-scene stories. Murrow was unable to secure a facility in the city to transmit his own report. He blamed his failure on NBC's exclusive contract with RAVAG, the Austrian broadcasting service. In fact, as Jordan later wrote to a colleague in New York, once the invasion took place, NBC's contract was moot, since the chiefs of Austrian broadcasting had been immediately dismissed by the Nazis. "Everything was upside down in the RAVAG building during those days, and if Columbia had only been on the job, they probably could have gotten the same treatment we did," wrote Jordan.

In bed with a fever back in New York, Paley was frantic that CBS was being trounced by NBC so conspicuously. His first instinct was to try to use his own influence to solve the problem. He had met the head of Austrian broadcasting the previous summer and regarded him as a friend. Paley placed a call to Vienna, but the man confessed he was no longer in charge and could do nothing to help.

Paley concluded that CBS needed a way to "not only get the news but dramatize it." At that moment, as he has recounted many times, "out of necessity and competition I invented the World News Roundup"—the model for broadcast newscasts for decades to come. By his recollection, he called Klauber at CBS headquarters to describe his vision of a series of reports from European capitals, switching quickly from one to the next. But Robert Trout, CBS's main news announcer at the time, recalled that the idea for the roundup emerged from an impromptu seventeenth-floor discussion Sunday morning, March 13: "Paul said to me, 'Why don't we put several of these reports together and just make one program?' Mr. Paley has an idea he thought of it. To me it was Paul. It came out of a dialogue between Paul and me. In the heat of it nobody thought it would become an institution."

Whether Paley deserves the credit for thinking of it, he seized on the idea. At first Klauber had to tell him that CBS engineers thought the plan was impossible. "Goddammit," Paley recalled saying, "there's no reason in the world I can think of why it can't be done. It has to be done. You go back at them." When Klauber called back, they had found a way. That Sunday night, March 13, at 8:00 P.M.—the very heart of prime time— Trout introduced the first roundup, with live reports from Murrow in Vienna, Shirer in London, and newspaper correspondents moonlighting as CBS broadcasters in Paris and Berlin. A senator in Washington chipped in as well with an analysis of events. "With fine careless rapture," said

Paul White, "we would flip from capital to capital via shortwave." The broadcast made a huge splash. Paley was elated. He asked for a second roundup two days later and still more after that. But he was unwilling at that stage to commit to a regular, much less a daily, roundup.

Indeed, even after CBS's triumph with the roundup, Paley fretted about the cost of news broadcasting. Following the *Anschluss,* Winston Churchill made one of his dramatically perceptive speeches in the House of Commons about the dangers ahead. Shirer was impressed and called Paley to ask if Churchill could repeat the speech on CBS. Paley, who considered Churchill an acquaintance, agreed to give him fifteen minutes, but when he added that CBS could pay Churchill only $50, Shirer was stunned. Churchill was making $1,500 a week from his syndicated newspaper column and commanded thousands of dollars for his freelance articles. Shirer complained that CBS's fee was insufficient. Paley replied, "Explain to Winston that it will be a sustaining program, that is, without commercials. Tell him fifty dollars is our standard fee for 'sustainers.' "

Churchill was delighted at the opportunity to appear on the CBS network, but upon hearing how much he would be paid, he responded, "Tell your boss I'll be happy to do it for five hundred dollars." Shirer thought that reasonable. CBS's profits for the year, after all, ran to $3.5 million. But Paley refused to pay it, and Churchill never made his speech on CBS.

In September 1938 the Nazis partitioned Czechoslovakia. This time Kaltenborn was at the anchor desk in New York. From CBS's Studio Nine he sat before a microphone, stitching together nearly two hundred reports from European capitals for eighteen straight days. He delivered more than a hundred analyses, pausing now and then to nap on a nearby Army cot. American listeners were riveted. Murrow and Shirer seeped into the national consciousness. Murrow emerged from his thirty-five broadcasts during the Munich crisis as a bona fide broadcaster and CBS lost no time in exploiting the publicity value of his new prominence. Before the close of 1938, *Scribner's* magazine had run a major article about Murrow, and *The Saturday Evening Post* had commissioned a profile of White. "It is very obvious," wrote one NBC executive to another at the time, "that Columbia is carrying on a well-planned campaign to get outstanding magazines to feature their efforts."

This time there was to be no turning back. In mid-1939, Paley authorized Klauber and White in New York and Murrow overseas to build a staff capable of covering the widening story. They turned to eloquent, sophisticated writers from the world of newspapers. Eric Sevareid, twenty-six years old, was an editor at both United Press and the Paris edition of the *New York Herald Tribune*. Elmer Davis, a freelance writer, and Charles Collingwood and Howard K. Smith of United Press had all been Rhodes Scholars. Murrow demanded "original, more reflective reporting" from his reporters, wrote David Halberstam in *The Powers That Be*. "He told his men that eight out of ten stories should be original and not patched by the wires. . . . He wanted thoughts and ideas, a sense of the issues at play and a sense of the texture of the country they were covering."

If these men did not have the necessary sonority for radio, they would learn. Most of them emulated Murrow's calm and dignified delivery and became known as "Murrow's Boys." Sevareid returned to the United States not long after he was hired and stood near Paley at a reception in Washington. Paley failed to recognize him. To his embarrassment, Sevareid overheard Paley boasting to the chairman of the FCC, "We've got a young fellow Sevareid, speaks like Ed Murrow." Sevareid turned to him and said, "I am Sevareid." As Sevareid himself recalled, he had no idea he had picked up Murrow's inflections. "I had been with him so much," he said.

Suddenly news was in demand. Listeners couldn't get enough of it. Advertisers wanted to be identified with it. In early 1939 the World News Roundup, appearing twice daily by then, acquired its first sponsor. "From now on we will be sponsored by Sinclair Oil," Murrow announced to his troops. "You will get seventy-five dollars each time we are on the air." Replied Sevareid, "Ed, we are recording this great human story. Is this right to take money from this oil company?" There was a moment of abashed silence. Then Murrow said, "You'll get used to it."

At CBS, news was now as lucrative as it was prestigious. Late in 1939, Kaltenborn wrote Shirer to tell him that the Camel cigarette company had bought a one-and-a-half-minute announcement following Kaltenborn's fifteen-minute program of analysis and preceding the evening Roundup. "It is completely separated from what precedes and from what follows. Yet the Camels people are paying for the entire fifteen-minute period in order to have the privilege of making this independent announcement. It is a new technique in radio advertising which may develop. Paul White told me the other day that at long last the News Department is completely paying for itself with sponsored news broadcasts. We have them now at all hours of the day." As Kaltenborn confided to Murrow, "My sponsor's sales are jumping."

Now Paley became the most ardent booster of CBS News. During the invasion of Czechoslovakia he had a radio with him at all times, always tuned to CBS. Journalist Quincy Howe credited his hiring to Bill and Dorothy Paley, who had heard his broadcasts on New York radio station WQXR. Paley permitted newscasts to be scheduled across the board at the same time each day, while newscasts on NBC suffered from poor time periods and erratic scheduling. "He had a real instinct for it," said Dorothy Paley. "The correspondents were really stimulated and encouraged by him. He talked about it a lot. He was excited about it. It was very important to him."

Paul White was an effective ringmaster for Paley's new organization. His refurbished newsroom conformed to the progressive image Kesten and Lescaze had fashioned for the network. The walls were beige, and White's office was sleekly modern, with rounded corners and plate-glass windows reaching almost to the floor. Sitting at his desk he could see the newsroom and the news studio, which also had plate-glass walls, and beyond into the control room and monitoring room where, sitting before small individual speakers, each slugged with the name of a foreign country, translators monitored foreign short-wave broadcasts. One executive, after a visit in the late 1930s, remarked that the CBS News setup had a "rather theatrical air . . . that undoubtedly makes it impressive to visiting writers."

Now that CBS News had a staff of its own, White, Klauber, and Paley laid down further standards comparable to those of the best newspapers. The news was to be edited and broadcast only by members of the CBS News staff. No outsiders were permitted to broadcast the news, even if it was sponsored. News analysis would be permitted, but only after news reports; and as in a newspaper's editorial page, the analysis would be clearly defined as such.

However, journalism was subordinated to the dictates of business in CBS's ban on the use of tape recorders—a policy on which Paley brooked no opposition. The rule was designed to protect lucrative entertainment programs on NBC and CBS: Paley and Sarnoff reasoned that if performers like Bing Crosby could record their programs, they might try to distribute them on their own, eliminating the need for network middlemen.

When CBS invoked the ban for news as well, Murrow and Shirer tried repeatedly to persuade Paley to change the policy. They pointed out that atmospheric conditions would prevent any number of live broadcasts from getting through. They told him that by recording events as they happened throughout the day, they could assemble a report that would bring listeners what newspapers could not: the sounds of troops marching in the morning, an ambassador's protest in the afternoon, a fiery speech by Hitler in the evening. Moreover, they urged that using recordings could enhance their ability to cover a war. "In order to broadcast live, we had to have a telephone line leading from our mike to a shortwave transmitter. You could not follow an advancing or retreating army dragging a telephone line with you," Shirer told Paley. "With a compact little recorder you could get into the thick of it and capture the awesome sounds of war." The argument, Shirer later wrote, "seemed so simple, so logical. But Paley was adamant."

Fortunately for CBS, Murrow, Shirer, and other CBS News correspondents were resourceful enough to catch at least some of those "awesome sounds" for their listeners. In so doing, they followed the precedent set by H. V. Kaltenborn, who had first broadcast battlefield sounds with a microphone during the Spanish Civil War. The CBS newsmen in London were helped by the fact that the nighttime bombings coincided with CBS's live broadcasts at 1:00 A.M. London time.

Murrow created indelible portraits of war for his listeners. "He was a natural," said Paley. "He just went on the air, and reported it." Murrow himself once said during the Blitz that "the strongest impression one gets of these bombings is a sense of unreality. Often the planes are so high that even in a cloudless sky you can't see them. I've stood on a hill watching an aerodrome being bombed two miles away. It looked and sounded like farmers blasting stumps in western Washington. . . . Even when the dive bombers come down looking like a duck with both wings broken and you hear the hollow grunt of their bombs it doesn't seem to have much meaning."

His style was conversational, and some of his most enduring impressions were personal—the "little picture," as his producer Fred Friendly would say years later. "There were no nerves. No profanities, and no heroics," he reported after interviewing a group of Royal Air Force pilots at the time of Dunkirk. "There was no swagger about those boys in wrinkled and stained uniforms. . . . A boy of twenty drove up in a station wagon. He weighed about 115 pounds. . . . His voice was loud and flat. His uniform was torn, had obviously been wet. He wore a pair of brown tennis shoes three sizes too big. After he'd gone I asked one of the men who'd been talking with him what was the matter with him. 'Oh,' he replied. 'He was shot down over Dunkirk on the first patrol this morning. He landed in the sea, swam to the beach, was bombed for a couple of hours, came home in a paddle steamer. His voice sounds like that because he can't hear himself. You get that way after you've been bombed a few hours,' " he said.

Murrow was known for his theatrical touches—the fat pause in his introductory "This . . . is London," the microphones placed at the feet of Londoners as they descend into air-raid shelters. Masterful at evoking a mood, he could analyze incisively as well. After a particularly bad stretch of bombings he sized up the British character:

There is still a sense of humor in the country. The old feeling of superiority over all other peoples remains. So does class distinction. There is great courage, and a blind belief that Britain will survive. The British aren't all heroes. They know the feeling of fear. I have shared it with them. They try to avoid thinking deeply about political and social problems. They will stand any amount of government inefficiency and muddle. They are slow to anger, and they die with great dignity. They will cheer Winston Churchill when he walks through block after block of smashed houses and offices as though he brought them great victory. During a blinding raid when the streets are full of smoke and the sound of the roaring guns they'll say to you, "Do you think we are really brave or just lacking in imagination?"

As the accolades grew and Murrow rose in the world, he took up the trappings of the good life, although he carefully kept his reserve. To the British, Murrow was a saint. Night after night he elegantly presented their point of view to his American listeners without seeming too much the advocate. They were grateful, and they embraced him. "His job would have made him socially acceptable anyway but this was special," said Robert Landry, an American reporter who knew him then. "He had incredible entrée. He had exactly the right style. Fred Bate [Murrow's counterpart at NBC] was more ordinarily socially acceptable than Murrow. But Murrow was special. He was so American that they even liked that. They wanted things American. If he had been more Anglophile in his style they might not have liked it. He seemed to come from the center of America."

When Paley visited London in August 1942, Murrow knew precisely what to do for him. Murrow's attentiveness was calculated. He had a history of ingratiating himself with older men, of knowing how to make them feel at ease. Paley, then in his mid-forties, was seven years Murrow's senior and already knew his way around the British capital. But Murrow introduced him to those he did not know.

Inevitably, the two men drew together. Neither gave away much about himself. "You could talk with Ed at great length and know a lot of his thoughts and impressions but he was always very guarded about talking about himself," said Landry. The same could have been said for Paley. Murrow and Paley both struggled to maintain control over inner turbulence. Their engines always ran hard, propelled by determination. "Even at the peak of fame and fortune, Ed couldn't sleep," said one longtime colleague. Murrow smoked constantly and drank coffee from morning until night. "He was exhausted," the colleague went on, "but the will was driving him on. There was a lot of anguish in him that he couldn't get out. He couldn't get close to individuals. It embarrassed him to show emotion. He wouldn't do anything that would make him look awkward."

Paley felt comfortable with Murrow, who was not so obviously educated as, say, Howard K. Smith or Elmer Davis. Murrow was accessible, not intellectual. His talent lay in his descriptive powers and his flair. Both Paley and Murrow excelled at subtle technique. Murrow also had the same kinds of instincts as Paley—the ability to size up situations, to get to the heart of the matter. Murrow's was "a kind of biting common sense," in the words of one former colleague at CBS. The clear-cut nature of World War II made the ideal connection. Murrow and Paley could sit comfortably on the same side of an issue when the fascism and anti-Semitism of Hitler and Mussolini were so loathsome. They could unite in CBS's role as the beacon for all right-thinking citizens.

In ordinary circumstances, Murrow would have had little interest in a man so steeped in the values of business as Bill Paley. Murrow's background put him on the side of the underdog, and he had an empathy for the impoverished that Paley admired only up to a point. But in the early years Paley needed Murrow, and he brought all his charm to bear on furthering their friendship.

Ed Murrow came along at the right time in Paley's life. His belief in broadcast news as a fundamental part of a democracy appealed to Paley, who had always considered himself a patriot and a believer in the American system. Yet Murrow's notions of broadcasting's role in national life went further than Paley's. Murrow believed that broadcast news should inform the citizenry not only about the accomplishments of government but about its problems and conflicts as well. Over the years Paley would have occasion to object to the presentation of such problems and conflicts on CBS's airwaves.

16

O N THE BALMY EVENING of July 13, 1937—an auspicious date for a man of reverse superstition such as Bill Paley—the magnificent London residence of Mrs. Laura Corrigan blazed with light and overflowed with merriment. Mrs. Corrigan, a wealthy American socialite who crashed London society in the early 1920s, had emerged as one of the city's leading hostesses. Her vulgarity, frequent malapropisms, and bright auburn wigs (worn to cover baldness from a childhood illness) caused her British acquaintances to dub her "The Big Wig of London." But these same people flocked to the lavish parties that she threw in houses she rented each June and July for the peak social season. In 1937 it was an opulent nineteenth-century mansion on Kensington Palace Gardens, also known as "Millionaire's Row." As usual, her ball was the most glittering party of the year.

Bill and Dorothy Paley were there that night—two months and a day past their fifth wedding anniversary. Dressed in their finery, they threaded through the crowded ballroom. Paley could count numerous friends in the crowd. One, Jay O'Brien, was dancing with a young woman Paley had not met. She was neither classically beautiful nor stunningly dressed. Twenty-five years old and five feet two, she had curly brown hair set neatly into marcel waves. Her face was gamine: snub nose, bright blue eyes. But she had a lovely figure that her Schiaparelli print linen ballgown showed to its best advantage. Her vivacity captivated him—but he also knew that she was, in the words of one friend "kin to everybody fine." "Jay," said Paley to his friend, "now it's my turn."

He stepped toward Lady Mary Dunn and off they whirled. He danced like Fred Astaire, she thought. And when she looked up at his "half moon eyes and lovely smile and lovely teeth," she was absolutely riveted. Paley was equally smitten. "Can you meet me tomorrow?" he whispered.

They met for a drink the next day, and the day after. On the third day he proposed. "Let's run away together," he said.

"Where would we go?" she asked.

"To India!" he replied. "We'd wait there until the scandal died down."

"We couldn't stay there for long," she said. "Where would we go then?"

"To Japan and China. We'd travel through the Far East and then we would go back to Kiluna and start a whole new life."

"Couldn't we live in Wiltshire?" she asked.

"No," he said. "There is too much to do in New York."

Mary knew that none of it was possible. The daughter of the fifth Earl of Rosslyn, a bon vivant who had gone through much of his fortune, she was married to Philip Gordon Dunn, a man who would eventually inherit a title as well as enormous wealth. He was the son of Sir James Dunn, the Baronet of Bathurst in New Brunswick, Canada, and a steel-manufacturing magnate. Mary had two daughters at home, aged four and two. Yet she had fallen in love. She and Paley continued to meet surreptitiously—for tea, for drinks—over the next ten days.

Like Bill Paley, who was interested in all the passions of aristocratic society, Lady Mary was an enthusiast—about horses, racing, gambling, opera, and books. Although she discovered that Paley was only moderately knowledgeable, she found him unaffected and considerate, and admired his enormous mental energy. Unlike so many others she treated him in a matter-of-fact fashion that he seemed to enjoy. After two weeks, she was convinced of his sincerity. Had she said yes, she was certain they would have gone to India. "I am not going to bed with you under any circumstances until you come away with me," he said.

The following month, the Dunns and the Paleys were in Monte Carlo at the Palais Hotel. One evening they were all gambling with a group of American and British friends. Dorothy, uninterested in gambling, went home earlier than the rest. Soon after, Philip Dunn asked his wife to come home with him. She told him she was on such a winning streak that she had to stay. He relented, and Mary and Bill Paley played baccarat side by side for several hours more. Mary's cousin, Eric Ward, the third Earl of Dudley, then asked them to join him for breakfast.

After breakfast the three strolled outside the casino. By now it was about five in the morning. Eric impetuously kissed his cousin, leaving a streak of lipstick from another girl he had bussed earlier. They were in a gay mood, and Mary suggested they take a swim. She and Bill were sitting in an open Fiat taxicab, holding hands; he had not kissed her yet. Suddenly there was a screech of tires. Philip Dunn, in his pajamas, jumped out of his car and looked at his wife. Seeing the lipstick on her cheek, he shouted, "Do you have to kiss every little Jewboy in Europe?"

Paley did not even flinch. With almost pathetic dignity, he said, "I'm sorry we're so late, but Eric insisted we have breakfast." Philip Dunn ordered his wife out of the cab and into his car. They had a screaming row, and when they arrived at the hotel, they found Paley waiting for them in the lobby. "Don't be cross, Philip," he pleaded. "There's nothing to be cross about except we are rather late." But Philip Dunn was implacable. He told his wife to pack and they left Monte Carlo immediately.

For the next seven months, Paley called Lady Mary from his office in the United States. She was disconsolate. She asked him to give her one of his possessions as a keepsake, and he sent her his favorite lizard belt. They had long conversations about divorce, while the Dunns continued to fight. Finally she said, "It's no good to go on playing. My children are too young to be deserted. I like Dorothy and don't want to hurt her." Paley, implying earlier extramarital gambits, told her she was special to him. "This time it's different."

Dorothy had no idea of Paley's unfaithfulness. He had strayed early in their marriage, indulging his old taste for showgirls. Other flings followed. The previous year he had been captivated by Zsa Zsa Gabor, a seventeen-year-old beauty newly arrived from Hungary. Paley proffered her marriage as well. But she considered him "just another distinguished suave man" and declined his offer, hoping for a more robust all-American husband.

Bill's peccadillos weren't the only symptom of trouble ahead. To those with a sharp eye, other hairline cracks were showing in the Paley marriage. When Dorothy corrected him in public, she was brisk and impatient, not gentle. Sarcasm had gradually crept into her manner. "She has developed the most unattractive, irritable, smart aleck manner," Alice-Leone Moats wrote in 1937. "She snaps Bill's head off every time he opens his mouth and goes around pouting all the time. Her idea of being funny is to stick a large bowl of roses under Bill's nose because he suffers from rose and hay fever. I said to Maggie Swope that I thought Dorothy seemed unusually nervous and irritable and she said, 'Oh, I think that's just the manner she's adopted.' 'All I can say,' I answered, 'is that it's a manner that is better not cultivated.' "

"Dorothy may have been a little too competitive. That might have affected him," said Marietta Tree. One evening at the Swopes' house in mid-1938 a group including Maggie Swope, man-about-town William Stewart, and Dorothy Paley sat up all night playing mah-jongg. Afterwards, Alice-Leone Moats wrote: "Dorothy has become such a fiend that poor Bill goes home alone every Saturday and Sunday night—a joke on him because he was always pleading with Dorothy to wait while he played backgammon."

Dorothy had grown resentful of her husband's need to control virtually every aspect of their relationship. All decisions about the household had to be his. She never forgave him for deciding to sell the home at 29 Beekman Place that was so dear to her. And she bristled when he insisted on keeping her to a strict allowance for clothing, other personal expenses, even charitable gifts. Paley was not as parsimonious as Averell Harriman, whose wife, Marie, used to complain about having to buy her own toothpaste. But in one effort to economize, Paley proposed that Dorothy's maid be fired while he kept his valet.

Paley also dictated their friendships. Whoever displeased him was banished, much to Dorothy's dismay. She was particularly fond of an American couple named Virginia and Brose Chambers whom they saw frequently in Paris. He was a lawyer who worked for Harriman, and she was an intelligent, enormously cultivated woman. In the late 1930s the Chambers, low on funds, had to return to the United States. Paley delivered an ultimatum: he and Dorothy were not going to see the Chambers any more because he found them tiresome. "In fact," recalled Dorothy, "they didn't have much money and he didn't think they were worth spending time with. Also, he didn't like Virginia much. She wasn't stylish or attractive. She was plump around the middle. He thought she was noisy and that she had a slave complex—which she did. She always wanted to do things for me. We stopped seeing them and it hurt them."

Paley banned the Swopes with the same finality after he had a falling out with Herbert. Not only did Paley prohibit them from visiting Kiluna, he instructed Dorothy to cut off Maggie, one of her closest friends. Shortly after Paley's decree, Maggie called Dorothy at Kiluna one Sunday and asked if she could come over. They met in Dorothy's dressing room. "Can't you and I at least be friends? We've been such close friends and it's such a pity," Maggie pleaded. "It's not possible," said Dorothy. "I can't do it. He is my husband."

Dorothy's discovery that she was unable to have children exacerbated the tension between the Paleys. Dorothy had finally become pregnant in 1937, only to miscarry after two months. A series of tests confirmed that she would not be able to conceive again. Both Paleys were deeply disappointed. The following summer—a time when Dorothy's irritability with her husband grew more pronounced—Alice-Leone Moats wrote that "Dorothy Paley and Dolly O'Brien do nothing but go around the countryside looking at babies. It seems to be a mania. She's apparently mad about babies, which is a most unexpected trait in her character. This has probably been accentuated by the fact that she, herself, can't have any."

In 1938, they adopted a newborn boy named Jeffrey and a year later an infant girl named Hilary. Paley was an indifferent father. He loved babies, but young children irritated him. Dorothy was not overwhelmingly maternal either. She tended to be severe, and held to the prevailing views on child rearing, which advocated an arm's-length approach. Yet she felt strongly about progressive education, and she was keenly interested in children, though it sometimes seemed she leaned too much on the help of experts in raising her own.

The children helped underscore the differences between Dorothy and Bill. In 1940, Paley selected a new home on East 71st Street, on the top floor of a town house. Clearly, it would be a pied-à-terre for Bill and Dorothy only; the children would have to remain at Kiluna full time. But Dorothy wanted to see more of them than just on weekends. In one of the few times in their marriage that she dared cross him, Dorothy consulted a child psychologist, who urged Paley to relent. The Paleys ultimately settled on a town house that could accommodate the entire family.

While Dorothy catered to Paley and ran her various households exquisitely, she was not quite attentive enough. "I never behaved as if the world revolved around him," she said. "Maybe that was a problem." Paley needed a woman who was slavishly devoted and who worked constantly to enhance him. Increasingly, Dorothy directed her energies to a variety of causes. She raised money to build a nursery school in Harlem, dragging in her new friend Marietta to help paint coat cubbies. She tapped their friends on behalf of the New School for Social Research, a progressive, liberal institution in Greenwich Village. Inevitably, she wanted to join the war effort. She asked Paley's permission to accompany Marietta to England. Paley would have none of it, even after Murrow interceded on Dorothy's behalf.

Arthur Hornblow, a Hollywood producer, used to say that Dorothy Paley "wore her brains on the outside." With time, her assertive ways began to annoy Paley. Sometimes her strong views suited him, especially her determined stand against the Nazis. After the invasion of Czechoslovakia he used to tell friends, "If Dorothy were there she would have held them off with bayonets." More often, he was displeased when she expressed opinions he did not like. Once at a party Dorothy fell into an argument with Averell Harriman over Charles de Gaulle. Dorothy insisted that de Gaulle would be a significant force in pulling France together. Harriman dismissed him on the grounds that he supported Communists. Later Paley rebuked his wife, telling her not to be so strong. Harriman was the expert, he said, and Dorothy had no right contradicting him. "She spoke her mind, and that's what killed it," said one longtime friend. "He says he wants people to speak their mind but in the end he has to prevail."

From the beginning Paley had relied on his wife's instincts about CBS personnel. "She would say no, no, and warn him about people," recalled Irene Selznick. "She was awfully good, very fast on the uptake." Yet as Paley gained confidence, he regarded her advice more as interference than assistance.

Dorothy's relationship with Murrow caused particular friction. Although she had encouraged the friendship between Murrow and Paley, she and Murrow were actually the kindred spirits in the early days. They shared the same political passions, and when they were together they could talk for hours. One evening before Murrow went abroad, he and his assistant, Helen Sioussat, dined with the Paleys in a Manhattan restaurant. "Dorothy went on and on with Ed," Sioussat recalled. "She was very knowledgeable. She was talking about public affairs, about newspaper articles, radio shows, biographies she had read." Dorothy and Ed continued their discussion en route to a nightclub on Central Park South. "Bill and I got tired of it," Sioussat went on. "We laughed and stopped and looked at the windows at Saks while Dorothy was bending Ed's ear."

"It goes beyond her being opinionated," said another longtime observer of them both. "She doesn't brook discussion, nor does he. One wonders how they survived. At the beginning they were probably so eager to please that they would back off or avoid problem topics. As time went on, that was impossible."

Dorothy occupied a dangerous role, particularly in a marriage to someone as proud and strong-willed as Paley. In a sense she had assumed a mother's function, teaching the social graces and the finer things in life, guiding him in judging character and sizing up situations. It may have been inevitable that Bill would rebel against her. "She understood him better than he understood himself, and was always willing to let him know it," said the wife of one of Paley's close friends. "It was not a pleasant thing for him. She always knew what was the right thing to do."

Paley caused Dorothy considerable heartache. Even as he was philandering, he could be wildly jealous. It was not a matter of love but possession, and perhaps projection as well. Sometimes at parties he would watch her talk to a flirtatious man. At home afterwards he would become enraged and make accusations. "He was always a hundred percent wrong," said Dorothy years later. "He was probably saying to himself, 'This is the way *she* should feel about me.'"

Dorothy learned the truth about her husband in the most publicly humiliating fashion. On March 8, 1940, a woman known as Johanna Stoddard committed suicide by leaping from the seventeenth floor of the Book-Cadillac Hotel in Detroit. She wore a gray dress and was swathed in a silver fox cape. Behind her she left $700 in cash and checks, fragments of romantic poetry and costly gowns, hats and underwear strewn on the bed. On the table, a solitaire game showed the ace of spades—sometimes known as "Death's card"—placed prominently in the center. A florist's card read "You're still lovely." Nearby stood an easel with paint and brushes. On one wall she had scrawled in red letters four inches high: EXIT SMILING. There was also a note:

Dearest Bill,

I just wanted to thank you for your kindness. You know how things were with me. I may have said things in desperation that I didn't mean. I hope you do not hate me, and, I mean, I'm sorry. I know you will understand and forgive me. I'm not well. My lungs are in a precarious state, where I have to be so careful.

I still love you, but I guess you were right. I only fought so hard because my heart hurt so. You've been very white about everything. I can only hope to emulate you and try to do something good with my life. I am very tired.

Goodbye darling.

Johanna

It was addressed to William S. Paley of New York, President of the Columbia Broadcasting Company.

When news of the suicide reached New York that day, Paley was distraught. First, he went home to Dorothy and confessed: Johanna Stoddard had presented herself as an aspiring actress. They had a brief affair that she tried to keep going despite his rebuffs.

Her real name (which Paley did not know) was Geraldine Kenyon Bourque. She had left her husband, an autoworker in Pontiac, Michigan, as well as an infant daughter, in 1931. "He was dreadfully upset, first because his unfaithfulness had been revealed and second that it was a scandal," Dorothy recalled. "He didn't have any feeling about her but he did feel bad. He had been to bed with her, so there was an association."

The explicit intimacy in papers left by Bourque was embarrassing to Paley as well. There were two long letters, unaddressed and undated, but unmistakably intended for him. "Darling," she wrote, "I have been thinking of how magnetic you were and how afraid I was of that magnetism . . . I discovered you to be a wonderful lover. Your words were caresses, a fever surged within me, but even in that heated moment I refused that which I craved so terribly. . . ." Another passage read: "I wish you were poor like I am, because then it would be so much easier. You are going to be away from me so much because you are very important and I am not."

The CBS public relations machinery moved into high gear. Klauber hurried over to the Paleys', where he spent the day composing a cover story for the press. In a statement that appeared the next day in newspapers across the country, Paley admitted to having met the woman a year earlier in a restaurant with a group of people. He said she had later written to him to say she had tuberculosis and needed help finding a job as an entertainer. He made a point of saying that he and Dorothy had talked to her several times, "trying to straighten her out, but she became more mentally disturbed all the time. Finally she began to write letters to me, declaring that she had developed an emotional attachment for me."

By this account, Geraldine Bourque had become a legitimate nuisance, yet Paley never notified any authorities about her. Instead, he said his lawyers had tried to contact her relatives and he had offered her medical attention, which she refused. He admitted to having heard from her last a few days earlier, when she told him she was going to Michigan.

Nobody who traveled in Paley's circles believed a word of it. At CBS, Stanton "never saw so many high-powered people in the elevators the day or two following the suicide, so there must have been something there." Niles Trammell, president of NBC, jokingly wrote to a friend that if something like that happened to him, he would make certain of two things: "the first—she would not have $700 in cash, and the second—we would refuse to make a statement."

Dorothy's trust was shattered. Not long afterwards, Paley came home with a large gray dog that he asked her to look after for a few days while its owner was away. Dorothy loved dogs and always had several in her household, but she thought his request odd. He was too exuberant, too solicitous. So, she did some detective work and discovered that Paley was having an affair with the dog's owner. "He was so happy and so dear, and that was why," said Dorothy.

She knew by then that Paley was a compulsive womanizer. "I don't know how tortured she was about his roving eye but there was plenty of it," said Irene Selznick. "She covered up, and he covered up." Mostly he went for classic mistress types—common, empty-headed, and pretty. Many were one-night stands. Dorothy tried to take a detached view, reasoning that his philandering was a symptom of his insecurity. Each new conquest, she thought, reaffirmed his attractiveness and desirability.

She continued to cling to their marriage, difficult though it was. The Paleys never had any public spats; they were too well behaved for that. Nor did Dorothy ever contemplate seeking a divorce. "I did confront him on a couple of occasions," she said. "I didn't like what he was doing, but I also recognized the inevitability in him. He could never be different."

17

WILLIAM PALEY, the man most associated with the power and glitter of television, at first mistrusted the new medium of picture and sound. He failed to grasp the potential and uses of television, and actively obstructed its development. He was like a horse-and-buggy driver who couldn't fathom the Model T. Television appeared as a relentless expense that would end by draining attention and resources from radio, his true love. If it had not been for the Paramount merger and Paley's competition with Sarnoff, and for the prodding of several executives who played on that rivalry, CBS might have stayed out of television altogether.

But the Paramount connection forced Paley to come to grips with television. A main reason for Paramount's interest in CBS was to control the industry as it emerged from its experimental stage. To moguls such as

Adolph Zukor, television in the home seemed as threatening as radio. But if television could be used by movie theaters, it might prove useful to the studios.

Paley's first pronouncements took this line. "It is hard to tell just how television will be handled," he told a St. Louis audience in 1929. But he predicted that it would be relegated to the movie houses "because of the size of the theater screen, which would make television more enjoyable, and the attractiveness of well-rounded programs presented in the theater."

In a newspaper article he was quoted as saying that television was not a stay-at-home medium: "Man is a social creature; he likes to rub shoulders with his fellows." Paley foresaw audiences flocking to movie theaters to watch news on live TV. And he predicted that the "great events in the world of sports"—the World Series, football, auto and horse races—would also be seen by millions of fans at theaters. "Perfections in the projection of motion pictures will play a large part in making television applicable to theater, rather than home, presentation," he concluded.

Sarnoff, on the other hand, understood. As early as 1923 he had informed his superiors at Marconi that television would be "the ultimate and greatest step in mass communications." At his urging, in 1928, RCA and NBC received a government permit for the first experimental television station in New York. With the futuristic call letter W2XBS, the station went on the air in July 1930 showing a fuzzy picture of the cartoon character Felix the Cat.

Sarnoff was dissatisfied with the technology, which relied on a whirling mechanical disc that frequently malfunctioned. He hired an émigré scientist, Vladimir Zworykin, a former communication specialist in the Czarist army who had experimented with television in Russia, and committed $1 million from NBC's radio earnings to develop an all-electronic television system. When the new technology was ready in 1936, NBC put on a public demonstration, using studios in the RCA Building and a powerful transmitter atop the Empire State Building, then the tallest building in the world.

CBS's first experimental station, W2XAB, had gone on the air Tuesday, July 21, 1931, a year after NBC. Its inaugural variety show ran from 10:15 to 11:00 P.M. that night, with sportscaster Ted Husing as master of ceremonies. New York mayor Jimmy Walker made the opening remarks, followed by the introduction of the "Columbia Television Girl"—Natalie Towers. The CBS chief engineer, Edwin K. Cohan, spoke on "What to Expect of Television," Kate Smith sang "When the Moon Comes Over the Mountain," the Boswell Sisters sang "Heebie-Jeebie Blues," and George Gershwin performed several of his famous songs. Significantly, Bill Paley was not even in town. Vacationing in Venice, he read a cable from Klauber reporting that the event was "a huge success . . . everyone delighted."

Over the next two years CBS telecast programs to approximately 7,500 crude television sets in the New York metropolitan area. But in February 1933 CBS discontinued its experimental effort. Paley decided to sit on the sidelines until it was clear that Sarnoff's promise of an electronic system could be fulfilled, which wouldn't happen until 1936.

All through the thirties Paley made his moves in television solely to keep pace with his rival across the street. "Sarnoff at RCA had his wary eye glued to the television future and grandly predicted moving pictures in every home; Paley was keeping his eye on Sarnoff," said Peter Goldmark, the brilliant Hungarian inventor hired in 1935 by Paul Kesten to develop television at CBS. Kesten, nicknamed "vice-president for the future" by his CBS colleagues, was eager to revitalize the network's interest in the medium. But Paley, Goldmark knew, "had mixed feelings about television. On the one hand, he thought it was much too expensive ever to be practical; on the other hand, he was persuaded to try again with an experimental station and take a chance that something might come of it." Only later did Goldmark learn that it was Kesten who "cushioned most of Paley's objections to my ideas and ultimately helped convince him to keep the company in television."

In July 1937, a year after television broadcasting resumed at NBC, Paley decided to build his own new television transmitter. His only instruction was that it was to be "bigger and better than RCA's" and that it was to top the magnificent Art Deco spire of the Chrysler Building—an example of Paley's flair for promotion. The CBS president also ordered construction of a television studio in Grand Central Station. All told, Paley earmarked nearly $1 million for television. "The urge to beat RCA, and its ruler, David Sarnoff," said Goldmark, was an "overriding force at CBS."

As usual, Paley was playing both sides of the fence. He and most of his executives remained skeptical of television's moneymaking potential. Klauber disliked the new medium, and he feared its hypnotic power. "Television is like eating peanuts," he once told a colleague. "You know why you shouldn't eat them, but you keep reaching for them." With encouragement from Klauber, Paley labored to keep television confined to experimentation. He urged the FCC to delay approving television broadcasting to the general public and permitting commercial sponsorship. The federal regulators accepted Paley's argument that radio might be damaged if they acted too hastily. The FCC's caution infuriated Sarnoff, who insisted that television had been tested enough; since the 1920s, RCA had spent $20 million to ensure that the new medium was technically feasible.

Sarnoff called his opponents "parasites," interested only in enriching themselves with profits from radio while impeding a medium that would put America in the technological forefront.

Sarnoff forged ahead on his own. In April 1939, NBC began a regular program service with a telecast of President Roosevelt opening the New York World's Fair. Also on display at RCA's Hall of Television were new television sets with screens ranging from five to twelve inches across. Every day visitors crowded around the sets to watch NBC's eclectic mix of programs transmitted to the fairgrounds from its studio in the RCA Building: snippets of operas, cartoons, cooking demonstrations, and travelogues, as well as live pictures of baseball games (Columbia vs. Princeton), wrestling matches, fashion shows, and skaters at Rockefeller Center caught by a roving bus equipped with cameras. Consumers began buying RCA's sets, richly priced from $200 to $600 ($1,900 to $5,600 in 1990 dollars), as soon as they rolled off the assembly line. Six months later, CBS launched regular broadcasts when its transmitter was completed. There were still fewer than ten thousand television sets in the New York area.

To cut costs, CBS concentrated on showing films instead of live programs. But among the fifteen hours transmitted each week was a scattering of programs featuring news, special events, documentaries, and sports. Gilbert Seldes, the prominent New York drama critic, was CBS's first director of television programming. By the early 1940s, some thirty staffers at CBS were at work on television, which was by then costing CBS about $750,000 a year. And still CBS was not on the leading edge. "Before the war we did the minimum to keep our television license," recalled Frank Stanton. "NBC was way ahead of us. Sarnoff was the visionary. He had the guts."

By 1941, the FCC was still blocking Sarnoff's plans, refusing permission that would allow the sale of advertising time on television. Its chairman, Lawrence Fly, saw RCA as a dangerous monopoly that would dominate television as it had radio. But after some pressure from Congress, the FCC at mid-year finally permitted commercials to be sold on television programs. By then even Paley could not resist counting the television aerials on rooftops whenever he traveled by car on business trips. As the numbers rose, so did the commercial possibilities. Once television sets were in widespread use, Paley grudgingly recognized that he might make back the large investment for programming in advertising dollars.

World War II abruptly halted television's progress. Manufacture of sets was suspended to ensure that electronic components could be used for national defense. In mid-1942, NBC and CBS reduced their weekly program schedules from fifteen to four hours of movies such as *This Is England, The Lottery Bride,* and *Words for Battle.* Paley, who was still fearful that television would kill radio, was relieved.

In 1928, Paley had seized on radio because he grasped its commercial power when the La Palina program pushed cigar sales to new heights. The CBS radio network had a shape that he could mold to suit his purpose. But television was more complicated, and its application difficult to imagine for a man who always demanded concrete proof that something would work. Like the movie men, Paley could not see beyond the obvious inferiority of the television picture to the theatrical screen.

David Sarnoff was an electronics man. He knew that the technology was at hand to make television a fixture in America's living rooms. Later, he would bitterly resent the adulation and power that Paley derived from television. Paley was just plain lucky. When the time was right, he had a system in place—a prosperous radio network—and a farsighted executive in Frank Stanton that made it possible for him to rush into television.

Paley's initial tentativeness played against a backdrop of other professional frustrations. CBS's expansion in the late 1930s had chipped away at his control of the company he bought and built. As the thirty-seven-year-old Paley embarked on his second decade in radio, his improvisational style seemed out of place. CBS had matured into a major corporation, streamlined and professional. Ed Klauber, Paul Kesten, and increasingly Frank Stanton were running the company with systems and routines that were alien to Paley's entrepreneurial individualism. As CBS got larger, Paley withdrew more and more from its daily operations.

Despite its financial success, classy public image, and new prominence in news, CBS Radio was stalled in the audience ratings; NBC still controlled nearly all of the most popular shows. And every week seemed to bring a fresh problem for Paley. His news commentators were beset by controversy. The regulators in Washington were once again bedeviling CBS and NBC, embroiling Paley in a battle so nasty and dispiriting that he ultimately would give up his position as CBS's principal spokesman. The tensions created by these fights put Paley increasingly at odds with Klauber, whose devotion to CBS could not compensate for his difficult personality.

Paley had exhausted all his stratagems in trying to make CBS first in the ratings. He had created stars, as well as stolen them; he had wooed advertisers relentlessly. Yet once he established a show, the advertiser would usually leap to NBC's more powerful network of stations. "It was a great frustration for Bill, and for everyone," said Frank Stanton. "We would work our hearts out to build the business and then lose it."

CBS paid no financial penalty for these defections, however. As the nation went to war, the government enacted an excess profits tax—with rates as high as 90 percent—to prevent profiteering. The tax was an incentive for businesses to cut profits by spending more on advertising. With plenty of sponsors to go around, CBS and NBC profits ran just about even. Remaining in second place only hurt CBS's image, and Paley's ego.

His discomfiture ran deep. In their desire to satisfy advertisers, NBC and CBS relinquished control over programming. The advertising agencies now made the decisions, not only about stars, scripts, and formats but about placement in the network schedules. CBS lost its hold over the area of Paley's greatest strength. He was addicted to the glamour of show business, and he could no longer feed his addiction.

In CBS's radio newscasting, the principles set down late in 1937 by Klauber and Paley were proving difficult to enforce among the network's independent-minded commentators. Paley's interpretation of the network's rules was neither consistent nor entirely understandable to subordinates. Certain opinions were grounds for dismissal; others, equally strong, he would permit. These confusions were further compounded by the war.

At the outset only Edward R. Murrow stayed comfortably within the rules for fairness. Murrow modeled his analysis on the commentaries on CBS given by his mentor, Stephen Duggan. His broadcasting style, says Murrow's biographer A. M. Sperber, consisted of "subtle, guarded advocacy, coupled with an awareness that the quiet, informed, 'objective' voice was often the best persuader." Kaltenborn, by contrast, was incapable of curbing his outrage over Hitler's expansion. Klauber continually tried to rein Kaltenborn in. "Just don't be so personal," he'd say. "Use such phrases as 'it is said,' 'there are those who believe.' " Kaltenborn tried, but admitted to Murrow, "I find myself going off the deep end every now and then. For a great many years, my radio listeners have expected me to express personal opinions."

In March 1939, Kaltenborn's style proved too much for his sponsor, General Mills, which dropped his program. The reason, a General Mills official explained candidly, was "the inescapable fact that no radio news commentator who is worth listening to can possibly avoid indications of his personal point of view, and we are rapidly approaching a time when our national problems will be reflected in violent political emotions. It is not, as we see it, a proper function for a company manufacturing and merchandising products for general consumption to involve itself publicly in such emotions."

Other advertisers too protested to Paley that CBS was trying to push the United States into war. Roosevelt dispatched the head of the FCC, Lawrence Fly, to complain about the network's coverage. Klauber sent

Fly packing, telling him that CBS would report the news as it saw fit. But Paley was spooked. The majority of Americans remained isolationist, and the government began making threatening noises about taking over broadcasting in the event of an emergency. In this tense atmosphere, when the very control of American radio broadcasting had suddenly become an issue, Paul White issued an internal CBS memo outlawing the word "commentator," which he said had come "to connote the expression of a personal or editorial opinion which is beyond the purview of those upon whom were called to analyze the news." Henceforth, the term would be "news analyst."

On September 3, 1939, England and France declared war on Germany. The pressure on American broadcasters increased when Stephen Early, the White House press secretary, publicly warned that radio was a "rookie" in handling war stories and must behave as a "good child." This patronizing yet ominous warning prompted Paley, Sarnoff, and their chief executives to hold a day of discussions about the role of the networks in wartime. Obviously intimidated, they declared their intention to return to normal programming as quickly as possible. "Those opposed to this view," the *New York Times* wrote the next day, "contend that radio is confronted with its first chance to cover a war in the 'public interest, convenience and necessity,' and should do it in a 'big way.' It was made clear yesterday, however, that this is the opinion of a minority."

After the meeting, Klauber issued a statement outlining CBS's policies on war coverage. He emphasized the need for objectivity, fairness, and factual accuracy. Newscasters, he said, should read calmly, without showing emotion or prejudice. The task of news analysts would be "to help the listener to understand, to weigh, and to judge, but not do the judging for him." CBS's policy, soon echoed by others in broadcasting, was, in the view of broadcasting historian Barnouw, "a kind of neutrality law for radio."

"Paley understood the power of CBS, that everyone listened to us," recalled Eric Sevareid. "There were admonishments. 'You are from a neutral country,' CBS executives said. 'You have to be a neutral reporter.' " At one point, Paul White cabled Sevareid that he had gone "furtherest limbward"—as far as he could go without crossing the line into forbidden commentary.

Kaltenborn's excesses continued to worry Paley, although the commentator's new sponsor, the Pure Oil Company, had few complaints. Pure Oil's sales were booming as a result of its association on radio with Kaltenborn, who had risen to folk hero status; in the Frank Capra film *Mr. Smith Goes to Washington,* Kaltenborn was the voice of integrity. Yet late in 1939, CBS told Pure Oil that there was no longer a quarter-hour available for the broadcast during the evening, when the male listeners likely to buy the company's products would be tuning in. CBS was relieved when Pure Oil began negotiating with NBC. In April 1940, Kaltenborn shifted networks.

CBS had played a neat trick, dropping the commentator without actually pushing him. But the network revealed its thinking later that year after conservative Republican congressman Karl Mundt of South Dakota attacked network newscasters for partisanship. Mundt raised the specter of greater government control over the broadcast of war news if the networks did not police themselves. To reassure Mundt, a CBS vice-president told him that Kaltenborn had been discontinued by the network "due to the fact that he was going to excess in the matter of exciting people's emotions about the war." Kaltenborn insisted that he had not been dismissed, and proffered as evidence a customarily bland letter of praise written by Paley ("We too have enjoyed the association throughout your years at Columbia") when he left.

As the European war progressed, Elmer Davis grew to be just as difficult as Kaltenborn. From 8:55 to 9:00 each night—a key spot in CBS's prime-time schedule—he read and commented on the day's top stories. Invariably, there would be fights between Paley and Davis over what Paley called the commentator's efforts to "get too much viewpoint in." Once every three to four weeks Paley would take Davis out to lunch and urge him to abide by the rules. But the problems with Davis never came to a head because in 1942 he left CBS to lead the newly created Office of War Information (OWI).

From a distance of 3,500 miles, Murrow was harder to control, and Paley was less inclined to curb him than he was other commentators. Murrow had begun to feel strongly that the United States should join the battle in Europe. In a March 9, 1941, broadcast Murrow was explicit: "The course of Anglo-American relations will be smooth on the surface, but many people over here will express regret that they believe America is making the same mistakes that Britain made. For you must understand that the idea of America being more help as a non-belligerent than as a fighting ally has been discarded even by those who advanced it originally. Maybe we should hear some frank forthright talk across the Atlantic instead of rhetoric but I doubt it."

Despite Murrow's undisguised effort to influence opinion, Paley issued no rebuke because Murrow was his fair-haired boy. What is more, opinion had begun to shift toward intervention, at least among the nation's movers and shakers along the Eastern seaboard. Murrow's reports helped turn the broader American public in that direction. By December 1941, when Murrow was honored by Paley at a star-studded formal dinner at the Waldorf-Astoria Hotel in New York, the CBS commentator's views were so widely accepted that he could comfortably declare that the war in Europe would be decided "along the banks of the Potomac." It was already clear that Murrow's image as a man of conscience honored CBS and Paley.

Barely a week later the Japanese bombed Pearl Harbor. America's declaration of war only increased tensions over commentary at CBS. Top network executives joined the war effort, enlisting the services of CBS personnel to produce government programs. CBS Radio playwright Normal Corwin teamed with Murrow in *An American in England,* a documentary/drama series to counter anti-British sentiment fostered by the reactionary "America Firsters," who opposed involvement in the war. Under the supervision of the Office of War Information, CBS broadcast news to Europe in eighteen languages. Even the highly rated Hummert soap operas introduced plot lines that encouraged Anglo-American comity. Inevitably, the line between authorized and forbidden opinion blurred even more.

In the summer of 1943, CBS presented an extraordinary broadcast, an "Open Letter on Race Hatred" that was laced with opinion. Paley allowed the program because its moving force was Wendell Willkie, the defeated conservative Republican presidential candidate of 1940, whose world travels had liberalized his views. The program dramatized the Detroit race riots that in June 1943 left thirty-four dead and more than seven hundred injured. It was written by one of CBS's top talents, William Robson. At the end, Willkie made an impassioned statement equating fascism abroad with discrimination against minorities in the United States.

Paley took a keen interest in the show from start to finish. He listened carefully as Robson played him a recording of the rehearsal, with everything but Willkie's concluding remarks. At various points Paley would mutter, "Caution here," or, "You're overboard there." Robson went back to the typewriter and another rehearsal was taped for Paley. After further changes, Paley gave the go-ahead. But he was still nervous. "I have a report from our man in Washington that the FBI had definite proof that the Negroes started the riot in Detroit," he told Robson. "How about that? You don't say it in your script." Robson pointed out that he lacked evidence to make such a statement. "Are you certain of your facts?" Paley pressed Robson, who replied that he was.

Still, Paley took no chances. He knew CBS affiliates in the South would be angered, and ordered that a recording of the program be previewed by the stations so they could decide whether to carry it. A number of Southern stations chose not to. The program was broadcast as scheduled, one of CBS's most honorable efforts.

Only a month later, CBS commentator Cecil Brown ran into trouble when Paley decided he was injecting too much opinion into his newscasts. After taking over from Elmer Davis in mid-1942, Brown had had periodic squabbles with CBS officials over the definition of editorial opinion, but he was not censured. Then on August 25, 1943, Brown rebuked President Roosevelt, accusing him of "failing to dramatize what we are fighting for." As a result, said Brown, enthusiasm among Americans for the war was "evaporating into thin air." His tone did not differ substantially from Murrow's criticism of the president two years earlier, but then again, Brown was not Murrow.

Two days later Paul White blistered Brown with a memo charging him with defeatism "that would be of immense pleasure to Dr. Goebbels and his boys." Unless Brown agreed to conform to CBS policies, the memo concluded, he should quit the network. The words were White's but the sentiments were Paley's.

Brown maintained that he was not editorializing, but the damage was done. CBS had attacked him. He had no choice but to submit his resignation, which he did quietly on September 2. Paley tried to disassociate himself from the dispute, writing a polite note accepting the resignation, and stating that Brown had made "some very valuable contributions to the advancement of the news service."

There the matter might have rested had not Kaltenborn delivered a speech several weeks later accusing CBS of censoring its news commentators. CBS countered with a full-page newspaper advertisement restating its policy against editorializing. In explaining the ad, White conceded that this policy had not been consistently enforced but would be applied strictly henceforth. He also said that the censorship row had nothing to do with the resignation of Cecil Brown.

The explanation for CBS's unusual advertisement, according to the *New York Post,* was that the network was "making a bid for new commercial sponsors and through its advertising was taking steps to assure them that it has not been promoting any one point of view." Only the day before Brown's disputed remarks, his own sponsor, Johns Manville, had canceled their contract because of his outspokenness.

Brown finally broke his silence to say that his departure was a direct result of censorship at CBS. In a letter to White that prompted headlines in the press, Brown said, "News policy as enunciated by you is not, as you suggest, intended to make CBS reporters neutral, passive spectators of this war, but to make them creatures of your own editorial opinion of what constitutes the news."

· · ·

Newspaper columnists at the time speculated that yet another factor in the Brown dismissal may have been CBS's wish to avoid controversy during its four-year-old fight with the FCC chairman, James Lawrence Fly. From the start, after his appointment by Roosevelt in 1939, Fly had launched a campaign against monopolistic practices at the networks. He and others in Washington were concerned that the networks dominated local stations and dictated the programs they broadcast. A former general counsel of the Tennessee Valley Authority, Fly, tall and lanky, with a Southern drawl, was the epitome of the idealistic, crusading New Dealer. He believed strongly in the competition of ideas as well as the diversity of outlets for news and information. Concentration of ownership and control were anathema to him.

A special three-man committee of the FCC had held hearings for six months in 1939, calling officials from networks and stations to testify. CBS sent 17 witnesses, whose testimony filled 2,180 pages of the 8,713-page hearing transcript. Paley's testimony alone accounted for 130 pages. Throughout, Paley and his fellow broadcasters had insisted that their networks were not monopolies. Broadcasting, Paley stressed, was a competitive business, a "tool of democracy" best regulated lightly if at all.

The White House had supported Fly, but the investigation made the administration jittery. By early 1940, radio broadcasters were lobbying vigorously at the White House and on Capitol Hill. RCA officials planted an article in the *Saturday Evening Post* that characterized Fly as a megalomaniac while Paley concentrated on ingratiating himself with Roosevelt. At the president's request, he surveyed the extent of Nazi propaganda while visiting broadcasters in South America. Before his departure in November 1940, Paley had made certain to flatter the president by congratulating him on his election to a third term. "Few things have meant as much to me, or have given me such full gratification," he wrote, "as the decision by the American people to have you lead us during the next four years."

At the end of 1940, Fly was sufficiently alarmed to tell Roosevelt that the networks "are prepared to seek the destruction of the Commission if any substantial network regulation is attempted." The following March, Fly sensed the pressure being brought on the White House by broadcasters and urged the president to authorize release of a new set of rules restricting network operations.

But Roosevelt balked, asked Fly to delay the report, and arranged to meet in mid-April 1941 with Mark Ethridge, vice-president of the *Louisville Courier-Journal* and general manager of the newspaper's radio station, WHAS, an important CBS affiliate. Ethridge, the former president of the National Association of Broadcasters, had come on Paley's behalf. (An appearance by Paley himself would have been too blatant.) In the brief meeting, Ethridge persuaded Roosevelt to put the regulations on the back burner.

Word of the White House maneuvering leaked to *Variety,* which reported that Roosevelt was "rumored" to have told Fly to put the monopoly report "back in the closet" in the interests of promoting cooperation with broadcasters in the nation's defense program. Fly knew that two years' worth of work was about to evaporate because of Paley's last-ditch effort.

Quietly, Fly pressed the commission to issue the new regulations anyway. Ethridge got wind of Fly's plans and begged the White House to stop the FCC. On a Saturday morning, May 3, 1941, Stephen Early called Fly to order that the regulations be withheld. "I'm sorry," said Fly. "They're already out." In fact, although the documents had been printed, they had not yet been distributed. Fly had lied to save the regulations, which appeared a few hours later.

Under the proposed rules, NBC had to divest itself of one of its two networks. CBS had to scuttle its "option clause" giving the network the right to take over any time period in a local station's schedule. Publicly, Paley charged that these actions would "torpedo" the existing structure of broadcasting and lead to government ownership. Privately, he wired Roosevelt his "hope that you will take steps to stay the damaging venture of the Commission." But once the regulations were out, Roosevelt could not call them back.

Now Paley took the lead in trying to discredit Fly and the FCC. He said the FCC had no legal right to make such rules and issued a thirty-three-page rebuttal outlining the gloomy consequences of the FCC's actions. "I fought like a steer," he later recalled. In lengthy, emotional testimony before Congress that June, he urged Congress to pass a new law for radio.

But Paley made two ill-conceived proposals that undercut all his previous and subsequent statements about radio regulation. Under the existing law, the FCC was only permitted to regulate local stations. Fly's monopoly report cunningly circumvented this restriction by saying the FCC would not license any station affiliated with a network that defied the new rules. In his testimony Paley protested that the FCC regarded the networks as illegitimate. To ensure their full legal rights, he said, the networks themselves should be licensed by the federal government. Paley added that fairness in the presentation of news and controversial issues should be a condition of licenses for networks as well as stations—a suggestion that may have had the unintended consequence of opening the door to the FCC's Fairness Doctrine of 1949, which forced broadcasters to provide contrasting viewpoints on controversial issues.

Paley's proposals surprised friends and foes of CBS and NBC in Washington. Even the FCC had rejected network licensing as too restrictive. In fact, it was Klauber who had conceived of the proposals, much to the dismay of several other CBS executives, including Joseph Ream, the CBS attorney. And Paley had such confidence in Klauber that he embraced his ideas and became their advocate.

The hearings were confrontational, with calls for Fly's resignation and threats of legislation or court action to strip the FCC of its powers. Yet in the end the networks' very structures undermined their own arguments. CBS predicted doom if its ability to take over local station time was eliminated, but NBC had never used this "option clause" with its stations. NBC said that losing one of its networks would be catastrophic, but CBS had prospered with only a single network. Even worse, Paley proved an ineffective witness. Klauber wrote all his boss's testimony, and while Paley rehearsed it enough to make a smooth presentation that would avoid embarrassment, he was unwilling to submit to the two or three days of mock questioning that he needed to be thoroughly informed. Paley chose to rely on his charm, and he lacked the facts to counter Fly effectively.

Afterwards, CBS and NBC consented to meet with the FCC to see if they could agree on modified rules everyone could live with. Over the summer of 1941, Paley, Klauber, and NBC president Niles Trammell met a half-dozen times with Telford Taylor, general counsel of the FCC. In presenting the network case, Paley's manner was freewheeling, even jaunty at times. He sprinkled his arguments with profanity and Broadway metaphors that struck Taylor as undignified. But when Paley grew angry he would hold his control and merely shake his head. Klauber, however, was a dark, dour counterpoint, whose obvious hatred of Fly's FCC erupted in furious outbursts.

After two meetings, Taylor presented a compromise. Instead of eliminating the option clause entirely, the FCC would adopt NBC's approach. The broadcast day would be divided into four parts; in each part, the networks could control three hours of a station's time. But Paley and Klauber, whose network would be hit hardest by any such change, were tough, argumentative, and finally unyielding. After several more fruitless sessions, negotiations broke off.

That autumn the FCC issued modified rules incorporating the option clause revision and dropping the requirement that NBC divest one of its networks—although Fly urged RCA to dispose of one network voluntarily. Two weeks later the networks filed suit to prevent the FCC from putting the rules into effect on the grounds that the commission had no legal right to issue them. The following January the Department of Justice filed an anti-trust suit against CBS and NBC, making the same monopoly charges as the FCC.

Meanwhile the campaign against Fly got nasty. Toward the end of 1941, Martin Dies, chairman of the House Committee on Un-American Activities, accused the FCC of harboring subversives. Early the next year Congressman Eugene E. Cox of Georgia called Fly "the most dangerous man in Washington" and compared his FCC with the Gestapo. Cox set himself up as chairman of a special committee to investigate the FCC, while another House committee held hearings on a bill to overturn the FCC's new rules. Throughout 1942, Fly was dragged repeatedly to hearings where he was attacked by Paley, Trammell, and other broadcasters. Fly was called a Communist and a menace to national security; Cox even tried to impeach him. It was an unprecedented harassment of a public official.

Then a vigilant FCC investigator discovered that Cox had been paid to help a radio station in Georgia obtain a license. After this conflict of interest was exposed, Cox resigned as chairman of the FCC investigation. The House bill died, and in May 1943 the Supreme Court upheld the FCC's right to regulate. Two months later, RCA sold its Blue Network for $8 million to Edward Noble, the owner of WMCA in New York, who had made a fortune manufacturing Life Saver candies. The new network was rechristened ABC.

The FCC's regulations loosened CBS's stranglehold on its stations, although the network still dominated large portions of the radio schedule. But breaking up the two NBC networks was a classic case of good intentions leading to bad policy. RCA's ownership of a second network had applied a gentle brake to commercial impulses. The Blue Network was an outlet for Sarnoff's high-minded ideas on public service. It was supported by profits from the mass market Red Network. The presence of NBC Blue forced image-conscious CBS to either match or surpass programs catering to selective tastes. Selling NBC Blue to a third party brought the collapse of this system in which self-interest helped preserve the public interest. ABC had to pursue mass audience programming to build its business, and all three networks became even more driven by commercial forces.

For Paley, the FCC rules were a severe setback. Fly had proved Paley's toughest adversary, fighting every maneuver and employing as much guile, power and stamina as Paley himself could muster. And Fly won— at a time when CBS had maximum leverage through its role as wartime propagandist. The regulations stayed. No new radio law was passed. Not only did Paley lose the battle, he had wasted an inordinate amount of time. He had always hated to go to Washington. It had been a colossal bother to prepare and make the presentations he so dreaded. Never again would Paley appear before Congress as CBS's representative.

He bitterly disliked Fly, but in later years Paley would sanitize his views. To one writer, he maintained that "we were pretty good friends" who met in Washington after hours for drinks and continuing debates. But to Fly's daughter Paley said, "Although we had quite a few meetings, all of them were formal in nature. . . . Unfortunately, perhaps, we had little or no social relationship." In the end, Paley could never bring himself to acknowledge that Fly had prevailed.

During this period Paley was subjected to public criticism, even ridicule, for the first time. Early in the battle, when Paley broadcast a defense of the networks on CBS, *Time* magazine reported that "it delighted Columbia executives that Mr. Paley had a bad case of microphone fright. Hovering around him in his office at Columbia's Madison Avenue studios in Manhattan were two production men, two vice-presidents, one engineer, and two page boys. There were duplicate microphones in case one broke down, a precaution not usually taken either with Jack Benny or President Roosevelt. Mr. Paley read quickly and nervously."

The protracted fight also provoked clashes between Paley and Ed Klauber. Klauber's proposals for network regulation and a fairness requirement were serious blunders that may well have contributed to Fly's victory. Much as he hated to own up to mistakes, Paley recanted the fairness requirement in one of his final congressional appearances in 1942. But he could never bring himself to mention again the licensing of networks.

Despite their differences, Klauber continued to dedicate himself completely to Paley and CBS. Klauber had virtually no life outside his job. Most evenings, after dropping Paley off at his house, Klauber would sit by the telephone in his apartment, ready to field questions and problems until CBS went off the air for the night. In return for his devotion, Klauber hoped only that Paley would regard him as a friend.

Yet Klauber and Paley dined together socially only once, and then only because Klauber tricked Paley into it. In the office one day Paley mentioned that his favorite dish was his mother's stewed goose. "Oh, we have that at home," Klauber said abruptly. "Isn't that funny," said Paley. "I've never had it anywhere else except my mother's." Klauber immediately invited Paley to have stewed goose at his home. Taking no chances, Paley arrived alone. Gladys Klauber tentatively served the stewed goose, and it was dreadful. She had no choice but to admit that she had never cooked it before; her husband had unearthed a recipe from an aunt. Paley,

of course, failed to see the poignancy in Klauber's invitation—that a subordinate would risk his wife's embarrassment in an effort simply to socialize with his boss. To Paley, it was all a "great joke. We had a very amusing
evening."

Such insensitivity reflected Paley's self-centered nature. But Paley had
also come to begrudge Klauber, who had become overbearing. "Klauber
had a facile mind, very far-reaching," said one executive who knew both
men. "He knew a lot about a lot of things. On occasion he made Bill feel
like a little boy, and Bill resented it." Paley began complaining that
Klauber was crowding him. Perhaps out of exasperation over Paley's indecision, Klauber had become more aggressive in asserting his authority.
When Paley was off on his frequent travels, Klauber had grown accustomed to taking control. Although at one time Paley had welcomed
Klauber's disagreement, now it was irritating. And when Klauber's high
standards stood in the way of commercial gain, Paley's patience wore thin.

Paley listened more closely to complaints that Klauber's coldness and
intimidation were undermining morale. "You've got to get rid of
Klauber," said Paley's attorney, Ralph Colin. "He's evil." Paul Kesten
made no secret of detesting Klauber, either. Nor could Klauber abide
Kesten; he found Paley's slick promotion man too eager to win at any
cost, and too fast and loose with the facts. For more than a decade Klauber
and Kesten had been locked in a power struggle over who would run CBS
under Paley. Everyone around them felt the intensity of their rivalry. "If
you wanted to walk out in the hall of the twentieth floor in those days you
took your umbrella and put your hat on it—if it didn't get shot off you
could go out," recalled Frank Stanton.

By 1942, Kesten prevailed over Klauber at last. That March Paley
quietly stripped Klauber of his executive vice-president's stripes, appointed him to the meaningless post of chairman of the executive committee on the board of directors, and made Kesten CBS's first general
manager. A year and a half later, without consulting the board of directors,
Paley called Klauber, then fifty-six, to his office late one August afternoon
and fired him. The next day a two-paragraph announcement in the *New
York Times* said that Klauber had resigned because of ill-health.

After Klauber left, Paley permanently sealed the door connecting their
two offices. Yet Klauber's summary dismissal could not be papered over.
Ralph Colin, no friend of Klauber's, was offended by the way Paley turned
him out. At the next board meeting, Colin criticized Paley for short-
circuiting the directors. Paley was loathe to admit publicly that he had
fired Klauber, but he did say in later years that Klauber became too "possessive," which "caused something of a management problem." What
Paley saw as possessiveness others read as Klauber's desire for his boss's

friendship—and for the sort of approval that might have mellowed the curmudgeonly Klauber. Working for Paley only worsened Klauber's bad traits. Paley's rejection plunged him into depression.

The day Paley gave him notice, Klauber invited Frank Stanton to his apartment. As the two men talked, Klauber's eyes filled with tears. "I gave my life to Bill," he said with a tremor in his voice, "and he never once invited me across the threshold."

18

D URING THE DIFFICULTIES and controversies of the late thirties and early forties, Paley had looked for any diversion he could find on foreign shores. There were frequent vacations and extended business trips abroad as well as heady stints in government service.

His journey in late 1940 to South America brought new professional opportunities while enhancing his personal prestige. Since the expansion of CBS into war-torn Europe was impossible, Paley conceived of starting a commercial network to the south. It would be his first entrepreneurial challenge since building CBS a decade earlier. He threw himself into the project with his customary brio, even arranging for tutors to visit the CBS Building to provide instruction in Portuguese and Spanish for interested employees. And when Roosevelt asked Paley to combine his visit to South American broadcasters with a presidential mission, the CBS president was deeply flattered.

Paley spent seven weeks in South America, accompanied by Dorothy, as well as his news director, Paul White, and Edmund Chester, director of CBS's short-wave activities. Not only did Paley line up prospective affiliates, he interviewed what he referred to as "many of the lesser lights, especially American and South American reporters" in his quest for information on the Nazi infiltration of Latin America. Paley turned on every ounce of charm. He persuaded sixty-four stations in eighteen countries to join his network. In a typical touch, he had the contracts not just printed but engraved—"the most beautiful contracts you ever saw."

CBS was free to make money from the enterprise, which was frankly designed to seal Pan-American friendship and enlist support in the event that the United States entered the war. Network activities in South America were to be overseen by the government's coordinator of Inter-American affairs, Nelson Rockefeller. The thirty-two-year-old Standard Oil heir had actually been recommended for his job by Paley, who had cultivated their friendship the previous summer during a vacation in Northeast Harbor, Maine. "An event of no small importance, for it was the beginning of his career in politics," Paley would proudly say of his Rockefeller recommendation. Paley had been eager to do a favor for Rockefeller, one of the richest and most socially prominent men in America. Three years earlier, Rockefeller had invited Paley, the voracious new collector of Matisse, Picasso, and other Post-Impressionists, to be a trustee of the Museum of Modern Art, which had been founded by Rockefeller's mother. A board membership at MOMA carried instant cachet in the upper reaches of New York society. The vice-president of the museum also happened to be Jock Whitney, the next-door neighbor who ruled the social world Paley still yearned to join.

CBS reaped a publicity bonanza from La Cadena de las Americas (Network of the Americas). *Fortune* magazine devoted six pages to Paley's triumphant blow-by-blow account of his negotiations, filled with lofty pronouncements ("We are far too prone to think of Latin Americans as a mass of black-haired, backward people who owe what security they have, in the midst of their well-costumed revolutions, to the Monroe Doctrine and North American cash") and photographs taken by the CBS president. It didn't much matter that NBC had already been operating an informal network in Latin America for several years; once again, Paley had taken an NBC idea and had done it with greater pizzazz.

In South America itself CBS's venture aroused criticism. Performers, advertising agencies, and even some stations complained that U.S. companies that spent millions of pesos on local radio advertising would turn to CBS instead. *Sintonia,* an Argentine radio magazine normally friendly to the United States, wrote: "Our artists don't realize they were being lured with pretty phrases about 'cultural exchange' . . . which, in reality, hide a clear intention to create unjust and traitorous commercial competition to our own broadcasting."

After considerable delay, the network was launched in May 1942 with seven hours a day of programs from New York in Spanish and Portuguese. It was CBS's most far-reaching and explicit foray into propaganda. "We did not slant the news," recalled William Fineshriber, who worked on the network. "We slanted everything else about the United States and entertained them with their singers. We used entertainment as the bait for news."

After the United States's entry into the war halted export trade, Paley was unable to make money from the venture as he had envisioned eighteen months earlier. But the public relations value of La Cadena de las Americas proved useful enough until the end of 1942, when the government took over the network for war broadcasting.

Paley's involvement in Latin America led the U.S. government to ask for his advice about policy in that part of the world. In January 1941, after he returned from his survey trip, he submitted a five-page memo to Roosevelt that included a bold course of action for the administration. Paley proposed that Roosevelt consider intervening in the event of any Nazi-backed takeover of a South American government—whether by a coup or behind-the-scenes maneuver. Under Secretary of State Sumner Welles took an understandably dim view of Paley's hawkish proposal, cautioning Roosevelt that the plan could only play into Nazi charges of Yankee imperialism. Better to concentrate on propaganda to counter Nazi influence, Welles said.

For Paley, an entertainment impresario and former cigar man, offering foreign policy advice was exhilarating stuff. It whetted his appetite for more power and influence. Less than a year later, on December 1, 1941, Paley secretly organized something he called "Department X," a group of university researchers charged with studying and analyzing everything being written on postwar planning. Over the next eighteen months, Department X would reduce more than one thousand documents and books into four hundred digests and five elaborate charts, all of which were submitted to government experts. The high-flown survey was designed not for planning at CBS—indeed, it was done entirely outside CBS, purely at Paley's initiative—but for nothing less than the national interest.

In August 1942 Paley was off again—this time without Dorothy—to London. Since the beginning of the year, the radio networks had operated under a policy of wartime censorship. CBS had rarely needed to submit a script to the Office of Censorship; the network had simply incorporated various government restrictions into its news broadcasts—bans on reports about the weather, troop movements, war production, and casualties. To see how these rules were working in the field, Paley decided to spend a month in London. He had not been there since 1939, before the start of the war.

His traveling companion on the Pan American clipper—Paley says it was pure happenstance—was Jock Whitney, an Air Force captain by then, on his way to London for a wartime posting. The two men spent most of their time playing cards during the flight. But there were new avenues of conversation as well.

Although Whitney and Paley seldom socialized, they sat across the table at Museum of Modern Art board meetings. Whitney had also worked since 1940 for Nelson Rockefeller as director of films for the Office of Inter-American Affairs. Whitney and Rockefeller were close enough friends for Rockefeller to have been a guest at Whitney's small wedding earlier that year to Betsey Cushing Roosevelt. Because of Rockefeller, Paley and Whitney had more in common than ever before.

Paley was met at Heathrow Airport by Randolph Churchill, who swept him into London for dinner with his stunning wife, Pamela. The daughter of a minor English peer, the eleventh Lord Digby, Pamela Churchill (her second and third husbands would be theatrical producer Leland Hayward and Averell Harriman) was already a legend at twenty-one. She had dark auburn hair, deep sapphire eyes, a shapely figure, and creamy skin. Men were bewitched by her solicitous manner and dazzling gaze. Unhappily married for less than three years, she and Randolph Churchill had been leading separate lives since the birth of their son, Winston II, in December 1940. For Bill Paley, the evening was the beginning of a long friendship that would include one brief passionate interlude.

After dinner the Churchills took Paley to a nightclub where they encountered Whitney. Whitney and Paley walked back together through the dark London streets to their hotel. Listening to Whitney talk that night, Paley felt that as a civilian he was left out—"I got the feeling that important matters had been negotiated on high."

The next morning, Paley was no longer the kid with his nose pressed against the glass. Former CBS lobbyist Harry Butcher, now an aide to Dwight Eisenhower, commander-in-chief of the Allied Expeditionary Forces, invited Paley for lunch with the general. Paley was excited but apprehensive. He worried that Eisenhower might put him on the spot by talking about what CBS could do to improve American and British public opinion about the war.

Their talk in Ike's apartment at the Dorchester Hotel avoided any controversial topics, however. It was entirely casual. "Bill much thrilled by the opportunity to talk war shop with the generals," Harry Butcher noted in his diary. Paley came away deeply impressed with Eisenhower. "He was one of the most effective men I had ever known in small groups," he said later. Paley noted his "confident manner, and absolute assumption that any right-thinking person would do exactly what he proposed. He seemed to get genuine approval from all others around him. He stressed teamwork and learned from others—little from books, I understand." Eisenhower, in turn, understood precisely how to ingratiate himself with Paley, giving the CBS chief a car and driver, a supply of scarce gasoline, and special papers that enabled him to travel freely throughout England.

For the next three weeks Ed Murrow, his star newsman, whirled Paley through London for breakfast, lunch, and dinner with dignitaries, including nearly every British cabinet minister. Murrow put on a big luncheon for Paley at the Savoy, and brought him around to his apartment

on Hallam Street to converse with "the boys," his talented cadre of correspondents. The newsmen reveled in the keen interest Paley took in them,
and the admiration between Paley and Murrow was transformed into
genuine friendship.

Paley's aristocratic friends from prewar days entertained him lavishly
as well. Duff and Diana Cooper threw a dinner party at the Dorchester.
The guest list included Prime Minister Winston Churchill and his wife,
Clementine; Brendan Bracken, one of Churchill's top aides; Ronald Tree,
a member of Parliament, and his wife, Nancy; and a famous beauty, Freida
Casamori. Paley's enduring memory of that dinner was having to excuse
himself to relieve his bursting bladder just as Churchill asked him to summarize the American view of the war in Europe. When he returned, Paley
could not disguise his nervousness as Churchill pressed him for a response.
The next day, London was atwitter with Paley's breach of etiquette; the
consensus was that Paley should have endured his discomfort and answered Churchill immediately.

Paley spent weekends visiting his old friend Olive, Lady Baillie at
Leeds Castle, and the Duke of Marlborough and his wife at Blenheim. He
met Lord Louis Mountbatten and Edwina, his alluring wife. Lord Mountbatten was about to leave for his post as supreme commander of Allied
Forces in Southeast Asia. Paley was taken with Edwina, who was half
English and half German. Her grandfather was Sir Ernest Cassel, a Co-
logne-born Jewish banker who had served as financial adviser to Edward
VII and become one of the richest and most powerful men in Europe.
Spirited and independent, Edwina had beautiful large blue eyes and a
come-hither smile. Several days after their meeting, Paley invited Edwina
to join him for dinner at Cherkley, the country home of press baron Lord
Beaverbrook. Beaverbrook tried to get Paley drunk and pump him for
information, but Paley held his liquor and later boasted that he had prodded Beaverbrook into spilling some choice indiscretions.

Lady Mary Dunn did not cross Paley's path during the trip. Their
romance was over; Philip had joined the Army, and Lady Mary had taken
up with a dashing commando named Archie Campbell. But she had remained friends with Bill and Dorothy, largely because Dorothy was ignorant of her husband's infatuation. Two years earlier the Paleys had taken
in the Dunns' two daughters, Nell and Serena, at Kiluna to escape the
bombing. Diana and Duff Cooper's twelve-year-old son stayed with the
Paleys as well. In early 1942, when the Dunn girls returned to England,
Dorothy sent along two enormous trunks of expensive new clothes that
would fit them for the next four years.

Everywhere he went Paley absorbed the patrician taste of his hosts,
working hard to give the impression of elegance without effort. He espe-

cially strove to emulate the Old World ways of Ditchley, the country home of Ronald and Nancy Tree. "Nancy Tree had the reputation of having the best taste of almost anyone in the world," Paley said later in a revealing statement. "I think I learned more about living and about the way things should look if they are to be beautiful and well run by my visits to Ditchley than almost any other way that I can remember. Every room was so comfortable-looking in its furnishings and yet beautiful. It wasn't pretentious. It didn't have a luxurious look but rather an elegant look. One of her great secrets was making everything comfortable, what she sometimes called 'studied carelessness.' . . . She had the knack of making a room look old or used . . . which is very, very difficult to do. She was a genius at that."

The closest Paley came to war was a visit to a Royal Air Force aerodrome in Cambridgeshire to watch Stirling bombers take off for a raid on Germany. Accompanying Paley in his chauffeured car was Norman Corwin, in London to produce *An American in England* with Murrow. They watched ten squadrons take off and waited tensely for six hours. When all the planes returned safely, Paley was tickled that the pilots regarded him as a lucky omen.

On the eve of his departure late that September, Paley gave an address on the BBC. He reported that anti-British sentiment was a problem in the United States, partly the result of rumors spread by German propagandists that American troops were encountering hostility in Britain. He pledged as an American broadcaster to "defeat and dispel" those rumors and report accurately on the war.

The next day Paley had one more quick meeting with Eisenhower. The general took the opportunity to underscore the importance of radio in shaping public opinion to back up the United States Army. Afterwards, Paley confided to Butcher that he had decided to enlist, "no matter how important other people think the broadcasting business."

Paley knew that he could perform a valuable service by heeding Eisenhower's plea and directing wartime broadcasting at CBS. He did in fact redouble the network's propaganda activities on his return. But his visit to London had convinced him that his service would only be properly recognized if he wore a uniform and went overseas. Jock Whitney was there. David Sarnoff, although still stateside, was already a colonel in the Army Reserve and had requested active duty. Even nearsighted David Selznick was clamoring to enlist as a private.

"Don't be an idiot," Dorothy said when Paley revealed his plan. "You are not a common soldier. There are other things in which you have expertise." Once again, Paley took his wife's advice and sought a post that would befit his position. He called on his old friend Robert Sherwood, the playwright turned speechwriter for Roosevelt who headed international operations for the Office of War Information under Elmer Davis. Nearly a year later, in the summer of 1943, Sherwood came up with an enticing position: consultant to the Psychological Warfare Branch of the Office of War Information. Paley would wear the uniform of honorary colonel and be sent to Algiers, Eisenhower's headquarters for his North African campaign and planned invasion of Italy.

Paley's assignment stirred controversy within OWI, however. In mid-September, OWI headquarters in Washington advised C. D. Jackson, a Time-Life executive serving as American director of OWI in Algiers, that Paley "is interested in working under your direction and has good relationship BBC." When Jackson received the cable he looked at Richard Crossman, his British counterpart, and asked, "What are we going to do with him? We already have someone running the radio operation." Given Paley's stature, however, Jackson had no choice but to meet the request. "Send Paley airborne," he cabled two days later.

Publicity over Paley's new post in subsequent weeks rankled Jackson, however. The following month Jackson cabled Sherwood at OWI in Washington asking for clarification of Paley's duties. He was concerned, he said, that Paley wanted to be a "freewheeling radio hotshot" rather than a cog in his organization. Jackson's worries deepened when he was subsequently told that Paley wished to bring along two aides, Davidson Taylor, a CBS executive, and Arnold Hartly as program manager.

Despite Washington's reassurance that Paley "understands thoroughly that he will be part of and subject to the authority of the Psychological Warfare Branch," Jackson urged OWI not to send the two aides along. "Feel strong and others here . . . concur that idea of Paley arriving with 'team' is bad," he cabled. "Do not believe either you or Psychological Warfare Branch should invite inevitable gossip and eventual newspaper comment that CBS is 'taking over' PWB radio here or in Italy." Not surprisingly, Paley and his team prevailed. They were scheduled to touch down in Algiers in mid-November.

With only a few months to prepare for his departure, Paley determined he would leave CBS in the hands of Paul Kesten. Indeed, it had been this need for haste that prompted the abrupt firing of Klauber that August. Paley dove into preparing for his departure. Louis Cowan, a successful producer of radio quiz shows who served in the New York OWI office, briefed him on the organization's operations. Paley toured the OWI studios and offices, peppering Cowan with questions about everything from engineering to programs.

Paley was not subjected to boot camp with ordinary GIs. For one week in November 1943 he trained at the sprawling Long Island estate, owned by the department-store tycoon Marshall Field, where the OWI had set up its "indoctrination school." There Paley pursued a regimen of courses on pamphleteering, intelligence gathering, and short-wave receiving, interspersed with gentle drills in muscle building. By the time he finished, a gold dog tag from Cartier, bespoke uniforms from London, and a special traveling staff were ready.

Paley's decision to join the war effort marked a turning point. He yearned to escape both his marriage and his network. The war represented a challenge, an opportunity to display his talents in a new setting. OWI was beginning to resemble a private club. It was filled with bright men from publishing, advertising, film, and radio, including Joseph Barnes of the *New York Herald Tribune;* Edward W. Barrett, editor of *Newsweek;* and John Houseman, CBS's talented producer and director. Many of them had Ivy League degrees and good social pedigrees. Their approval was desirable. Without the financial and regulatory pressures of CBS, Paley could return to his hail-fellow ways of the cigar business and early radio days. He had witnessed the freewheeling atmosphere of wartime London. He intended to have fun—and to take stock of his life and work.

19

TO REACH ALGIERS, Paley and his travel escort, an OWI official named Philip Hamblet, had to fly from New York through Miami, Brazil, Dakar, and Marrakesh. Paley nearly failed to make it past Brazil, where his layover lasted several days. Anxious about the delay, he had such trouble sleeping that he did what came naturally: he took a strong sleeping pill. Shortly after he dropped off, Hamblet learned that their flight was due to leave in an hour. Paley was out cold, so Hamblet had to pack his companion's belongings, dress him, and haul him to the airport. Paley did not awaken until they were airborne.

Paley was intrigued by what he called the "lush, strange charm" of Algiers. He did not even complain about the seedy hotel where his unit was billeted. In his effort to be one of the boys, he could scarcely afford to act superior. However, he quietly inquired where he might rent an apartment.

One of Paley's colleagues, a lieutenant named Matt Adams, had found a lovely home on the outskirts of the city where he lived with his two superiors, C. D. Jackson and Edward Barrett, Jackson's deputy. When

Adams asked him to join them, Paley agreed eagerly. They nicknamed the house "Villa Adams" and fell into a carefree life. An Arab boy arranged for a barber to visit each morning to shave the men; the boy also brought them a fresh chicken, a cut of beef, or other scarce foodstuff. A French-woman known as Madame bought their groceries and prepared their meals. She was an outstanding cook; Paley later said her dinners were the best he had at any time during the war. Still, they were never quite enough for the ever-hungry Paley, who raided the icebox at all hours of the day and night.

At OWI headquarters, Paley occupied a makeshift office with a crate as a desk and boxes for filing cabinets. Jackson assigned him to help establish a radio network in Italy to transmit broadcasts from Armed Forces Radio. The purpose of the network was to lure Italian listeners with entertaining programs interspersed with propaganda—just the sort of arrangement CBS had used for its South American network.

As in his first days at United Independent Broadcasters in New York, Paley had a reputation to overcome. This time he was a big shot who was expected to chafe under orders and to try to intimidate his superiors. But, as before, Paley surprised them all. They had no way of knowing how smooth and ingratiating he could be. At forty-two, he took on the air of a young man so unassuming that he could be challenged by an office boy. His new colleagues found him reserved, even shy. They were flattered when he fraternized easily with men below his rank at the Officer's Club bar. They were impressed by his eagerness, by how quickly he caught on to any task he was assigned, and by his way of discreetly pushing to get a job done.

Paley had been in Algiers only a few weeks when he was sent on a mission to southern Italy to consult with his new superior, Hamilton Smith, about the fledgling radio network there, a linkup of stations in Palermo, Bari, and Naples. In a note to Smith sent on ahead, Jackson revealed that his initial fears about the CBS man had vanished. Jackson knew that Paley would have good ideas about making popular radio programs, and he urged Smith to take his advice freely. Jackson also grasped the subtle nature of Paley's effectiveness. "Of Bill Paley's competence there can be no question," he wrote, "but I would like to add that he is also one of those rare individuals who doesn't have to throw his weight around to establish himself as a bigshot. Therefore I know he will be able to make his experience felt without demoralizing the boys who have been working at our particular problem for what they consider a long period of time."

Paley arrived in Bari on Italy's east coast just after a German bombing raid had blown up Allied ships in the harbor. Most of the city's inhabitants had fled to the mountains, and Paley was touched when the station never-theless arranged a live radio concert in his honor. He worked with the head of Radio Bari to draw up a prototype for a programming schedule, and then made the rounds of other stations where he proposed various improvements in programming.

Overall, however, his work was peripheral. Until the Allies broke through the German line beyond Naples, much of Italy was still beyond the reach of Allied radio propaganda. Returning to Algiers, Paley was reduced to the more mundane tasks of drawing up organizational charts, writing reports, and shuffling paper. Still, he remained respectful, even deferential. Given his preference for the quick phone call to the lengthy memorandum, these tasks must have taken uncharacteristic patience. Even when Jackson gave him vaguely patronizing orders—"I hope you will find it possible to send frequent detailed reports to America about radio in Italy and here. . . . People in the field, including myself, always forget that the home office knows nothing except what they get at the end of a cable line" —Paley complied without complaint.

The exhilaration of war boosted his spirits. He was not only meeting with but also socializing with Eisenhower, whom he greatly admired. Paley's ebullience was evident in a telegram to CBS executives after he had been abroad for two months: "Think might be interested in my broadcast-ing experience over here without . . . unions, legislation and so forth. Very pleasant, but how I miss those commercials."

Naturally, he found romance as well. She was a pretty blonde named Peg Pollard, also newly arrived from the United States. C. D. Jackson assigned her as Paley's administrative aide, and Paley began pressing his attentions from the moment she walked into his cluttered office. She had wangled an assignment at OWI in Algiers to be with her husband of eighteen months, Richard Pollard, a photo-journalist assigned to the Sig-nal Corps who would later rise to be photo editor of *Life* magazine in its heyday. That she was married only enhanced Peg's allure to Paley. He often invited her to lunch and dinner, and she usually went with him; since husbands and wives were not permitted joint military assignments, Peg and Dick had to avoid being seen dining out together. When Paley gave a party or a dinner, Peg served as his hostess.

They worked together from eight in the morning to eight at night. He was businesslike in the office but never demanding. Friendly and solic-itous, he charmed her with his attentiveness. At the end of the day they rode down the elevator together, and he would wrap his arm around her and say wistfully, "Oh God, another day has passed." Over dinner, he avoided talking about CBS, preferring to gossip about wartime social life and the people they worked with. He led her to believe that he and his wife were divorced. "He was sexy, he really was," she recalled. "He had a way of approaching women, a way of looking at me. I liked him, but I loved my husband."

Typically, Paley would not accept a rebuff. In late January 1944 he asked his old friend, Eisenhower aide Harry Butcher, if he could arrange a transfer to London where Eisenhower was moving his headquarters. The transfer order came through quickly: Paley would join the Psychological Warfare group that would help prepare for *Overlord,* the planned invasion of France across the English Channel. His new position would be chief of broadcasting within the Psychological Warfare Division of the Supreme Headquarters, Allied Expeditionary Forces (SHAEF). Paley went directly to Peg Pollard. Would she come with him? When she said no, he asked why. "My husband is here," she replied. "May I make a suggestion?" he countered. "Why don't you divorce your husband?"

She stayed in Algiers, and Paley moved on. Once he decided to leave, he was eager to be in London as soon as possible. But he drew a low priority in the flight assignments and was frustrated to learn that he faced a wait of several days. Paley could not resist using his influence with a high-ranking friend in the Air Force to get on a special flight the next day to England. He still had his knack for revising the rules when the old ones proved wanting.

Shortly after Paley's arrival, a young attaché from OWI named Guy Della Cioppa appeared in his suite at Claridge's Hotel to brief him on *Overlord.* Della Cioppa carried a sheaf of secret documents—maps of planned landings at OMAHA and UTAH beaches, as well as the phony landings designed to deceive the Germans—that he spread out on the floor of Paley's sitting room. Paley nearly overwhelmed him with questions. Several weeks later, Della Cioppa was named chief of tactical warfare for radio operations for the First Army, reporting to Paley.

Paley's first two principal tasks in London were to supervise broadcasts to Germany and Occupied European countries, and to prepare radio messages to accompany the Allied invasion of France on D-Day. Within days of his arrival he plunged into the bureaucracy of the Office of War Information. He drew up organizational charts and attempted to streamline operations. His first appointment was one of his CBS executives, Brewster Morgan, to head the new American broadcasting station in Europe, ABSIE, which had been in the planning stages for more than a year and was due to start operation at the end of April. He put Davidson Taylor, another CBS executive, in charge of programming, and dragooned an old friend from New York, Stuart Scheftel, to prepare the first broadcasts from liberated France.

As in Algiers, Paley won over subordinates and superiors alike. "He had a sort of mystique among the younger American personnel," said W. Phillips Davison, then an American private serving under Paley. "He looked terribly young. He was also modest and democratic."

In his eagerness to serve his country, Paley fit easily into the hierarchy. "Straighten out with Phil Hamblet where Maury Pierce should have desk space," C. D. Jackson ordered early in February 1944. Paley not only complied, he shuffled his entire department so they were all working under one roof.

"He used his power effectively and gracefully," said Guy Della Cioppa. "He gave us a stature, spirit and affection. He didn't just point a finger and say, 'Do this.' Psychological warfare was not deemed that important by the military, and Bill Paley's presence and determination lifted the whole spirit of the unit."

Although all planning since 1942 had called for a separate American radio propaganda organization run by OWI, Paley proposed combining the British and American operations broadcasting to Germany and German-occupied countries. While he understood the British instinct to keep the BBC's identity separate, the inefficiency of two organizations irked him. Paley wrote a long letter suggesting the amalgamation to Brendan Bracken, Britain's minister of information and an acquaintance from pre-war days. A press baron and Churchill crony, Braken was the sort of powerbroker Paley could readily reach.

"Radio broadcasting is an arm of warfare just as are guns and bullets," Paley stressed.

> When it comes to guns, bullets, and the like, we have shared, with each other, all our resources so that each country could have what it needed most. . . . In radio here in Europe, we suffer a serious lack of facilities. You, on the other hand, through your admirable foresight, have in operation very full means for the carrying on of radio warfare. Were it possible for us at this time to make up part of our deficiency through some satisfactory sharing arrangement with you, we would not only be doing a better and more efficient job, but PWB [Psychological Warfare Branch] would, at the same time, be in a much better position to carry on this very important work, which we must do once the Continent has been invaded.

A week later Bracken turned him down on the grounds that decisions would be slowed by a combined command, leading to delays and a weakened radio service. Nor did Bracken accept Paley's alternate suggestion that the Americans be given more time periods on the BBC's service to Europe. (At that time only 107 of the BBC's 1,100 weekly programs were set aside for American broadcasts.) Paley felt stung and complained bitterly to John G. Winant, the U.S. ambassador to the Court of St. James's. Paley found Bracken's reasoning not only unduly bureaucratic but unrealistic "in the light of the small percentage of time we occupy in the total schedule and the importance to the Allied cause of taking full psychological advantage of the sizable role America is playing in the war."

Ambassador Winant presumably went to bat for Paley, because the BBC finally agreed to double its allocation of time to the OWI programs. Paley characterized the decision as "quite a coup," achieved by "some rather fancy infighting." In his memoir he boasted that he was "the OWI hero of the hour."

Paley grew impatient with the frequent bureacratic struggles at the Office of War Information. He proposed that a separate "creative" group be established outside conventional channels to brainstorm about propaganda ideas—the psychological warfare that was the meat of his own work in London. Jackson enthusiastically took up the idea and included Paley in the group of five men. "They have all been selected for their imagination as well as ability," Jackson wrote to his superior, General Robert A. McClure.

Paley was involved in both "black" and "white" propaganda that accompanied the advancing Allied armies. "Black" propaganda was information sent out under false pretenses: misrepresented facts and outright lies. It was transmitted by a phony German radio station located in a secret compound outside London. At the outset, the station broadcast accurate information to gain the confidence of the German troops. The information was derived from intelligence operations and often got on the air before bona fide German stations broadcast it. Announcers on the phony station built up their credibility by reading letters to loved ones seized from captured German soldiers. Only after the invasion, when battle action disrupted communications, would the bogus German station start to broadcast lies.

No stranger to the art of shading truth, Paley was fascinated by black propaganda. He worked closely with Richard Crossman, a brilliant Englishman who would later serve as a member of Parliament and editor of *The New Statesman*. Crossman, who had spent a lot of time in Germany and spoke the language fluently, proved so clever at such propaganda he was nicknamed "Dick Double Crossman."

"One of the basic elements in all successful propaganda is the skillful use of the truth," Paley recalled, a tenet that applied as well to CBS's more successful public relations gambits. "If your listener ever catches you in a lie, you are ruined." Paley discovered that "the truth was useless if it was not believable. An Allied leaflet early in the war told German soldiers about the good conditions in American prisoner-of-war camps. Although it was entirely truthful, the Germans found it preposterous." He also learned that "to deny a lie put out by the enemy only gave it greater currency. It was usually better to reply by implication or try to direct attention elsewhere."

Paley oversaw a series of recordings made by Eisenhower, King George VI, and leaders of European governments-in-exile for broadcast on D-Day to bolster resistance forces in the occupied countries. The recordings were made in secrecy and locked in a vault. Eisenhower's recording contained a serious glitch that is the subject of one of Paley's favorite anecdotes. As Paley recalled it, Robert Sherwood was in Paley's office one day reading transcripts when he discovered a passage in which Ike seemed to be urging his listeners to endanger their lives needlessly. Paley took the credit for overcoming Ike's resistance and persuading him to re-record the message, eliminating the dangerously ungrammatical sentence.

Davidson Taylor remembered the episode differently. He said he spotted the error and persuaded Paley and his boss, General McClure, to listen to it together. Only then did Paley focus on the problem. In General McClure's presence, Paley vowed that he would convince Eisenhower to do the recording over.

As D-Day approached, Eisenhower realized he needed more help in planning for radio broadcasting. He asked for the best communications expert in America, and the War Department summoned David Sarnoff to Europe. Sarnoff arrived in London on March 20, 1944—a full two months after Paley—and checked into a fine suite at Claridge's. His pleasure in his new surroundings disappeared, however, when he heard that the suite's previous occupant had been Paley, who had moved into an even more impressive one. Still, Sarnoff could take comfort in knowing he was a genuine colonel, while Paley was only a civilian working as an "assimilated" colonel.

The next day Sarnoff met for the first time with Eisenhower and was as impressed as Paley. (It is a tribute to Eisenhower's shrewdness that he would so quickly befriend the two leaders of American broadcasting.) Ike deputized Sarnoff to put together an American radio station powerful enough to reach all the Allied forces throughout Europe after the invasion. In addition, Sarnoff would oversee all radio communication between SHAEF headquarters and the invading armies.

Like Paley, Sarnoff proposed that the British and American broadcasters combine their transmissions to the Continent. But when Sarnoff heard of Brendan Bracken's resistance, he went straight to the top. In a meeting with Winston Churchill, Sarnoff carefully outlined the problem. Churchill told Sarnoff he sympathized with Bracken's preference to keep the BBC separate, but Sarnoff managed to persuade the prime minister to overrule his minister of information on the grounds that the Allies must be united across the board.

Ironically, Sarnoff faced opposition to this plan from none other than Paley, who evidently lost his fondness for the idea once Sarnoff took it over. One of Sarnoff's aides, Walter R. Brown, recalled that "Paley objected strongly because the arrangements did not fit in with his plans for broadcasting to the enemy." When Sarnoff and Paley met to discuss the matter, added another of Paley's aides, "they were really going at it." But Paley came around, said Brown, and "agreed that the central plan was the only one that would be secure."

20

OFF DUTY, "Colonel" Paley occupied a well-appointed suite at Claridge's, the elegant Mayfair hotel of rose brick and wrought-iron balconies that accommodated so many American officers it became known as "Little America." He had a sitting room with a sofa, two armchairs, a writing desk, and telephone; a large bathroom; and a huge bedroom off the bathroom. His personal valet was in attendance. In later years Paley would insist that he had lived in a flat several blocks away, off Grosvenor Square on South Audley Street. It was, he said, a modest three-room place, on the top floor of a four-story building, that belonged to a beautiful woman who rented it to him and his roommate, the playwright Robert Sherwood. Curiously, not even his closest aides could recall such a flat, nor could Sherwood's widow, who said her husband always stayed at Claridge's. Paley's colleagues did remember the luxury in which he lived at Claridge's.

Throughout the war, evening dress was mandatory for dinner in the hotel restaurant, where Paley could choose from such delicacies as cold salmon trout with ravigotte sauce, lobster with rice and creamed lobster sauce, fresh asparagus, minute steak floridor, and crab lutecienne, accompanied by the finest vintage wines. It was hardly a life of deprivation, and once Paley had all his staff in place, he played more and worked less. "He was floating around London while we were doing all the work. He wasn't knocking himself out," said one staff member.

Paley adored the camaraderie he found in London. His fondest memory was of a stag party at CBS correspondent Charles Collingwood's flat that ended in a drunken free-for-all with one guest clinging to a lamppost to stay upright. "Everything that happened that night was funny," Paley said. "It was that everyone loved each other, and it was just a brawl, a great big lousy brawl, but it was one of those nights in my life that was very outstanding."

The only damper on American high jinks in wartime London was the "Little Blitz" of March 1944, in which the Germans launched V-1 rockets against England. The new generation of guided missiles buzzed loudly on approach but were silent before impact, terrorizing the populace. Paley made it a point to appear fearless. While other guests at Claridge's went down to the cellar each night, Paley remained in his suite with the curtains drawn to protect him against flying glass. In time he would gauge the reaction of others to the bombings as a means of sizing up character: "It was interesting to find out who could take it and who couldn't. The people you thought were very strong would come into my office and ask to be transferred somewhere else because they couldn't stand the bombing. Then some skinny little guy would have great strength and not be bothered by it at all."

Paley expanded his circle of friends among the aristocracy, New York socialites, and American Army brass circulating through London. Tommy Hitchcock, the famous American polo player idolized by Jock Whitney, had a flat on Grosvenor Square where he threw parties for members of the top echelons of military and civilian society. Whitney, who had been Hitchcock's flatmate, had left for North Africa just as Paley arrived in England.

Paley's new acquaintances were enchanted by him. "He was easy, warm, full of energy and curiosity," recalled Simon Michael Bessie, who was also attached to the Psychological Warfare Division. One unlikely friend was George Backer, former editor of the *New York Post* and husband of Dolly Schiff, owner of the newspaper and a member of one of New York's prominent German-Jewish families. The Backers and the Paleys had met at the Swopes' but had not been close friends. Not only was Paley outside Our Crowd, said Bessie, "he didn't think Jewish." Backer, an officer in Psychological Warfare, was fiercely intellectual, but he got on with Paley because he found him open to ideas. Paley, said Bessie, "was not an intellectual. He was a doer, not a meditative type, but he had an aesthetic side—a sensitivity to painting and to arts in general."

Paley's friendship with Murrow deepened as well. "Bill and Ed met frequently," recalled Murrow's widow, Janet. "They became close friends. My impression was Ed knew a great deal about England and Bill didn't know as many people. As far as Ed was concerned, it was flattering to have the president of the company as a friend. He found Bill a very affable person."

London was "a romantic place, very romantic," Paley confessed years later. "It was sort of like the normal, conventional morals of the time were just turned on their ear because of the urgency. . . . The normal barriers, you know, to having an affair with somebody were thrown to the four winds. If it looked pretty good, you felt good, well what in Hell was the difference? And it was very light and bright, a fast-going kind of time."

For someone as powerful and wealthy as Paley, it was hard to know where to begin the amorous adventures. But an obvious start in those days was with Pamela Churchill, by then all of twenty-four years old. Randolph, from whom she was separated, was serving with the British Army, leaving her free to work her charms on a succession of American men. She set up a salon in London where she entertained generals, prominent journalists, politicians, and other dignitaries. "Unless you were a high-powered journalist or important in some way, you weren't very welcome there," said Janet Murrow, who never returned after her first chilly visit. Paley and Murrow, however, were two of Pamela's most frequent guests.

"Pamela's parties were very, very good," Paley recalled. "She was extraordinary in the way she took care of her men. She called me up once and said, 'What are you doing about liquor? I know it's hard to get.' I said, 'I don't know where to get any. Could you take care of it?' The same if you needed a car, she would say, 'Call this place or that place. Anything you need or want, please call me.' That made it all very cozy and welcoming."

Paley was doubtless as keen on seducing Pamela as she was eager to add him to her list of conquests. They had a short-lived affair, described by one of Paley's closest friends (and arch rival of Pamela) Nancy "Slim" Keith, as "a little slap during the war—a stop and a tickle." Paley in later years would titillate his girlfriends by admitting he had bedded Pamela but would go no further. "I never discuss the women with whom I have been intimate," he teased one friend in later years when she pressed for details.

Lady Mary Dunn had the misfortune to witness Pamela's attachment to Paley at its most intense. Paley had invited her to dine with him several months after his arrival. At the time, she was living on a farm outside the city. Perversely, she arrived at Paley's suite dressed in slacks and a jersey, the clothes she had worn that afternoon to milk the cows. Although she had run through another infatuation since Paley, Mary still felt a lingering attraction. After they had talked together for a quarter of an hour, the door opened—without even a knock—and Pamela breezed in, looking exquisite. She began fussing over Paley in a proprietary manner. Although Bill and Pamela had been an item for several months, Mary had not known about it and was overcome by jealousy. After enduring ten minutes of Pamela Churchill's performance, Mary rose to her feet and left, as she later said, "sour as a bit of old rhubarb."

But the Churchill-Paley affair was more convenient than romantic and it readily settled into a long-standing relationship of mutual admiration. "Very few people really impress Pamela," said Richard C. Holbrooke, an assistant secretary of state in the Carter administration who befriended Pamela in later years. "For Paley she has more than respect. It's almost fear. She said she thinks Bill Paley is the toughest man she knows."

After Paley, she flitted from Averell Harriman, who was more than twenty years her senior, to Ed Murrow. Like Paley, Pamela Churchill refused to be inconvenienced by the presence of a spouse. Rather than suffer the humiliation, Janet Murrow returned to America. Her coolness coupled with her husband's guilty conscience eventually brought the Murrows back together—a profound defeat for Pamela, who was in love with the dashing CBS correspondent.

Paley meanwhile had hooked up with Edwina Mountbatten, whose husband, Louis (known to all his friends as Dickie), was in Burma as supreme commander—Eisenhower's counterpart in Asia. "Cheer up," Dickie had said in one of his letters to Edwina. "Don't mope. See some of your friends, Bill Paley for example." Edwina, by then forty-three years old, presided over a salon at her home on Chester Street that surpassed in importance Pamela Churchill's gatherings. Because of Mountbatten's position, matters of state were routinely discussed by Edwina's guests, who included Winston Churchill, Max Beaverbrook, and Eisenhower. The well-connected Paley, by now involved in the *Overlord* mission, fit in perfectly.

"She wasn't in love with Bill, but she liked him, much as she liked the other boys," said Stuart Scheftel. It was easy to see how a fling with Edwina would appeal to Paley. "Highly intelligent without being intellectual, elegant and vital rather than conventionally beautiful," says her husband's biographer, Philip Ziegler, "Edwina blazed in London society with a fierce brilliance which alarmed some and dazzled almost all. Restless, egocentric, intolerant, she was rarely a comfortable person to be with, yet equally was never boring." Like Paley, she was hedonistic and promiscuous; she threw herself into pleasure.

Late at night Paley and Edwina could be spotted together coming out of the Psychological Warfare offices, and they were seen frequently over dinner in fashionable Mayfair. Given Paley's high profile and the important position of her husband, some high-level members of the British government finally told her that the affair was getting too well known. They broke it off, but Paley still maintained an affection for her; later, after returning to the United States, he would send her lipstick, perfume, and other luxury items.

As in later years, Paley kept his women in categories. The Edwina Mountbattens and Pamela Churchills he would wine and dine. But at the same time he carried on below stairs with women who lacked the social standing of his "official" mistresses. "I always felt," said one friend from those days, "that he was torn, and that he felt he didn't deserve to be on the same level with the very social ladies." In London he began a romance with Marian, his British secretary, who bore more than a passing resemblance to Peg Pollard. Like Peg, Marian was married, but her husband, a British officer, was stationed in the Far East.

Marian, a brunette in her mid-twenties with pale skin and a shapely figure, was "well educated and quite pretty," according to one of Paley's fellow officers. "She wore her uniform briskly as the British women tended to do." In later years Paley would boast to a girlfriend that he hired Marian "because he loved how she looked." She was, said a fellow officer who watched the relationship develop, "a sex object for him." Paley purposely kept their relationship sub rosa because she worked for him, and, as his fellow officer put it, "he was enough in the public eye to worry about it."

In mid-June, a few weeks after D-Day, Paley went to France with C. D. Jackson and a Psychological Warfare contingent. There he learned that OWI needed additional loudspeakers to call German troops to surrender. When General McClure sent Paley to Washington to secure the equipment, Paley went straight to Army Chief of Staff General George Marshall, who promptly supplied the speakers.

While stateside in the summer of 1944, Paley traveled home to New York. His mission, as he later recounted it, was to ask Dorothy for a divorce. In his memoir he said that after reflecting on his life, he had concluded that his marriage "was no longer a success." Before those words were published, however, he had said privately that his marriage "had not been a success"—an important distinction, since the phrase he crafted for public consumption implied that the marriage had gone sour, not that it had been a mistake. Paley recalled that when he broached the subject with Dorothy, he was amazed to find she did not feel as he did and would not agree to a divorce.

By Dorothy's account, her husband did not ask her for a divorce during his three-week visit that summer, but it was obvious to her that he was in an agitated state. "He didn't know what he wanted to do with his life," she recalled. "He was depressed. He said, 'I'm not sure I want to go back to CBS. I don't know how life would be.' I said, 'This is not the time to make a decision. You are going back to England.'"

21

HIS LIFE WAS AT LOOSE ENDS when Paley returned to London in August 1944. From there he traveled to Paris, the new headquarters for Psychological Warfare, where he took a suite —rather more modest than his lodgings at Claridge's—at the George V Hotel. He also had the use of a luxurious apartment in a penthouse on the rue Barbet de Jouy, on the Left Bank. It was owned by the wealthy Palm Beach socialite Charles Munn, who had asked Paley, as an old friend, to look after it. Paley brought back Munn's two maids from Brittany, and used the apartment to entertain. When Duff Cooper arrived as British ambassador with Diana, Paley threw the first of many lavish dinner parties there. The arrangement suited Paley perfectly. At the George V he could blend with his military colleagues in a comfortable suite, while at the Munn apartment, as he later said, "I could live in great splendor whenever I wanted to."

The atmosphere in Paris—where as a young man he had prowled the brothels—was even more hedonistic than London. American officers filled the barroom of the Ritz Hotel, drinking and picking up girls. "All the girls were playing a part," said Paley, "because they must have done the same thing with the Germans. If you were an American and you were in uniform, it was anything you want! They just appreciated you so much. That was a wild time."

Paley had even greater responsibilities in Paris than in London. He continued to supervise "black" propaganda, which by then was being broadcast from the powerful transmitter of Radio Luxembourg, liberated by the Allies in September 1944. And he was put in charge of drawing up guidelines for German newspapers, magazines, radio, book publishing, film, theater, and concerts after the anticipated Nazi surrender.

Paley's unit worked sixteen- to eighteen-hour days preparing the German manual. He delegated the main job of assembling the chapters to two aides, Guy Della Cioppa and John Minary, an attorney from Chicago with the rank of captain. Minary impressed Paley with his care in drafting documents and his understanding of the political implications of the words he was attributing to Paley. He was bright, with a sense of humor, endless patience, discretion, intense loyalty, and self-effacement to the point of invisibility. Here was a man, Paley realized, with the requisite qualities to be his majordomo after the war. For four decades Minary would devote his life to serving Paley's interests, whether it meant talking to the Paley children about their trust funds, dispensing money from Paley's foundation, running interference with the CBS board over Paley's perquisites, or firing a lazy parlor maid.

While Paley declined to get involved in the nuts and bolts of writing the German Information Services Manual, he remained accessible to his subordinates. He came to the office every day, sometimes for many hours, other times only briefly. His junior officer, Phillips Davison, termed him a good boss: "He didn't make unreasonable demands and if he did, he was in there working too. He got work out of people and didn't kick them around."

Davison was also struck by Paley's caution in making decisions: "My job was to draw up staff studies and policy documents. Most of the people I got signatures from were perfunctory. Paley was always very careful before he signed anything. Sometimes he asked questions and always read the documents. His caution contrasted with the usual assumptions that the officer responsible knew what he was doing. Maybe that came from CBS, where if he made the wrong decision it cost a lot of money."

Getting the manual approved required considerable political maneuvering among various factions, which Paley accomplished with finesse. "Bill Paley as chief coordinator of redrafting has done a wonderful job and has called forth the loyal cooperation of all sections here," wrote an OWI official named Tommy Thompson to Edward Barrett. By mid-March 1945 all the necessary signatures had been obtained.

Around the same time, Paley's superior officer, General McClure, offered him a colonel's commission. As civilians, Paley and his colleagues were never entirely accepted, yet they enjoyed the flexibility of remaining outside the miliary structure. Paley said he balked at first at McClure's offer, only to be convinced by George Backer that he needed a commission to take command of the military officers who would be working for him in Germany. "I need not tell you that we are proud of our first unassimilated colonel," Edward Barrett wrote in a congratulatory note. "Roy Lord [an American colonel in charge of communications] was over for lunch today and he had the highest sort of praise for the work you have done for him. I might say the opinion was unanimous."

By all appearances, Paley was delighted with his new status. When he arrived in Paris the previous August, the doorman of the George V Hotel greeted him with "Bonjour, Col-o-nel Paley." Paley, in guidebook French, replied, "Jean, je ne suis pas Col-o-nel. Je suis *Monsieur* Paley." It took several such exchanges for the doorman to get the message. On the day Paley was commissioned, Jean greeted him with "Bonjour, Monsieur Paley," to which Paley replied, "Je ne suis pas monsieur. Je suis *Col-o-nel* Paley," and broke into a big grin. But Paley's mood fell short of complete satisfaction. David Sarnoff had already been commissioned a brigadier general the previous December. Paley expressed his irritation to William Shirer that Sarnoff held the superior rank.

Shortly after receiving his commission, when the Information Services Manual was almost completed. Paley collapsed and was rushed to the American Hospital in Paris. Doctors gave him a shot of strong sedatives, which knocked him out for nearly two days. In his hypochondriacal fashion, Paley thought he had had a heart attack and insisted that he be tested and retested when his diagnosis was not borne out. Paley's physician told him he was suffering from "complete exhaustion." One of Paley's colleagues, back in the United States for a visit soon afterwards, told Dorothy that her husband had a "nervous collapse" as a result of extreme anxiety and tension. "Were the pressures that great?" Dorothy later mused. "I don't know. The odd thing was that it was the culmination of a wonderful time."

Paley had been racing to finish the information manual. He had been operating for the first time within a rigid military command structure. And a month earlier, in February 1945, one of his colleagues had written that "Bill Paley reports terrific pressure to get back to his own affairs." His doctor told him to rest for several weeks, but Paley insisted on returning to work after just one week in bed.

As the German troops retreated, the Psychological Warfare contingent pushed into Germany. On VE-Day, Paley was in a small hotel in Heidelberg with Richard Crossman. They cooled a bottle of wine under a water tap and drank to the victory. The next day, May 9, 1945, sobered them beyond their worst imagining when they reached the Dachau concentration camp shortly after it was liberated.

The truth about the camps was well known by then. Murrow's broadcasts from Buchenwald the previous month had described the horrors in stomach-wrenching detail. But seeing it firsthand was for Paley "a terrible trauma." At the crematorium he saw some two hundred bodies "piled up like garbage." Years later Paley vividly described seeing an SS officer try to escape and watching a young American Army captain hand his pistol to a camp survivor. The survivor raised his thin arm but could not fire the gun, so the captain took it back and executed the SS man. "I had seven people at least die right in front of me while they were walking to get some food," Paley said. "You couldn't describe it. It was awful."

Given Paley's already fragile mental state, the experience must have been shattering. From the day in his childhood when bullies chased him down the street because he was a Jew, he had grown a shell against his various brushes with anti-Semitism. But Dachau forced him to confront the most ghastly consequence of such prejudice. Privileged and relatively sheltered during his war years, Paley had witnessed only one bombing in London: he saw men and women still sitting in restaurant chairs after having been killed by flying glass. Dachau was a view of death of a different order.

Not long afterwards, the Psychological Warfare Division settled into a school compound in a little town outside Frankfurt called Bad Homburg. Here the atmosphere was vastly different from Paris or London. The American and British contingent stuck together and had little to do with the Germans, for whom Paley had nothing but contempt.

Although Paley spoke no German, he had enormous control over the populace as supervisor of the de-Nazification of all German media. "I was running a far bigger network than I ever dreamed of heading as a civilian," he said. "I was in charge of every newspaper, magazine, radio station and theater in Occupied Germany. The Germans were so hungry for information and entertainment that my empire made a fortune for the Army. It was the most exciting period of my life as we weeded the Nazis out of the communications media, pumped in fresh democratic ideas and personnel, and generally remade the German mind until we felt they could take over their communications themselves."

The power infected Paley; he saw his responsibility as nothing less than an "empire." It fueled him to work harder than he had before. Each day he would assemble his staff of thirty broadcasters for conferences in the biggest room at headquarters. There they worked together trying to fill each quarter hour of the German broadcasting schedule. Paley tapped into his old entrepreneurial skills with new vigor. "I was impressed by the way he seemed to grasp the nitty-gritty—all the aspects of the operation," said Phillips Davison. "He provided a really centralized direction to it. He was a prodigious worker. He was there all the time. I rarely went to his office and didn't find him. He wasn't a playboy at all in this period as he was before."

Despite his new rank, Paley never affected the manner of a superior officer. He voiced surprise when a regular Army man, a Captain Fitzgerald, insisted that Paley draw his $800-a-month military pay. (As a civilian, Paley had been a dollar-a-year man.) Paley called everyone by his first name and maintained a jovial air. He thrived on the creativity of the men from Hollywood and Madison Avenue who surrounded him.

With Billy Wilder, the Hollywood director, he formed an instant bond based on their love of food and on endless games of gin rummy. Paley secured a pass to the generals' PX, where he obtained beautifully marbled hunks of steak. He dispatched Wilder, a German Jew who had fled to the United States before the war, to secure rich black German bread, butter, and eggs from local farmers by bartering cartons of cigarettes. The two men met often in the kitchen of Paley's rented villa—a gloomy place with large rooms stuffed with Biedermeier furniture upholstered in dark fabric. Using a broken toaster, Paley and Wilder improvised a grill for their steaks. "Over and over we would fix up very festive and good-tasting dinners," Wilder recalled. "He did a lot of the cooking and he ate with tremendous enjoyment. The Germans have a word, *essen,* which means to eat. They also have *fressen,* which means to devour. That suited him much better, but the food had to be good."

Marian, Paley's secretary and lover, had stayed in the shadows in London and Paris, but their relationship intensified in Bad Homburg. Paley shared his villa on the outskirts of town with Davidson Taylor and Guy Della Cioppa. The two men had rooms at one end of the house and Paley occupied a suite at the other end. Conveniently, Paley's bedroom could be reached by a back staircase. Although Marian was assigned to a women's dormitory, many nights she stayed with Paley. Early in the morning a German maid would arrive to make tea, which she discreetly left outside the bedroom door. Shortly afterwards, Marian would depart by the rear staircase.

Only a few of Paley's colleagues knew about Marian, who was unfailingly polite and proper outside the boudoir. From time to time one of Paley's subordinates would invite her to have a cup of coffee. "Oh no," she would say, "I am waiting for Mr. Paley"—or, after his commission, "Colonel Paley." Ever the respectful secretary, she never called him "Bill" or otherwise hinted at their intimacy. This was the one time during the war that Paley kept up an exclusive romance; but then again, Bad Homburg lacked the highborn ladies he could pursue in Paris and London.

Even after the war, he would remain loyal in his fashion to Marian, sending her the same kind of bagatelles (silk stockings, candy, perfume) that he sent Edwina Mountbatten. Once Paley asked one of his aides at CBS to buy Marian a negligée. The aide found one with a feather boa for $100, which Paley promptly mailed to her in England. Like so many other incidents in his life, Paley's dalliance with Marian assumed greater significance over the years. When he was in his eighties, he described Marian to one girlfriend as "the woman I fell madly in love with. I was insane for her. She was a great beauty." Their relationship only ended, he said, when Marian told him that she had to rejoin her husband on his release from a Japanese prisoner-of-war camp.

World War II left Paley feeling that "life had never been so exciting and immediate and never would be again." He was, in fact, shaken from top to bottom by the experience. His state of mind during this period can be seen in the doodles he compulsively made during meetings. Two of them, retrieved by an aide from a wastebasket in Paley's office at Bad Homburg and saved for more than forty years, were given to the author. One is signed "W.S.P.," the other simply "P."

Bursting with energy, sexual preoccupation, and a fear of death, the provocative symbols in these drawings suggest something of Paley's psychological turmoil. They are sad images that still manage to suggest hope, and even a touch of self-deprecation—a contradiction entirely within Paley's intricate character. Like his life, these drawings are crammed with incident.

Two experienced psychologists were asked to analyze Paley's sketches independently without knowing his identity. Both said that in the absence of an interview they could make only suggestive interpretations. In reading some of the symbols, their views diverged. To the Jungian analyst, a pot sprouting three flowers suggested the Oedipal triangle; an art therapist saw it as a decoration in a hostile environment. Yet both came close enough on the most significant imagery. They concurred on key personality traits, as well as on the forces that seem to have shaped Paley from his youth through early middle age.

Conflict and discomfort form one major theme. There are strong images of death and warfare: stick figures fighting, a variety of weapons, and a menacing skull, which may be the vivid face of mortality Paley saw at Dachau. Most disturbing is a tethered camel that is defecating. The animal is pierced through the neck by an arrow and beset by bugs, an image that conveys torment and possible self-disgust at being so shackled.

Phallic and anal imagery predominates as well—a large bullet exploding from an elongated cannon, an arrow hitting a bull's-eye, a saber penetrating a belt, a prominent penis on the camel, the rump of a pig, and a rear view of a monkey with a long curling tail. Such symbols of aggression suggest uneasiness, perhaps anger, in Paley's relations with women.

The oddity is that these are juvenile symbols drawn by a man in midlife. Had they been the work of an adolescent, they could have signaled the normal defensiveness—the need to assert power—of that age. And there are other similar juxtapositions, pictures of what Jungians call *puere eternis*—the eternal boy. Paley had drawn a schoolboy, for example, with mismatched legs. One leg appears to be slender and female, the other a muscular but truncated boy's limb. The Peter Pan image is echoed by a beanie perched incongruously on a camel.

By his own admission, Paley had a turbulent relationship in his youth with his mother. He grew angry at her for her harsh and exclusionary treatment after the birth of his sister, yet he continued to yearn for her attention. As a boy he feigned illness and inflicted minor injuries on himself so he could stay home from school. As a man he became a Don Juan, with a special taste for married or otherwise attached women.

These ambivalences may have found their way into his wartime drawings. Boats gliding through an ocean could signal a need for a refuge, a longing to return to his mother or to someone who could take care of him. Yet the only overt female image is of an Arab woman veiled from head to foot.

Balancing all the negative symbols in Paley's drawings are signs of hope, perhaps showing determination to overcome and move on. Despite the overall instability, they are not aimless. A pyramid in the center of one drawing has a small door and window, perhaps indicating a means of escape. A radio microphone next to the healing image of a snake may portend CBS's role in helping Paley reshape his life. Even the ghastly skull is floating on, rather than submerged in, a large tub of water. A fear of death may be present, but so may be the will to prevail. There are a few lighthearted touches as well, especially a little top-hatted valet attending the camel.

One is struck by the meticulous detail, the product of someone highly intelligent who takes in everything but seems not to notice. The variety of the images shows a mind that goes nonstop, seeks many interests, and finds little repose. The intricacy hints the compulsiveness of a perfectionist who will leave nothing to chance. Without structure, he feels uneasy; everything must be sorted out carefully before he says or does anything. The psychologists call him a "defended person," who needs to be in control, presenting only what he wants to present. Yet he can sustain mystery and knows how to hide the rich undercurrents of his life.

Those who came to know Paley during the war were mystified later when his subordinates at CBS characterized him as aloof and imperial. His wartime colleagues failed to understand that they knew him out of context. No longer in command, he was part of a military machine with numerous superiors to please. He was tested in a way he never had been at CBS, where he held all the power. During the war he strove to make his mark. He was compelled to be conscious of his effect on others. If he treated subordinates badly, he ran the risk that those whose approval he wanted might think ill of him.

As Paley neared the end of his wartime rite of passage, he resolved to change the way he worked and lived. He had a new appreciation of CBS as a worldwide communications medium. He had seen his network from a distance and through the eyes of others. He knew he had to recapture the power he had ceded to the advertising agencies before the war. He realized that he had to remove himself from the troubles with the federal regulators that had plagued him in the late thirties. And he saw that he must do something about television, which unnerved him.

CBS ennobled Paley in the war years, conferring on him a new personal power. Because of his network's role in reporting the war—particularly through the words of Edward R. Murrow—Paley had been lionized as never before, and he intended to build on that prestige. The upper-class English way of life deeply impressed him. He revered the English aristocrats as "civilized and intelligent," and professed never to have seen their streak of anti-Semitism. The English, he once said, "weren't so stupid as to make distinctions. The anti-Semitism in [America] is eight times worse than it is in England." During his stint in London he had been able to examine at close range over a long period the genteel, graceful style he wished to perfect for himself. It would be more rarefied and subtle, but less stimulating than in his prewar life. And Dorothy, whose challenging ways had proved too vexing, would have to go.

3

———

THE

Raider

———

22

D OROTHY PALEY WAS SHOCKED by her husband's behavior when she welcomed him home in early September 1945. "He was still recovering from his breakdown," she recalled. "He had always had a tic but it was exaggerated to an extraordinary degree. He was extremely depressed. He just sat and made faces. He didn't want to talk much, and he didn't want to go out. He was a very different person." His two children, Jeffrey and Hilary, by then seven and six, hadn't seen their father for nearly two years. They were at once fascinated and frightened by the way his face moved, and rapidly learned that the violent twitch meant tension, which could burst into anger. When Dorothy consulted a doctor for advice, he suggested that she prod her husband to get out among his friends. So the Paleys went through the motions of a social life.

But only days later Paley was off to Colorado Springs, where he set out to reshape his life in solitude. The first step, he decided, would be to insist on a divorce from Dorothy. With that decided, he went to California to visit David Selznick, his closest friend, by now the producer of a string of hit films. Selznick had separated from his wife, Irene, just a few weeks earlier.

Selznick's zest bolstered Paley. Here was a kindred spirit who had made the same decision about his personal life. The two men laughed and caroused. Once again Paley felt happy. He left California with his resolve strengthened.

Back in New York, he sought out his attorney, Ralph Colin, asking him to confront Dorothy about a divorce. Offended, Colin told Paley to do it on his own. Finally Paley pulled himself together and told Dorothy he no longer wanted to be married; he wished to be unattached. Dorothy refused to free him, although by then she was well aware of Paley's indiscretions overseas.

Some months earlier Ralph Colin had confided, with considerable dismay, that her husband had been "carrying on" with Edwina Mountbatten and Pamela Harriman. "Do you think I was surprised?" recalled Dorothy. "I had had thirteen years of dames. I knew this was his illness. There were always girls. He never stopped. It was absolutely pathological. So now I knew about Edwina and Pamela. What was the point to know more? What difference would it make? There was not going to be a cure for him. I knew it was beyond his control. So I had accepted it, knowing it must have caused such guilt because there was so much lying involved. But I didn't feel it seriously impinged on our relationship. That was also a period when every man was unfaithful and most of the women. It was more accepted."

In her husband's absence Dorothy herself had taken up with Anatole Litvak, a journeyman Hollywood film director. "Anatole was the kindest, most wonderful person . . . unselfish, caring, a lovely lovely person," said Dorothy, "but I had no intention of marrying him."

The Paleys entered a stalemate lasting several weeks. Behind closed doors they argued, but maintained a polite facade for company. When Irene Selznick arrived at their door in late September, they greeted her warmly, and assured her they would take care of her. The eagle-eyed Mrs. Selznick wasn't fooled one bit. "I don't care what you do, but be careful about appearances," she cautioned Dorothy.

Paley offered to escort Irene to the theater the following week. "The show I want to see more than anything is *Carousel*," he said eagerly. "I'll wear black tie and we'll go to El Morocco and you will be the Merry Widow."

The morning of her "date," Irene Selznick received a cryptic warning from Dorothy: "You'd better dress warmly tonight. You might be standing on a corner because Bill is going to be late picking you up. He thinks he has Michael [their chauffeur] but he doesn't because I am using him. I am going to the opera with Mr. Litvak. Don't you dare get a car or call Bill and warn him or I'll never speak to you again."

That evening, Paley called Irene Selznick's room at the Waldorf-Astoria. Breathless, he said she should meet him at the corner of 50th Street and Park Avenue, next to the hotel. She made no comment and waited patiently as it grew later and later. When he finally arrived, he was pale but they saw *Carousel* and went on to El Morocco as planned. Irene had never seen Paley so tense. Just as the food came, he turned to her and said, "I feel ghastly. Do you mind if we call it a night?"

After dropping her off, Paley continued out to Kiluna Farm. He never slept under the same roof with Dorothy again. Her date with Litvak had been designed to arouse her husband's jealous streak and entice him back, but, compounded by her appropriation of the chauffeur, his cuckolding was the justification he needed for a separation.

More than forty years later, Dorothy had no memory of the events so vividly recalled by her friend Irene. "I can't remember going to the opera with Tola," said Dorothy, "and I can't remember a conversation about taking Michael for the evening." But Dorothy did acknowledge that Irene had been there when Paley walked out, and that Litvak had been a source of contention. "Oh, he used it against me," she said. "Naturally he was going to use anything. How lovely to be able to have the fall from grace and make it useful."

Once Dorothy realized her husband had finally left her, recalled Irene, "she was tough as hell for a day or two. Then she cried and cried. The way it happened and when it happened gave Dorothy a tremendous jolt. As crazy as he was, as hard to please, as demanding, she hated to give him up. They were a remarkable couple."

Paley took an apartment at the St. Regis, only blocks away from his CBS office. Under the ownership of Vincent Astor, the elaborately decorated hotel was the epicenter of all that was fashionable and lively.

Joining the escapist mood, Paley avidly pursued his pleasures, squiring showgirls and socialites. On a yachting trip to Cuba with David Selznick and Selznick's new girl, the actress Jennifer Jones, and theater impresario Leland Hayward and his wife, Margaret Sullavan, he visited Ernest Hemingway and Martha Gellhorn. Their house guest was twenty-nine-year-old Nancy "Slim" Hawks, the honey-haired *Harper's Bazaar* model then married to film director Howard Hawks (she would later marry Leland Hayward, and British banker Sir Kenneth Keith). Paley lost no time making a play for Slim.

"He was funny. He laughed a lot. He was very agreeable. And he was a full-blown sexy man," she recalled. "He made me feel divine. He wanted me to come on the boat with them. I said, 'I have to go to California. I am married and have a baby.' He called me later that fall to ask me to Kiluna for Thanksgiving. I said, 'I have my own family and we have our Thanksgiving together. I am a married lady.' He said, 'You will be very well chaperoned.' " She declined, and he took the defeat gracefully.

But behind the vivacity, Paley was depressed and distracted. His wartime aide, Guy Della Cioppa, who had joined him at CBS, recalled his boss's moodiness: "I knew the whole thing with Dorothy was brewing when we were overseas. Everybody talked about their wife and family but he never did. Even when he came back to the States, he didn't. He was a lonely man then. He would ask me occasionally to go to dinner with him. For the first six months after he was back, my impression of him was disintegration. He didn't seem to have the old spirit. He was faced with problems at CBS. And he was beginning to worry about television heavily."

Paley's personal life overwhelmed his attentiveness to business in the months after his return. When Elmer Davis decided to return to news broadcasting after his stint leading the Office of War Information, his agent, Jap Gude, wrote to Paley, whom he had known from the early days of CBS: "Dear Bill, Elmer Davis is back in circulation. . . . You should know everyone is after him. He belongs where he started—where we would like him to go. Meantime we are under pressure. Please give me a call. We will talk about it with you or anyone else."

But Paley was in Colorado contemplating his future. He had left Gude's letter behind, ignored or unread. Either way, his inattention was unusual. News was a hot commodity, and an illustrious commentator was a big catch. Yet Gude never received a reply from Paley, so he began negotiating with NBC, ABC, and the Mutual radio network. In each case, the presidents of the networks appeared personally to entice Davis.

Finally Gude called Paul Kesten, who seemed oddly detached. Instead of calling Gude back, Kesten sent over a corporate lawyer to present terms for a deal. It was a perfectly good offer, but halfhearted compared to the other entreaties. With Paley incommunicado, the gesture was doubtless the best Kesten could do without clearance. After all, Paley had tangled with Davis many times about his outspokenness before the war, and even Kesten couldn't know how Paley would react to the newsman's return.

Gude called Davis to relay CBS's offer. "Don't bother," said Davis, who had received a copy of Gude's note to Paley and was wounded that Paley had not even replied. "We will make a decision about one of the other networks and forget about CBS." Davis went to the fledgling ABC network.

When Paley learned of Davis's defection, he was furious that CBS had been dealt such a blow by its small competitor. He blamed Gude entirely. Years later Ed Murrow would tell Gude, "You know, Bill Paley has never forgiven you for taking Elmer Davis away from CBS."

When he returned to the office from California in late 1945, Paley still seemed to be drifting. While abroad he had decided to permit Paul Kesten, by then forty-seven years old, to continue running the business day to day. Kesten would be promoted from executive vice-president to president, and Paley, at age forty-four, would become chairman, thus removing himself from the daily headaches.

On the very day of his return to CBS from Europe, September 4, 1945, Paley had given Kesten the news. To Paley's astonishment, Kesten not only turned him down, he wanted to leave CBS. Paley ascribed Kesten's response to health problems. "I found out that the poor fella had been very ill, just hanging on by the skin of his teeth," Paley later said. "He just shook his head and said, 'I'm not up to it but I have someone who I think is.' " Paley's recollection is exaggerated; only two months after their meeting, the *New York Times* ran a glowing profile of Kesten, who scarcely seemed to be "hanging on by the skin of his teeth." Indeed, Kesten would continue to work actively into the mid-1950s.

In fact, in addition to his arthritis, Kesten had the beginnings of emphysema, which he concealed from everyone. But it was a minor element in his thinking. Kesten had decided he could not work with Paley. Their views of the company's future were too much at odds, and he could not tolerate the pressure of Paley's intrusions.

Kesten had been spoiled by his wartime tenure. At the outset, he had run CBS with the assistance of three executives: Frank Stanton; Frank White, the chief financial officer; and Joseph Ream, the corporate lawyer. When the trio proved unwieldy, Stanton's two colleagues suggested him as second-in-command. Under the new organization, Kesten oversaw programming and news, and Stanton was in charge of research, sales, public relations, building construction, maintenance and operations, as well as the company's radio stations in Washington, Boston, New York, Minneapolis–St. Paul, Chicago, St. Louis, and Los Angeles.

Kesten and Stanton took radio advertising to new highs; fully two thirds of the network's time was sold commercially, compared with one third before the war. The two executives also developed a strong plan for television. They knew that 85 percent of CBS revenues came from the company's own radio stations, and they recognized that television stations would be even more lucrative. After careful study they had homed in on the cities where CBS could establish the strongest television stations.

Even before his return to the States, Paley had begun brooding about how to take the CBS Radio network into first place over NBC. Shortly after VE-Day, Kesten sent Paley a fifteen-page single-spaced letter outlining his vision. CBS, he said, should abandon mass programming and concentrate instead on catering to an elite audience of highly educated and cultivated listeners. In other words, Kesten wanted CBS to be as classy as its clever publicity had claimed. The network already had a good head start. CBS was revered for the quality of its news organization. Norman Corwin, William N. Robson, and other writers had taken radio drama to new heights. Their work was creative and infused with a social conscience. "Perhaps it will strike you, Bill, that I've merely expressed briefly the things we've told ourselves we've been—or wanted to be—these many years," wrote Kesten.

The proposal was a profoundly pragmatic effort to surmount NBC's advantage. Kesten knew NBC would maintain the edge in pursuing the mass audience because its stations could reach so many more listeners. The less powerful CBS lineup could more readily accommodate a smaller, more select audience.

That subtlety eluded Paley, who thought that Kesten's plan really amounted to "giving up the fight against NBC and giving up a national cross-section radio network for a narrower, specialized network of dubious potential." Anything less than winning the largest audience represented defeatism to Paley.

His own plan was a scheme based on control of talent and programming. In the summer of 1945 he had sent Kesten a handwritten letter from Germany that he began while riding in the military command car. The "Command Car Letter," as Kesten and Stanton called it, laid out the broad outlines of Paley's principles for programming the radio network.

Instead of buying programs produced by advertising agencies, CBS would develop the programs on its own—either by building them around new talent or by buying the rights to existing programs. This would require substantial financing to increase facilities and staff within CBS, but Paley felt that the payoff would give his network a new kind of advantage and foster stability. By owning the talent, Paley could prevent the defections that had thwarted his success before the war. It would no longer matter how much stronger the NBC network was. Once NBC's affiliated stations saw that CBS controlled the most appealing shows, they would defect and affiliate with CBS instead. As with many of Paley's ideas, it was simple yet revolutionary.

According to Frank Stanton, Paley's rebuff of Kesten's scheme must have come into play in his refusal of the CBS presidency. "Since Paul and I shared so many things, the fact that he didn't talk about it must have meant he was hurt," said Stanton. "It was the kind of thing that would have cut him deeply, although he never mentioned that as a reason he didn't want to stay on."

At a welcome home reception in CBS's 52nd Street studio the Friday after Paley's return, Paley—still in his colonel's uniform—took Stanton aside. "Are you going to be working tomorrow?" he asked. "Oh sure," said Stanton. "Let's have lunch," said Paley. Stanton assumed Paley was gathering the company's top brass together in the office to discuss their new television plan. "You know how to get to my place?" Paley asked. "Oh yes," said Stanton, shifting gears quickly and figuring they were meeting at Paley's town house on East 74th Street. Paley was so offhand and cryptic, though, that Stanton began to wonder.

That evening, Stanton called Kesten and said, "I guess we're having lunch with Bill." "You are. I'm not," replied Kesten. There was no sharpness to his voice, only a frankness that signaled that Stanton was about to walk into something big. The only further information Kesten gave Stanton was directions for reaching Kiluna Farm.

Stanton rented a car and drove out to Manhasset the next day (his wife had not been invited). In the drawing room at Kiluna, Stanton caught his first glimpse of Paley's private world. About a dozen socialite friends were there, apparently to give Stanton the once-over. Stuart Scheftel was among them. "I got the impression that Bill didn't know Frank Stanton at all. He wanted to know what I thought," Scheftel recalled.

Dorothy presided over one of her impeccable meals—Paley's dramatic exit from her life was still a month away. After lunch Paley said, "Gee, I sort of feel like taking a walk. Anybody else feel like coming with me?" Stanton had caught on to Paley's oblique approach by now. Although it was pouring outside, Stanton understood the invitation was meant for him. Besides, he had found the social chitchat around the Paley's large dining room table tiresome. So he said, "I wouldn't mind taking a walk, too."

The two men strolled across the terrace, around the formal garden, to the swimming pool where they sat on a bench under an umbrella.

"I want you to take over as president of CBS," Paley said. Stanton was speechless.

"Don't you want it?" Paley asked.

"But Mr. Paley, you don't even know me."

"No, no," said Paley, "I know a little bit about what you've done, and I'd like you to consider taking it on."

"It's a pretty important job. I'd like time to think about it," Stanton ventured. Why wasn't Paley tapping Kesten, the logical choice for the job? Paley said simply that Kesten had turned him down and had suggested Stanton.

Although Paley said he intended to stay on as chairman, Stanton got the impression that his boss wanted no role in running the company. Emboldened, Stanton asked how they would divide the responsibilities. "Don't pin me down. Quite frankly, I don't know," said Paley, echoing the misgivings he had expressed to Dorothy. "I don't know whether I'm going to stay in broadcasting. I don't know whether I'm going to go into government. I don't know what I'm going to do. I want you to take the company and see what you can do with it." The hint of annoyance in Paley's voice signaled Stanton to probe no further.

As they walked back to the house in the drenching rain, Stanton said he needed a week to ponder the offer. When they reached the double Dutch back door, Paley leaned over to unlatch the bottom half. "You'll take care of the announcement on Monday," he said, assuming that no one could refuse him.

"But I thought I had a week to think about it," said Stanton.

"Oh yes," said Paley with a smile. "Then you'll let me know." Stanton guessed that meant he would have time to deliberate.

The following Monday, Stanton met Kesten in the CBS boardroom; the room was like a tomb, unlighted and still. Stanton recounted his Saturday visit to Kiluna. "You ought to be president," he told Kesten. "Let me be your number two. Let me do the things you don't want to do or don't like. If you don't want to travel or are not up to it physically, let me carry the burden." Stanton tried to coax Kesten to change his mind.

Under pressure, Kesten finally opened up. The fact was, he admitted, he was incompatible with Paley. He could not deal with Paley as his boss. As an example, Kesten cited the advertising campaign he had recently conceived for the network. Kesten had been high on the campaign, especially the artist who had done the graphic work. But Paley picked at the proposal until Kesten knew he had to go another route. Kesten realized he could not tolerate that kind of interference.

Stanton rented a Plymouth and took Ruth to New England for three days to contemplate his future. At thirty-seven he had been thinking about leaving CBS to establish his own research company; he felt he was ready to run his own show. Yet the challenge of CBS—for all Kesten's misgivings about Paley—was too alluring. With Ruth's encouragement, he decided to take the job.

But when he returned to his office, Paley had left for his holiday retreat in Colorado. For the next four months, while Paley was in California with Selznick, and then in Cuba, Stanton heard nothing further about the CBS presidency. "I was all dressed up and ready to tell him I was his boy, and he wasn't there. Months went by and I never saw him. I didn't know what was going on. I thought he had a change of heart," Stanton recalled.

Then, on Christmas Eve, 1945, Frank Stanton was leaving the office in the late afternoon. Everyone else had gone home early, and Stanton thought he was the last one in the building until the elevator door opened on the executive floor. There was Bill Paley, his arms brimming with packages. He was with a tall, attractive woman wearing a mink coat that nearly brushed the floor. It was Minnie Astor, the wife of Paley's friend Vincent Astor, and sister-in-law to Paley's neighbor, Jock Whitney.

"Gee, where have you been?" said Paley. "Haven't seen you for some time." He was warm and friendly, and Stanton felt thoroughly perplexed.

After some disconcerting small talk, Paley finally said, "Been expecting to hear from you."

Stanton replied, "Well, I've been expecting to hear from you, too."

"You want to talk about it now?"

When Stanton assented, Paley asked Mrs. Astor to wait while the two men conferred briefly in his office.

Stanton explained that since he had heard nothing further about the job, he had concluded that Paley changed his mind. If that was the case, Stanton reassured him, he would certainly understand. "Oh no," said Paley. "I've just been waiting to hear from you." Typically, there was more to the interval than Paley let on. From afar, Paley had been watching Stanton work, reserving the right to rescind his offer. But he had been pleased by Stanton's intelligence and imagination as an executive. Curiously, Paley would later claim to have worked closely with Stanton during the months of his conspicuous absences.

At the CBS board meeting in early January 1946, Stanton was officially named president of CBS. But it was the annual shareholders' meeting on April 17 that truly portended things to come. Before the proceedings began, Ralph Colin said to Stanton, "Are you all set?"

"Sure," replied Stanton breezily.

Colin looked at Stanton hard. "You know Bill isn't coming to the meeting?" he said.

Stanton wheeled on him and said, "What do you mean, he isn't coming?"

"Didn't he tell you? He wants you to run the meeting."

"No," said Stanton with a small sigh, "he didn't tell me."

Nervously, Stanton presided over the first order of business, the election of new directors. A woman shareholder raised her hand. "I nominate Barbara Cushing Mortimer." Stanton shifted uneasily in his seat. He recognized the nominee's name. She was a girlfriend of Bill Paley. "Why does this have to happen to me?" Stanton thought to himself. He accepted the nomination, and it was seconded. "Ouch," Stanton wrote in a note to Joe Ream, who was seated next to him. "Can we nominate someone else?"

Ream raised his hand and nominated Larry Lowman, Paley's friend and a vice-president of the company. Stanton knew he had the proxies and could control the voting, so he was no longer worried. But he did glance toward the back of the room where Lowman sat, shaking his head no. Lowman knew all about Paley and Barbara Mortimer, and he was not about to run against her. Just as vigorously, Stanton shook his head yes. Lowman was elected. After a few days he resigned, permitting the board to elect a replacement.

It had been a discomfiting test, a case of Paley having fun at the expense of the wonder boy from the Midwest. But Stanton's experience at the first annual meeting taught him a crucial lesson about his boss. He realized that Bill Paley did not want to hold responsibility unless he chose to.

23

————

"MRS. MORTIMER JR. Heads Choice of Ten Best Dressed Women," announced the *New York Daily News* on January 21, 1945. The article gushed that a "home-bred heiress, Mrs. Stanley Grafton Mortimer Jr," had come "out of nowhere, as it were, to cop the great clothes-horse sweepstakes." Two years later Mrs. Mortimer was destined to win another contest, with an even bigger prize: Bill Paley.

The fashion upstart was called, incongruously, Babe—a name readily associated with blowsy blondes. But this Babe was delicate, the ultimate in refinement. She was tall (five feet eight inches) and graceful, her posture perfect. Her voice was gentle—not so low as her sister Betsey's—and touched with a New England crispness. She could look meltingly sweet or icily elegant.

Taken separately, her features were imperfect: the lips too thin, the nose sharply aquiline, the jaw a trifle large. But with her dark, flashing eyes, sculpted bone structure, luminous skin, and long, Modigliani neck, the elements came together as a work of art.

"Babe" was not a diminutive for Barbara. It stood for "Baby," her position in the family hierarchy. She was born in Boston on July 5, 1915, the fifth of five children. She had two sisters, Mary Benedict (Minnie), ten years her senior, and Betsey, seven years older. There were two brothers as well: William, born in 1903, and Henry, born in 1910. It was Minnie who named her youngest sister, since her mother had given up. "Barbara" was Minnie's favorite doll.

Although Barbara Cushing grew up in Boston, she stood outside that bastion of Yankee aristocracy. (In later years people often referred to her family as the Cushings of Boston, wrongly implying a Brahmin entitlement. Her parents, Katharine Stone Crowell and Harvey Williams Cushing, came from Cleveland, Ohio.)

The youngest of ten children, Harvey Cushing was born on April 8, 1869. His father, Henry Kirke Cushing, practiced medicine, as had his grandfather and great-grandfather. A nineteenth-century workaholic—not one vacation in forty years—Dr. Kirke, as Harvey's father was called, presided over a strict and puritanical household where the back of a hairbrush was a common punishment. But he saw a promising spark in his youngest son and singled him out for favored treatment.

A small and fiercely determined boy, Harvey applied himself in school, ranking near the top of his class. At Yale he excelled academically and—to his father's dismay—played superior baseball as well. Later, at Harvard Medical School, Harvey Cushing displayed the single-minded drive and energy that would help forge a new and demanding medical specialty. He sequestered himself in a boardinghouse, called himself "the leper," and toiled over his lecture notes and books to the point of exhaustion.

Still, he found time to court Kate Crowell, a girl he had known since childhood. Like Harvey, Kate was from Midwestern pioneer stock. Attractive, witty, outgoing, and popular, she had been educated in the East at Miss Porter's, an exclusive girls' school in Farmington, Connecticut, and was an avid reader. In her company Harvey "entered easily into all the youthful pleasures around him," recalled Mary Goodwillie, a family friend.

Harvey was wiry and handsome, with the erect carriage and mien of a patrician. His face was narrow, with deep-set dark blue eyes and a beaked nose. He dressed meticulously; even in the operating room he wore a perfectly pressed gray tunic with military-style collar and surgeon's cap that looked tailormade. He was vain to the point of knowing which profile showed to best advantage in a photograph.

At twenty-three, he extracted an extraordinary promise from Kate: they would be married, but their engagement would not be announced for ten years so he could establish himself in medicine. Wrote one of Harvey Cushing's biographers, John Fulton, "The prolonged courtship which followed unconsciously stimulated Harvey in his work—unconsciously but most powerfully—for he was now determined to rise to the top, not for himself alone, but to please the girl he loved so tenderly. . . ."

After Harvard and a year at Massachusetts General Hospital, Cushing went to Johns Hopkins and pioneered neurosurgery along with a handful of other doctors. He married Kate in 1902; over the next eight years in Baltimore she bore his first four children. In 1912 he moved his family to Boston, where he became a professor at the Harvard Medical School and surgeon-in-chief at Peter Bent Brigham, Harvard's new teaching hospital.

Like his father before him, Harvey Cushing was totally absorbed in medicine. His brief periods of spare time were spent in the company of intellectuals such as James Ford Rhodes, a historian; M. A. DeWolfe Howe, editor of the *Atlantic Monthly;* and Bliss Perry, a Harvard English professor, at "The Club," the Saturday Club, and the Tavern Club, three of Boston's most prestigious dining clubs. (Conspicuous by its absence was a membership in the Somerset, bastion of the old Yankee aristocracy.) Cushing seldom socialized with his Harvard colleagues, although he often invited interns to dinner, where he delivered long, hypnotic monologues accompanied by graceful gesticulation.

Throughout his energetic career Harvey Cushing performed more than two thousand brain-tumor operations, devoting an average of four days a week to operating. Wearing tennis shoes for comfort, his legs throbbing from the effects of a circulatory disease called vascular polyneuritis, he stood for four hours without resting. Yet he thrived on pushing himself to the limit. Cushing's skill and patience were legendary, and his discoveries through pathologic studies greatly advanced the study of neurology. When he began operating on brains in the early 1900s, 70 percent of his patients died; at the end of his career, the mortality rate was 7.3 percent.

Harvey Cushing endured the ultimate—and now legendary—test one morning in June 1926. Preparing to remove a tumor from a woman's brain, he was told that his eldest son, Bill, had been killed in an automobile accident. A pre-med student at Yale, Bill had been the favorite son, the repository of his father's hopes. To his younger siblings, Bill had been a surrogate father, "the pivot around which we all revolved and the star in my mother's life," according to Betsey. Bill's death was the family's greatest tragedy, yet when Harvey Cushing heard the news, he unflinchingly transmitted some instructions to the authorities and proceeded to operate for four hours. Cushing's colleagues only learned of his son's death after the operation had been completed.

Cushing expected his children to be as precise and disciplined as he was. "Perfectionism," said Betsey, "was drummed into us." He insisted the children take cold showers each morning and hung "No Smoking" signs in their rooms. (He, however, chain-smoked two packs daily.) The children often went for days barely catching a glimpse of their father. He usually visited them only two weekends each summer at their house in Little Boar's Head on the New Hampshire coast. Still, his children held him in awe and were suitably intimidated. When Minnie and Betsey were in their teens, he intercepted all their calls from young suitors. Even if the phone rang as early as eight-thirty in the evening he would tell the caller gruffly, "She has gone to bed."

Kate was the buffer; whenever her husband came down too hard on the children, she would remind them, "One day you will be proud of him." Sadly, the more glamorous he became, the plainer she seemed. As she aged, she grew as round as a muffin. But Kate—or Gogs, as she was always known—was bright, able, and determined, and she knew her own mind. Her steadiness and keen sense of her domestic responsibilities kept the family running smoothly.

"Just as Harvey was a genius in his profession, so was she a genius in managing the perfect home for such a man," said Mrs. Albert Bigelow, a neighbor. "He could always come back from the terrific strain of his work at the hospital to a peaceful home and a serene wife who had intelligent understanding, a grand sense of humor, and who supplied the creature comforts which only a good housekeeper can provide."

Harvey was undemonstrative. He only took Kate on a handful of his numerous European trips. Formal social functions bored him, and Kate had to expend enormous effort to persuade him to accompany her to balls and banquets. Harvey was penurious with the household budget as well.

Kate took to smoking cigarettes surreptitiously because Harvey felt it was unseemly for women to smoke. One day she was smoking at home when her husband arrived unexpectedly. She extinguished the cigarette in the palm of her hand rather than suffer his sharp rebuke. "That," said her grandson, William Cushing, "showed how tough she could be."

Indeed, Gogs was hardly a pushover. "Mrs. Cushing had a strong nature and a quick temper that matched her husband's," wrote Harvey Cushing's biographer, Elizabeth Thomson. "But this perhaps was the salvation of their marriage—this and a love for one another that was long-standing and deep-running and strong enough to withstand the impact of two highly motivated individuals working out a life together."

Inevitably, Kate grew weary of her burdens and numerous disappointments. Not long after the end of World War I, after eighteen years of marriage, she poured out in a letter what she had been unable to say to her husband face to face. After his return from war duty, she wrote:

. . . you didn't seem to need us much. Your visits to Little Boar's Head grew fewer. Wait for vacation—we waited. The vacation was four days. It was hard to make the children understand. Something in me was hurt to the core. Perhaps it was my heart—ever since then I've been trying to build a shell around it so that it shan't be so hurt again. Don't let me do it. Don't kill the love and tenderness that I have always felt for you.

In fact, Cushing was devoted to his wife and drew from her emotional support far more than anyone suspected. He was subject to severe attacks of depression; when his mood plunged, no one could speak to him. His dependence on Kate was evident in his letters to her. "Please don't feel that the game is up," he wrote in a large, agitated scrawl—a departure from his customarily small, precise hand—from a Philadelphia hotel room after walking out following a row.

No one—not even you and I—can (tho' I cherished once the thought
that we could) live together and have so few outside diversions and so
many inside griefs without getting a little weary. I knew how hard you
were trying this afternoon to pry open my shell but I had reached the
point where I was incapable of helping. I wish you had persisted instead
of leaving me as you did without a touch. I would have been less
miserable tho no less undeserving of it. I want to come back to you. I
love you.

Under Harvey and Gogs, the Cushing household may not always
have been placid, yet it was spirited and happy overall. The Cushings
never lacked material comforts or sufficient funds for vacations, private
schooling, and a small staff of servants. But the Cushings were not rich.
Harvey earned good fees from his practice, and inherited a comfortable
stipend from his father and grandfather's real estate investments. However, Cushing plowed a substantial amount of his earnings back into the
clinic and laboratory he operated at Harvard. An atmosphere of New
England frugality imbued the Cushing household. One year, for example,
Minnie would get the new coat and the piano lessons. The next year would
be Betsey's turn, and on down the line.

They lived in a large yellow house with many gables, at 305 Walnut
Street, in the shady Boston suburb of Brookline. A white picket fence
stood out front. Behind the house were a formal garden and tennis court.
"The combination of her appreciation of fine materials with a nice sense of
utility and function always resulted in an attractive and gracious setting,"
wrote Elizabeth Thomson of Kate's home. "In every room there were
photographs and objects of art and sentiment which expressed the personality of the occupants and made the house look hospitable and 'lived in.' "

It has been said that Gogs Cushing once announced, "My girls will
all marry wealth in this country or titles abroad." Whether she so baldly
articulated it or not, she had one overriding mission in life: to prepare her
daughters to marry well, to create a world for their husbands, to keep their
men happy by doting on them. Socially, she was ambitious. But she
wanted to get the girls out of Boston, where their prospects were limited
by their lineage. And she aspired not only to social position but to enough
wealth to give her daughters more independence than she ever had. "She
was obsessed about their having enough money," said Connie Bradlee
Devins, the daughter of an old-line Boston family, who would become
Barbara's secretary.

Of the three Cushing girls, Barbara held the most promise. She
started out in life being called "Henry" by her siblings, because she so
closely resembled her next-eldest brother. But as soon as Barbara had a

say in the matter, she nicknamed herself "Odeal." In this guise, she pretended she was a waitress serving her sisters and brothers their lunch and dinner. Their parents regarded this as frivolous and forbade the children from acknowledging the nickname.

A streak of whimsy endeared Barbara—the name "Babe" didn't stick until later, when she moved to New York—to everyone. During her girlhood she had two imaginary friends named "Mr. and Mrs. Brick." She carried the fantasy to great lengths, always making room for them on the sofa when she sat down. Like her father, Barbara was artistically gifted; her drawings of fairies resembled those of the Victorian illustrator Arthur Rackham. Her liveliness and friendliness were infectious as well. "Barbara is wildly excited and everywhere at once," Minnie wrote Harvey from a European cruise when they were children.

She was a pretty child, but her looks stopped short of beauty because her teeth were a trifle prominent. After she had her teeth straightened in her early teens she emerged as a stunning young woman. She had Harvey's distinctive nose, his lithe physique and natural grace, and Kate's generous jaw and penetrating black eyes.

As Barbara grew older, she developed a dignified reserve. "Barbara was very self-contained," said Eleanor Mittendorf, a school friend. Ever eager to please, she studied conscientiously at the Winsor School in Brookline. At fifteen she moved on to Westover, a fashionable finishing school in Connecticut. Her only spark of misbehavior—a smoking habit developed in her teens—was approved by her mother and carried out behind her father's back.

Barbara was Harvey Cushing's favorite. She called him "Va" or "Fadie" and strove to make him happy. When Barbara was only fifteen, her father took it upon himself to operate on her: she had a small benign tumor on her neck. The procedure was risky and delicate because of the growth's proximity to the jugular vein and crucial facial nerves. During the operation he nicked the vein but proceeded, in the words of his granddaughter Kate Whitney, "cold as ice." His incision did not even leave a scar. When she graduated from Westover and won every prize, her sister Betsey recalled, "I looked at Father and the tears were running down his cheeks."

During a vacation after her sixteenth birthday with her mother and Minnie at Elkhorn Ranch in Montana, Barbara took pains to send her father careful descriptions. "Some great black clouds overtook us," she wrote in a sophisticated, rounded hand, "and it began to pour. The rain came down so hard. It was as though someone was pouring Niagara Falls through a sieve. . . . We could see way off in the distance, through little wisps of clouds, the ranch, with smoke coming out of the chimneys. . . .

Va, you'd love it, especially the mountains, we have tried in vain to paint them."

Barbara knew best how to tap the playful streak in the great Harvey Cushing. Once when the writer and educator Archibald MacLeish came to visit, Barbara bounded into the living room, sat on her father's lap, and called him "Daddy dear"—which none of the other children would have dared say. He squirmed with embarrassment and stumbled to explain that his daughter was not as daffy as she seemed.

But Barbara, like her sisters and brothers, was deeply saddened by her father's separate life. "We all miss you awfully Dear papa," she wrote to him when she was just eight years old. "Stay home with me. and Don't go earning money. We'll just do Something funny. I'll give you my Pennies..and I'll give you my shiny Buckle. I'll arrange all for you."

It was clear that Barbara learned her mother's lessons in attentiveness at an early age. As she and her sisters matured, they would fulfill Gogs's ambition by attracting the most desirable men of their generation.

24

BABE GRADUATED from Westover in 1933, and made her debut at the Ritz-Carlton in Boston the following year. The hostess for the dinner dance, attended by four hundred guests, was her sister Betsey, who by then could afford such an extravagance.

Betsey had been the first Cushing girl to make an illustrious match. In 1930, at age twenty-two, she had married James Roosevelt, a Harvard Law School student, the eldest son of the governor of New York, Franklin D. Roosevelt, who was soon to be president of the United States.

It was a lucky thing, too; Harvey Cushing had been nearly wiped out by the stock market crash in 1929. Even the trust fund established for his family was lost after Cushing's Boston bank collapsed. When Harvard offered him a pittance of a retirement pension in 1932, the esteemed Cushing, sixty-four then, wrote to the president of Yale: "I may have to start in afresh as a wage earner, which is not easy at my time of life." Yale promptly offered him a professorship and laboratory with a generous stipend.

At eighteen, Babe flew into the social whirl of debutante parties and evenings in New York. "You might tell son Franklin that the next time he takes Barbara to a night club, whether or not he allows photographs of the fact to be taken, all will be over between us," Harvey Cushing wrote FDR. "When will you ever become old enough to realize that the new generation goes to a Night Club instead of Sunday School?" Roosevelt replied.

A year later Babe was in a serious automobile accident while riding home from a party on Long Island. According to legend, her young man had run into a tree while staring at Babe. But whichever way he was looking, he was drunk. All of Babe's front teeth were knocked out, requiring extensive dental bridgework and reconstruction of her jaw. Afterwards, perhaps out of envy, acquaintances claimed Babe's face was made even more perfect by the plastic surgery. In fact, the dentist used photographs to reconstruct her teeth as they had been—including one front tooth that her top lip didn't quite cover.

Babe took her misfortune with grace. When her nieces came to visit, she covered the black and blue lower half of her face with a chiffon handkerchief so she wouldn't alarm them. Years later, in a ballroom filled with black lights, a friend looked over at Babe's smile and saw only a black hole. "Why don't your teeth light up?" the friend cried. "They're all false!" said Babe with a giggle.

In 1935, Babe secured an entry-level job at *Glamour* magazine because she wanted to be with her sisters in New York. She commuted from New Haven for a while, then moved to a Manhattan apartment in a luxury building that she shared with a friend, Priscilla Weld, another well-bred Boston girl who was working at *Good Housekeeping*. Babe yearned to be independent and was drawn to the wide-open social life of New York.

She quickly became a sensation, but not exclusively on her own. Rather, she was part of a powerful trio. Babe, Betsey, and Minnie were known throughout Manhattan—and even beyond—as "the Fabulous Cushing Sisters." Babe by then was in her early twenties, Betsey in her late twenties, and Minnie in her early thirties. Betsey was the most ladylike and sensitive-looking. She had blue eyes and a fair complexion; her delicate features were pretty, but not as dramatic as Babe's. Minnie had fine, thin features as well, but was the least attractive. Her teeth and nose were prominent, and she seemed more angular than her sisters. She was quite tall, though, which made an impression.

With their dark wavy hair parted identically on the left and falling just below the neck, the Cushing girls were seen everywhere together. "The three of them had enormous sense," recalled Diana Vreeland. "They had the sort of minds that were curious about beautiful things. They had a basic sense of taste, a basic look about the bones in their faces. They were built like Americans. There was a moment when they were extraordinary."

All three Cushings displayed a carefully cultivated ability to please men. They were not regarded as flirts, but rather as natural, charming, and thoroughly feminine. They dressed smartly, projected an air of elegance, and knew how to enter into the fun. Their breeding showed in every way. They were even nice to women, especially to women; they knew that important women gave the parties and set the social rankings.

The triumvirate was not without calculation. "I remember Babe leveled with me once," recalled Alice-Leone Moats, a member of their circle in those days. "She told me their mother said early on, 'The three of you stick together. That is where your strength is.' So they hunted together." Moats was one of a minority who remained unimpressed by the Cushings. "They weren't interesting but they had talent," she observed.

For the most part, they were devoted to and protective of each other. "Betsey could be rough," said the fashion photographer Horst, who knew all three sisters. "She was demanding and the opposite of Babe. Betsey could be rivalrous with anybody. She could be imperious. She was never easy, but Babe was easy." Later in life Betsey would divulge her competitive feelings about Babe to E. J. Kahn, Jock Whitney's biographer: "Babe was always the glamor girl and I was always the crumbum except when I was away from her. Babe was a perfectionist. Compared to her, I always felt inadequate." Fortunately, Betsey redeemed herself with a rollicking sense of humor and an ability to kick up her heels.

Minnie was everyone's favorite. Older and plainer than the others, she was sweeter as well. "She has her happiness safe inside," her mother once said. Babe always felt closest to Minnie. As a girl, when someone asked her which sister she liked best, Babe would say, "Minnie, of course. She wears chartreuse green, and she wears lipstick." Unlike Betsey and Babe, who could be aggressive, Minnie was unfailingly gentle. As the eldest, Minnie also tended to be more serious, the most intellectual—and the least conventional.

The first to bolt from Boston, Minnie pioneered New York as a career girl, moving into a cold-water flat on Madison and 59th with her old friend Kay Halle. Despite her meager circumstances, she soon managed to hook up with a man even more desirable than Jimmy Roosevelt.

In 1935 she became the mistress of Vincent Astor, the forty-four-year-old heir to a $70 million real estate fortune, one of the richest men in the world. Known as "Ghastly Astor" to his enemies and V.A. to his friends—with the exception of Minnie, who called him "Winsie"—Astor owned a Georgian house at 130 East 80th Street, a villa in Bermuda, and Ferncliff, a 3,000-acre estate in Rhinebeck, New York.

In business, some regarded him as a daring thinker, but the overwhelming view of his personality was far less complimentary. He was notoriously juvenile, a practical jokester with a penchant for rubber pretzels and iron hot dogs. He could be moody as well as tyrannical. When he felt depressed, he would ride on one of the miniature railroads he installed in Bermuda and at Ferncliff.

It was Babe who was the most beautiful and glamorous of the Fabulous Cushings. She moved to *Vogue* magazine in 1939 as an editor in the fashion department, where she worked under the legendary fashion editors Edna Woolman Chase and Carmel Snow. She also befriended Diana Vreeland, fashion editor at rival *Harper's Bazaar*. Babe's phone rang off the hook all day, but mostly with social calls. She went out to lunch with beaux, and drifted off to the fashion collections. "You never knew where she was," said her secretary, Connie Devins. "Everyone always ran up and down the halls saying, 'Where's Babe?' "

Babe's salary was small, and she never kidded herself about having a real career. Her ambition, like that of her entire generation, was to marry and have children. She was talented enough to design clothing or fabrics, perhaps even to paint or sculpt, but Babe knew as well as anyone that *Vogue* valued her looks and style above all else. Through the lens of Steichen or Horst, she looked like the quintessential fashion magazine editor. To Horst it seemed that Babe still had a lot to learn in those days: "She stood out. But she was not like an actress. She held back and was afraid of the camera. She was not that confident."

But she was a beautiful clotheshorse. Instead of merely wearing clothes, Babe seemed to carry them on her graceful frame. *Vogue* once said she had "the tight high buttocks of island women who have carried things on their heads all their lives." Her wardrobe budget was modest—$50 a month—yet she dressed with extraordinary chic, using such elegant touches as a little solid gold evening bag with her initials traced in small jewels. Restraint was essential to her style. She pulled herself together with simplicity, and she knew how to use the element of surprise. "She would come in to *Vogue* wearing a red linen suit and a pink blouse," recalled Despina Messinesi, a longtime *Vogue* editor. "It was the first time I ever saw that."

Like Bill Paley, Babe Cushing was a keen student. She set out to pick the brains of those who knew about things that would improve her. "She wanted to know all about fashion and things in Paris. It was all brand new to her. She was learning and didn't make a fuss," recalled Horst, who used to dine with Babe regularly in New York bistros in the early days. Horst had lived in Paris for many years, where he had formed a close friendship with Coco Chanel. Paris was the center of the fashionable world, and Babe needed to understand it. "Tell me," she would say, "why is it that Chanel dresses look the way they do?" Still governed by Bostonian propriety, she framed many questions as "could one?" and "should one?" But it was clear to Horst that Babe yearned to be more daring.

If a refined, fashionable woman could have street smarts, Babe fit the bill. When her friend Susan Mary Jay (later to marry the prominent newspaper columnist Joseph Alsop) wanted to work at *Vogue* in 1939, Babe shrewdly advised her on how to shape her writing sample. The somewhat preposterous topic was "The Future of the Open Toed Shoe." After discovering that Edna Woolman Chase, *Vogue*'s editor-in-chief, was partial to open-toed shoes, Babe dictated an enthusiastic essay to Susan Mary, who got a job as a receptionist. Several months later she and Babe found themselves at the New York World's Fair, floating in evening dresses from parachute harnesses for the fashion photographers. They were paid $75 an hour.

Babe was no intellectual, as she knew all too well. "She had trouble with language," recalled Connie Devins. "She could be quite inarticulate unless she was telling a story about somebody. She spoke in pretty simple sentences. She was a classic boarding school girl who never learned very much. I don't think she read. But she was smart enough to be a very good listener and she asked good questions. She knew when to keep her mouth shut, when to be background, and when to be a hostess. She had a knack of knowing where she belonged."

For all her glamour, Babe retained a down-to-earth niceness; she was neither cool nor aloof. Susan Mary Alsop recalled that Babe "was too much of a lady to be a snob. She was funny, too—extremely funny, quick —not a wit in the Dorothy Parker sense, but awfully funny, a mimic. But, as she was shy, she didn't like holding forth. She preferred to have everyone around her and to throw in droll comments which had everyone rolling on the floor."

Babe kept some distance from her many male admirers. She had a certain wariness about men, which some thought stemmed from her mother's difficulties with Harvey Cushing. Babe may have also understood that a lot of men simply loved being seen with her; her attention fanned their egos. "She was savvy. She knew how to please a man, how to make him think he was the most attractive man who ever walked," said Connie Devins. "I used to listen to her talk to all the beaux. It was like listening to Garbo. She had more men in love with her." Jean Pagès, a French illustrator for *Vogue,* was so infatuated with Babe that he could speak of nothing else. Iva Patcévitch, who took over *Vogue* after Condé Nast died, was also an ardent admirer, as was Bobby von Moltke, a Danish playboy living in New York City.

The man who succeeded in capturing her was far less worldly, although he was beautiful—clean-cut and chiseled as a Greek god. Stanley Grafton Mortimer, Jr., was a New York blueblood, a graduate of St. Mark's School who had followed the customary lockstep to Harvard, where he met Babe in his sophomore year. They caught up again at parties in New York, much to the delight of her mother, who had been appalled by Babe's foreign suitors. By all accounts, Babe genuinely loved Stanley.

Mortimer was high-WASP aristocracy, and the family wealth had deep roots. His father, a descendant of John Jay, first Chief Justice of the U.S. Supreme Court, was renowned more as a rackets champion than as a retired Wall Street broker. Stanley's mother was the former Katherine Tilford, daughter of Henry Morgan Tilford, a founder of Standard Oil of California. Through her, Stanley stood to inherit at least $3 million.

The Tilford-Mortimer clan had Tuxedo Park, a fashionable enclave near New York City, as its home base. There, Henry Morgan Tilford's widow was the reigning dowager. For forty years her annual debutante dinners before Tuxedo Park's Autumn Ball determined which girls were approved for New York society.

Babe was as captivated by Stanley Mortimer's good looks and charm as by his pedigree. He was a party boy who put in time working for Ruth, Roth & Ryan—an advertising agency more popularly known as Riff Raff & Ruin—and spent many afternoons at the exclusive Racquet and Tennis Club on Park Avenue. As a couple, Babe and Stanley turned heads. "He was the boy next door. Everything was correct," said Diana Vreeland.

The Mortimer-Cushing wedding on September 21, 1940, was one of the big events of the social season, held at a home Gogs Cushing rented in East Hampton, Long Island. In a nice touch of understatement, the only attendants were Betsey Roosevelt's two daughters, Sara and Kate. Harvey Cushing never lived to see his favorite child marry. He had suffered a fatal heart attack in late 1939.

Babe and Stanley settled into a small triplex apartment in an East Side brownstone. They didn't have heaps of money—old Mrs. Tilford left him $50,000 when she died in 1941—but there was enough to hire a maid and a cook. They filled their home with elegant (inherited) furniture. Babe took on most of the decorating herself, settling on a red, green, and white color scheme. She spent her spare time scouring antique shops for bargains in French and Victorian pieces, antique enamels, china, and ornate bottles. "She adored beautiful objects," Diana Vreeland recalled.

The Mortimers entertained frequently and well. Like her mother, Babe served daily afternoon tea. She abhorred cocktail parties, preferring dinner followed by songs around a piano. It was an old-fashioned New York society life, with nights out at mystery movies and plays. Right on schedule, Babe "retired" from her glamorous job to have a son, Stanley

III, in 1942, and a daughter, Amanda, in 1944. In 1943, however, she returned to *Vogue* as an occasional model.

During these years, the well-married Cushing sisters took off. Minnie had finally landed Vincent Astor, who agreed to a small wedding at Gogs's house only six days after the Cushing-Mortimer ceremony. The three sisters all hired George Stacey, New York's premiere interior decorator; in the words of decorator Billy Baldwin, "those girls had a kind of monopoly on taste."

Hovering behind the scenes, Gogs enlarged her cozy embrace to include her daughters' New York friends, who were enchanted by her. "She was the most charming woman," said Leonora Hornblow, a friend of Babe's. "She was terribly interested and would want to know all about you—how you met your husband, all about your children. It wasn't nasty curiosity. You would feel you were the most important creature. She had lived only to sit with you."

It was Gogs who had put her foot down and persuaded Vincent Astor to make an honest woman of her eldest daughter. When Betsey's marriage to James Roosevelt broke up in 1940, Gogs came to the rescue and set her up in the building next to her own apartment on East 86th Street. Each week she would have Betsey and her two daughters over for dinner with Minnie, Babe, and her children. Gogs sat in a chair and read everyone fairy tales. One fairy tale came true in 1942 when Betsey wed the fabulously wealthy Jock Whitney.

In 1943, Stanley Mortimer joined the Navy and went to the Pacific. On his return in 1945, he had changed. He was drinking heavily and was subject to sharp mood swings. "He would drink when he was on a high, which would throw him into orbit," recalled Connie Devins. "Babe was still crazy about him but she couldn't handle it." On May 29, 1946, Babe divorced him in Florida, charging him with being "habitually intemperate from the voluntary use of alcoholic liquors." He gave her a $40,000 trust fund to support their two children, who remained in Babe's custody.

Well before her divorce became final, Babe had taken up with the recently separated Bill Paley. He always professed to have first noticed Babe at a dinner party in the fall of 1946. That is clearly untrue. Not only was she celebrated and thus a perfect target for his alert eye, but according to Dorothy, in 1942 and 1943 Babe and Stanley took a house on Shelter Rock Road in Manhasset near Greentree, Jock and Betsey Whitney's estate next to Kiluna. Minnie and Vincent lived up the road as well. "Babe and Stanley were at the house quite often," said Dorothy.

By the time of the CBS annual meeting in April 1946, when Babe was jocularly nominated for the CBS board, there was no doubt that she was seeing Paley regularly. So, for that matter, was Janet Stewart, the stunning high-society widow of William Rhinelander Stewart, a wealthy man-about-town from an old New York family. When *Fortune* magazine described the membership of New York high society in 1937, it had singled out a "Regency Council" of seventeen, including Will Stewart and Jock Whitney. The Stewarts had been such good friends of Bill and Dorothy that the two couples spent many Christmas holidays together. But with Will dead and Dorothy out of the picture, Janet launched a hellbent pursuit of Paley. She even loaned him some of her china and silver to replace what Dorothy had taken away from Kiluna.

Watching Paley conduct the two romances was a favorite parlor game in New York society. Two beauties, one brunette, the other pale blond: which one would he choose? Temperamentally, Janet was Babe's opposite: conspicuously bright, opinionated, almost pedantic. "Bill always wanted the best," said Horace Kelland, a friend of the Cushing sisters. "It mattered a great deal to him that Janet was Mrs. Will Rhinelander Stewart. She was comfortably fixed, and her father, Mr. Newbold, had owned and published *The Washington Star*. It was a terrible decision to make: the sister of Mrs. Vincent Astor and Mrs. Jock Whitney, or the widow of Will Stewart."

As Paley debated, Babe went to Paris in the summer of 1946 to model the new collections for *Vogue*. She could not have been too smitten with Paley, because she proceeded to have a romance with a handsome diplomat named Elim O'Shaughnessy. "Babe was enchanted with Elim, who fell head over heels and pursued her with tenacity," said Susan Mary Alsop, who was in Paris at the time. "He kept asking her to marry him. She said no, but finally at Orly airport in the waiting room she gave up and said yes." When she returned to New York, Babe called Susan Mary. "For God's sake, get me out of this. I'm not in love with him," she said. "He's nice-looking and intelligent but I'm not in love." (Others who knew O'Shaughnessy said Gogs Cushing had disapproved because he had no family money.) On Susan Mary's advice, Babe hastily wrote him a letter calling it off.

Paley renewed his courtship of Babe and dropped Janet Stewart. "Everyone expected him to marry Janet," said Alice-Leone Moats. "But Bill said, 'No, I have left one bossy woman. I don't want to take on another.'" Paley began to visit Babe at the 86th Street apartment she shared with Gogs. When Babe had an attack of phlebitis and was hospitalized for a month, Paley visited her every evening. She sat in bed, wrapped in tulle, looking like a portrait by Watteau, and he arrived with dinner for two in a warming container. For each visit, he consulted with a chef from one of his favorite restaurants to concoct the perfect menu. One snowy evening her friend Marietta Peabody Fitzgerald came unannounced for a visit and found Bill and Babe necking in the hospital bed. When Babe recovered, Paley picked out a Cadillac for her, took her to the car dealership, and embraced her outside the back door of the showroom.

Babe was flattered by Paley's elaborate attentiveness, although her mother was suspicious. Paley's wealth was impressive. In 1946 his holdings in CBS alone were worth $9.8 million, and his income from salary and dividends that year was $805,623. But Gogs had reservations because of his background. "I don't know whether she tried to deter or moderate or expedite," Irene Selznick recalled, "but she knew she could sure keep an eye on it. She did after all have a house in Manhasset. And Betsey was right next door."

Babe was never madly in love with Paley. Rather, she found him fascinating. He wasn't as classically handsome as Stanley Mortimer, but he was attractive enough. She was drawn to Paley's vitality and lightning responsiveness. She found his complications alluring compared to Stanley's simplicity. She could see that something was going on at all times with Paley; the lights were blazing, the mind was ticking. "She knew all about Stanley Mortimer," said Leonora Hornblow. "Bill Paley was exotic. She couldn't get to the bottom of him. There were these secrets."

Not long after his ardent courtship began, Babe ran into Connie Devins. "You've got to tell me what he's like," Connie said. "How does an American Jean Gabin grab you?" Babe replied. (The French film star played the lead in Jean Renoir's *Grand Illusion* and was known for his masculinity more than his good looks.) Babe also wrote one of her infrequent letters to Susan Mary Alsop in Paris, to tell her that she was going to marry Bill Paley: "In he comes at the end of a hard day. He always has something new to tell me or a little present to cheer me up."

But no marriage plans were made until suddenly, on July 24, 1947, word leaked out that Bill Paley had granted Dorothy a $1.5 million divorce settlement in Reno, Nevada. A month earlier Dorothy had taken her children to nearby Lake Tahoe, where she established residency in order to sue Paley for divorce on grounds of desertion. She was joined there by her friend Marietta, who was filing for divorce from Desmond Fitzgerald and planning to marry the Englishman Ronald Tree. The two women and their children lived together in a chalet on the lake that cost Dorothy $5,000 for six weeks.

The settlement—and the size of the check—came as a surprise. Dorothy and Bill had been in a nasty struggle over their separation. "He was cold as ice," recalled Dorothy. "He couldn't have been more unpleasant. It was the worst period of my life. There was nothing nice about it. All his worst qualities were exposed." Once when Dorothy had taken the children to Florida for a holiday, Paley dispatched a truck to their home on 74th Street and removed most of the paintings. He refused to declare his net worth and sent a lawyer to Dorothy suggesting that she move out of the house and into a smaller apartment. At one point David Selznick tried to intervene because he thought Paley was being too stingy with his proposed settlement.

According to one friend close to the couple, Paley did not intentionally inflict pain on Dorothy, "but when he causes pain he puts himself first. He doesn't relate to the other person's dilemma. He doesn't mean to inflict harm but his fears prevent him from recognizing the feelings of others."

Amid the disputes, in January 1947, Dorothy learned that she had breast cancer. She was only thirty-eight. She had a radical mastectomy and stayed at Columbia Presbyterian Hospital in New York for more than a month. Paley came once for a short visit after the surgery, and he sent her a record player and some records. "He knew he had had enough of the marriage," said one close friend. "But when she got cancer, guilt complicated his feelings."

The eventual divorce settlement seemed generous enough, but from it Dorothy had to pay all the schooling and expenses for the children. Moreover, she had to take $125,000 of the proceeds and buy the 74th Street house from Paley (who had bought it for $75,000 six years earlier). She kept her bedroom furniture from Kiluna and her jewelry; he kept all the paintings except those he had given to her during their marriage, including an exquisite Degas. She retained custody of Jeffrey, nine, and Hilary, eight, who would see their father on holidays and for a month in the summer.

Dorothy was devastated by the divorce. Many of their friends spurned her and chose to side with him. "You don't exist," Dorothy recalled. "It has nothing to do with you. It is entirely circumstance. People are interested in where the power and money sit." "Her taste didn't change. Nothing changed," said Marietta Tree, who managed to remain friends with Dorothy, Bill, and Babe. "But she just wasn't married to Bill anymore."

Dorothy pulled herself together quite effectively, however. She married (and later divorced, after seven years) a Wall Street stockbroker named Walter Hirshon, and she dedicated herself to philanthropic causes, serving for many years on the board of the New School in New York City.

Bill and Babe were married on July 28, 1947—three weeks after Babe's thirty-second birthday. Bill Paley was forty-five years old, and one newspaper account of the wedding noted that he was "the first Cushing son-in-law who is not socially prominent." Years later Ralph Colin told Frank Stanton that on the eve of the wedding he had drawn up a prenuptial agreement that Babe and Bill signed.

The ceremony, presided over by Supreme Court Justice J. Edward Lumbard, Jr., was at Chester House, Gogs Cushing's shingled "cottage" on the Whitney estate. Afterwards there was a reception out back on the veranda, with its Doric columns, latticework pergola, and vista of broad lawns and trees. The guest list was short—fewer than twenty-five family members and a handful of close friends: Babe's two sisters, their husbands, and Betsey's two daughters; Babe's two children; Gogs, Goldie, and Sam; Blanche Levy (Leon was on a business trip); Babe's brother Henry and his wife; Jack Baragwanath and his wife, Neysa McMein; Ed and Janet Murrow; Paley's faithful factotum John Minary; and Sidney "Spivey" Spivak, a young man who hung around the Cushing sisters. Only days before the wedding, Babe called society photographer Jerome Zerbe, who flew down from Nantucket to take a series of candid shots of the festivities.

Babe wore a simple pale silk shirtwaist with a jewel neckline, capped sleeves, embroidered belt, and calf-length full skirt. Her ears sparkled with pearl and diamond earrings matched by a bracelet on her left wrist. Her hair was parted neatly in the middle, swept off her forehead, and held in place by a wreath of tulle. Paley wore a dark double-breasted suit. A gold identification bracelet glittered on his right wrist.

The atmosphere was pleasantly informal. Some guests perched on white rattan furniture while others lounged on cushions scattered on the brick terrace. Vincent Astor (wearing his Brook Club tie as always) stretched his "grasshopper legs" on the lawn and chatted with Neysa McMein. Even Sam Paley flopped down on a needlepoint cushion under a tree to talk with Betsey Whitney and her brother.

Gogs, wearing a flat-brimmed hat trimmed with silk pansies, clowned with her new son-in-law and looked thoroughly pleased. Bill fed wedding cake to Babe from a Chinese export porcelain plate. And he feigned horror when Jock Whitney presented him with a ten-inch-high wooden corral surrounding a miniature bride and groom. Hanging over the rails of the corral were five glamorously dressed dolls—ladies who lost in the Paley wedding sweepstakes.

Four days later, on August 1, Bill and Babe set sail on the *Queen Elizabeth* for a honeymoon in England, France, Italy, and Switzerland. Their luxurious suite on the A-deck overflowed with flowers for the bon voyage party. They sailed away from a pier on West 50th Street, leaving behind a row of gleaming ocean liners along the Hudson River. Among the 2,243 passengers who waved goodbye from the deck that afternoon were Cary Grant, the English playwright Frederick Lonsdale, designer

Hattie Carnegie, Arthur Hornblow, the Hollywood producer, and his wife, Leonora. The celebrities banded together and took turns every evening giving a dinner party in an elegant private dining room. Each host tried to outdo the others by ordering the most imaginative menu.

By day Babe sat in one of their two well-located deck chairs—marked Paley 1 and Paley 2—and read novels. On the first afternoon Babe and Leonora Hornblow met Louis Marx, the toy-manufacturing king, who was so enchanted that he gave them each a solid gold yo-yo. Every day thereafter Babe and Leonora would take a spin around the ocean liner, twirling their yo-yos and giggling like schoolchildren.

After spending some time in London, the Paleys traveled to Paris, where Duff Cooper, the British ambassador to France, and his wife, Diana, had them to tea—a gesture that Paley resented because he expected a more grand welcome for Babe. On the Riviera they stayed in the Hôtel du Cap d'Antibes, a mecca for the international crowd, that sat "like a frosted cake at the top of a small hill above the bland, blue sea."

Toward the end of their honeymoon Paley gained some notoriety by winning one million francs playing baccarat at the Monte Carlo Casino. At his side was his old friend Olive, Lady Baillie, who announced, "In all my years at Monte Carlo I have never seen such a shoe."

To friends who saw them that summer, Bill and Babe seemed the dream couple. Each time he looked Babe's way, Bill beamed with pride. He was simply thrilled to be married to her. They were too self-contained to act like lovebirds, yet they took genuine joy in each other's company. His little-boy enthusiasm seemed to spark her streak of exuberance.

On March 30, 1948—eight months after Bill and Babe's hurry-up marriage—Babe bore their first child, William Cushing Paley. The infant weighed six pounds, and there was no mention of his being premature. Gogs said only that he was "a quiet, small baby." The arrival of the Paleys' son, however, seemed to indicate what had only been hinted at the previous July: that Babe had been pregnant by Paley when they were married. (Two years later, they would have a second child, Kate.)

The wedding would doubtless have come off anyway. It signified destiny fulfilled on both sides. Babe had found the wealthy and powerful man she had been bred to marry. While it may not have been apparent at the time, Paley's temperament was also similar to her father's: brilliant, vital, energetic, egocentric, demanding, domineering, and charming on his own terms. And Paley had found the perfect antidote to Dorothy. Babe's beauty and social standing—"the ultimate glowing Gentile," in the words of one friend of Babe—greatly enhanced his position in life (in his memoir, he entitled the chapter about his courtship and marriage to Babe

"Triumph"). Babe was also trained to look up to her man, to flatter him, and burn incense for him.

Had Dorothy Paley thought about it back in 1942, she might have imagined what a woman like Babe could offer a man like Bill Paley. That year, when the Paleys heard about Jock Whitney's marriage to Betsey Cushing Roosevelt, Dorothy said, "Oh, he will be so bored." "No, he won't," responded Paley. "He will have everything the way he wants it."

25

AS A BROADCASTER, Bill Paley had a simple formula for financial success. Though it seems obvious today, it was groundbreaking in radio days. He believed that a network should be free and independent. Its shows should appeal to a wide popular audience and occasionally cater to minority tastes. Plots should be believable and uncomplicated, and audiences should identify with the characters. Above all, the network should do everything it could to find and nurture stars.

Paley's "Command Car Letter" in 1945 to Paul Kesten had revealed his determination to be first in the ratings by gaining control over stars and shows. By the mid-1940s, with Frank Stanton in place as president and running the company day by day, Paley was free to pursue his vision with single-minded zeal. He established a programming department to develop mass appeal shows, especially comedies—the core of NBC's success. He appointed his aide-de-camp from World War II, Davidson Taylor, then forty-one years old, to be CBS's chief of programming. Experts who had helped shape NBC's success also came aboard: Cy Howard, formerly a scriptwriter for Jack Benny in Hollywood; Irving Mansfield, who produced the Fred Allen show for four years; and Hubbell Robinson and Harry Ackerman from the ad agency Young & Rubicam.

Each Tuesday at 10:00 A.M. when Paley was in town, he assembled what he called his program planning board for a report on the progress of new shows. He sat at the head of the table, with Frank Stanton at the other end. Flanked by the chiefs of programming, promotion, sales, and research, Mr. Paley, as he was called, was attentive and asked questions sparingly. He did most of his talking after the meetings, speaking individually with program executives. That was his chief method of staying in touch.

In 1946, Paley introduced four CBS-produced half-hour radio shows. He put them on the air while he sought sponsorship. Instead of permitting advertisers to take over production, Paley offered only to sell the commercial time, theorizing that a successful CBS-owned show could serve as the anchor for an evening's schedule. Each show was supposed to deliver an audience big enough to keep the surrounding programs from defecting to NBC.

Accustomed to calling all the shots, advertisers resisted Paley's plan. But he refused to budge, and in a matter of months they began to see that Paley's format could serve their interests as well. CBS-produced programs cost less and were also less risky for the advertising agencies. By the end of 1947 CBS was producing thirty-six of its own programs, fifteen of which had commercial sponsorship.

The extrovert Cy Howard formed a close bond with Paley. Howard would bound into programming meetings, acting out the various parts in the shows he proposed. Paley regarded him with amusement but also recognized Howard's talent. Howard and his colleagues were encouraged to take the initiative.

"Bill Paley gave me my head," recalled Harry Ackerman, a CBS production executive. "I overreached and made deals without his knowledge. Once I picked up the Joan Davis show, and Hubbell Robinson was shaken when I hadn't checked with him or with Bill. In my presence, he called Bill to tell him, and Bill just said okay. I think Bill respected people capable of decisions. He was inspirational. If he liked something and was sure, he was immediate. If he was not sure, he asked probing questions. If you wanted to go ahead and he didn't have serious disagreement, he said 'Go.' "

It took Paley's programmers less than a year to come up with their first hits and potential stars. Cy Howard developed "My Friend Irma," a "dizzy dame" show, and "Life with Luigi," about a bumbling Italian immigrant. Harry Ackerman discovered a red-haired comedian named Lucille Ball at the Stork Club in New York and signed her to star in "My Favorite Husband," based on a story he read on the train from New York to Hollywood. Ackerman also put Eve Arden in "Our Miss Brooks," a comedy about a wisecracking high school teacher.

While Frank Stanton's portfolio did not include radio entertainment shows, he was responsible for launching CBS's biggest star of this period, Arthur Godfrey. Stanton first heard Godfrey announcing on CBS's affiliate in Washington, D.C., in 1941. Beyond the requisite deep voice, Godfrey had a folksy sincerity that made his commercial pitches unusually persuasive. Stanton brought him to CBS's station in New York as host of a show introducing aspiring young performers. Although no sponsor even nibbled after thirteen weeks, Stanton persevered until the audience embraced Godfrey.

After Godfrey took off in New York, Stanton shifted him to the radio network. At his peak, Godfrey could be heard on two different nighttime shows as well as a morning program. He singlehandedly pulled in $6 million a year in advertising, earning the nickname "Mr. Columbia."

Although Paley appreciated Godfrey's value to the network, he never warmed to the popular entertainer. "Godfrey was never accepted by the people on the West Coast," said Stanton. " 'Why do you have this jerk?' they would say to Bill. I always thought Bill looked down on him because he came out of local radio. Besides, Godfrey was irreverent, insolent, and difficult. But maybe most important to Bill was that Godfrey had no style."

Irritated by Paley's unconcealed disdain, Godfrey took public pokes at the CBS chairman. Speaking to a group of auto executives and advertisers in Detroit in the late 1940s, he really let fly. "The best way to get ahead in radio is to let it be known—a year or so before your contract runs out —that you're going to switch to NBC," he said. "I started the rumor— my contract has two years to go—and ever since have had lunch every two weeks with Paley. I worked for that bastard fourteen years before that [in fact, it was only eight] and never even saw him."

CBS steadily inched up on NBC, which still lacked a programming department of its own. "NBC just sat there," recalled Stanton. "They would take this or that program produced by the advertisers." NBC executives continued to believe that the network's stronger stations and greater reach were sufficient to attract the best programming and keep the stars in line.

At year's end in 1947 two new CBS shows had joined radio's top ten —"Arthur Godfrey's Talent Scouts" and "My Friend Irma." But Paley felt impatient. "I know a good comedian when I hear one," he told an interviewer that year. "The only trouble is that too many are on NBC." In May 1948, when Paley received a memorandum from an NBC vice-president crowing about his network's dominance, he decided to go on the offensive. It was time to raid, as he had done in the thirties. But this time, he needed to make sure that NBC could not snatch the performers back.

Paley's approach arose out of a routine lunch in his private dining room at 485 Madison with Stanton and Lew Wasserman and Taft Schreiber, two top executives of Music Corporation of America, Hollywood's largest talent agency. MCA represented two of NBC's most popular stars, Freeman Gosden and Charles Correll, the creators of "Amos 'n' Andy."

Paley could have the show, Wasserman said, if he agreed to pay for it somewhat unconventionally.

Since the tax rate on incomes above $70,000 was 77 percent, Wasserman suggested that Correll and Gosden incorporate and sell CBS their company's physical assets—the characters and scripts for their shows—for $2 million plus a share of the profits from future shows. The amount paid by CBS would then be considered a capital gain and taxed at a substantially lower rate of 25 percent. Moreover, Correll and Gosden would continue to receive regular salaries from CBS for their performances. The two stars stood to make far more at CBS than they ever could at NBC. And as owners of the show, CBS could tie up the performers in long-term contracts.

Paley loved the idea. It was tidy, ingenious, and gave him total control. But was it legal? To the delight of CBS, the Bureau of Internal Revenue readily approved the deal.

In September 1948, Paley triumphantly announced that Amos 'n' Andy had joined CBS after nineteen years on NBC. "Strangely," wrote David Sarnoff's biographer, Kenneth Bilby, "Sarnoff did not respond to his competitor's provocation." At that moment, Wasserman returned to Paley and suggested the same sort of deal for the king of radio, Jack Benny.

Benny had appeared briefly in the early days on CBS but had been dropped by his sponsor, Canada Dry, for taking potshots at their soda. Although Benny had been a mainstay on NBC since 1932, he was not entirely happy. He felt NBC took him for granted; the network never bothered taking out ads for his program when the prime-time season began each fall. Even more wounding, Sarnoff didn't deign to socialize with Benny when the comedian traveled to New York. "Jack is a loyal guy," recalled his former agent Irving Fein. "He once said to me, 'If I had dinner with Sarnoff once in a while and lunch once a year, I never would have wanted to leave NBC.' "

The price for Benny's departure was steep: $2.26 million to buy his company, Amusement Enterprises, plus salaries for the services of Benny ($10,000 a week) and his co-stars. But Paley agreed instantly. He had been careful to maintain a sizable hoard of cash at CBS—$10 million in 1948—by keeping dividends low, and the company had taken out a $5 million loan from the Prudential Insurance Company as a backstop.

When Wasserman informed Batton Barton Durstine & Osborn (advertising agency for the Benny show) about the deal with CBS, Ben Duffy, BBD&O president, was wild with anger at the prospect of losing the security of NBC. He tipped NBC president Niles Trammell, who rushed to the West Coast to match the deal. The NBC chief was a courtly southerner, with an infectious sense of humor. Like Paley, he knew how to please and flatter performers. He easily convinced Benny to make a capital gains arrangement with NBC.

"Benny's $4,000,000 NBC Deal: Web Forestalls Raiding by CBS" was the page-one banner headline in *Variety* on November 10, 1948. According to the article, Trammell had engineered "radio's most fabulous deal to date" by offering to buy Benny's company for $4 million—nearly twice Paley's offer. At that very moment, *Variety* reported, Trammell was on the West Coast "wrapping up final details" in a deal that had been made with "the reported blessing" of David Sarnoff.

In fact, Sarnoff had expressed misgivings. He was worried about MCA's stipulation that the network not submit details of the deal to the Bureau of Internal Revenue for three months. Sarnoff felt that NBC needed government approval before signing the contract. Even more worrisome were statements made by Senator Styles Bridges, Republican of New Hampshire and chairman of the powerful Senate Appropriations Committee, on November 12. He questioned whether the capital gains sales by top radio performers were "a dodge to escape income taxes," and asked the Bureau of Internal Revenue to explain why the arrangements should be legal.

While NBC negotiated with Benny in Hollywood, *Variety* crowed about CBS's defeat and Paley stewed. If only he could speak directly to Benny. Paley quietly dispatched one of his executives, Manie Sacks, to the West Coast. An old friend of Ike Levy, Sacks was head of the popular music division at CBS Records. Before that, he had been a talent agent and had a close relationship with the Bennys, especially Jack's wife, Mary Livingstone. Whenever Jack and Mary came to town, Sacks had arranged for the limousines, decorated their hotel suites with flowers, and planned Mary's shopping itinerary.

Sacks visited the Bennys and persuaded them to hear Paley out before Jack signed anything. Paley subsequently called Benny, reaching him at the home of George Burns in the middle of a dinner party. Paley the charmer emphasized the great importance he attached to performers, whom he called CBS's most treasured assets. Flattered, Benny agreed to meet Paley in California as soon as he could hop a plane. Sarnoff heard of Paley's departure but did not follow him to the coast. Wrote Bilby, "That would demean his stature as an industrial tycoon." When Paley arrived with Ralph Colin, Benny had gone off to a rehearsal, but Wasserman was ready to deal.

Niles Trammell had flown back to New York only hours earlier, summoned by Sarnoff, he said, to reconsider the tax question. He left behind the latest NBC contract, written by teams of lawyers over the previous three days. With Benny's permission, Wasserman offered the

NBC contract for CBS's signature. After a close reading, Paley and Colin pronounced themselves satisfied and signed it, changing NBC to CBS throughout the document.

It was by no means certain, however, that the Benny deal would pass muster in Washington. On November 24, *Variety* reported from Washington that Jack Benny "is likely to find he will not be allowed to take a capital gains tax cut but will have to pay the much larger personal income tax on his arrangement. Revenue Department's approval of the Amos 'n' Andy thing has had both public and private repercussions. . . . Within the secrecy of the Treasury Department itself there is understood to have been quite a ruckus over the approval given Freeman Gosden and Charles Correll to sell themselves and their show to CBS."

With the capital gains deal, CBS bought Benny's company; but the American Tobacco Company, Benny's sponsor, still held a five-year contract for his services as a performer. Vincent Riggio, the president of American Tobacco (he had taken over from the legendary George Washington Hill several years earlier) was thus entitled to specify where Benny would appear. The deal engineered by MCA was contingent on Riggio's approval of CBS as Benny's network.

Ben Duffy of BBD&O held firm in his opposition to any switch from NBC. He said he risked losing a substantial number of listeners because of the weaker collection of stations on CBS. Riggio felt compelled to follow Duffy's advice, especially since the tobacco chief was anxious about the capital gains flap. He and his board met in an all-day session on November 19 to consider the consequences of the CBS arrangement. "Riggio looks askance at his star radio salesman playing around with capital gains propositions," *Variety* reported afterwards.

But the old-time tobacco man had a strong bond with Paley, himself the son of a cigarmaker. Indeed, people who saw them together were struck by Riggio's similarity to Sam Paley. When Paley bypassed Duffy to call Riggio at his apartment, Riggio was receptive. All Paley wanted was a meeting where he could assemble all the participants from American Tobacco and BBD&O and make his case. Riggio agreed to convene the group the next day.

For all his earnestness, Paley failed to convince Duffy and his colleagues that a massive publicity blitz would ensure as many if not more listeners on CBS. They would only agree if Paley consented to pay American Tobacco $3,000 a week for every lost rating point for the rest of the company's contract with Benny. Paley was boxed in. To capture Benny he had to strike a deal with potential financial pitfalls. "Our neck was way out," Stanton recalled. "I was really scared we could not pull it off. Seven o'clock on Sunday had not been a hot time period for us and it was for

NBC." Even more worrisome, CBS could reach fewer homes at that hour because of NBC's stronger stations.

On November 26, CBS announced the Benny defection during a station break. The news sent shock waves through the broadcasting industry. "Getting Benny away from NBC seemed like getting Quebec away from Canada, so fixed had he been, and for so long, in the heaven of that richer and bigger network," wrote CBS radio dramatist Norman Corwin at the time.

Paley's persistence played an undeniable role in the Benny triumph. "If it had not been for my personal telephone call to Benny that night, I would not have been in Wasserman's office when Trammell of NBC had walked out," he said later. Technically, the boast was correct. But once again Paley could not share credit. It had been Manie Sacks, after all, who paved the way for that phone call and revived the deal when it was all but dead.

Paley also benefited from David Sarnoff's blind spot about the importance of talent. Trammell had been desperate to match the CBS deal. He had even gone before the RCA board. "We will lose major talent," he told them. "The deal might be repugnant to us, but there is nothing dishonest about it." But Sarnoff ultimately balked at using NBC's superior resources to counter Paley's raids. Beyond the tax questions—and given the rumblings from Washington, they were significant—Sarnoff believed that paying such sums to performers would set a bad precedent. It might, he felt, establish a star system that would give performers too much leverage over their network bosses.

"Leadership built over the years on a foundation of solid service cannot be snatched overnight by buying a few high-priced comedians," Sarnoff said at RCA's annual shareholders' meeting in 1949.

According to legend, ten days after the Benny deal captured the headlines, David Sarnoff called Paley. "Why did you do this to me, Bill?" Sarnoff supposedly asked. "I thought we had an agreement not to raid each other's talent." After a long pause, Paley is said to have replied, somewhat sheepishly, "I needed them." Paley denied making the comment, but Ike Levy said he was in Paley's office when the exchange took place.

The CBS chairman's response sounds utterly characteristic. CBS and NBC did have an agreement in the 1930s not to raid each other. But Paley violated that pact with his wooing of Major Bowes and others in 1936. Since then, raiding had become fairly routine. Immediately after the war, NBC picked off several promising CBS shows—"The Hit Parade," "Take It or Leave It," "Ozzie and Harriet." But the magnitude and boldness of

Paley's 1948 offensive was so great that Sarnoff could well have called him to account for it.

CBS used all its promotional savvy and an estimated $100,000 to hype the Benny debut on January 2, 1949. Benny was heard in guest spots on one CBS show after another. He even said a few words between halves of CBS's broadcast of the Rose Bowl game. CBS leaked the fact that Paley had taken out several insurance policies on Benny—including one for $150,000 with Equitable Life in Philadelphia—to protect the network's investment. Paley was said to be so concerned about his prize talent that he received daily bulletins from the West Coast on Benny's health and how many hours he slept the previous night.

Benny's initial ratings were even better than expected: 27.8 percent of the nation's homes with radio sets versus 24.1 when the show was on NBC. Stanton won a contest among CBS executives by guessing that Benny would score 27.2.

But the Bureau of Internal Revenue marred CBS's triumph with a ruling against Benny's capital gains deal. "An 'I told you so' atmosphere has permeated NBC headquarters," reported *Variety*. Even worse, after two months of initially high ratings, the audience for the Benny program slipped enough in March 1949 to compel CBS to pay American Tobacco a rebate of $34,000. Another rating slide during the last week in April cost the network an additional $15,000.

Still, the Benny glow was of immeasurable worth. Paley loved Benny and his show, and the comedian luxuriated in Paley's attention, even briefly introducing a character named "Mr. Paley" who appeared in several shows. Once Paley himself made a cameo when Benny did a sketch about a testimonial dinner. As "Mr. Paley" paused in his speech praising Benny, the comedian wisecracked about how the words failed to meet his high expectations. "It was so ridiculous," Paley said years later, "but it went off quite well."

After snatching Benny, Paley set his sights on Bing Crosby, who years earlier had left CBS for NBC and then ABC. When Crosby became available late in 1948, Paley paid $1 million for 25 percent of Crosby's company, which controlled his radio and film activities. In the process, CBS committed itself to finding a sponsor willing to sign an ironclad contract with Crosby for three years. Chesterfield agreed to pay $40,000 a week for Crosby's show—roughly $1.5 million for each thirty-nine-week season—and Paley had "the Groaner" in hand.

In the following months CBS plucked off even more NBC stars: George Burns and Gracie Allen, Edgar Bergen, and Red Skelton. As with Benny and Crosby, Burns's move to CBS took him back where he began in the early 1930s. It was no coincidence that all the deals were brokered by MCA or that George Burns was one of Jack Benny's closest friends.

Contrary to the mythology, none of these defectors tried the capital gains gambit. "Cap Gains Nipped by CBS-Benny Nix," reported *Variety*. Besides turning down the Benny deal, the Commissioner of Internal Revenue announced his intention to close the door to capital gains arrangements for the services of radio performers. In this new climate, performers were inclined to play it safe. ("Words were passed to 'lay off if you don't want to get into a D.C. jam,' " as *Variety* put it.) Benny was ultimately vindicated in a higher court, which ruled that performers could be corporations subject to the capital gains tax; but in the early months of 1949 no one could predict that outcome.

By March 1949 CBS Radio had nine of the top fifteen radio programs, and by the end of the year twelve of fifteen. For the first time in twenty years, CBS led in the audience ratings. Moreover, twenty-nine CBS-owned radio shows were fully sponsored. *Variety* called the achievement "Paley's Comet." Without a doubt, it was the biggest upheaval in broadcasting since Paley bought CBS in 1928.

Sarnoff responded by earmarking $1.5 million to develop some thirty new radio programs to replace NBC's losses. Opposite Jack Benny, NBC placed the popular bandleader and game show host Horace Heidt, with an amateur hour akin to Arthur Godfrey's. It bombed—though curiously enough, CBS later stole Heidt and tried him out in a television version in 1950. NBC sensibly locked in its biggest star, Bob Hope, with a fat contract, but the network never regained its leadership in radio.

Starting a program department to develop shows in house was one of the smartest moves Bill Paley ever made. "Truth to tell," Paley acknowledged privately, "I did not see the future very clearly. What I saw was stuck under my nose daily. We were second to NBC entertainment, and since I am combative by nature, this situation was intolerable. We were not masters of our own programming. And we did not own our own on-the-air talents. We were functionaries, middle men, not prime movers."

Likewise, the Paley Raids of 1948 and 1949 were a brilliant strategic maneuver. For an initial investment of less than $6 million to win over Gosden, Correll, Benny, and Crosby, Paley provoked a small stampede of other valuable personalities. In the space of five months he nearly wiped out NBC's roster of top talent. The raids displayed more vividly than ever Paley's persistence, his cunning, and his refusal to play by the book. They gave CBS a leadership position that meant greater profits and power.

Paley's postwar moves also signaled a shift away from prestigious, money-losing programs. Now that the networks bore the risks of producing costly programs, they felt compelled to think only in commercial terms, calculating which concepts and stars would produce the biggest audiences for their advertisers. The CBS department devoted to high-quality experimental drama withered. The network barely even tried to sell cultural and public affairs programs for sponsorship. The few remaining high-toned programs were shunted into less desirable time periods, while prime listening time overflowed with escapist entertainment.

The coming of television hastened the change. With higher production expenses, television programs had to score quickly to earn their keep. As one reporter noted after interviewing Frank Stanton in the late forties: "TV is radio's baby and right now the baby is biting papa's hand—and will eventually bite it off. The paradox of the situation is that the prime requisite for nursing TV into a healthy state—with the lure that it promises to pay off better than radio has—is a radio system that can carry the load. . . . The big reward for all this star stealing, Stanton estimates, will be a $6.6 million increase in gross business in 1949, with about $1 million more net." In fact, CBS in 1949 made $105.4 million in gross revenues—$7 million more than in 1948. But net income dropped from $5 million to $4.2 million, largely because of TV development costs.

No one felt the pain of the CBS transformation more poignantly than Norman Corwin, the celebrated radio dramatist. Corwin encountered the Paleys by chance in November 1948 on a transcontinental train ride from Pasadena to New York by way of Chicago. On the second evening of the trip, Paley invited Corwin to join him in the dining car. At that moment, Corwin knew his radio career had ended and a new era had begun: "You know," Paley said as he ate his salad, "you've done big things that are appreciated by us and by a special audience. But couldn't you write for a broader public? That's what we're going to need more and more. We've simply got to face up to the fact that we're in a commercial business, and it's getting tougher all the time. If our programs don't aim to reach as many of the 90 million radio sets in the country as we can possibly get to tune us in, why then we're not really making the best use of our talent, our time and our equipment."

As Corwin tried to absorb Paley's words, the CBS chairman said, without expression, "Jack Benny is coming over to us." He was letting Corwin in on a secret, for the announcement had not yet been made to the press, although *Variety* had been filled with rumors about the negotiations.

"A different Paley," Corwin mused. "War and the competition of NBC had apparently changed his thinking." Ten years earlier when Corwin arrived at CBS, the network had reserved blocks of hours every week for unsponsored programs that were created and produced under the rubric of "public service." In the printed rate schedule, a breakdown of the broadcasting week that every CBS salesman kept tucked in his coat pocket, such programs were blocked in green and bore the legend: "Reserved from sale." The Sunday afternoon concerts of the New York Philharmonic occupied this green zone, as did Corwin's programs.

While Corwin and Paley ate their dinner, Corwin thought it over: "The network, as its top men told me more than once, had never been interested in how my programs rated, for the shows were obviously never going to command majority audiences, and there was no thought of selling me to a sponsor. I was generally scheduled opposite Bob Hope, the highest rated program on the air—not as a sacrifice, not as a bone thrown to the dogs, but because all of us at CBS felt that Hope's and my audiences were mutually exclusive.

"The handwriting was on the wall, as far as radio was concerned. It was now spelled out in fresh ink, in Paley's hand. I knew what 'broader public' meant. I knew that to set out with the express aim of 'reaching as many sets as possible' would mean studying to write soap opera, or gags, or programs of towering innocuousness. Just how I was to command that broader public, Paley left to me. He was simply describing the new look."

Corwin returned to his seat, two cars behind the Paleys. He sat in the dark, aimlessly watching the distant lights and the blur of trackside trees. "Where the hell indeed was I?" he said to himself. "I had never written a stage play, a movie, a novel, a short story. I was a radiowright—a new species. And according to some critics, best of the breed. But it was clear now that my outlet, the far-flung and pervasive Columbia network, was no longer a Champs-Elysées down which I could walk, run or skip as I had done in the past. . . . I was on a train going east on no particular business, without portfolio, without a target . . . feeling uninspired, worn from the pace, sorry for myself, certain of the death of my medium, dull from Scotch, and unnecessary."

26

THE LEGEND of Paley's Comet is built on a misconception. Paley undertook the talent raids to strengthen radio, not to push into television. The raids were designed to establish him, at last, as the undisputed leader—in radio.

"I never heard Bill talk about using the stars for television at all," recalled Frank Stanton. "For him in those days it was all radio. His postwar idea was simply to get control of radio programming. He never talked about television. He didn't see the light until well after the early days. The odd thing is that he had an enormous love affair with Hollywood, and you would have thought television would have been the way to get into the action for him. But he didn't pick stars with any idea about leaping into television."

Indeed, a *Business Week* article written in the early fifties outlined Paley's plan: "CBS wanted to make sure radio audiences wouldn't go over to television by default. If CBS had the best entertainment and showmanship, it could keep a lot of its circulation *despite tv*." So intent was Paley on saving radio in the 1940s that he dispatched executives to make speeches, hoping, said one, "to slow down the progress of television, trying to indicate the virtues which were uniquely those of radio."

Paley knew television was coming. But as in the thirties, he wanted to delay its arrival as long as possible. "Bill did not want television," said Stanton. "He thought it would hurt radio. It was also a question of money, as far as he was concerned. He didn't see any profit in TV at all. Bill was concerned about the bottom line, that we couldn't afford television, that it was too costly." NBC's David Adams saw further calculation in Paley's attitude: "When TV was getting started, Bill Paley turned his back on it and thought there was money to be milked out of radio." When Stanton prepared his first big meeting in 1947 to discuss a five-year plan and budget for television, he urged Paley to attend. "We are talking about spending a lot of money and you ought to be there," said Stanton. But Paley begged off, claiming an overbooked schedule.

Paley credits himself with more vision than anyone noticed at the time. "I had a very strong feeling that television was right behind us and we started to think about how we could make the transition," he told one interviewer in the mid-1970s. "It became obvious to me at least that some of the important personalities in radio could become important personalities in television, so we made an extra drive to get associated with these important personalities."

This recollection crumbles on the record. Of the stars Paley stole in his famous raids, the only one CBS built into a durable top-rated television performer was Jack Benny. On television, "Amos 'n' Andy," although as popular as ever, was appallingly racist. Two years after its first appearance in June 1951, CBS ceased production under pressure from the National Association for the Advancement of Colored People. (CBS would continue to profit from "Amos 'n' Andy" until 1966, however, through the sale of reruns to local stations.) Looking back, Paley seemed perplexed about the network's loss of a program that he said was "more popular in black neighborhoods than it was anyplace else."

Although Edgar Bergen had made a successful appearance on a televised NBC variety show back in 1946, CBS did not move him to television until 1956. Even then, he lasted barely a year in prime time as a quiz show host. Later he was switched to daytime. Red Skelton made a hit on CBS Radio, but NBC grabbed him back and introduced him on television in 1951. He soared to fourth in the TV ratings. CBS recaptured Skelton in 1953, and he made the list of the top fifteen shows in 1955. Burns and Allen moved to television in 1950 and had a long run, although they failed to penetrate the top fifteen shows. Bing Crosby waited until 1951 before making his first guest appearance on television. But he hesitated to star in a weekly television series until 1964, when ABC cast him in a short-lived situation comedy.

Despite the TV failure of most of its purloined talent, CBS finally captured ten of the top fifteen prime-time television shows in 1955, supplanting NBC as the number-one network. CBS's biggest TV hits grew out of ideas and stars developed within its own programming department. "Our Miss Brooks," for example, made a seamless transition from radio to television.

In 1948, Ed Sullivan's famous television variety show, originally named "Toast of the Town," was the brainchild of Charlie Underhill, the soft-spoken, prematurely gray chief of programming for television at CBS. Sullivan, a celebrated columnist for the *New York Daily News,* had appeared on radio in a dime-a-dozen gossip show. Underhill tapped Sullivan to be master of ceremonies in a summer replacement show that the Ford Motor Company consented to sponsor.

Sullivan was an artless performer, with his high-pitched nasal voice, awkward gestures, bungled introductions, and peculiar grimaces. Paley objected immediately to Sullivan's gauche mannerisms and wanted to remove the show after the first week in June 1948. But he deferred to Underhill and the president of the television network, Jack Van Volkenburg. The CBS chairman bought their argument that if the show worked, it would fill an entire hour on Sunday night; moreover, with Sullivan's extensive show-business contacts, there would be an endless supply of new and varied talent. They were right. As time passed, Sullivan's odd chemistry caught the viewers—who perhaps felt sorry for his inept performances—and his show became a national institution.

Paley liked Arthur Godfrey even less on television than he had on radio. Godfrey made the jump early, in January 1949, by simply setting up a camera in his radio studio for a simultaneous radio and television broadcast. A second-rate musician and a hopelessly amateurish actor, he mugged for the camera. He sweated. He muffed his lines. But he was an informal, comfortable guest in the living room and his very lack of slickness contributed to his appeal. Much to Paley's surprise, Godfrey soon

had two top-rated television shows in prime time and one in daytime—
reaching as many as 80 million people a week.

Late in 1951, Jack Van Volkenburg arrived unannounced at Frank
Stanton's door. "I have a helluva piece of talent in my office," the CBS-
Television president said. "I need your authorization to sign him." Stanton
had an important luncheon appointment with a client and asked if he could
see the performer after lunch. "No," said Van Volkenburg. "It's Jackie
Gleason and he is drinking heavily and I'm afraid he's going to pass out."
Gleason's contract with the Dumont Network was about to expire, and
the comedian wanted to come to CBS. It would cost CBS at least $50,000
a week per show for thirteen weeks guaranteed—later raised to $66,175,
making it the network's most expensive show at the time. In other words,
CBS would have to pay Gleason more than a half million dollars even if it
could not sell the time to an advertiser.

"My God, what if we can't sell him?" exclaimed Stanton, who knew
that his small television network had only begun to run a modest profit.
Signing Gleason could push them back into the red. "The only way we
can get Gleason is this deal," said Van Volkenburg. Stanton had seen
Gleason's variety show, "Cavalcade of Stars," on Dumont during the
previous two years and he understood his star potential. "Okay," he said,
and went to lunch.

The deal was sealed without Paley, who was away from the office for
long stretches in those days. When he returned, he asked Stanton, "What's
new?" "We've signed a helluva talent, Jackie Gleason," Stanton replied.
"Who's he?" asked Paley. Stanton described the portly comedian's galaxy
of memorable characters such as Ralph Kramden, The Poor Soul, Reggie
Van Gleason III, and Joe the Bartender. "Who bought him?" Paley asked.
"We haven't sold him yet," Stanton said quietly. "I suppose if we don't
sell him we can pay him off," Paley said. "No," replied Stanton. "We
have to play him even if we don't sell him." "Who was so stupid to make
that deal!" Paley thundered.

For months CBS tried to sell the new Gleason show. No sponsor
came forward. Every time Paley met Stanton, he opened the conversation
with "Have you sold . . . what's the name of that guy?" Finally, only
weeks before the debut in September 1952, the head of CBS-Television
sales, William Hylan, sold the show in twenty-minute segments to three
different advertisers. A year later Jackie Gleason ranked in the top ten, and
by 1954 he was in second place.

When Gleason became the most watched man on television during
the 1950s, Paley gave him the store—starting with an $11 million deal for
two years that included a house in Peekskill, New York. During negotiations with Paley and Stanton, Gleason was usually so drunk he would

drop his head on the table and fall asleep before the entrée. But on the air, he was a winner, and Paley indulged him. When Gleason wanted to take the show to Miami so he could play golf every day, CBS financed the move, which included a private train to take Gleason and his cast to Florida in style.

Bill Paley adored Lucille Ball's radio show, "My Favorite Husband," but he nearly lost her in the switch to television. When CBS executive Harry Ackerman suggested that Lucy consider television, Lucy and her husband, Desi Arnaz, a Cuban bandleader, decided to set up a company to produce television programs on their own. Naturally, they wanted to share in the rights to any televised adaptation of "My Favorite Husband," which portrayed Lucy as the zany wife of a Midwestern banker. Lucy also wanted Desi to play her husband in the TV version. Ackerman conveyed their wishes to Paley, who turned them down, claiming that Lucy had worked in radio for a salary and could continue to do so in television. Paley was skeptical that viewers would accept a husband with a strong Latin accent, and he had little confidence that Desi could act.

To prevent Lucy from leaving CBS, Ackerman offered Arnaz a generous contract to star in a radio game show called "Win Your Vacation." After coaxing the show's host, Johnny Carson, to step aside, Ackerman revamped the show for Arnaz, calling it "Your Tropical Trip."

Lucy and Desi proceeded to develop a television situation comedy, "I Love Lucy," on their own, spending $5,000 to fund the pilot in 1951. The plot revolved around the antics of a harebrained housewife constantly scheming to show her husband, a Cuban bandleader, that she belonged in show business too.

Philip Morris bought the show through Milton Biouw of the Biouw advertising agency. "I have Lucy under lock and key for television," Biouw said when he called Frank Stanton one morning. Biouw was looking for the best possible time period and television station lineup for his client. "We'll put it on Monday night," said Stanton impulsively. "You don't have any stations," said Biouw. At the time many cities had only one television station, an NBC affiliate. When Stanton called, pleading for Monday from 9:00 to 9:30 P.M., he managed to pull together a string of strong stations that he offered Biouw in a handshake deal that afternoon.

The following autumn "I Love Lucy" zoomed into third place in the ratings; by October 1952 it held first place. For more than two decades Lucille Ball would triumph as the screwball queen of television comedy— wide-eyed, wacky, innocent, even poignant. She specialized in hilarious sight gags: brawling in a vat of unpressed wine grapes; getting pinned to a kitchen cabinet by a giant loaf of bread; frantically dipping chocolates on an accelerating assembly line. Lucy's shows were always inventive, and somehow believable.

According to Paley's account, Lucy's TV show was hatched one day in 1950 when he met with the actress. Paley delighted in recounting how she lamented that her marriage couldn't last if Desi continued to travel as a bandleader while she performed on television without him. She told Paley she wanted to have a baby, which would not be possible if she were kept apart from her husband. If CBS did not include Desi in her show, she would refuse to do it. "Under duress," Paley recalled, "I said we'd have to find a place for him, 'We'll put him into your show.' " At that moment, said Paley, he directed Lucy's writers to come up with a television format.

While that meeting doubtless took place, Paley's role doesn't square with the recollections of others involved. Lucy and Desi had had to scrape together their own money to produce a sample show; Ackerman held Lucy and Desi in CBS Radio until Paley saw their filmed presentation; Stanton worked fast to prevent NBC from taking the series away. Because Lucy and Desi had developed the show themselves, their new company, Desilu, held complete financial control—far more than they would have had if Paley had accepted their original bid for a piece of the action.

The legend that Paley had a large hand in developing "I Love Lucy" and other CBS-Television shows was the handiwork of CBS's masterful public relations machine. The press gobbled up everything the CBS flacks threw its way. *Variety* built up the Paley myth in the late 1940s, often crediting him with theories that his colleagues never heard him mention. The network PR department succeeded in portraying him as a broadcasting superman. After CBS signed Crosby, for example, *Variety* announced: "Paley and his missus blew the coast for his Manhattan citadel, where more spectacular deals are being brewed."

"As any executive in his position would, Bill Paley took credit for starting Lucy—as if he did the work," said Harry Ackerman. "He did make the decision to go ahead. But I can't think of his discovering a piece of talent or buying an idea." The hoopla generated by CBS's programming triumph over NBC produced headlines about Paley, and before long the boss apparently came to believe his own press clippings.

27

T HE FIERCEST FIGHT for dominance in the early days of television involved the technology for color pictures on the home screen. Spanning more than a decade, the struggle was interrupted twice by war and punctuated by unpredictable rulings from the Federal Communications Commission. Mingling ego, jealousy, pride, and greed, the effort to control color television threw David Sarnoff and William Paley into a strange role reversal, each adopting the other's tactics. When the end came in the mid-1950s, NBC and CBS had paid dearly, both financially and in lost man-hours. It would take still another decade before color television sets would be commonplace in America's living rooms.

In 1940, twenty-five years before color television came into its own, CBS had a color technology ready to go. It was the inspiration of CBS's resident inventor, Peter Goldmark, then thirty-three years old.

The slender, intense Goldmark, son of a hatmaker father and a musician, had been intrigued by the moving image since his boyhood in Budapest. When young Peter wasn't practicing on the piano and cello, he was building makeshift film projectors and simple radio receivers.

The family moved to Vienna in the 1920s, where Goldmark studied physics at the Physical Institute. In 1926 he bought his first do-it-yourself television kit. It cost the equivalent of $22 and had a screen one inch high and half an inch wide in front of a disc pierced with hundreds of holes. When the disc was spun rapidly behind an image caught by a camera lens, light filtered through the holes and was changed into electronic impulses by a photoelectric cell. A synchronized receiving disc filtered the light and dark impulses onto the viewing screen, creating a rough image. Goldmark patiently waited until after midnight when the BBC broadcast an experimental video signal: "My first televised image, a dancer . . . flickered nervously because the pictures were transmitted at too slow a rate for proper reception. . . . Here was a moving picture transported by electric energy through space from London to Vienna."

After completing his studies, Goldmark moved to England, where he helped set up a television department for a radio company in Cambridge. But the Depression brought his efforts to a halt and he emigrated to New

York in 1933. Like Frank Stanton, who would later become his chief promoter and protector, Goldmark wrote letters to the networks offering his services. Late in 1935, Kesten responded after reading an article on television by Goldmark. He offered the twenty-eight-year-old a job developing the medium at CBS for $100 a week. Goldmark came aboard in January 1936—just three months after Stanton's arrival.

Goldmark was attractive, glib, and gifted. (In the late 1940s he would develop the LP record, CBS's greatest technological triumph, which brought in tens of millions of dollars.) He was also an effective advocate. Once described as "part child and part tyrant," he was passionate, and Paley responded to passion. Goldmark's vision and charisma prompted Kesten, Stanton, and Paley to place their faith in his ability to develop a color technology, which they saw as a relatively inexpensive way to catapult CBS to prominence in broadcasting.

Goldmark became a true believer in March 1940, when he saw his first color film—the extravagant *Gone With the Wind*. Inspired, Goldmark started to tinker in CBS's tiny laboratory on the tenth floor of 485 Madison Avenue. With Kesten's encouragement, he developed a rudimentary color system that he showed to Lawrence Fly, chairman of the FCC, the following September to stir up interest at the regulatory agency.

Goldmark's model for color television was in part an adaptation of the old mechanical spinning disc devised for black and white television in the 1920s. But unlike the outmoded black and white disc system, Goldmark's approach melded the wheel with electronic transmission and reception. On the screen, the system delivered remarkably true colors.

Goldmark attached green, red, and blue filters to a disc driven by a motor inside the camera that captured the video image. This wheel sent out the colors in sequence—first red, then blue, then green—in what became known as the field sequential system. These were received in the television set, where they were blended through another revolving color filter to form the entire spectrum. Goldmark recognized that the wheels were an interim step; they would be replaced by color tubes in the television set and the camera as soon as those components could be developed.

In December 1940, Goldmark unveiled his first color images—a series of slides of a Spanish dancer on a TV screen three inches wide—to Paley, Kesten, and Klauber. All three urged the inventor to continue his work. The following June the FCC permitted CBS to broadcast in color on an experimental basis. Six months later the experiments were abruptly suspended after Pearl Harbor.

In 1944 Goldmark approached Kesten again for permission to develop a color system with even greater clarity. Instead of transmitting in the VHF—very high frequency—portion of the broadcasting spectrum (where black and white television was broadcast), Goldmark proposed designing CBS color for the UHF—the ultra high frequency portion. Clearer pictures could be achieved in UHF, which also had space for seventy channels (14 through 83) as opposed to twelve in VHF (2 through 13). Kesten gave the green light, and Stanton enthusiastically backed him up.

"I absolutely believed in Goldmark's color system," Stanton recalled decades later. "It worked beautifully. Peter wanted it in UHF for greater fidelity to picture quality. It would be superior to picture quality of today . . . so what Kesten was embracing in Peter was not only color but higher-quality color that would have given a better presentation in the home."

By the time Paley returned from the war in the autumn of 1945, CBS had 120 people working on color in its labs, including 50 engineers, scientists, and physicists. Their workplace occupied two floors of the CBS Building and was elaborate enough to include a glass-blowing facility and machine shop.

That winter, Kesten got Goldmark and Paley together for their first lengthy discussion about Goldmark's system. Paley listened "with an air of mixed impatience and interest and quickly told us that he loved the idea," said Goldmark. "I would discover that love and hate with Paley were emotions that quickly followed one another. . . . Paley, of course, could use a blockbuster device. Competition was then intense for audiences." Goldmark did not understand, however, that, according to Stanton, "It was fashionable to be interested in television but not to be in it to where it was going to cost you a lot of money. That was part of the attitude of the period." Prodded by Kesten, Paley told Goldmark to press ahead.

CBS color would not work on existing television sets, but in 1945 only six thousand or so sets were in use—mostly in bars. The prospect of consumer resistance seemed unlikely, and CBS color was there for the asking. It was simple, and significantly less expensive to produce than other possible systems. Paley understood that CBS stood to make money —perhaps as much as $50 million in royalties—by licensing other companies to manufacture TV sets using the new CBS system. For a relatively small investment of $2 million, CBS could not only cash in but be seen as the leader in an exciting new technology. An added bonus for Paley was the chance to trump Sarnoff at his own game.

But by Paley's later account, he was skeptical about color, which was opposed by manufacturers of black and white sets. He only concurred with Kesten and Goldmark, he said, to avoid undermining the work of his subordinates.

Paley's excuse was a predictable reflection of his chronic ambivalence about television. His concern about the high cost of shifting from audio to video gave CBS a curiously schizophrenic character in the late forties and early fifties. Mighty radio and infant television inhabited different worlds at the company. In those days CBS advertising salesmen carried calling cards engraved "Sales-CBS Radio" with "Television" typed underneath as an afterthought. Two separate program planning boards met at 485 Madison Avenue—on Tuesday for radio, on Thursday for television. Until the early 1950s, Paley didn't attend the television planning board.

"Television wasn't on Bill's plate," said Stanton. "It was more electronics and stations than programming in the beginning, and someone had to look after it." Stanton had grown passionate about television's possibilities during the war as he watched the reactions of visitors to CBS's experimental station in Grand Central Terminal. When Kesten retired in August 1946, Stanton became the new CBS man "in charge of the future." Thus Paley continued to rule radio and Stanton oversaw television.

After careful study during World War II, Stanton made plans to build CBS television stations in Boston, Los Angeles, San Francisco, and Chicago—prime markets with enormous room for growth. Along with the CBS station in New York, these cities would form the core of a television network. Stanton applied to the FCC for licenses in the four key cities and staked out properties for CBS studios and transmitters.

But Stanton's effort to develop a television network foundered on his simultaneous quest for color. In September 1946, CBS asked the FCC for permission to broadcast its color system commercially. That month Rosell Hyde, a member of the FCC, confided to Stanton that his fellow commissioners were puzzled by CBS's apparent mixed message—promoting a new color system and at the same time applying for black and white television station licenses. Hyde advised Stanton that dropping its license applications would help CBS's campaign to have its color system accepted. He assured the CBS president that as soon as color was approved, CBS could easily renew its request for station licenses. Unwisely, Stanton acceded to Hyde's suggestion and withdrew the black and white applications.

By the time Frank Stanton testified on behalf of CBS's color system in December 1946, the network had conducted some 200 demonstrations in a fifth-floor suite at 485 Madison Avenue for more than 2,700 representatives of government, industry, and advertising. His testimony was compelling. The CBS colors were bright and true in sample telecasts shown to federal regulators. Network officials had cause for optimism. They eagerly awaited the FCC ruling, which was due the following March. To their utter amazement, the FCC vetoed CBS's request. No color system, in the view of the commissioners, was yet ready for approval.

The man behind CBS's stunning setback was Paley's arch rival, David Sarnoff. Sarnoff, the great technical visionary of broadcasting, was using every resource at his disposal to block a new technology. CBS's bold move to bypass black and white television and plunge headlong into color threatened his master plan for developing television in America. The stakes were huge: by the end of World War II, Sarnoff had spent $50 million to develop his own all-electronic system for black and white television.

In 1940 Sarnoff had been well aware of Goldmark's experiments with a field sequential system for color transmission. But he could not believe that anyone would take Goldmark seriously. Sarnoff was impressed neither by the simplicity of Goldmark's approach nor by his use of electronic components. All Sarnoff could see was what he regarded as an outmoded design that could only impede his own plans.

During one of his occasional lunches with William Paley that year, he warned the CBS chairman that he was getting in over his head by tackling color. "Forget it," said Sarnoff with his customary bluntness. Then he disclosed that his scientists had tested what he considered the only workable color technology: an electronic scanner that would transmit dots of color simultaneously rather than in sequence. But the color and the fidelity had been murky. "True" color, said Sarnoff, was still years away. Paley chose to ignore Sarnoff's patronizing advice.

Because of the wartime ban on set manufacturing, Sarnoff had to postpone his mass introduction of black and white television. The FCC opened the door again in 1945 by authorizing twelve VHF channels for black and white broadcasting and approving the UHF spectrum for color experimentation. During the war years Sarnoff had thought about television incessantly, meeting at every turn with European broadcasters. He was convinced, according to Kenneth Bilby, his biographer, "that television would reshape life in the century's second half to a point never attained by print or voice communications. . . . He saw the new medium in life transforming terms. . . . He saw himself as destiny's instrument."

But Sarnoff's timetable for television had more to do with financial rewards than lofty notions of destiny. He wanted first to saturate the market with his black and white sets, then years later to introduce his sophisticated all-electronic color sets. Under the RCA system, existing black and white sets could receive both color and black and white images. Eventually consumers would want to buy the new RCA color sets, but in the meantime they would not have to throw away their black and white sets as they would if CBS prevailed. By 1945, however, RCA's color technology was as primitive as it had been in 1940. Sarnoff had made no effort to refine it.

As CBS made its first postwar moves toward color, Sarnoff focused entirely on getting RCA black and white televisions into as many homes as possible. The end of World War II was an ideal launching time for television. The postwar economy was humming, and with more products coming off the assembly lines, advertisers looked to television as a powerful way of reaching consumers. Those consumers—young couples with their growing families—were drawn to television as a magical form of entertainment in the home.

The first RCA sets appeared in stores in September 1946. Their small, round-cornered screens were fitted into huge cabinets, often of mahogany or walnut. By the end of the year Sarnoff had sold ten thousand sets for $385 apiece ($2,566 in 1990 dollars).

Whereas CBS dropped its applications for key television licenses while waiting for the FCC color ruling, NBC concentrated on building a television network. As its nucleus, Sarnoff authorized construction of RCA-owned stations in Los Angeles, Chicago, and Cleveland. He constantly urged NBC's radio affiliates to invest in the future by building television stations. "You are the generation that created radio," he told them in a stirring speech during the late 1940s on the boardwalk in Atlantic City, "and in doing so you have provided an enormous service to the country, changed the culture of the United States and you did very well by yourselves. You enriched yourselves. . . . Seldom is it given to one generation to have such an opportunity to rise again, but now before you is that opportunity in television—a larger, richer, broader opportunity than ever existed in radio."

CBS was utterly unprepared for Sarnoff's black and white invasion. Network officials could only hope that approval of CBS color by the FCC would stop Sarnoff in his tracks. But Sarnoff had the CBS leaders outflanked in the realm they thought they knew best: publicity. Concerned over a growing positive perception of CBS color in the press, Sarnoff launched an aggressive negative campaign in 1946.

He complained about the inferiority of the CBS color system, calling it a "horse and buggy" technology. In countless speeches and press conferences he claimed that CBS color could only be seen on a small screen (in fact, the CBS system could work on a large screen, as soon as a larger picture tube was developed). Sarnoff also emphasized that the incompatibility of CBS would render black and white sets in the American home worthless.

Sarnoff was backed up by his fellow manufacturers, who were eager to cash in on the black and white boom. Allen B. Dumont, a pioneering television set manufacturer and owner of important early television stations in Chicago, Pittsburgh, and Washington, D.C., came up with a vivid symbol of CBS's faulty technology: a wheel six feet in diameter that he displayed during an FCC hearing to show what would be needed to see CBS color on a large screen. "It was phony," recalled Frank Stanton, "but that didn't matter. The damage was done."

It may be that Sarnoff had planted sufficient seeds of doubt among the FCC commissioners to explain their decision in March 1947 against CBS color. But the RCA chief also appeared to benefit from a special pleading inside the commission as well.

The following autumn, the chairman of the FCC, Charles Denny, moved to RCA as a vice-president. "It smelled," said Stanton, who was given the impression by NBC president Niles Trammell that Sarnoff had offered Denny the job as a quid pro quo. The outcry over the apparent conflict of interest prompted Congress to amend the Communications Act several years later to prevent any FCC commissioner from working for a broadcaster for a year after resigning.

In 1947 black and white television began to explode with sales of 179,000; the following year sales soared to one million. At the end of 1948, David Sarnoff and Allen Dumont issued glowing New Year's predictions in *Variety* about the "terrific momentum" for television in the year ahead. In 1949, RCA introduced a new ten-inch table model for $269.50, and more than 2 million were sold.

CBS meanwhile struggled to catch up. It trimmed its color research and scrambled to reapply for VHF stations in San Francisco, Boston, and Chicago. Early in 1948 Stanton expanded CBS's black and white television broadcasts from twenty hours over five days a week to thirty-eight hours over seven days a week—virtually all of it live—and ordered construction of two 700,000-cubic-foot television studios to transmit programming from Manhattan's Grand Central Station.

The following September the FCC dealt CBS yet another blow. Inundated with applications for competing frequencies, the commission froze the licensing and building of new television stations. CBS's hastily submitted reapplications were caught in the huge backlog. The company was left with just one company-owned station in New York and a short string of television affiliates. Forty-nine television stations were then operating around the country, most of them allied with NBC. The prospects for television at CBS looked grim indeed.

While CBS had its hands tied, NBC operated a thriving television network. Week after week, against feeble competition, NBC captured nine out of the top ten television programs. "CBS could count on only New York, which is why I had to scramble for 'I Love Lucy,' " explained Stanton. Indeed, much of Stanton's time during those years was consumed by scrounging for affiliates and trying to find stations for CBS to buy.

At first he bought part interest in several stations owned by newspapers in Washington, Los Angeles, San Francisco, and Minneapolis to establish some strategic footholds. Late in 1950 he paid $334,000 to buy KTSL in Los Angeles at a sheriff's sale of the estate of Paley's old friend Don Lee. CBS renamed the station KNXT.

During this period Paley clung to the belief that radio was CBS's best hope. But time was proving him wrong. Network radio hit its peak in ratings and advertising sales in 1948. It then began to decline as television caught on, and sponsors and stars fled to the new medium. For a while, Paley was able to counter this trend by exploiting the 1948 talent raids. CBS Radio advertising revenue actually continued to grow until 1950. By 1951 *Variety* was calling it a "bargain basement medium." Everyone seemed to recognize that network radio was dying a slow death—everyone, that is, except Bill Paley.

28

AMID ITS SETBACKS in television, CBS managed to pull off a technological triumph that rankled David Sarnoff for years: the development of the long-playing record. Shortly after VJ-Day in 1945, Peter Goldmark had begun to wonder whether several existing technologies could be combined in a new way to make listening to recorded music more enjoyable. He conceived of slowing down the speed, from 78 revolutions per minute to 33⅓, and increasing the number of grooves in the record from eighty to more than two hundred. He used discs made of Vinylite instead of brittle and heavy shellac, and increased fidelity with a lightweight pickup arm and small stylus devised by an unsung CBS engineer named William Bachman. Instead of four minutes of sound, Goldmark designed the new records to run for at least twenty-five minutes on each side.

By the end of 1945, Paul Kesten had approved Goldmark's plan for developing the system at a cost of $100,000. Unknown to Goldmark, Kesten had to lean on a reluctant Bill Paley to spring the funds. "The LP," said John Hammond, a longtime CBS Records executive, "was done without Bill Paley. Either he didn't understand it or didn't see the future in it."

Under tight security in CBS's tenth-floor laboratory, Goldmark supervised experiments to perfect the long-playing record. When Stanton took over supervision of the CBS labs, he continued financing the experiments out of corporate funds. Paley's only awareness of Goldmark's work was through Stanton's barebones briefings.

Finally, in the spring of 1948, Stanton invited Sarnoff for lunch to show him CBS's innovation. Stanton set up an RCA LC-1 professional speaker in his office; he wanted superior sound for the LP, and to flatter Sarnoff, he made certain the speaker was the General's brand. Atop the speaker was Goldmark's prototype LP turntable. As Stanton and Sarnoff walked into Stanton's office for coffee and cigars, the turntable was already spinning. Sarnoff watched Stanton walk over to the turntable and drop the stylus onto the record. Biting off the end of his cigar, Sarnoff listened intently. The RCA chairman tried to make light of CBS's achievement by noting that his company had already produced 33⅓ rpm records. When Stanton told him this record could play twice as long as RCA's, Sarnoff became visibly upset.

"I can't believe little Columbia Graphophone invented this without my knowing about it," said Sarnoff, trying to belittle CBS Records by using its original corporate name. Stanton then offered to share the CBS technology with RCA. His maneuver was partly selfish: he wanted to avoid a fight as draining as the color television battle. "We would want to pay our way," said Sarnoff. Stanton explained that royalty payments were unnecessary, since the LP combined preexisting elements that had been refined and did not require a patent. Stanton's only request was that CBS be permitted to announce the new long-playing record twenty-four hours ahead of RCA in order to receive credit for its development.

Stanton reported to Paley that Sarnoff seemed genuinely interested in the technology. But Paley was lukewarm about it. According to Goldmark, Paley thought that only classical music connoisseurs would be interested in longer-playing records. He wondered where the profit would be with such a small audience. But he liked the idea of sharing the technology with RCA to cut the risk. To prod Sarnoff into joining forces, Stanton arranged a formal demonstration of the LP at CBS.

Sarnoff arrived at CBS with a group of sixteen engineers. They crowded into the paneled boardroom with Paley, Stanton, Goldmark, and an assortment of other CBS executives and engineers. Paley demonstrated the 33⅓ record juxtaposed with an old 78. The difference in clarity alone was dramatic. Sarnoff congratulated Paley.

Though clearly impressed, Sarnoff said he needed more time to consider CBS's invitation to join in making and selling the LP. Paley knew CBS had a winner, and he enthusiastically embraced the LP. On June 21, 1948, CBS unveiled its new product at a press conference. Later that year Sarnoff announced that RCA would go with its own innovation, a small

45 rpm record, instead. He was too proud to accept that CBS had devised a superior technology. Two years after that, RCA adopted the LP as well.

As usual, Paley's memory of his role in the LP contradicted the accounts of others. He never mentioned his misgivings about a limited market. And Paley said that he had been the one to preview the LP over lunch for General Sarnoff two days before the demonstration in the CBS boardroom. Paley may have played the LP for Sarnoff on his own, but Stanton had been there first.

Decades later, Stanton took emphatic pride in his guidance of the LP: "I caused it to be taken from a glimmer in Goldmark's eye to the finished product." Echoing John Hammond, he added: "Bill was pleased with the LP but he had no role in its development. He stepped in at the very last minute." At the time, however, Stanton politely drew back, declining to seek rightful credit for his role. A move of that sort would only antagonize Paley.

Back in favor at CBS because of the LP, Goldmark pressed ahead with color television. During 1948 he worked behind the scenes developing a new CBS color system—this time in the VHF band—to utilize existing black and white sets with special converters. When he invited the FCC commissioners to see his latest breakthrough, he succeeded in stirring their interest.

In 1949 the FCC reopened hearings on color broadcasting. CBS's converter system—a $50 adapter and a $100 device to fit in front of the screen—was awkward at best. Yet in October 1950, after nearly a year of hearings and 11,718 pages of testimony, the FCC approved the system. "Paley the impatient anti-technologist found himself with an exclusive franchise in a device made by the latest technological research," as Goldmark put it.

The commissioners concluded that the RCA system, with its inferior color and picture quality, had barely progressed in four years. Even Sarnoff had to admit that on his system "the monkeys were green, the bananas were blue, and everyone had a good laugh." The FCC was won over by CBS's natural colors—especially the flesh tones—and clear pictures. The commissioners felt that the system's quality and simplicity outweighed the incompatibility and relatively small picture size.

So, just as CBS's radio revenues were beginning to dive—in 1951 the network would be forced to cut some of its advertising rates for the first time—the company seemed poised to push its color system against RCA. Stanton went on the offensive. Speaking on CBS Radio, he accused the network's critics of making misleading statements about the so-called mechanical nature of the CBS color.

"It would be difficult to find a more negative triumph . . . a championship dive with no water in the pool," wrote *Fortune* magazine of the FCC decision. By 1950 Americans owned more than 3 million black and white television sets. RCA and nearly all the other manufacturers vowed to continue producing televisions using RCA's black and white system. They refused to make either CBS color sets or adapters for black and white sets. The only exceptions were a handful of small firms—Tele-tone, Celomat, Muntz, and Belmont—who joined forces with CBS.

Sarnoff sued the FCC, contending that its order "contravened" the opinions of industry experts and threatened the $2 billion black and white television industry. In March 1951, Paley, Stanton, and Goldmark found themselves seated in the paneled chambers of the U.S. Supreme Court. Directly in front of them were Sarnoff and his executives. As the arguments proceeded, Sarnoff turned to Paley and said, "Bill, we could have avoided this headache if I had hired Peter in the first place." The following May the Supreme Court let the FCC decision stand.

On June 25, 1951, CBS presented a "gala premiere" of its first commercial colorcast, starring Arthur Godfrey, Ed Sullivan, Faye Emerson, and Patty Painter, "Miss CBS Color." With a characteristic CBS nod to class, George Balanchine's New York City Ballet performed Ravel's *La Valse*. Bill Paley and Frank Stanton appeared, and so did Wayne Coy, the chairman of the FCC. Throwing impartiality to the wind, Coy praised the "hour of triumph" for CBS color. Trouble was, only twenty-five television sets (out of 10 million in the country) were equipped to watch CBS.

Ten days earlier CBS had taken a risky step intended to rectify that imbalance. The company agreed to buy the Hytron Radio and Electronics Corporation of Salem, Massachusetts, a manufacturer of television sets as well as tube components for radios and televisions. Instead of cash, CBS gave Hytron $18 million of CBS stock—620,000 shares, or 26 percent of CBS's total holdings. (Paley's share at the time was 13.3 percent). Hytron's owners, two brothers named Bruce and Lloyd Coffin, were invited to sit on the CBS board. Lloyd put people off with his high collars and taciturn manner; the more casual and loquacious Bruce spoke for them both.

Bill Paley has always said that the success of his first acquisition, CBS Records, nudged him into television set manufacturing. If CBS could diversify so effectively once, why not try another arena outside the government-regulated realm of broadcasting? "Electronics," Paley bragged at the time, "is more dynamic than oil."

Peter Goldmark called the move Paley's "secret ambition. . . . Despite his jet set executive veneer, Paley secretly admired Sarnoff's propensity for empire building, his Horatio Alger adeptness in creating an industry."

Frank Stanton attributed Paley's motive more to a wish to best Sarnoff on all fronts, "to be king of the hill." At CBS, said Stanton, the talk turned to manufacturing "because we thought having a manufacturing arm was part of being a broadcaster. That's what RCA had, and we had a monkey-see-monkey-do attitude." It had not escaped CBS's notice that RCA had the luxury of drawing on profits from its radio and television manufacturing to plow into television programming, while CBS had to finance its television development entirely from CBS Radio profits.

Paley always disavowed any connection between the CBS interest in Hytron and the FCC's approval of CBS color in October 1950. The timing, Paley insisted, was "coincidence." Stanton, however, conceded that the FCC decision was "part of the environment. There is no question it was part of the mix that influenced us." Indeed, with the major set manufacturers arrayed against CBS, the only hope—albeit slender—for developing CBS color lay in making sets with the CBS name.

Stanton had been keen on set manufacturing from the start. He wanted to buy the holdings of Allen Dumont, who owned a top-quality television manufacturing company as well as three strong television stations. Stanton even took Paley on a tour of Dumont's plant in New Jersey. But Paley was uncomfortable with Dumont, a chilly character with few social graces.

A Wall Street investment house brought Hytron to Paley's attention, pushing the company as an inexpensive way to enter the television set business. Paley and Stanton assigned Goldmark and Adrian Murphy, then head of CBS Television, to investigate. The two CBS officials returned with an enthusiastic report. They cautioned, however, that neither Hytron's television sets nor its vacuum tubes were first-rate. Goldmark expressed confidence that by using CBS's staff of engineers, Hytron could turn out a better product. Both Paley and Stanton believed that CBS's promotional flair and the magical CBS name could contribute to the product's success. "I went along with Hytron because I thought we could turn it around," said Stanton.

Once CBS got into the venture, however, Paley balked at approving a large enough budget for research and development. "Bill's fundamental mistake was that he only went halfway," said Stanton. "He saw an opportunity to make a modest operation into a big thing. But he wouldn't accept that it took money—probably double the price of the acquisition—if we were going to be in the big leagues. Everyone else was doing much better work. I still think that with enough capital we could have become an important factor."

Looking back, Paley would explain Hytron away by saying, "We didn't know very much about the manufacturing business, and much more importantly, we didn't care about it, you know, it wasn't our cup of tea." Yet Bill Paley cared deeply about Hytron in the early months. He and Stanton traveled out to Hytron's Long Island City plant in Paley's limousine. They fussed over designs for knobs and dials, and the finishes and styles of cabinets on the forthcoming CBS-Columbia television line.

Paley could not grasp the idea of lead-time in manufacturing a physical product. Final decisions on the design of products sometimes had to be made a year in advance; Paley's experience in radio had narrowed his time horizon to that of a four-year-old. He was accustomed to ordering last-minute changes in shows as the actors walked through the studio door, and felt uncomfortable in a business that left no time for such improvisations. As Goldmark said later, "Paley was not programmed for a long-term investment. He was an impatient man."

While Paley and Stanton fiddled with knobs and bezels, David Sarnoff prodded his engineers to work eighteen-hour days, seven days a week, perfecting an electronic RCA color system to present to the FCC. On July 13, 1951, he demonstrated the result in public—to great acclaim. Both Paley and Stanton attended the demonstration. Afterwards Paley told friends that he was impressed by the "tremendous improvement" of the RCA system, although he considered CBS color to be superior. But the men at the top of CBS knew their technology faced a significant threat.

In the fall of 1951—more than a year after the United States entered the Korean War—the federal government asked manufacturers to stop producing color television sets on the grounds that they used materials needed for the war. CBS was thus prevented from launching twenty hours a week of color telecasts in October and thwarted in its very reason for purchasing Hytron—the production of color television sets.

The suspension saved CBS from unleashing a full-scale enterprise based on its increasingly outmoded color technology. Had CBS gone forward, it would have had to produce 1 million color sets and absorb losses of at least $100 per set for an indefinite period. "It was the luckiest thing in the world," Stanton would say years later. "It was a graceful way of getting out of color manufacturing."

RCA took advantage of the hiatus by continuing to pour black and white sets into the market while fine-tuning its color system. CBS tried a pathetic counterpunch by pushing a line of second-rate black and white sets. It was too little, too late. RCA and other entrenched companies had a virtual lock on the market.

The obvious inferiority of the CBS sets enraged Paley. "I thought everybody concerned, right from the beginning, had agreed with the principle that CBS-Columbia television receivers were to be designed to match the best in the field," he carped in a long memo to Stanton late in 1951. Paley was suffering from the convenient amnesia of the powerful. He and Stanton had known going in that Hytron's sets were not top-line. The Coffin brothers were tightfisted New Englanders who wouldn't waste their money on research. Their method was to wait until someone else introduced a product. If it worked well, the Coffins would copy it and undercut its price.

Increasingly, Paley turned his venom on the Coffin brothers for selling him a bill of goods. During one meeting in a St. Regis conference room, Paley grew agitated listening to bleak sales reports from the Hytron executives. "You want it back. Buy it back," he snapped to Bruce Coffin. By 1953 Paley had tossed the Coffin brothers off the CBS board.

In March 1953 the government lifted its ban on manufacturing color TV sets. At that moment, 23 million black and white television sets were in use. Within weeks, Stanton announced that faced with such overwhelming numbers, CBS would scuttle its plans to develop color television. "The boat," said Stanton, "had sailed." The following December the FCC fixed the much-improved RCA system as the color standard.

That same year, however, CBS saw its first profit from the television network that Frank Stanton had assembled piece by piece. After buying the Los Angeles station late in 1950, Stanton coaxed Paley in March 1951 into offering $28 million to buy ABC. The scheme—conceived by Stanton while waiting for a plane at Chicago's Midway Airport, and approved enthusiastically by Paley during an hour-long phone call the next morning —was intended to give CBS control of ABC's three television stations in Chicago, Detroit, and San Francisco. CBS would then resell ABC's stations in New York and Los Angeles as well as its radio and television networks for $20 million.

Stanton and Paley met with Edward Noble, chairman of ABC, in early April to discuss the proposed transaction. But the FCC hinted at its disapproval of the deal to Stanton; so CBS bowed out and ABC was sold instead to United Paramount, which owned a chain of movie theaters as well as a Chicago television station. In a complicated sleight-of-hand, CBS ended up paying $6 million for Paramount's Chicago station as part of the deal.

The negotiations leading to CBS's purchase of a Chicago outlet created bad blood between Paley and Leonard Goldenson, the president of United Paramount who would become chairman of ABC. Shortly after the ABC-CBS deal fell apart, Stanton arranged a meeting in Ed Noble's suite at the Waldorf-Astoria. Paley was there, as was Ralph Colin. CBS knew that once United Paramount and ABC got together, they would have to dispose of one of their Chicago stations. After analyzing the market, Stanton recognized that the Paramount outlet was more desirable. In the five-and-a-half-hour meeting with Noble, he made CBS's preference clear and Noble agreed to let CBS have Paramount's station for $5 million.

When Goldenson heard of Noble's pledge, he exploded. "Are you out of your mind?" he exclaimed. "By what right can you do that?" An imperious man, Noble had no doubt he was within his rights. Goldenson told CBS that the deal was off unless the price was raised to $10 million.

Two weeks later, Noble held another meeting with the CBS executives in his Waldorf suite, this time with Goldenson and his attorneys on hand. Paley, Stanton, and Colin heatedly objected to Goldenson's tactics. Finally, CBS consented to raise the price for the Paramount station to $6 million, and Noble agreed to cut his price for ABC to $24.5 million. As a measure of CBS's lingering distrust, Colin went into an adjoining room and drafted their agreement on the back of an envelope. According to Stanton, Paley felt for years that Goldenson tried to welch on a deal.

Paley places himself front and center in his account of this crucial transaction. He claimed that he was the one who struck the deal with Noble for the Paramount station. Later, when the forces from CBS met with Goldenson over the disputed price, Paley recalled "raising hell" and forcing Goldenson to take $6 million.

To the contrary, said Goldenson, "Frank Stanton was really running that show. He was the dominant factor, and he made a steal. I told him that afterwards. Our station was already earning $1.5 million a year, and the ABC station was still losing money." Indeed, Stanton's calendar shows him to be the lead negotiator with both Noble and Goldenson throughout the spring of 1951.

As soon as the FCC lifted its four-year freeze on television station licenses in April 1952, CBS lost no time in assembling a network equal in size and strength to NBC. CBS dedicated its new $7 million Hollywood production and office facility, Television City, on November 15, 1952, and broke ground on a $2 million TV headquarters in Washington, D.C.

With each new expense, Paley's apprehensions about television rose. "I went through $60 million in developing TV," said Frank Stanton, "and the board was getting nervous. Before we came out of the red in 1953, Bill was very anxious. He kept wondering when this would change. There was a period when television was very iffy." At one point Stanton even thought of spinning off a new company, CBS Television, financed by a public offering of stock. But the board wouldn't hear of it. Years later, Paley called the early days of television "a big crap shoot."

With a year or so of the television network's first black ink, Paley embraced the medium wholeheartedly. By 1956 the CBS Radio network,

Paley's pride, was losing money. But the strapping television network was making a profit and CBS was riding high, with twelve out of the top fifteen shows. Two years later, CBS finally had its full complement of five television stations that the FCC permitted each network to own—for a total cost of $30 million. The final two purchases were KMOX-TV in St. Louis for $4 million and (closer to home) WCAU in Philadelphia.

In 1946 Ike and Leon Levy had sold their radio holdings to the *Philadelphia Bulletin,* at that time the city's leading newspaper. Like Bill Paley, Leon Levy was a radio man to the bone; he didn't want to spend the money necessary to develop television. The *Bulletin* built a modern new television station on the outskirts of the city and sent an emissary to Stanton proposing a sale to CBS. On hearing that Stanton had agreed to pay $18 million and was prepared to go as high as $28 million, Paley told him he was crazy. Paley was mollified when Stanton pointed out that the deal included a large tract of prime real estate as well as a radio station. After assorted write-offs and depreciation, the effective cost was only $8 million.

Years later Paley was unforgiving—and unfair—in blaming Stanton for CBS's failure to line up a television network before the license freeze back in 1948. "The fault," he said, "lay in our poor judgment in not having a fallback position in the event our color system failed."

Many critics echoed Paley's displeasure, charging that CBS had paid inflated prices for its stations. In retrospect, $30 million ($135 million in 1990 dollars) for four stations seems like a bargain—especially given CBS's subsequent gusher of television profits. Moreover, CBS picked up stations after they had begun showing a profit; most television stations broke into the black in 1951. Had CBS built the stations on its own, it would have had to absorb several years of deficits. So while NBC had a head start with its own stations, in the end its advantage didn't count for much. CBS's programming flair took the network to first place, where it stayed.

Throughout these years of growth, Hytron stuck to CBS like a painful burr. Worn down by what he called the "persistent headache" the venture gave him, Paley ordered the television-set-manufacturing business shut down in July 1956. He kept vacuum tube production going until it was overrun by the deluge of Japanese transistors. In 1961 Paley would close what remained of Hytron. The total loss over ten years: $50 million.

Hytron stained Paley's pride. He was embarrassed at having backed an inferior product when his public image was so associated with quality. The setback changed Paley: his questioning intensified; he became less surefooted. "The fact that he made so costly a mistake has weighed on him all the time," said Ralph Colin. "He is forever uncertain."

"The outstanding flop in the record of CBS," Paley called Hytron at one point in the late 1970s. He held Stanton accountable for failing to make the silk purse out of the sow's ear. Stanton was certainly guilty of excessive optimism—even arrogance—about CBS's manufacturing and marketing capabilities. Unlike Paley, Stanton the basement tinkerer was absorbed by technology and engineering. He had a greater bias for manufacturing than Paley did. And when the business fell apart, Stanton was too proud to admit defeat. The major villain in Paley's eyes, however, was Peter Goldmark and his recommendation. Paley chose to ignore not only Goldmark's caveats in his original report on Hytron but his own failure to make the necessary bold moves at the outset.

It took some fifteen years for CBS to recover from the decision Paley and Kesten made in 1940 to press for color television. But whatever their motives, it had been a visionary move, and it had made sense at the time. At the end of World War II consumer acceptance seemed possible, and incompatibility between CBS and RCA sets was barely an issue. Even when the market was flooded with 3 million black and white sets in 1949, Paley and Stanton's continued devotion to CBS color was understandable —at least to anyone who knew Peter Goldmark. His messianic zeal was infectious. "You always know what Peter tells you is gospel," Paley told *Time* magazine as late as 1950—although years later Paley would rebuke Stanton publicly for his "blind devotion" to Goldmark during the forties and fifties.

The technical excellence of CBS color also dovetailed perfectly with the CBS corporate ego—Paley's insistence on being regarded as first and best. "It was the best quality you could get in color," said Paley. "We were interested in having the best color system that could be developed." Moreover, for much of the struggle Paley had the press behind him, portraying CBS as a David battling the RCA Golaith.

It seems ironic that Paley, the dealmaker, the supersalesman, the man Goldmark described as an "anti-technologist," would lose by staking himself to a gold-plated technology before a demand for it existed. Paley had no fingertips for the mechanics of television; his instincts failed him. Yet he allowed himself to be swept along. Paley was not fully engaged in CBS during this period. He was often absent when key decisions were made. And even when he was involved, his ambivalence about television clouded his judgment and sent confusing signals to his subordinates.

But Paley, as so often, had the last laugh. He and Sarnoff each had returned from World War II to pursue an obsession. Paley's was to master his network's fate by controlling radio programs. Sarnoff's was to make television a reality after years of dreaming and experimenting. As it turned out, Paley's talent raids and program development ended by saving CBS Television. He may have thought he was building radio, but his gut—the visceral, even primitive, love for stars and shows that figured in every move he made—was to give his fledgling television network an advantage Sarnoff would never match.

29

"IF YOU WANTED to imagine a person to take the job of the most important broadcaster in America, you could not have done better than to invent Ed Murrow," Bill Paley once said. "He had it all, and more." Yet on Murrow's triumphant return to the United States after World War II, Paley made a misstep with his star correspondent that tarnished both men and resulted in eighteen months of unhappiness for Murrow.

CBS News correspondents had enjoyed an easy, friendly relationship with Bill Paley during the glamorous war years. In the postwar period, he grew more distant and formal. The exception, as always, was Murrow, whose relationship with Paley became more complicated but no less intense. Even before the war, Paley gave Murrow leeway to express his opinions on air, while firing others—Cecil Brown, H. V. Kaltenborn— for the same offense. Murrow's privileged status was further enhanced by his fame during the war. Murrow had done so much for CBS that he seemed to have a bottomless reservoir of goodwill.

Murrow wanted to build on his position and become a stateside commentator after the war. Campbell's Soup was willing to sponsor Murrow in a fifteen-minute radio newscast; his salary would be an ample $2,500 a week. But Paley had other ideas. The CBS chairman invited Murrow to New York in December 1945 to convince him to become a top executive, CBS Radio's first vice-president for public affairs—in effect, president of CBS News. Paley stressed the opportunity to consolidate the organization Murrow had built during the war, to launch new programs, to have power and influence beyond the role of newscaster. Moreover, Murrow would report to Paley alone. Paley would even allow Murrow's contract to stipulate that if Paley ever ceased to be chief executive of CBS, Murrow could go elsewhere.

Although flattered by Paley's attention, Murrow resisted at first. The newsman had misgivings about the coming of television and Paley's strategy of seeking a mass audience. Murrow also felt guilty about vaulting over Paul White, who had run the news department at CBS so ably for many years. Paley told Murrow he didn't think White had the depth necessary for the job; in fact, White's flippant attitude had already scuttled his chances for advancement.

Paley understood that he could appeal to Murrow's deep sense of loyalty and friendship. Over dinner at a Manhattan restaurant and a glittering weekend at Kiluna, Paley cajoled and pleaded with the brooding newsman. At one point Murrow wrote his wife in London that he feared Paley would be "sore" over a rejection. Finally Murrow accepted, but only conditionally: he would take the job for a year, and then consider resuming broadcasting if Campbell's Soup still wanted him.

Why would Paley reroute the career of CBS's most famous broadcaster? It was, after all, like taking a twenty-game winner in his prime and moving him to the front office. Paley said he feared that Murrow might lose his popularity with the war's end; he told Stanton that he thought Murrow had been drained by his wartime experience and needed a break. But there was something more complex at work. Both men felt diminished on their return from London, where they had been American heroes. Now they were back to the less exalted mission of making money for the network—or at least Paley was. Murrow remained a romantic symbol. For Paley, there may have been an element of jealousy. With one move, Paley took away Murrow's visibility and put him under his thumb.

Paley's oft-stated reason for the move was that he saw Murrow as a promising executive who could provide leadership and draw on his overseas experience to guide decisions about news coverage. Paley had been impressed by Murrow's selection of his team in Europe, his "sensitivity about people and how good they could be. . . . He stood for integrity. He stood for honesty. He stood for accuracy. He was a man who looked good, who spoke well, and people were attracted to him." To take such a man and place him near the top of the corporate ladder showed precisely where Paley's priorities were: the top executive was more important than the top journalist.

Moreover, Murrow's presence in a key executive position would be good for CBS's image at a time when the network was being severely criticized. The public appetite for broadcast news declined after the war. As advertisers clamored to sponsor entertainment shows, Paley responded by nudging CBS's news programs from prime viewing hours to peripheral time periods where advertisers could buy time cheaply. But CBS and its rivals moved too quickly into highly commercial programs after performing a public service during the war years. What followed, according to Jack Gould, was an outpouring of "more diverse and insistent criticism of radio than the industry had experienced in the whole of its previous 25 years."

The FCC launched a major study of how radio stations were failing to live up to their obligation to provide public service programs. The results, delivered in a fifty-page report known as the Blue Book, were released in March 1946—not so coincidentally, the same month Murrow took over as CBS's vice-president of news. The Blue Book not only documented the scarcity of public affairs programming, it attempted to define what the Communications Act meant by "public interest, convenience and necessity." In a radical move, it proposed that broadcasters offer programs in certain categories—education, news, discussion, and religion—to keep their licenses.

For more than six months Paley stayed conspicuously silent in the face of this bold assertion of the government's power over radio programming. What accounted for such restraint, given Paley's record of opposing even the smallest governmental encroachment? On the personal side, Paley was busy divorcing Dorothy and courting Babe. And when he appeared at CBS, he devoted his attention to gaining control of radio entertainers and their programs. His mind was tightly focused on beating NBC in the ratings. But mostly he had no stomach for taking on Washington, so he let others in the industry—chiefly Justin Miller, president of the National Association of Broadcasters—do it for him.

The broadcasting lobby ferociously fought the Blue Book, charging that the government was acting as censor. The FCC retreated, and by the fall of 1946 it was clear that the Blue Book would be, in the words of Erik Barnouw, nothing more than "a statement of principle, of mysterious status," not a guideline for the industry.

In October 1946, when the threat had disappeared, Paley weighed in with an address to the National Association of Broadcasters. It was his first speech after the war—and one of only a half-dozen public statements on important broadcasting issues delivered from 1945 to 1960. (Stanton, by comparison, made speeches and testified as an industry spokesman during that period no less than three dozen times.)

Paley lashed out at radio's critics, deriding most of their objections as self-interested and sensationalistic, the posturing of "snobs preaching to fellow snobs." Paley's caustic tone turned downright anti-intellectual when he announced that he had no sympathy for "some critics who apparently want public discussion programs, political talks, symposiums, social controversy and so on to take the place of popular entertainment." Doubtless he was unaware that a key consultant to the Blue Book was Charles Siepmann, a former official of the BBC, who was Murrow's soulmate and confidant.

Having settled his scores, Paley turned statesmanlike. He reminded his fellow broadcasters that they had all been guilty of "advertising ex-

cesses" in the "competition for economic survival." And he pointedly
announced CBS's plans to improve the quality of public affairs and educational programs.

Thanks to Ed Murrow, CBS had plenty to offer. Murrow had
launched an array of new programs, including "You Are There," a re-
creation of historical events; "CBS Views the Press," a review of daily
newspapers; and "As Others See Us," an analysis of foreign press coverage
of the United States. As his programming centerpiece, Murrow had taken
CBS's nascent radio documentary unit and beefed it up with big budgets
($100,000 per program) and talented producers. He scheduled a dozen
programs on topics such as race relations, health, and housing. When the
first of these, "The Eagle's Brood," about juvenile delinquency, was
broadcast, Frank Stanton wrote to Charles Denny, chairman of the FCC,
that "the type of promotion we are putting behind these public affairs
programs is an effort to build the largest possible audience." The documentary series earned CBS yet another burst of favorable publicity.

Paley knew it made sense to indulge Murrow's idealistic visions for
news programming. Chief among these was Murrow's conviction that the
networks should broadcast editorials. Since 1941, the FCC had a policy
called the Mayflower Doctrine prohibiting broadcasters from advocating
a point of view. But the FCC had indicated a willingness to reconsider
Mayflower, and Murrow wanted to nudge the regulators along. By taking
a position on vital events and issues of the day, Murrow argued that CBS
could make a great contribution to public affairs. At first, Paley went along
with him.

With Paley's permission, Murrow hired Russell Davenport, a writer
and editor from *Life* magazine, who devised an elegant plan to surround
CBS editorials with commentaries from prominent liberals and conservatives. The overall effect would be electronic editorial and op-ed pages.
When Davenport submitted the proposal in February 1947, Paley summoned all his top brass—Stanton, Murrow, attorney Joe Ream, and Davidson Taylor, then head of programming—to a meeting at Kiluna. Paley's
support for the idea vanished when Stanton and Ream played to his instinctive caution by arguing that CBS should wait for the FCC to overturn
the rule first. Paley also accepted Stanton and Ream's contention that CBS
had no right to tell its affiliated stations what their editorial position should
be.

Two years later, the FCC would in fact repudiate the Mayflower
Doctrine and permit stations to express their viewpoints as part of a "rea-
sonably balanced presentation"—a decision that became known as the
Fairness Doctrine. At that time, Paley would hail the FCC reversal of
Mayflower and announce CBS's intention to broadcast editorials "in its

own name." As a practical matter, CBS would do so only three times—twice on broadcasting issues.

Murrow, who had been in charge of news for less than a year, took his first setback with Paley badly. He viewed it, according to his biographer A. M. Sperber, as "a lost opportunity . . . a memory that rankled." By then Murrow could also see the future of CBS more clearly. His highly touted radio documentary series had limited appeal; even his wartime popularity was not enough to pull news back from the fringes of the schedule. And despite CBS's reversals in developing color television, the emphasis was shifting to that medium as RCA sets inundated the market. "Ed had some ideas on how news should be run, but as he went along he was aware of the commercial pressures on television," said Janet Murrow. "Ed would have loved it if Bill had taken up the cudgels and done something different with television."

Murrow confided his anxieties about television to Michael Bessie, a wartime colleague Paley tried to hire for CBS News. Television had different values, Murrow told Bessie in an effort to dissuade him from taking the job. Instead of putting a premium on educating and uplifting, television was turning into an instrument for entertainment. "I don't think you have the temperament. I'm not sure I have," said Murrow.

The political climate further soured Murrow's mood. "He had a sense of a darkening cloud, a premonition of things to come," said Janet Murrow. The Congress elected in November 1946 was dominated by Republicans for the first time since 1930. Its conservative bent grew out of the rabid anti-communism sweeping the country. Since 1945 the Soviet Union had installed Communist governments throughout Eastern Europe and seemed poised to do the same in Greece and Turkey.

In February 1947 Britain asked the United States to help defend the Mediterranean by providing financial aid to Greece and Turkey. Congress approved the aid overwhelmingly, spurred on by Truman's argument that the United States was obliged to support governments trying to resist communism—a position known as the Truman Doctrine. At CBS, commentator William Shirer, who years later would write *The Rise and Fall of the Third Reich* and other best-selling books, used his Sunday afternoon news analysis program to take issue with the Doctrine and criticize the government of Greece, which he saw as repressive and undemocratic. Shirer's views on the Truman Doctrine defied the conventional wisdom and were considered liberal at best, leftist at worst. The next month, top executives of the J. B. Williams Company, the shaving-cream manufacturer that sponsored Shirer's program, told CBS they wanted to replace Shirer with another commentator. "They were in fact disenchanted with Shirer's liberalism," Frank Stanton acknowledged years later.

CBS officials cited a vague dissatisfaction with Shirer's performance and the program's declining ratings—knowing full well that all news shows were losing their audiences. Murrow told Shirer that CBS would try to find him another sponsor; until then, Shirer would go "sustaining." Not only did Shirer balk at the pay cut, he insisted that he stay in his time period. The CBS sales department went to work trying to find another way to accommodate the Williams Company. But Shirer decided to force the issue. The following Sunday, March 23, he said on the air that he was losing his sponsor because a soap company had the power to decide who could be heard on radio. Afterwards Shirer told reporters that his liberal views were the cause. His most intent listener that afternoon was William Paley, sitting in his Kiluna living room with a group of weekend guests. They immediately jumped on Paley for allowing Shirer on the CBS network; Paley had heard about Shirer's left-leaning views from his conservative friends before. Now he was infuriated by Shirer's public insubordination.

The following Monday, Paley called a meeting with Murrow, Stanton, Davidson Taylor, and Bill Gittinger, head of sales. "Bill [Paley] was sore," recalled Stanton. " 'Get him out of the time period,' Bill said. At first Murrow defended Shirer. He wanted to be on his side. He defended him on the grounds of loyalty and all Shirer had done for CBS. But Bill would hear none of it and Murrow caved quickly."

Paley's position hardened when a cordon of pickets surrounded CBS headquarters at 485 Madison that day and protest telegrams arrived in his office. They were signed by writers Dorothy Parker and Arthur Miller, as well as Paley's old pal Robert Sherwood, and the poet Archibald MacLeish, whose work had been heard on CBS Radio. Suddenly Paley was yanked from the background into the spotlight, and he hated it. The following Friday he had to meet for nearly an hour with a delegation led by the editor of *The Nation,* the left-leaning weekly.

Murrow went through his own unpleasant contortions. He issued a statement denouncing Shirer's assertion of advertiser interference in CBS's decisions about news broadcasters, but his argument had a hollow ring. CBS had been influenced by advertisers before. General Mills's disapproval of H. V. Kaltenborn and Johns Manville's cancellation of Cecil Brown's contract were only the most conspicuous precedents.

Within CBS, Murrow complained that Shirer was writing his commentaries out of newspaper clippings and neglecting to do the necessary reporting. "Shirer's program was a newsman's news program," said Frank Stanton. "It was listened to by opinion leaders and policymakers. In a sense the argument that he hadn't been working hard was Murrow finding a rationale for what he and Paley did." Indeed, that year Shirer's program won several prestigious Peabody awards.

For all his internal criticism, Murrow loathed bringing bad news to Shirer. "He said he didn't think it was fair," recalled Stanton. "It was a personal relationship, and he hated having to tell his old friend he had to get out of his time period." Together, Murrow and Shirer devised a compromise, a statement informing the press that Shirer would have a new sponsored time period. With Shirer in tow, Murrow took the document to Paley's office for his approval. Paley coldly turned it aside. "As far as I'm concerned," he told Shirer, "your usefulness to CBS has ended."

The following Sunday, the last day of March, Shirer announced his resignation from CBS on the air. The episode opened a small crack in the bond between Paley and Murrow. Unaccustomed to losing control of any situation, Paley resented the maelstrom of bad publicity and the spectacle of pickets descending on his office. Murrow had not only failed to shield Paley, he had forced the final confrontation with Shirer.

Murrow felt sickened by the rupture with his old friend. His disenchantment with his role at CBS became obvious. "Being an executive was painful for him," recalled Stanton. "He was certainly making cracks all the time." In the late spring of 1947, Paley gave Murrow an opening. "I have a strong feeling you want to go back on the air," Paley said to the newsman. "I can tell you're sort of miserable." Murrow answered that he would only return to broadcasting if Paley ordered him to. Paley knew this gambit of Murrow's: "I'll do it if you order me to" was a phrase Murrow used a lot. "Okay, Ed, I order you to," replied Paley, and Murrow broke out in a grin.

In fact, Murrow had selected a spot on the schedule even before he and Paley engaged in their small charade. Ward Wheelock, owner of the advertising agency that handled Campbell's Soup, had asked Stanton during a luncheon meeting if Murrow was ready to return to the air. Stanton quickly invited Murrow to join them after lunch, and Murrow just as quickly expressed enthusiasm for anchoring the nightly newscast, "Edward R. Murrow and the News," under Campbell's sponsorship.

Murrow resigned his executive post on July 19, 1947, and was replaced by Davidson Taylor, whom Paley had been eager to remove from entertainment programming. Despite the public relations value during the Blue Book controversy, Paley's appointment of Murrow as a high-ranking executive had been a mistake. Murrow had initiated some notable programs, but given his closeness to Paley, he might have done so anyway as a broadcaster. Otherwise, Murrow failed as an executive. His major initiative, editorials on the air, had fallen flat; he found administrative work burdensome; and he hated the dirty business of firing people. Yet other than acknowledging Murrow's distaste for firing people, Paley never admitted that Murrow wasn't suited for the job.

For all their ideological differences, Paley and Murrow kept up the social link they had formed during the war. Virile, magnetic Ed Murrow, a man who could make smoking a cigarette seem like the height of romance, became, in a way, another bauble for Paley. Like Paley, he wasn't to the manor born, but Murrow acquired the bearing—as well as the bespoke suits from Anderson & Sheppard of Savile Row, shirts from Bertollini in Rome, shoes from Scotland—to shine in the most elegant social circles. The Murrows visited Kiluna periodically for house party weekends. "He was like a conflagration," recalled Slim Keith, by then a close friend of the Paleys, "a very high flame burning inside." Murrow fell in with the routine: the croquet and the swimming, the dinner party repartee and the all-male after-dinner poker games wreathed in smoke. But despite his years hobnobbing with British aristocracy, Murrow never really warmed to the Kiluna crowd. He was far more comfortable in the company of men and women of accomplishment. When Paley asked Murrow to take a house in Manhasset on the Kiluna property, Murrow declined. "Ed felt that it would be a mistake," recalled Janet Murrow.

Babe and Bill also visited the Murrow country home in Pawling, New York. These were quieter times in a more subdued setting, where Paley and Murrow would go off together and hunt in the rough fields surrounding Murrow's white colonial home. At work, Murrow and Paley had lunch together every two weeks. "He never made a move without talking to me about it," Paley boasted.

Paley made much of having singled out Murrow as an exception to his unwillingness to mix business and personal relationships. It has often been said that Stanton felt jealous over the social relationship between Paley and Murrow, although Stanton purposely kept aloof from Paley outside the office. When Bill and Babe Paley got married in July 1947, Murrow was the only CBS man among the select group of guests. Paley's failure to include Stanton became a symbol of their social distance and gave rise to an anecdote that had Paley asking Stanton to lend him a movie camera to take films of the wedding, which he explained was to be strictly a family affair. Afterwards, when Paley gave Stanton the film to be developed, Stanton was supposed to have felt hurt when he saw Murrow in the frames.

Although Stanton would later remark: "I don't know whether I was upset or not about not being invited," he said the business about the movie camera was "pure fiction. I don't even know whether there were movies taken. Where that got started I don't know. Ralph Colin might have been the source of the stories about unhappiness." As Paley's personal attorney, Colin secured the judge to perform the ceremony and then was galled when Paley did not include him. Colin considered himself Paley's superior socially and intellectually. He later said that Paley was "intentionally insulting" and showed a "lack of sensitivity and bad upbringing, a lack of values." On the wedding day, Colin showed up in Stanton's office to propose a sarcastic toast to the bride and groom.

Far more irksome to Stanton than their social relationship was the unconventional working arrangement between Murrow and Paley. Even after Murrow left the executive suite, he could go directly to Paley whenever he wanted, bypassing Stanton and others in the chain of command. This indulgence on Paley's part caused strained relations between Stanton and Murrow. Each begrudged the other's access to Paley. "Ed wanted to go around all organizational structures," said Stanton. "Whenever he wanted to get one past me, he would call up Bill and come up the back stairs and Bill would see him."

Murrow's dislike of Stanton was obvious. "Stanton never talked adversely about Murrow," recalled CBS commentator Eric Sevareid, "but there was some kind of resentment by Murrow having to do with Stanton working the top floor." Whenever anything went wrong, Murrow blamed Stanton, never Paley. "I think Murrow transferred some of his frustration to Stanton," said former CBS correspondent Howard K. Smith. "Rather than criticize Paley, whom he loved, he criticized Stanton, who represented the establishment. Many times, it was actually Paley who was bearing down on Murrow." Not surprisingly, Murrow's open animosity got back to Stanton, further deepening the rift.

Paley feigned innocence. "They could not get on with each other and I never could have straightened that one out," he said years later. "I think Stanton did not approve of the idea of Murrow's going over everyone's head in his dealings with me . . . and perhaps Murrow did not like the idea that I was so close to Stanton. I could never quite figure it out."

Of course Paley had it figured out perfectly. It was in his power to make the Murrow–Stanton relationship work, and he chose not to. Perhaps, as so often, he simply wished to avoid a disagreeable situation. Perhaps he could control both men more effectively by keeping them apart. "Bill and I talked about it," said Stanton. "He shrugged his shoulders. He didn't want to get into a fight with Ed."

"I hold Bill Paley to blame for not letting Ed Murrow and Frank Stanton get along," said Fred Friendly, Murrow's longtime producer. "They were the two white knights, each handsome, each a leader. They were very good for CBS. A great leader would not have tolerated the strained relations between the two men. It was somewhere between hatred and indifference. When I see executives played off one against the other, it is a sign of an insecure leader. Stanton and Murrow should have been pulling together. It is a sign of Bill Paley's inadequacy that it didn't happen."

30

MURROW'S RETURN to the airwaves in the autumn of 1947 coincided with the first stages of an orchestrated scare over Communist subversion. Early that year the House Un-American Activities Committee had stepped up its probes of alleged traitors in government, business, organized labor, the film industry, and universities.

Writers, actors, and journalists seemed especially vulnerable to charges that they were closet Communists. During the 1930s, many of them had embraced communism for its hard line against fascism, only to reject it after the Nazi-Soviet non-aggression pact of 1939. Viewed in light of Soviet postwar expansion, these sympathies were deemed treasonous by the right-wing politicians who moved into powerful positions following the 1946 elections.

In April 1947, three former FBI agents who called themselves American Business Consultants, Inc., launched a weekly newsletter entitled *Counterattack*. Intended to expose Communist infiltration of broadcasting, the newsletter quickly gathered an extensive subscriber list at the networks and among prominent advertisers such as DuPont and General Motors. Advertisers fearful of associating with anyone undesirable sent a steady flow of complaints to the networks. Whenever CBS newscasters seemed too liberal for the prevailing mood, Bill Paley heard about it. Given the choice between losing advertising revenues or standing up for his correspondents, Paley usually went for the buck.

Even before the first issue of *Counterattack,* Bryce Oliver, a former radio commentator, wrote in *The New Republic* that individual radio stations as well as the CBS and NBC networks had dropped two dozen left-leaning correspondents under sponsor pressure in the previous year. "The networks have been growing more and more worried about 'opinion' on the air," wrote Oliver. "Radio's resistance to ideas seems mainly opposition to liberal ideas. Pressure to 'tone down' news which is sympathetic to organized labor and to Russia has increased rapidly in the last few months."

The House Un-American Activities Committee opened widely publicized hearings on subversives in the film industry in October 1947, temporarily diverting attention from the networks. But by mid-1949 the
spotlight was back on broadcasting. *Variety* reported that the "red scare
. . . has grabbed a stranglehold in television. The pervading fear of becoming tainted with any shade of red has reached such a point among the
television networks and ad agencies that any actor, writer or producer
who has been even remotely identified with leftist tendencies is shunned."
Blacklists, *Variety* reported, were now used routinely in the radio and
television industries. When CBS fired one of its directors, Betty Todd,
after she pleaded the Fifth Amendment before an investigating committee,
Counterattack urged its readers to write Bill Paley praising the CBS action.

Paley was caught up in his famous talent raids in 1948 and 1949. But
shortly after snaring Jack Benny late in 1948, Paley indicated to Norman
Corwin that he was not oblivious to the Red scare. "There is going to be
a terrible wave of reaction in this country," Paley said. "No place will be
safe for a liberal. Why, I went to a board meeting on Wall Street a little
while ago and to my surprise and embarrassment, I found myself congratulated on all sides for getting rid of Bill Shirer." Corwin thought to himself, "CBS was known as a liberal network, I was a liberal writer, and
now, he had said, no place was safe for liberals."

Only weeks later Corwin received a new contract from CBS under
which the network would take a 50 percent cut of profits from Corwin's
programs instead of 10 percent. Corwin rejected the network's harsh
terms. "I was under no illusions," he said. "The climate would not have
been comfortable for me at CBS."

In February 1950, Senator Joseph McCarthy delivered a speech in
Wheeling, West Virginia, charging widespread Communist infiltration in
the State Department. Public hearings called by the Tydings Committee
to investigate the charges brought forth a torrent of accusations by Mc-
Carthy. His demagoguery stirred Murrow, who used his radio newscast
to question McCarthy's evidence.

The broadcasts prompted numerous letters of complaint to Murrow's
sponsor, Campbell's Soup. In May 1950, Campbell's told CBS it would
stop sponsoring Murrow's radio newscast at the end of June. The soup
company wished to use the hour for a music show. But instead of agreeing
to shunt Murrow to a new time period as he had Shirer, Paley held his
ground. Meanwhile, CBS sales vice-president Bill Gittinger rounded up
new sponsors. The fact that Murrow's show had high ratings helped his
cause immeasurably; the fact that the newscaster's name was Murrow
helped as well.

Political pressure on the networks took an uglier turn with the publication of a 215-page booklet called *Red Channels* in June 1950. Assembled by the men responsible for *Counterattack,* it received wide distribution on Madison Avenue and at the networks. The slender volume contained a list of 151 prominent TV and radio journalists and entertainers who allegedly had Communist leanings. Among the names: Norman Corwin, William Shirer, Leonard Bernstein, and CBS documentary producers Robert Lewis Shayon and William Robson, as well as broadcast journalist Howard K. Smith.

The Red scare wasn't the only source of contention. Murrow's stand on the Korean War provoked a clash with Paley that dwarfed their earlier disputes over network editorials and William Shirer. Following the North Korean invasion of South Korea in June 1950, President Truman sent American troops to help turn back the Communist invaders. Murrow went to cover the story. When he arrived in early July, he supported the U.S. position; the alternative, he believed, was betrayal and appeasement reminiscent of Munich in 1938. But one month on the ground changed his mind. The fighting was chaotic, with South Koreans in retreat everywhere. Murrow decided that the U.S. command under General Douglas MacArthur was a bungle, and that American lives were being lost unnecessarily.

During World War II, Murrow's loyalty had never come into question. The issues were clear to Murrow, a classic moralist who saw only black and white, and his views were shared by the public. Korea, an undeclared war, was far murkier—a civil conflict in which battle lines evaporated. It was a war without strong popular backing.

On August 14, 1950, Murrow sent a dispatch to New York from Tokyo condemning the judgment of American commanders. Not only did his words challenge the Army's prohibition against "unwarranted criticism," they ran counter to Murrow's own avowed policy of not editorializing on the air. Ed Chester, CBS's director of news, read the transcript of the radio broadcast on the teletype and immediately went "up the back stairs" to Frank Stanton's office. "He told me the gauntlet was down," Stanton recalled. Stanton held the broadcast without consulting Paley, who was away from the office.

When Paley returned, he was furious with Murrow for transgressing the government's wartime press rules. Paley believed that those in authority knew more than mere reporters. In his view, Murrow had no right to question MacArthur's strategy. (Indeed, only a month later Murrow's judgment would seem hasty; with his brilliant landing at Inchon, MacArthur succeeded in splintering the North Korean Army and retaking all of South Korea.) Murrow, equally enraged over CBS's "censorship," flew back to New York for a well-publicized showdown with Paley. The September 6 issue of *Variety* carried a story noting "considerable speculation around CBS as to what transpired" between Murrow and Paley when Murrow "confronted Paley upon checking in at headquarters."

Paley stood by Stanton, who had decided before the meeting that if Paley vacillated he would have to leave CBS. Paley went beyond simple support, taking ultimate responsibility and killing the broadcast. After a heated argument, Murrow retreated. "It was one of the most serious differences ever really between us," Paley later said, recognizing that Murrow "felt it was a lack of faith on my part." As Paley later recalled it, "The hurt just stood out on his face."

By then CBS was on the verge of its own hunt for Communist sympathizers, a capitulation to incessant pressures from advertisers. At first, CBS had stood firm. In a statement to *Counterattack* in October 1950, CBS asserted that "through our control of programs on the air, we believe we have made Communist infiltration impossible." But, recalled Frank Stanton, "the fact that we had policies to prevent influence in programs didn't satisfy them."

CBS's solution to the problem, devised by attorney Joseph Ream in mid-December 1950, was to require all 2,500 network employees to sign a "loyalty oath" asking whether they were or had been a member of the Communist Party or any other group that advocated the overthrow of the U.S. government. If an employee had belonged to a subversive organization, he had to "provide a convincing 'explanation' that his membership was not meaningful." Ream adapted the CBS oath from a questionnaire President Truman had authorized for the civil service in March 1947. The American Bar Association, the American Medical Association, and the National Education Association had instituted their own loyalty tests as well.

A genteel Southern conservative who had come to CBS from Wall Street, Ream hit upon the oath, he later said, because "it was obvious to me we were losing business because we were the most liberal network." If CBS could demonstrate that its people were blameless and its politics bland and neutral, the advertisers would be assuaged and CBS would continue to prosper. Surprisingly, the first person Ream consulted about his idea was Murrow. After questioning the First Amendment implications, Murrow gave the oath his imprimatur. "Murrow," said Ream years later, "was as much an anti-Communist as anyone I knew, stemming from his experience in the war." Ream then submitted the oath to Stanton, who approved it "right quick." "I went along with it. It wasn't something I was proud of," said Stanton.

As was so often the case, Stanton did not clear his decision with Paley, although he informed the chairman promptly after the fact. "I told him that we were doing it," said Stanton. "I didn't get a yea or nay. He didn't step in and say, 'Don't do it.' "

Only a handful at CBS refused to sign the oath, although many who signed found it repellant. "I was disgusted with the whole charade," said William Leonard, who would eventually become CBS News president in 1979. "I was ashamed of CBS for what we all considered to be abject knuckling under." One employee resigned on principle. Of nearly two dozen who admitted to Communist ties, all were investigated and some fired. Winston Burdett, one of "Murrow's Boys," owned up to past Communist associations and was hauled before a Senate committee. He disavowed his connections, and CBS kept him on. Howard K. Smith, another of "Murrow's Boys" who had joined the Labor Party in college, was saved from firing because he was posted abroad.

CBS was not certain everyone was telling the truth. Early in 1951, Ream launched a second, more invidious program—a political screening for CBS employees suspected of Communist leanings. He had one assistant, a former FBI agent, Alfred Berry.

While the loyalty oath had been public and straightforward, the new screening process was secretive and arbitrary. Working from lists supplied by *Counterattack* and advertising agencies such as Young & Rubicam, Ream and Berry ran down leads with the FBI and sources on Capitol Hill. As an ex-FBI man, Berry knew how the Bureau's lists had been assembled and how people had been identified by the Justice Department. In many instances, CBS's information was more complete and up to date than that of the amateur vigilantes at *Counterattack*.

The CBS men kept files on those who seemed suspect and told producers and executives who had to be eliminated from CBS programs. When producers submitted names of writers they wanted to use, Berry or Ream would simply reply, "Sorry, we can't clear." Even guests on network talk shows had to be vetted in advance. It was, in effect, McCarthyism in microcosm, and the entire industry took its cue from CBS. If an actor appeared on CBS, he had obviously passed muster. "CBS and blacklisting became synonymous," declared a report on the phenomenon by John Cogley for the Fund for the Republic in 1956.

The results could be devastating. One day CBS News chief Sig Mickelson got a call from Joe Ream about Alan Sloane, who wrote religious broadcasts for CBS. Sloane had signed the loyalty oath, revealing no subversive associations. But when Mickelson went to visit Ream, the attorney pulled out a paper stating that Sloane had been a member of the Communist Party. Ream told Mickelson he had to get Sloane off the program.

In 1952 Ream retired, in part because the blacklist experience "took something out of me." Ream's replacement was Daniel T. O'Shea, who had been brought in by Paley in August 1950. Trained in the law at Harvard, O'Shea was a sentimental Irishman who loved a tough fight and hewed to the far right in politics. For a number of years he had been a top aide to Paley's friend, David O. Selznick.

O'Shea served as CBS's "security officer" for three years, a zealous crusader for the cause. He investigated every CBS program and made regular trips to California with his lists of forbidden actors and writers. Within the company he was known as "vice-president in charge of treason," the keeper of "the black book that didn't exist." His methods were mysterious, his comments cryptic. "You really didn't know who had what evidence," said Sig Mickelson.

CBS sometimes failed to defend employees who were the targets of right-wing tormenters. The most tragic of these was Don Hollenbeck, who from 1947 to 1950 had anchored one of Murrow's pet radio programs, "CBS Views the Press." The *Counterattack* forces began smearing Hollenbeck as early as 1949. Their attacks continued even after he switched to anchoring a late evening newscast on CBS. Jack O'Brian, television columnist for the Hearst press, kept up the harassment, repeatedly calling Hollenbeck a Communist. CBS News shamefully kept a discreet distance. Finally, in the summer of 1954, Hollenbeck cracked under the strain and committed suicide. Belatedly, Paley tried to uphold Hollenbeck's honor by ending CBS's use of Hearst newsreels on its television newscasts.

Bill Paley would later say that CBS had done nothing to "abridge the rights and freedoms of our employees." The son of immigrants, Paley had always prided himself on his patriotism. Yet this time he somehow had it turned around. Perhaps he had been listening too much to his conservative friends, but he seemed oblivious to the fact that CBS's political screening was a reprehensible violation of basic civil liberties. CBS routinely invaded the privacy of its employees and dismissed them on little more than rumor and innuendo. "Yes, it was a blacklist," acknowledged Frank Stanton. "I wince when I say it, but that's the case."

Paley's sense of patriotism also led him to permit cooperation between the Central Intelligence Agency and CBS News in those days—making CBS, in effect, an instrument of American foreign policy. He permitted CIA operatives to screen CBS news film, to eavesdrop on conversations between CBS news officials in New York and the field, and to debrief CBS correspondents on their return from overseas assignments. Paley was aware that CIA agents from time to time operated as part-time CBS correspondents. He even permitted the CIA to use his own Paley Foundation to funnel money to CIA-sponsored projects abroad.

Throughout this period, NBC was engaged in the same sort of witch-hunting. "NBC had a blacklist that I tore up toward the end of the Mc-

Carthy era," said David Adams, former vice-chairman of NBC. "There was cross-checking between NBC and CBS," said Frank Stanton. "There was a sharing of information."

Stanton stood on the front lines, having approved both the loyalty oath and political screening. Frank Stanton, not Bill Paley, received the irate letters from advertisers addressed to CBS . . . the Communist Broadcasting System. But Stanton, who would later be celebrated for his integrity and rectitude, should have known better. "We were not as courageous as we should have been," he admitted years later.

Paley managed to remain comfortably removed from the dirty business going on at his network. Only occasionally did he find himself pulled into decisions with blacklist overtones. Once at a program planning meeting attended by Paley, Stanton, and a handful of other executives in the early 1950s, Sig Mickelson proposed a program featuring Lillian Hellman, who had been a Communist Party member in the 1930s. "Nobody said, 'Forget it,' but it was eased over," recalled Mickelson. "The message was, 'Better look for someone else.' " In 1953, Murrow asked Paley to intercede when Al Berry ordered that journalist Theodore White—a sharp critic of the corrupt regime of China's Chiang Kai-shek—be barred from appearing on a WCBS program called "This Is New York." Paley refused to get involved, and White never appeared.

Recalled Sig Mickelson, "He stayed quite remote, in line with his tendency to keep himself from anything unpleasant." But Stanton kept Paley informed. "He was aware of it all. I didn't hold anything from him," Stanton confirmed. "When we had infrequent lunches or meetings, we talked about it. He would grimace at the conversation about the blacklist. He was perfectly happy to have me there, taking care of it."

Yet the fact remains that Paley—the man who had stood up to Father Coughlin's demagoguery in the early 1930s—approved every move to appease the witch-hunters two decades later. His office was a mere three doors down from Dan O'Shea's, and Paley sanctioned O'Shea's kangaroo-court methods. Sometimes when Sig Mickelson questioned the inclusion of a name on the CBS blacklist, O'Shea would reply, "The chairman wants it this way so you better do it."

The refusal of Paley and Stanton to take a stand against the vigilantes did no honor to them or CBS. Not only were they unwilling to jeopardize profits, they feared antagonizing the FCC and the Congress, which were controlled by forces sympathetic to blacklisting. Although they knew that the supposed Communists and fellow travelers posed no threat whatsoever to the nation, Paley and Stanton found it expedient to hire only those who were politically neutral. It was easier to go along than to fight.

Yet Paley never owned up to what CBS was doing. He never even accepted the term "loyalty oath." He called it, variously, an "in-house questionnaire," a "mild questionnaire," a "very small step," a "simple thing." He also refused to admit the existence of the political screening, omitting it from his memoirs and all other recollections of the period. "We didn't have a blacklist," Paley insisted, ignoring, as was his habit, the overwhelming proof to the contrary.

4

THE
Hedonist

"**B**ILL PALEY Won't You Please Come Home?" . . . "Where Is Paley?" Such headlines appeared at intervals in *Variety* during the postwar years—small but significant expressions of the broadcasting industry's concern about Bill Paley's perplexing habits as CBS's top executive.

More conspicuously than ever, Paley was the absentee landlord as he took longer and more frequent vacations—his customary month to six weeks in the summer, two to three weeks in the sunshine each month from December through March, plus periodic shorter trips.

Paley had been having trouble immersing himself in CBS since his return from World War II. As he approached his fifties he seemed in the throes of a midlife crisis. Although he was as hard-driving as ever, he had been feeling the stresses of the broadcasting business for two decades. The aggravations of the Red scare and the complications of television pushed him even further away. The triumphant Paley Raids were behind him, and he was now unwilling to make the hard transition from entrepreneur to manager.

Frank Stanton had observed Paley's restlessness and disconnection for several years and found it perplexing. But Stanton was even more surprised one day in 1950 when Babe Paley arrived at his office unannounced. She went straight to the point. "We've got to do something about finding something interesting for Bill to do. He's bored." Stanton later told a friend he was concerned about Babe's plaintive tone.

Some months later, President Harry Truman called Stanton, whom he had come to know two years earlier through their mutual friend, Leonard Reinsch, an executive for Cox Radio in Atlanta. The day after Franklin Roosevelt died, Reinsch had dragooned Stanton to Washington to help draft the new president's speeches to the armed forces and a joint session of Congress. During the following week Stanton shuttled between New York and Washington, joining a group of advisers who ate sandwiches in the White House Cabinet Room while writing Truman's appointment announcements and rehearsing the new president for his first press conference. Since those hectic days, Stanton had dropped by the White House

on numerous occasions to visit Truman, who also met periodically with
Stanton when he came to New York. It was a warm, informal relationship, with ample room for inquiries from Truman about candidates for
important posts.

When Truman told Stanton he was looking for someone to head a
commission to analyze the nation's natural and material resources, Babe's
words about her husband drifted back. Afterwards, Stanton told Truman's
appointments secretary, Matt Connally, that Paley would be perfect for
the post. Connally said slyly, "Are you trying to get rid of him so you can
run the company?" "No," said Stanton, somewhat taken aback. "I think
it might interest him, and it would be a shame not to use his talent."

Connally relayed the message to Truman, who asked for help from
Stuart Symington, then chairman of the President's National Security Resources Board. Symington also happened to be a Manhasset neighbor,
cousin to Jock Whitney, social friend, and frequent Paley golfing companion (along with James Forrestal, then Secretary of Defense, and Charles
Payson, Jock Whitney's brother-in-law). But when Symington called
Stanton—knowing nothing of his catalytic role—the CBS president was
prudently noncommittal about Paley's availability. He knew if he responded enthusiastically it would look as if he were trying to push Paley
out.

In the summer of 1950, Symington approached Paley, appealing directly to his patriotic streak, pointing out that the Korean War had raised
the possibility of shortages in minerals, metals, and oils. The president felt
the need for a sweeping look at these resources, coupled with recommendations for their use well into the future. Paley was startled by the request,
mostly because he couldn't fathom its origins, despite his golfing relationship with Symington. "Precisely why this acquaintance should have led
Symington to hit upon me was beyond me," Paley said years later. With
a laugh, Paley turned down Symington's flattering but puzzling overture.

Soon afterwards Symington arranged for Paley to visit Senator Lyndon Johnson in Washington. Johnson (by then a friend of Frank Stanton's
as well) entreated Paley to take the job. Also on hand that evening was
Sam Rayburn, the Texas congressman who was Speaker of the House. As
Johnson prodded Paley, Rayburn, engrossed in a televised wrestling
match, glanced up and said, "I agree." But Paley felt out of his element;
he told the men he knew nothing about minerals and metals except as an
occasional armchair investor.

In late November, Symington set up a meeting between Truman and
Paley in the White House. Truman made his case seriously and intently.
Paley offered the standard demurral, but Truman countered, and it was
clear that Paley could refuse no longer. Although reassured by Truman's

pledge of as much cooperation and money as the commission would need, Paley left the White House feeling dazed and anxious.

The White House announced on January 22, 1951, that Paley would head a five-man group, known as the President's Materials Policy Commission. He would receive no compensation save a small amount for expenses. He would go immediately to Washington and take a leave of six months from CBS—a commitment that in fact would stretch to eighteen months.

Why would Paley make such a move? Frequent vacations were one thing, but how could he divorce himself during this crucial moment in the development of CBS television? The FCC had approved CBS's color system only three months earlier, and CBS was fighting off RCA's effort to reverse that approval. In the coming months CBS would argue and win its case for color before the Supreme Court, buy the Paramount station in Chicago, lay the groundwork for the CBS-Television network, and buy Hytron, the television-manufacturing company. Important new TV stars such as Jackie Gleason and Lucille Ball would be launched by the network, which would also present its first commercial color telecast. It would be a period when CBS would formulate many of its basic policies for televising entertainment and news programs. But Paley savored the idea of top-level government service. It took him closer to the realm of Averell Harriman and further from the cigar factories of his youth.

The Washington niche also offered a convenient escape from the witch-hunting miasma and may have simultaneously played a role in CBS's move into blacklisting. In late December 1950, *Variety* had raised the "intriguing question" about the "motivating factor or factors" that led to CBS's loyalty oath. Specifically, *Variety* wondered whether Paley's then-rumored return to government service had prompted the network to clean house. "CBS in projecting itself as the most liberal of all networks," *Variety* said, "was branded by some . . . as the Red Network." With the loyalty oath, Paley was "apparently determined to erase such stigmas."

To help ease Paley's move to Washington, Stanton gave him guidance on prospective commissioners and staff members. Stanton knew Paley would need a top-notch writer, so he proposed Eric Hodgins. An engineer from the Massachusetts Institute of Technology, Hodgins was also a former managing editor of *Fortune* and had written a witty best-selling novel, *Mr. Blandings Builds His Dream House*. Paley leapt at the notion. Hodgins was "thunderstruck" but called Stanton to say he had to decline because he knew nothing about the subject. "Eric, don't be a damned fool," Stanton said, and hung up the phone. As usual, Paley appropriated the idea of hiring Hodgins as his own.

Lyndon Johnson suggested George Rufus Brown, a Texas crony who

headed Brown & Root, a large contracting firm, as one of the commissioners. The others were Arthur H. Bunker, a former director of CBS who
had moved from investment banking at Lehman Brothers to head a minerals company called Climax Molybdenum; and Edward S. Mason, an
economist who ran Harvard's Graduate School of Public Administration.
Paley also hired Philip Coombs, an economics professor at Amherst College, as his executive director.

"It was no accident that the majority of commissioners were Republicans," said Coombs. "And they were not just ordinary Republicans but
important figures. We were likely to come out with controversial policy
recommendations for government and industry. If you had a bunch of
flaming liberals, you wouldn't be taken seriously. It was pretty hard to
make an attack on Bunker, who was a fund-raiser for Republicans. Some
might call that calculation, I called it common sense."

After moving into the commission's spacious suite in the White
House Executive Office Building, Paley's initial problem was attracting a
first-rate staff for his relatively short-term operation. He fell back on his
old CBS strategy: create an atmosphere of quality and make the Materials
Policy Commission *the* place to be in Washington. "We're going to play
this very cleverly," he told Coombs. "We're not going to take the first
people who come along. We're going to really aim for a very high-quality
organization. If we get three or four top people, they'll attract a lot of
other people. But if we start out with three or four considered to be
ordinary, that'll be the end of our effort to put together a first-class team."
Paley's idea worked, and before long he had assembled a staff of some 140,
supplemented by such superior consulting companies as Arthur D. Little.

Paley devoted himself completely to the commission during its first
six months. Instead of public hearings, he, Hodgins, and Coombs met
informally with industry leaders and other experts two or three times a
week. They sent out questionnaires and commissioned special studies. In
weekly staff meetings, Paley impressed his underlings with his fair-mind-
edness and humility. "He was pleasant and unassuming," said Harry
Kahn, a staff member at the time. "He was suffering a twitch. When he
talked his eyelids went up and down, but it didn't seem to disturb him and
he handled it well."

Although many on the staff had heard about Paley's reputation for
toughness, they saw none of it. He treated them deferentially. "He made
it clear that he was not the expert," said Kahn. "He was learning like
everyone else." As in World War II, Paley understood that he had pulled
people away from important jobs to work for him. They were making a
sacrifice, working long hours for the public good. He had to treat them

well. "He created an atmosphere where people felt appreciated," said Coombs. The Paleys even threw a party for the staff members at the Shoreham Hotel.

After four months, Paley informed Truman that the commission's job would take a year beyond the six months originally planned. Truman replied within twenty-four hours that he wanted the best possible report. "Take as much time as you need," the president wrote. "Money is no object."

Truman kept his word. By the end of eighteen months, the federal government would spend around $900,000 for the work. The president also opened doors for Paley by telling his cabinet officers that they should make personnel and information available to the commission.

The only seriously divisive issue among the commissioners was the 27½ percent oil depletion allowance, which permitted oil companies to take substantial tax write-offs for investing in oil wells. This was an important economic issue, and Hodgins and Mason, the commissioners most attuned to public policy, believed that the allowance would have a damaging long-term effect. They saw it as an enormous tax loophole for the wealthy that loaded too much investment money in oil at the expense of other resources. Coombs also strongly advocated a substantial reduction if not outright elimination of the allowance.

Paley, however, shaped the commission's recommendations to favor continuation of the prevailing allowance. The reason, Paley later said, was its usefulness as an incentive to stimulate domestic oil production. Hodgins had a different and somewhat more cynical view of Paley's rationale: "Messrs Paley, George Brown, and Arthur Bunker, being men of considerable wealth, were quite sure that the 27½ percent depletion allowance was merely the manifestation of what providence had intended all along. Professor Edward Mason of Harvard and I being peons of the commission . . . in pocketbook, felt very strongly that we should criticize this depletion allowance. . . . Mr. Paley was extremely anxious for a unanimous report, and in the face of this wholly understandable desire and in the force of such overpowering dollar opposition as Professor Mason and I encountered, we rather let this go."

For the first year Paley worked four days a week on what quickly became known as "the Paley Commission." He cut down his time in the Executive Office Building only during the last several months. He devoured hundreds of pages of material, often staying up to three in the morning to finish reading a study. Most days he would have lunch with Coombs and Hodgins, listening intently as they discussed the latest report on electric energy or copper production or water conservation. "Bill Paley would tell us it was the best, most intensive short-run education he had gotten," said Coombs. "I saw not only curiosity but a certain joy. When something interesting came along, it would stimulate and excite him."

The Paleys rented a house in Georgetown and entertained the city's most influential figures. Babe was thrilled. "She loved being in Washington," said her friend Susan Mary Alsop. "At dinner parties she was always interested. She followed the news. She was hungry for it."

Paley kept in touch with CBS, dipping in and dipping out as he had in previous years. Most weeks he would spend his Fridays at 485 Madison Avenue en route to Kiluna. He made regular phone calls to Frank Stanton and key programming executives. Sometimes he communicated daily, at other times weekly. When Stanton came to Washington on business, the two men would usually get together.

From time to time, Paley brought CBS concerns to his new Washington colleagues. Coombs, whose expertise was industrial organization, was fascinated by Paley's descriptions of the competition between CBS and RCA. When Paley asked him what he thought of CBS—as the CBS chairman often did when he encountered men with specialized knowledge —Coombs gave Paley what he later characterized as a "lecture on the subject of industrial structure." Coombs pointed out that RCA was vertically as well as horizontally integrated; RCA's ability to make radio and television sets gave the company strength. Not long after that discussion, Paley seized on the ill-fated idea of buying Hytron. "My views weren't the cause," Coombs said years later, "but they may have softened him up."

Paley was justifiably elated over the commission's five-volume report, titled *Resources for Freedom,* which was issued in June 1952, a few months before Paley's fifty-first birthday. Ten thousand copies were printed at a cost of $55,000. "Bill Paley was so proud of it," recalled Howard K. Smith, then serving as London bureau chief for CBS News. "He had me send lots of copies to his friends in England. I saw him as a rich man aching to do public service in a conspicuous way."

In accepting the report and its seventy-eight recommendations, President Truman told Congress, "I do not believe there has ever been attempted before such a broad and farsighted appraisal of the material needs and resources of the U.S. in relation to the needs and resources of the free world."

In thoughtful, even eloquent terms, the report looked ahead to 1975 to project and analyze the growing demand for raw and manufactured goods and the shrinking resources to meet those needs. It noted that the United States faced an ever-increasing raw materials deficit. The commission failed to foresee the growth in environmental concerns, and it underestimated population growth and the magnitude of consumer demand for durable goods such as automobiles, air conditioners, and, yes, even television sets. But its essential conclusions were prescient. Paley proved himself adept at the long-range view.

The commission correctly predicted global energy shortages and recommended research into and development of alternate sources such as oil shale, nuclear power, oil and gas from coal, solar energy, and hydro energy. Among other measures, the report urged the development of automobiles that could get 25 to 28 miles per gallon, a proposal that would not be seriously considered until the "energy crisis" of the mid-1970s. Recycling scrap and synthesizing new materials such as plastic also figured prominently among proposed solutions.

The most controversial aspect of the report irked conservative and protectionist politicians. The commissioners dismissed the notion that the United States should strive for self-sufficiency. Instead, they concluded that America should seek materials of the lowest possible cost to ensure a continuing rise in its standard of living and assure reliable sources of essential resources. The report urged the government to negotiate agreements with developing and underdeveloped nations rich in materials. These relationships would not revive colonial exploitation, but would help "resource nations" develop their own economies. To accomplish those goals, the report recommended elimination of high protective tariffs and laws that discouraged investment abroad.

The report drew high praise in the press. In an editorial, *Life* magazine drew parallels with Alexander Hamilton's acclaimed *Report on Manufactures* in 1791. *Fortune* magazine featured a long excerpt, calling the report "one of the greatest, most readable government documents of the century." *U.S. News and World Report* put Paley on its cover that August and ran a seven-page interview with him.

Some conservative forces grumbled that the commission took too liberal a stance. They saw the report as a government effort to subject the materials industry to excess planning and control, and viewed the tariff recommendation as an attempt to undercut American industry by subsidizing low-wage workers overseas.

Typically optimistic, Paley expected the federal government to act on the commission's work and develop strong policies. But the report was badly timed, appearing amid the Eisenhower-Stevenson presidential campaign. Paley not only visited Arthur F. Burns, head of Eisenhower's Council of Economic Advisers, but he wrote twice to the new president, urging him to put its proposals high on his agenda. Despite his friendship with Eisenhower and many others in the new administration, Paley's efforts were unsuccessful. "Perhaps Eisenhower's people did not want to do anything or build on anything the previous administration was responsible for," Paley said later. "That is the only explanation I can think of for the inaction." It didn't help that Truman and Ike were personally distant.

Paley tried to keep the cause alive by funding an organization called Resources for the Future, which was eventually absorbed into the Ford Foundation. He assigned his star newsman, Edward R. Murrow, to anchor a documentary entitled *Resources for Freedom*. In the film, which was televised in January 1954, Murrow deferentially interviewed all the commissioners, including his boss. Paley made yet another pitch for government action: "The only cause for alarm would be if we closed our eyes to the threat of creeping scarcities and higher costs and pretended that somehow the materials problem would blow over. It won't. . . . The materials problem is everybody's problem."

Four months later, nearly two years after his report was issued, Paley found himself in a Senate hearing room testifying before the special Subcommittee on Minerals, Materials, and Fuels Economics. He had dutifully refreshed his memory on the report's salient points, and had a lengthy statement prepared by aides. He also brought along Dr. Edward S. Mason to fill in any blanks. He approached the task with his usual trepidation; he had not endured a congressional hearing since his unsuccessful battles with Lawrence Fly back in 1942. But this time would be different. He had come to defend a piece of work that filled him with pride.

His appearance turned out to be difficult, to say the least. For nearly four hours Paley fielded a barrage of hostile and often unfair questions from Senator George W. Malone, a conservative champion of Nevada mining interests, flanked by senators from Idaho and Wyoming. Malone had evidently been seething for two years over the Paley Commission's strong anti-protectionist tilt, and all his venom came pouring out. Malone also happened to be one of the most steadfast supporters of the Red-baiting senator, Joseph McCarthy, who only three days earlier had appeared on CBS to rebut a scathing indictment of McCarthy by Edward R. Murrow.

Malone insulted, needled, contradicted, and patronized the CBS chairman. "I think you are improving," he said at one point when Paley slightly modified a point. Unaccustomed to such treatment, Paley kept his composure, soldiering through despite numerous interruptions. He held his position and spoke with palpable feeling. It was a bravura display of Paley's strength, his determination not to be bested, and his courage.

Paley had no reason to regret his preparation. When Malone skewered him on his ignorance, the facts in question were generally beyond the scope of the Paley Commission study. But Paley had made one crucial strategic error. Before the hearing he had neglected to visit the members of the committee on Capitol Hill—a gesture that was routine for Frank

Stanton but beneath Bill Paley. As a result, the CBS chairman had no ally to reprimand Malone when he was out of line.

Paley was shaken. "I don't know how you can go down there and do that," he said when he caught up with Stanton afterwards. More than ever, Paley was willing to cede Stanton what he called the "Washington beat." It scarcely seemed to matter that the role of spokesman for CBS had already conferred great power and status on Stanton. Paley would not appear before Congress again.

32

HAVING PROVED his creative skills again in government service, Paley might logically have found new stimulation at his company's emerging television network. Instead, he directed his energy toward lighter pursuits: decorating, collecting furniture and art, and hobnobbing with high society.

The importance of these sidelines to Bill Paley cannot be underestimated. "When he talks about his attainments he talks not in professional terms but in terms of satisfaction with his social achievements," said Truman Capote, a confidant of Bill and Babe Paley during that period. "He is a bit of a name dropper—royalty for example." Paley was known to display his photo albums to guests, ostensibly to show his prowess as a photographer, but the names and places could not fail to impress: Picasso and Babe; former British prime minister Anthony Eden with Bill and Babe at Cap d'Antibes; Bill taking a stroll with Queen Elizabeth and Prince Philip.

The CBS chairman grew fabulously rich in the postwar years. Since much of his evolving identity—at least among his friends—derived from his wealth and its stylish emblems, making money became a kind of religion for him. "If you have spent your life pursuing money, you don't know of anything else," said one intimate of the Paley family. "Enough is never enough. You have to keep it going or you'll get eaten up. He was hardly going to get eaten up, but he acted as if he might." Fleur Cowles, the second wife of *Look* publisher Gardner Cowles and a friend from those days, compared Paley to "one of the cats of the jungle. He prowled around in search of moneymaking."

Paley continued to diversify his holdings by whittling down his percentage of ownership in CBS—from 18.7 percent at the end of World War

II to 10.5 percent by the end of the 1950s. Yet in that same period Paley's CBS holdings rose in value from $9.8 million to $38.6 million, and his annual income from his CBS salary, bonus, and dividends increased from $805,623 to $1.4 million. In addition, he had considerable earnings from an investment portfolio overseen by a retinue of advisers.

With Dorothy before the war, he had sought fun and escape; but his companions, though some had wealth and titles, were chosen for their cleverness, intelligence, or talent. As he grew richer, Paley's world grew smaller. In the postwar years he seemed to concentrate on climbing the social ladder in America and Britain. His world was the realm of Jock Whitney and Alfred Gwynne Vanderbilt, of dukes and viscounts, of beautiful, decorous women and dashing gentlemen, where bloodlines and social standing were all. "They will get rid of every Jew," an old friend of the Paleys from a prominent Jewish family predicted after Bill and Babe's marriage. That was not quite true; the Paleys remained friends with the Selznicks and the Goldwyns, but they seemed to be the exceptions.

Most of Paley's postwar friends fell short of his intelligence and achievement. Some were not even that rich. But all had high social positions and a certain degree of stylishness. Many were silly and artificial. Their company was undemanding, and there was little competition for attention. Paley's new acquaintances shared his material and social preoccupations, and he could dominate their activities and conversations. They were drawn by his magnetism, not to mention his money and power. He was a tycoon, not a boring businessman but a glamorous gentleman, a breed apart.

By his early fifties, Paley's black hair was streaked with gray at the temples. But he remained vigorous and attractive—broad-shouldered and well built at nearly six feet and 180 pounds. His dark brown eyes and brilliant smile flashed as disarmingly as ever. He appeared a good ten years younger than he was. After his years in London and the example of his brother-in-law Jock Whitney, the fine points of upper-class manners were now second nature.

Appearances became paramount. "The Paleys were social climbers," said Charlotte Curtis, who watched their ascent. "Their friends narrowed. They began to live on a predictable circuit. They went to all the right functions in New York." They became the most-sought-after but unapproachable couple in New York. "If you were giving an ideal dinner party, the Paleys would be invited," said the social columnist Suzy (Aileen Mehle) in the mid-1970s. "They dress up anything they touch. Putting her in a room is like putting in a bouquet of flowers, and he dresses it up too because he has money and power, and style and charm when he wants to." For the most part, the Paleys exchanged dinner-party invitations with their tight circle of friends. Since their pied-à-terre in New York was too small to entertain large groups, Bill and Babe gave private parties in the ballroom at the St. Regis hotel. There were forty guests at one dinner in honor of Dame Edith Sitwell.

The Paleys cultivated their aloofness. No one but close friends could reach them on the phone; otherwise, a letter was mandatory. Although they went out virtually every night in New York, they seldom appeared at fund-raising benefits or other stops on the party route. "We never go to balls. I think they're just hell," Babe once declared. "My husband dislikes them as much as I do." Occasionally they might grace a symphony or opera opening, but even then they tended to enter by a side door—at Babe's insistence, Truman Capote once said, to avoid the flashbulbs. "Her husband objected," said Capote. "He *wanted* to be seen by the photographers." Babe seemed to wrap herself in mystery less out of calculation than a craving for privacy. When she went to a restaurant with friends, she avoided the front banquettes where the maitre d' would place his most ornamental customers. Instead, she would request a table to the side.

This life must have been a disappointment for Babe, who had married Paley in part to escape high society and enter a more adventurous world of movie stars, producers, directors, and writers. "The people he liked were the people they saw," said Susan Mary Alsop. "In the early days Bill had been perfectly bored by Long Island society. But then after the war he got amused by those people and their counterparts in Europe. Babe had a sharp mind and was interested in his CBS connections. But he had done all that. He had got through that period when the house was filled with writers and intellectuals. He got bored with that. He wanted glamour. Because of Babe's devotion to Bill, she did exactly what he said." Said Irene Selznick, "To Bill, it was up and up."

The focal point of the Paleys' social life continued to be Kiluna, where every weekend was a house party for four or five couples. "If I don't keep the house full on weekends, I couldn't live with him," Babe once indiscreetly confided to a CBS executive, echoing Dorothy's lament. Each Saturday morning, Paley would rise early and eat breakfast alone in his room. (His guests generally preferred to sleep in.) Sitting on his bed amid newspapers and a bulging briefcase, he would work the phones for several hours before disappearing with his chums for a round of golf at the exclusive Links Club. In the words of *Time* magazine, he "competed tensely and excitedly"—usually "clobbering" his opponents—an innocent bit of news magazine hyperbole given his 15 handicap.

Weekend cronies included his neighbor Leland Hayward, the theatrical producer (who would be stolen from his wife, Slim, by Pamela Digby Churchill); millionaire banker Watson Blair, whose parents owned one of the most beautiful homes in Palm Beach and whose wife, the former Josie Cutting, was from an old-line New York family; Long Island socialite Tommy Choate; stockbrokers Roy Atwood and Joseph Sheffield, both longtime pals of Jock Whitney; and Walter N. Thayer, an attorney and business associate of Whitney's.

Whitney, of course, stood at the top of Paley's list. Just being around Whitney exhilarated Paley. "My brother-in-law Jock Whitney," he would say, running the words together as if they were one, whenever he brought Jock around CBS. "Bill's friendship with Jock had a great deal to do with everything," said Diana Vreeland. "The Whitneys never particularly got anything from Paley, but his importance was from being related to them," said Alice-Leone Moats. For his part, Jock Whitney greatly admired success in business. "Jock would naturally adore someone like Bill Paley who was doing something," said Charlotte Curtis.

E. J. Kahn commented that "a lot of people took Jock to be a kind of lightweight—polo, horse racing, money, all that—but he wasn't. I suspect that Paley, quite apart from being his brother-in-law, recognized this and appreciated it. They were probably very lucky to have found and profited —obviously not in a monetary sense—from each other."

Paley was more outgoing than Whitney, but both tended to be reticent and private. Underneath, Whitney was every bit as strong and authoritative as Paley. "Utterly sure of himself and terribly shy," was how René d'Harnoncourt, a director of the Museum of Modern Art, characterized Whitney. Their membership on the MOMA board led them to share in one of the great troves of the century: Gertrude Stein's collection of thirty-eight Post-Impressionist paintings, most of them by Picasso. Years earlier Stein had refused to donate her collection to the museum, but when MOMA officials heard the paintings would be available for sale, they assembled a syndicate of buyers, including Whitney, Paley, and David and Nelson Rockefeller. Each man put up $1 million and pledged to give some of the works to the museum during or after their lifetimes. Paley later called the transaction "almost a steal."

On the golf course, where they spent a lot of time, Whitney and Paley regressed into a juvenile joking rapport. But Paley never ventured into Whitney's select world of polo and breeding racehorses. Nor did he learn Jock's difficult and arcane sport of court tennis—a favorite game of French, English, and American aristocrats over the centuries. It was an exclusive sport, with less than a dozen courts in the United States. Whitney's father had been so hooked on the game that he had his own court built at Greentree, where Paley would sit in a row of red felt thrones and watch Jock play.

It is a measure of Paley's idolatry that he embraced so many of Whitney's friends and elements of his lifestyle. He even convinced CBS to buy Whitney's private plane. To Paley, Jock Whitney embodied the ultimate in American masculine style. Yet Whitney's influence was less in matters of taste than in the way he operated. "Bill," summed up Walter Thayer, "liked the way Jock lived."

A gentle rivalry flecked their relationship as a result. Once while watching television with Whitney at Greentree, Paley wanted to change the channel. "Where's your clicker?" Paley asked, figuring Jock would have a remote-control switch at his fingertips. Jock calmly pressed a buzzer, and his butler walked up to the TV set to make the switch.

The only blemish on their friendship was the attitude of Betsey Whitney. She remained cool to Paley—either out of mistrust or snobbery, or perhaps a little of both. Betsey's friends often remarked on one incident when her dislike took a spiteful turn.

It was during a dinner she and Jock gave at Greentree for Lord Mountbatten, who had recently commissioned a movie of his life. Betsey tried to coax Paley into buying the film for CBS. But Paley showed little interest in such an uncommercial project, despite his Anglophilia and his old affair with Edwina. Betsey was visibly miffed. At her direction after dinner, the butler produced a half-dozen candies on a dish. Paley dove for them with his usual avidity. He swallowed one, then another. "Betsey," he said. "What are these?" "They're the dog's treats!" she replied with a gleeful laugh. Aghast, Paley was said to have checked in with his doctor the next day.

David Selznick was one of Paley's few prewar intimates to make the postwar cut—even as the friendship between Selznick and Whitney, his *Gone With the Wind* business partner, cooled. "Betsey didn't like David," Irene Selznick explained. "She thought he was a bad influence—gambling, staying up late, playing. So she kept him away." Babe had no such sway over her husband. Even if she had, it is difficult to imagine how Paley could have spurned the charismatic, larger-than-life Selznick, the man Alfred Hitchcock once called "charmingly ruthless." "David didn't love Bill the way he loved Jock," said Irene Selznick. "He was fond of Bill, enjoyed him, looked forward to his company. David was very aware of Bill's faults, but he liked his brightness and enthusiasm and met him more than halfway."

Prominent among Paley's friends on the other side of the Atlantic was Loel Guinness, scion of the prominent British banking family, former Royal Air Force flyer, and member of Parliament, who inherited a considerable fortune in the late 1940s. "I don't think Loel read a book or bought a good painting in his life," said Lady Mary Dunn. "He was just rich— and he inherited that."

Michael and Jeremy Tree, the sons of the same Ronald Tree whose ancestral home at Ditchley had so impressed Paley during the war, ranked high among Paley's friends as well. Lusty and indiscreet, Jeremy Tree was a friend of British royalty and managed Jock Whitney's racehorses in England. Michael Tree was an amateur portrait artist who worked at Christie's auction house, and his wife, Lady Anne, was a close friend of Babe. The Tree brothers called Paley "Dads" and kept him amused with their teasing chitchat. "Michael is funny," said Slim Keith. "If the material isn't there, Michael makes it up. He makes Bill laugh, and what Bill wants to do more than anything is laugh."

Paley was equally transfixed by David Somerset, cousin and heir to the tenth Duke of Beaufort. Somerset, called "the Dazzler" by Paley's American friends, was renowned for his narcissism; if there was a lull in the dinner conversation, it was said that he would catch his reflection in a soup spoon. "David and Bill were wicked together," said Lady Mary Dunn. "Even Babe was made to laugh by their conjoint malice. They were always funny and unforgivable."

The Paleys also mingled with the Duke and Duchess of Windsor, Baron Guy de Rothschild, Lord Victor Rothschild, and Judy Montagu Gendel, a well-born Englishwoman who was one of Paley's few homely female friends. If Paley hankered for an old-fashioned English breakfast, she would show up the next morning dressed as an Edwardian maid to serve him kippers, haddock, kidneys, bacon, eggs, and porridge.

Whatever their own financial status, upper-class Englishmen of the period seemed to find wealthy Americans irresistible, and Paley's British friends doted on him. "To them, he was the ideal successful American dream," said Horace Kelland, who moved to London during the postwar years. Paley in turn was flattered by their attention. "He loved having such instant entrée into British society," said John Pringle, a friend from London and the Caribbean. "He had more good friends in England than America."

In America, Paley "had a shield around him, a number of men who had to give top performances," noted M. Donald Grant, former chairman of the New York Mets (the team owned by Jock Whitney's sister, Joan Payson). They were the court jesters, ever ready to complete a golf foursome, quick with the badinage and practical jokes. They usually had little money of their own; they existed to make bored rich men laugh.

First among Paley's courtiers was Jack Baragwanath, the mining engineer and legendary raconteur. Fourteen years Paley's senior, "Handsome Jack," as Baragwanath was widely known, had cut a dashing figure in New York society for several decades. A trim six-footer, he wore his dark hair slicked back and had a pencil mustache. After studying geology at

Columbia University, he had spent more than a decade in the roughneck world of South American mining camps before returning to New York. In the early twenties he married the illustrator Neysa McMein, a darling of the Algonquin set for her prowess at parlor games and croquet. It was through Neysa that Baragwanath and Paley first met. Before the war they had seen each other at Swope and Harriman house parties, but they never became friends in those days, primarily because Dorothy did not consider Baragwanath suitable company.

Baragwanath was often vulgar and licentious, yet he managed to ingratiate through his infectious wit. Shortly after Paley's marriage to Babe, when the Paleys and the Whitneys cut through some brush separating their properties and constructed a 125-foot road, Paley named it "Baragwanath Boulevard," and it was dedicated with great ceremony. Handsome Jack had arrived. "Jack would say two words to Bill and send him into paroxysms of laughter," said Slim Keith. Baragwanath helped play host to Paley's many guests, keeping them company when Paley was otherwise occupied. Paley relished Baragwanath's earthy tales of his unconventional life in South America and of randy encounters with attractive women. (Eventually Baragwanath compiled his tamer stories in a book of sketches published by Doubleday.)

Baragwanath was flagrantly unfaithful to his wife, boasting a string of vacuous young women. One writer characterized his way with women as "bluff, hearty, a little teasing, and more than a little suggestive . . . he never got over the rebellious thrill of recounting and embellishing his sexual adventures." During the 1930s Baragwanath had been renowned for a "freedom week" each summer, when he and his friends would entertain a different group of women—sometimes including high-priced call girls—each evening. They cavorted together indoors and out, and the women often posed for nude photographs.

Like Paley, Baragwanath was self-centered and hated to be alone. He relished entertaining his powerful friend but never challenged him. Paley loved recounting how Baragwanath drove him crazy by singing, humming, and mumbling "Chiquita Banana," a particularly irritating television commercial. Paley retaliated by placing a tape recording of the jingle that played continuously in a locked cabinet in Baragwanath's office while Baragwanath tried in vain to find the key. Baragwanath roared at Paley's lame jokes and tricks, like the time Paley sold his friend some cast-off suits, overcharged him by $400, and wrote a refund check in disappearing ink. Less well known was Baragwanath's other important role, that of helping to arrange Paley's extramarital trysts.

Paley rewarded Baragwanath well for his services. When Baragwanath's career as a mining engineer fell apart, Paley let him live rent-free at

Kiluna in the stucco cottage with green shutters and small arched windows that was attached to the tennis house. For the next several years, Jack and Neysa, who was by then frail and ailing, spent many evenings together with Bill and Babe. "After Neysa died, Jack came to every meal at Kiluna," said Slim Keith.

Paley even invented a job for his friend in the company that oversaw the Paley family investments. At the time Paley was putting large sums in oil and minerals, diversifying his holdings outside the broadcasting business. "I thought I'd make him happy and make a little money for me too, so I hired him," Paley said. When Baragwanath was ill at the end of his life, Paley remained a true friend, paying for a full-time nurse to care for him in his apartment on East 56th Street in Manhattan.

A more notorious jester was Truman Capote, who befriended the Paleys in January 1955 on a trip to Jamaica. Their only intimate drawn from the literary world, he was thirty years old at the time—twenty-four years younger than Bill and nine years younger than Babe. The Southern-born writer had been widely celebrated for his short stories and first novel, *Other Voices, Other Rooms*. Capote had a knack for self-promotion and social advancement, cozying up to a group of high-society women—Babe Paley, Gloria Guinness (wife of Loel), C. Z. Guest, Slim Keith, Pamela Churchill, and Marella Agnelli. A flamboyant homosexual, Capote idolized the women he called his "swans" for their grace and beauty.

He belonged more to Babe than Bill, serving as her intellectual mentor, telling her what books to read (Proust, Wharton, Henry James), sharpening her conversational skills, boosting her self-confidence. His charm and intellect impressed her; she considered him a soulmate, her one refuge from the banality of Long Island society. He in turn looked to her for the fine points of decorating and upper-class manners.

"At first Bill was appalled by Capote," said Irene Selznick, recalling the writer's fey mannerisms, pronounced lisp, and baby face with its fringe of blond bangs. "Then he was amused. This was early fresh Capote—still dewy-eyed, not so spoiled and bitchy, still talented and inventive and quick and ambitious socially." Paley called him "Tru-Boy" and appreciated his ability to keep the conversation sizzling at dinner parties with caustic gossip and unconventional pronouncements delivered in his best high-pitched manner. "Capote," said Michael Tree, "was a rich man's Pekinese."

Capote had an open invitation to Kiluna. According to Leonora Hornblow, a periodic guest with her husband, Arthur, "he was there every weekend he chose to be." For some two decades Capote accompanied Babe and Bill on countless trips to the Caribbean and Europe. Most of the time Paley paid his way.

Capote's relationship to the Paleys was almost too peculiar to be categorized, though it was part entertainer, part psychiatrist, and part intimate friend. He cultivated them, they cultivated him, and each side milked the relationship to the hilt. Yet Capote was also very much the indulged child who, incidentally, took up more of the Paleys' time than their own children did. He thought nothing of having the great Bill Paley curl up on his bed for a chat. After meals Capote often sat to one side of the living room with Babe, their heads pressed close to share gossipy revelations too choice for public consumption. They would giggle together, and Babe would talk to him as if he were one of the girls.

At Kiluna, Paley and his friends passed the time in a state of perpetual frivolity. The Whitneys, Vanderbilts, and Paleys formed a softball team for weekend play; during each game, butlers stood at the ready, holding silver trays filled with cold drinks. Croquet continued as a popular diversion, as did swimming and poolside lounging in the warm months. There was always a fierce backgammon tournament in one of Kiluna's ground-floor rooms, a match in the indoor tennis house, and in the evenings a preview of a new film.

In the company of his friends, Paley projected unflagging optimism and exuberance. He was fiercely loyal. "I'll bet you never heard a nice person say anything bad about Bill Paley," said Henry Mortimer, a brother of Babe's former husband and a longtime friend. When told that many who worked for him had less than flattering views, Mortimer rejoined: "No, I meant *nice* people. People like *us*." What he meant, of course, was the *right* people.

Dinner-table talk at the Paleys' was designed to entertain the master of the house—always the center of attention. "He had a low tolerance for conversation not focused on what he wanted to talk about. . . . Whoever was worth his salt in Bill Paley's eyes spent time amusing him," recalled one frequent guest at their table. Titillating stories about the rich and famous formed one leitmotif. "He always liked talking about little jokes, small occurrences in life, badinage," said Michael Tree, whose inside scoops about British aristocracy (especially who was sleeping with whom) made tasty conversational morsels. Paley gave as good as he got, telling tales about events in his life and people he dealt with in the early days of his business. "He would tell funny stories, not deep stories," said John Pringle, "nothing that divulged relations with his family."

Food was an endless source of discussion at Kiluna. "You could always get a sparkle if you talked about a marvelous dish," Pringle went on. Paley delighted in regaling his guests with his culinary adventures, like the time he was driven seventy-five miles to patronize a famous chef in Normandy. That day Paley ate not one but two lunches—the first lobster, the second roast duck—and on his return to Paris that evening downed another multicourse dinner.

Paley preferred to steer conversation away from television whenever possible, although he privately solicited the views of Jock Whitney. Despite Whitney's pedigree, Paley considered him to have good instincts about the lowbrow medium. Whenever the subject came up in company, however—usually as the question, "Why can't American television be more like British television?"—Paley would say that no one would watch it. "Only one thing was on his mind: money," recalled Horace Kelland, a frequent visitor and close friend of Babe in those days. "The dollar was one thing, taste was another." From time to time Paley would try to impress his friends by showing them a program of which he was particularly proud. "There would be an embarrassed silence," recalled Kelland. "We would say, 'Oh God,' and he would defend it. He would say we didn't know what the public wants."

"It was a cardboard world," said one Paley intimate from those days. "Nobody talked about real things or concerns. You had to be funny, lighthearted, and entertaining. That was the idea of good form." Even discussions about politics, or about art, had to assume a jocular tone.

Yet Paley was not fundamentally a frivolous man. He was serious about his business; he believed in what he was doing. His preference for levity may have been partly an escape, so that "he didn't have to use his brain, a total change," in the view of Marietta Tree. Paley himself once noted that he wished to avoid his father's habit of discussing "business problems" around the dinner table. Less obvious was the danger of an argument arising from a serious topic. Paley had a temper that few saw but everybody sensed.

For all their affection, Bill Paley's friends were also wary. They understood the limits of what could be discussed and how far he could be pushed. They learned to bend to his whims. "There is a touchy no-man's-land with people like Bill you cannot go into," said John Pringle. "He was a very demanding person. There could be no fuck-ups. If you were going to do something, he expected it to be done. But he never gave the impression of being unattractively demanding. He would be grateful. If there was any irregularity with Bill Paley it was that while whatever he said at the time he meant, he could be hurtful when he changed his mind later. You could be taken to the sky by Bill and dropped on your ass. That was his enthusiasm. And there was no excuse for your coming to him with something absurd." Even people just as prominent as Paley, like Katharine Graham, chairman of *The Washington Post,* treated him with kid gloves. "Bill does not have a high degree of patience," she said. "You didn't want to bore him. He really always wanted things to be perfect."

Friends formed vital links on the Paleys' travels abroad. The couple spent a month each summer with Loel Guinness and his wife, Gloria, at Piencourt, the Guiness home near Deauville in Normandy, and cruised the Mediterranean on the Guinness yacht. Other stops on the Paley summer itinerary included Mautry, home of Baron and Baroness Guy de Rothschild in Normandy, and vacation homes owned by assorted friends in France and the Greek Isles. One summer the Paleys rented a home on Ischia; another year they took a house on Capri for a month. Paley often made a detour to Baden-Baden, where he took the waters for his health just as his father had done.

In London they stayed at the Connaught, which Paley now preferred to Claridge's because of its dark-paneled intimacy and pseudo-exclusivity; no one unknown to the management could get a room. When Jock Whitney served as ambassador to the Court of St. James's, the Paleys stayed at the ambassador's residence. In Paris, the Paley suite at the Ritz Hotel overlooked the Place Vendôme. Occasionally Bill and Babe would stay with Brose and Virginia Chambers. Banished during the Dorothy era by Paley, they had come into money after the war, bought a charming home in Paris that had belonged to Cole Porter, hired a splendid chef, and were happily restored to Paley's charmed circle. Virginia Chambers went to great lengths to help Bill and Babe find the most exquisite and tasteful things on their Parisian shopping expeditions. Virginia's "slave complex," denigrated by Paley when it was directed toward Dorothy, was acceptable when applied to him.

The Paleys seldom traveled alone. With Vincent and Minnie Astor during the summer of 1952 they visited the Chantilly chateau rented by Susan Mary Alsop, then married to William Patten, an attaché at the American Embassy in Paris. Two summers later Bill and Babe took New York socialites Rosie and William Gaynor to Paris. Michael Tree and his wife shared a house one summer with the Paleys in Greece. Leland Hayward and his wife, Slim, joined them in Hawaii one year, and another time in Venice, where, said Slim, "Babe and I shopped like two drunks, buying shoes and fabrics."

The admiration of his high-status friends meant a great deal to Paley. "He does the things that people need to do to work at friendships. He has good manners," said Carter Burden, who was married for a time to Babe's daughter Amanda. Paley took particular care in selecting gifts for his cronies. Jack Baragwanath, for example, had often regaled Paley and his friends with tales of the toucan, a bird he saw in Brazil; he had claimed that a banana could go through a toucan's digestive system by the count of twelve. One year Paley went to elaborate lengths to secure a toucan for Baragwanath's birthday. The bird was finally wheeled into the Kiluna dining room with a shawl covering its cage. At the unveiling, Paley and Baragwanath laughed uncontrollably.

Paley's extravagant favors were legendary. When Leland Hayward's son Bill had to be flown to Menninger, the famous psychiatric clinic in Kansas, Paley offered the use of the CBS airplane, a DC-3 equipped with a bar and plush seats that he called "my airplane." Once during one of David Selznick's financial crises, Paley gave his friend a signed blank check and said, "You fill in the amount." On hearing that Katharine Graham was hospitalized with pneumonia, Paley sent homemade soup to her room every day and gave her his house in the Caribbean to use for her recuperation.

Paley's pals reciprocated with their own grand gestures. Loel Guinness built a kitchen on his yacht next to Paley's appointed room so Paley could snack on chicken wings in the middle of the night. John Pringle, whose family owned a resort in Jamaica, endeared himself to Paley by importing ten pounds of Paley's favorite chopped chicken liver from the Stage Delicatessen in New York. He surprised Bill, Babe, and Truman Capote by serving it in a covered silver dish. Baragwanath once had a bench built at Kiluna for Paley with a plaque inscribed wryly: "To Bill Paley from his only friend, Jack Baragwanath."

It was to please his friends as much as himself that Paley lavished extraordinary time and attention on his homes. After he and Babe were married, they began a series of Kiluna redecorations that continued over the years—with the assistance of interior designers Syrie Maugham, Billy Baldwin, Sister Parish, and Stéphane Boudin, among others. Out went the red and green chintz. In came the signature Maugham pallor—chalky white and gray Danish canvas walls with a fleur-de-lis design for the drawing room. Other additions included bibelots, the porcelain and gold vase-lamps, the large-leaf plants in cachepots, the throws draped over the end of a tufted yellow damask sofa, the piles of pillows, the fine French furniture ("FFF"), which Baldwin claimed at that time were "a signature of taste, of fashion, and absolutely a must."

Paley's bedroom was redone in green patterned chintz. Babe filled her bedroom across the hall entirely with French period pieces—of ebony, gilt bronze, and lacquer. She had a weakness for anything associated with Louis XIV, XV, and XVI. In her bathroom, Babe installed a tent ceiling of sheer white fabric. There was also an Empire carved and gilt-wood clock in the form of a black Indian woman, wearing a gilt feathered head-dress and skirt, with a white enameled clockface.

Stéphane Boudin gave the dining room lacquered Chinese red walls (a direct copy of the dining room owned by Olive, Lady Baillie in the Bahamas, except that hers was green). Carefully placed around the room was an assortment of Meissen porcelain figures of lions, palm trees, swans, and horses, as well as urns and decorative boxes. On the dining-room table stood a pair of Louis XIV ebonized wood and gilt-bronze *torchères*, more than four feet high.

Decorating was a joint effort; both Bill and Babe took it very seriously. In quest of a French commode for the Kiluna drawing room, the Paleys invited Billy Baldwin to join them during their holiday in Paris in the summer of 1954. Bill and Babe offered Baldwin an all-expenses-paid week on the condition that he accompanied them each day on the search. "Bill had the strong idea of collecting for a name," Baldwin recounted, "and he was determined to find what he wanted in Paris.

"Bill had the strength of ten, and it was great fun to go to all the terribly expensive and fashionable antique shops with them and find everyone staring at Babe," he went on. Finally, at a well-known antiquarian, Paley spotted a black lacquer commode with a price that Baldwin termed "absolutely staggering." The dealer told Paley that the commode would make his drawing room "the most important room of New York." Paley agreed and pronounced the piece "magnificent." Baldwin, however, described it as a "whore." Paley disagreed at first, then reluctantly went along with Baldwin.

Several days later they visited a woman in Versailles with a houseful of superb furniture, most of which was destined for the Palace of Versailles on her death. In the middle of her salon was a French commode that Baldwin later said was "to die for," but it was not for sale. The woman had already turned down offers from Aristotle Onassis and Stavros Niarchos—which only whetted Paley's appetite. "There was Bill Paley literally down on his knees with tears in his eyes pleading with her to sell it to him, but getting absolutely nowhere . . . Bill just couldn't believe it," recalled Baldwin.

Baldwin also had a strong hand in the New York pied-à-terre kept by the Paleys for more than two decades. The three-room suite on the tenth floor of the St. Regis hotel had a sweeping vista up Fifth Avenue. The drawing-room walls were covered in shirred brown and pink chintz. The French furniture was upholstered in apple green velvet and pale stripes, with needlepoint pillows scattered about. A Venetian bronze clock hung from the ceiling over a Sicilian needlepoint rug. Throughout the room, Babe placed miniature bouquets of red roses, pinks, and baby's breath.

In the early 1950s the Paleys paid $120,000 for a vacation house in Round Hill, a fashionable resort in Jamaica where Noël Coward also had a home. A pavilion surrounded by three bedrooms, the house sat on an outcropping of rock with a breathtaking view. It was designed for comfort more than style, offering simplicity on a grand scale. The bamboo furniture was done in a chintz of reds, yellows, pinks, and oranges, with big, soft pillows. The day before the Paleys arrived for one of their two or three prolonged winter visits, a butler would bring their luggage, unpack, fill the house with flowers, and arrange all the latest magazines on tables.

The Paleys spent the least amount of time—usually several weeks during the summer—at their camp on Squam Lake in New Hampshire. They had bought it completely furnished and called it Kiluna North, suggested by Frank Stanton when Paley offered $5 to the person who could come up with the best name. (Paley sent Stanton his $5 in the mail.)

The rambling weathered wood house with robin's-egg blue shutters stood in the middle of a pine forest, near the lake. Its spacious pine-paneled living room was filled with clusters of comfortable wicker chairs and sofas covered with quilts. A large artificial flower arrangement that Babe bought for $75 sat near the gaming table, and the bar was fully stocked with alcohol and soft drinks. On various side tables were pictures of Babe taken by the stylish fashion photographer Richard Avedon—a contrast to the homey informality of the surroundings. A dozen servants attended the household indoors and out. The Paleys kept the house for about a decade before they gave it to Dartmouth College in honor of Paley's aide-de-camp John Minary, a Dartmouth graduate. It was just as well for Babe, who never quite trusted Bill alone in New York during the week while she and the children remained at Kiluna North.

It was in their quest to create perfect living environments that Babe and Bill shared their happiest moments. Admittedly a shallow pursuit, they could commune on matters of taste and style that conveniently crowded out the vexing problems of family life and their own increasingly apparent incompatibility.

Sailing down the Dalmatian coast one summer on Alexander Korda's yacht, Bill and Babe spent every moment of their trips ashore shopping together. "She was always in antique shops, with him right behind," said Slim Keith, "and he was in art galleries with her right behind." But unlike Dorothy, Babe had little say about Paley's art acquisitions. When he bought from the Gertrude Stein collection, Babe served as his proxy because he was ill at home, but he dictated her choices.

Some members of high-WASP society continued to eye him suspiciously as an outsider. Joan Payson once warned M. Donald Grant, "Watch out for Bill Paley. He'll take the gold right out of your teeth."

Anti-Semitism was more overt in this rarefied world than in Paley's prewar crowd. The patter on the golf courses where Paley played included ethnic and racist jokes sometimes told within his hearing. "Many of those men reeked of intolerance and racism," said one intimate of Paley's. "That he put up with that showed how badly he wanted to be accepted."

As in Philadelphia, Paley had problems with exclusive clubs, despite his prominence. The most embarrassing incident—because it became so widely known—was his rejection by the Metropolitan Club in Washington in the early 1950s. Philip Graham, publisher of *The Washington Post* and Paley's seconder, was dismayed to learn that the club had requested that Paley's name be withdrawn. Graham asked Frank Stanton to find out why. Stanton asked around and confirmed his worst suspicion: it was because Paley was Jewish. Stanton summarily withdrew from the club.

Other exclusions were more private but no less wounding. Although Jock was his sponsor, Paley was turned down for membership in the golf and tennis club on posh Fisher's Island in Long Island Sound, where the Whitneys had a vacation home. "One reason for Squam Lake was that they couldn't go anywhere else," said Jeanne Thayer, wife of Walter Thayer. "That has to affect someone with long antennae like Bill."

Some hurts Paley never even knew about. One year the Village Bath Club opened across Shelter Rock Road from Kiluna. Figuring it might be a convenient place for her children to play, Babe walked over and introduced herself to the manager. "I live across the way," she said. "How do I join?" The manager gave her an application which she filled out.

When she got no reply, she called John Minary, who contacted John "Tex" McCrary a public relations consultant and radio personality who lived next to Kiluna. McCrary called the developer and said, "Why can't Bill Paley's kids belong to that club?" The developer replied, "It's restricted. There's not a Jew in the whole set-up." McCrary realized that if he pressed his point and forced the membership, the Paley children could suffer. With some difficulty, he explained the situation to Babe. "Don't tell Bill," she said.

Another summer Babe asked her friend Susan Mary Alsop to help the Paleys get established in fashionable Bar Harbor, Maine. Susan Mary made some inquiries but never heard anything back. Only later did she find out that her own mother and Marietta Tree's father, the Right Rev. Malcolm Peabody, had prevented the Paleys from being admitted to the Bar Harbor Club. Susan Mary was furious when she heard her mother say, "But we can't have Jews." Babe was gracious enough never to bring up the matter again.

Having been burned several times, Bill and Babe avoided other WASP watering holes such as Hobe Sound, Saratoga, Newport, and Palm Beach—where, ironically enough, Paley's parents settled for their retirement. Sam and Goldie belonged to a Reform temple in West Palm Beach and opposed building one in Palm Beach proper for fear of worsening the anti-Semitism there. But Sam helped found the Palm Beach Country Club when he was barred from membership at the Gentile-only clubs.

Still, Bill and Babe were accepted in some highly desirable places. He belonged to the River Club in New York City and the Links on Long Island, where he was one of the few non–Gentile members. Either by choice or self-protection, Paley never became much of a clubman. His reaction to anti-Semitism continued to be denial and deflection—unlike David Sarnoff, who railed against real and perceived anti-Semitic slights. Had Paley confronted anti-Semitism, he would have upset the odd equilibrium he had created for himself. Paley did not, after all, overtly deny being Jewish. He simply assumed the WASP mantle and left it to others to draw their own conclusions.

In the end, the closed doors did not matter. The Paleys were exclusive enough to transcend club memberships. In Kiluna, Round Hill, and Squam Lake they created their own club with their own rules. They determined who could belong and could take solace in leaving behind those who spurned them. With Paley's money and power, and Babe's captivating glamour, they knew few limits.

33

BABE PALEY devoted her life to creating a perfect world for her husband, just as she had been trained to do in her mother's well-ordered household in Brookline, Massachusetts. But the role was an immense strain; the most beautiful and blessed woman in America became progressively unhappy. It was not easy to please a man as demanding as her husband. "She had the wisdom to know that Bill Paley wanted control and order around him—and that it should look effortless," said Tex McCrary.

She ran Kiluna with extraordinary precision and organization, supervising a staff of twelve—butler, cook, kitchen maids, three parlor maids, valets, a chauffeur with a tendency to hysterics, and a dwarflike houseman who carried the wood and did the marketing. Supplies were kept in a basement storeroom: huge boxes of paper towels, toilet paper, detergent, and other staples. When something was needed in Manhattan, the houseman transported it in the Paley station wagon. On his return trip he brought bags of laundry and the Kiluna laundresses spent the week washing and ironing Paley's custom-made shirts as well as sheets and table linens. All was in readiness every Friday.

Babe pampered guests even more elaborately than Dorothy. No one had to unpack or pack. Baths were drawn by servants, and any item of soiled clothing was whisked away, washed, ironed, and folded neatly in the guest's dresser. The bedrooms offered every comfort and convenience: fruit and flowers, piles of new books and magazines, and three newspapers each morning. The bathrooms were stocked with countless bath oils and colognes. "They lived on a level of luxury I never met in England before the war, and I had been to quite a few grand houses like Blenheim," said Lady Mary Dunn, who came to visit several times. "They ran it in a way that money didn't seem to count. You could hardly get into the bedroom for the flowers."

Babe understood full well that, as her friend Leonora Hornblow put it, "Bill Paley lived for his stomach." He woke up thinking about what he was going to eat. He was voracious at breakfast, often tucking into steak or lamb chops. Wherever he was (at home, on the CBS plane, or in the office) Paley snacked incessantly. On an average day he might consume as many as eight meals—breakfast, lunch, and dinner, as well as five mini-meals. "Mr. Paley cannot be twenty minutes without eating," said one former household employee. When the Paleys began traveling frequently to the Bahamas, Paley's valet, John Dean, would exclaim after serving endless drinks and honey buns to Paley that "I was the only man who walked to Nassau."

The food at the Kiluna table met Paley's lofty, almost obsessive standards. Truman Capote used to joke about Babe's "baby vegetables, unborn vegetables" decades before they became chic. Often she went out of her way to secure special delicacies to please her husband: once she had the chauffeur take her to Kennedy Airport to pick up a freshly shot fowl that she had flown in from overseas. "Babe thought nothing of going down to Chinatown herself to get him the right tidbit," said her friend Natalie Davenport, an interior designer. The bounty of the Sunday morning breakfast invariably attracted a large crowd: lamb chops, hash, steak, fish, pancakes with bacon crumbles on top, and Paley's favorite sausages brought from Country Host, a gourmet shop on Lexington Avenue in Manhattan. Many of the menus used by Paley chefs came from Gogs Cushing's recipe book.

Up at Squam Lake, Babe took pains to have an abundance of local produce on hand, including corn picked just before it was tossed in the pot. Babe kept toothpicks at every place and challenged the guests to see how many ears of corn they could eat with just one pat of butter. (At her husband's urging, Babe was conscious of the dangers of a fatty diet even in those days.) After the meal, Babe would say, "Okay, now everybody can pick their teeth." When a friend once asked, "How could you do that?" Babe replied, "It's better than having everybody sitting around talking to each other with corn between their teeth."

Babe planned their Caribbean trips like the Normandy invasion, ordering food from grocers and specialty shops in New York, making a master list with everything from avocados and artichokes to a half-dozen different kinds of lettuce. The veal had to come fron Leonard's, a top Manhattan meat market. The staff crated it all and packed it in the CBS plane.

The Paleys usually entertained two sets of guests in the islands. The first set would stay for a week and leave on Sunday. The next day the second group would arrive for a week-long stay. During the second week everything would be repeated (the menus, the activities) exactly as it had been during the first. "Mrs. Paley didn't want any loose ends," said onc former employee. "She wanted to keep Mr. Paley happy. He wanted everything to run smoothly."

She worked hard at anticipating Paley's needs. She made time to read books and briefed him on what was current and choice. She selected imaginative gifts for him such as a vintage cigar store Indian and a long wooden antique lounge chair from India for his CBS office. She was never a minute late when meeting him.

Tranquility was her goal at all times. "Babe wasn't combative at all," said Carter Burden. "She could not tolerate ups and downs." Burden learned about her aversion to confrontation firsthand. When he was forging a career as a liberal politician patterned after Bobby Kennedy, Burden challenged Paley about the amount of worthless drivel appearing on the CBS network. Babe's son Tony chimed in to support Burden, and Paley defended himself passionately, although not angrily. "Later Babe told me she was shocked and horrified," said Burden. "She said it was the worst thing that could happen. I think Bill actually enjoyed it."

Because she was so preoccupied with order and calm, Babe's rare expressions of strong opinion raised eyebrows. After seeing the musical *My Fair Lady,* in which CBS had a sizable investment, Babe announced that she found it old-fashioned and boring; the criticism vexed her husband. Perhaps as a consequence of such misfires, Babe feared intellectual discussions. There were no reproaches or discouraging words from Babe to Bill in the presence of others. She avoided comments or situations that might diminish him—quite the opposite of Dorothy's bursts of superiority. "Babe always built him up, told him how wonderful he was," recalled Natalie Davenport. "When he came in from a golf game, she would say, 'Oh honeybun, I'm so glad you're back' and give him a big hug," said Jeanne Murray Vanderbilt, a longtime friend.

Babe carefully followed Bill's lead. During the opening of the television season each fall they would stay home and eat their dinner on trays in front of the set, watching the new shows on all three networks. Not a great fan of television herself, Babe nevertheless knew she had to keep her husband company. When Paley tired of their house in Jamaica in the late 1960s, he sold it for $250,000—a tidy profit of $130,000—and built a new one next to the exclusive club at Lyford Cay in the Bahamas. He preferred the temperature there and found the climate more congenial for playing golf.

Closely supervising the design of the house, Paley spent $50,000 alone on studies of the tides and erosion to determine the best placement. "He picked the spot he wanted," recalled his friend Walter Thayer. "It was swampland that he filled in. I remember tramping around in it with him. He had the vision to see how lovely it would be." For a housewarming gift, Thayer paved Paley's driveway with crushed oyster-shell gravel in a shade that complemented the surrounding foliage.

Whatever her reaction to losing her adored home in Round Hill, Babe turned her attention to making their new "cottage" even more beautiful. Although Paley didn't participate in decorating, she kept him abreast of her progress. She always had him in mind when making her choices.

With the help of Natalie Davenport, who was a decorator at the prestigious McMillen Company, Babe filled the spacious open living room with early European furniture. There were Jacobean commodes and armchairs with blue and white tapestry seats, overstuffed sofas and chairs upholstered in a lively blue and white print, and a white rug with a blue diamond design. A large custom-made white bookcase held row upon row of blue and white china, and two Delft chandeliers formed the centerpiece of the room. The dining room had an exquisite red-lacquered Chinese table, and each bedroom was furnished in a different style. Beyond the French doors in the living room was a porch covered in a fur rug that led out to the pool. Babe planted tuberoses around the outside of the house so that the tropical breeze would fill the air with their fragrance.

The Paleys were proud enough of their surroundings to permit the occasional magazine photo spread. But otherwise the details of their private life were protected. Babe was not permitted to speak to reporters except about the most inconsequential subjects—her favorite flower or the designer of a given dress—and then only infrequently. "Babe was careful not to include anyone from the press at their dinner parties for fear they would write something," said Charlotte Curtis. "She was very circumspect." Paley reacted fiercely to any betrayal or invasion of their world, as Paley's old wartime boss C. D. Jackson discovered in the late 1940s. Jackson's employer, *Life* magazine, had written a snide story describing Babe and her sisters as gold diggers. Paley regarded the article as almost sinful disloyalty on Jackson's part. "Really C.D.," Paley wrote. "How could Time Inc. have stooped to such a low order of journalism? It took a decent and useful family and deliberately insulted and belittled it. . . . You've heard me on this score in the past when I've had the '*Time* treatment,' but I want you to know that my resentment then was of no account compared to what it is now."

As for Babe, it was best that she remain a goddess in the public eye, aloof and mysterious. She knew that her looks were of paramount importance to Paley. She once told Natalie Davenport that she had stopped setting her hair before she went to bed because "that was time reserved for him and he didn't want her doing her hair at night." It was often rumored over the years that Babe wore night makeup so she would appear flawless in the morning. That was not the case, but her first act on awakening, she said, was to "put on her face." Afterwards she would climb back into bed to wait for her husband to arrive from his bedroom, usually in his pajamas, to discuss the day's plans. "She wanted to be beautiful for him when he came to see her," said a former servant.

Once Michael Burke, then a CBS executive and later president of Madison Square Garden, arrived early one morning at the Paley apartment for a business meeting. He was surprised to be greeted at the door by Babe in her robe. "You are the only man who has ever seen me without my makeup," she said with a laugh. "Even my husband hasn't." Women friends who glimpsed the beauty of her freshly scrubbed face wondered why she bothered with such elaborate artifice. "Her skin was luminous," said Leonora Hornblow. "She would have been beautiful in sackcloth and ashes."

Babe did everything she could to enhance her beauty, and after consulting beauticians and hairdressers, she learned to apply makeup artfully in only ten or fifteen minutes. "She knew all the tricks," recalled a former governess for the family. "She talked to me about my makeup. She gave me a little bottle of foundation that must have cost $100." At one point she was a devotee of Ernest Laszlo and his cream facial treatments; at other times she patronized Janet Sartin's Park Avenue salon.

When strands of gray began to appear in Babe's hair she agonized about what to do. Kenneth, her hairdresser at the time, advised her to stay natural, using only a rinse to prevent yellowing. On her travels she took along the bottles of rinse, which she would mix before handing them over to hairdressers with meticulous instructions. Envying her distinctive silver tones, droves of women imitated the look. But Babe was never entirely comfortable with her decision. She often considered changing the gray, and one hairdresser after another talked her out of it. "She was a perfectionist, and she was insecure," said a former hairdresser. "She questioned everything over and over again."

She seemed to be forever on a diet, although she was thin as a stick. "These marvelous dinners would come out and she would have about two bites of everything," recalled one of her friends. "She was always dieting to look the way he wanted her to look."

Her friends insisted that Babe was not conspicuously vain. "I imagine she had a face-lift," said Irene Selznick. "Everyone else did. But the vanity of just looking at herself, the enchanted look some ladies have when they catch their reflection, I never noticed with Babe. Nor was I aware of the mirror coming out all the time."

More than her beauty, Babe's style elevated her above her peers. High-society women followed her slavishly in everything she wore. On her way to lunch at La Grenouille one day, she removed her scarf because it was too warm and tied it casually to the side of her handbag. Within a month, this "look" was copied everywhere. After fourteen years on the best-dressed list—thirteen of them at the top—she was named in 1958 to fashion's Hall of Fame since she was "above annual comparison." She was the first society figure to patronize Halston when he was designing hand-painted chiffon caftans. Other favorite designers were Valentino, Mainbocher, Givenchy, Galitzine, Fabiani, Chanel, Norell, and Charles James, whose dramatic red velvet and satin evening dress she wore in *Vogue*. Paley took an active interest in his wife's wardrobe, as she did in his. "She was involved with his ties," recalled John Pringle, "and he was involved with her skirts."

What set Babe's style apart was its apparent effortlessness. At five feet eight she always looked streamlined in a size six or eight. There was an understatement and modesty in her elegance. Her clothes seemed to have been created expressly for her. She didn't spend a fortune on a new dress every week. She mixed her clothes judiciously and hung onto items she liked; she could wear the same gray flannel slacks for twelve years and get away with it. She said that neatness, "which is grooming, after all," was the key to dressing well. Even members of her family never saw her look frumpy or messy. "She was immaculate in blue jeans and loafers," recalled her niece, Kate Whitney.

Babe also knew precisely how to create a stir—by coming down the staircase at Kiluna, for example, wearing a black Mainbocher evening dress with ruching at the hem. Inside the ruching she had sewn tiny bells that heralded her arrival, and she walked in bare feet. "This was not affectation, it was effect," said a guest who was there that evening. "She was smiling. There was no one else there at that moment but my husband and me." Whenever Babe entered a room, she had the impact of a movie star. Once the CBS London bureau was rendered speechless as everyone stared at her perfection. Babe was wearing a navy blue A-line coat with a little black collar, black gloves, black shoes, and what one observer called "an amazing gray bouffant hairdo." "Much of her terrific presence was learned," said one of Babe's male confidants. "She was a wonderful self-creation."

Beginning in 1950, when Bill set up a trust fund of CBS stock in her name, Babe had an annual income—at its peak in 1977 it was $157,000—to spend on herself, primarily for her wardrobe and costume jewelry. When it came to real jewels, however, Paley paid. Babe owned more than $1 million worth of baubles from New York's finest jewelers—Cartier, Tiffany, Harry Winston, Van Cleef & Arpels, Bulgari, and Fulco de Verdura, an Italian duke in the jewelry business. Most of her jewelry sat in a bank vault, especially after thieves stole $190,000 worth (including a $75,000 emerald ring and $50,000 diamond necklace) from a safe at Kiluna in the early 1960s. Whenever Babe wanted to wear something from her collection, her secretary and a secretary from Paley's office were dispatched to the bank; they would sign for the piece and ride back to the apartment in his limousine. One of her favorites, a ring set with one cabochon emerald of 30.92 carats and 34 round diamonds weighing 7 carats, she would pin to the back of her dressing-room curtain for safekeeping. She hid her pearls inside a hollow monkey statue in her bathroom.

Among her other valuable trinkets were a necklace of thirty-one emeralds, weighing approximately 700 carats, with a diamond clasp; a ring set with one cushion-shaped canary diamond, weighing 21.25 carats; a pair of earclips set with two pear-shaped polished emeralds of 44.48 carats and thirty-four round diamonds; a pearl necklace of thirty-nine strands, some two hundred pearls apiece, thirteen diamond rondels—with eight diamonds in each—and six diamond balls, each of which contained thirty diamonds; and a gold bangle bracelet set with fifteen marquise diamonds, forty-three square diamonds, and multiple round diamonds.

Paley's gifts to Babe, including two full-length coats of Russian sable, were calculated to underline his stature and image. Paley wanted a wife without peer to show how successful he was. He wore her like a medal.

"She knew it was important for him that she was the best dressed," said Natalie Davenport. "I once remember when Russian blouses were in, I said, 'Oh, they're so unflattering.' She said, 'But I have to have one.' She had to keep up the reputation." Babe herself feigned indifference when she told *Women's Wear Daily,* "Lots of women go overboard on clothes. It's terrible on style and pretty bad on men's pocketbooks, too. Once you get where you're going, you forget what you have on, so why fuss?"

Others felt that Babe's stylish position meant far more to her than she let on. "She let Charles James dress her for a spectacle," said Tex Mc-Crary. "She didn't want to be fashionable. She wanted to be *fashion*. She wanted to be the North Star." Truman Capote claimed that Babe envied Loel Guinness's wife, Gloria, for seeming to be even more chic. (Gloria, known in New York as "the Ultimate," wore such a large ring on her right hand that she could not find a glove to fit.) And there is ample evidence Babe was passionate about her clothes. Instead of going to the couturier collection in July, she would wait several weeks so she could visit the salons alone. On her trips to Yves St. Laurent's grand salon, she would request that all the clothes be laid out on the floor rather than shown to her on models. That way, she could see how the pieces related to each other.

Babe was pathologically organized about her wardrobe. Adjoining her bedroom at Kiluna was a large dressing room with walls, valences, and shades of mustard yellow chintz covered with stripes and flowers. Behind the walls were four hidden closets, opened by a key. Two of the closets contained fifty-two drawers (in four rows of thirteen each). Three more closets were hidden behind another wall, and there was also a huge walk-in closet with four areas for hanging. During Dorothy's day, the walk-in closet had been a fireplace.

Mirrors covered the inside of all the doors to the hidden closets. Babe lined her fifty-two drawers with paper of pale blue stripes and pink roses. Each drawer had a typed label in a brass holder, categorizing Babe's belongings in the most meticulous fashion: slips, step-ins, long-sleeved knee-length nightgowns, day stockings, black slips, petticoats, evening bras, girdles, all-in-ones, wool vests and pants, black bras, cotton pants and bras, thin socks, heavy socks, wool shawls, silk nightgowns, old chiffon nightgowns, nylon nightgowns, new nightdresses, cotton nightgowns, thin nylon nightgowns, winter nightgowns, winter pajamas, wool bed-jackets, flowers, white socks, belts, handkerchiefs, silk squares and hand-kerchiefs, chiffon scarves, scarves (square and long), scarves (square) silk and cotton, white silk gloves, colored gloves, sports gloves, black gloves, short colored gloves, evening bags, jewelry boxes, traveling bags, lingerie cases, collars, cuffs and dress accessories, cotton gloves, woolen gloves, sweatshirts, blue jeans, ski mittens.

Babe's sense of style had a pronounced impact on Paley. "With Babe he learned a great deal about furniture, china, style of living, and clothes. All that was part of her job," said Horace Kelland. "She made him more

glamorous," said Diana Vreeland. She certainly helped him feel comfortable in a world that was not his own. He once confided to Charlotte Curtis
that he made more mistakes about taste than Babe did. Under her influence
he learned to handle himself more carefully in dealing with his high-society
friends. He absorbed her ironclad rules of etiquette ("Always write your
thank-you notes the night you return home from a party"). "She raised
standards generally in every area of his life," said Slim Keith. "His thinking and heart and soul as well as taste."

Her attempts to please him were poignant. "She always had a little
gold pad next to her place at dinner," said Carter Burden. "If someone
mentioned a book, or if something went wrong with the service or meal,
she would jot it down." Leonora Hornblow recalled that sometimes after
a dinner party Babe would approach the women who flanked her husband.
"You were sitting next to Bill," she would say. "What did he eat? Did he
like it? What did he say?" When Paley came down to the house in Lyford
Cay for the first time after Babe had finished decorating it, he told her,
"It's just beautiful. I am so thrilled." "You really like it?" she asked. "It
was so touching because she was so pleased," recalled Natalie Davenport.

Yet somehow her efforts were never enough. Even after she had
triple-checked the guest lists and slaved over the seating arrangement for a
dinner party, he thought nothing of rearranging it all when he came in the
door. "He had no consideration for the time and effort she had put in,"
said John Backe, who would become president of CBS in the late 1970s.
"He would say, 'This is bad. It's crazy. It doesn't work. Let's do it this
way.' "

Paley could be inconsiderate in other ways. One summer they rented
a house on Capri for a month. Both Babe and Bill fell in love with the
place. After the first week, Paley had an idea. Before they left the United
States he had ordered Babe an extravagant necklace from Fulco de Verdura. "Which would you rather have?" he asked her. "I can cancel the
necklace and buy this house." Babe chose the house, so he canceled the
necklace. Afterwards, when Paley encountered some problems on the island, he got angry and decided they should leave early. "Poor Babe," said
Horace Kelland, who was with them, "she didn't get the necklace or the
house."

Paley tended to be stingy about family expenses, which were paid
through his personal business office, run by John Minary, the one exception being Christmas shopping, which Babe charged half to her own account, half to Bill's. After years of running the household on her own,
Babe asked Bill to hire a private secretary to help her. He initially refused
but finally relented. Interviewing a candidate for the job, Babe balked
when the woman mentioned a salary figure. "I don't know," Babe said.

"They [Minary and his minions] have a policy of not paying too much." Paley, recalled Carter Burden, "would go through periodic economy drives and John Minary would come in and cancel Babe's magazine subscriptions." This pressure made Babe money-conscious, for all her jewels and designer dresses. She would try to cut costs and search for bargains at Ohrbachs. Or she would brag about money saved on floral arrangements by buying artificial flowers.

Naturally, Capote had a theory about Paley's penny-pinching. "You know, he liked keeping the budget low because it made her more dependent and more supplicant to him," Capote said. But Babe's old friend Slim Keith took a more benign view. "Most men of means have tremendous waves of parsimony," she explained. "He never cut back on anything significant." But in the end, Paley's reputation for stinginess with his family stuck. "You hear again and again how tight he is," recalled one longtime observer of the Paleys. As an intimate of the Paley family put it, "His generosity depends on who you are and where you come from. If he is unwilling to let a grandchild get one hundred shares of stock, God knows what he is capable of."

Bill Paley was as spoiled as a man could be. "He took everything for granted," said Natalie Davenport. "His every little wish was taken care of. He knew Babe would keep trouble from him." This pampering made him even more self-absorbed. "Anybody who wishes to be waited on and have the way paved for him that much is boorish," said one of Babe's friends. "Bill Paley is one of those people who take, take, take." But, like Paley's employees, Babe dared not cross the master. He did everything he wanted and rarely had to do anything he disliked. Nobody had his way more than Bill Paley.

34

PALEY'S CHARM masked his narcissism—and underlying insecurities. He appeared to be easygoing but was not. His efforts to keep his private life under wraps stemmed from a fear of exposure. "He needed to control everything, because if he couldn't control, he was afraid," said one Paley family friend.

Paley would carefully hold his thoughts in reserve, counting on others to weigh in first. He would be unlikely to say, for example, "I think the CBS program schedule is in terrible trouble. I am so stumped about what to do. I have been thinking about these alternatives. What is it that you would do?" Instead, he might say, "CBS's program schedule doesn't seem very good to me. The programs just don't seem up to par." His indirect approach was self-protective and somewhat manipulative, but it had the benefit of seeming polite and socially correct.

Paley's inability to share credit was another reflection of his narcissism. It did not occur to him that anyone else could have had a role in his success. His convenient memory and capacity for self-delusion screened out contradictory details. "He could talk himself into things," said one man close to the Paley family. "He wouldn't back down if he believed something. Nothing could change his mind." If anyone took him on, Paley was never at fault. "He was not a self-analytical basket case," said a former girlfriend. "It was all steel. He wanted what he wanted, but if he didn't get it, you were the selfish one."

One tipoff to Paley's insecurity was his deep-seated suspicion. "He didn't trust a lot of people. He would always think someone wanted something," said Frank Stanton. This may have bothered him; he marveled at the easygoing ways of Jock Whitney. "I've often wondered how that came about," Paley said. "When you have that much money, you're apt to be suspicious all the time of others' motives."

Paley revealed his vulnerability through defensiveness and anger. "He could hide his peculiarity with some people," said Irene Selznick, "but others saw views of him neither you nor I can imagine. I think there must have been moments of rage that I tremble to think of . . . the anger from his vitality and drive and will . . . or when he was being contradicted." Another intimate of the Paley family observed that the tripwires for his anger could be surprising: "He would latch onto something casual in conversation and make a big deal out of it. It was hard to figure. He obviously felt threatened. His image seemed in danger of being tarnished, which is important to someone so dependent on others for his self-worth."

Truman Capote told his biographer Gerald Clarke of one particularly chilling outburst. In Venice, the Paleys and Capote had been to dinner with an Italian count and his wife. Although the couple had seven children, it was widely known that the count was homosexual. Still, he had danced the entire evening with Babe, provoking a fit of jealousy from Paley, whom Capote called "the most jealous person I've ever known in my life."

Back in their hotel, Paley lashed out at Babe, who dismissed his complaint with "Oh Bill, don't be such a bore." "There's something going on between the two of you," he insisted. When Capote backed up Babe, Paley wheeled on him: "What the fuck would you know about it?"

"Well," said Capote. "The fuck I would know about it is that he's gay, and all the affairs he has are with men."

"I know a lot of guys who go around pretending that they're gay and they're fucking everybody's wife from here to Maine. It's just an act. I don't believe he's queer at all," Paley replied.

Capote said that Paley was so infuriated he began throwing furniture around the room. Capote and Babe fled to an adjoining bedroom and locked the door. "And he wasn't drunk!" recalled Capote. "He was just in a fantastic rage! He is a very violent man." Paley later denied the incident, but the intensity of his jealousy has been well documented.

The man who filled his wartime doodles with juvenile symbolism remained the wounded child. Paley always felt unloved and was himself incapable of genuine love, which requires give and take as well as trust. "I think I do not like the idea of depending on others," he said in one moment of unwitting revelation. "I don't feel safe. When I find myself becoming dependent on one particular person, I start to worry about what would happen if he or she were no longer there and about who could take his or her place."

The real casualties of Paley's narcissism were his children. Superficially, the Paley family had a nice symmetry—three girls and three boys arranged in three sets of pairs. There were Jeffrey and Hilary, the two children Bill and Dorothy had adopted as infants in 1938 and 1939; Amanda and Tony, Babe's two children from her first marriage; and the two children by Bill and Babe—Billie, born in 1948, and his younger sister Kate, born two years later. Jeffrey and Hilary lived with their mother, but they saw their father every other weekend for Sunday luncheon and spent several weeks in the early summer each year at Kiluna. When they were young, Dorothy sent nursery school teachers along to supervise their activities.

Paley treated his children much as he dealt with his top executives. In each case, their absolute dependence shaped his manner toward them. He had little concern about the effect he was having on them. What counted was that they knew he was in charge. John Backe once saw how Paley's tyranny played out in the family when he overheard a phone call between Paley and his son Billie: "It was the roughest language I ever heard from father to son. He said, 'You don't know what you're doing. You never have.' He was very angry, yelling, screaming. I offered to leave and he said, 'No, stay.' He totally emasculated the kid. I came out of our meeting in a cold sweat over the wedge he drove between himself and that boy."

"The temper," said one family intimate, "made the children careful. He could be mellow and comfortable at one time or just explosive and terrible another. It was terrifying for those who were dependent on him emotionally or economically. They just wanted to please him."

Unlike Dorothy, Babe did not oppose Paley's insistence that the children grow up at Kiluna. Bill and Babe spent most weekdays at their Manhattan pied-à-terre. Its small size (only three rooms) made it strictly for adults only. Even at Kiluna, Tony, Amanda, Billie, and Kate lived apart, occupying the five-bedroom cottage that was separated from the main house by a game room. The cottage had its own living room and kitchen, as well as a playroom in the attic adjoining the bedrooms for the cook and nanny who oversaw the children.

When Bill and Babe were in residence, they remained remote from the activities of the cottage. Most of the time the main house overflowed with friends, the phone never seemed to stop ringing, and the driveway was filled with cars. If the Paleys happened to be at home and no guests had alighted, they would have an occasional family meal.

Conversation at these gatherings was circumscribed and superficial. "It was a matter," said a participant, "of getting by." Paley treated the girls as if they had not a brain in their heads. They joked with him and ribbed him, but only up to a point. As with guests, conversation centered on Paley or a subject he knew best—usually food, the safest terrain for all concerned. Political discussions were off-limits. Art was permissible, but since the children knew so little, Paley usually ended up delivering a lecture on his paintings. There were no general discussions about school. (That subject was reserved for periodic one-on-one luncheons the children had in Paley's office.) And always, in the background, the television competed with the children for Paley's attention; he kept the set in his library going all the time. "Nobody expressed anything in our family," recalled Amanda. "We didn't really talk to each other. There was such a separation of children and parents."

The Paleys were away from New York nearly a third of the year, usually without their children, although they did take them abroad several times. On vacation at Squam Lake, adults and children went their separate ways. Paley was rarely there during the week but often flew up in the CBS plane with a crowd of guests for the weekends. He spent his days playing golf at the Bald Peak Colony Club on nearby Lake Winnepesaukee. As at Kiluna, the children dined apart whenever guests were around.

A stern, distant father, Paley tolerated his children, but he was not affectionate toward them or involved in their day-to-day lives. Many years later he would admit: "I put much more attention on Babe." He was rigid when it came to his children—the boys in particular—with a strong sense of duty but little paternal warmth. He seemed to want to be a good father, yet he did not know how.

Paley stressed the need for self-discipline, hard work, and the folly of taking money for granted—a noble but decidedly mixed message from such a lover of luxury. Unlike his own father, who helped his son's career in every way, Paley did all he could to discourage his sons from going into his business. He never explained his reasons to them, leaving them to feel rejected and inadequate. His rationale, he would say to friends, was an abhorrence of nepotism. "I didn't think it was fair to have them work at CBS," he once said. "If it was a small company, that is one thing. But it was a large public company. If one of my sons succeeded they would say it was because of me. If not, people would be nice to him for the wrong reasons and it would hurt the company."

Other factors may have come into play as well. Given his need for absolute control, Paley felt uncomfortable with the idea of relinquishing his power over the company he built. Perhaps more important, he feared the embarrassment that would occur if one of his heirs failed to make the grade—like David Sarnoff's son Bobby at RCA.

Paley's expectations for his children were hard to discern, since he appeared to mistrust them. He once told a member of his family that he could count on his friends because they didn't want anything from him—implying that his family sought to use him. When he and Dorothy were wrangling over their divorce settlement, she said at one point, "The children should be provided for outside me and outside child support. They should have something that is theirs." Paley responded, "I see no reason for that. How do I know what they'll be? Jeff may grow up to be a Communist." Paley organized trust funds for Jeffrey, Hilary, Billie, and Kate that gave him total control over the assets. Babe likewise set up trusts for Amanda and Tony. Most of the children's money was tied up in CBS stock.

The times Paley did seek out the company of his children, it was on his own terms—if he decided to organize a family picnic, for example. "He was an overpowering father," said John Pringle. "He wanted them to do the things he wanted to do." Occasionally Paley took his daughter Kate into the office to watch the pilots—sample episodes of television series. "He would ask my opinion of them and then not listen to it," said Kate years later. "I was never right. My strategy was to pick out the ones with the best-looking guys. He could never see my insight in that direction."

Paley fancied himself as paterfamilias, not family dictator. In his own mind he did the right things as a father. As the children grew older and went away to school, he never forgot a birthday. His secretary would send the birthday card, or Babe would send the gift. But Paley himself could not be counted on to pick up the phone and call with a birthday wish. His fantasy, said Dorothy, was that "all his children behaved beautifully, thought he was tremendous, adored him as a father, looked to him for guidance in all subjects, and would all be successful in some nebulous way." In Paley's 418-page memoir, there are only seven sentences mentioning his children. "All six brought the wonderful joy of childhood and youth to our home and our lives," he concluded stiffly.

"I was amused by an article in a magazine in which Bill talked about what a wonderful father he was," commented Janet Murrow. "That is something the children ought to say, not Bill." In public, his loyalty to family never wavered. Not long after Kate's birth in February 1950, he and Babe were in Hollywood having dinner at Romanoff's, the famous show-business watering hole. Paley was seated next to the wife of a CBS executive. "You must be thrilled to have two little children," the woman said to Paley. "Oh yes," he said. "I love babies, but I already have two children." "I know," said the woman, "but they are not your own." At that, Paley's normally affable face froze and he stared icily at the woman. "Madam," he said, "they *are* my children." Whenever his son Billie came to visit him at his office, Paley made a point—much as he did with his own father—of giving him a big hug and kiss in front of the secretaries.

There was little identification with Jewish religion or culture in the Paley household. All the children went to schools where the student bodies were predominantly Gentile. But Paley did arrange through the Jewish Theological Seminary for a rabbi to visit Kate and Billie every weekend for several years to instruct them in the Old Testament. He also advised Jeffrey and Hilary to expose themselves to Judaism because their boarding schools only taught them about Christianity. Paley suggested that they both meet with the head of the Jewish Theological Seminary; but he did not push the idea and neither of them followed up.

The Paley children seemed uncomfortable with the choices their father made for them and the lifestyle he gave them. Paley's youngest daughter, Kate, used to keep track of the length of time it took for a cigarette ash to stay in an ashtray before a servant whisked away the cinders. "It was hard to be average, which is what I wanted more than anything," Kate said. "In high school, I used to hang out with Willie Hearst and Edsel Ford. They were in the same boat and we understood each other."

When Billie Paley was at boarding school, he was embarrassed by the large limousine his parents used on visits. Babe tried to explain this to Bill, but he was incredulous. "It wasn't so much that Bill was snobbish, it's just that he was so accustomed to that kind of luxury," recalled Susan Mary Alsop. "Once Babe got it through his head, he found a smaller car to take them there. He had forgotten what it was like to be an ordinary American middle-class father."

Paley's inconsistency—charm one minute, toughness the next—kept his children off balance and strained his relations with all of them. They never knew what to expect. In emotional situations, he absented himself. "As a father, he was charming but rather lazy," said Susan Mary Alsop. "In moments of crisis, when someone failed an exam or wanted to run away, he would hand it to Babe. . . . He could be insensitive without meaning to be."

Jeffrey and Hilary, who came to Kiluna as visitors, were the least touched by their father's presence. Relations were strained between Jeffrey and Bill, and Paley thought Dorothy had poisoned their son against him. Jeffrey, an excellent student and a good athlete, went to Dalton and Fieldston in New York and later to the exclusive Taft School in Connecticut. During his prep school years at Taft he competed on championship basketball teams; his achievements were even mentioned in accounts in the *New York Times*. Yet Paley saw his son play basketball only once, when he attended a Father's Day. Otherwise, Paley's sole visit to Taft—a mere two-hour drive from New York—was for graduation.

Paley tried to fulfill his duty by guiding Jeffrey in choosing a college. Father and son visited Harvard and Yale together, and Paley encouraged Jeffrey to attend Yale because of the Cushing and Whitney connections there. Jeffrey selected Harvard, where he performed well, graduating with a B- average. But after a year at Harvard Law School, Jeffrey decided to drop out. Paley was furious. He told his son he lacked discipline and the ability to see something through.

The clash was one of many during Jeffrey's adolescence and early adulthood. Jeffrey had resisted boarding school, even to the point of deliberately failing an entrance exam at Lawrenceville, but he finally went to Taft at his father's insistence. For all of Jeffrey's achievements, Paley constantly found fault with him. Jeffrey, who strove for his father's approval, rebelled when he failed to receive it and grew increasingly critical of his father's values and ideas. He was, said one man close to the Paleys, "fighting the world." Paley's friends saw him as a difficult young man with a chip on his shoulder.

Jeffrey's decision to pursue a career in journalism after leaving law school only intensified the friction with his father. Although CBS polished its image with broadcast journalism, probing reporters always made Paley nervous—and Jeffrey was just that sort of reporter. He worked for five years on the *International Herald Tribune* in Paris, which was owned in part by Jock Whitney. "He really enjoyed that experience," said Dorothy, "but it was difficult for him. He never had any recognition from his father, not a word of praise." Still, Jeffrey tried to use his newspaper experience, plus a year he spent with Granada Television in London, as a springboard to join CBS News in the early 1960s.

When Jeffrey asked for help, Paley promised to find him a position. Months went by until Jeffrey discovered that his father had "forgotten" the request. Paley finally placed Jeffrey for a summer in the news department at WCBS, the network's flagship station in New York. It was a disaster. "He heard nothing but criticism from Bill," said Dorothy. "It was clear Bill didn't want him there."

After that, Jeffrey withdrew further from his father. He turned from journalism to take a master's degree in economics at the New School for Social Research, then lived a quiet, almost ascetic life in New York working as an investment adviser.

Hilary Paley had a somewhat easier time with her father. She was female, pretty, and she tried hard to get along with him. Tradition-bound in his attitudes, Paley did not have to wrestle with any expectations for his daughter's success other than marriage and children.

Hilary was a picturebook child with blond hair and an upturned nose. "Her beauty pleased Bill enormously," recalled Dorothy. After attending the Riverdale Country School in New York, Hilary went away to the fashionable Shipley School on Philadelphia's Main Line. Like her mother, she attended Bennett College for just one year. She had not one but two debuts. The first, under a pink-and-white-striped tent in the garden at Kiluna, was given by her father. Three months later her mother gave her a dinner dance at the River Club.

By then the distance between Dorothy and her daughter was becoming apparent. While Dorothy had intellectual appetites, Hilary had none. "She was always a trial," said her mother. Hilary was strong to the point of toughness; she could swear like a trooper, and slash with cutting remarks. But she had an appealing liveliness, and she adored a good party.

Hilary worshipped her father, but she could never be certain how much he loved her. More than anything, she wanted to be Babe Paley. "That's one way of getting to the father," commented Dorothy. Hilary was considerably closer to her stepmother than to her own mother. "Hilary was not the same type as her mother," said Marietta Tree. "I could see how she and Babe would get on." "She would talk about Babe as if she were talking about the queen, whose affection and esteem she sought but was not sure she had," said a friend of Hilary's.

Hilary loved glamour and the trappings of clothing and jewelry. "She was like that from infancy," said Dorothy. " 'Is that real gold?' she would say." As a young woman, Hilary would arrive for Squam Lake visits with a wardrobe of clothing far too fine for the rustic atmosphere. She would sit on a boudoir chair in her room dressed in a silk negligée, her hair perfectly coiffed, wearing heavy makeup and smoking a cigarette. "She seemed very out of place," recalled Marguerite Platt, who supervised the children one summer at Squam Lake and Kiluna. Emulating Babe, Hilary took a job with *Vogue* magazine after college and married a stunningly handsome man, J. Frederic Byers III, whose blood ran nearly as blue as that of Stanley Mortimer. Byers was descended from the founders of Byers Steel and W. R. Grace & Company, a WASP pedigree that brought Paley's wholehearted approval.

Of the four children who lived with Bill and Babe, her two children by her marriage to Stanley Mortimer were the easiest. Young Stanley, nicknamed Tony, the older of the two, was handsome and blessed with a sweet disposition. He was Babe's favorite, the child with whom she had the closest relationship. When Babe was alone with the children, Tony often assumed the paternal role and helped her with discipline. He was a good student at Green Vale, a fashionable private academy on Long Island, and St. Marks, later graduating from Harvard and receiving a law degree from the University of Virginia as well as an MBA from Columbia University. Yet for all of Tony's good looks, ability, and achievements, he never drew close to Paley. Their dealings were edgy at best, in large measure because of the closeness of mother and son.

Amanda was two years younger than Tony, who gave her the nickname "Ba" when he was unable to pronounce "Baby." Raven-haired and dark-eyed, she inherited her mother's looks. "Babe worried about Ba," said Susan Mary Alsop. "She was so beautiful." Perhaps too beautiful. The relationship was difficult and aloof. Babe dictated, and Amanda retreated into shyness. The teachers who accompanied Jeffrey and Hilary to Kiluna each summer remarked to Dorothy Paley about Amanda's sadness; they could not understand how she could have been so ignored.

"Ba was cute as a button but her personality didn't emerge," said Irene Selznick. "She was very contained. One didn't have a notion of the shape of her personality." Amanda was raised, another friend once said, "to act dumb—mainly to get a man." To her contemporaries she was quiet, modest, unobtrusive, and sweet. Underneath, however, was an iron will. She had a strong, inquiring intelligence that she tried to fulfill even as she doubted her ability to do so.

After graduating from Westover, where she was sent in Babe's footsteps, Amanda made her requisite debut at Kiluna and went on to Wellesley. Three days after her arrival at college, she had a blind date with Shirley Carter Burden, Jr., a Harvard senior and the great-great-great-grandson of Cornelius "Commodore" Vanderbilt. Burden was tall, blond, and handsome. He was not only rich and social but glamorous as well. His mother was Flobelle Fairbanks, a former actress and first cousin to the dashing Douglas Fairbanks, Jr.; his father was an investment banker and photographer who lost his Social Register listing when he married Flo-

belle. Carter Burden had grown up in a Beverly Hills mansion, surrounded by movie stars and dating their daughters, including Geraldine
Chaplin.

Amanda fell for him instantly—as he had anticipated she would.
Their love affair was, in fact, quite calculated. It had been contrived by
Carter and his Harvard chum, Bartle Bull, a well-to-do New Yorker.
Both men viewed Amanda as a desirable catch. "They went after
Amanda," recalled Belinda Breese, who later married Bull. "They orchestrated the seduction. She was a very pretty, naive, sweet little girl. Bartle
went on and on about how they had done it." The following year Carter
and Amanda became engaged, and Amanda dropped out of Wellesley to
prepare for her marriage—a move that only intensified her feelings of
inferiority about her intelligence. (She would become, like Babe, an earnest autodidact, taking courses all over New York and reading vora-
ciously.) After the engagement, Flobelle Burden and Babe Paley met for
the first time over lunch at the Colony. Each spent the entire meal raving
about the qualities of the other's child and downplaying her own.

Amanda and Carter were married on June 14, 1964, at St. Mary's
Roman Catholic Church in Roslyn, Long Island; Amanda adopted Carter's Catholic faith. He was twenty-three and she was twenty. It was an
enormous wedding, with a dozen bridesmaids, two flower girls, and nineteen ushers. Mainbocher designed Amanda's wedding dress and Cecil Beaton took the photographs. The Kiluna reception took place under a
pistachio green tent filled with pink and white flowers. Babe adjusted her
own and Amanda's makeup to counteract the unflattering green glow that
made every other woman feel vaguely unattractive.

"Their marriage was all so perfect, and so romantic," recalled Irene
Selznick, who was Flobelle Burden's best friend. "It took people a while
to catch on. They didn't know who Carter was. Carter wasn't even
Carter yet. It was exciting to watch. They were young and so unsophisti-
cated."

They burst onto the New York social scene with one party after
another at their elegant apartment in the Dakota on Central Park West.
On weekends, Carter and Amanda had the run of the Kiluna cottage,
where they would entertain their own house guests. They were known,
variously, as New York's No. 1 Fun Couple, the Fashionable Savages, the
Moonflower Couple, and the Young Locomotives. Less than two years
after the marriage, *Vogue* ran a ten-page feature on the Burdens in their
Dakota digs entitled "The Young Joyous Life."

Amanda emerged from the chrysalis to become a star. Halston called
her "the most beautiful girl going." She nudged out Jacqueline Kennedy
at the top of the best-dressed list. Designers flocked to have Amanda

display their clothes on her slender frame. She became a fixture in *Women's Wear Daily*.

With her marriage to Burden, Amanda soared in her stepfather's estimation. Bill Paley was crazy about Carter, who had enormous charm, not to mention social prominence. "To Bill, there wasn't anybody like Carter," said Irene Selznick. "I never saw anything like Bill's infatuation with Carter. Carter loved Bill, too. He lapped up the attention. Bill loved Carter's appetite, his desire to learn, to know. He was exactly ready for Bill. Suddenly Bill was a great stepfather, and Amanda blossomed."

In many respects it was a marriage that mirrored Bill and Babe's. Amanda devoted herself to her husband's well-being. Kitty Hawks, Slim Keith's daughter and a close friend of Amanda, described Amanda's wifely role as "her job, and that's how she wanted it." Together, Amanda and Carter pursued fine furniture and bought Abstract Expressionist art. Carter became intrigued by women's fashions. Amanda grew passionate about fine French cuisine.

Fueled by Carter Burden's ambitions, they lived at a level of luxury unlike any of their contemporaries—even down to the somewhat bizarre butler who accompanied them on weekend visits. "Carter was from California, so we figured that explained a lot," recalled Belinda Breese. But the desire to be like Bill Paley came into play as well. "They simply had an overabundance of taste," Truman Capote told a reporter in 1972. "The truth of the matter was that most of those tastes were Carter's. Carter was the one who was saturated with the Paley way of life." But somehow Amanda and Carter did not quite carry it off. After several years on the New York social scene, they seemed shallow and silly. They had violated Bill and Babe's cardinal rule of social cachet: Amanda and Carter were overexposed.

To protect their deteriorating reputation, they made a 180-degree turn toward the serious pursuit of noblesse oblige. They moved to an apartment in the staid, old-money River House on the East Side. Amanda dedicated herself to volunteer work. Carter graduated from law school at Columbia University and quickly became one of New York's brightest young liberal politicians. Wearing a pin that said "I am Carter Burden's Wife," Amanda campaigned avidly when he waged a successful race for the New York City Council. They seemed destined for great things—perhaps, it was murmured, even the White House.

Throughout these years Amanda's friends could see that Babe was jealous of her dazzling daughter. "Her mother was extremely competitive with Amanda," said one source close to the Paleys. "When Amanda started doing all the things Babe did, it made it worse between them." And even with her beauty, Amanda had found it difficult growing up in the shadow of the great Babe Paley. Whenever Babe came to visit her daughter at Westover, Amanda's awestruck friends would wait by their dormitory windows for the Paleys' chocolate brown Bentley to arrive: first a long, slender arm would emerge, a lighted cigarette curling smoke from the holder poised in hand, and then the long legs would swing out the door as the girls watched wide-eyed. And then in due course Amanda was expected to be her mother's daughter in every way—especially by her young husband. On the first day of their honeymoon in Paris, Carter was upset when their room had not been stocked with Perrier. "I didn't know I was supposed to do those things," Amanda said as he stalked out and didn't return for six hours. "I assumed you were your mother," he later explained. It was only the beginning of the considerable strain Amanda would feel from Carter Burden's expectations.

But Amanda's problems paled compared to those of her half sister, Kate. "She is the most wounded of all the birds," commented one friend of the Paleys. Kate resembled her father, but what was rugged and appealing in a man was merely plain in a girl. "She had big black eyes and that was it," said Irene Selznick. Still, she was lively and responsive, and during her earliest years Bill Paley doted on Kate.

But when she was three years old, fate dealt her an unspeakably cruel blow. During a family vacation in Cap d'Antibes, Kate began to lose her hair. "It was horrible, like a nightmare," recalled her sister Amanda.

By the autumn every hair on Kate's body had fallen out. She was a victim of alopecia universalis, a rare and inexplicable disorder often associated with severe stress. Then, as now, there was no certain cure. Some doctors suggested at the time that the loss came from an emotional disturbance. Amanda, for one, linked the alopecia to the departure in the early summer of Kate's favorite nanny. "The nurse was pretty mean to the rest of us," recalled Amanda. "She whacked us with brushes, but she was close to Kate."

The Paleys consulted one specialist after another. "Babe went crazy," said Tex McCrary. "She turned to everything—faith healing, you name it. It was a traumatic experience. She was horrified, terrified, mystified. It was more than a mother's concern. It was a helluva thing for Babe." David Selznick became obsessed with the problem. "What he put Bill through," recalled Irene Selznick. "He used to give Bill hell, explain what should be done, tell him, 'What the hell use is power and money and imagination if you don't use it?' He kept saying that Bill should use all his resources to find a cure, go to China, to India, try any possibility. He drove Bill awfully hard for years. Then he finally reached a point of diminishing returns. He eventually gave up."

Some of the attempted cures bordered on the bizarre. For a time Kate had to sit in the sun on the terrace at Kiluna while a nurse rubbed bear grease on her head. Babe did what she could to mitigate the trauma. She hired James Masterson, a leading psychiatrist, to work with Kate. She found the best wigs money could buy and took Kate to Kenneth to have them cut and styled in a private room at the salon. Throughout her childhood, Kate wore her dark brown wigs Buster Brown style, with long bangs that obscured her lack of eyebrows.

None of her siblings could bring themselves to discuss in any depth what was happening to their sister. From time to time Amanda or Tony or Billie would take note of an embarrassment that had befallen Kate, or some new cure, but none made an effort to take care of her. "It was a strange household," recalled Amanda, "so fragmented and wacky. Our parents weren't there, and when they came, we were all clamoring for attention. There was no bonding among the kids. We were all looking out for ourselves."

Understandably self-conscious about her affliction, Kate became increasingly shy and acutely sensitive. If someone patted her on the head, she would instinctively pull away. "She was eager to please, very thoughtful," recalled Marguerite Platt. "She loved to play games. She was a happy, laughing child, but if the wig fell off, she changed completely. She would hide and not come out. She would get frantic and very upset, and wouldn't show her face until the wig was on perfectly. Once I was able to talk to her about it. I said, 'Don't worry, you will have lots of boys interested in you. They will like you for what you are. They won't bother about your not having any hair.' She burst into tears and said, 'No, they won't. No boy will ever like me.' "

When awkward moments arose, Babe worked to build up Kate's confidence. One summer when Kate was ten, she and the other children spent several weeks with their parents at the Hôtel du Palais in Biarritz. Babe asked her friend Susan Mary Alsop to send her daughter over to spend the night with Kate. The ten-year-old Anne knew nothing about Kate's condition. At bedtime, the girls were placed in separate rooms. When the governess brought Kate to say goodnight to her friend, Kate was wearing a turban. Anne mischievously yanked the turban off Kate's head, and Kate burst into tears. When Babe arrived moments later to find her daughter crying and Anne blushing, Babe said, "You know, Anne, Kate is so wonderful about this. Let's talk about it." They talked it through and then Babe said, "Let's tell a story and have some fun." The next day at the beach, Babe took her daughter into a cabana and when they re-emerged Kate was wearing a bathing cap. After Kate had finished swimming, her mother whisked her back to the cabana, after which Kate appeared in a beautifully brushed wig.

It may be that Babe's insistence on such perfection, however well intentioned, exacerbated her daughter's anxiety. Perhaps, had Kate been able to acknowledge her trouble frankly, she could have been more at ease. "Kate cast a shadow over the family," said Marguerite Platt. "Mrs. Paley was so desperately trying to help her, but it was hard to know what she could do right. Because of who Babe was and what she looked like, I could see that Kate would always resent her. Living in that family put too much pressure on Kate. I wished I could take her out of that family. Babe would have had to have lived a different life to accommodate Kate."

Although she was far from beautiful, Kate had her mother's luminous skin, splendid posture, and long-limbed, graceful figure. With makeup, she was able to accentuate the bone structure in her long face. By her teens, Kate's looks could be best described as exotic. She was very bright, and promisingly artistic, with a strong hand and a keen eye. She performed well in school at Green Vale and at Madeira, a posh girls' boarding school in Virginia. Babe tried, after her fashion, to stay in touch with her daughter. Whenever Kate went to Washington to visit Susan Mary Alsop, Kate would call her mother at Kiluna. "Oh Kate," Babe would say, "Mrs. Alsop says you are in tearing form."

When Kate reached coming-out age, her parents gave her a dinner at Greentree, Jock and Betsey's Manhasset home, followed by dancing at Kiluna to Peter Duchin's orchestra. Newspaper accounts referred to the event as a "near-debut" and a "nondebut" in keeping with the mood of the times (the party was held shortly after the assassination of Robert F. Kennedy in June 1968). Later that year Kate enrolled at the Rhode Island School of Design, but she never completed her course of studies.

Inevitably, a gulf grew between Babe and her daughter Kate. How could a daughter so afflicted have failed to resent a mother who embodied such perfection? "There was a strong rebellion," said Carter Burden. "You go against the person you care about most." For seven years Kate had virtually nothing to do with her mother or father. "Kate practically disappeared and bad-mouthed Bill and Babe all the while," said Leonora Hornblow. She traveled a great deal, dabbled in painting, and joined the demimonde of Manhattan's downtown artistic community. She seemed to grow more comfortable with her condition; she even painted portraits of herself without her wig and showed them to friends.

Occasionally Kate would call home, and Babe would invite her for tea. But at the appointed time, Kate failed to show up. When she turned twenty-one she tried to invade a trust fund in her name established by Sam Paley, but her father blocked the move, and she threatened to sue. Eventually, she did succeed in prying loose some of her inheritance.

During the estrangement, Richard Salant, then the president of CBS

News, was surprised one day when Kate arrived with the daughter of a neighbor to play tennis on his court. "When she heard I worked for CBS, she stopped playing tennis and unloaded," Salant recalled. "She said her father was a monster, cruel and selfish."

Kate's older brother Billie suffered in his own way, and brought his parents just as much heartache as Kate did. During childhood, he was a handsome combination of his parents, with black hair and Babe's flashing dark eyes. "He was very good-looking," said Leonora Hornblow. "He could have been an Arabian prince." He was an appealing child with a kind heart; he used to give away so many of his toys that his parents became alarmed. Without quite realizing it, Bill and Babe made their son feel he was odd—a sense that Babe compounded when she sent him away at age seven to a special camp to correct his left-handedness.

Shy and nervous, Billie bit his nails to the quick. Babe tended to indulge him and forgive his misbehavior too readily. But like his siblings, Billie's bids for attention were largely ignored. When Paley took his children on several European trips, Billie eagerly followed his father, tasting and learning about food at his elbow.

But for the most part, when Paley took notice of his son, it was with a torrent of criticism. "I remember when Billie was sixteen years old," recalled one of Babe's friends. "I was visiting Babe, and Billie came out to say hello. He had long hair at the time. When he left to see some friends, Babe said, 'Thank God. When Bill sees him with that long hair, he goes crazy.' With Billie it was pick, pick, pick. Bill never let up on him."

Later, Billie began raising hell. "I spent all kinds of time getting young Bill out of trouble," said Ralph Colin, Paley's attorney. "He once drove his car into a police car in Manhasset." Billie was a miserable student, shuttling through a succession of day and boarding schools and ending up at an unaccredited school in Switzerland from which he never graduated. "Billie got himself kicked out of schools intentionally. He wanted attention. His father responded by making an effort to find another place for him," said one Paley family intimate. Thus, without a high school diploma, Billie was enrolled in Rollins College in Florida, where he stayed only a few months.

"I was a strange child," Billie himself admitted in 1977. "My parents thought I was crazy. I was sent to a psychiatrist when I was ten, got kicked out of schools, started smoking dope when I was sixteen, and didn't have many friends." He told a reporter, "My father and I never really got along. I was too weird for them to believe. And of course I wasn't a success. I was different, that's all. I didn't want to alienate my parents. I love my parents, but I hated them, you know? I just left."

Billie escaped to Europe, where he and a friend made a movie "based on the surrealistic viewpoint of two adolescent boys searching for meaning. It was highly autobiographic. It gave vent to all our fantasies and strangest thoughts." He "picked up a heavy amphetamine habit" in Spain, and was introduced to the "hash cure" in Morocco. "It was lovely," he said. "You just stay stoned the whole time."

As a combat cinematographer in Vietnam in the late 1960s (a posting secured by his father) Billie became a regular heroin user and was nearly court-martialed for protesting against the war. Instead, he was assigned to complete his tour by sweeping floors in the photography labs.

Back in the States, Billie dropped out of sight—the most extreme gesture in his lifelong effort to avoid being associated publicly with his famous father. For four months he lived the life of a hermit in Piney Point, Maryland. He rebuilt an old sailboat with a friend and sailed around the Florida Keys, working as a dolphin trainer, yacht broker, construction worker, photographer, and door-to-door salesman—sustained all the while by income from two trust funds. During his stint in Florida he bought a gold hoop earring for $5 and had his left ear pierced so he could wear it at all times. "It's a symbol of freedom," he said. "It's there to keep me from being too serious, to remember that I am a gypsy at heart."

In his own troubled way, Billie revealed himself as much a bundle of contradictions as his father. His decision to live alone on Florida beaches was a variation on the dream hatched by his father and grandfather of moving to an orange grove. "I've spent a long time living in as frugal a manner as possible, trying to find myself," Billie said in the mid-seventies. "I gave up the material things in life to discover what I really wanted. I spent a lot of time alone . . . I love solitude." Yet in the next breath he could profess his fondness for parties, fine food, and enjoying himself. "I love myself," he told an interviewer. "I'm a hedonist. I'm having more fun than 99.8 percent of the world."

Not surprisingly, Paley appeared awkward around this rebellious, immature extension of himself. "He has always been stiff with Billie," said one close friend. "Billie must have felt badly he didn't have a less uptight father. Sometimes when they were together it seemed like they were being introduced for the first time."

Had Babe asserted herself, she might have made a difference in the lives of the Paley children. But she kept her distance—a genuine weakness in her character. Perhaps she had no choice. Perhaps she remembered all too well her own father's domineering ways and wondered if her mother might have fared better by making more of a life with him.

In any event, Babe did the opposite of what her mother had done. In deference to her husband's demands, Babe devoted little time to the sustained nurturing and schooling of her children. Her daughters spent most of their time with governesses, so they rarely had a chance to see what Babe did and how she did it. Consequently, the domestic knowledge that had been Gogs's forte was not passed along in any systematic way.

"Bill put pressure on Babe," said one man close to the Paleys. "Every decision had to do with being with the children or with him. One or the other. It was no secret that he was willful." "She wanted to be a good parent, but I don't think children interested Bill," said Marietta Tree. "She was always ready to do what he wanted to do. She often felt she was neglecting the children."

Babe's natural reserve may have played a part as well. One of her friends once described her as "warm but not tactile. She was not a toucher. She would never pick up and hold her children, for example, and they suffered from the lack." With more than a trace of bitterness, her daughter Amanda would later tell friends that Babe disliked giving goodnight kisses for fear of mussing her hair and makeup.

Babe felt guilty over spending so little time with the children. When trouble arose, her first instinct was to send them to therapists and psychiatrists rather than to confront the problems on her own. "She once told me she did all the wrong things," said one of her friends. "There were too many Christmas gifts to compensate for the guilt."

Behind the platonic and publicized ideal of Babe Paley was the private Babe, disappointed and unappreciated, pained and self-pitying. One of Babe's problems, in the view of Leonora Hornblow, was that "she was extra-super-sensitive. She didn't have that extra skin—the calluses—the way most people do. Criticism was painful to her."

Disillusion with her marriage set in quite early, according to her friends. "She wanted Bill heart and soul, and he didn't give himself heart and soul," said Marietta Tree. "He loved Babe and always will, but she wasn't the focus of his life. Nor was anybody. That was very hard for Babe to accept." Her feelings, according to Capote, boiled down to betrayal. "After three years of the marriage she really almost wanted out," Capote once confided. "She thought that he'd married her more for her sister and brother-in-law than for herself, the idea that with her came, you know, Mrs. Whitney and Mrs. Astor, I mean, he was getting the whole family." She sensed, in effect, that she was his possession, the most valued among the precious objects in his ever-expanding collection.

Babe struggled to conceal the pressure of pleasing her husband. "There was a streak in everybody's mind about that marriage," said Diana Vreeland. "They weren't born for each other. They were not ideal. But happiness like sun blazing in a room was not Babe's disposition. She was private and didn't radiate that easily. And if she were troubled, there was no way she wore it on her sleeve." Truman Capote once told Babe that she should consider managing Bill Paley's life—overseeing three households, tending to his every need—as a job, purely and simply. "Her life with Bill was not easy at all," recalled her friend Horace Kelland. "She had to put on a marvelous face."

And the signs of strain poked through. She could be nervous and high strung in a manner that was sometimes surprising. "She wasn't a hundred percent certain," said Kelland. "That was part of her charm. You felt not unpleasantness but pressure on her. If the food was not quite right he would say, 'This is ghastly.' . . . He was not that certain, either. He was under pressure, too. When you marry someone as he did, to get the best, you think she is going to know and be certain about everything."

Babe suffered from severe migraine headaches every four to five months that lasted two or three days. "You could see them coming on," said Slim Keith. "The blood vessel on her forehead would begin to pound. Then it was tippy-toe time and darkened rooms." Babe once told Marietta Tree that she thought the headaches resulted from her anxiety about neglecting the children. To smooth out the edges, Babe took Miltown tranquilizers, and she regularly saw a psychiatrist.

The one person who witnessed Babe's troubles at close range was her sister Betsey, to whom she periodically ran in tears. Once when a floor lamp at Kiluna got damaged, Paley demanded that it be fixed on the double. While Babe was trying to get it repaired, she had to leave for Europe with Bill. When they arrived home, Babe was still so nervous about the lamp that she called Betsey from the airport to find out if the repairs had been completed. Betsey reported that they had not, so Babe said, "Run over to Kiluna and get it out of the house. I don't care what you do with it. Just get it out of his sight."

Although Betsey was less celebrated than Babe, it had become clear that she got the better of her sister in marrying Jock Whitney: old money, high status, the grandest of American homes, and a husband who was devoted to her and her children. But when Babe was in pain, the two sisters pushed aside all rivalries, and Betsey's natural coolness toward Bill Paley would turn to resentment. Much of the time, Paley's infidelities were the source of Babe's unhappiness. Betsey took strong exception to his constant philandering. "Betsey," said Irene Selznick, "was for the straight and narrow."

"Bill was always flirting with everyone," recalled Jeanne Murray Vanderbilt. "He was on the make. Babe was so nice. She always tried to invite pretty women he would like to look at. But I guess he never stopped —on the side, during the week. The atmosphere was like that. You could sense what was going on. I remember when George Abbott would bring an attractive young actress around. Once or twice these girls told me Bill had asked them for their phone number and called them."

So capable of subtlety in other areas of his life, Paley made clumsy sexual advances. During the summer after her divorce from Alfred Vanderbilt in 1956, Jeanne Murray Vanderbilt was surprised to get a call from Bill Paley. Babe was in New Hampshire, and Paley asked Jeanne to join him for dinner and a movie at Radio City Music Hall. At the end of the evening, Paley made a pass, which she rejected. "Babe was my friend!" she recalled.

Babe had little choice but to keep her reserve and take pleasure from the freedom and wealth that came with being Bill Paley's wife. She lived luxuriously, and most of the time this was enough. "I think he gave her joy," said Leonora Hornblow, "and he took joy from her company." Capote once said of Babe and Bill that she "loved loved loved him and hated hated hated him." Yet Paley was too fascinating for that simplistic analysis, despite the trials that his narcissism presented for Babe. "She loved loved loved him and sometimes was hurt hurt hurt by him, but she didn't hate hate hate him," said Slim Keith. "She loved him. She saw him as a riveting man."

35

LARGELY IN PALEY'S ABSENCE, CBS Television grew apace. As top entertainment shows shifted from radio to television, so did the news operation. TV News at CBS expanded from 14 full-time staffers in 1950 to 376 six years later. During that time the annual budget rose to $7 million. Television, with its complicated electronic equipment, simply required more personnel and cost more than radio; CBS-Television newscasts lost some $10 million a year through the 1950s.

The news expansion was not a philanthropic gesture: CBS, along with NBC and ABC, had to continue presenting news and public affairs to serve "the public interest, convenience and necessity" mandated by the Communications Act. Yet for all the growth and the regulatory demands, CBS News programs were confined to the edges of the television schedule, out of prime viewing time, just as they had been in postwar radio.

Like Paley, Murrow the radio man had mistrusted television at first. But Paley's wariness stemmed from commercial considerations. He had harbored no doubts, however, about television as a medium for news programming. Back in 1948, he wrote in the *New York Times* that "Television offers keener insights than printed or spoken words alone can provide." He predicted that "if tomorrow's politician's words are honeyed and plausible, we shall know whether his facial expression contradicts them."

Murrow never shared Paley's optimism on this score. While recognizing its potential power, Murrow fretted about television's inherent deficiencies. He understood that the radio audience was forced to concentrate on words and ideas without the distraction of images. The television camera served to limit rather than expand news coverage, to put a premium on "visuals" instead of explanation and analysis. He saw radio's superiority as a medium of greater public service and intellectual force—a distinction that eluded Paley.

Murrow made the jump to television in the autumn of 1951 when he converted his radio magazine program, "Hear It Now" to "See It Now." The mission of the new weekly half-hour program was to bring depth and intelligence to a medium that had shown little capacity for either. It was designed to be a sort of *Life* magazine of the airwaves that would capture significant stories in documentary style.

"See It Now" was created by Murrow and his producer, Fred Friendly, who came out of radio in Providence, Rhode Island. A big man of oversized appetites and enthusiasms, Friendly was creative, passionate, and energetic, as much a dramatist as a journalist.

"See It Now" won high praise from the start, although it did not attract a large audience. Each week it delved into one or two stories, homing in on what Friendly liked to call "the little picture" to explain larger issues. In December 1951, shortly after its debut, "See It Now" took a swipe at Senator McCarthy in a brief piece showing the senator as a haranguing interrogator. But otherwise the program avoided the subject of McCarthyism and blacklisting, concentrating instead on safe topics.

Prodded by colleagues, Murrow finally focused on witch-hunting in October 1953 with a program on Milo Radulovich, an Air Force lieutenant who had been asked to resign as a security risk because his father and sister were supposedly subversive. "See It Now" found no evidence for the accusation and Radulovich kept his commission. Five months later, Murrow and Friendly decided to take on McCarthy, whose influence and popularity were at their peak.

Close as he was to Paley, Murrow cunningly kept quiet about his plans to unmask McCarthy. Since the Radulovich broadcast, Alcoa Aluminum, the sponsor of "See It Now," had come under pressure to drop Murrow, who had been attacked by conservative columnists for one-sided reporting. Affiliates of CBS had also complained about the newsman's supposed liberal bias. Murrow could not be sure how Paley and Stanton would react to a McCarthy report. "We tried to keep it a secret until the last minute," said Friendly.

Only two months earlier, in January 1954, "See It Now" had focused on another conservative senator, John Bricker of Ohio, and his efforts to cut back the president's power to make treaties. The program featured a debate between Bricker and Democratic senator Estes Kefauver. Afterwards, Bricker cried foul, claiming not only that Kefauver had been allotted more time, but that Bricker had not known he would share the stage with an opponent. As the chairman of the Senate committee with jurisdiction over broadcasting, Bricker blistered Stanton. The senator—a McCarthy supporter and longtime Murrow hater—claimed that Murrow's producer had lied to him, and threatened investigations into network practices. Bricker's threats sunk in. Stanton agreed to give the senator more time on another broadcast of "See It Now," which infuriated Murrow.

Memories vary on exactly when Murrow called Paley to brief him on the McCarthy broadcast: Friendly and Paley said it was March 8, 1954, the day before the scheduled Tuesday night program; Stanton and another executive, Louis Cowan, insisted it was the afternoon of the broadcast. "Are you satisfied it is accurate?" Paley asked after Murrow outlined the program. Murrow assured him that it was. "Will it cause a big stink?" asked Paley. "Yes," answered Murrow, who offered to screen the program for Paley before it went on the air. Paley declined, but he added that McCarthy might want time for a reply. "Why don't you offer McCarthy the time yourself?" Paley said. "That way it won't look like you are bending in to him." Paley's suggestion was really a command in shrewd psychological disguise. Before airtime Paley called Murrow. "I'm with you today, and I'll be with you tomorrow," he said.

Despite his brave words, Paley was nervous. He knew McCarthy was capable of coming after Murrow—and CBS. Paley watched the program that Tuesday night in his suite at the St. Regis Hotel with Babe and Leland Hayward and his wife, Slim. "His support of Ed was total," recalled Slim. "I was so thrilled by it, and we all were." When Murrow signed off, the Paleys called him. But it was Babe, not Bill, who spoke to Murrow and told him how good the program was. Cautious as ever, Paley was putting some distance between himself and Murrow. Paley did talk directly to Stanton. The two men agreed that while it had been a fine show, they had to "batten down the hatches."

The program exposed McCarthy by hanging him on his own words through footage skillfully edited to show the pattern of his demagoguery. Murrow heightened the impact by pointedly characterizing McCarthy's techniques, and concluded by stating that "this is no time for men who oppose Senator McCarthy's methods to keep silent. . . . The actions of the junior senator from Wisconsin have caused alarm and dismay amongst our allies abroad and given considerable comfort to our enemies." From beginning to end, it was all-out advocacy journalism.

As such, it was enormously effective—the most dramatic evidence to date of television's power. In the aftermath, CBS logged some fifteen thousand letters and an equal number of phone calls overwhelmingly supporting Murrow. Thousands of telegrams to Alcoa also sided with Murrow. But McCarthy wrote the sponsor as well to threaten an investigation. Conservative columnists lashed out at Murrow, alleging Communist connections in his youth.

"The day after the broadcast they tore the roof off the building," said Paley, who called Murrow to say, "We're in for a helluva fight. Is there anything he can get you on?" Murrow assured him there was not, but Paley wanted to be safe. "Let's get our own people to dig into everything you ever did and find out if there is anything vulnerable," Paley suggested. With Murrow's assent, CBS hired the prestigious law firm, Cravath Swaine & Moore, to conduct the probe. The lawyers found no skeletons.

Paley and Stanton had to act fast to explain the network's position. In response to an inquiry from *Newsweek,* they issued a statement on March 17 that essentially rewrote the rules. While reaffirming CBS's obligation to separate editorial opinion from presentation of the news, the two executives added a new wrinkle in the case of documentary programs where "the expression of opinion or editorialization might take place."

CBS, according to Paley and Stanton, could "delegate responsibility for the program content and for the expression of opinion (if any) to one of its staff members. It is careful, of course, not to delegate such responsibility except to one in whose integrity and devotion to democratic principles CBS reposes complete confidence." Murrow, by implication, happened to be a man of such integrity and devotion. Paley would later call the Murrow program "exceptional," insisting, "we gave him carte blanche to develop an editorial opinion. . . . We changed our policies in connection with certain matters that we thought were of vital importance to the future and health and security of the country."

Paley's explanation is little more than an ex-post facto rationalization. "We were trying to make the best out of what was a violation of policy," Stanton said years later. "It wasn't all a cover-up in the way we answered *Newsweek.* But had the program been put to us in advance, we would have insisted on due process for the other side. The broadcast was not balanced."

Paley felt compelled to reaffirm the principles of CBS's objectivity even more forcefully in a full-dress speech delivered two months after the McCarthy broadcast. Titled "The Road to Responsibility," the speech was a group effort involving lawyer Richard Salant and speechwriter Robert Strunsky as well as Paley and Stanton. But, as in the past, Paley was establishing himself as the policy maker. Preparing for the speech commanded his attention for weeks.

Paley was hailed for his sensible, calm, and serious approach to the volatile issue of fairness and balance, and for his call for greater "courage and performance" in covering public affairs on television. Jack Gould wrote in the *New York Times* that the speech was a "turning point in broadcasting's evolution," prompted by "a corporate soul-searching on the whole matter of television's place in the field of news and public opinion." Paley, years later, would characterize his remarks as nothing less than "the bible for news operations in this country."

Throughout the days between Murrow's attack and McCarthy's reply, Murrow met with Paley and Stanton to discuss strategy and work on the Cravath investigation. Paley suggested that when Murrow spoke after McCarthy's statement, he should say that history would judge whether he or McCarthy had better served his country. It was a suggestion in which he would take justifiable pride.

By Paley's recollection, he met with Murrow daily, for hours on end. The memory was, like many others, an exaggeration. "Certainly after the broadcast Bill and Ed had contact," recalled Stanton. "But we weren't holding Ed's hand every day. It was an unusual period, but there was no council of war."

The televised reply damaged McCarthy even more than the original Murrow attack. Looking awkward and pasty in poorly applied stage makeup, McCarthy raged about Murrow's alleged subversion and repeated his accusations of Communist influence in government. "You saw him in action and you know he was a very wild sort of guy and not very fair and you sort of got the feeling, like, 'God, we've been following this guy and just look at him now,' " recalled Paley. "It was the beginning of McCarthy's downfall."

In the following months McCarthy went over the line by accusing the Army of harboring Communists as well. The Senate held televised hearings in which McCarthy's irresponsible charges fell apart, costing him the support of his colleagues. For thirty-six days in April and May the hearings were carried live, courtesy not of CBS but of ABC. With its lucrative schedule of soap operas, CBS wasn't about to give up the time. ABC, however, had virtually no programming during the day. ABC won plaudits for its public service, and the hearings drew large audiences, which helped the network attract new advertising support. "It wasn't

Murrow who killed McCarthy," said Jack Gould. "It was ABC's decision to put the hearings on. That was the exposure that did it." Ironically, Paley's speech calling for greater responsibility by broadcasters in news and public affairs came on the heels of his decision not to broadcast the hearings.

Twenty-five years after the fact, Paley argued that CBS deserved the credit for bringing down McCarthy. "We covered the hearings, you know," he told TV talk show host Phil Donahue. "We covered that with television and that also I think was another step that brought about Mc-Carthy's downfall. Remember that fellow [Joseph] Welch, the lawyer, who was defending the defense, brilliant man and he was, you know, just marvelous and I used to look at it and it was like seeing the best drama I ever saw in my life. And McCarthy, I think, just showed himself for what he was more and more all the time."

Even though Paley inflated CBS's role, the network was instrumental in dismantling McCarthy. Many of Murrow's colleagues felt he waited too long to take on the Wisconsin demagogue, and Paley would admit, many years later, that the timing "might have been six months earlier." But at the time, he was just as happy that Murrow held off. President Eisenhower's two appointments to the Federal Communications Commission in 1953, John C. Doerfer and Robert E. Lee, were friends of McCarthy, and Doerfer was busy investigating McCarthy's suggestion of Communist tendencies among television stations that failed to carry McCarthy's speeches. Eisenhower himself—a friend of Paley's from wartime days—had declined either in the 1952 presidential campaign or afterwards to criticize McCarthy.

When Murrow did go on the attack, it helped defuse the negative publicity CBS had drawn with its blacklisting. It was another classic case of CBS having it both ways, in perfect Paley style. "CBS—villain to those who reject blacklisting—can always point to its Ed Murrow when the criticism gets too hot. When criticisms of Murrow start to mount, the network can point with pride to the tight shop its security officers run," said the Cogley Report on blacklisting in 1956.

As McCarthy collapsed, so did the network blacklists. Dan O'Shea would leave CBS in mid-1955. Formerly forbidden writers and actors found work on the network. And Ed Murrow was once again a genuine hero.

The McCarthy broadcast marked the peak of Murrow's postwar influence at CBS. But while Paley did not waver in his support, the experience made him uneasy. "In spite of the genuinely favorable public reaction, 'uncomfortable' would be too mild a word to describe the relationship with Ed Murrow at about that time," said William Leonard. Paley continued to worry about protests from advertisers concerned about consumer boycotts. "Bill Paley was proud of the McCarthy broadcast but more retroactively," Fred Friendly recalled. "He was proud but determined it wouldn't happen again." It was inevitable that Paley would make sure Murrow could never again put the network on the line.

In the fourteen months following the McCarthy broadcast, Murrow went out of his way to test Paley's resolve by continuing to report on sensitive topics. In January 1955, he interviewed J. Robert Oppenheimer, the scientist in charge of developing the atomic bomb who had just lost his federal security clearance because of Communist associations before the war. The two men had a thoughtful exchange about government secrecy and the role of the scientist, threaded with criticism of the administration's growing control of research. Dan O'Shea, in his waning days as CBS's blacklist enforcer, objected vigorously to the broadcast. Sensing another possible confrontation, Murrow asked Paley to screen the interview. Paley, who normally avoided involvement in news programs before the fact, took a look and agreed to let the program appear intact. Afterwards, right-wing critics once again attacked the network for being too liberal.

There were other controversial programs on such topics as book burning and the involvement of the Texas statehouse in a land scandal. In May 1955, Irving Wilson, president of Alcoa Aluminum, called a luncheon meeting with Paley and Stanton. Wilson told the CBS men that Alcoa wanted to reach more consumers by advertising on entertainment shows rather than on public affairs programming. "My very private reaction was that Alcoa didn't want to take the heat," said Stanton. "Wilson put it to Bill and me as a readjustment of his ad planning, and he was so genteel and general that we couldn't argue." After the lunch, Paley let out a big sigh. " 'Just one more problem,' it seemed to say," Stanton recalled.

Although McCarthy was no longer a threat, CBS had no shortage of critics. Numerous CBS affiliates had been complaining about the Murrow program for months. "They were unhappy with some of the broadcasts. The station managers were reflecting the view of their country clubs and their local client lists," according to Stanton. Moreover, in early February 1955, John Bricker, the conservative senator from Ohio, had launched a new effort to regulate the networks. Stanton was convinced that Bricker's actions stemmed directly from his experience with "See It Now" a year earlier. "When CBS squeezed Bricker's toe, I was the guy who got slugged," Stanton said later. "Bricker had me down for hearings and everything else."

Paley was eager to minimize the political controversies stirred up by "See It Now." The program occupied a valuable slot in prime time that could fetch far more revenue if filled with an entertainment show. After a discussion with Stanton, Paley invited Murrow and Friendly to his office in early July 1955, ostensibly to tell them of a wonderful new opportunity. He offered to expand "See It Now" to a full hour and give them more resources. Of course such an ambitious effort needed more preparation time as well. It would be better, Paley said, if the program ran eight to ten times a year. Friendly and Murrow, exhausted by their battles with sponsors and the front office, acquiesced. In the process, they lost more than forty slots on the air per year. Not even CBS's shrewdest newsmen were immune to the classic Paley soft sell.

36

T HE REMOVAL of Murrow's weekly forum signaled the ascent of Frank Stanton as the dominant force at CBS News. The first moves had actually come within months of the McCarthy broadcast. In August 1954, Stanton combined the news and public affairs departments of radio and television under the direction of Sig Mickelson, who had come to New York from the CBS station in Minneapolis several years earlier. Chief among Stanton's twelve directives for the news division's operations was a newly created editorial review board consisting of Paley, Stanton, Mickelson, and other corporate executives. Henceforth, news policy would be set by this group.

That same month Stanton appeared on CBS Television to deliver the first network editorial. He took the Senate to task for barring radio and television journalists from committee hearings debating whether to censure Joseph McCarthy. Although Stanton had spoken out often on broadcasting issues, this was the first time he had served as the network's spokesman on matters of news and public affairs.

Inside and outside the company, Stanton was now clearly the day-to-day decision-maker for CBS News. He served as chairman of the weekly meetings of the editorial review board, which Paley rarely attended. (Paley stayed abreast by reading agendas and minutes.) "In the 1950s Paley pulled away from the news department," said Sig Mickelson. "His interest formed a jagged line, but essentially it was a decline, essentially backing away." Even the annual year-end luncheons Paley hosted for "Murrow's Boys" were discontinued. Alexander Kendrick, a veteran correspondent, pointed out that "toward the end of the fifties, Paley was usually in Jamaica for the holidays."

In 1957, when CBS wanted Nikita Khrushchev for an interview on "Face the Nation," Stanton supervised the negotiations. "Bill was not involved at all," recalled Stanton. "He didn't know it was coming." Afterwards, President Eisenhower and Secretary of State John Foster Dulles criticized CBS for allowing a Soviet official to appear unedited on American TV. Bolstered by widespread praise for the interview in the press, Stanton fought back by taking out a full-page advertisement in the *New York Times* lauding CBS's journalistic enterprise.

Initially, Paley said little about the broadcast. "I got the idea he wasn't happy, but he was always careful in how he exercised his displeasure. He wouldn't say he was angry," said Stanton. The CBS president defended the interview in an address to the National Press Club in Washington. "As the praise in print picked up, he was happier by the hour," Stanton said. In the end, Paley backed up Stanton by issuing a memo to the CBS organization calling the interview "one of the most outstanding broadcasts ever carried on radio and television." That fall the Radio and Television News Directors Association gave Stanton an award for his achievement.

A few months later CBS broke ground again—once more at Stanton's behest and without Paley's involvement. During a meeting at the Rand Corporation think tank, where he was chairman of the board, Stanton conceived of a broadcast that would assess relative American and Soviet technological capabilities in light of the Soviet Union's launching of the Sputnik satellite. Called "Where We Stand," it appeared in early January 1958, followed by a CBS editorial urging viewers to end their complacency and renew their commitment to innovation lest the Soviets surge ahead.

The editorial was read on air by Howard K. Smith—significantly, Murrow was nowhere in sight—and written by CBS's editorial board under Stanton's guidance; Paley, who was away much of the time during the months preceding the broadcast, attended none of the meetings. Filling him in before the broadcast, Stanton could see that Paley was less than enchanted—"He didn't like it but he didn't object." Although some in the administration took issue because CBS was focusing on American weakness, the program and editorial were not controversial.

Paley's chief involvement at CBS News was his continuing irritation over expressions of personal opinion on the air—purported violations of CBS standards that were called to his attention by friends, business associates, and government officials. To Paley, journalists were an increasingly troublesome breed.

The views of both Howard K. Smith and Eric Sevareid antagonized Paley during the fifties. CBS executive Richard Salant usually transmitted Paley's displeasure to Smith, whose fifteen-minute Sunday afternoon broadcast was laced with commentary. At Paley's direction, an editor was installed in Washington to put the blue pencil to the correspondent's analytical pieces. Both Sevareid and Smith objected, and Sevareid asked to see Paley. During their luncheon meeting, Sevareid argued that CBS needed to provide facts and solid opinion, but Paley would have none of it. "Paley wouldn't yield an inch," said Mickelson. "Eric came out defeated and baffled by it. Paley's attitude was so hard and fast."

The inevitable blowup came in August 1956 when three American reporters defied an edict by the U.S. State Department and accepted an invitation to visit Communist China. One of the reporters was William Worthy, of the *Baltimore Afro-American,* who signed on as a stringer for CBS. Only one of his broadcasts got through, but it disputed the administration's view that Mao Tse-tung's regime was on the verge of collapse. Deputy Under Secretary of State Robert Murphy complained to Paley. Testifying later before the Senate Foreign Relations Committee, Murphy characterized Paley as an "old friend" to whom he had made a "simple inquiry."

When Worthy came back to the United States, Sevareid debriefed him and prepared a radio report criticizing the State Department. CBS killed the piece, and Sevareid gave his copy to a friendly senator for inclusion in the *Congressional Record.* This not only amounted to insubordination in the eyes of CBS; Sevareid had turned over proprietary information. Paley summoned him for a dressing down. "I'm going to have this out with the old man," Sevareid told Murrow, who tried to go along but was barred from the meeting. "You have broken a commitment," Paley told Sevareid. "There is no such thing as total neutrality," Sevareid countered. "What did you want me to say when Russia invaded Hungary? Was I to sound neutral? I couldn't. If I did, I wouldn't have an audience in two months. You can't be an intellectual eunuch."

Paley refused to budge and Sevareid felt despondent. "Maybe I've been too long with CBS," he said. Paley's silence signaled that he wanted Sevareid to resign. "But I simply sat still and Paley sat still and nothing happened. I don't know why Paley didn't fire me. We never talked about it again," said Sevareid.

The newsman had backed down; thereafter his commentaries were more temperate, prompting Paley to characterize them years later as "fair, honest and well-founded," never mentioning the dispute over the Worthy report. "I rode along because of my nature," Sevareid acknowledged. "I was more interested in elucidating than advocating."

Murrow had broadcast a report siding with Worthy as well. But instead of killing his broadcast, CBS settled for a reprimand. Murrow later admitted he had violated CBS's policy prohibiting reporters from taking sides in a controversial issue.

On the surface, Murrow appeared to be thriving with his new hour-long program, now mockingly known on Broadcast Row as "See It Now and Then." His four-year-old celebrity interview program, "Person to Person," was popular with viewers although an embarrassment to news purists. He made the cover of *Time* magazine in September 1957. But *Time* had caught its subject past his peak and on a downward drift.

Murrow had resigned from the CBS board of directors in October 1956 because of a potential conflict of interest in negotiating a new contract, part of which involved the network's purchase of "Person to Person" for a fat fee. In truth, Murrow felt uncomfortable in the boardroom. He had been a member since 1949, when he was proposed by Stanton to give news and public affairs a "place at the table." "It was another way of nailing him down," said Jap Gude, Murrow's friend and agent. In the seven years that followed, Murrow contributed so little that fellow board member and Paley in-law Ike Levy used to calculate how much each utterance was worth—$5, $15, $25—based on his director's compensation of $200 per meeting. "Ed would sit at the end of the boardroom table with Ike Levy and they would doodle around and joke instead of paying attention to the important matters at the meeting," recalled Joe Ream. "They didn't show proper respect for what was going on, and I don't think Bill Paley particularly appreciated that."

Troubles continued apace on the air as well. In January 1956, "See It Now" ran a program highlighting the problems of small farmers. Murrow was careful to include Secretary of Agriculture Ezra Taft Benson, the devout Mormon who carried out Eisenhower's attempt to dismantle New Deal farm policies by reducing crop subsidies. Benson disputed "See It Now's" contention that the new policies were pushing farmers off their land. Afterwards he complained that the program was unbalanced and demanded more time to clarify the administration's position. Mickelson assured Fred Friendly that the request would be rejected. But Paley overruled him, bowing, Mickelson later said, to pressure from the Eisenhower administration. Benson got a half hour of his own on CBS. Murrow was so angry he composed a letter of resignation that he never submitted.

"See It Now" could not seem to hold a sponsor. General Motors, the original advertiser on the hour-long version, had dropped out even before the first program in the fall of 1955. Pan American Airways sponsored a few installments, then withdrew. After the first year in the new format, Paley shifted the program from prime time to Sunday afternoon.

In March 1958, Paley and Murrow had their final rupture over "See

It Now." It involved a trivial provocation that Paley took far too seriously. In fact, Paley's response reflected his cumulative ill-will toward "See It Now"—and toward Ed Murrow. The program addressed the prospect of statehood for Alaska and Hawaii, an innocuous enough subject. But perhaps for the sake of drama, it focused on the views of right-wingers who saw the two prospective states as havens for Communists. One proponent of statehood called an obscure Republican congressman from upstate New York, John Pillion, "crazy" for holding such beliefs. Pillion asked for equal time to refute.

Mickelson considered the request unwarranted. In a meeting with Paley, he argued that the program was sufficiently balanced. But Paley, Mickelson recalled, "was cold and stubborn. He just didn't yield. He wouldn't give up. I argued with him for two hours." Paley insisted that the program flagrantly violated CBS standards of fairness. In fact, far more was at stake. "Paley was distressed by Edward R. Murrow and wanted to let him have it," recalled Mickelson. "By this time he was getting irritated by the 'See It Now' business." Paley ordered Mickelson to tell Murrow and Friendly the request would be granted. Stanton ducked, staying at a distance. "I was short-circuited when Bill got involved," he said later.

Murrow wrote another angry letter. Rising to Paley's bait, he rashly demanded to be let out of "See It Now" by the end of the year. In May 1958, Murrow and Friendly met with Paley in the rarefied surroundings of the chairman's office. Paley, dressed impeccably as usual, sat behind his chemin de fer table. Murrow had removed his jacket; he wore his trademark red suspenders and his shirt was open at the neck.

The three men talked about ways to avoid a Pillion situation again. But the discussion heated up quickly. "We had a terrific argument," Paley recalled. "I just said, 'Listen here, now. We have the right and we have the responsibility to decide for ourselves who should and who shouldn't be getting reply time. The person doing the broadcast should not be the final arbiter on a question of that kind.' "

Abruptly, Paley told them that "See It Now" was being taken off the air. When they protested, he snapped the trap shut, citing Murrow's letter. "But I thought you and Fred didn't want to do 'See It Now' anymore," he said. When Murrow asked incredulously whether Paley really wanted to destroy such a valuable program, the CBS chairman punched his own stomach and uttered one of his most celebrated lines: "I don't want this constant stomachache every time you do a controversial subject." Countered Murrow, "It goes with the job." Murrow, said his wife, was "pretty burned up when Bill said that he couldn't stand the effect Ed's programs had on his stomach. It was the only time I can remember that Ed was really furious with Bill. He said, 'Well, that's just too bad.' "

Paley's displeasure went deeper than stomach pains, real or metaphorical. Although Paley never said so explicitly, Murrow—and to a lesser extent Smith and Sevareid—angered the CBS chairman because they so consistently nettled the Eisenhower administration. Not only were Eisenhower and Paley friends of long standing; Paley had a political ambition that Eisenhower had the power to fulfill: a prestigious ambassadorship in Europe.

Paley's admiration for his amiable former commander had continued unabated after the war. "Ike was a hero to him," said one of Paley's former wartime aides. "Bill was awed by Ike's importance as a commanding general." Paley admired and identified with Eisenhower, whose smile was every bit as winning as Paley's. Both men shared a simple, unintellectual approach to problems and relied on the force of personality—quiet charm and confident optimism—to get their way. Eisenhower, like Paley, praised the virtues of consensus and was far more calculating than he appeared.

When Eisenhower had been named president of Columbia University after the war, Paley lost no time asking him to join the CBS board. Paley cited CBS's various connections with the university and pointed out that Nicholas Murray Butler, Eisenhower's predecessor, had served on corporate boards. "The actual time for meetings," Paley noted reassuringly, "is not great. . . . The first Wednesday of each month we convene at 2:30 and we are seldom at it after 4:30."

Although Eisenhower turned him down, Paley renewed the invitation in 1948, sweetened by the proposal that Eisenhower appear in a series of broadcasts on CBS. A sponsor was waiting in the wings, Paley said, and if Eisenhower was unwilling to receive a fee, the sponsor would contribute money to Columbia for scholarship funds. "I feel strongly that you should have a regular platform for the discussion of some of the serious issues confronting the country," Paley wrote, "and for the expression of definite ideas on these issues whenever you feel you want to express them." When it came to powerful men such as Eisenhower, Paley seemed more than willing to suspend his rule of neutrality.

Again, Eisenhower demurred, but soon afterwards he reciprocated by inviting Paley to join the Columbia University board of trustees. Paley eagerly accepted, but according to his own recollection the nominating committee turned him down because he had been divorced. When an embarrassed Eisenhower asked the committee members to reconsider, they admitted they had been mistaken and invited Paley aboard. Curiously, a letter from Eisenhower to Paley at the time made no mention of Paley's divorce as a reason for delay. "The vacancy is in sight," wrote

Eisenhower, "but the former trustee involved is so old and ill that we are proceeding as delicately as possible."

Paley's intimates—namely, Jock Whitney and his friends—formed the nucleus of wealthy Eastern establishment Republicans who prodded Eisenhower to run for president in 1952 after Ike had left Columbia to serve as NATO commander in Europe. That February, Eisenhower gave in to their urgings. Although Paley was on the periphery, he felt confident enough the next month to write a letter offering some advice. Eisenhower's name had been entered for and won primaries in New Hampshire and Minnesota while he was still abroad, and many of Paley's cronies were entreating the general to return home. Confessing himself an "amateur in the field of political strategy," Paley took an intriguingly contrary view.

It would be better to stay away until the Republican nominating convention in July 1952, he wrote, because "the Eisenhower movement is based on a combination of factors—including your absence because of heavy duties and responsibilities overseas—and . . . these factors have produced an end result which is working and working damn well. Why change the formula?" Paley's view showed characteristic caution as well as his philosophy of leadership at CBS: create a mystique by remaining in the distance. In the end, Paley said, "your qualities, plus some sixth sense, usually lead you to the right answer." In this case, the answer was politely to disregard Paley's advice.

When Eisenhower kicked off his campaign with a press conference in his hometown of Abilene, Kansas, Paley made one of his few overt interventions in CBS's coverage of his friend. He ordered CBS News to televise the press conference live, at some expense. Unexpectedly, the Eisenhower advisers objected because of their boss's discomfort with television cameras. When CBS pointed out the trouble it had taken, they relented.

During the campaign Paley was a visibly enthusiastic supporter of the Republican cause. Jock Whitney, who contributed significant funds to the campaign, served as finance chairman of Citizens for Eisenhower. Although Paley did not actively raise funds, he was an informal consultant. Walter Thayer, Whitney's aide, visited Paley in his office once or twice a week to brief him on campaign strategy and solicit advice. "Bill would help on campaign issues, how to present them, what use to make of radio and television," Thayer recalled. "We would swap ideas. He was keenly interested. His advice was to narrow the issues and give the people a clear choice." Paley's private advice was especially valuable because 1952 marked the first television campaign. Eisenhower's use of "media events," stressing images over substance, was crucial to his victory over Adlai

Stevenson, whose fondness for words and ideas was incompatible with television.

Paley felt far more comfortable as an Eisenhower booster than he had been as a New Deal poseur before the war. Sam Paley was a lifelong Republican, and Bill Paley settled easily into the moderate wing of the Grand Old Party. He was a man of wealth and a businessman to the core. "He was very much under the political influence of Jock Whitney," recalled CBS newsman Walter Cronkite. But Paley kept his partisanship quiet. "Henry Luce wanted to change the world," said Fred Friendly. "He cared about China and Europe and was a geostrategist. Bill Paley didn't consider himself that, but he did want to see Eisenhower elected."

Shortly after Eisenhower's victory that November, the president-elect offered Paley a job as secretary to the cabinet. "You'll be the one man around here who can come into my office at any time without knocking," Eisenhower said with evident pleasure at the generosity of his offer. "Any time you have to see me, I'll be here to see you. It's an important job and I think you can do it." But the post evidently didn't measure up to Paley's expectations, and he declined rather abruptly, explaining that he was too busy. The newly elected president felt bruised. Nearly a decade later a remorseful Paley wrote to Eisenhower in hopes of redressing his "awkward" rebuff. Paley explained that he had told one of Eisenhower's subordinates that he could not take the job. Had the subordinate transmitted the message, said Paley, he "could have spared you the business of making the offer and me the hardship and embarrassment of saying no." When Eisenhower unexpectedly broached the subject, Paley had only been able to give superficial reasons that "sounded selfish and lacking appreciation of your offer."

Paley considered Eisenhower to be "more than just a political friend, a true friend." They played golf and bridge together, and Paley dutifully sent birthday telegrams, long-playing CBS records, and words of encouragement. "I am more convinced than ever," he told Eisenhower early in 1955, "that your long-standing personal philosophy, which is now emerging in correct and dramatic terms, represents the best course for the party and the best course for the country."

As the reelection campaign geared up in 1956, Paley became more politically active. Early in January he wrote a long and passionate letter to the president proposing a major foreign policy address. It was time, Paley said, for the leader of the Free World to counteract the assumption of the Communists that democratic nations would disintegrate and communism would triumph. He urged Eisenhower to assert that the Communist nations would eventually fall apart because they failed to satisfy the "inner needs and desires of men"—the natural craving for freedom. Such a speech "could well predict that the first peoples to throw off the shackles of Communist totalitarianism will be those who have known liberty and freedom in the past."

Eisenhower sent Paley a thoughtful, appreciative reply. Paley's ideas had appeared in previous presidential speeches, and Eisenhower acknowledged the merit of pulling them together into a full-length address. Reading over the two letters for the first time years later, Walter Thayer commented, "They don't surprise me a bit. You cannot have a better picture of Bill's philosophy than this, and Eisenhower would listen. It was typical of both of them—Bill's concern about the image Ike portrayed and his views of what was going on in the world and in Moscow, as well as Ike's awareness of his own idea of how to deal with it."

After the election, Paley dashed off an exultant letter. Not only was Eisenhower's personal popularity crucial to the victory, but the president had succeeded in convincing Americans to share his philosophy. "How overjoyed I am that our country will have the benefit of your leadership during the next four years," Paley wrote.

In December 1956, Eisenhower nominated Jock Whitney as ambassador to the Court of St. James's, the plum coveted by Paley. At the same time, the president sent word to Paley that he was thinking of naming him ambassador to France. Stanton discussed the feeler with Paley, who expressed interest. Quietly, Paley hired a tutor and began taking French lessons. Then, recalled Stanton, "the circuits went dead." Stanton made discreet inquiries in Washington and learned that Eisenhower had retreated because he feared criticism over having brothers-in-law in two critical European posts. Paley was crushed, but declined to raise the matter with Eisenhower himself. "Ike," said Stanton, "let Bill down."

Paley's frustration was felt at CBS. The men at CBS News knew that Paley blamed their liberalism at least in part for his inability to become an ambassador. Murrow continued to have the most liberal profile of all. In the 1956 campaign, Murrow had lost his journalistic bearings by secretly coaching Adlai Stevenson on television techniques behind the scenes. "Bill Paley disapproved of Ed because Ed angered Eisenhower," said Howard K. Smith. "Paley expected much for himself with the Eisenhower administration, and it did not happen."

37

I F "See It Now" signified television at its best, the quiz show represented the worst of the new medium. The first big money show, "The
$64,000 Question," surfaced on CBS in early June 1955. In a twist of
irony, it appeared in the slot just before "See It Now," which less than a
month later lost its weekly berth. That unfortunate juxtaposition foreshadowed the intersecting fate of Murrow and the quiz mania in the years
to come.

There was nothing about the start of "The $64,000 Question" that
could have predicted the hold it would have on the national consciousness.
It was produced by Louis G. Cowan, who had made his mark by creating
"Quiz Kids," a popular radio show. Six feet three, with horn-rimmed
glasses, Cowan was a man of sensitivity, cultivation, enlightened liberalism, and inherited wealth. His brainchild for CBS, however, was unabashedly crass: Two contestants vied to answer increasingly difficult
questions for ever greater amounts of money, beginning at $2 and going
to an ultimate jackpot of $64,000. Cowan injected an additional gimmick
by "casting" his contestants. He sought ordinary people with unlikely
specialties: the cobbler who was an opera aficionado; the gynecologist who
knew all about food and cooking; the jockey with expertise in art.

Paley asked that the drama be intensified by putting more levels en
route to the jackpot. "It would be a much better program," he said, "if
you put in platforms—one at $16,000, for example, and one at $32,000—
where the contestants would stand or step aside. That way you have
suspense. Will this person come back? Will this person step aside or stay
on?"

Stanton's demographic research indicated that the show appealed to
as many viewers at the top of the socioeconomic spectrum as at the bottom. For a mass audience program to have that many upscale viewers was
unusual. Lou Cowan had a worthy rationale. He believed that the show
would celebrate knowledge and give people an incentive to learn. But its
genuine appeal, as his wife, Polly, often argued, was the glorification of
greed.

As such, the quiz show meshed perfectly with the materialism of the
times. The postwar economy was booming, and wages were rising rap-

idly. Consumers bought homes, cars, household appliances, novelties, and luxury items. Installment debt reached new heights. And television advertising both celebrated and fanned the buying binge. When quiz show winners marched off with their loot to splurge on Jaguars and mansions, they were fulfilling the American Dream—a dream defined by television.

"The $64,000 Question" was an instant success, supplanting "I Love Lucy" as the top-rated show. Sales for the quiz show's sponsor, Revlon, rocketed as well. That year CBS passed NBC as the number-one network with better ratings for ten out of fifteen prime-time shows. Quiz show imitators sprang up on all three networks: "The $64,000 Challenge," "The Big Surprise," "High Finance," "Dotto," "Treasure Hunt," "Giant Step," and more. NBC's hottest version, "Twenty-One," launched in 1956, raised the stakes by removing the limit on prize winnings.

For the networks, all this activity translated into huge advertising revenues. At CBS, net revenues had increased more than fourfold since the beginning of the decade—from $87 million in 1950 to $354 million in 1956. The revenue boom was also fueled by a revolution in the way commercial time was sold. As the television audience grew, the cost of sponsoring an entire half-hour- or hour-long show increased dramatically. Smaller advertisers found themselves shut out of television, and larger advertisers wanted to find a way to reach viewers on a greater variety of programs.

An inventive solution to these problems was devised by Sylvester "Pat" Weaver, who came to NBC in 1953. He created three shows for the network: "Today," "Tonight," and "Home." Instead of selling them as programs, he sold their commercial time by the minute. Within a year, CBS began selling its time on the same basis.

"Spot" selling opened up television to a greater number of advertisers and generated huge demand for ad time. Unfortunately, the demand greatly reduced the remaining non-sponsored programs—the once-great proving ground for venturesome ideas. More than ever, the emphasis was on commercial shows that attracted large audiences. It became somewhat easier to sells news and public affairs programs to several advertisers instead of one, thereby spreading the risk. But such programs were a low priority for advertisers.

In the late 1950s, the quiz shows nearly did the networks in. The seeds of the trouble had been planted in 1956, when Senator Bricker's year-long campaign culminated in threats from the Justice Department of anti-trust action against the networks. Having taken control over programming from advertising agencies after the war at Paley's direction, CBS now felt pressured to hand that control to independent program producers. In so doing, CBS hoped to defuse Washington criticism that the networks had become too powerful.

The first hints of quiz show improprieties came in a *Time* article in April 1957 that the networks chose to ignore. Five months later, Herbert Stempel, a disaffected contestant on "Twenty-One," told NBC officials that his opponent, Charles Van Doren, had been fed questions in advance and that the producers had told Stempel to give wrong answers. The producers denied the charges to the NBC executives, who chose not to mention the accusations to their superiors.

In August 1958—three months after Paley had canceled "See It Now" —the quiz show scandal blew open when Edward Hilgemeier, a stand-by contestant on CBS's "Dotto," revealed that one of the show's contestants had been coached. Stempel went public with his accusations of fraud on "Twenty-One" as well. Stanton immediately launched an investigation and kicked "Dotto" off the air—actions that Paley heard about after the fact.

Both the Manhattan District Attorney's Office and the U.S. House of Representatives followed with their own probes. The next fourteen months brought one revelation after another of widespread quiz show rigging by the independent producers. Coming on the heels of Mc-Carthyism and the blacklists, these were the darkest possible days for the networks, casting the integrity of television even further into doubt.

In the middle of this crisis, on October 15, 1958, Edward R. Murrow threw an incendiary bomb. Speaking to the annual convention of the Radio and Television News Directors Association in Chicago, Murrow cited the "decadence, escapism and insulation from the realities of the world" that characterized television. He castigated the networks for squandering their "powerful instrument of communication" in the pursuit of profits. To make up for their sins, Murrow urged the networks to make a "tiny tithe" to increase news and public affairs programs. "This instrument can teach, it can illuminate," he said. "Yes, and it can even inspire. But it can do so only to the extent that humans are determined to use it to those ends. Otherwise it is merely wires and lights in a box." More than anything said before, Murrow's words exposed the hypocrisy of Paley's effort to have it both ways—to cut back on public affairs in the push for greater profits while expecting CBS to be regarded as the premier news network.

During the preparation, Murrow kept his speech even closer to the vest than he had the McCarthy broadcast. This time he was taking on his boss, mentor, and friend, William S. Paley, not some demagogic senator. He showed his draft only to Friendly, who asked, "Do you want to hit him that hard?" Yes, Murrow said, he did. He knew he would enrage Paley but, recalled Janet Murrow, "Ed had given up the idea of making an impression any other way."

The day of the speech, Murrow released a copy of the text to Mickelson, who brought it to an editorial board meeting. Paley took the first look. He read it, said nothing, and passed it along to the others. "He was very cool," recalled Mickelson. "He must have been a superb poker player." But everyone in the room could recognize his icy fury. "He is fouling his own nest," said Paley at last.

Paley had certainly known Murrow's beliefs for a long time. But for the man who symbolized CBS to most viewers to hit the networks when they were down seemed an unforgivable act of disloyalty—regardless of how wounded he was over Paley's cancellation of "See It Now." "It was a direct attack on me," Paley would later say. Not only was he hurt by the speech itself, but by Murrow's decision to withhold it from him.

Years later Paley described his subsequent treatment of Murrow as "very peculiar." In fact, it was completely in character. He knew Murrow expected, even desired, a showdown. Paley refused to give it to him. He said nothing then, or ever. Paley's silence only deepened Murrow's bitterness. Except for one poignant visit some years afterwards, Bill Paley and Ed Murrow "never had a civil conversation after October 1958," said Fred Friendly.

Firing Murrow would have been too messy, but Paley could freeze him out. When the assignments went out for election night coverage, Murrow learned that he was demoted to reporting regional returns. "He got an office memo telling him what he was to do," recalled fellow newsman Robert Trout. "It was absurd. It was an insult, and it was an insult in the way he was told. But he was like a soldier. 'I'm a reporter,' he said, 'I'll accept my assignment.' It was a public humiliation."

Early in 1959 Lou Cowan, whose quiz show success had propelled him to the presidency of CBS Television, tried to nudge Paley into considering Murrow's proposals. Cowan informed his chairman that CBS had achieved record profits in 1958 and then suggested that more money could now be invested in experimental programs. "What is the point of being number one," he asked, "except to seize the opportunities that leadership offers?" Paley ended the conversation abruptly. Later that month, Murrow was granted a leave of absence at his request amid considerable speculation in the press about his standing at CBS.

But events forced CBS into pushing more resources toward news and public affairs even as Murrow was winding down. The quiz show disclosures were intensifying, and the network study committee at the Federal Communications Commission was homing in on stringent new ways of regulating ABC, CBS, and NBC. The networks had to do something dramatic.

CBS formed a "special committee" of five executives, including Richard Salant and a rising network star named James T. Aubrey, to study the damage to the network's reputation. In early March 1959 they submitted a fifty-eight-page report to Stanton, recommending an allocation of nearly $1 million for a "strong and continuing public relations campaign" that would "overcome the impression that CBS management does not care enough about any of its responsibilities except making a profit." The committee advocated continued use of CBS's high-quality "nonbroadcast 'face' " through such means as compelling graphics. "Charges of shabbiness or backwardness are consistently belied by CBS's appearance, as a result of its high standards," the report noted. In addition, the committee proposed that CBS bolster its image by announcing a series of regularly scheduled news specials in prime time.

Two months later Stanton unveiled the series, which would begin as a monthly and switch to weekly in a year or so. "CBS Reports" was "salvaged," in the words of CBS newsman William Leonard, "from the wreckage of the Edward R. Murrow–Fred Friendly 'See It Now.' " Significantly, Murrow was not the centerpiece, although he would be brought in as a participant during his leave of absence. Stanton chose Fred Friendly as executive producer. During all the deliberations, Paley was nowhere in evidence—partly by choice but mostly by circumstance.

That May, Paley's legendary hypochondria reached an alarming point when he decided that a chest cold was actually lung cancer. It began quite innocently when Paley was playing golf at the exclusive National Golf Links in Southampton with Jock Whitney, Walter Thayer, and their stockbroker cronies Roy Atwood and Joseph Sheffield. Paley came down with a chest cold that naturally sent him scurrying to a local doctor, who suggested bed rest for several days.

Back at Kiluna, still fretful about his condition, Paley called his Manhasset physician, William Messinger, who ordered an X-ray and later told Paley he saw a shadow on the film. Paley flew into a swivet about the possibility of a tumor on one lung and sought further opinions. He called Babe's doctor, Connie Guion, who assembled a team of specialists, including Dr. Frank Glenn, head of surgery at New York Hospital and a onetime student of Dr. Harvey Cushing. At Glenn's direction, Dr. James Moore, a nose and throat specialist, inserted a bronchoscope into Paley's lungs to snip some tissue for a biopsy. Dr. Glenn told Paley that further exploratory surgery might be necessary as well.

Moore's probe with the bronchoscope revealed that Paley's lungs— after some forty-four years of four packs of unfiltered cigarettes a day—

were dark purple instead of glistening pink. Moore told Paley that if he could see his own lungs, he would never smoke again. At that moment, Paley had a cigarette cupped in his hand. He held it up to the doctor, announced that it would be his last, and dropped it into a bowl of water. When Paley told Babe of his vow, she was skeptical to say the least. "Oh, for God's sake, you'll never quit," she said. But Paley was so frightened that he kept his pledge.

Several days later he returned to New York Hospital for further examination by a lung specialist, who ordered additional X-rays. These pictures were compared to routine X-rays taken over the years by Paley's former Manhattan physician, Dr. Milton Rosenbluth. All the X-rays showed the same shadow—although Paley had never heard any expression of concern from Dr. Rosenbluth. Meanwhile, the biopsy had shown no evidence of malignancy.

The team of eight doctors huddled for a consultation and summoned Paley to hear Dr. Glenn present their report. He said that most of the doctors believed there was nothing to worry about. However, Glenn, who evidently understood the demanding ways of his patient, added that a few members of the team felt there might be a problem. "We would not feel very comfortable taking any chances with you," Glenn said with classic understatement. He recommended that Paley's chest be opened and explored (with today's high-tech diagnostic tools, a CAT scan would have served the same purpose). If a tumor was present, it would be removed.

The operation was scheduled for the following Monday, and Paley was ordered to spend the weekend in the hospital. He was paralyzed with fear, but incapable of sharing his anxieties—even with Babe. Reading was no help. He got little comfort from the lung surgeon. When Paley asked him how he dealt with patients when the news was bad, the physician betrayed more than a little annoyance by answering, "Mr. Paley, in your case, I haven't made up my mind yet."

The surgery involved a huge incision across Paley's chest and the removal of three ribs. The doctors found nothing and sewed him back up. In the process they discovered that Paley's diaphragm was paralyzed on the right side and had pushed up his right lung, resulting in the shadow on the X-ray. It was a condition he had apparently had for some time.

Instead of feeling relieved, Paley plunged into a depression that would last a year. He went to Biarritz with Babe for the summer to convalesce. But rounds of golf and festive luncheons with friends failed to cheer him. "I would be myself for a while," he recalled, "and then this blanket would come over me." With Babe, he was frequently irascible and sometimes downright nasty. To explain his behavior, he decided that he was really two Bill Paleys: when he was feeling chipper, he was William; when he was depressed, he called himself Guillaume.

By the following fall, the networks' crisis of credibility was once again at full boil. In September, Congress passed a law codifying the Fairness Doctrine promulgated earlier by the Federal Communications Commission. The networks found the gesture threatening; it compelled them to put opposing viewpoints on the air when they presented strong opinion. The FCC was also considering a new proposal that the networks be licensed. And the House of Representatives swung into its final round of hearings on the quiz show scandal.

Frank Stanton had to defuse the crisis, and once again he did it without consulting Paley beforehand. Caught in the grip of his depression, Paley was even further removed psychologically from CBS than usual. He remained in the shadows, acquiescing to nearly every decision made by Stanton.

The CBS president chose to make amends for the quiz shows at the Radio and Television News Directors annual meeting where Murrow had issued his jeremiad the previous year. Stanton confessed that the networks had let the American people down, announced his plans to cancel CBS's remaining five and a half hours of quiz shows, and pledged to take a "hard look" at everything on the network. "We accept the responsibility for content and quality and for assurance to the American people that what they see and hear on CBS programs is exactly what it purports to be."

When Jack Gould of the *New York Times* called Stanton later for details, the CBS president said that devices like canned laughter and phony studio applause would have to go, as well as any rehearsing on news and public affairs programs. Did that include "Person to Person," Murrow's recently concluded celebrity interview program? Yes, Stanton said, "Person to Person" had relied on the sort of advance questions that would no longer be permitted.

The next day, Murrow's office in New York read him Gould's follow-up in the *Times* over the telephone to London, and Murrow hit the roof. He gave an interview to United Press in London denying any impropriety on "Person to Person," and dismissing Stanton as ignorant of television and radio production techniques. Murrow's attack made page one of the *New York Times*.

It also shattered a promising truce between Stanton and Murrow that had been reached only four months earlier, on the eve of Murrow's departure for his sabbatical. The two men had talked far into the night in Stanton's office, killing a bottle of Black & White Scotch together. They spoke of friends and ideals and matters that had nothing to do with broadcasting. "We were purring like kittens," said Stanton. "Just a couple of guys sitting around talking about the things we would change. I remember him getting out of the car on Madison and walking the half block down to his home and saying goodbye to me in the warmest way."

Now, back at headquarters, Paley and Stanton were furious that Murrow was once again dragging CBS through the mud. Paley wrote a long and angry letter to Murrow that strongly implied Murrow should leave CBS. "He didn't flat out ask Ed to resign," recalled Stanton, "but he put his thoughts in such a way that you could interpret that he was asking for a resignation." When Paley showed him the letter, Stanton cautioned against sending it. "We are suffering from 3,000 miles of separation," Stanton said. "We don't deserve another explosion on Page One."

Stanton had written to Murrow as well, pointing out the importance of corporate unity and the need to adhere to the principles Stanton had espoused in his speech. As Paley read over Stanton's letter, his response was typically indirect. "Bill was uncomfortable with it," recalled Stanton. "He didn't say not to send it, but I could tell he had had his bellyful so I didn't." Nor did Paley send his letter.

Instead, both CBS chiefs acceded—with considerable misgivings—to an offer by Ralph Colin to visit Murrow in London. After hours of discussion, Murrow and Colin agreed on a statement that fell short of an outright apology. Murrow reaffirmed the integrity of his show, but conceded he had reacted too harshly, without benefit of all the facts, and endorsed the new CBS policies.

Colin returned to New York to hash it out with Paley and Stanton. The CBS chiefs wanted an outright apology that Murrow was unwilling to give. With Paley, Colin, and CBS's outside public relations adviser, Earl Newsom, on the sidelines, Stanton called Murrow in London. While Murrow's statement was scuttled, the conversation cooled off both men. Paley, however, refused to come to the phone. "Bill was still pretty angry," recalled Stanton. "I can't recall his words, but I was more willing to let bygones be bygones." Paley would have no further communication with Murrow for the duration of his sabbatical.

Stanton felt relieved that Paley had backed him up as he had in previous controversies with Murrow. "He was doing what a CEO should do," Stanton said later. "He was supporting a person who had made a policy decision. I would have been hurt and surprised and angry if he had undercut me." Paley in fact had some misgivings about Stanton's stance. He had disapproved of Stanton's inclusion of "Person to Person" in his remarks to Jack Gould. But, Paley would later say, "I could not stand by silently and allow Murrow or anybody else to attack a CBS president in such a way."

RIGHT William Paley as a toddler, the son of cigarmakers who came to America in the late 1800s. BELOW At age nine (front row, far right) with the neighborhood children on Marshfield Avenue in Chicago, where the Paleys established a small cigar factory in the barn out back.

"With Bill's appetites, there could never have been enough affection or adoration."

1

2

3

4

LEFT William Paley's parents, Goldie and Sam, in later life. BELOW A cigar store on Chicago's West Side similar to the one where Paley was born.

"I was determined to show my mother, to prove myself not only to her but to anybody else who found fault with me."

5

WILLIAM S. PALEY   Z B T
"Bill"   *"La"*   *"Pop"*
5204 Overbrook Ave., Philadelphia, Pa.
Wharton

Western Military Academy; entered from University of Chicago (2). Assistant Manager Swimming and Water Polo (3), Manager (4); Associate Business Manager "1922 Class Record;" Junior Week Committee; Wharton Smoker Committee (3); Jubilee Week Committee (3); Undergraduate Council Election Committee (3); Minor Sports Committee (4).

RIGHT University of Pennsylvania yearbook, 1922. BELOW As president (front row, center) of his fraternity, Zeta Beta Tau, 1922.

"I was half student, half playboy."

6

7

9

10

FACING PAGE William S. Paley as CBS president in the early 1930s. TOP LEFT Edward Klauber, Paley's first second-in-command, 1939. TOP RIGHT Paul Kesten, CBS's slick promotion whiz, succeeded Klauber as Paley's number two. RIGHT A celebrity by 1938, Paley was caricatured by Zito.

"I gave my life to Bill, and he never once invited me across the threshold," said Klauber.

BILL
PALEY

11

LEFT Bill with his first wife, Dorothy Hart
Hearst, on their honeymoon in Hawaii, 1932.
BELOW Bill and Dorothy at Kiluna Farm in
1941, with their son Jeffrey, front, flanked by
children of British friends who lived with them
during the war.

*"There is no question in my mind that Bill was the
love of my life."*

RIGHT Dorothy's style and intellect had a significant impact on her husband in the thirties and forties. BELOW Paley on a winter holiday in Canada, 1934.

"You could see them floating up and up. They were gobbling everyone right and left."

FACING PAGE At Bad Homburg, Germany, in 1945, Colonel Paley with future CBS executive Davidson Taylor (left), Hollywood director Billy Wilder (center), and aide-de-camp Guy Della Cioppa (kneeling). RIGHT With Edward R. Murrow at the peak of the newsman's fame as a wartime broadcaster from London. BELOW Flanked by Freeman Gosden (Amos) and Charles Correll (Andy), the targets of the first Paley raid on NBC in 1948, which cost CBS $2 million.

"Life had never been so exciting and immediate, and never would be again."

17

18

19

20

TOP With his radio stars, comedians
George Burns (left) and Gracie Allen
and Jack Benny (far right) with his wife,
Mary, in 1952. BELOW With Lucille Ball
in 1949.

*"I never heard Bill talk about using the stars
for television at all. For him in those days it
was all radio. . . . He didn't see the light
until well after the early days."*

21

22

TOP With Frank Stanton (far left), Arthur Godfrey (left) and Wayne Coy, chairman of the FCC, at CBS's first color telecast, June 1951. RIGHT The man in the middle between Edward R. Murrow and Frank Stanton, 1946.

"I hold Bill Paley to blame for not letting Ed and Frank get along. They were two white knights, each handsome, each a leader."

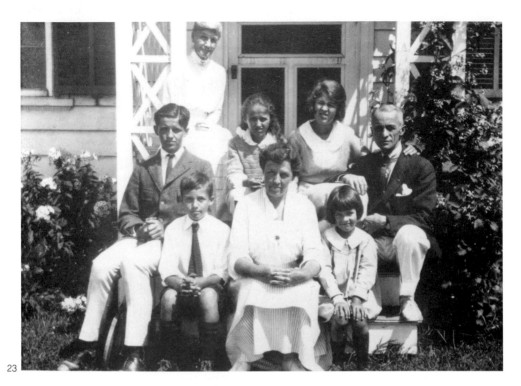

23

24

TOP Barbara (Babe) Cushing, Paley's second wife, and her family in the early 1920s. Front row: Henry, Mrs. Kate Cushing (Gogs), Babe. Second row: Bill, Betsey, Minnie, and Dr. Harvey Cushing. CENTER Society figure Stanley Grafton Mortimer, Jr., Babe's first husband, in the early 1940s. BOTTOM Babe with Tony and Amanda in 1944.

"Babe was warm but not tactile. She was not a toucher. She would never pick up and hold her children, for example, and they suffered for the lack."

25

ABOVE The Fabulous Cushing Sisters:
Babe, Betsey, and Minnie in 1937.
RIGHT Babe after being voted one of the
world's ten best-dressed women.

*"She was savvy. She knew how to please a
man, how to make him think he was the most
attractive man who ever walked. I liked to listen
to her talk to all the beaux. It was like listening
to Garbo."*

28

Bill and Babe's wedding, July 28, 1947, at
Chester House on Jock Whitney's estate. TOP
LEFT Bill and Babe with Sam (far left), Goldie
(to Babe's right) and Gogs. TOP CENTER John
Minary, Paley's factotum, and Blanche Levy,
Paley's sister. TOP RIGHT Flanked by his other
brother-in-law, Vincent Astor (left), and court
jester "Handsome Jack" Baragwanath.
LEFT Edward R. Murrow with Jock Whitney,
Paley's new brother-in-law. RIGHT Paley
feeding cake to his glowing bride.

*"Bill Paley was exotic. Babe couldn't get to the
bottom of him. There were these secrets."*

29

30

31

32

FACING PAGE Babe in the St. Regis living
room designed by Billy Baldwin. She was
as much a decoration as the fine French
furniture. RIGHT With Truman Capote,
"a rich man's Pekinese," on a Caribbean
holiday in the 1950s. BELOW The Paley
children on a rare family vacation abroad,
at Cap D'Antibes in 1953: Billie (lower
left), Kate (lower right), Amanda (upper
left) and Tony (upper right).

*"It was a strange household, so fragmented
and wacky. Our parents weren't there, and
when they came, we were all clamoring for
attention."*

34

35

LEFT At Kiluna North, the Paleys' vacation home on Squam Lake in New Hampshire, Bill basks in Babe's attention. BELOW With Aline, the Countess of Romanones, in Spain during the 1960s. FACING PAGE Babe in a tranquil moment at Round Hill, their estate in the Caribbean.

"They lived on a level of luxury I never met in England before the war, and I had been to quite a few grand houses like Blenheim."

LEFT "Jungle Jim" Aubrey, president of CBS Television from 1959. He was dismissed in 1965. BELOW Paley with another heir apparent, Arthur Taylor, before their blow-up.

"Paley was constantly undoing what we had done for the previous two weeks. It was humiliating—all the second-guessing, the coming back from a trip and redoing everything."

39

40

RIGHT Paley with CBS President Frank Stanton, the man who ran the company for 27 years, at CBS headquarters (Black Rock) on its completion in 1964.
BOTTOM Paley with John Backe, the first designated chief executive officer, in the late 1970s.

"The only way you could ever tell that Frank Stanton was angry was when the back of his neck was red."

44

FACING PAGE Bill and Babe in front of the restaurant immortalized in the scandalous Truman Capote roman à clef that riveted Manhattan high society. ABOVE Babe in her beloved dell garden at Kiluna, the Paleys' Long Island estate.

"She complained that she had knuckled under, that she had done too many things that he wanted her to do. Everything that she harbored against him came out. She knew she was dying. She didn't have anything to lose."

45

46

TOP LEFT With Evangeline Bruce, for a time the leading contender to be Paley's third wife. LEFT With millionaire widow Brooke Astor, a frequent escort to balls and dinner parties. FACING PAGE, TOP LEFT With the elegant Marietta Tree, his favorite member of the CBS Board of Directors. FACING PAGE, TOP RIGHT With old friend Slim Keith. FACING PAGE, BOTTOM At Iranian embassy party with Henry Kissinger, Casey Ribicoff (left) and Gloria Guinness.

"He always had a roving eye and a groping hand. Just as he is about food, money, belongings, power and glory, why couldn't he be the same about sex?"

47

48

49

50

51

52

TOP LEFT With daughter Hilary Califano TOP
RIGHT Amanda and Carter Burden as "New York's
Number One Fun Couple" during their 1960s
heyday. LEFT Tony Mortimer, Babe's favorite, and
his wife, Siri. FACING PAGE, TOP LEFT With his
daughter, Kate (left) after her conversion to born-
again Christianity, and Amanda. FACING PAGE, TOP
RIGHT Son Billie Paley as an aspiring restaurateur,
1977. FACING PAGE, BOTTOM Son Jeffrey Paley and
his wife, Valerie, in 1989.

*"Nobody expressed anything in our family. We didn't
really talk to each other."*

53

54

55

56

57

TOP In his office at Black Rock, with its antique chemin de fer card table and paintings by Toulouse-Lautrec, Derain, Picasso, Vuillard and Rouault, an atmosphere of "studied casualness." LEFT Gauguin's *Queen of the Areois* in the living room at 820 Fifth Avenue, his Manhattan duplex.

"He had that lovely impeccable taste that only common people can have."

58

TOP With CBS directors Michel Bergerac,
Harold Brown, Walter Cronkite and Roswell
Gilpatric. RIGHT In 1980 with Tom Wyman,
the only successor to supplant Paley as
chairman. BELOW With Laurence Tisch, Diane
Sawyer and Don Hewitt in 1987.

*"When I step down, will I be invited out to
dinner?"*

59

60

61

62

TOP With Frank Stanton following
their rapprochement in the early
1980s. LEFT In front of his Museum
of Broadcasting after its opening in
1976.

*"The failure of various successors
magnetically drew him to Stanton, who
looked so much better by comparison."*

RIGHT In his office with CBS President Laurence Tisch in 1986. BELOW With Tisch at the presentation of CBS's prime time schedule in 1987.

"I feel so sorry for Bill Paley and Frank Stanton. Larry Tisch is breaking up the company and eating it himself."

65

In the entrance foyer at 820 Fifth Avenue, with his treasured Picasso *Boy Leading a Horse*.

"Life was not meant to be devoted to the acquisition of money, followed by a lazy life of leisure. I knew that life was meant to be lived to the fullest, day by day, to the very last one."

Paley took stronger exception to Stanton's proposed banishment of canned laughter and prompted studio applause. At the urging of Jack Benny, who felt his show would be adversely affected, Paley raised his objection with Stanton. "I just don't think we ought to have that," Paley said, and Stanton quietly complied, conceding he had gone too far.

The quiz show imbroglio finally wound down in November 1959 after Charles Van Doren made a dramatic confession at a congressional hearing. The following month, Lou Cowan resigned as president of CBS Television under intense pressure from Stanton. Cowan had not appeared before the congressional committee due to a flare-up of phlebitis, and Stanton had borne the brunt of the congressional wrath instead. Stanton and Colin were convinced that Cowan had to have known about the misdeeds on his old show, "The $64,000 Question," and that he had purposely avoided testifying about it. "He grew up with quiz shows," said longtime CBS public relations aide Kidder Meade. "He understood the Hollywood mentality."

Others, notably Richard Salant and William Paley, believed strongly in Cowan's innocence. Years later, Paley would say that Cowan was "smeared rather badly." Paley had always liked Cowan. Before Cowan became president of CBS Television, Paley had enjoyed kicking around program ideas with him, and indulged Cowan's efforts to second-guess the programming department. But once Cowan was a top executive, Paley grew less enchanted with his administrative talent; while Cowan was a great talker, he didn't always deliver.

As for Stanton, it was clear to him that if Cowan hadn't known about the crooked goings-on at the quiz shows, he should have. So when Stanton told Paley that Cowan had to go, the CBS chairman raised no objection. "He knew it was something that had to be done," said Stanton. "Paley vanished to the Bahamas," said Cowan later, "and never returned my phone calls."

As Cowan's replacement, Stanton appointed James Aubrey, whom he had been grooming for months. By now, Paley's absence from the company had become so conspicuous that it was the occasion for *Variety* to ask, "Where Is Paley?" "In a crisis," said former *Variety* reporter Robert Landry, "Paley was always out of town."

Paley didn't grasp that the quiz scandals stemmed from the very nature of commercial television. "We had given very little attention to quiz shows because they were so successful and problem-free," he would say many years later. But more than anything it had been Paley's insistence on ever-higher ratings and profits that pushed the producers over the line. What Paley concluded from the quiz scandals was the need for the networks to reassert control by supervising their programs more closely—an idea close to his heart.

Murrow returned to CBS headquarters from his sabbatical in May 1960. In the following months he narrated some notable "CBS Reports" broadcasts, including "Harvest of Shame," a chilling exposé of the treatment of migrant workers. But he was going through the motions; "Harvest of Shame" was the work of its producer, David Lowe.

Paley and Murrow had little contact. "As Ed became more of a national figure and created controversies for Bill, the distance grew between them," said Frank Stanton. Their social relationship had ended several years earlier. Now, even in the office, they rarely met face to face. No longer was Murrow special; he was just a cog in the CBS news machine.

Murrow's bitterness was palpable. Over drinks with his colleague Blair Clark after their radio broadcasts, Murrow would complain: "I don't think I can get through to Bill anymore." Said Clark: "Ed was so reserved he never expressed a longing for anything, but he thought things were going to hell." "When Ed was on the way down," recalled Charles Collingwood, perhaps the closest to him of Murrow's Boys, "it was a very poignant time. He felt it bitterly and sometimes expressed it in an outburst of bitterness. He told me, 'They'll use you up and burn you out and throw you out.'" Wounded as he was, Murrow declined to criticize Paley directly. "He never lost his fascination with Bill Paley," said Howard K. Smith.

Shortly after the election of John F. Kennedy in November 1960, Murrow got a call from the president-elect: would Murrow be interested in heading the United States Information Agency? Kennedy had actually already offered the job to Stanton, who suggested Murrow. The newsman was interested, but before he made his final decision, he sought out Paley as so often in the old days.

Stanton was in Paley's office when Murrow arrived. Murrow explained the job offer and said he was inclined to take it. Paley saw the opening as an opportunity. Without offering any specifics, he assured Murrow he would have a place at CBS "forever." But he quickly moved on to advise Murrow that he should insist on being a member of Kennedy's inner circle of advisers. Afterwards, Paley expressed surprise over the offer, and Stanton filled in the background. Still, Paley said that he wouldn't have guessed that Murrow would take such a job, heading a government bureaucracy. A week later Kennedy announced the appointment.

Murrow did his last CBS broadcast on January 31, 1961. In the autumn of 1963 he was diagnosed as having lung cancer and underwent a three-hour operation. To ease his recuperation, he and Janet moved to La

Jolla, California. Early the following month, Bill Paley came to visit. The two men had seen one another intermittently since Murrow's departure. But this was the one moment that genuine warmth returned to their relationship. They had lunch together, laughed about old times, and Murrow took Paley sightseeing. Paley offered to take on Murrow as a programming consultant.

Back in New York, doctors found that the cancer had spread to Murrow's brain. They removed a tumor and treated him with radiation. He could barely speak, his body was wasted, and he wore a stocking on his head. Paley dutifully made numerous visits to his bedside. But it was by no means certain that Murrow had forgiven him. On one of his last visits, Fred Friendly said to Murrow: "Ed, I don't know yet who the good guy is—Bill Paley or Frank Stanton." Murrow, who had blamed most of his troubles on Stanton for so many years, paused and said, "I don't know either. You may have to rethink the whole thing." In April 1965, Murrow died.

In later years, Paley found comfort by glossing over their estrangement. "We were very close friends to the bitter end," he said. "I guess he was one of the closest friends I ever had." When pressed about what happened between them, Paley preferred to blame Murrow's unhappiness on the necessary restrictions of television and a nostalgia for the more freewheeling days of radio. On a personal level, Paley said, "It was very difficult to have an intense controversy with Murrow. He was tight and very unemotional." Paley even considered Murrow to be something of an ingrate: "My God, I gave him his nest egg. Ed was never a happy person."

At bottom, the rift occurred because Murrow brought too much controversy and too little money to CBS. "With Ed, Paley got to the point where he didn't want to be bothered," said Robert Trout, an old friend of Murrow's. " 'Why do I put up with this?' Paley said to himself. Ed was endangering the profits. 'It was a great thing to make profits,' Ed said, 'but why do they need to be so much bigger every year?' Because Paley demanded it. He knew Murrow was still a good man, but the price was too high. In the end, Bill Paley wanted to make a lot of money and keep a lot of money."

"Murrow had a cool, disabused view of power and the people who had it," Blair Clark once said. "He had a detached overview of everything around him." But when Murrow sensed a gross betrayal of principles on Paley's part, television's most famous newsman lost that "cool, disabused view." In the end, Murrow was forced to tell Paley precisely what he thought he was—a greedy businessman. Nothing could have hurt more.

5

THE

King

38

BILL PALEY and Frank Stanton had few common interests, no natural chemistry. Theirs was a relationship built on convenience and necessity: each instinctively recognized that his own weaknesses were the other's strengths. Over the years, they were amiable and rivalrous by turns. They were wary of one another, each privately disapproving of how the other lived. Without their shared devotion to CBS, Paley and Stanton might well have disliked one another.

Each used the other for his own ends. Stanton wanted operating control of CBS, and Paley wanted someone to operate it for him while he maintained ultimate authority. Stanton's behind-the-scenes role in Paley's appointment to the Materials Policy Commission showed Stanton's understanding of his boss, and—despite his protest to Truman's aide—his self-interested desire to hold Paley at bay.

For all his absenteeism over the years, Paley tried to keep Stanton under his control. To Paley, Stanton was a kind of corporate Jeeves, the man who took care of the details, cleaned up messes, and could be counted on always to do the correct thing. Paley knew Stanton's rectitude would reflect well on CBS. Paley also knew that the work stimulated the midwesterner, almost to the point that he could not get enough of it. Stanton's seven-day work weeks more than matched Paley's abundant energy in the early days of CBS.

Paley and Stanton had a working cordiality, but they were so dissimilar that they could never be close. Superficially, the two men cut handsome figures as CBS chiefs, Paley now in his fifties, Stanton in his mid-forties. They were nearly identical in height, and both had resonant, broadcast-quality voices. Stanton had the edge in meticulousness: his closely cropped flaxen hair was so perfectly parted that he was jokingly referred to as "The Veronica Lake of CBS." Paley's dark, English-tailored suits tended to be more conservative, while Stanton favored showy touches such as shirts of robin's-egg blue. But Stanton carefully balanced the flash with a professorial mien. His jaw often clamped on a pipe that he miraculously kept glowing with a single light.

Stanton was impeccable in behavior, manners, and judgment. He was more conspicuously brainy, more sensitive, more orderly, and decidedly more intellectual than Paley. Stanton's reading list for one month in 1948, published in *The Saturday Review,* included Mencken's *The American Language, Mona Lisa's Mustache* by T. H. Robsjohn-Gibbings, Kinsey's report on male sexual behavior, *The Big Sky* by A. B. Guthrie, Jr., and *The Age of Jackson* by Arthur M. Schlesinger, Jr. Yet Stanton remained, in the words of *Time* magazine, "just a country boy with a Madison Avenue gloss"—a plow-ahead, honest, smart businessman with technocratic habits.

Paley had become the ultimate stylish tycoon, living the glamorous high life. He was charming in society and iron-willed, even ruthless, around CBS. As he grew older, Paley relied more on his instincts, although he was far more cautious—particularly after Hytron—than his legend would have it. "Rat smart," CBS executives called him behind his back, mindful of the rat's cunning resourcefulness and sense of survival. He grew more and more arbitrary. Stanton knew, along with everyone else at CBS, that one flick from Paley could whip him into line.

Paley spent much of his office time on the phone. He loved nothing better than pushing a button to talk to one of his programming executives, reading him a comment about a show from a torn and crumpled note. At the end of the year Paley's correspondence and memoranda would fill two file drawers to Stanton's twenty. Paley usually dictated his correspondence. His memos tended to be brief, sometimes running only two to three lines. They focused largely on suggestions about programs, such as changing an actor or adjusting a plot line.

Yet in crucial negotiations, Paley could still sit for hours, working his way through fine points of a contract until he had bargained all to his satisfaction. When Richard Salant was assigned to draft Paley's "Road to Responsibility" speech in 1954, "he told me in general what to say, but I was amazed at how meticulous he was. Every sentence, phrase, and comma he would struggle through and improve. It was tortuous. We spent a week on it, and it was a helluva speech."

Paley loathed presiding over the annual CBS shareholders meeting— the one opportunity for mere mortals to hector him. Each year he would spend days diligently reading briefing books and rehearsing his performance with aides. An effective actor, he could handle questions and answers in a smooth and ingratiating manner that disguised his annoyance with the whole exercise.

His wartime aide, Guy Della Cioppa, served as Paley's CBS factotum —keeping his boss's schedule down to the minute, drafting letters and speeches, researching the backgrounds of individuals or companies requesting favors, looking into the sort of airplane CBS should buy, even calling Jock Whitney's office to find out where he got the leather top for his new Cadillac. Paley's secretaries prepared files of clippings from newspapers for him each day, and carefully underlined all items of interest in the trade bibles, *Variety* and *Broadcasting* magazine. Number-one secretary Elsie Simmons sometimes needled him by composing memos in rhyme to remind him of his many appointments with doctors and dentists.

Paley seemed more impatient than ever with hierarchy. Stanton recounted confidentially to a magazine reporter in 1949 that Paley "often hands out jobs to underlings in the elevators without consulting department heads. Having 'Spoken to God,' the underling proceeds to work with vigor; the department head, having had no orders, gets mad at Stanton for letting Paley practice his idiosyncrasies. Then, reports Stanton, when he brings up the question to Paley, the boss gets an amazed look on his face and can't understand why he has to go through channels."

Being CBS president made Stanton more systematic than ever. His memoranda were stamped with an array of options for action—Regret; Appropriate Action; Background; FYI; File; Note in Return; Reply Direct; Return to Sender; Suggest Reply; To Discuss; Comment or Recommendation; Copy to FS; Urgent—one of which he would circle for the receiver's attention. He kept a yearly diary, bound in red leather with a gold embossed label, which fit into a black case. Each page was covered with lists of cryptic abbreviations and notations in Stanton's precise hand; those that he had disposed of were crossed out neatly in red pencil. Whenever he had a business meeting over a meal, he kept a notebook and pencil by the side of his plate.

Stanton reorganized CBS in 1951 to create three separate divisions for radio, television, and laboratories. (He would later expand it to seven entities, each a small corporation with its own president and officers.) Characteristically, Stanton's scheme derived not from a burst of inspiration but from careful study. "I just looked up Alfred Sloan's old memorandum on how to organize General Motors into decentralized parts, and the course was clear," Stanton recalled. When he told the chairman of his plans, Paley gave him the go-ahead and asked no questions.

Shabbiness and sloppy work were anathema to Stanton. Every time he visited the CBS headquarters in Los Angeles, workmen would repaint the red banisters; Stanton wanted them to look fresh. Once a fellow broadcaster received a letter from Stanton on new CBS letterhead. Feeling mischievous, the recipient measured the letterhead and discovered it to be off-center by a few millimeters. He wrote to Stanton, pointing out the mistake, feigning dismay at the CBS president's sloppiness. Stanton wrote an amusing reply, announcing that he was going to have the entire stock of stationery destroyed and the engraver fired. "I had the feeling he actually was a bit annoyed," the man said later.

Stanton's office was designed by Florence Knoll, the doyenne of modern office decor. It epitomized his preference for sleek and modern efficiency. One entered through a black-lacquered door. His desk was a slender slab of black Bavarian granite. Behind it, a teak credenza contained three telephone lines; controls for a radio, television, and record player; and an intercom. The facing wall, also of teak, held three television sets, a bar, file cabinets, and bookshelves.

Mies Van Der Rohe created the four Barcelona chairs with tan leather seats, as well as a glass cocktail table, and there was a pair of teak chairs by Hans Vegner. The floor was carpeted in an unobtrusive dark gray, wall to wall. The pictures included a drawing by Léger, a white wood relief by Arp, a geometric painting by Josef Albers, and an oil by Pierre Soulanges. Stanton also had bronze sculptures by Giacometti and Marini.

His idea of relaxation was arriving in the office on Sunday wearing a sports coat. He survived on little sleep, usually five hours a night. His workday began late in the evening when he would read the *New York Times* and watch the late news before retiring at 1:00 A.M. Upon awakening at six, he would tune in the morning news; his home had a television set in every room. Some mornings he would have a business breakfast in a suite at the Ambassador or St. Regis Hotel. En route to and from work, Stanton kept tabs on his network with a portable screenless television set that enabled him to hear the audio on all CBS programs.

Stanton was in the office by 7:30 or 8:00 A.M., and by the time everyone else arrived at nine or ten, he was miles ahead. One reporter offered this description of Stanton at work in 1951:

> By 10 o'clock the pressure is rising and Stanton has begun to weave, attack, and duck with a precision that most observers have described as brilliant. When the telephones are at full blast, he is often on two or more lines at once. . . . While talking he sometimes makes notes, which he usually tears up at the end of the conversation. The act of making them helps stamp the information on his mind. . . . During the afternoon and at night (8 o'clock is the average time of departure) Stanton usually has the television set turned on with the sound eliminated. When spotting a scene that he wants to hear, he flicks a switch and brings the sound in. When the television is running silently, he sometimes turns his radio on. One CBS executive was startled to realize after a brief and satisfactory conference that during the course of it, Stanton had been following a television show, a radio program, had taken a couple of telephone calls and had dictated a fast memo.

CBS was Frank Stanton's life. On trips to England, he would sit in a room at Claridge's and watch British television for several days, taking notes. His social life was curtailed by his willingness to work every weekend. His wife, Ruth, often joined him on those quiet days. She would sit and read, and they would have dinner together at a nearby restaurant.

If one incident typifies Stanton's devotion to CBS to the exclusion of his own pleasure, it was New Year's Eve in 1952. During the Christmas season, the playwright George S. Kaufman had made a comment on a CBS comedy show that the sponsor, the American Tobacco Company, considered sacrilegious. American Tobacco demanded Kaufman's removal, and Stanton wanted to keep him on. The situation was at an impasse by New Year's Eve, when Stanton and his wife set off for New Hampshire to celebrate their twentieth wedding anniversary. Midway through the eight-hour drive, Stanton seized on a possible solution: CBS would take the time period from American Tobacco and keep Kaufman on the air while it sought a new sponsor. After a truncated celebration, the Stantons returned the next day so he could meet with CBS lawyers.

It was in business meetings that the contrasts between Paley and Stanton were most noticeable. Paley, recalled programming executive Harry Ackerman, "was the kind of man who came in each morning and would reach into his pockets and put on the table twenty-four pieces of paper, including napkins. I think of him not so much as nervous as having the quickest intelligence—constantly on the alert, constantly thinking, one jump ahead, with crinkling, shining eyes, zeroing in on the next question."

On his desk, Paley had an ashtray stenciled with a message that inadvertently revealed his own turn of mind: "Serendipity: The art of finding the unusual or the pleasantly unexpected by chance or sagacity—Horace Walpole." Paley's approach to problem solving in meetings seemed undisciplined and haphazard. "His mind was not well trained; it was self-indulgent," said William Leonard, a longtime CBS News executive.

Programming was the perfect speciality for Paley. It was the only area of the business where the answers were a matter of opinion; Paley did not have to study or think in any orderly fashion. His only responsibility was to screen the pilots and offer his judgments.

Paley could, in fact, see things that eluded others—the off-key costume, the woman with the slightly too aggressive manner. At one point Amos 'n' Andy introduced a character who seemed an instant success because he got more laughs than anyone. When Freeman Gosden asked Paley for an assessment of the show, Paley criticized the new character. Perplexed, Gosden said, "But this guy is getting the biggest laughs of all." Paley persisted, saying the man lacked believability, would not sustain the interest of the audience, and was jeopardizing the program's main characters. Gosden took the character out.

Since his earliest days at the network, Paley had created the illusion of a consensus that was in fact *his* consensus. "His control was never in doubt," said Jack Schneider, a longtime CBS executive. "He was just toying with people. He knew he could cut your head off, but he would pretend he presided over a parliament."

Paley didn't initiate; he tended to react—to an idea, a suggestion, a crisis. He would jump from point A to point Z, hop back to F, and ultimately find the solution somewhere around point C. If the most logical conclusion did not match his intuition, he would say, "That doesn't make sense," and dismiss the cold facts of research. Paley's intuitive leaps kept his subordinates off-balance, and his digressions were often wasteful and annoying.

Sometimes, close students of Paley detected a pattern behind the apparent chaos. "We would show him a pilot," recalled Robert Wood, a former CBS-TV president, "and he would say everything was wrong. He would move from the negative to the less negative and then to what was good about it. That way, if it failed, he could say, 'I told you so,' and if it succeeded, he could say, 'I told you so.' He circled every possibility, which heightened our anxieties."

Paley was, of course, the master of calculation. "He didn't do things inadvertently," said one longtime board member. "He was in complete control. I have seen him play dumb and hide behind obfuscation. He would give himself time to regroup. It was one aspect of his genius." After seeming to lose track of a conversation, even to the point of appearing to doze off, Paley would exclaim, "Say that again!" Suddenly it would be apparent that Paley had heard everything, and had even scribbled notes to himself. If he lost interest in a topic, he dropped it; he would never feign interest to be polite as other executives might.

Paley listened selectively, and remembered the same way. He could block out what he did not want to know, or, recalled programmer Oscar Katz, "If you put on a flop, he would never forget it. Whenever it would come up he would note it." Paley had terrible trouble remembering names —of his subordinates and of television show titles in particular—which was disconcerting to those around him. "At a program board meeting in the 1950s, Paley brought up a show he'd seen on ABC—'77 Sunset Boulevard,' " recalled Oscar Katz. "I said, 'That's "77 Sunset Strip," Mr. Paley.' He said, 'Whatever is its name, it's pretty interesting.' That meant that CBS should do something like it. Two weeks later he said, 'Have you seen that show on ABC—"77 Sunset Boulevard"?' He remembered that he asked me but once again he forgot the name."

Paley had a boxer's instinct for weakness. "Bill told me once, 'Watch out. Always be concerned if their voice drops and ask them to repeat it,' " recalled former CBS programming chief Michael Dann. The unnerving question out of left field was a crucial part of Paley's strategy. Once he zeroed in on the soft spot, he would drill at it relentlessly. "If something got in him, it didn't make a difference what it was," said William Leonard, "he had the quality of shutting out everything else."

Despite his diminishing share of the company—some 11 percent— Paley acted the omnipotent owner. If he wanted to explain something, he did; if he chose not to, he didn't. It was unnecessary for him to follow any pattern. Paley's manner in meetings was what Marietta Tree admiringly called "controlled aggression." His imperious conduct made people automatically regard him as the Boss. In fairness, the only person he had ever worked for—other than his volunteer jobs for the government—was his father, so he lacked a full appreciation of the fear that a boss might inspire. Paley did not have to exercise his power overtly; his mystique came from the perception of that power. "Many people who own their own business are less apt to be as independently proprietary as Paley," said David Hertz, a management consultant who worked closely with Paley. "His attitude was that anybody who didn't like it could get out." If Paley wanted to find out something, he would do so by his insistent prying.

Although he abhorred difficult or messy situations, Paley was strong enough to face reality. "He was very much a realist, more than he would ever show," said one close aide. "He would cut down to why something didn't work. He would discover the reality." Unfortunately for those just below him, he would take out his displeasure on them when confronted with bad news.

Paley thought in concrete, literal terms. When one of his executives offered him an elaborate concept, he tuned out. "If Bill Paley wanted to fire someone, he would tell Stanton to do it," said David Adams, former vice-chairman of NBC. "If he wanted to express a complicated idea, he would have Stanton say it." Paley made his shrewdest analyses in light of his own experience. Every solution came down to a few essentials: Does it help the bottom line? Does it work? Is it practical? Is it in the CBS image? Bill Paley kept his mind blissfully uncluttered.

Stanton held enough details in his head to give Paley a month-long migraine. Stanton's approach to problems was rigorously logical. He made decisions quickly, dissecting them piece by piece in orderly fashion. He also had unusual retentive powers. One day Paley's aide Guy Della Cioppa walked unannounced into Stanton's office. "Frank," said Della Cioppa. "Just a minute," said Stanton. Della Cioppa paused, then passed along some information. "Why did you ask me to pause?" Della Cioppa then asked. "You know you can train your mind as you can train a muscle," said Stanton. "I opened a file drawer in my mind so that what I was just doing was well organized. Then I closed it and opened another for you."

The word among CBS executives was "When you go in to see Bill Paley, you'd better know all the facts because he is sure to ask you something you haven't thought about. When you go see Frank Stanton, it doesn't make any difference. He already *knows* all the facts." Stanton had always made it his business to know more about a problem than anyone else. He once revealed that the key to his survival at CBS was "by staying a step ahead of everybody"—presumably including Bill Paley.

Stanton managed to elevate himself above the grubby world of commercial television. In his own way, he created an image for himself every bit as carefully as Paley did. Stanton came to represent the highest aspirations for broadcasting and earned widespread respect among politicians and businessmen. Inside the company, he concerned himself with proposing and developing a scattering of high-toned television series such as "Playhouse 90." Outside CBS, he was a trustee for important institutions such as Sarah Lawrence College and the National Citizens Commission for the Public Schools. He joined the boards of the American Management Association and the Business Council, a group of chief executives. Stanton also served on numerous corporate boards, partly for the prestige but also to learn how other businesses worked.

From 1939 to 1942 Paley was a member of the Pan American Airways board, but only for social reasons. His friend Cornelius Vanderbilt Whitney, Jock's cousin, lured Paley at a time when airlines were a glamorous novelty. When Whitney fell out with Juan Trippe, Pan Am's chief executive, Paley resigned from the board. He would later say that he declined to join corporate boards for fear of creating a conflict of interest with CBS News. His reason may have been heartfelt, but it gave him a useful excuse. And he declined to impose such a restriction on Stanton.

The truth was, Paley found the world of business tiresome. He shied away from appointing hard-nosed businessmen to the CBS board. He rarely talked about business in social settings. "Occasionally, if a man in the room had a connection to the broadcasting business, Bill would talk to him, but it would be very short," said Marietta Tree. Paley fraternized with a handful of powerful tycoons, all of whom had great flair, charisma, and social cachet—men like Italy's Gianni Agnelli and Greece's Stavros Niarchos. But standard-issue businessmen were little Babbitts far beneath him. He could not be bothered to learn about their operations. He took the aristocrat's view that to serve on the board of a business was somehow to be in trade.

Likewise, although Paley was obsessed with his public image, he did not share Frank Stanton's interest in mingling with members of the press. Many Saturday mornings Stanton had breakfast with Jack Gould, the influential TV critic for the *New York Times,* and lunch with George Rosen, *Variety*'s lead reporter on the broadcasting industry. Stanton genuinely enjoyed these relationships, while Paley took the classic view of high society: journalists were untrustworthy lowlifes, and it was best to keep one's distance.

Both Paley and Stanton shied away from simple comparisons casting Stanton as analytical, cerebral, and intellectual, and Paley as instinctive, intuitive, and impulsive. Those characterizations contained truth but Stanton said they were "overstatements in both directions. We were closer than many people realize." Both men chose to emphasize their mutual concern with taste and quality for CBS. Asked to compare himself to Paley, Stanton once noted with evident restraint, "I'm curious. He is reasonably curious. He's not mechanical. I am. He's musical. I'm not. He has a sense of theater. I don't. He's not so much interested in how things work."

Each man professed to admire in the other man the qualities he himself lacked. Paley often said he respected Stanton's organizational ability, his correctness, his equanimity, and his relentless commitment to CBS. When someone suggested back in 1953 that Stanton's dedication to his work seemed to be an escape mechanism, Paley rose to his defense, dismissing any quasi-psychoanalytic suggestion of compulsion in Stanton's behavior. "I can't imagine what Frank might have to escape from," said Paley. "I've never known such a well-balanced man or one who's more stable emotionally. If it's any one thing, it's his curiosity that drives him. He's always wondering about something—and won't rest until he's got the answers."

Stanton was awestruck by the magic of Paley's charm; for some time it obscured his appreciation of Paley's shrewdness and brilliance. "He had such facility in his personal relations in business," Stanton remarked. "He was a smooth piece of work. He could charm the birds right out of the trees. I used to think there was an awful lot of luck in what he did. But I learned that there was a lot more skill than I first gave him credit for."

Stanton could not understand Paley's ability to drift in and out of the company, and his unwillingness to bear down in a sustained way. And Paley was bothered by Stanton's unflappability. "My uncles used to get red when they got mad, but Stanton gets white," he once complained to a CBS executive. Stanton seemed to wear his integrity too conspicuously on his sleeve for Paley's taste. But most of all, Paley believed that Stanton did not know how to live. To Paley, Stanton was hopelessly square.

Like Paul Kesten, Stanton found release from office tensions in fast
cars. At various times he owned a Muntz Road Jet, a black 1952 Porsche,
and a black 1959 Ford Thunderbird with the right front seat and chrome
removed. Sometimes when he was on business trips he would have one of
the cars sent to his destination so he could drive it on the open road.
Stanton was also a skilled amateur photographer who owned numerous
cameras, lenses, and filters, and made prints in his own darkroom. He
liked to park his car on an obscure Manhattan street and spend the afternoon exploring an area of the city he had never visited before.

Even after two decades in New York, Frank and Ruth Stanton were
private people who tended to keep to themselves. When they ventured
out, it was for a quiet dinner or evening at the theater with some friends.
Ruth was Frank Stanton's closest confidante, a sensible sounding board for
any number of office problems. "She knew more about the company than
anyone else," Stanton said years later.

Together, the Stantons decorated their first apartment at 25 East 83rd
Street, four rooms that *Time* magazine called "tasteful and precise, resembling a wing of the Museum of Modern Art." In 1956 they bought a
handsome brick town house on East 92nd Street in Manhattan and spent
many hours working on the decor—down to the frosted glass with a
thistle pattern that they designed for the hood over their kitchen range.
The Stantons filled their home with an eclectic array of soft Victorian
furniture, Art Nouveau pieces, Tiffany lamps, and modern art, which they
collected avidly. Their early favorites included Jackson Pollock, Piet Mon-
drian, and Henry Moore, who became a close friend.

Stanton's taste in art and furnishings did not impress Paley. "It's easy
to do a modern office," Paley once told a reporter. Babe used to bring
friends around to Stanton's office when he was away. They would giggle
about how crazy it was because it was so modern.

Paley was forever making suggestions to Stanton about leisure. Take
time off, he'd advise, visit this or that European capital. One year the
Stantons relented and toured Europe for an entire month. They didn't
always follow Paley's advice, however. When Paley urged Stanton to
build a home near Kiluna and later in Jamaica at Round Hill—as he had
asked Murrow—the Stantons declined on both counts. "I made it a condition when I agreed to be president of CBS that I not socialize with Bill,"
Stanton would say years later. "I told him he could have me any time
during business hours but not after. I was determined not to be in the
position of Colin and Klauber and to a lesser extent Kesten, who longed
to be accepted by Bill outside the office. I didn't want to be part of that
world."

Stanton's explanation seemed somewhat disingenuous, if not defensive. One could argue that Stanton was more self-contained than Paley, that Paley needed the constant stimulation and adoration of New York high society to ward off his demons and boost his self-esteem, and that Stanton found such company superficial and empty. While that may have been true, Stanton was also socially insecure. He felt safest on corporate ground.

Despite his sophisticated understanding of design, architecture, and modern art, Stanton never felt comfortable with Paley's crowd and what they stood for. Both men had arrived in New York lacking connections to the schools, clubs, and resorts that were the touchstones of "the right people." But Paley shut the door on his modest origins and transformed himself through invention and determination into a facsimile of the Eastern establishment. Stanton could not; he was unable to escape being the son of a high school woodworking teacher. It was easier for Stanton to retreat rather than risk rejection or, even worse, mockery.

Stanton's rebuffs of Paley's various social overtures deeply annoyed Paley. The emperor of CBS had benevolently extended his hand, and Stanton had turned away. Perhaps Stanton understood correctly that Paley's efforts were born not so much of friendship as of power. But nothing rankled Paley more than Stanton's refusal to invite him to his home.

The Stanton town house was such a sacred hideaway that Stanton once considered buying a professionally decorated apartment in a fashionable building and using it solely for entertaining. Still, he did invite several close friends, including the pollster Elmo Roper and William Golden, a CBS graphic designer, to his home from time to time. His stubborn insistence on not including Paley among the select few—even after Paley had entertained the Stantons in his home any number of times—was an obvious cut. Over the years Paley bitterly complained to others about the slight, once calling Stanton a "closed-off, cold man."

Perhaps as a result, Paley would later insist that he had consciously devised a rule against socializing with his employees, Stanton included. It was a decision, Paley would say, that "came rather naturally. I could see the dangers of socializing with my office associates . . . I feared the one-dimensional kind of existence it might lead to and the risk of encumbering my business affairs with my social ones. This separation was more or less understood and accepted at CBS and became a long-standing way of life for me."

The trouble was, Paley selectively breached his own rule. Larry Lowman had always been a crony as well as an employee. Edward R. Murrow became a social friend, as did Goddard Lieberson, an executive of CBS Records since 1939. Paley's willingness to socialize with these men made his distance from Stanton that much more noticeable. "There were certain kinds of people he liked being around," said Sheryl Handler, president of Thinking Machines Corporation, a small company Paley invested in. "If you were that kind of person and you were at CBS, you were around him. He always knew what he liked and didn't like. He wasn't going to do something for the form of it." In Murrow and Lieberson, Paley saw attributes that elevated both men above the average CBS executive; both were trophies that Paley eagerly displayed to his friends.

Of the two, Lieberson came closer to intimidating Paley. British born, handsome, and exceedingly cultivated, Lieberson was a trained musician and accomplished composer who created piano and chamber music as well as choral versions of texts by James Joyce and Ezra Pound. He dressed elegantly, spoke Japanese, practiced calligraphy at his desk. His wife, Brigitta, was a ballerina with the stage name Vera Zorina. She had previously been married to George Balanchine. Lieberson was a more sophisticated epicure than Paley; among CBS executives it was agreed that Lieberson employed the better chef.

Unlike Stanton, Lieberson had standing in worlds that greatly impressed Paley: society and culture. At the very least, he was Paley's social equal. Babe adored Lieberson, and loved to join him periodically for lunch and dinner. Lieberson knew everyone; he was knowledgeable without being overbearing. Revered in classical music circles, Lieberson brought prestige to CBS through his contacts. He produced a groundbreaking series of recordings of Arnold Schoenberg and Aaron Copland, and helped keep Igor Stravinsky afloat when the Russian composer was strapped for cash. Béla Bartók was one of his good friends.

"Bill Paley learned an enormous amount from Goddard Lieberson," said John Hammond, for many years Lieberson's colleague at CBS Records. "Like Paley, Goddard was unconventional." According to Brigitta, "Bill had a receptive mind, and he listened to Goddard."

Lieberson was a Paley-style charmer, adept on the dinner-party circuit. He also approached business much as Paley did: he did not kill himself at the office, and he focused his energy on his performers. Lieberson was Jewish, but he never tried to mask his heritage. Paley, who could not bring himself to utter a Yiddish phrase, must have marveled at Lieberson the aesthete tossing off one bit of slang after another.

When Paley described Lieberson in a 1979 autobiography, the lavish encomiums might have applied to himself: "brilliant . . . a legend in his time . . . extraordinary human being . . . handsome . . . elegant . . . dapper . . . sense of good taste." Paley's summary of Stanton in the same volume was more pointedly subdued and distant: "reserved . . . articulate . . . willing . . . imaginative . . . structured . . . cool . . analytical . . . rigid."

At bottom, Paley and Stanton's relationship was "always at arm's length," said Dorothy Paley. "It was strangely impersonal." They could never openly acknowledge the unbridgeable distance between them. Had they been genuinely fond of one another, they might well have averted the power struggle that would entangle them both in the years to come.

39

PALEY AND STANTON did not assume the classic Mr. Inside–Mr. Outside relationship so common between corporate presidents and chairmen, where one man operates inside the company and the other deals with the outside world. At CBS, each man was Mr. Outside in his sphere of influence, Paley in Hollywood, Stanton in corporate and political circles. William Leonard said that "Frank seemed to handle Paley in much the way a wily prime minister would deal with an equally shrewd, erratic—but absolute—monarch."

If Stanton had not agreed with Paley on the overall goals for the company, the two men could never have co-existed. Stanton might have had high-minded principles about programming, but he understood Paley's ground rules for a mass medium. When Paley decided to scuttle one of Stanton's few forays into programming, "Playhouse 90," Stanton buried his own feelings and went along with the Boss. But more often than not, the two agreed on what was appropriate for CBS. "There were pilots we saw together that I felt were cheap and below standard," said Stanton. "Frequently Bill would say the same thing I was going to say."

Stanton's first rule for dealing with Paley was to keep him informed, but not too deeply. With a careful eye toward controlling the information, Stanton had all areas of the company reporting to him; programming executives reported to both Paley and Stanton.

Outside CBS, Stanton had an extensive network of informants on Capitol Hill and in the federal bureaucracy. "He knew what was going on in Washington before I did," recalled Eric Sevareid, a veteran Washington-based correspondent. "He was always one step ahead. He was so closely informed it was amazing."

When Paley was away, Stanton kept a running tab of notes on what he thought would interest Paley. He would then send the chief a series of chatty memos, four to five pages. Each paragraph was a single sentence. These sentences covered the status of various projects, gossip about the industry, and tidbits about executives and board members. If Paley wanted more detail, he asked. Above all, Stanton kept Paley's trust by giving him straight answers.

Stanton also briefed Paley thoroughly after his trips, a task that could not have been easy. Said CBS attorney Joseph Ream, "Bill's technique of asking all sorts of questions around a subject would make the other guy think, 'This should be obvious.' If you are working like a devil and want to get something done and have to go back to the beginning and explain each square one by one, it is not much fun."

Although Stanton was only seven years younger than Paley, the two men assumed a father-son manner marked by Stanton's unwavering filial respect ("Mr. Paley") in the presence of their subordinates. As Klauber had been a father figure to Paley, so Paley became one, at least in the early years, to Stanton. At that stage, Stanton knew he was learning as he was going along.

In meetings, Stanton submerged his ego, never taking issue with Paley. As he grew more experienced, he learned to reflect an opposing viewpoint by attributing it to others—by saying, for example, that this or that constituency would object to a particular policy. When Stanton expressed his own opinion, it was to agree with the Boss. When he disagreed, he occasionally signaled his feelings to close colleagues by raising his eyebrow, rolling his eyes, or giving a wink as if to say, "Oh no, here he goes again."

This behavior disappointed CBS executives who counted on Stanton's support. They felt he was cowed by Paley. With the exception of Joe Ream in the earliest days, Stanton declined to confide in anyone about his private dealings with Paley. Stanton was too fearful that any explanation would be misunderstood, taken out of context, and leaked. "Everyone always wondered what Frank Stanton said to Bill Paley afterward," said Fred Friendly.

In fact, Stanton talked hard in private with Paley, often arguing points forcefully. Counting on Paley's tendency to have second, third, and fourth thoughts—the so-called 540-Degree Club, meaning a completion of the circle and halfway round again—Stanton would try to hold his position until Paley fell into line. (Stanton's successors lacked this patience). When Stanton first proposed stock options for top CBS men, for example, Paley objected, complaining that the plan cut into his own position. Confronted with Stanton's persistence, Paley grudgingly agreed.

Other times in those one-on-one sessions Stanton would push as far as he could and then fold in the face of Paley's implacable resistance. He would never try to circumvent a final decision of Paley's "It was no use arguing against a maximum leader," said one of Stanton's successors. "No matter how bright or wonderful your arguments were, it was psychologically intimidating."

In part, management principles governed Stanton's approach. He felt it was wrong for CBS's two leaders to disagree in the presence of subordinates. "Nothing would disrupt an organization more quickly than word of disagreement at the top," he said.

If Paley opposed a plan of action put forth by Stanton in a meeting, Stanton would wait until the two of them were alone together. "Let's sleep on it," he would say. Later, in Paley's office, after Stanton had systematically presented the facts, the CBS chairman usually came around.

"In private, Frank Stanton could talk to Paley without Paley losing face," said Jack Schneider, a former president of the CBS broadcast group. "If he argued with Bill Paley in public in a big meeting and Paley took a position that was untenable, Stanton couldn't get him to change his mind. He couldn't put Paley in a position of backing down. It was better for Stanton to remain silent and keep his powder dry."

Stanton handled Paley masterfully when CBS ran into problems. He positioned himself as the pessimist in order to fully prepare Paley for the worst outcome. Paley, the chronic worrier, found himself in the optimist's role, assuring Stanton that CBS would prevail. When CBS did win the battle, Paley was doubly pleased.

Early in his career as CBS president, Stanton learned how to set small traps to capture Paley's interest. In 1946 Arthur Hull Hayes, the head of CBS's radio station in New York City, suggested to Stanton that the station begin the broadcast day with a new morning news and information program two hours earlier than the station's customary 9:00 A.M. kickoff. Stanton was enthusiastic, and the two men spent long evenings at each other's homes working up a proposal.

They took the idea to William Hylan, head of sales for the CBS radio network. Hylan knew that Paley tended to look down on the stations and was only interested in programming for the network, so he concocted a scheme. Paley was due to come to Hylan's apartment for cocktails after work, and Hylan suggested placing the proposal on the coffee table in his living room. When Paley arrived, he spotted the report on the table, picked it up, and asked Hylan what it was. Hylan told him, Paley leapt on the idea, and directed Hayes to implement it. Had Paley received a formal proposal from Hayes, a mere station man, he might well have spurned it.

Paley relied heavily on his extensive sources outside CBS, often to the chagrin of his colleagues. Jock Whitney, Walter Thayer, and David Selznick were the most trusted members of Paley's kitchen cabinet. In later years Paley would say that he and Selznick agreed never to do business together. But in fact Paley talked to Selznick in the late forties about having the producer supply CBS Television with two-reel films. The "negotiations" took the form of discussions when the two men were touring Europe, Selznick on a honeymoon with Jennifer Jones, and Paley on a prolonged vacation with Babe. Nothing ever came of the talks.

More frequently, Paley would return from a weekend with friends brimming with bits of information that he thought could apply to CBS programs. In luncheon meetings with Stanton the following Monday, Paley would run through various suggestions he planned to make to his programmers. These were often strange conversations—observations on foreign policy mingled with complaints about the quality of this or that show that had been prompted by small digs from friends. Sometimes Paley's comments would throw well-developed plans into momentary chaos. If, for example, Paley had accepted a proposal but subsequently heard something in conversation that cast doubt, he might try to rescind his approval.

After a while, Stanton could tell who had been visiting Kiluna by the kinds of questions and requests Paley made on Monday. Stanton also learned that once Paley's enthusiasms had dissipated, he rarely followed through. Paley did not embrace the views of outsiders any more than he did his own men, but his use of personal contacts created the feeling that he listened more closely to them. It became an annoyance, creating an undercurrent of ill-will.

When the mood struck him, Paley would constantly challenge—even badger—his second-in-command. During most of Stanton's twenty-seven years as president, few others were subjected to Paley's full-court press. The one exception was the head of programming, who knew that Paley's involvement came with the territory. Paley was frequently on the phone to the programming chief, and when the CBS chairman sat in on programming meetings, he usually took over.

In every other respect, Paley remained detached from the CBS troops. "He was above everyone," recalled Sal Ianucci, a former CBS executive. "He played that to the hilt. Dealing with him, you were dealing on a different level. He never said anything personal to anyone."

Not only did Paley avoid small talk, he rarely handed out compliments. "Bill was never able to convey appreciation the way Frank Stanton could," recalled Kidder Meade. "I don't think Paley could do it. He could be gracious and polite on occasion. He could fill the air with praise. But Frank Stanton could convey appreciation." Once when an aide wondered aloud why Paley had declined to thank an executive for a superior performance, Paley said simply, "That's his job. I expect him to do well."

Executives at CBS were wary of direct contact with Paley. Everyone feared him and some hated him. "You knew at any moment if you did not perform, no matter how, you might lose your job because Mr. Paley was not satisfied," recalled one former executive. "If you had any contact with Mr. Paley at all, you were in some jeopardy." The longer Paley was around a subordinate, the less he tended to trust him. With Paley, a man might begin with 100 percent support, drop to 80 percent, then 40 percent, and at some time be declared expendable.

Program executives ran the greatest risk of incurring Paley's displeasure because of their regular contacts with him. Junior programmers saw him twice a year in big meetings; higher-ups met him more frequently in smaller groups and fielded phone calls. "Paley wouldn't yell at you, particularly if you were down the line," said veteran programmer Michael Dann. "He was not difficult to be with because of his personality. When he wanted to be, he was one of the most charming, exciting people to be with. But he was difficult because he wanted to talk about weakness. You wouldn't talk about good things. It was always tough."

Goddard Lieberson was the only executive who dared cross Paley publicly. Taking advantage of his special relationship, he veered dangerously close to mockery. Once at a meeting to discuss the performance of CBS Records, Paley referred to a page number of a document and announced he didn't understand a particular figure on the page. Lieberson peered over his bifocals at the page and said, "I'm looking at page 9 but I don't see that figure." Paley restated his question, and Lieberson again said he was mistaken. Knowing that he was being needled, Paley gave up. In such situations, Paley indulged Lieberson because he liked him so much.

While Paley was inaccessible, Stanton kept an open door. He offered a cordial and warm ear to unhappy subordinates, generous with both his time and his advice. "He is what he is," Stanton once advised a dispirited Robert Wood after a meeting in which Paley sharply questioned the performance of CBS Television. "He has confidence in you, but he has a different way of getting at things. Don't let it upset you. I am always at your side."

Because Stanton had day-to-day contact with the executives, he made virtually all recommendations for advancement or demotion, even when it came to Paley's cronies. Goddard Lieberson was such a free spirit that Stanton had difficulty taking him seriously at first. When he passed Lieberson over for the presidency of CBS Records in the early 1950s, Lieberson expressed his disappointment to Stanton directly. The CBS president told him that if he showed some managerial and financial flair in addition to his capability with performing artists, he would get the job next time. Stanton made good on his promise in 1956, and Lieberson became one of CBS's most able executives.

As he had with Ed Klauber, Paley left the business of firing to Stanton. "Paley didn't like the impression of firing," said one former CBS executive. If Paley became disenchanted with an executive, he would quietly signal thumbs down to Stanton. Many times Stanton tried to soften the blow by giving an executive a less visible spot in the company or a sinecure while the man looked for work elsewhere. When dismissal was inevitable, Stanton either did it himself or delegated the job.

Davidson Taylor, for example, had been through World War II with Paley as one of his aides. A sensitive Southern gentleman, Taylor was a musical scholar who had joined CBS Records before the war. In that capacity he had commissioned American composers for CBS radio; Aaron Copland dedicated a piece to him. After the war Paley appointed Taylor vice-president for CBS programming. When Taylor failed to come up with a schedule to Paley's liking, Paley directed Stanton to narrow Taylor's portfolio to news and public affairs programs.

But Taylor was equally ill-cast there. He lacked the toughness to deal with the strong personalities in CBS News. Hubbell Robinson, then head of programming, began crowding him, and Taylor mistakenly thought Paley would be his protector. By then Paley was growing impatient. When Robinson suggested firing Taylor, Paley gave the order and Taylor moved quietly to NBC.

It also fell to Stanton to motivate and reward subordinates for top performance—a paternalistic role that he carried far beyond the call of duty. Stanton gave his senior executives their own private dining rooms and seats on the CBS board to enhance their prestige in the eyes of the world. He designed generous bonus and incentive plans to encourage their best work. If someone did a job well, he sent a note with a "smile" drawing; if he was disappointed, he drew a frown. When CBS was crippled by a union strike, Stanton supplied the picketers with coffee; after the strike was over he arranged to have overtime checks delivered by hand to the executives who had replaced the striking workers.

Stanton's thoughtfulness won the loyalty of many CBS men. He was forever sending clippings, books, and items of interest to employees; he knew far more about their likes and dislikes than anyone imagined. When CBS programmer Harry Ackerman was planning his first visit to Paris, Stanton wrote a ten-page letter listing every gallery and restaurant, even indicating which should be seen by moonlight. Before a dinner with a group of CBS executives and their wives, Stanton noted all the food preferences of his guests and organized separate menus specifying seafood for one man, steak and chocolate ice cream for another.

By channeling everything through Stanton, Paley never had to show his hand. It mattered little to Paley that he remained distant from so many at the company he built. If something failed, Stanton was the fall guy; if it was a success, Paley could take credit—an astute if not terribly admirable strategy. "Frank Stanton would tell you the bottom line. Even if Paley was right there, Stanton would do the talking if there was tough news to deliver," said Sal Ianucci. "It was like Paley was functioning in Frank Stanton's head, and his words were coming out of Frank Stanton's mouth. In large groups Paley didn't want confrontations, and he didn't want to deliver bad news."

Paley shunned a great deal of CBS's day-to-day business. Although restructuring the company into divisions helped preserve CBS's position in radio and built its strength in television, Paley's avoidance of such administrative matters was predictable. More surprising was his lack of involvement in areas close to his heart. Design and image, for example, had preoccupied him since CBS's earliest days. Yet once Stanton took charge, Paley removed himself from those questions as well. It was Stanton, not Paley, who oversaw the development of television's most enduring symbol, the CBS Eye.

The Eye was conceived by William Golden, a graphic designer who came to CBS in 1937. In 1951, Stanton asked Golden to create something that would give the new CBS-TV network a distinctive identity on the air. Golden first offered the letters CBS superimposed with an oscilloscope. "Too weak," Stanton said. Then Golden came up with two versions of the Eye. The moving image showed a series of concentric "eyes." As the camera zoomed in, the iris of the eye clicked open and shut to reveal coming attractions. In the still photograph, an eye appeared against a cloud formation.

Stanton loved the image, with one qualification: the clouds had to go. He ordered the simplified Eye emblazoned on everything having to do with CBS Television: studio marquees, press releases, trucks, cameras, theater curtains, studio walls, matchboxes, cufflinks, ashtrays, and neckties. The Eye was so effective that although it was never used as a corporate logo, it became inextricably linked with the company.

About a year after its introduction, Paley expressed misgivings about the Eye. "He was not unhappy with it," Stanton recalled, "but he didn't care whether we continued it. He just didn't think much of it." Paley planted doubts with Golden as well, who suggested to Stanton that he try something new. "Just when you're beginning to get bored with what you have done is probably the time it is beginning to be noticed by your audience," Stanton told Golden. At Stanton's insistence, the CBS Eye stayed.

Both Paley and Stanton were quite contented at first with their relationship. "I let Frank Stanton run the company," Paley would say years later with imperial certitude. "I had complete confidence in him and allowed him to get recognition. I think he felt he got it."

Paley had carved out a life for himself that was not too demanding—a kind of semi-retirement, with enormous leisure and just enough anxiety to keep it spicy. "Paley was shrewd," observed Jack Gould, longtime TV critic for the *New York Times*. "He had it organized to the point where the only phone calls he got were the ones he wanted." Paley did exactly as he pleased. He was smart enough to know that the stimulus of the small amount of responsibility he wished to carry was enough. He knew he could count on Frank Stanton, who walked the fine line of being deferential enough to avoid Paley's anger and assertive enough to gain his applause and confidence.

"It worked out fine for CBS," recalled Kidder Meade. "It really put Frank Stanton in the seat as de facto chief executive officer. . . . The company was running smoothly. It was a source of great pride, and Bill Paley had the good sense to let it run on its own. He understood that his type of entrepreneurial thing for a company ranked 70 on the Fortune 500 was not the way to go. It was good sense, but it was convenient too."

To much of the outside world, Frank Stanton, not Bill Paley, was Mr. CBS. In Washington, Stanton made headlines fighting for broadcasters' independence and got favorable treatment for CBS. He was better prepared and more eloquent than his counterparts at the other networks. He knew every senator and congressman. His speech, conduct, and look gave CBS a personal dignity that had little to do with what was appearing on living-room TV screens. Stanton's contribution to CBS's image was incalculable.

There was no more clear-cut evidence of Stanton's unusual stature than when *Time* magazine put him on its cover on December 4, 1950. It was twelve years after Paley had appeared on *Time*—but an extraordinary feat for a second-in-command. "A lot of people I knew thought I was chief executive officer and Paley was chairman," Stanton recalled. "I think if there was anything I wanted to do with the company and I proposed it, there was a pretty good chance I could go ahead and do it . . . Bill and I had a modus operandi that would permit that. I knew his interests and he knew mine."

Significantly, for the first decade of Stanton's presidency he drew a higher salary and bonus than Paley. In 1946, Stanton's first year in office, he made $94,010 in salary to Paley's $65,000. By 1955, Stanton's salary and bonus had risen to $281,522, compared to Paley's $225,000. Because of his CBS holdings, which were worth $19.2 million by the mid-fifties, Paley made considerably more than Stanton in stock dividends: $786,132 in 1955. By that year Stanton also had a comfortable CBS stake worth nearly $4 million that yielded $151,168 in dividends.

As a barometer of corporate status, however, other chief executives kept an eye on relative salaries. So when Fred Borch, the chairman of General Electric, wanted to inquire about buying 80 percent of CBS in the mid-1950s, he scheduled a lunch with Frank Stanton. "You are talking to the wrong person," Stanton told him. To which Borch replied, "I know Paley owns the stock, but he's not running the company." "Yes he is," said Stanton. "He makes the decisions." Stanton the loyal number two knew he had to say those words—but he did not completely believe them.

During the first decade Stanton and Paley had worked together, the true nature of their partnership was masked. Paley allowed Frank Stanton to build an entirely new business at CBS. As Stanton recalled years later, "Who else had the opportunity to take a new medium, television, and plot its future and be there at each step of the way? Some days it was so interesting that if they had not paid me, I would have almost paid them to do it."

In his series of corporate restructurings of CBS, Stanton solidified his own power and further isolated Paley. For all Stanton's efforts to conceal Paley's lack of knowledge from subordinates, they began to lose respect for the CBS chairman. Paley's erratic involvement in the company seemed arrogant. Because he was so often absent, CBS executives began to regard him as a dilettante, seriously out of touch with his own company and lacking Stanton's dedication. Paley suffered by comparison to his dynamo president, "the boy wonder of the networks," as one newspaper called him. Some even thought Paley silly and mocked him behind his back, imitating his twitch and other mannerisms.

"While Bill Paley was away, CBS began to be a major factor," said Richard Salant. "It grew in Bill Paley's absence. By the mid-1950s Frank Stanton was the industry leader. Bill Paley had to feel left out. There was something new in the atmosphere of CBS."

Stanton loved his job too much; he got used to running CBS. He was a force, with a substantial constituency among Washington powerbrokers and a high profile in the broadcasting industry. People bowed to Frank Stanton, who took his statesmanship seriously. He had mastered the mechanics of the job. "I am running the show," he said to himself. "Why am I not in charge?"

Paley was in a box. Stanton was a kind of national treasure, a hero too powerful to dislodge. Besides, Paley needed Stanton; he made the machine run and understood many of the complexities that eluded Paley. But as Paley recognized this dependence, he grew to resent Stanton. Paley hated to admit being dependent on anyone.

Paley had come out of World War II as a true statesman of broadcasting on the strength of the contributions of Murrow and his colleagues at CBS News. Yet in his quest for pleasure and convenience Paley had allowed that reputation to dissipate. "I withdrew," Paley explained years later. "I just didn't have as much reason to be out front or to be stating the company's position." He had gone beyond delegating: he had abdicated. He had given Stanton too much running room and had ceded too much power and prestige—outside CBS and within it as well. The GE chairman's overture suggested as much, and so did Paley's friends, who began chiding him for permitting Stanton to make a bigger salary.

Thus the CBS Proxy Statement for 1956 contained a small but telling number—a glimmer of an essential turning point in the relationship between Bill Paley and Frank Stanton a decade after it began. That year, for the first time, the two men had identical salaries, $300,000 in 1956, and they would both earn $299,807 the following year. Significantly, the salary adjustment coincided with the year Paley shut down Hytron's failed television operation—a misstep he bitterly blamed on Stanton. From that time on, Paley began insisting on symbolic equality with Stanton. Their offices were designed to measure the same square footage down to the inch. They were driven around town in identical limousines. When the two men were together, there was no denying where the power was, despite Stanton's fame and visibility.

Still, Paley's work habits continued much as before, and Stanton continued to pilot the company in the chief's absence. Stanton persevered at CBS because he assumed that when Paley reached the mandatory retirement age of sixty-five in 1966, he would hand over the reins to his number two. In 1956, Stanton was asked to head the University of California. Intrigued, he took a week off to tour all nine campuses without anyone knowing—Paley included. Stanton even calculated that the job could give him a springboard to run for the U.S. Senate. Confident in his future at CBS, he turned the offer down. By that time Stanton was essentially trapped—by his ambition, by the perquisites of his job, and by the belief that one day CBS would be his to run on his own.

40

W HEN PALEY EMERGED from his postoperative depression late in 1960, he was fifty-nine years old. Like Rip Van Winkle, he found the world had changed at CBS. James Thomas Aubrey, Jr., the youthful network president appointed a year earlier following the quiz show scandal, had taken over programming, and Stanton controlled everything else. Paley saw that in effect he had become a supernumerary, and he was determined to reclaim his empire.

His first step was to assume an active role in areas he had avoided for years: news and corporate image. This brought him onto Stanton's turf and created inevitable friction.

"If Paley had not gone off to war and then removed himself from CBS during its explosive growth—if he had worked alongside Frank Stanton—everything would have been much better," said Richard Salant. "Paley was a lot like a father who had gone away for many years and left his wife to bring up their baby. The baby grew up to be a sensation, but Papa had very little to do with it. He came back and said to the mother, 'But it's *my* baby.' "

"It was a difficult relationship with Bill," recalled Stanton. "As he got older, he reentered the company. . . . He had not been involved for years. My problem was that he resented the fact that people on the outside said to him, 'What do you do?' Also he discovered what an important force television had become, and he wanted to be part of it. He wanted to be running the company, but he didn't want to do it."

Paley recognized the tension, although he felt Stanton had no right to complain: "When I finally started to come back under full steam, I think it created some strain between Stanton and me, which was natural since he had gotten used to making most of the decisions." In Paley's view, Stanton had received sufficient recognition; now it was his turn.

During 1960, Stanton had been an especially visible advocate for CBS News. He had lobbied vigorously in Washington to set up a series of four debates between Richard Nixon and John Kennedy. (Congressional action was needed to temporarily amend the Communications Act.) Although Paley understood the importance of the debates, he showed no interest in helping set them in motion.

Stanton sensed Paley was preparing to move back into CBS operations. Yet he also caught flashes of Paley's old restlessness. Perhaps Rome would serve the double purpose of redirecting Paley and placing him at a comfortable distance from CBS. But unlike 1950, it was impossible for Stanton to operate sub rosa. He had to make the suggestion to Paley; yet he could not appear to be trying to push Paley out.

Stanton visited Robert Lovett, an old Washington hand and loyal member of the CBS board of directors. "Wonderful idea," responded Lovett. "Good for Bill, good for the country." Just to be safe, Stanton ran

But Paley avoided any overt grab for power that year, partly because he was involved with the presidential campaign as a partisan. Paley contributed $25,000 to the Nixon campaign, a substantial sum that represented his still-unrealized hope for an important diplomatic post. "Bill was involved once removed in supporting Nixon," said Paley's friend Walter Thayer. "He was helpful in developing programs and ideas."

After the fourth presidential debate in October, Herb Klein and other Nixon aides sensed that their man was gaining on Kennedy and urged him to consider a fifth encounter. The Nixon forces held a strategy session for the candidate and some two dozen advisers in the Waldorf-Astoria Hotel. Paley and Walter Thayer both felt strongly that Nixon should do another debate; Paley even had data from CBS showing Nixon's progress. But a weary Nixon deflected the arguments and left the meeting.

Afterwards, Paley sent a message through Thayer asking Nixon to reconsider, but Nixon refused. Years later Paley credited himself with pressing the idea single-handedly. "I gave Nixon advice which if he had followed would have caused him to win the race against Kennedy," he boasted to former CBS newsman Daniel Schorr.

Ironically, Paley's longing for an ambassadorial post was nearly satisfied by the winner of the 1960 election. In December, Vice-President–elect Lyndon Johnson called his old friend Frank Stanton for suggestions about candidates for the ambassador's post in Italy. As in 1950 when he proposed Paley for the Materials Policy Commission, Stanton found himself in a ticklish situation.

Stanton sensed Paley was preparing to move back into CBS operations. Yet he also caught flashes of Paley's old restlessness. Perhaps Rome would serve the double purpose of redirecting Paley and placing him at a comfortable distance from CBS. But unlike 1950, it was impossible for Stanton to operate sub rosa. He had to make the suggestion to Paley; yet he could not appear to be trying to push Paley out.

Stanton visited Robert Lovett, an old Washington hand and loyal member of the CBS board of directors. "Wonderful idea," responded Lovett. "Good for Bill, good for the country." Just to be safe, Stanton ran the idea past two other board members, who also endorsed it. The next day at lunch in Paley's dining room, Stanton made the proposal. "What do you think Babe would think?" Paley asked. Stanton said he thought Babe would be happy in Rome: "She's conscious of fashion, and Italy is a fashion center." Paley said he would have to think it over. After lunch Stanton had reached the door when Paley called out softly: "Frank." Stanton turned. "Thank you," said Paley. "It was," Stanton said years later, "the warmest thanks I ever heard from him."

Lyndon Johnson had told Stanton he had forty-eight hours to secure a reply from Paley. Two days passed, and Stanton heard nothing. Paley never mentioned the idea again, and Stanton never raised it. "It was not the kind of thing you wanted to bring up," Stanton would later explain. "I figured he didn't want to talk about it."

Stanton knew his man. Whenever Paley did not want to deal with something, he simply ignored it. But Stanton was bruised nevertheless. "He told me he felt unappreciated," said Michael Burke, a CBS executive at the time. When asked about the offer decades later, Paley would only say that Rome "wasn't a central, important place."

In any event, Paley was caught up in his reinvolvement with CBS News. News programs were flourishing at all three networks as penance for the sins of the quiz scandals. Some TV critics even called the early sixties the "Golden Age of the Television Documentary." Richard Salant spoke of "maximum hysteria on Paley's part about news." In 1960, NBC's evening news anchor team, Chet Huntley and David Brinkley, passed CBS's evening newscast anchored by Douglas Edwards in the audience ratings. "It drove Bill Paley wild that Huntley-Brinkley were ahead," said Salant.

That August, Paley made his displeasure known at a management conference in Atlantic City. He asked Sig Mickelson, then president of CBS News, to think about replacing Edwards. "How about Walter Cronkite?" Paley wondered.

The Missouri-born Cronkite had been a correspondent for UPI during World War II and had come to CBS to cover the Korean War. As anchor of CBS's political convention coverage since 1952, Cronkite had proved a smooth, compelling television presence. But during the fifties, Cronkite had somewhat diminished his journalistic reputation by anchoring the docu-drama "You Are There," a re-creation of historical events, and by appearing on CBS's first foray into breakfast-hour television, "The Morning Show," where his partner was a lion puppet named Charlemagne.

By 1960, Cronkite had redeemed himself as the chief correspondent on the well-received CBS public affairs series "Eyewitness." But Mickelson told Paley that he and his subordinates were "not now convinced that Cronkite is the right person." The news chief assured Paley that CBS had begun an extensive talent search among anchors of local newscasts around the country. Paley replied that Edwards's replacement should be a qualified, knowledgeable newsman who could give the newscast greater credibility and stature.

Over the following months no one, it seemed, could make a decision about the Edwards show. In December 1960, Stanton shook up CBS News by revamping the old CBS News editorial board into a CBS News executive committee and installing his protégé, Richard Salant, then a CBS attorney, as its chairman. Two months later, Salant replaced Mickelson as president of CBS News.

At this point, Stanton still had the upper hand in news, and his choice of Salant annoyed Paley. Salant was sardonic and bright—a little too sharp and fast for Paley. He was also a protégé of Ralph Colin, whose prickly temperament was beginning to grate on the CBS chairman.

"Bill was not supportive of Salant," said Stanton. "He never felt comfortable with Dick. He didn't try to block the appointment, but he didn't greet it with enthusiasm." Salant himself was aware of the awkwardness. "The whole process of conversation with Bill Paley was difficult for me," he recalled. "I didn't feel that I was making myself understood to him or that I understood him. He threw me."

Paley attended the news executive committee meetings as intermittently as he had those of the editorial board. But he began hosting news luncheons each Tuesday for Stanton, Salant, and his general manager for news, Blair Clark, a blueblood heir to the Coats and Clark thread fortune. These were disconcerting sessions in which Paley devoted his time to quizzing Clark, a former Harvard roommate of President Kennedy with impeccable connections in New York media and social circles.

"Paley wasn't interested so much in the CBS News programs as he was in who was doing what to whom in the papers around the country, who was going up and down," Clark recalled. "It was all rather gossipy. Paley asked questions about the industry. It was mostly about personalities. I had the impression of someone who really wasn't in a substantive way concerned about the form of the news. He wouldn't exactly say, 'Tell me the latest gossip,' but it was clear that he wanted to hear it. I went to all the dancing parties at the White House and I would tell him about them. He was bright and quick but he didn't read much. I was struck by this: he wasn't much interested in political things like the Bay of Pigs or the civil rights movement. There was no real attention to what was going on."

Salant took a more benign view of Paley's superficiality in these meetings, pointing out that "he didn't really need our gossip. He had lots of ways of picking up information. What he was trying to do was to let us know he was interested in CBS News."

During these lunches, Stanton said little. He concerned himself far more with the CBS News executive committee, where he and Salant worked out standards for the rapidly expanding television operations of CBS News. "Some policies started with me, and some started with Dick," said Stanton. "I don't remember sitting down and discussing them with Bill because they had to do with day-to-day operations."

As in the past, Paley continued to intervene in CBS News when he spotted violations of his rule against editorial opinion. He was most often distressed about Howard K. Smith, who frequently expressed his views in news reports from Washington. Smith felt he was within bounds, especially since so many exceptions had been made for Murrow. "How Bill Paley thought his policy could be strictly enforced after Murrow's program about McCarthy, I don't know," said Blair Clark. "People like Howard Smith said, 'If Ed Murrow can do it, why can't we?' "

In the spring of 1961, Smith completed a documentary on racial tension in Birmingham, Alabama, that Murrow had started before leaving the network. As his conclusion, Smith quoted Edmund Burke: "The only thing necessary for the triumph of evil is for good men to do nothing." The quote resembled the famous close to Murrow's McCarthy broadcast: "The fault, dear Brutus, is not in our stars, but in ourselves"—just the sort of editorializing that Paley had vowed to keep out of CBS News programs.

Shortly before the documentary was to appear in May, Smith did a radio report on the situation in Birmingham. He accused President Kennedy of failing to live up to his promises and quoted Burke. When Paley heard it, he was livid. CBS's Southern affiliates were raising hell, and Paley thought Smith had been grossly unfair. Blair Clark ordered the quote stripped from the television broadcast. Smith angrily demanded an audience with Paley to lodge a protest.

Several months later, Paley summoned Smith to lunch in New York. In preparation, Paley asked Smith to send a memo outlining his understanding of CBS's policy on fairness and balance. Instead, Smith wrote about his duty to enlighten the public by giving it informed opinion on issues of the day.

Stanton, Salant, and Clark silently bore witness at Paley's dining-room table while Paley and Smith argued. "It wasn't a reasoned discussion of balance and fairness," Clark recalled. "It was more like Paley saying, 'How can you think that isn't opinion, Howard?' and Smith saying, 'You have a right to your opinion, Mr. Paley. Either I am right or you are, Mr.

Paley, and I know I am right.' " What irritated Paley more than anything was Smith's statement that journalists had an obligation to lead the country since the president was not doing so.

Paley's exasperation finally boiled over. He yanked out the memo Smith had written. "I've read junk like this before," he said, throwing the offending document across the table. "Maybe you ought to try something else." As usual, Paley could not bring himself to say the words, "You're fired," but Smith correctly concluded that he was out. The newsman pushed back his chair, said, "I think this lunch is over," and left the room.

Paley would later insist that Smith "wasn't driven off the air. He and I had a difference of opinion . . . I never fired him." Even though Paley periodically came down hard on his newsmen, he "always liked to be on the side of the journalistic troops," said Salant. Once again, Paley wanted to have it both ways. "When it came to unpleasant acts he always distanced himself," said Salant.

In early 1962, Paley turned his full attention to the Douglas Edwards broadcast. For his first year on the job, Salant had been reluctant to move too fast on Edwards's replacement. But Paley was now eager for a resolution. Salant and his deputy Blair Clark favored Cronkite.

As devil's advocate during the Tuesday news luncheons, Paley sometimes stunned subordinates with his questions. "How about Roger Mudd? How about Dan Rather?" he asked at one point. Though both were promising young correspondents, Mudd had been aboard less than a year and Rather was brand new. "It was almost a dialectical procedure on Paley's part to force us to say why we were for Cronkite," recalled Blair Clark. "Paley was looking at it in terms of casting. It was amazing that Paley looked at everything in terms of casting."

Paley decided on Cronkite that March—although, as the newsman learned years later, Paley's friend Truman Capote disliked Cronkite's screen presence and urged Paley not to use him. The following year, Paley gave his blessing to Salant's hard-fought battle to expand the newscast from fifteen minutes to a half hour. Still, it would take four more years for Cronkite to overtake the entrenched Huntley-Brinkley team in the ratings.

On both Cronkite's appointment and the expansion of the news, Stanton and Paley were in accord. But Paley's jealousy of Stanton's prominence was becoming increasingly obvious inside and even outside the company. As early as May 1961, Paley publicly reasserted his position as CBS's leader when he addressed the annual conference of CBS-TV affiliates for the first time. His themes, as in the past, were the need for broadcasters to be as free of regulation as possible and to exercise responsibility in their programming. He proudly cited the "great tradition" of such drama series as "Studio One" and "Playhouse 90" and promised an expansion of "CBS Reports."

The timing of Paley's remarks was unfortunate. Only four days later, on May 9, 1961, President Kennedy's new chairman of the FCC, Newton Minow, made a mockery of Paley's defense of television. Addressing the National Association of Broadcasters, Minow blind-sided the networks by denouncing the poor quality of television, calling it a "vast wasteland." Although Paley registered no immediate reaction, he traveled to Washington that fall to meet with Minow. He wanted to know, he said, why Minow and Stanton couldn't get along. Minow explained that while he often disagreed with Stanton, he admired and respected the CBS president. Paley seemed unpersuaded. "I have the sense," he said with evident disapproval, "that you and he are having trouble."

Paley had even more difficulty disguising his irritation with Stanton in 1962 when a delegation from the International Radio and Television Society asked the CBS chairman to accept their Gold Medal award. Trouble was, they had first approached Stanton, who directed them to Paley's office. When the group told him they had already spoken to Stanton, Paley understood instinctively that he was playing second fiddle. He turned them down and abruptly dismissed them.

Puzzled, the group returned to Stanton and asked him to reconsider their initial offer. Stanton went to Paley. "Are you sure you don't want this award?" he asked. "No," Paley said petulantly. Stanton knew Paley would have gladly accepted it had he been asked first.

Once so smooth in anticipating Paley's reactions and feelings, Stanton was beginning to misread his boss. One of CBS's many acclaimed documentaries in 1963 was a three-part series called "Storm Over the Supreme Court." Shortly after the final part appeared in June, Arthur Goldberg was nominated to the high bench. He asked CBS if the program could be shown at a dinner for him in Washington. Fred Friendly, who produced the series, told Stanton that a CBS spokesman was needed at the dinner. Stanton said Paley wouldn't be interested and suggested Friendly take the honors.

The morning after the reception, Friendly encountered Paley in the hallway and told him about "all the nice things that had been said about CBS the night before."

"Who introduced the program?" Paley asked.

"Why, I did," Friendly replied.

"What right did you have to represent CBS at that dinner?" said Paley. "Mrs. Paley and I should have been there."

Recalled Friendly, "It was the beginning of my understanding that Bill Paley wanted to be identified with the victories of CBS News. Murrow had grown too big for Bill Paley. Now Frank Stanton had too."

Because Paley's work habits continued to be erratic, Stanton could hardly avoid maintaining a high profile in news. When John F. Kennedy was assassinated in November 1963, Paley was on a holiday in the South of France. Stanton immediately wiped all commercials from CBS. This outraged Robert Kintner, president of NBC, who called Stanton and screamed at him. But NBC and ABC quickly followed suit; at the end of the four days of commercial-free coverage, the three networks had lost around $4 million apiece.

It was not until the second day that Paley checked in with Stanton for a briefing. Paley made numerous suggestions, none of which was useful because he was simply too far from the scene. Overwhelmed with keeping CBS's coverage together, Stanton was unusually curt with Paley. "He was second-guessing at every turn," recalled Stanton. "He was hearing things and basing his questions on what he was hearing."

Stanton later realized how slighted Paley had felt. "He was wistful about missing it," said Stanton. "He didn't like being away from the action, so he cut short his trip." Paley told Stanton that his friends couldn't understand why as CBS chairman, he had not been there, in the middle of the coverage. The following month the *Gallagher Report,* a trade newsletter, noted that Stanton "was annoyed at Paley, who was abroad during the Kennedy assassination . . . Stanton made the right decisions."

In February 1964, Paley asserted his authority over CBS News in a most painful way for Stanton. Angered that Cronkite had failed to catch up with Huntley-Brinkley—the half-hour newscast had been on merely six months—Paley demanded that Stanton fire Salant. The new president of CBS News, Paley said, would be Fred Friendly, Murrow's old partner who was the producer of "CBS Reports."

Paley felt comfortable with the expansive and dynamic Friendly. Both men worked emotionally and instinctively; they were two of a kind. Unlike Murrow, whom Paley once called "tight and unemotional," Paley saw Friendly as a "man of great vigour who loved to shout and carry on. It was easier to argue and have a kind of verbal duel with someone like that."

The more time Paley spent with Salant, the less he liked him. "Dick was a hair shirt to Bill," explained Stanton. "When he thought something through and took a position, he was almost unassailable. On occasion Bill was more simplistic and emotional than analytic. To be confronted with facts was not always a happy situation for Bill, and Salant stood up to him.

Another factor was that Fred Friendly was a doer. He had more moxie than Dick and he was a very persuasive guy."

Stanton was in torment when he summoned Salant. He told his friend he needed him in Washington because government relations were growing more complicated. Heartbroken, Salant looked Stanton in the eye. "Is this yours or his?" asked Salant. "It's mine," said Stanton. Fifteen years would elapse before Stanton would admit to Salant that Paley had sacked him because of the ratings. "I was devastated by my participation in that situation," explained Stanton.

The following July, Frank Stanton stayed away from a national political convention for the first time since 1948. Bill Paley was the top man for CBS at the Republican National Convention in San Francisco. He sat at Friendly's elbow, questioning, prodding, and putting enormous pressure on the new CBS News president. Everything seemed to go wrong.

On July 10, CBS News correspondent Daniel Schorr broadcast a report from Munich that Barry Goldwater, the Republican nominee, was traveling to Germany. During his stay, said Schorr, Goldwater would meet with right-wing German politicians. Goldwater denounced the report as unfair and false. He was going to Germany, he said, but he was not planning any such meeting. Paley demanded that Friendly fire Schorr, but Friendly resisted, explaining that he couldn't punish a correspondent so severely for one error. Several days later, Schorr made a correction on the air. But Paley held a grudge against Schorr for the incident and bad publicity. "It never fell out of my mind," he later told Schorr.

CBS's convention coverage was awful, and everyone was at fault. Cronkite talked too much. Friendly and his deputy, William Leonard, directed the coverage badly. "I could hear them," Cronkite later said, "shouting at each other in the control room." While Cronkite was slow and windy, NBC's Huntley and Brinkley sparkled. NBC trounced CBS in the ratings.

Paley, who loathed losing, convened a meeting in New York. "Bill was sore about everything," recalled Stanton. "We took a beating and he wanted action." "What the hell happened to Walter?" Paley asked Leonard and Friendly. As the two newsmen struggled to cover for Cronkite, Paley bore in. Wasn't it true that Friendly and Leonard had planned to have Cronkite on less? "Well, sir," answered Leonard, "that was the idea but Walter sort of, I guess you could say, resisted it." "You mean he would get what amounted to an *order* and he wouldn't obey it?" Paley snapped. Once again, Leonard tried to defend Cronkite. "Who can replace Walter?" Paley asked suddenly. "Right now. We can't have people who won't take orders, and anyway it's not working."

Friendly and Leonard tried to dissuade Paley, but he was relentless. "What about Roger Mudd and Robert Trout?" Paley said. The casting had potential: a bright young correspondent, wry in the Brinkley style, teamed with Trout, an old hand. Stanton urged Paley to give Cronkite another chance. "He was headstrong," recalled Stanton. "He wanted to get rid of Cronkite. He felt the world had moved on and Walter was old-hat."

Several days later, Paley had his "consensus." Mudd and Trout would anchor the Democratic Convention in August. When they broke the news to Cronkite, Friendly and Leonard never told him it had been Paley's idea. In the end, Mudd and Trout fared no better in the ratings than Cronkite, who was back on the air for CBS on election night. Paley never voiced any regret over the upheaval he caused, nor did Stanton ever remind him of his objections.

41

ONE REASON Paley had so much time to meddle in news during the early 1960s was his virtual exclusion from programming by TV network president James Aubrey. Once, in Aubrey's first year, Paley had made a halfhearted stab at reasserting his influence over the entertainment schedule. In a long memo in August 1960, Paley complained that Aubrey had failed to include any cultural programs on his list for the 1960–61 television season. He reminded Aubrey that CBS had always highlighted a few such offerings to reaffirm its reputation as the quality network.

Aubrey ignored the memo—a response that Paley would later rationalize by saying, "I was still in my recessive period after the operation. It may be that I did not altogether get my way for some time."

That was an understatement. For the next four years Paley seemed in thrall to Aubrey, the embodiment of WASP traits he so revered. Aubrey was "conventionally good-looking, no surprises," wrote Merle Miller in the early 1960s in *Only You, Dick Daring!*, a wickedly biting memoir of the television business: "high cheekbones, a wide mouth, a straight, assembly-line nose, the unrevealing blue eyes, and imperial brows . . . a tall man, a little over six feet, and he has a flat stomach. . . . He has a hearty, disinterested handshake, and he carries himself with the air of a man used to authority and a lot of pushups." Aubrey was, in the words of *Business Week,* "the coolest of the cool." But there was even more to his allure for Paley than that. Aubrey's daring streak appealed to Paley. Ever since the early days in Philadelphia when he had befriended gangsters, Paley had been fascinated by men—and women—who lived on the edge.

Born to privilege and wealth, James Aubrey grew up in prosperous Lake Forest, north of Chicago, where his father was a successful advertising executive. Aubrey and his three brothers went to Exeter and Princeton. In college he played end on the varsity football team, belonged to Tiger Inn, a top dining club, and graduated cum laude in 1941 with a degree in English. During World War II he attained the rank of major as an Air Force test pilot.

In 1948 he got a job at CBS's radio station in Los Angeles. He advanced quickly and joined the network's West Coast programming department. In 1956 he jumped to ABC, where he helped devise a string of action shows that gave the third-ranked television network its first successful programming lineup. In 1958 he sent a message to Frank Stanton: he wanted to return to CBS. Stanton immediately hired him as his executive assistant.

Aubrey occupied an office between Stanton and Paley and dazzled the entire twentieth floor with his intelligence and ability. He was, as one executive said at the time, "slick as silk, smooth as glass, adaptable as plastic, and very very good at what he sets out to do." Aubrey noticed immediately that Paley conducted his business dealings almost entirely "on his persona."

Whether by design or by instinct, Aubrey mirrored many of Paley's traits. His luminous smile gave him unstoppable charm, but this outward affability masked a steely interior. He dressed impeccably and expected perfection. He argued brilliantly, often withholding his opinions while coaxing others to express theirs. He combined fiscal restraint with a showman's flair—he was consumed with winning, as he said, "not by a foot but by a mile." He disdained and avoided the press. Above all, he focused obsessively on the heart and soul of network television—programming. As Paley had so often done, Aubrey made suggestions about every element, from a sit-com character's personality to a piece of furniture on the set. Aubrey was five days shy of forty-one when Stanton made him president of the network.

By the time Paley had bounced back from his surgery and depression late in 1960, Aubrey was so entrenched, and so manifestly capable, that Paley could not afford to intrude. "How did Aubrey get all that power?" wrote Miller in his memoir. "There was a vacuum and Aubrey stepped into it." While Paley could be paralyzed by second thoughts, Aubrey flaunted a cocky certitude. "Bill was caught up in Aubrey's success and didn't want to do anything to disturb it," Stanton recalled.

The Aubrey juggernaut was making CBS and Paley richer than the CBS chairman had dreamed. From 1959 to 1964, CBS profits nearly doubled—from $25.2 million to $49.6 million—and CBS stock split two-for-one in the five years Aubrey headed the network. During the same period, Paley's CBS holdings shrank slightly (from 10.5 percent in 1959 to 8.6 percent in 1965) but grew in value from $38.6 million to $87 million.

Aubrey was a workaholic, routinely logging twelve-hour days, six days a week. He would watch as many as a half-dozen movies on weekends—always with an eye toward casting a possible television series. On flights to the West Coast, he could breeze through three books. He saw every new play and nightclub act.

A physical fitness fanatic, he exercised each morning at Nicholas Kounovsky's Manhattan gymnasium, where he was known for standing on his head longer than anyone else. "I could picture Aubrey exercising with bar bells," wrote Merle Miller, "but never working up a sweat." He brought his golf score into the low 70s by playing eighteen holes at 5:00 A.M. for six months straight.

Paley's programming catechism found its most ardent advocate in Aubrey. Network executives, Aubrey said, could not afford to choose programs based on what appealed personally to them. "We try to cultivate objectivity," he once said, knowing that if he put a show appealing to the lowest common denominator on the air, "maybe the head of a corporation won't watch it, but his customers will."

His formula for success was simple—and simpleminded: "broads, bosoms, and fun," as a colleague put it in a memo leaked to a congressional committee. He jettisoned all live drama and moved entirely to filmed weekly series in two categories: inane comedy and fast-action adventure. With hits like "The Beverly Hillbillies," "Petticoat Junction," "Green Acres," and "My Favorite Martian," CBS surged ahead of NBC in popularity. In the 1962–63 television season, CBS had eight of the top ten television programs, seven of them comedies. It was CBS's most shameless excursion down the low road.

Aubrey was the first network president to control all aspects of the programming process. He read scripts for every show and even demanded —sometimes at considerable cost and inconvenience—that entire scenes be reshot. When the respected playwright Garson Kanin conceived a weekly drama about a sophisticated Broadway press agent named Mike Bell ("an extra dry martini—five parts savvy to one part sentiment, with a little onion for flavor"), Aubrey transformed "Mr. Broadway" into a cheap action show. "Mike Bell must be a hero in the traditional, even conventional sense," Aubrey wrote in a memo to the producer. "He must be the agent of all the action. It is particularly important for Mike to be in physical danger."

Except as a rubber stamp, Paley had little part in deciding what programs appeared on CBS's airwaves. He professed dismay at some of Aubrey's choices (although he did nothing to stand in the way) and was apparently incredulous in 1962 when Aubrey and his executives outlined a show about a suddenly oil-rich family from the Ozarks that moves into a mansion in Beverly Hills. "What the hell *is* this?" Paley whispered to Stanton, who reassured him that it was probably just a "one-joke show." Paley "genuinely disliked 'The Beverly Hillbillies,' " Aubrey recalled. "But he put it on the schedule anyway."

Years afterwards, Paley insisted that he loved the show; how could he admit to loathing such a success? "I thought it was beautifully done," he said. "It was very funny. I saw nothing wrong with it at all. I wasn't the least bit ashamed of it."

At first, Aubrey and Paley got on well. With his prep school and Ivy League bona fides and membership in such exclusive Manhattan men's clubs as The Brook, Aubrey could hold his own with Paley's socialite friends. They played golf together and Paley invited him to Kiluna. They shared a penchant for philandering as well, and prowled together in New York and Hollywood. "Bill and I used to date the same girls," recalled Aubrey, "and send the same girls bouquets." By 1963, Aubrey had divorced his wife of nearly twenty years, the actress Phyllis Thaxter. Paley, of course, continued to have it both ways by staying married to Babe.

As Aubrey grew more successful and powerful, he became insufferably arrogant. His charm vanished, replaced by cruel and high-handed behavior. "You're through," he said abruptly to program executive Hubbell Robinson during a meeting one day in 1963. The veteran programmer thought Aubrey meant only that Robinson's presentation was over. "No, Hub, you're through. You're finished," Aubrey repeated. "I've already talked to Paley. I accept your resignation. He accepts your resignation." As if the incident were not savage enough, Aubrey relished recounting it to associates.

Aubrey did not bother to mask his ruthlessness as Paley did. The former test pilot was known for his icy calm, a capacity for growing "colder and colder" as the pressure intensified, in the words of one former subordinate. "Jim had no fear level," recalled Robert Wood, who headed CBS's station in Los Angeles when Aubrey was network president. "Nothing you could do would frighten him, physically or intellectually. He was an enigma, a different kind of person, a loner. When he wanted to do something, he would do what needed to be done." Once when he was flying with Aubrey from New York on a TWA Constellation, Wood looked out the window to see that one engine was on fire. He shook Aubrey awake to tell him. "Goddamn it," Aubrey said, "don't wake me again until all four are on fire."

In one chilling scene in his book, Merle Miller captured Aubrey's powerful presence. As the actor Jackie Cooper described his ideas for a proposed weekly series, "Aubrey received this information without comment or show of emotion. . . . He lowered his muscular body into a regulation leather chair. He placed his highly polished black shoes on top of a low table. . . . After awhile what might, I suppose, have been construed as a smile lingered briefly near his lips."

Aubrey was widely feared and loathed. When John Houseman called Aubrey "The Smiling Cobra," the sobriquet stuck, as did "Jungle Jim." "Aubrey was two people," recalled Oscar Katz, who was one of his programming vice-presidents. "You never knew which he would be. At times he was the best executive, at others the worst."

In 1963, Aubrey switched Jack Benny out of his coveted Sunday evening time period after his ratings began to slip. Aubrey did not himself notify Benny, who called Paley to get the decision reversed when he was informed. When Paley returned the call, Benny declined to take it. "Jack was uncomfortable," said Irving Fein, Benny's agent at the time. "He didn't want Bill Paley to turn him down. He had thought it over and figured Paley had okayed the decision." Benny's instincts were correct. Aubrey had presented his decision to Paley as a fait accompli, leaving Paley feeling hurt but unwilling to override him. When Benny's handlers objected to the rescheduling, Aubrey let the comedian's option lapse and Benny returned to NBC, where his ratings plummeted against "Gomer Pyle," a goofy service comedy on CBS. "Aubrey turned out to be a genius," recalled Fein. "He let Benny bomb. After that, the Paley-Benny relationship dissolved. Jack was very bitter about Bill Paley."

Aubrey's cavalier ways offended some big advertisers—among them Campbell's Soup, Lever Brothers, and General Foods—as well as stations affiliated with CBS. On visits to station owners, Aubrey would walk out of meetings and leave town without telling anyone. Once when Stanton questioned him about such behavior, Aubrey said, "They don't mean anything, those dumb shits." "Once he got a strong power base in the company, he went bananas," said Stanton. "He was rude to affiliates, showed contempt for advertisers, and was rude to talent. Lucille Ball couldn't say his name without calling him an SOB."

Eventually, Aubrey began mistreating Bill Paley. In programming meetings he would either ignore Paley's comments or express impatience. "Aubrey was a very sharp guy," recalled Stanton. "There were things going on in the industry that he knew and Bill didn't know because Aubrey was so immersed in Hollywood. He didn't have the patience to bring Bill up to speed, but it was unkind to act that way in front of others." One producer recalled being in Aubrey's office when Paley called to question a show. In the most superior manner, Aubrey said, "Billy, you worry about the finances, I'll worry about the programs," and hung up. Remarkably, Paley tolerated the impoliteness for a time. "They were snotty remarks, put-downs," Stanton recalled. "It was upsetting to Bill. In the meetings he made no issue of it, but he remarked on it afterwards. He took it because he had genuine hopes for Jim."

Paley felt he could not afford to cross someone who was riding so high. In June 1963 the closely read *Gallagher Report* called Aubrey the "hottest top management property" in broadcasting. By the spring of 1964, Aubrey was taking credit for single-handedly masterminding CBS's success. *Business Week* put him on its cover, calling him the "undisputed arbiter of what America sees on its TV screens" and "the most brilliant executor of the CBS system." The article barely mentioned Paley and didn't even include Stanton. The *New York Herald Tribune* credited Aubrey with having "absolute power" at CBS and the "final say" in all its programs. *Time* called him "Mr. CBS" and *Variety* dubbed him "TV's St. Peter."

At the same time, the Hollywood gossip mill began raising questions about Aubrey's personal and professional behavior. He was notorious for his girlfriends, wild parties, and bursts of reckless behavior. One evening during that period Aubrey invited a program producer to a Los Angeles Dodgers game. Aubrey also brought along John Reynolds, a straight-arrow CBS executive. En route they stopped off at the home of another CBS programming man, who had two women in tow, both dressed in black with fur stoles and stiletto heels. After several rounds of drinks, the group piled into two cars. "We went down Sunset Boulevard at ninety miles an hour with Jim driving," recalled the producer. "He was drunk. He would come up as close as he could and brush against another car. 'You can't get killed,' he said. 'You just scare them.' "

On April 16, 1964, *Hollywood Closeup,* a scandal sheet, alleged in an "Open Letter to William S. Paley" that Aubrey was taking kickbacks from producers, particularly Keefe Brasselle, a longtime friend of Aubrey's who ran a small company called Richelieu Productions. Aubrey had just contracted to put three Richelieu series on CBS without even seeing pilots. Brasselle, an actor with few credits, had virtually no experience as a producer. When CBS ignored the charges, *Closeup* editor Jaik Rosenstein wrote to E. William Henry, chairman of the FCC, in early July. Despite some misgivings about the reliability of Rosenstein—who berated Henry in another letter late in August—the FCC contacted CBS for comment in September. Stanton immediately appointed Ralph Colin to launch an investigation.

While Colin quizzed CBS executives about the financial arrangements between Brasselle and CBS, Stanton hired a New York City police detective to put a tail on Aubrey. He discovered that Aubrey used a chauffeured Chrysler limousine that was owned by Filmways, a television producer. Moreover, Aubrey was sharing an apartment on Central Park South paid for in part by Filmways. Stanton visited FCC chairman Henry in Washington to share the findings informally. He told Henry that although he was disturbed by the conflicts of interest, they fell shy of illegal kickbacks. After CBS submitted a formal report in mid-December exonerating Richelieu and Aubrey, the matter was dropped by the FCC, which seemed content to let the network clear its own man.

But doubts lingered at CBS. Mindful of the questions raised about Aubrey, Paley had already begun to make some noises about programming. He was tired of winning high ratings with cheap shows; Aubrey continued to resist him on sprinkling the CBS schedule with token symbols of quality. The one exception had been a courtroom drama, "The Defenders," which Paley had muscled on the air after Aubrey kept it on the shelf for a year. "Aubrey's making a serious mistake," said one advertising executive early in 1964. "He isn't 'tithing.' Paley and Stanton, when they were calling the shots, always plowed about 10 percent back into image, goodwill, public service, that sort of thing. Aubrey isn't willing to do that. He's got to make every buck in sight."

Unfortunately, Paley managed to look foolish while trying to take a stand on a show he considered beneath CBS's somewhat tenuous dignity. Titled "The Munsters," it revolved around the misadventures of a family of feckless monsters. Although the premise seemed silly, the show was clever—and quite funny. When Aubrey touted "The Munsters" at the programming meetings in the spring of 1964, Paley tried an end run to keep it off the schedule. He summoned Michael Dann, Aubrey's chief programming executive, to his office. The CBS chairman had nearly debated Dann into submission when Dann summoned his associate, Oscar Katz, who proclaimed the show an "instant hit." When Paley asked for evidence, Katz pointed to his stomach and said, "Intuition." "You used the only argument I can't answer," said Paley.

But Paley kept pushing. Shortly before the 1964 television season began, he called Dann to say, "We can't let 'The Munsters' go on the air. It isn't CBS. It's not our kind of show." When Dann objected that he had nothing else to fill the time slot, Paley growled, "Fix it as best you can," and slammed down the phone. Dann could do nothing, so the program went on as planned and got a big audience. The next day at lunch Paley said to Dann, "I wonder what would have happened if I hadn't made that call. Obviously you changed the pilot. I think it's much better." Dann explained later, "We hadn't changed a frame, but the ratings had changed the situation."

Such episodes hardened Aubrey's contempt for Paley. "I have to do it for the chairman," he would say in the presence of producers. "He doesn't know anything about it, but I have to humor him." At one point in 1964, Paley and Stanton decided that CBS should set up a task force to study the pay television business. Stanton asked Michael Burke to invite Aubrey to join the effort. "I don't want to talk about it," Aubrey said to Burke. "But the chairman and Frank Stanton want you to be part of it," said Burke. Shot back Aubrey: "Fuck you. I don't want to talk about it." Burke tried for the next fifteen minutes to argue with Aubrey, who finally said in exasperation, "We have missed the boat on pay television. Bill Paley and Frank Stanton are old farts. Why don't you move to the twentieth floor and we'll take over the company." Burke recalled some years later, "Frank's and Bill's antennae had to pick up those sounds."

There had been rumors of Aubrey's larger ambitions at CBS. In November 1964 the *Gallagher Report* said that Aubrey was angling to take Stanton's job. A few weeks later, Stanton and Aubrey were both working late. As they left the office, they decided to walk up Fifth Avenue together. Passing by the Pierre Hotel, Aubrey suggested a nightcap. They stood at the bar, and Aubrey dropped a bomb. He had been talking, he said, with a group of Wall Street investors who were willing to buy a majority interest in CBS, installing Stanton as chairman and Aubrey as president. "It's time to kick the old man out," Aubrey said. Stanton was shocked. "I'm not the guy to play that game," he said. As they walked up the avenue to their homes, Stanton felt that he and Paley had been crudely betrayed. "I knew the cord had to be cut," recalled Stanton. "Aubrey had to go."

Aubrey had already started to self-destruct. His fall schedule was in tatters as NBC and ABC pulled even in the ratings with CBS. In mid-December he made an unprecedented midseason realignment of fourteen shows, replacing the biggest losers (including two of the three Keefe Brasselle shows) with reruns of movies. His arrogance had driven him not only to select many of his fall shows without the benefit of pilots, but to forgo making replacement programs.

In late January 1965, Paley and Stanton accompanied Aubrey to Hollywood to set the 1965–66 schedule. After those assembled watched the pilots together, Aubrey, acting as ringmaster, displayed the new schedule on a big magnetic board and then declined to take questions. From the back of the room Paley said, "Aren't we going to discuss anything?" "No," said Aubrey. "That's our programming for the year." Paley had never before been humiliated in front of his staff. Driving to the airport with Stanton, the CBS chairman was livid. "We've got to get him out of there," he said. It was not so much an order as an expression of anger. But Stanton—who had not told Paley what he had heard at the Pierre Hotel bar—knew he was free to oust Aubrey.

For Aubrey's replacement, Stanton settled on John "Jack" Schneider, who had come up through the company's "farm system." Like Aubrey, he was handsome and charming, but his geniality was genuine, and he had shown good leadership as the head of CBS stations in Philadelphia and New York. By mid-February, Stanton told Paley he was preparing to fire Aubrey and appoint Schneider. Paley agreed, but grumbled that he didn't even know Schneider.

The first hints began to leak that Aubrey was in trouble. *Newsweek* reported on "persistent rumors that he will soon leave the network. . . . If Aubrey is maneuvered out, some have suggested it will be because he has besmirched CBS's image. Others, perhaps cynically, see his cardinal sin as the loss of ratings supremacy." But both Stanton and Paley would have been willing to give Aubrey time to improve CBS's position. "Ratings," Stanton later said, "were not the issue."

"He could not handle his own success," Paley commented. "Power went to his head and bedazzled his common sense." "Things add up in one's character," said Stanton, "like barnacles on a ship. Eventually, they stop the ship."

On Wednesday, February 24, Aubrey flew to Miami to attend a forty-ninth birthday party for CBS comedian Jackie Gleason the next evening. After the Gleason bash, Aubrey was reported to have attended yet another wild party. Many in the television industry interpreted this incident as the proximate cause of Aubrey's departure, but in fact Stanton and Paley had already agreed to it.

On the afternoon of Friday, the twenty-sixth, Stanton called Aubrey in Florida to request a meeting at noon the next day to discuss a "serious" matter. He then summoned Schneider. "We're flying Aubrey up here, and I'm going to fire him tomorrow," Stanton told him. "I want you to take the presidency of the network." Schneider was surprised, but he accepted instantly. Fearful of leaks, Stanton told Schneider he could not return to his office. Instead, Stanton dispatched his own limousine to send Schneider to his home in Connecticut.

The next morning, Stanton got a call from Paley, who was in traction at the Regency Hotel, where he and Babe were living while their new apartment on Fifth Avenue was being renovated. "Are you sure you want to go with Schneider?" Paley said. "I think we should consider Bill Hylan [a longtime CBS sales executive]. Maybe we shouldn't really let Aubrey go."

"It's too late, Bill," Stanton said. "I have the announcement here in my hand."

"But have you thought this through?" Paley asked.

Stanton tried to remind himself of the 540-Degree Club.

Patiently, Stanton listened to Paley's misgivings. "Bill had been willing to overlook a lot because Jim had such an impact on our profits," Stanton commented later. "I think Bill would have put off firing him if I hadn't had a replacement." Despite Paley's doubts, Stanton went ahead as planned. "It was a wild, tense morning because of Bill's indecision," Stanton acknowledged.

Shortly before noon, Aubrey arrived at Stanton's office. He sat in a chair directly in front of Stanton's desk. "This is a difficult meeting for both of us," Stanton began, "but we have to part company. This is no reflection on your record, but rather a problem with how you have gone about your business." Stanton declined to elaborate, not wanting to get into a prolonged discussion. At that moment, tears flooded the eyes of The Smiling Cobra. "Does the chairman know?" Aubrey asked.

"Yes, he knows," said Stanton.

"Could I see him?"

"He's laid up with a bad back," Stanton said.

But Aubrey insisted. Stanton picked up the phone. "Bill, Jim would like to see you," he said. "Is he there with you?" Paley asked guardedly. Stanton could tell Paley was nervous, but the CBS chief agreed to meet with Aubrey as soon as possible.

The meeting between Aubrey and Stanton lasted only fifteen minutes. As soon as Aubrey left, Stanton called Paley to fill him in. Remembering their difficult conversation earlier in the day, Stanton pointedly added that when Aubrey asked for another chance, he had refused. Stanton also told Paley that Aubrey had been reduced to tears. "I'm sorry you have to see him," Stanton said, "but I couldn't deny him the call."

An hour later, Paley called back. Aubrey had not arrived—although the distance from CBS headquarters to the Regency was a five-minute walk. Stanton began to worry. He called the security men in the lobby, who said they had seen Aubrey come in, but they hadn't seen him leave. "Search the building!" Stanton told them. Stanton went to Aubrey's office and found it empty. By now Stanton was frightened; he worried that Aubrey had committed suicide. Stanton opened a window and peered out at the building's setbacks. A half hour later the phone rang. It was Aubrey. He was on his way to see Paley. He had taken a walk in Central Park to clear his head and regain his composure.

Calm and confident once again, Aubrey made a strong pitch to reverse Stanton's decision. Had he known of Paley's earlier indecision, he might have pressed even harder. "You know, I deserve it all," Aubrey finally said. "I'm sorry. I wish to hell you'd give me another chance but I know you won't. And I'll tell you one thing: I'll never say one bad word about CBS or you." For all of Aubrey's insults and misbehavior, Paley never lost his admiration. He recalled Aubrey as "magnificent in defeat . . . standing there tall, physically fit and handsome . . . he was a strong, well-disciplined man."

After a four-year stint as president of MGM in the early seventies, Aubrey settled into a life of seclusion, making low-budget movies with titles like *Savage Heat* and *Deathstone*. Graying but still firm and fit, he operates out of a small house off Sunset Boulevard. His second-floor office has bare floors, a desk, a shabby sofa, and an alert Doberman sitting in the corner. In the late 1970s, Aubrey and Paley met once for lunch after Paley's memoir was published. When Paley asked if Aubrey had read it, the exiled CBS man replied, "You know I don't read fiction."

Paley had begun to reassert his control over programming the day before Aubrey was fired. That Friday morning, shortly before lunch, Paley called Michael Dann, the programming vice-president, who had not heard from him in months. Suddenly, out of the blue, Paley was asking Dann his opinions of various shows on the new program lineup for the fall. "What does Jim think about the Polly Bergen show?" Paley asked.

"Jim thinks it will go well, and I do too," Dann said.

"You don't sound convinced," said Paley. "What would you put in?"

There was something in Paley's voice that suggested an order rather than a genuine question. Dann couldn't figure out who frightened him more at that moment, Paley or Aubrey. "NBC just canceled Shirley Booth in 'Hazel,' " said Dann. "It is predictable, but it has a good audience. It could buy us a year."

"I'll call you back," Paley said.

A half hour later Stanton called. "Buy the Hazel show from Screen Gems and cancel the Bergen show," he told Dann. Terrified but exhilarated, Dann called Sal Ianucci, CBS's vice-president for business affairs. "Sal," he said, "the old man is back."

42

P ALEY HURLED HIMSELF back into CBS's programming schedule, which Aubrey had left in shambles. He also became deeply involved in the increasingly glamorous realm of corporate acquisitions as he entertained notions of creating a vast and diversified CBS empire.

"From 1965 on, Bill Paley became the living, acting, vital force I knew him to be," recalled programming vice-president Mike Dann. "Every single night or morning he would be on the phone with me about ratings and how we were doing. I would call him between eleven and midnight if I had a problem, or if he had a problem he would call me. Many times I would be shopping in White Plains on a Saturday morning and I would phone him from a booth. We would discuss the Friday night ratings and programming problems."

Paley was enchanted and amused by Dann, who was short, round— almost elfin in appearance—with a high-pitched voice and exuberant personality. "We called Mike 'the Screamer,' " recalled Emily Greene, a long-time CBS executive assistant. When Dann emerged from behind his enormous desk, recounted Merle Miller in *Only You, Dick Daring!*, "I kept thinking of the desk that Chaplin sat behind in *The Great Dictator.*"

During their meeting, wrote Miller,

> Dann was answering telephone calls, receiving verbal messages and documents on crinkly paper from several secretaries, crinkling and studying the documents, noisily opening all the drawers of his desk and noisily closing them, passing a box of King's Ransom cigars, suppressing a yawn or two, not suppressing a yawn or two, packing and unpacking and repacking a dispatch case that was open near his desk.

Dann understood the sort of programming balance that Paley desired —the need to drop in a classy production of *Death of a Salesman* with Lee J. Cobb to counterbalance the weekly grind of witless comedies. But he was far more cynical than Paley. When asked once by the owner of a CBS affiliate what was in store for the fall season, Dann cracked, "Same old crap." Dann, however, followed the whims of his boss. He grasped the nuances of the care and feeding of William S. Paley.

Jim Aubrey had instituted the custom of marathon screening sessions —reviewing dozens of pilots—for several days each February prior to setting the new prime-time schedule. During Aubrey's reign, Paley had been a bystander. Now he was a presence.

His subordinates eyed him carefully during these sessions, always aware they were on trial even though he affectionately referred to them as "the boys." He was often restless during the screenings, which began at 9:00 A.M. and ended at 6:00 P.M. When his back hurt, he lay down on a special sofa installed by the programming department in the screening room. On his lap he kept a bound book (reproduced by CBS at a cost of more than $5,000) containing photos, credits, and story lines for each show. Paley liked to scribble in the book, glancing only occasionally at the screen. Close by, Mike Dann placed a heap of Paley's favorite deli sandwiches—served warm on the best bread available.

"If Mr. Paley didn't like a show, he would fidget a lot," recalled veteran programmer Alan Wagner. "If he liked it, he was quiet and took notes." Paley thought nothing of talking through a show that bored him, or if he was really bored, walking around, grabbing a pickle, and chewing on it. Mysteries with complicated plots often confounded him.

"If something was bad, he would go through the roof," recalled Dann. "He could berate you all the way through the pilot. If it was pretty good, he would say, 'I don't think you can keep it up through the series.' " Once in a while, Paley would proclaim, "Good job," but he would never say, "You've got a winner." The worst judgment was when he left the room.

Programmers were constantly unnerved by Paley's instinct for the bull's-eye. "If there were a show, for example, where you had done nothing but fight with the director and you were unhappy with the direction," recalled Oscar Katz, "you would screen it for Bill Paley, and the first thing he would say would be a criticism of the direction. You would think to yourself, 'How did he know?' "

If anything, Paley was more inclined than ever to play it safe and keep the profits pouring in. At one point Dann was interested in buying "Civilization," a BBC series that had been highly praised in London. It would cost $250,000, and Dann planned to run it early Sunday evening. Paley said, "Nice show but we can't afford it now." Dann knew that CBS could well afford it, but Paley simply did not want to write the check.

"The operative force in Bill Paley's life was to buy the best and gamble the least," said Mike Dann. "CBS never pioneered because Paley believed totally in building a better mousetrap, not inventing the first.

Remember, the taking of Jack Benny was not a risk. The perception of Paley as a risk taker is all nonsense."

Paley's instincts about performers were more unshakable than ever. He decreed that singers Julie Andrews and Leslie Uggams were not television stars. He hated Peter Falk in a short-lived 1965 series about a lawyer called "Trials of O'Brien." Falk played the character as a talented professional with sloppy personal habits. After every episode, Paley would call Dann to say, "How can you have that cockeyed fellow with a toothpick in his mouth, and where did he get that dirty raincoat?" Paley was right; the TV audience was not quite ready for an anti-hero. Six years later, Falk successfully re-created the character as a detective named Columbo on NBC.

Paley refused to be complacent about CBS programs. He seemed to watch everything that appeared on the air, and the moment something went wrong, he was sure to be on the phone. Paley had the disconcerting habit of catching a show at 8:00 P.M. in New York and assuming his programmers on the West Coast were watching it simultaneously—forgetting that they were on Pacific time.

In September 1965 he tuned in the opening episode of "Rawhide," a six-year-old show about a cattle drive in the Wild West, and was incensed by what he saw. Eric Fleming, the star of the series, had died earlier that year. Instead of replacing Fleming, Dann's subordinate Perry Lafferty had promoted Clint Eastwood, the second-in-command, to be trail boss. Lafferty also "modernized" by adding some blacks to the cast. Still unaccustomed to Paley's new involvement, Lafferty had not bothered to alert the chairman about the changes. Paley called Dann in his Hollywood office to say he couldn't stand Eastwood in the lead. Dann finally convinced Paley that he couldn't respond until he saw the show when it aired three hours later.

Back in New York, Paley braced Lafferty. "What's going on with 'Rawhide'?" Paley asked sternly. When Lafferty tried to explain, Paley looked at him with utter disapproval. The viewers didn't like the changes any more than Paley, and "Rawhide" had to be canceled at the season's end.

Paley could be paternal about hit CBS shows, defending them to the end. By 1967, "Gunsmoke," the long-running CBS western, had lost its appeal to the Saturday night audience and Dann recommended its cancellation. Paley resisted, "kicking and screaming," recalled Dann, but finally capitulated to the sales department's conclusion that the show could not be sold successfully. At that point Paley left for a two-week vacation in Lyford Cay. Several days later he called Dann. "I haven't been able to sleep at night," he said. "We've got to get 'Gunsmoke' back. Let's switch it to

Monday night." Recalled Dann, "Shows became like a part of his family if they were successful." Dann made the switch, and "Gunsmoke" held a place in the top ten for five more years.

Occasionally, Paley's personal feelings would cloud his programming decisions. When CBS introduced "Medical Center" in the late 1960s, with Chad Everett playing a young doctor teamed with an older chief of staff, Paley called Dann to complain. "Build up the older star," he said. "Why?" asked Dann, knowing the appeal Everett had to viewers. "Would you let a young doctor like that operate on you?" asked Paley. "Paley liked older men in control," commented Dann.

For all of Paley's demands and dark looks, his new generation of programmers relished the attention he gave them and their work. "He was good at supporting you and putting the emphasis where the emphasis should be," said Mike Dann. "He gave me the best people, he always allowed the biggest program budget, and when the going got toughest he would hold me up. If I had a problem, the first thing he would tell me was, 'Settle down. We can lick it. Just relax. It isn't that bad.' Then he would outline the problem. He would say what to do about the writers, the producers. The only way to really get to him was by being a crybaby. You never got into trouble with Bill by telling him about a problem you were having, but God help you if he discovered it on his own."

Performers clamored for Paley's attention as well. Even in his periods of corporate inactivity, he made a point of traveling to the West Coast once or twice a year. Most of the time Babe accompanied him. With maid and valet attending and suitcases stuffed with dinner jackets and evening dresses, the Paleys would take a spacious suite—their favorite was bungalow 21—for ten days or so at the Beverly Hills Hotel. Sometimes, if Paley had an overwhelming craving, they would stop for Cantonese food at the Beachcomber Restaurant en route from the airport. In the evenings, at a local watering hole such as Romanoff's or Chasen's, Bill and Babe would preside over bountiful dinner parties. The Paleys in turn would be feted at the homes of stars and studio executives.

In meetings with his performers, Paley was suitably attentive; some observers detected more grudging tolerance than genuine admiration. One producer called Paley's attitude "impersonal love." But he always praised them and asked if they were happy. He was invariably well briefed, quizzing his program executives before each encounter with a star. If a complaint was coming, he would know about it ahead of time.

For their part, the CBS stars were deferential; they understood and respected Paley's power. Once when Danny Thomas was coming to a meeting at CBS, he panicked when he realized he didn't know Paley well enough to call him "Bill." He thought "Mr. Paley" seemed inappropriately formal. His solution: Thomas called Paley "chief."

Only a few performers declined to have much to do with the CBS chairman. Bing Crosby kept his distance. Red Skelton wouldn't even take a phone call from Paley, who was known to consider Skelton uncouth—despite his ranking in the top fifteen shows for a decade and a half. CBS stars pointed to the case of Arthur Godfrey to demonstrate that one stood up to Paley at one's peril. Back in the early days of television, when Paley criticized his television show as too static, Godfrey mockingly read Paley's comments on the air. Then he turned to the camera, wiggled, and said, "Is this movement enough, Mr. Paley?" Paley later got his revenge by having Godfrey fired.

Paley was selective about the talent he socialized with. In fact, the list of performers he knew only casually or not at all far outnumbered those he could call friends. "He didn't want to see some because they were boring or they fawned on him," recalled one former programming executive. He had little to do with such big CBS stars as Ed Sullivan, Jackie Gleason, James Arness, Robert Young, Richard Boone, Raymond Burr, and Andy Griffith.

A radio man at heart, Paley stayed close to the stars who came out of radio after the war. Lucille Ball was an enduring favorite, as was George Burns. Until Aubrey ruptured their relationship, Paley adored Jack Benny as well. Even after "Amos 'n' Andy" left the air, Freeman Gosden—the more urbane of the pair—remained a friend of Paley's. "Bill liked Freeman and Freeman almost worshipped Bill," recalled Stanton. "I remember how happy Freeman was when Bill told him the name of his shirtmaker and tiemaker in Paris. Freeman made a beeline to France." What Paley's pets had in common, besides their popularity, was an ability to make him howl with laughter.

As time went on, Paley did get to know and like some of his pure television stars. Danny Thomas, Carol Burnett, and Doris Day all made the cut. But he seemed to enjoy the company of glamorous film stars like Cary Grant and Barbara Stanwyck most of all.

Occasionally Paley invited CBS performers to visit him back at Kiluna for the weekend. Goodman Ace was more like a stand-up comic than a guest; he would spend several hours entertaining Paley and his socialite friends before sitting down to eat. Freeman Gosden could fracture a dinner party by re-creating his old characters, jumping from one voice to another. Truman Capote claimed that Babe had a list of CBS people she would not tolerate in the house and that Paley invited CBS entertainers rather grudgingly: "He would say, 'We have to have Jack and Mary Benny to dinner,' and they did, and obviously she didn't seem to be very pleased about it."

Because of Paley's image of showmanship, top writers and producers gravitated to CBS. They knew programming was a high priority and that they could get decisions out of CBS. Those who met Paley were struck by his level of involvement, his knowledge of such arcana as scheduling and plot lines. Instead of budgets he talked about character believability, keeping the focus on what would work for the viewer. "That part of the world lives on impressions," said Stanton. "Bill sprinkled magic dust on CBS."

By the end of 1966, CBS had bounced back smartly from the discomfiting moment in April 1965 after Aubrey's dismissal when Paley faced his shareholders to explain why CBS's earnings had dipped. He had blamed CBS's lagging prime-time ratings (CBS had only five out of the top ten prime-time shows, compared to nine a year earlier) and—rather crassly—the high costs of "unscheduled news coverage" of Sir Winston Churchill's death and civil rights unrest in the South. Although revenues for 1965 were nearly $700 million, net income had dropped to $49 million from $49.6 million the year before. But by the end of 1966, CBS revenues surged to $814 million, and net income leapt to $64 million. Once again, CBS had eight out of the top ten prime-time shows.

Wall Street was not as impressed as it should have been. These were the go-go years of corporate diversification, and the money men were eager to see CBS earn its stripes as a full-fledged conglomerate. All three networks felt pressure to expand their horizons and move away from regulated businesses that might be subject to big profit swings and new restrictions from Washington. CBS also had large amounts of cash that it had to invest to avoid heavy taxes. Paley knew that acquisitions could fuel CBS's growth and add to its stock price. What was more, buying companies would take him back to the heady deal-making atmosphere of his early years at CBS.

In 1961, Paley and Stanton had commissioned a study by Harbridge House consultants in Boston to show them the way to diversification. The report, delivered in 1962, recommended that CBS derive no more than half of its income from broadcasting. The most compatible businesses for CBS to buy, according to the study, would be in communications, entertainment, and education—a sensible enough course.

In the summer of 1962, Paley and Stanton tapped Michael Burke as their first vice-president in charge of diversification. A prep school graduate and an All-American halfback at the University of Pennsylvania, Burke came equipped with good looks and glamour. He proved a charming and capable impresario. Burke, who had run several CBS offices in Europe, spent his time exploring companies and briefing Stanton and Paley in meetings every Thursday in the boardroom. But he didn't have enough clout for the job. Only Stanton and Paley had the heft to get a deal moving, and Paley quickly got caught up in the excitement of the chase.

"Paley called me three to six times a day," recalled Burke. "Things would cross his mind. 'Why not buy Time, Inc.?' he said one day in the early sixties. So Frank and Bill and I had lunch with Jim Linen and Andrew Heiskell [president and chairman of Time, Inc.]. It was a lively lunch. We agreed it was a great idea, but it would never be allowed by the Justice Department."

Paley initiated some merger inquiries out of pure curiosity. "He frequently looked at other companies like Time, Inc., and thought they were doing it better than we were," recalled Stanton. "He was interested that way in IBM. So I had conversations with Tom Watson." When it became clear that IBM was only interested in buying CBS, Stanton backed off.

Stanton had been thinking of expanding into print journalism even before the consultants recommended it. As early as 1960 he had approached Malcolm Muir, editor of *Newsweek,* about buying the magazine from the estate of its principal owner, Vincent Astor—Paley's former brother-in-law—who had died in 1959. Stanton thought the $15 million price tag seemed cheap. But Paley said no, and Phil Graham, who ran *The Washington Post,* bought *Newsweek* in 1961. When Graham committed suicide in 1963, Stanton made a run at the Post Company.

Stanton's dream was to buy the newspaper and let Paley run it. "I thought it would involve him in Washington in an important way," said Stanton. "TV has impact, but on a day-to-day basis you can't match print for its impact on policy." Stanton approached Fritz Beebe, the attorney for Graham's widow, Katharine, who said she did not know if she wanted to keep the paper or not. Beebe subsequently told Stanton she might be interested in selling. Then Stanton asked Paley. "I couldn't get him to respond," Stanton recalled. "He wouldn't join the issue."

Stanton continued to make overtures to other communication companies. He had discussions with Paramount, McGraw-Hill, and Curtis Publishing. Each time Paley declined to bite. By the end of 1963, CBS had $85 million in cash on hand, and it had considered and rejected some seventy-five possible purchases.

In July 1964, Paley stunned Stanton with the news that he had decided on CBS's first acquisition. He wanted to buy 80 percent of the New York Yankees for $11.2 million (CBS would eventually buy out the remaining 20 percent for $2 million). Unknown to Stanton, Paley had made his first overture back in May 1963 at the Deepdale Golf Club when he was playing a round with his old friend Dan Topping, co-owner of the Yankees. Paley had casually asked if Topping would ever consider selling the ball club, and Topping replied that he was negotiating with a prospective buyer.

The matter rested there until early July 1964, when Topping called Paley to ask if CBS was interested. Paley said he was, and the two men began negotiating. At that point, Paley brought Stanton in. "The first meeting I went to with Bill and Topping, I didn't know an earned run from an error," Stanton admitted. "I wasn't a baseball person." Sitting on CBS's board, however, was an avid "baseball person," Joe Iglehart, an owner of the Baltimore Orioles. Iglehart spurred Paley on, and when the deal was completed, he sold his interest in the Orioles so he could stay on the CBS board.

CBS announced the deal in early August, prompting howls of protest from other baseball owners suspicious of CBS's motives. Stanton went to Boston (Paley had no intention of involving himself in such a contentious situation) for a special meeting of the American League members. For an entire day they cross-examined him before agreeing to approve the purchase. Stanton was so persuasive that afterwards, he recalled, "some of the owners figured that it had been my idea. It was an ironic situation. But I did support the purchase. It wasn't that much money, and it had the potential to enhance CBS."

Still, why did a man as prone to caution as Paley make such an odd first move? The Yankees organization was no communications or education company, although it did entertain its fans. Paley had little feel for sports. CBS had recently paid $28.2 million for the rights to televise National Football League games for two years, but that had been Aubrey's idea, and Paley had agreed reluctantly.

After buying the Yankees, Paley said regally, "It's a good investment." Pressed, he added, "There's more leisure time in this country and a percentage of it will be spent at ball parks." Some time later, Paley told Fred Friendly that his motivations were rooted in his childhood, when he shagged balls for free tickets to Chicago Cubs games. "All my life," he told Friendly, "I wanted to own a baseball team, and that's why I bought the Yankees."

Most of all, Paley wanted the Yankees because they had class. In the previous decade they had won the American League pennant nine times. The Yankees' aura of quality fit CBS's self-image as the Cadillac of the networks.

Paley relished the novelty of baseball's glamour. He brought Babe to the games, where they entertained socialite friends like Tommy Tailer and Winston Frost in a private dining room in the stadium. Burke, who Paley put in charge of the Yankees, would take the boss down to meet the players. "He was like a ten-year-old child," Burke recalled.

In 1965 the pressure on CBS to move beyond broadcasting intensified. The FCC proposed that the networks relinquish half of their prime-time programming to the control of sponsors and independent producers. Yet Paley hung back from a major move. His next few acquisitions were as unlikely as the Yankees.

That year the company paid $13 million for the Fender electric guitar company, and in July 1966, CBS bought Creative Playthings, a manufacturer of expertly crafted educational toys, for $13.5 million. In each case Paley emphasized that CBS was pursuing its goal of buying top-quality companies in their fields. But beyond that, they had no connection to the goals set out by the Harbridge House report. Harbridge had identified music as an area CBS understood, and Paley tried to explain that Fender was a "compatible product" because it had to do with music. In fact, Fender was a manufacturing company with a product that was sold through specialty stores—a tenuous relationship even to CBS Records.

As with programming, Paley was buying the best and gambling the least. He invested in established companies with successful track records, companies that felt right and seemed to have little down side for CBS. "He was a spender of money," said management consultant David Hertz. "He would buy a company and probably pay too much. But he didn't see it as a risk. To take a risk, you know you are taking a risk. Bill doesn't gamble. If he thought something was a risk, he wouldn't do it."

Throughout their acquisition dances, Paley and Stanton kept a discreet distance and avoided stepping on each other's toes. If Stanton was disappointed that Paley declined to act on his proposals, he didn't show it. And he certainly played loyal soldier on the Yankee purchase.

Close aides saw small indications of Stanton's unease, however. Like a mastiff trained on a choke collar, Stanton had always leapt instantly when Paley snapped the leash. But the leash tightened as Paley became more vigilant about his power, and Stanton was starting to growl. Although Stanton could win over Paley more often than he lost, his frustration began to show. "One thing that I think got Frank down was Paley's concentration on what was wrong as opposed to an acknowledgment of what was right," said Robert Wood. Slowly, almost imperceptibly, Paley did to Stanton what he did to so many executives throughout his career: he wore him down and made him smaller.

43

T HE MOST BITTER battle between Bill Paley and Frank Stanton had nothing to do with any programs—news or entertainment— that CBS put on the air, or even with a proposed expansion of the company. Rather, it concerned a new headquarters for CBS. It was to be a sleek, sophisticated symbol of CBS quality, and it was enormously important to both Paley and Stanton. For four straight years it consumed the two men; they exchanged as many memos about plans as on any other subject in their time together. They squabbled over the smallest details. They wounded and infuriated each other. The outcome of the struggle served to deepen the divisions between the two men.

Stanton had been pushing for a new CBS building since the mid-1950s. After scouting a number of sites, he had persuaded Paley to buy a piece of land on Sixth Avenue and 52nd Street. Stanton, the onetime aspiring architect, also had definite ideas about the building. He wanted to avoid the skyscraper cliché, a "Coca-Cola bottle with setbacks," and he was set on having Eero Saarinen do the design. A friend of Saarinen's for some years, Stanton liked the Finnish-born architect's imaginative and varied designs; Saarinen didn't just repeat successful formulas.

On November 21, 1958, Stanton introduced Paley to Saarinen at lunch. Calm and understated, with a wry sense of humor, Saarinen was capable of engaging charm. But in Paley's presence, recalled Stanton, "he froze." Paley was cool to Saarinen but agreed to let the architect work on plans.

For the next two and a half years, Paley could not make up his mind about the building. During part of that time he was recuperating from his surgery and depression, but even when he came out of it, he was uncertain. "I was never sure what Bill wanted," recalled Stanton. "The things I proposed, he wasn't excited about. He didn't say no, but he sure as hell didn't show me any sign of wanting to go ahead. We were on dead center."

In March 1961, Saarinen presented a mockup to Paley and Stanton. It was restrained and orderly, simple and modern. Paley hated it. In every respect the design reflected Stanton's taste. A dispirited Saarinen started over, but Paley's continued indifference gnawed at Stanton and Saarinen, a perfectionist who took his work very seriously. What's more, Stanton was irritated that CBS was paying interest on an empty lot.

Finally, Stanton invited Paley for a talk in his office on Easter Sunday. Stanton pressed for a decision, but Paley wouldn't commit himself. "If I could assure you that *Vogue* magazine would shoot a spread with its models in front of the building, would you do it?" Stanton asked in exasperation. Paley brightened. "Yes!" he said, then took it back. But in Paley's instinctive response, Stanton understood one source of his indecision: he worried that the building would not get the kind of attention he wanted it to have.

Not long afterwards, during a discussion with Paley and Stanton, the normally placid Saarinen lost patience and accused Paley of wanting to do a "chintzy" building. Paley got up and left the meeting. From the hallway, he summoned Stanton. "I don't want to have anything more to do with that man," he said.

Stanton prepared to tell Saarinen that CBS would buy out his contract. He asked the architect to come to New York for a meeting. After dinner the night before Saarinen was due to arrive, Paley went to the small room next to Stanton's office where several cardboard models of the building were set up. The next morning he called Stanton. "Let's talk some more," he said. Paley had turned the 540 degrees. He liked Saarinen's original design. What Paley had dismissed as too austere was now strong, beautiful, and timeless. Why the turnaround? Stanton never knew, and Paley never said.

To lock Paley in, Stanton proposed a shrewd compromise. He would oversee the building's exterior, and Paley would be in charge of the interior. Stanton was so eager to get moving that he gave up his dream of having Saarinen design all the furniture. While vacationing in Spain in July 1961, Paley sent a telegram giving the go-ahead. Shortly thereafter, Eero Saarinen died. Fortunately, Saarinen's chief designer, Kevin Roche, was able to take over, and the building proceeded as planned. Rising thirty-six stories, it comprised a series of vertical slabs interrupted by dark-tinted windows. The exterior was sheer, devoid of setbacks or ledges.

Naturally, Paley tried to change the terms of his compromise with Stanton. Both Saarinen and Stanton had settled on black granite for the facade; Stanton had brought a swatch of dark gray Harris tweed to their first meeting to suggest the color and texture he wanted. Saarinen liked the idea of black as a contrast to the ubiquitous glass box. But Paley seemed uneasy. After Paley and Stanton visited the mockup Roche had built in New Rochelle, New York, Paley said, "I know why Eero wanted it black: because he knew he was dying."

Paley pressed for pink granite, which, Stanton later learned, had been

Babe's idea. Stanton finally persuaded Paley that pink simply would not work. After months searching for the right granite, collecting samples from around the world, Stanton found the ultimate selection, a rough stone of charcoal gray, at a quarry in Quebec.

Although Paley claimed to have visited the mockup in New Rochelle thirty times, he ended up ceding to Stanton the entire design of what became known as "Black Rock." "With his energy, Frank stole the building from Paley," said Robert Wood. Stanton even ended up overseeing the interior. The design firm selected by Paley did three sample offices, all of which were unsatisfactory. Stanton suggested his good friend Florence Knoll, and Paley capitulated.

Stanton and Knoll selected the furniture and the rugs, the wall coverings, even the 899 plants and the flower arrangements that would be changed daily. Stanton picked out such details as the typeface for the elevator numerals and supervised the selection of prints for office walls. A committee including Paley, Stanton, Colin, and several museum directors chose the major artworks, including paintings by Vasarely, Soulanges, and Pollock—reflections of Stanton's hard-edged taste, not Paley's.

There was one conspicuously defiant exception to the Stanton standard: Bill Paley's office. It was even more richly traditional than before, with dark green carpets and mahogany period pieces, and paintings by Toulouse-Lautrec, Derain, Picasso, Vuillard, and Rouault covering the dark green walls. "Slightly overripe," was how John Hightower, former head of the Museum of Modern Art, characterized the room. "It was as if Bill Paley were saying, 'This is mine. Frank Stanton doesn't affect my taste. My cave is my cave,' " said Jack Schneider.

When it was completed in 1964 at a cost of $40 million, Black Rock was a triumph of elegance and simplicity, one of New York's most distinctive skyscrapers. But as it won awards and kudos from critics, CBS executives could sense Paley's resentment. "To my mind the coldness between Frank Stanton and Bill Paley began with the building," said Robert Wood.

During the construction, Stanton conceived a publicity gimmick for the new building, a concert by the New York Philharmonic in the excavation. He and another executive presented the idea to Paley at a meeting. A few days later, the other executive asked Stanton where it stood. "It's over," said Stanton. "The chairman doesn't want it." Reading between the lines, the executive concluded, "It was because it was Frank's building. It was clear to me what was behind Paley's resistance: vindictiveness and tension." Eventually, Paley overrode his anger by taking the lion's share of the credit for Black Rock. "Bill did what he did to almost everybody who worked for him," said another top executive. "What they did became his."

The autumn of 1964 marked a low point in relations between Paley and Stanton. That September, Stanton was scheduled to go on a fact-finding mission to Vietnam as an adviser to the U.S. Information Agency. "Why are you going?" Paley asked him one day with evident disapproval. The question had nothing to do with Paley's feelings about the war; both he and Stanton were still firm supporters of U.S. intervention. Stanton knew Paley was simmering because he saw one more instance of Stanton getting all the attention.

At a lunch soon afterwards, Paley and Stanton found themselves disagreeing on one matter after another. When Paley vetoed a reception Stanton was planning for advertising agency art directors to unveil a mural on the new twentieth floor of Black Rock, Stanton blew up. "Well," he said angrily. "Maybe we should part company and you should bring Walter Thayer in to run the place." Paley ignored the remark and moved to another subject as if nothing had happened.

Stanton was still smarting when he returned from his mission to give a grim oral report to President Johnson and his secretary of defense, Robert McNamara. Stanton wanted to brief Paley as well, but Paley "expressed no interest," recalled Stanton. "He never asked me once about what I had seen or what I had learned."

By now the rifts between Stanton and Paley were surfacing in meetings and hurting morale. Everyone had always recognized the fundamental differences between the two men, but for nearly twenty years they seemed otherwise complementary. As Paley moved through his seventh decade, however, Stanton's usefulness became threatening. Paley's surgery and depression surely played a role, as did his sense of Stanton's growing desire for the top job. "It was in the atmosphere," said Richard Salant. "Stanton and Paley were at odds. I don't think Frank realized how this permeated the organization. It was felt at many levels."

Michael Burke recalled a rare Saturday morning session when he, Paley, Stanton, and Goddard Lieberson were discussing the music business. Stanton and Lieberson had a strong disagreement. As they argued, "Bill Paley got more and more nervous. He was shifting in his chair, walking the room. He was exaggeratedly nervous. Suddenly he spoke very sharply to Frank Stanton to rein him in. The meeting broke up after that. Both Goddard and Frank hustled out. Paley and I were left there. He was very disturbed. He said, 'I hated to do that. I've never reprimanded Frank Stanton in front of anyone else.' "

CBS executives like Burke and Schneider found themselves mediating between the two top men. One of the most perceptive go-betweens was management consultant David Hertz. "Frank would have one view," recalled Hertz. "Since he knew I would talk to Bill, he made sure I understood his view, which I would pass along. Then I would go back to Frank and say, 'Bill said not this or that.' I was probably privy to more of the nitty-gritty of these disagreements than those on the inside. They were often small issues—technical matters or talking about some individual. But neither man liked to take them up face to face. Neither had the stomach for confrontation. They went out of their way to avoid it. When they reached difficulty, Frank would retreat into a sulk and glower. He got very angry. Paley could not afford to retreat. He just ignored it."

Michael Burke viewed Paley and Stanton as two injured egos incapable of forgiving each other: "Frank was warm and sensitive. He could be hurt. One saw him hurt by Bill Paley. Frank felt he did a superhuman job of being president of CBS, and he began to feel Bill didn't appreciate all he did. But Bill's ego was bruised. He would talk to me in an easy way. He said, 'What the hell does Frank want? Everyone thinks he runs the place anyhow.' Bill thought Frank was stealing his thunder."

That fall there were rumblings in the press about Stanton's uncertain future with CBS. In September 1964 the *Gallagher Report* speculated that Stanton would take a cabinet post if Lyndon Johnson was reelected in November. In October, *Variety* elevated the rumor to near certainty, citing Stanton's "acute case of Potomac fever," and noting that at CBS there was "little left to intrigue him. . . . For several months now the Stanton visibility has been receding while Paley has assumed stage center." *Variety* observed that recently Paley had been making corporate announcements, while "all corporate releases heretofore were dual or only Stanton."

Johnson made the expected overture in November. The president invited Stanton to a secret meeting at the Johnson ranch in Texas. Accompanying Stanton were Thomas Watson of IBM and Donald Cook, chairman of American Electric Power. Over the course of the evening, Johnson took each man on a walk to discuss cabinet posts. He offered Stanton under secretary of state as well as secretary of health, education and welfare. Stanton declined both, and Johnson struck out as well with Watson and Cook. "He was petulant," recalled Stanton. Johnson sent the three men home on Air Force Two and arranged for them to be dropped off at a remote part of Kennedy Airport outside New York to avoid leaks.

Stanton had turned down the offers because he was still convinced he would run CBS when Paley retired in 1966. Moreover, at that time, Aubrey was beginning to crumble, and Paley would need Stanton's steady hand. Given all the trouble Paley was causing, Stanton might understandably have been tempted that evening in November over the bar of the

Pierre Hotel when Aubrey had suggested seizing the company from Paley. Instead, Aubrey's brazen disloyalty drew Stanton back toward Paley. But even then, Paley and Stanton could not close ranks entirely. That much was evident in Paley's resistance to Stanton on the morning of Aubrey's dismissal.

During the year preceding Paley's anticipated retirement in September 1966, his signals to Stanton were more conflicting than ever. In the spring of 1965 he ordered CBS's chief of public relations, Kidder Meade, to orchestrate a campaign to beef up the Paley image. The first payoff was a glowing seven-part series on Paley in May by Bob Considine in the *New York Journal-American* called "Live from New York—This Is TV's Bill Paley." Each part began on page one and was accompanied by prominent headlines and large photos. The stories were filled with gushy encomiums such as "Paley has kept his equilibrium throughout this unprecedented period of ruckus in the annals of the slickest and most successful operation of its kind in the world."

When the *Gallagher Report* took note in June of Paley's image-making campaign, Stanton showed particular concern about any slights Paley might be feeling. "Would it be possible to have someone crawl through the past two years of *Gallagher Report*s and pull out all references to me?" Stanton asked Kidder Meade.

Not long afterwards, Paley broached the idea of his retirement with Stanton for the first time. It was September 1965, the eve of Paley's sixty-fourth birthday. Stanton had set the rule of sixty-five for retirement back in the late 1940s to clear out some older owners and managers of radio stations and make way for young men in middle management.

The rule had come up in conversation previously only once, when Stanton asked Paley if CBS should consider retirement at sixty-five for board members as well as employees. When Paley quickly disagreed, Stanton asked why. "My father is on the board and I don't want him to think I am trying to push him off," Paley said. At the time, Sam Paley was in his mid-seventies and a relatively inactive board member. Still, Stanton assured Paley that the rule would make an exception for current board members. Paley continued to resist, so Stanton dropped the idea.

When Paley brought up the retirement rule in September 1965, his manner puzzled Stanton. At first, Paley seemed direct: what did Stanton think about the chairman retiring the following year? Stanton cagily replied that it was entirely up to Paley. "You know," Paley said, "I never agreed with you on that age sixty-five retirement program." His tone was mildly jocular, but it flipped suddenly into suspicion.

Paley told Stanton that Earl Newsom, a public relations consultant to CBS and to Paley, had approached him recently to suggest that he retire and hand over the company to Stanton. "It was obvious that Bill thought I was working through Newsom to get him to retire," Stanton recalled. When Stanton said he had never heard about Newsom's overture, Paley seemed skeptical.

Meanwhile, Stanton's ten-year contract with CBS was due to expire at the end of 1966, prompting the board's finance committee—Paley, Joe Iglehart, Robert Lovett, William Burden, and Leon Levy—to begin discussing terms for a new employment agreement. In January, Stanton received a memo from Paley that confirmed Paley's unwillingness to leave the company at sixty-five and Stanton's need for a title to reflect his duties.

The memo, to be ratified at the February 9 board of directors' meeting, proposed that at the request of the board, Paley remain chairman and devote himself to "planning and development." Stanton would assume Paley's title of chief executive officer, with responsibility for all of CBS's operations. Jack Schneider, president of CBS Television, would be promoted to the new position of group vice-president for broadcasting, in charge of the television network, CBS News, CBS Radio, and the CBS-Television stations.

"It came out of the blue," recalled Stanton. "It took me by surprise. He just sent it into me and said he would like to talk about it." When the two men did discuss the plan, Stanton uncharacteristically overplayed his hand. Stanton said he was displeased with the terms of his retirement in the proposed new employment contract. He wanted more money, his settlement to be based on a formula taking into account the number of years he had been president.

On February 8, Paley sent Stanton his latest version of the announcement incorporating several suggestions from the finance committee and requesting Stanton's final thoughts. The chairman also asked Stanton to have the memo copied and distributed to the press immediately following the board meeting. Stanton had only a few changes: substituting the word "realignment" for "reorganization" of the CBS management; modestly editing out Paley's reference to Stanton's superior work as CBS president; and rather poignantly inserting "the" before his new title of chief executive officer. Everything seemed smoothly on course.

The next day, the CBS directors assembled for lunch at one-thirty in the CBS boardroom on the thirty-fifth floor of Black Rock. They arranged themselves around the long French walnut table, surrounded by paintings by Ben Shahn, Georges Rouault, Jean Dubuffet, and Ben Nicholson. Everyone was in place except Paley. After several minutes, Winnie Williams, Stanton's secretary, entered the room and whispered in his ear. Stanton excused himself and told the other directors to begin eating.

He hurried to the chairman's office, where Paley was waiting. Paley told Stanton that he wanted to table the proposal for Stanton to become chief executive officer because there were still too many details to work out in Stanton's contract. "Let's wait and talk about it later," Paley said. Mystified and disappointed, Stanton nevertheless assented without comment. Paley had one more request. "He wanted to be kept on as chairman and asked how he could have it formalized," recalled Stanton, who said he would ask Joe Iglehart to make the motion at the meeting.

The two men then went to the boardroom where they joined the luncheon. "It was one of the most dramatic things I ever saw," recalled Richard Salant, who as a corporate vice-president served as secretary to the board. "The only way you could ever tell that Frank Stanton was angry was when the back of his neck was red. That day it was flaming. Afterward I asked Frank what had happened and he said, 'Bill couldn't go through with it.' "

When the board meeting ended, a memo went out to CBS employees and the press from Stanton, not Paley, disingenuously announcing that the directors had adopted a resolution "asking Mr. Paley to continue as Chairman of the Board beyond the time when he would normally retire. Mr. Paley, I am happy to report, accepted the Board's proposal." In addition, Stanton announced Schneider's promotion. The only word in the memo that Stanton could truly claim as his own was "realignment."

Stanton was "shattered," Ralph Colin said later. "I knew how hard it was on Frank when he didn't get the CEO," recalled Robert Wood, "but I never saw him lose his composure." Jack Gould recalled that when Stanton gave him the news, he sounded "shaken." Gould's subsequent article in the *New York Times* contained nothing about Paley's change of heart and said only that both Paley and Stanton were withdrawing somewhat in favor of Schneider and other younger executives. It was, at best, a fig leaf for Stanton.

Paley never again mentioned the chief executive officer title to Stanton. In retrospect, Stanton wondered if he had miscalculated by pushing the finances of his contract. Paley had made a benevolent gesture, and when Stanton proved insufficiently grateful, the chairman had evidently gotten angry. "If I had taken the cookies when they were being passed," Stanton mused, "if when he first talked to me I had said, 'Fine,' maybe things would have been different. But I'm not so sure the CEO would have gone through anyway. I couldn't second-guess him. He was too complex."

Six years passed before Paley gave a clue to what he had been thinking. On that occasion Paley and Stanton were discussing several candidates for president of CBS when Stanton said, "I have never come back to the meeting when you were talking about making me CEO." Paley paused for a beat and said, "I couldn't bring myself to do it."

Paley chose not to acknowledge his turnabout on February 9 publicly. In his 1979 memoir he skirted the issue by saying that he had "tried at one point" to secure a chief executive role for Stanton but that it "did not work out." But his version of the February board meeting is pure invention. "It was a spontaneous request by Joe Iglehart for me to stay past sixty-five," Paley said. "I never would have gone to him to ask. And when the board asked me, I felt that I had some things and ideas within me that I could contribute to CBS, that CBS needed me."

Years later Stanton would rationalize that the CEO title was not that important to him, but the fact was, his whole career had pointed toward achieving it. After the big letdown, why didn't he simply walk out the door? He was immensely successful in his own right; he could have readily secured a CEO job at another major corporation. He had been on the cover of *Time*. He was recognized in the business world as the man who ran CBS day to day. And he had plenty of money.

But he was still a small-town midwesterner from a Methodist up-bringing, in thrall to Paley and the glamour of a company he had dreamed about as a boy. When he ran into the wall, he didn't have it in him to leave. He had become the ultimate corporate man. And because of Paley's cunning, Stanton could still delude himself that the boss might yet come around. "Paley wouldn't have been so cruel as to cut Frank off completely," said Dick Salant. "Even though Paley couldn't go through with it in 1966, Frank could hope that he would still get the job." It was too soon to recognize what later became so obvous: that Paley would hang on forever at CBS.

To add to the already turbulent atmosphere at CBS in early 1966, Fred Friendly, president of CBS News, kicked up an embarrassing controversy over Schneider's appointment. Accustomed to dealing only with Paley and Stanton, Friendly was furious that he was now expected to report to Schneider—whom Friendly felt lacked the proper experience to supervise the news division. Privately, he lodged a protest that Paley dismissed.

The same week, CBS took a block of time from its daytime schedule to carry testimony from the Senate Foreign Relations Committee on U.S. policy in Vietnam. After two days of television coverage, Schneider balked at giving over six more hours to the testimony of George Kennan, the veteran diplomat. When Friendly watched NBC covering Kennan while CBS showed a rerun of "I Love Lucy," the CBS News president angrily lodged protests with Paley and Stanton.

Paley was vacationing in Nassau, so Stanton tried to cool Friendly down. Having reached an impasse, Stanton and Friendly agreed to meet again the following Monday morning. During their meeting, Jack Gould arrived unexpectedly. In his hand was a letter of resignation written by Friendly. Stanton was outraged that Friendly had given the letter to Gould before the situation was resolved.

After Friendly left Stanton's office, the newsman's attorney tried to persuade Stanton to let Friendly stay. When Stanton asked about the letter, the lawyer said, "Don't worry, Fred can ask the *New York Times* to back off." "You're crazy to think Gould would pull back," said Stanton. The CBS president called Paley, who was equally incensed by Friendly's behavior.

Paley telephoned Friendly in his office to vent his anger. Not only had Friendly broken his word, he had the nerve to quote Edward R. Murrow in his letter. "You had no right to do that," said Paley. "He is dead."

Stanton immediately proposed that Richard Salant be appointed to succeed Friendly. Paley was no more enamored of Salant than he had been five years earlier when Stanton had named him news president the first time. Salant had misgivings of his own. He would only agree to be named acting president. "I want to get some notion that the difficulties between you and Bill have been resolved," he told Stanton.

Paley subsequently came up with a candidate of his own, recommended by kitchen cabinet member Walter Thayer. He was Richard Clurman, chief of correspondents for *Time* magazine. Clurman had three meetings at CBS in mid-March—with Paley and Stanton; with Stanton alone; and with Schneider and Stanton. He was encouraged enough by these sessions to alert his superiors at *Time* that a CBS offer might be forthcoming. But Stanton meanwhile was busy talking Paley out of Clurman and boosting Salant. Stanton was helped by Cronkite and Sevareid, both of whom urged Paley to rehire Salant as well.

Finally Paley acquiesced—doubtless out of guilt over having thwarted Stanton's ambitions at the recent board meeting. In April, Stanton asked Salant to assume the job permanently. "We have resolved our differences. Everything is fine now," Stanton told Salant. "I wanted to believe it," Salant said later. "So I took the presidency of CBS News. But the symptoms were still there."

44

AS BILL PALEY became more involved in CBS, he drifted farther from Babe. By the mid-1960s the Paleys hit a turning point. Not only had he reached sixty-five, but Babe had passed fifty. For both of them, it was a period of doubt and searching, a time to set new ground rules for their relationship. They continued to dominate their exclusive social circuit, entertaining exquisitely at their various homes. But their routines grew rigid and stale. Increasingly, Bill and Babe Paley led separate lives; they had not had sexual relations for well over a decade. Each of them seemed to be setting the stage for the final act.

At bottom, Babe remained a "nice New England charming girl," in the words of her friend Horace Kelland. But in public she was absorbed with keeping up appearances. She was an icon, Bill Paley's perfect jewel, and the role was a demanding one. "She never changed at heart, but she did a lot on the exterior," said Kelland. The pressure showed in her near-incessant smoking; by now she was up to more than two packs of L & M's a day.

Over the years Babe tried to shake the habit—eight times by her husband's count. She kept her cigarettes in a 24-carat gold and black leather case designed by Schlumberger and always used an ivory holder with a filter. "She wouldn't have had a cigarette touch her hands," said her daughter Amanda. As with everything, Babe made her vice part of her style, smoking elegantly and fastidiously—almost unobtrusively. "Maybe it was the cigarette holders," recalled Walter Thayer's wife, Jeanne. "But I never really noticed her smoking."

Truman Capote, who knew her faults better than anyone, once wrote that "Mrs. P had only one fault; she was perfect; otherwise, she was perfect." *Vogue,* which lionized her the most, understood the effort required to maintain her public image. "She makes excellence look easy," the magazine noted in 1967. "To give backbone to kindness she asks most from herself. To care for what is worth care, she weeds the careless from her life. She is the most inscrutable of American women because she knows the root paradox: to be serene means working like the Devil."

Living with Bill Paley was even more of a strain. "He wore her down," said the photographer Horst, who had studied her face since her early days at *Vogue*. "He was a bit too much in command. She was not happy. He kept her too busy. 'Look at the list of what I have to do,' she would say." Yet to her family, Babe betrayed none of her growing unhappiness with her husband. "I never heard a cross word," said Amanda. "It was the way she was brought up. She never criticized Bill except once when she called him 'Delinquent Dads.' "

Perfectionism became an obsession. "She ran establishments, not families," said Jeanne Thayer. "She had to do so much, spend so much time preserving this little world, this capsule of their lifestyle, just to suit Bill. The idea that they had to import flowers and food to the Bahamas from the United States—no one else did that. Bill wanted the atmosphere to be perfect wherever they were."

Relations with her children weighed on Babe as well. By the late sixties, she and her husband were estranged from their two youngest children, Kate and Billie, who were then entering their twenties. Kate was living the Bohemian life in lower Manhattan. Billie had entered his drifting and drug abuse phase by this time. Babe remained distant from Amanda, who was a star on the New York social circuit.

But she did draw closer to Tony. Mother and son spoke every day, and on many evenings he would join her for a drink. She favored him financially as well, lending him $114,000 so he and his wife could buy and furnish an apartment on the Upper East Side. But the more she leaned on Tony, who was as handsome as Amanda was beautiful, the more resentful Paley became. He not only begrudged the time she gave her son, but the confidences that she obviously shared with him. "Tony knew all," said one Paley family intimate, "and Tony and Bill had a stormy time as a result." Babe couldn't even enjoy the one strong relationship she had among her children.

Ironically, in 1965, just about the time when the children had all left home, the Paleys bought a new apartment in New York. Unlike the small pied-à-terre the Paleys had maintained for two decades when the children were relegated to Kiluna, this apartment had room for all. More to the point, the twenty-room duplex at 820 Fifth Avenue overlooked Central Park and had the scale required for grand entertaining. Not content with just one decorator, the Paleys enlisted four to design one of the most elegant apartments in New York.

Billy Baldwin re-created their old St. Regis living room as an intimate library, complete with the antique needlepoint rug and the Venetian bronze clock suspended from the ceiling. On the walls of shirred brown and beige chintz were Picasso's *The Pink Lady,* Matisse's *Odalisque,* and two small paintings, one of two women by Vuillard, the other a reclining nude by Bonnard. Stéphane Boudin lined the apple green entrance foyer with mahogany shelves arranged with books and delicate statuary. Behind the large round table in the center, covered with magazines and piles of books and a huge vase of flowers, was Picasso's masterpiece, *Boy Leading a Horse.* Sister Parish and Albert Hadley did Babe's bedroom. A painter worked for five months applying eighteen coats of paint—six different shadings just for the base, plus glazing. They made the living room lemon yellow, and covered the dining room with Chinese floral wallpaper in peach and yellow.

The tables brimmed with objects selected by Babe from the most expensive Manhattan antique shops and obscure Parisian flea markets. There was also a profusion of flower arrangements, but Paley's treasured art collection was what really distinguished the apartment. The living room alone held Van Gogh's *Washerwoman at Arles,* Toulouse-Lautrec's *Montmartre Madam,* Bonnard's *Still Life,* Rousseau's *Vase of Flowers,* Monet's *Deux Roses sur une Nappe,* and Gauguin's *Queen of the Areois,* transplanted from Kiluna.

In her stylish new base of operations, Babe fell into a routine quite distant from her husband's. Moments of togetherness, with laughter and cozy confidences, were a rarity. Most mornings she awoke at seven— unusually early by the standards of society ladies. After she and Bill had eaten separate breakfasts in their bedrooms, they would sit down for what amounted to a business meeting to review their agendas for the day. Then Babe would scan the newspapers, call her friends, and take her bath.

Babe went out every morning, usually before ten. "She once told me she liked to get out early because she wasn't ready to listen to the complaints of all the help," said her friend Jeanne Murray Vanderbilt. Sometimes Babe was driven to the Art Students League on West 57th Street, where she took classes in drawing, painting, and sculpture. (Working out in a fashionable gymnasium was never part of her day. She considered exercise tiresome and openly acknowledged her ineptitude at sports. If she felt even the slightest bulge on her thin frame, she would diet rather than do a single calisthenic.)

Babe was one of the original Ladies Who Lunch—a ritual in which eating takes second billing to gossiping with chums at glamorous New York restaurants such as La Côte Basque and La Grenouille. She gave small luncheons for her friends at home as well. In the afternoons, she would frequently cruise the city's exclusive stores.

"She was always shopping," said one of her former servants. "She Christmas-shopped all year. She always had a purpose. There were certain places that she had to get to first. She was always trying to find things before her sisters did. She went to a lot of antique shops like Freddie Victoria. And she loved to buy costume jewelry."

On Mondays and Fridays Babe visited her hairdresser—for years Kenneth, then later Monsieur Marc. At Monsieur Marc's Madison Avenue salon she would have a surprisingly hearty lunch: perhaps a smoked salmon and cream cheese sandwich and a bottle of beer from William Poll's gourmet shop nearby. During her hours at the beauty salon she avoided the confessional conversation favored by many women. When she wasn't asking practical questions about hair and makeup, she read novels. "She was a person to get on with it," said one of her hairdressers. "She always had a book. There was never any 'do nothing' time for her." Babe did have a tendency to leave her books and reading glasses behind, to be retrieved later by one of her servants.

It all sounds sybaritic, and in many respects it was. But interspersed throughout each day were tasks and chores dedicated to her husband's well-being. His expectations were always on her mind. At home in the late afternoons, she would consult with her personal secretary and various servants before embarking on the evening's activities. "She was mired in household duties," recalled one friend. "Babe worried about the help all the time."

In earlier years, Babe's devotion had been easier to understand. She was enthralled with Paley, perhaps even genuinely in love with him. But as she reached middle age, love had turned into convenience. The marriage now rested on habit, creature comforts, and a shared social life. Her identity too had changed: to the public she had become Babe *Paley,* and she was content with the status that the name conferred. She craved a tranquil life, a luxury that her fear of Paley's rage made impossible. But Babe Paley knew she had made a Faustian pact. To be admired in public, she had to endure in private her husband's belittling demands as well as his infidelity. Only later would she come to grips with what she had given up.

For companionship, warmth, and fun, Babe counted on a devoted circle of friends, male and female. Those closest to her included fashionable society women such as Jeanne Murray Vanderbilt, C. Z. Guest, Josie Blair, Katherine "KK" Auchincloss, Janie Choate, Louise Melhado, Françoise de la Renta, and Slim Keith. Although Irene Selznick had divorced Bill's close friend David, she stayed an intimate friend of Babe. Unknown in society circles but close to Babe nevertheless was a girlhood friend, Marion Osborn, who lived high on a hill overlooking the Hudson River in upstate New York.

Babe also had a coterie of single men, platonic companions known for their urbanity, wit, and entertaining gossip. Called variously "walkers" or "laughing men," these friends included Horace Kelland, whose father, Clarence Kelland, had made a fortune writing adventure novels about the West; Peter Glenville, the English stage and film director; and

Charles Ryskamp, for years director of the Pierpont Morgan Library in New York. Also among them was Truman Capote, who ingratiated himself so skillfully that Babe opened up to him as a confidant.

Babe's friends provided a crucial release. "I was so at ease when I was in her company," said Jeanne Thayer. "With Bill and Babe together, the atmosphere was more formal." With Babe it was fun, if admittedly superficial. Conversation ran to clothes, decorating, and stories about mutual friends—about which she could be surprisingly outspoken, given her reticence around her husband. "She had very distinct opinions about who she liked and who was a bore," said Diana Vreeland.

Babe also found an outlet for her own wit and talent for mimicry. "He didn't like it when she was funny," recalled one of her close friends. "He wanted a certain amount of attention paid to her but not too much." Her manner was more playful when she was with her friends. "After dinner in Nassau she would knock on my door and say, 'Let's go for a midnight swim,' " recalled Horace Kelland. "She loved spontaneous fun. She was at her best in sneakers."

When Babe wanted to escape the pressures of the Manhattan whirl, she would visit Marion Osborn. With Marion, she felt no compulsion to have every hair in place. They would talk about old friends and old times, about flowers and gardening, and Babe's travels. Babe rarely discussed her husband except to say he was busy or to mention some place they were planning to visit on vacation. "I remember once," recalled Osborn, "when she came for a visit. We had a huge Newfoundland dog named Barnaby. I remember her sitting on the steps for the longest time, just hugging Barnaby."

Babe was thoughtful and solicitous of her friends. In some ways, she was more maternal with them than she was with her own children. With friends, no servants or demanding husband could stand in her way. "She was always thinking about her friends and how their lives were going. She would call up and say, 'How are things?' She had great loyalty and sensibility and thoughtfulness," said Osborn. "She was interested in everything about you," said Aline, the Countess of Romanones, whom the Paleys used to visit in Spain. "She had an odd sort of mother superiorness with me," recalled Slim Keith. "She would say, 'Nancy, I'm not going to let you do that, not unless you have someone to go with you.' She was all filled up with prim advice."

She gave her friends beautiful gifts. "KK" Auchincloss kept a small primitive watercolor from Babe on a table in the living room of her home in Maine, and Jeanne Vanderbilt proudly displayed two bibelots: a bronze and gilt sculpture of a blackamoor under a palm tree, and a porcelain cat. Babe handed down many of her beautiful clothes to Marion Osborn.

When Susan Mary Alsop and her husband, Joseph, were divorcing, Babe called her at once. "How are your finances?" Babe wanted to know. Susan Mary assured her they were fine, but Babe replied, "I don't believe you are well off. If you ever need money, you know where to come."

Babe's "laughing men" occupied an important place in her life. Because they didn't pursue her sexually, they never threatened Paley, but her relationships with them fulfilled a special need. Because they were men, they could compliment her and attend to her in a way that women could not. Nor did she feel the glimmer of competition that occasionally intruded on her friendships with glamorous women such as Gloria Guinness. She felt safest with these men—especially Capote, who babied her, idolized her, and in his odd way, wanted to *be* Babe Paley.

Babe was fundamentally old-fashioned: private, circumspect, and proper. "She rarely complained. She rarely said anything about what she was feeling," said Horace Kelland. "But I always knew when she was unhappy. She would ask you to go out driving with her in a car, and you knew she wanted to do it for a reason. She would be quiet or just not want to talk." A conversation about the intimacies of her marriage, said Slim Keith, "would not have occurred between us—about how active her sex life was. I never would have asked her about it. She never would have asked me. It wasn't part of our friendship."

Yet Babe told Truman Capote everything. He was the magician of gossip. He would disclose deeply revealing facts about himself—many of them, it turned out, untrue—in order to elicit the secrets of others. Babe naively trusted him. Capote knew all about the sterility of her marriage. She told him that she and Bill Paley stopped having sexual relations in the early 1950s. "It was since the birth of the last child, Kate," recalled another male friend in whom she would confide later in her life.

How did she cope with all those years of sexual rejection? During the sixties, there were wispy rumors of one or two fleeting affairs. Capote said Babe had a romance for several months with an American ambassador to an Eastern European country. Other friends talked about a time during the sixties when Babe seemed smitten with Jean Lambert, of the European banking family. He was good-looking but, surprisingly, rather humorless. "With him it was more a question of mutual interests than anything else," said Horace Kelland.

Babe even thought briefly of leaving Paley for Lambert. While she was weighing what to do, she called an old friend, a single man, and asked him to accompany her on a ten-day trip to France. "During the ten days she never mentioned Bill Paley once," the friend recalled. "Clearly to me she was a friend having a problem. But she asked only one leading question: 'How much do you have a year?' She said, 'Could I live on that much?' She was thinking that if she divorced Bill, how much she would need. Bill Paley never forgave me for that trip. I'm sure he thinks she poured it out to me. But she only wanted to be with someone comfortable.'' In the end, Babe was too dominated by and too dependent on Paley to go through with a messy divorce.

By nearly all accounts she remained otherwise faithful—more out of fear than anything else. Paley was, after all, fiercely possessive. "If he had known she seriously looked at another man, he would have acted like a Mafia don," said one of Paley's close friends. "I would not think she got in very deep," said Irene Selznick. "It was too risky. Bill was too clever, too threatening. She was a very bright woman with good instincts."

Many of Babe's friends believed that her sexual isolation from Paley never particularly bothered her—that she slipped quite easily into celibacy. Even as a young girl she had remained somewhat aloof from the men who pursued her. Partly this was a residue of Gogs Cushing, whose life with a self-absorbed husband led her to instill a suspicion of men in all her daughters. Carter Burden, who became close to Bill but not Babe, said Babe "had trouble with men. She viewed them as oppressors and villains."

That view seems extreme, but whatever the reason, Babe was not especially flirtatious; there was never even a hint of sexual advance. *Time* magazine once said she had a "coolly amiable glance that makes men instinctively straighten their ties." "She wasn't a woman who burned with lust," said Leonora Hornblow. "There wasn't honey in the honeycomb. She wasn't predatory."

Other friends went farther and concluded she was asexual. "I don't believe she minded the infidelity because she didn't like sex that much," said one woman friend from England. "She would have minded more if she had liked sex. It let her off the hook." Kelland felt she was "disinterested up to a point. Every woman, especially a beautiful woman, loves to be loved and admired. She was that. But she didn't look for a bedfellow. She was searching for affection and admiration."

Still, being spurned by her husband had to have hurt her pride. "It was very tough on her because he wasn't interested in her in that way anymore," said one close friend. "It wasn't that she denied him. He just lost interest. It must have been wounding." Her self-image seemed to suffer as a result. "She was so chic and so stylish and so beautiful," said a friend. "But she felt she did not attract men."

To Paley, Babe's friends were a relief. They diverted her, kept her at a distance, and afforded him the freedom to chase women. Jack Baragwanath, who often served as Paley's decoy—feigning a date with a woman Paley was after—once told his longtime friend Alice-Leone Moats that "Bill was never faithful to Babe for one single, solitary day."

Paley was as lusty and indefatigable as Babe was cool and proper. His conquests were on the order of models and starlets, even shopgirls in expensive stores. On visits to Hollywood, said Michael Dann, "Paley was fucking around, but he was discreet." His women tended, according to one friend, to be "sexy but tarty-looking." Brains were certainly not a prerequisite.

From time to time a famous name would surface. There were rumors in the sixties that Paley had an affair with Marilyn Monroe. Babe even braced him about it, threatening to pull out of a planned trip to Hollywood because it would involve attending a party with Monroe. Paley was able to convince his wife that he had never had anything to do with the famous star. Babe accompanied him to the coast after all, but they stayed away from the party. The link with Monroe was an instance where Paley's legend as a Lothario ran ahead of reality.

The truth, of course, could be found in his anonymous liaisons. Even when he lingered for more than a quick dalliance, Paley was not about to set up a woman and keep her in style. He lacked the generosity, and he never wished to create a serious rival to Babe. That may have given her comfort. And for him, along with the best art and the best clothing and the best network, he owned the best woman, one who was devoted to him. "It was the mores of a court," said one close Paley observer. "If the King goes to bed with an actress, the Queen doesn't bother about it."

Perhaps it was the memory of Johanna Stoddard, the woman who created a scandal for Paley by leaping to her death in 1940, that made him careful about his infidelities. Although he flirted openly and cadged phone numbers from girls at parties, he otherwise kept fairly quiet—except to Capote and a few others—about his assignations.

Still, *Babe* knew what he was up to, and at times he simply could not control his predatory impulses even in her presence. Once when Bill and Babe were in London, Kelland invited them to lunch at his flat in Eaton Square. "I thought, 'Bill loves pretty girls,' so I asked the prettiest girl in London, Camilla Mavroleon," recalled Kelland. "Babe was furious because Bill was so attentive to Camilla. He called Camilla [who was married] for weeks afterward trying to make a date. As usual he was very persistent. Babe was cross as two sticks at me."

Paley's pursuits had misogynist overtones. Said one friend, "He was not a woman-lover; he was a womanizer." His were not affairs of the heart. Whether he was motivated more by sex or ego is hard to tell, but there is no doubt that he had a teenager's enthusiasm. Twenty years after the fact, he would boast to a girlfriend about a particularly thrilling assignation he supposedly had in the sixties. Standing at the counter in Cartier's on Fifth Avenue one day, he noticed a beautiful woman nearby. When

Paley returned to his office, the salesman from Cartier called. "There was a woman standing next to you," said the salesman. "She would like to give you her telephone number." Paley took it and called her immediately. She refused to give him her name, but told him to come to her room at the Plaza Hotel. "If you will never try to reach me again, I will spend the afternoon with you," she said. Paley agreed and hurried to the Plaza. Recounting the tale to his 1980s girlfriend, Paley said the afternoon was "wonderful, a total fantasy, she was gorgeous."

By the 1960s both of Paley's parents were in their eighties. He remained respectful, but from them too he was distant. Goldie and Sam rarely visited Kiluna, but Bill and Babe would see them several times a year in Florida. Goldie once recalled, however, that her son would not stay with them; he preferred hotels. "We want independence," Goldie explained it away. "We all feel that way."

At CBS board meetings, Sam was deferential toward his powerhouse son, seldom speaking up and never taking a strong position. "There were times when I know Sam felt he was neglected and he thought Goldie was neglected," said one board member. "But parents often see it one way and children another. In board luncheons and everything else, Bill was solicitous toward his father."

Sam had suffered his first heart attack in 1958, which left him weakened. In March 1963 his heart failed, and he died at the age of eighty-seven. Goldie, according to her grandson Robert Levy, "never missed a beat. She was out with people, very active. She moved to a smaller house and did it all over." Sam left an estate of $20.6 million after taxes. He gave nearly $12 million to Goldie, $500,000 to his sister Sophie and her children, and $100,000 to various household employees. Bill and Blanche Paley each got $2.4 million in trust. Bill's trust fund was earmarked for his four children, but he retained control. The William Paley Foundation received $1.3 million worth of CBS stock, and another $1.3 million in CBS stock went to the Samuel Paley Foundation—also controlled by Bill Paley.

Paley immediately set out to use nearly $1 million of Sam's money to carve out an elegant Manhattan oasis of trees and waterfalls on East 53rd Street. Nicknamed a "vest-pocket park," it was dedicated to Samuel Paley's memory; indeed, it was originally to be named the "Samuel Paley Plaza." But by opening day in 1967, Sam's name had disappeared and William Paley was calling it simply "Paley Park."

For a time, the park was a limited but intense obsession. Paley fretted about the foodstand, changing hot dog brands no less than three times. He made frequent inspections to taste the coffee, hot dogs, and danish pastries, and to poke around the greenery. One of Paley's "prize possessions," according to his public relations man, Kidder Meade, was a bound volume containing five thousand names of people who signed a roster during the first few months the park was open, "thanking him for making the place available." Paley received congratulations for his contribution to the city, culminating in the chairmanship of Mayor John Lindsay's Task Force on Urban Design.

Paley suffered a severe blow when David Selznick had a fatal heart attack in June 1965 at age sixty-three. He heard the news on the radio in the early evening as he was dressing for dinner, and he wept unabashedly. Selznick, his dearest friend, had deliberately concealed his heart condition from Paley since its diagnosis a year earlier. Selznick was afraid that his hypochondriacal friend would worry constantly and that their relationship would be forever altered. He may have been right, but his secretiveness only heightened the shock when Paley lost his irrepressible pal so suddenly.

After Paley had regained his composure, he called Irene Selznick. "Are you all right?" he asked. She assured him she was fine, but he insisted on taking her to a party at "21" that evening. "For Chrissake, you're not going to stay in your apartment alone," he said. "Babe and I will pick you up." As an afterthought he said, "Jeezus, a heart attack, can you believe it?" "The secret is out. He had heart trouble," replied Irene, who along with their son Danny had monitored Selznick's condition and consulted cardiologists. Paley's tone changed immediately. "Don't you dare tell me he had heart trouble," Paley growled. "I was his best friend, and if I say he didn't have heart trouble, he didn't." When Irene insisted, Paley nearly shouted, "Why do you have to have it your way?" "It's not my way," replied Irene. "Let's not discuss it. You can have it any way you want."

When the Paleys picked up Irene, she sat in the backseat with Babe and Paley sat beside the chauffeur. As they pulled up to "21," Paley whipped around and said, "I called Connie Guion [Babe's doctor] and asked her whether David had heart trouble and she said no. I hope that satisfies you." Irene said nothing. She knew Paley well enough to recognize that he would insist on his version of events because it fit with his notion of his friendship with Selznick. She was not prepared, however, for Paley's subsequent behavior. At dinner, Paley, who was seated next to Irene, did not turn to speak with her once. "It took an awful lot to get through that evening," said Irene. "He should have had his face roundly slapped."

In the following days, Paley refused to back down although, commented Irene, "of course he knew the truth." The closest he came was to dispatch Jock Whitney twice to ask Irene if she was "sore." Under great pressure, Paley wrote a touching eulogy that Cary Grant read at Selznick's funeral. "I didn't think he could string six words together," said Irene. "Bill was as astonished as anyone."

It was not until a year later that Paley redeemed himself in Irene's eyes. She was at Kiluna for the christening of Amanda and Carter Burden's first child. It was sunset on a Sunday afternoon, and Paley pulled Irene aside. "I can't stand it," he said in a choked voice. "Sunday sunset. I think of David." Paley began to weep. "I loved him so," he said as tears poured down his cheeks. "Oh God, how I loved David! I didn't cry when my own father died, but how I cried for David. You know what's so awful? My conscience bothers me. The last time David came to Kiluna, I didn't know he had heart trouble, and I put him on the third floor. If I thought he never again would spend the night here, I would have made him more comfortable. I grieve over it."

Irene remembered the spring weekend well, and she told Paley that before Selznick went, he had called her to say, "If Bill Paley finds out about my heart, I never want to see him again as long as I live." When David arrived at Kiluna, Irene got yet another call, this one distinctly surreptitious. "Bill has put me on the third floor. What shall I do? I can't make it," he said. Irene advised him only to go upstairs once, at bedtime, and only to spend one night. She told him how to climb the stairs to avoid strain. Afterwards, Selznick boasted to Irene that he had avoided detection.

Now as the great Bill Paley wept, Irene comforted him, putting aside his callous treatment of her on the day of David's death. "You never guessed David's secret," she said. "You gave him proof that he had fooled you. You couldn't have given him a nicer present." With that, Paley's guilt lifted.

With mortality—and his legacy—at the back of his mind, Paley not only threw himself into CBS, he grew more involved at the Museum of Modern Art, where he had served as a trustee since 1937. Following his $5 million donation to the museum's fund-raising drive, Paley was elected president of MOMA in January 1968. Although it was a voluntary position, he had the powers of a chief executive. The prestige of his association with the Modern counted a great deal to Paley, who despite his lofty status still craved respectability.

Unlike his pro bono work during the war and for the Truman administration, Paley now held a volunteer job of considerable visibility. He had, after all, designated the Modern to receive at least part of his art collection upon his death. Once in a position of authority he was unable to contain the autocratic approach he used at CBS. Even in the genteel precincts of the Modern, Paley was inescapably Paley.

In May 1969, Paley convened a meeting with a group of past presidents and chairmen of the museum board, including David, Blanchette

(John D. III's wife), and Nelson Rockefeller, as well as William Burden, who also served on the CBS board. On a number of occasions Paley had run afoul of the museum's director, Bates Lowry, who had been appointed shortly before Paley assumed the presidency. Among other perceived faults, Lowry had ignored recommendations on fund-raising from Walter Thayer, Paley's friend and the museum's newest trustee. At the meeting Paley argued that Lowry was a poor administrator, and the small coterie of influential trustees agreed that he had to go. It fell to Paley to do his own dirty work and fire Lowry, a task that he would have delegated to a trigger man at CBS.

Backed by the power elite, Paley proceeded without consulting the full museum board. "It was typical of Bill to get on with it," noted Frank Stanton. "It had to be done, so he said, 'Let's do it.' " When Ralph Colin, who was also a MOMA board member, got wind of Lowry's dismissal, he was furious. Colin was a stickler for procedure, and at a subsequent meeting of the museum board he boldly reprimanded Paley for flouting the rules. Other board members, notably John de Menil, board chairman of the oil engineering and electronics firm of Schlumberger, Ltd., and a prominent patron of the arts, agreed that Paley had acted abruptly, but no one was as vociferous as Colin. Paley felt the sting of disapproval in the press as well. "Has MOMA gone network?" cracked one museum official to the *New York Times*. It was the first time the tough side of Bill Paley had showed itself outside CBS, and there were no paid minions around to protect the chief.

Behind the pointed disagreement between Colin and Paley was an undercurrent of resentment on both sides. A meticulous scholar who studied and documented his own extensive collection of Impressionist art, Colin never felt Paley was sufficiently knowledgeable about either the Modern museum or his own collection. One source of Colin's impatience was Paley's tendency to use Arthur Tourtellot, his speechwriter, as a proxy in museum business. Colin also resented what he regarded as social snubs from Paley that dated back to his exclusion from Paley's wedding to Babe in 1947. Especially annoying was a reception at an art gallery when Paley forgot the name of Colin's wife, Georgia, a Manhattan interior decorator. For his part, Paley began to see Colin as a "prima donna." The CBS chairman was irritated by Colin's habitual criticism, which seemed to sharpen over the years. "Ralph had an obnoxious personality," said Kidder Meade. "He was always whining and complaining."

After Colin's public rebuke at the museum board meeting, Paley's patience ran out. He summoned his adviser of more than forty years to his office at CBS. It was time, Paley said, to end their professional relationship. Paley told Colin he was going to hire another personal attorney and would brook no further discussion. Taking his cue, Stanton subsequently replaced Colin's firm as lead counsel with Cravath, Swaine & Moore, the class of the field. Some months later, Paley agreed to meet with Colin again. Colin told him he was upset that their friendship had suffered. To which Paley was said to have replied, "Ralph, you were never my friend. You were my lawyer."

Paley has denied saying that. Colin just as emphatically has insisted that his account is true. Those who knew both men well throw the weight of truth toward Colin. "It is conceivable to me that Bill Paley would fly off the handle and say, 'You weren't my friend,' said Kidder Meade. "Colin could get anyone on edge." Still, added Meade, Colin was "heartbroken and distraught when Bill dumped him."

Paley might have anticipated Colin's bitterness. What the CBS chairman did not predict, however, was Colin's vindictiveness. No one—not Klauber nor Kesten nor Dorothy nor Murrow nor Stanton—had turned on Paley as directly and vehemently as Colin did. For years afterwards, Colin recounted the story of the museum blowup to anyone who would listen. And those nine words, "You were never my friend. You were my lawyer," took on a life of their own. They became a symbol of Paley's brutality even to those who had served him long and well.

45

ALWAYS ACQUISITIVE in his personal life, Paley went on a corporate shopping spree in the late 1960s. "Bill would go away and sit on the stern of Gianni Agnelli's yacht," said Jack Schneider. "He would hear Agnelli talk about buying things. And Paley wasn't buying anything. So we got phone calls, or when he came back for a board meeting, he would say. 'What can we buy?' Then we would spend ninety days chasing down acquisitions before we could do business again. All because he wanted to be a player."

Trouble was, Paley was a little like Babe stopping in at Freddie Victoria on her rounds of favorite antique shops. He accumulated corporate knickknacks and window-shopped with avidity, but he shrank from the main chance. To Wall Street analysts, he seemed a man incapable of advancing beyond small-time deals. In 1965, *Forbes* quoted critics who called CBS "overly cautious" and wondered whether Paley and Stanton "deep down didn't have the hunger." Paley had been offered some good opportunities to take the plunge into a big-time communications company, but he still seemed haunted by the $50 million loss on Hytron, CBS's doomed foray into television set manufacturing in the early 1950s. Now his instinctive caution was showing through his bold public image. He needed to prove himself with a big and impressive move.

At $280 million, CBS's purchase in April 1967 of Holt, Rinehart & Winston, Inc., was certainly big enough—the highest price to date paid for a public company ($1.09 billion in 1990 dollars, which seems puny compared to $25 billion for RJR Nabisco). The Holt deal came to Paley through a contact on Wall Street, and he fastened onto the book-publishing company with a fervor that was absent when Stanton had urged him first to buy publishing house Houghton Mifflin and then Random House only months earlier. Paley had talked to Random House chief Bennett Cerf, an old friend, on several occasions, but in the end, CBS had lost out to RCA as Paley dithered.

Holt, Rinehart was a first-class organization, right in line with Paley's quality profile. The company was a leading publisher of textbooks, although its fiction and non-fiction lists had withered. The perception lingered on Wall Street that Paley had paid too much—thirty-eight times earnings. Whether or not Paley overpaid, it is clear that CBS had fallen into the old trap of judging a company on past performance rather than on future potential.

"Bill Paley enjoyed doing his deals too much," said David Hertz. "He was outwitted most of the time because he didn't want to lose. You have to be able to walk away, and once he decided he wanted something, Bill Paley didn't want to walk away. You would say, 'You are paying too much,' and he would say, 'No, this is a very valuable business. We will make it up in the profit stream.' "

Paley's other major move to diversify in 1967 seemed to have greater possibilities, but it was riddled with unforeseeable problems. It began in 1966 when Paley proposed that CBS produce feature films. In the earliest days of television, when CBS was starved for new material, Paley had talked to Selznick and others about buying the rights to air movies on CBS after they had appeared in theaters. But he had never taken the plunge, except for one deal that went sour in 1950 and prompted the seller, in-law Ike Levy, to resign from the CBS board and sell his CBS stock.

After that, Paley had shied away from films on CBS. In part, he believed that movies on television were "uncreative." Television, he said, should offer only home-grown programs. Paley also resisted following the lead of Sarnoff's NBC, which had taken to showing feature films out of desperation. As late as 1963, when Aubrey arranged to pay Paramount $40 million for some two hundred films from its library—a virtual steal—Paley vetoed the deal.

Only when Aubrey's schedule fell apart in the fall of 1964—and when NBC's movies caught on with audiences—did Paley finally agree to buy the rights to one hundred films from various studios for roughly $30 million. At that point he began to worry that the supply of feature films would run short, and the price would skyrocket. Paley assumed that if CBS made films for showing in theaters they could automatically be presented later on the CBS network, neglecting to consider that the actors, directors, and producers of such films would demand that NBC and ABC bid for them as well to ensure the highest possible price.

Paley was indulging in a fantasy that had its roots in 1929, when Adolph Zukor offered him a job as his assistant at Paramount. Paley had been friends with Hollywood moguls and producers since the thirties. "He always figured if they could do it, he could do it better," said Jack Schneider. "He thought he was Mr. Showbiz."

Paley was further emboldened by CBS's success over the previous decade as a producer of Broadway shows. In 1955, Goddard Lieberson had convinced Paley to pay $360,000 for a 40 percent ownership in the musical *My Fair Lady*. The show became one of the biggest hits on Broadway, earning CBS more than $33 million. In subsequent years CBS put money into more than forty shows—with an eye primarily toward securing the rights to make original cast albums. CBS made a profit on about 25 percent of the shows it invested in, including such hits as *Camelot, Mame, Cabaret,* and *Bye Bye Birdie,* whereas on average only 10 to 12 percent of shows that open on Broadway are profitable. (Paley turned down *Fiddler on the Roof* as "too Jewish.")

Paley credited Lieberson that CBS had scored so well on Broadway, so he felt strongly the CBS Records chief should lead the company's move into producing films for theatrical release as well. But Lieberson was highly skeptical of Paley's scheme, as was Stanton. They told Paley that CBS would fail unless it was willing to become a major studio. Paley, the master of trying to have it both ways, insisted that CBS could successfully operate on a smaller scale. "Goddard," recalled Stanton, "was too crafty to get involved in that."

Toward the end of 1966, Paley got exasperated with the nay-saying of Lieberson and Stanton. On a Saturday afternoon he called Jack Schneider, CBS's group vice-president for broadcasting. "I want to be in the feature film business," Paley said. "We ought to be there. Get us in." Recalled Schneider, "That was the charter. There was no business plan at all."

On Schneider's recommendation, CBS paid $9.5 million in February 1967 for the Republic Corp.'s seventy-acre film studio in North Hollywood. Out of that investment grew Cinema Center Films, a motion picture enterprise dedicated to producing about ten films a year for some $3.5 million per film.

Paley's pride in the new division was evident when he convened a dinner at Chasen's in Los Angeles for CBS executives. To Paley's right was the wife of Gordon Stulberg, newly appointed president of Cinema Center Films, and Stulberg was seated next to Babe. But despite his enthusiasm, Paley did not get personally involved in the film business as he did in TV programming. He never read a script or picked a film. Movie making for the big screen was an unknown quantity to him; he felt more comfortable leaving it to others.

Every six to eight weeks Stulberg would brief the chairman in New York. Paley asked questions as he did in TV programming meetings, but he was much more tentative. "He reacted in a curious sort of way," Stanton recalled. "He was never quite clear whether he was for or against something. In broadcasting you could at least figure out what he wanted, but nobody was ever sure what he wanted in movies."

One dilemma was how different Cinema Center Films should be from television programming. The first CBS film, *With Six You Get Eggroll*, starring Doris Day, convinced the Hollywood community that CBS only cared about making fluffy films that would one day end up on television. To counteract that perception, Stulberg proposed filming *The Boys in the Band*, a controversial Broadway play about homosexuals. "What better way to get their attention in Hollywood than to have a movie that began, 'Who do you have to fuck around here to get a drink?' " recalled Jack Schneider. Although Paley initially balked at the choice, he finally consented on the grounds, said Stulberg, that CBS had to "set up a distinct CBS motion picture personality."

Over the next several years, CBS made a creditable string of films, including *The Reivers*, starring Steve McQueen; *A Man Called Horse*, with Richard Harris; and *April Fools*, with Jack Lemmon and Catherine Deneuve. Its biggest artistic success was *Little Big Man*, Arthur Penn's film starring Dustin Hoffman. But because the film went way over budget at $9 million, it was not a commercial success.

Stulberg never heard anything, yea or nay, from Paley either about how the films were made or sold. "That was how he set it up," said Stulberg. "He was sensitive about asserting his control." Only once did a faint criticism drift back: when Paley showed his friends at Kiluna a CBS film called *Royal Hunt of the Sun*, based on the Pulitzer Prize–winning play by Peter Shaffer, half of the guests fell asleep. Judging by the film's sorry performance at the box office, most moviegoers had a good snooze, too.

Paley knew that CBS was not being taken seriously by the powerful theater owners, a failing that could prove disastrous. Unlike a studio, which had its own marketing and distribution business, CBS had to rely on outsiders to sell its movies.

Paley involved himself only briefly in the search for a distributor. Charles Bluhdorn, chairman of Gulf & Western and owner of Paramount, was interested. Schneider and Stulberg set up a meeting in Paley's office. The round-faced Bluhdorn came on with typical exuberance. He threw his arm around Paley's shoulder, and the CBS chairman visibly winced at the premature familiarity. "We have to get together more and soon," said Bluhdorn. "I'll have my wife call your wife and set up a dinner." Paley looked stunned and said, "Yes, you do that." He was polite, but, said Stulberg, "it was the shortest meeting on record." Afterwards Paley said nothing. "It was clear what he thought," said Schneider. "Revulsion." Which was too bad, because having Paramount distribute CBS's movies might have given them a crucial boost.

As the losses mounted, Paley grew irritated. "We didn't distribute or exploit our movies well," conceded Schneider. "Paley would say, 'Why isn't it going better?' The division was losing money. From the beginning it was almost assured to fail without a major distributor, but he never shared any responsibility for its failure." Just as with Hytron, Paley lacked the boldness that could have brought success.

In mid-1970, Paley shifted overall responsibility for CBS films from Schneider to Lieberson—who was none too pleased. Eighteen months later, Stulberg left, and Paley decided to shut down Cinema Center Films. Out of twenty-seven films, CBS had lost money on twenty—a total loss of some $30 million. Nor had CBS's films done much for the CBS network. Beginning in the mid-sixties, first NBC and then ABC had successfully developed movies made expressly for television; when those "telefilms" became top ten hits, CBS followed suit. "Cinema Center was disposed of with the concurrence of the board," said Courtney Brown, a CBS director at the time. "We began to feel that Bill didn't know much about making money outside broadcasting."

By that time, Holt, Rinehart was proving less profitable than CBS anticipated, and the investment in the Yankees had gone completely sour. In 1966 the once-dominant team had dropped to last place; it finished fifth the next two years. Only in 1969, when the Yankees climbed to second, did the team make a profit. In 1973, CBS finally sold the ball club to a group headed by George Steinbrenner for $10 million.

Paley would later insist that tax deductions enabled CBS to make an overall profit of $5.4 million on the Yankees. Michael Burke, the team's president, said that even with the write-offs, it was at best a wash for CBS. "Bill Paley was determined not to have it look like a bad deal," said Burke. But $10 million was less than the $13.2 million CBS paid nine years earlier, and sportswriters and their readers didn't sit around calculating tax write-offs. Combined with the mediocre performance of the Yankees during those years, the investment was a public embarrassment. In the business community, it symbolized CBS's inability to diversify.

While CBS was frittering away its mountain of cash from broadcasting, companies like Gulf & Western and Transamerica were growing smartly through shrewd acquisitions. Throughout this period Stanton gave wide berth to CBS's investments. Diversification was Paley's sandbox, and Stanton decided to let him play in it alone. Rather conspicuously, Stanton avoided getting involved in CBS's movie-making venture. Only one effort at diversification caught Stanton's attention—a costly mistake that further alienated Paley and dredged up his bad memories of Hytron and the color television debacle.

Once again, Peter Goldmark played the maverick inventor, with Stanton his stalwart champion. Tinkering in his labs at CBS, Goldmark came up in 1960 with a new device using miniaturized film to play pre-recorded black and white films on a television set—a revolutionary notion that was years ahead of its time. That fall in a budget meeting Goldmark asked for $75,000 to develop the device. Paley looked up from his doodling at the end of the boardroom table and asked for Stanton's opinion. Knowing that CBS might eventually diversify into the educational field, Stanton noted that the device could be used for education. But when Goldmark pointed out its possible application in the home, he detected Paley's instant disapproval. The chairman dropped his pencil and simply said no. "His tone," recalled Goldmark, "was edged with so much finality that everybody present became suddenly still."

Despite Paley's fear that the device, called Electronic Video Recording or EVR, posed a threat to network broadcasting, Goldmark found seed money from the U.S. military to develop a prototype. The Monsanto chemical company offered to fund the machine's development and pay a royalty to CBS. In the spring of 1964, Paley once again vetoed the idea of home use, but Stanton encouraged Goldmark to explore educational applications.

When Goldmark showed Paley a prototype the following year, the chairman's enthusiasm flickered briefly. "Marvelous," he proclaimed. "I want the best man on it." On that basis, Goldmark brought in IBM to manufacture the EVR players and sell the cassettes that would be made by CBS. Then, without warning, Paley scotched the project in the summer of 1965. Executives at IBM, said Goldmark, thought CBS "erratic" as a result. They had obviously never before encountered the 540-Degree Club.

Several months later the *New York Times* published a front-page story about EVR, and a consortium of European investors with interests in publishing and electronics offered to pay the development costs, with CBS receiving 20 percent of the profits. Upon hearing of the proposed arrangement, Paley shifted gears again. "EVR must be good," said Paley. "Why should we be just a minority partner?"

Even Goldmark was flummoxed. He tried to persuade Paley that CBS was protecting itself from risk by taking such a small position. But Paley was "smelling profit for the first time." Goldmark said that to take a larger role, CBS would have to put up significantly more money and show considerable patience. "Bill, Peter may have a point," Stanton said gently. But Paley was adamant. He insisted that CBS take 50 percent.

Through a series of mistakes made by CBS negotiators, several key partners dropped out. Even worse, Paley's guidelines for marketing the machine placed CBS in a Catch-22. To avoid even the hint of competing with television, Paley wouldn't let CBS put any money into software for the machine. But without films or other programs to watch, consumers were not interested. A year after the EVR was unveiled in 1968, technical problems held back its production at the manufacturing plants. Moreover, videocassettes and videodiscs were on the horizon, threatening obsolescence for the EVR. In 1970, CBS lost $14 million on the venture, and Paley, recalled Goldmark, was "hopping mad." Two years later Paley shuttered the EVR operation.

Frank Stanton may have been too taken with what he would later call "an ingenious invention," essentially a transitional technology en route to the enormous business in videotape cassette recorder/players that the Japanese would build in the 1980s. An understandably embittered Peter Goldmark contended that "EVR was on the brink of spawning a new series of industries, but Paley fought it, almost as though possessed of a death wish. Instead of opening a new world, Paley closed it."

Paley's obstructions and vacillations may have inadvertently limited CBS's losses, although one could argue that had he been willing to make a big enough commitment, CBS might have adapted to videotape and moved to the forefront of the home video boom. But Paley shied from the risk. "Bill Paley didn't have the guts to spend the money to really make an investment in technology," said David Hertz. In the end, Paley blamed both Goldmark and Stanton for the EVR episode.

By the early 1970s, Stanton was concerned about CBS's tarnished image on Wall Street. He took aside Ray Klemmer, CBS's man of the moment in charge of acquisitions, and asked: "How are we going to keep the chairman from buying more companies?" Stanton instructed Klemmer to put the brakes on Paley, to steer him toward thinking about long-term planning.

"I was on my way out," recalled Stanton, "but I was concerned that Bill was just interested in buying companies helter-skelter. It got very frustrating for me, so I wanted him to think about the direction of the company—and if he was going to acquire a company, how to stay with it, which he never did because it wasn't his style. He would just let it drift away from him."

46

FROM THE MOMENT Bill Paley reneged on his promise to make Frank Stanton CEO, the two men's co-existence was strained. Stanton continued to do his job conscientiously, running much of the company and providing counsel when Paley asked. But those who knew him saw a change. Paley's betrayal had broken his spirit—at least as far as CBS was concerned. He had learned that in Paley's world, even the president of CBS was a hired hand. He coasted toward retirement, hiding his bitterness from all but a few. "In the evening, Frank would sit in my office and pour out his frustration," recalled one former top CBS man. "He would come out of meetings and his face would be red and splotchy. He would say, 'You wouldn't believe what he did to me today.' "

In February 1967, after more than a year of negotiations—amid repeated rumors that he might leave CBS—Stanton signed a new contract, designating him a senior executive of CBS until 1971, two years shy of his sixty-fifth birthday. After that, CBS would employ him as a consultant until 1987. His salary jumped in 1967 from $150,000 to $200,000—as did Paley's. Bonuses to Paley and Stanton were identical that year, as usual: $160,000. Only in their CBS dividend income was an imbalance evident. Paley received $2.5 million to Stanton's $455,000.

In the years that followed, Stanton would experience one final spurt of hope that he might, if only for a few years, run CBS as his own. At Stanton's suggestion in February 1969, Paley brought Jack Schneider up to the thirty-fifth floor to serve as CBS's executive vice-president, with an eye toward his assuming the presidency when Stanton retired. As part of the reorganization, Paley again toyed with the possibility of naming Stanton as chief executive. But once more Paley was unable to relinquish the title.

One reason Paley had briefly reconsidered elevating Stanton was his own hope, following Richard Nixon's election in November 1968, that he would finally be rewarded by the Republican party with an appointment as ambassador to the Court of St. James's. "It would have been the ulti-mate ratification," said Jack Schneider. "It would have evened him up with Jock Whitney."

Paley felt he had been "generous" in giving $25,000 to Nixon for his unsuccessful run in 1960. But he had made no contributions after that because he felt that television had become too closely tied to the political process. Still, Paley remained active behind the scenes in Republican poli-tics. In 1962, Paley was among a group of Republicans who met with Nixon and urged him not to make the run for governor of California that he ultimately lost, prompting the notorious "You won't have Nixon to kick around anymore" speech. In 1967, Paley helped found the Ripon Society, a maneuver that identified him more closely with the moderate Eastern forces represented by Nelson Rockefeller than with Nixon's more conservative California cadre.

Early in the 1968 campaign, Nixon aide Ray Price brought Nixon, Paley, Whitney, and Thayer together for a lunch to "get reacquainted." Not surprisingly, at the Republican Convention in Miami that year, Pal-ey's loyalties remained with Rockefeller. In a penthouse suite at the Eden Roc Hotel, Paley, Whitney, and Thayer watched the proceedings non-stop on three televisions and drank bottles of Château Lafite. Paley changed channels with a clicker monogrammed in gold and grumbled about Nixon's triumph over Rockefeller.

After Nixon was elected, Paley nevertheless felt that his many years of loyal Republican service put him in good position for a patronage prize. It was testimony to how little he understood Nixon or politics. Or perhaps it was something more basic: for a lifetime he had demanded loyalty from others without ever grasping that it might one day be demanded of him. Toward the end of 1968, he dispatched Walter Thayer to advance the Paley cause to Peter Flanigan, who was fielding ambassadorial appointments. Flanigan's father, Hap, a New York banker, had been close to Paley in the Eisenhower days. In January 1969, Nixon did what any president would do—he gave the plum London posting to an unwavering friend, sup-porter, and contributor, in this case Walter Annenberg, owner of *TV Guide* and *The Racing Form*.

Paley was doubly defeated because he felt himself superior to rough-diamond Annenberg. "He was so galled," recalled a former CBS execu-tive. "He would have been psychologically willing to accept that he didn't get it because he was Jewish. But then that damned Annenberg got it—and he was Jewish." Recalled Flanigan, "There were a number of people who were disappointed when Bill Paley didn't get it."

Annenberg's arrival in London that April provoked widespread resentment among the British. Many thought him unqualified, and newspaper reports ridiculed his stiff pronouncements and lavish lifestyle. There was talk, toward the end of the summer, that perhaps Annenberg should be quietly replaced.

For a moment, London again seemed within reach. Frank Stanton was attending an affiliate advisory board meeting in Hawaii when he got a call from Arthur Tourtellot, Paley's speechwriter and adviser. "Bill has been offered the Court of St. James's," Tourtellot said. "You have to come back for the announcement, because you will be taking the CEO spot." Lest he unduly alarm the participants at the meeting, Stanton took care not to leave abruptly. By the time he returned to New York, recalled Stanton, "it had all gone away."

As Nixon was considering Paley for the London post, the Nixon White House declared war on the networks over their critical coverage of the war in Vietnam. In mid-October 1969, Jeb Stuart Magruder, a White House aide, wrote a memo outlining a broad campaign to use the FCC as well as the IRS and the Justice Department to intimidate CBS, NBC, and ABC. Several weeks later FCC chairman Dean Burch took the unusual step of calling Frank Stanton to ask for a transcript of CBS commentary following a speech by the president. And in mid-November, Vice-President Spiro Agnew attacked the networks in a speech in Des Moines, Iowa. He noted the enormous power held by television journalists, "a tiny, enclosed fraternity of privileged men elected by no one and enjoying a monopoly sanctioned and licensed by the government."

By that time, Paley had abandoned his earlier effort to identify himself with CBS News. Once again its chief spokesman, Stanton attacked Agnew for trying to bully the networks. Paley said nothing publicly, although, Stanton recalled, "Bill didn't disagree with me. He knew I felt that someone in the industry had to stand up to Agnew."

Paley preferred to avoid the emerging controversies of the Nixon years, and he knew Stanton continued to have current understanding of the policy and power of CBS News—areas where Paley still felt at sea. Stanton gladly took on the problems. News was the one remaining area at CBS where he could derive personal and professional satisfaction, without interference from the boss.

Because of Paley's invisibility, the administration adopted a schizophrenic attitude toward CBS that explains why Nixon would have even contemplated Paley for a prestigious appointment at such a contentious time. "Within the White House everyone thought Bill Paley was a great friend," recalled Herb Klein, then Nixon's communications director. "He was seen as a lord of the industry who kept himself separate. There was no animosity centered on Paley, because everyone felt he wasn't controlling the direction of the news. But everyone in the White House felt CBS was against them. Their anger was aimed at Frank Stanton and Walter Cronkite and Dan Rather [then CBS's White House correspondent]. The general feeling was that CBS was the most anti-administration, the most anti-Nixon of the networks."

For the next two years, Stanton concentrated on CBS News. He shielded CBS News president Richard Salant and his correspondents and anchormen from an array of White House complaints—much as he had done during the presidency of Lyndon Johnson. There was no way he could know that this would lead to further problems with Paley.

In February 1971, CBS aired a documentary called "The Selling of the Pentagon," a hard-hitting exposé of the Defense Department's $30 million propaganda operation. The White House and conservatives in Congress denounced the program as a "hatchet job," prompting a House committee to investigate. In April, the committee issued a subpoena to Frank Stanton for CBS's "outtakes"—film unused in the final program. Stanton refused, charging Congress with attempted censorship.

Throughout the spring, Stanton stood his ground, even as he was called to testify before the House Interstate and Foreign Commerce Committee. Before the session began on June 24, committee chairman Harley O. Staggers, a conservative from West Virginia, asked Stanton into his office. "We can solve this if you let me look at those outtakes," he said.

"No," said Stanton. "Then let's get down and pray," said Staggers, dropping to his knees. Stanton declined to join him, and Staggers's face reddened in embarrassment.

On July 1, Staggers and his commerce committee voted to cite Stanton for contempt of Congress. If the House of Representatives followed its customary procedure and supported the committee's recommendation, Stanton faced prosecution by the Justice Department and conceivably a jail sentence.

Suddenly CBS was the stuff of front-page headlines, and Stanton was the hero—praised in editorials from coast to coast as a staunch defender of the First Amendment. Just as suddenly, Paley entered the fray at CBS, insisting that he be included in strategy sessions. Ever since February, Stanton had been keeping Paley posted through memoranda. But Paley had been busy traveling, a month here and a month there, and he had neither taken a position nor asked to participate in the fight. On June 24, when Stanton testified to the committee for four hours, Paley was no-where to be seen.

Paley's passivity had perfectly suited Stanton and Kidder Meade. Part of the challenge CBS faced was that "The Selling of the Pentagon" had problems. The producer had spliced different sections of an interview together to appear as the answer to one question. Still, it was crucial for CBS to hold the line on editorial freedom. The strategy devised by Meade was to have "one person out front as the symbol, the ideal. Frank stood for the First Amendment. He was a pure person. People couldn't say he was up to hanky-panky or part of the jet set. In getting public opinion organized, we needed a leader."

Such distinctions were lost on Paley, who only saw that Stanton was covering himself in glory. Paley's friends, especially Jock Whitney, began to mock his invisibility. "Jock made jokes at Paley's expense," recalled Meade. "He used to kid Paley about letting Frank Stanton do all the work."

"This doesn't look good," Paley said to Meade in early July. "I feel totally left out. I have devoted my whole life to CBS, and I don't like feeling excluded." Both Stanton and Meade tried to bring Paley into the planning, although their annoyance showed. "So much had gone on that he didn't know," recalled Stanton. "It was embarrassing to stop and ex-plain things." Just to show he was involved, Paley sent out a memo—written mostly by Meade—on July 9 stressing the importance of resistance to congressional pressure as a "matter of duty."

When Paley insisted on playing a more active role, Meade advised him to stay on the sidelines. Without telling either Meade or Stanton, Paley went to Washington to lobby Carl Albert, Speaker of the House. Paley chose an obvious target without realizing that Albert lacked the strength to make a genuine difference. Even worse, Paley had in his back pocket a compromise ready to offer Albert. "Fortunately, Bill didn't know enough and neither did the Speaker," recalled Stanton, who was keeping tabs on Paley's movements through one of Albert's aides, John Brademas (later to be a congressman, and then president of New York University).

Paley's foray to Washington was silly but harmless. CBS mounted an enormous lobbying effort, using managers of its affiliated stations to lean on their congressmen. And Stanton did some effective missionary work of his own on Capitol Hill.

The Sunday before the House was scheduled to vote on July 13, Emanuel Celler, a Democratic congressman from Brooklyn who chaired the Judiciary Committee, called Stanton at home. "I think you are going to get killed," Celler said. "You don't have the votes. The White House and Staggers have gotten to the committee chairmen, and most of them are with Staggers. Find a way to give Harley Staggers something." Stanton replied, "I don't know how you give away a little bit of the First Amendment."

The next day Lawrence O'Brien, then chairman of the Democratic National Committee, called Stanton. "The White House isn't helping you because they are sore at CBS," said O'Brien, echoing what Stanton had heard earlier from House Republican leader Gerald Ford. At O'Brien's urging, Stanton met with Wilbur Mills, the Democratic chairman of the House Ways and Means Committee. In the middle of their meeting in Mills's office, the congressman went to the House floor and postponed the vote for a day. Mills announced that he would not support the contempt citation, and he and Celler worked throughout the day to turn the other committee chairmen around. Staggers, beginning to feel the tide change, railed against what he called undue pressure by CBS on Congress. By a vote of 226 to 181, the House rejected the contempt citation—the first time the legislature contradicted such a recommendation from a committee.

Paley seemed more annoyed than ever after CBS's triumph on Capitol Hill. He grumbled over the editing techniques used in "The Selling of the Pentagon," and he questioned whether CBS's defense of a flawed program was worthwhile. "Frank Stanton made a mistake in taking such a strong position," he told a group of CBS executives. "It gave me a pain in the stomach." Stanton understood why Paley hated seeing his number two in the limelight. But the CBS president felt wounded by Paley's criticism and disillusioned that the chairman was ready to compromise the fundamental principles of journalism.

During the next crisis, Paley jumped to take charge. In October 1972, the CBS Evening News scheduled its first major assessment of the Watergate political scandal. Since the mysterious burglary at Democratic party headquarters four months earlier, newspaper reports, primarily in *The Washington Post,* had uncovered a pattern of improper and illegal acts linked to the White House.

Because of the intricacies of the revelations, CBS decided to devote two unusually long segments on the Cronkite newscast to the story. The first, which took up two thirds of the program, aired on Friday, October 27. Stanton saw it on the 6:30 edition that was fed to some stations around the country. He called Paley to say he should watch the 7:00 edition and anticipate some flak from the White House. Paley, recalled Stanton, seemed "indifferent." Stanton watched a second time and felt pleased by CBS's effort. He went home somewhat surprised that the White House had not called. Paley, however, did call that evening. "He was negative," said Stanton. "He thought it was much too long."

The next morning presidential aide Charles Colson called Stanton, who was out. Colson then dialed Paley and blistered him. Paley had encountered Colson's complaints about "anti-Nixon bias" before, during a meeting with Stanton at CBS in 1970, as well as through periodic phone calls that Paley had largely ignored. Stanton had fielded complaint calls from Colson as well; afterwards, he usually called Herb Klein. "Frank would be puzzled, but he would be mad," recalled Klein. "He would talk about the threats but he didn't feel threatened."

Colson was more exercised than usual in his call to Paley on October 28—only days away from the 1972 presidential election. CBS had reason to be especially sensitive. The previous April, Nixon's Justice Department had filed an anti-trust suit against the networks, and the FCC was debating whether to force each of the networks to sell its complement of five local stations.

"Colson talked to me for a long time," Paley recalled. "He was pretty vicious." Colson later claimed that Paley apologized and assured him that he would look into the second installment, due to be aired on Monday evening. Paley contended that he promised Colson nothing but agreed to check into certain points because some White House complaints had mirrored his own concerns.

The following Monday, Paley convened a meeting with Stanton, Richard Salant, and other top CBS executives. Paley never mentioned the Colson call, but he was extremely agitated. He insisted that the segment had been too long and had violated CBS standards by mingling fact and opinion. Although Stanton remained silent during the entire meeting, which lasted several hours, Paley said his longtime second-in-command agreed with him completely.

Stanton, in fact, disagreed. A decade after the fact he would admit to Salant that he had felt proud of CBS's blending of published material and original research. He agreed with Paley only about the length of the piece. "I didn't share Bill's concern over the Watergate piece," said Stanton. "At the time it didn't seem that important . . . I didn't object because I didn't have an answer. Bill did all the talking. It happened before I left the network. I had other things on my mind."

Salant did his best to defend the program, but Paley conceded nothing. Although Paley did not explicitly refer to the second part, Salant knew the chairman well enough to decipher his message: shorten the segment, or even better, kill it. "Bill Paley is the master of never giving an order, but he could make himself perfectly clear," said Salant. He knew he could not drop the second part. But he saw some merit in Paley's argument that another lengthy piece could short-change the other news of the day. When the meeting concluded, Salant felt confused. He had been mystified by Paley's manner any number of times, but never before had he been so unnerved.

Back at the CBS News offices, Salant postponed the second segment for a day and worked with the evening news producers to shorten it. "They knew I had been on the carpet with Paley," said Salant. "They knew I was troubled when I said, 'I hope I feel this way because I am fair and honest.' " The segment ran at seven minutes instead of the planned fourteen—a superficial summary minus the detail that could have given it muscle.

The next day, Salant received a scalding memo from Paley. The chairman objected to the length of the second part, the "mixture of allegations and facts," and the use of names and photos that "left a strong impression of guilt." The piece, said Paley, was "unworthy of our fine traditions." During a subsequent one-on-one lunch, Paley made his points even more vehemently to Salant.

But it was not until Charles Colson gave a speech in Maine in mid-November accusing CBS of "McCarthyism" that Salant began to suspect that Paley had come under pressure. "My antennae went off," recalled Salant. "Colson's criticism was not so different from Paley's criticism. I was never sure whether Paley did what he did because Colson bullied him or because he was persuaded something was wrong. If I had known Colson was behind it, I wouldn't have touched part two."

Among the rank and file at CBS News, Paley stood accused of buckling to White House pressure and inappropriately meddling in the content of a news program. Virtually everyone below Salant believed that the chairman had explicitly ordered part two to be cut and watered down. Paley hated being portrayed as the overbearing censor, just as he had been shaken by similar confrontations with Murrow, Shirer, and others before and since. "Paley put great store in what history would say about him and what the press said about him," explained Salant. "He wanted to look good in his entertainment instincts and in his support of news."

For years afterwards, Paley found himself denying the accusation of censorship to one reporter after another. On one occasion, he claimed not even to have known a second part was coming—although it had been announced on the air after part one. In 1977 he called the second part a "complete surprise. . . . If I had known about it I don't think I would have done what I did." To further buttress his case, Paley frequently reiterated Stanton's support for his position.

Given Paley's history of sensitivity to editorial commentary, his concerns seemed genuine enough. He was likewise reflecting his innate bias toward those in power—in this case, Nixon and the Republicans. But Paley erred both in his handling of Colson—whom he reassured perhaps too much—and Salant. The impression of censorship was deepened by Salant's rattled demeanor in front of his subordinates. It may be that Stanton would have fared no better than Paley with the prickly Colson. But had Stanton dealt with Salant, he might have skillfully negotiated the fine-tuning of part two.

At the time of the Watergate imbroglio, Stanton was in the midst of what he would later call a "very unhappy, dark period." By then Paley had thrown him into the deep freeze, and Stanton's new contract, signed the previous year, had slammed the door. Stanton had been forced to step down as president in 1971, to become vice-chairman until his retirement on March 31, 1973. For the next fifteen years, he would be a consultant to the network at a salary of $100,000 a year plus office space, a secretary, and other support and services (including a limousine) that he had enjoyed as CBS president.

Paley's contract originally stipulated that he too would continue as a senior executive only until March 31, 1973—six months before his seventy-second birthday—after which he would continue as a consultant on the same basis as Stanton. But in 1972, Paley changed the terms of his employment to read: "until such date as Mr. Paley shall cease to be a senior elected officer of CBS." In other words, Paley would continue to lead CBS as long as he wished, while Stanton had to retire on schedule.

Paley would never repent forcing Stanton out. Decades later he would exclaim imperiously to a writer for *M* magazine, "So what! If he had been made chairman, I would have had to get out. I didn't want to get out. And I guess Frank didn't want to retire. There's no use having these retirement rules, unless you act on them accordingly. I'm the only exception."

Starting in 1971, Stanton's principal function was to help Paley find and train his successor. Jack Schneider's stint as presidential hopeful on the thirty-fifth floor had ended badly. When he moved up early in 1969 at age forty-two, he had Paley's unequivocal blessing. Schneider had run the broadcasting business beautifully. NBC had finished the ten-year conversion of its network to color programming in 1965—resulting in losses of some $6 million a year—and advertisers and audiences began to shift toward colorful NBC. Schneider had spent his first months as network president devising a plan to convert CBS to color telecasting. Paley initially resisted. "If we go to color telecasts, we'll only help RCA sell television sets," he said, "and I'll be damned if I'm going to help the General do that." With Stanton's help, Schneider turned Paley around, and color enabled CBS to solidify its dominance in the audience ratings.

By 1969, CBS's venture into movie production had not yet come apart, and Schneider seemed to be managing that enterprise well enough. He had impeccable relations with the Hollywood community, and he was eminently presentable: amusing, quick, well dressed, and so fastidious he carried his own Twining's teabags in his pocket. "He was a good leader," recalled Sal Ianucci, who worked as a West Coast executive for CBS. "He knew where the game was—in programs—and he let the experts run things. He was great at parties, a good-looking guy, and he gave great meetings."

In close proximity to Paley, however, Schneider's stock fell. He was a little too breezy for Paley's taste; he tended to make impetuous statements. Paley began to mistrust him, suspecting that he was not entirely forthcoming. "Their relationship lacked a deferential quality on Jack's part," said Bob Wood.

Although he lacked the meanspiritedness of Aubrey, Schneider succumbed to making fun of the boss for being out of touch. Both he and Bob Wood referred to Paley as WISP—the sound made by pronouncing his initials as a word. "He made it obvious to Bill that he knew more about Hollywood than Bill did," recalled Stanton. With Paley weighing on him from above, it was perhaps inevitable that Schneider would one day lose his cool.

Toward the end of 1969, the two men were meeting in the boardroom with a group of other executives. Paley rode Schneider unmercifully, pounding him with questions and complaints about the smallest details. As everyone was leaving, Paley said to Schneider, "Have you got a minute?" Schneider returned, and Paley apologized. "Oh, bullshit," said Schneider and stalked out, infuriating Paley. "Bill drove Jack to distraction," said Stanton.

Schneider kept his position for more than a year afterwards, but he could sense Paley's hostility. "He didn't like me anymore," said Schneider. "I tried not to take it personally because he was disappointed with everyone eventually." So in 1971, Schneider came to Stanton. "Send me back downstairs please," he said. That July, Schneider returned as president of the CBS Broadcast Group, and the position of corporate executive vice-president was abolished.

By that time, both Stanton and Paley were well along in the hunt for a successor. Paley had concluded that CBS needed a different sort from either Frank Stanton or Jack Schneider. They were good administrators, but they were mere broadcasters. CBS was now a $1 billion corporation with an array of businesses. Like ITT, the model conglomerate of the day, CBS needed someone who understood diversification and could handle complicated financial machinations.

After considering several attractive Wall Street prospects, among them the investment-banking wunderkind Dan Lufkin, Stanton and Paley zeroed in on fifty-year-old Charles T. "Chick" Ireland, a Yale-trained lawyer and senior vice-president of ITT who previously ran the Allegheny Corporation holding company. Here was the genuine article, a veteran of the acquisition game who had learned at the feet of the master, ITT's Harold "Hungry Hal" Geneen.

Jerry Roche, an executive recruiter, brought Ireland to Stanton in July. Ireland had already accepted a job as president of an insurance company in Texas, a commitment he dropped the morning after his four-hour conversation with Stanton. Stanton was impressed by Ireland's integrity and, after three more long interviews, convinced by his track record and ability as well. Without hesitation, Stanton called Paley on his holiday in Baden-Baden to say he wanted to send Ireland over for a meeting.

After their first encounter, Paley telephoned Stanton to ask why he had bothered sending "that guy" over to see him. Forty-eight hours later, Ireland called Stanton from Kennedy Airport. "I blew it," he said. It seemed that Paley simply did not like the man's style. Ireland was a Marine Corps veteran, bright and tough, outgoing and vigorous, but rough around the edges—a stocky type who wore a T-shirt to play tennis. Chick Ireland was decidedly out of place in the glamorous surroundings at Baden-Baden.

When Paley returned to New York in early September, however, he called Stanton. "Who was that guy we looked at?" he asked. Ireland was summoned to CBS where, said Stanton, "Bill fell in love with him." What turned Paley? Back in the corporate realm, he was bedazzled by the ITT mystique and persuaded that Ireland had the strength to whip CBS into a tighter, more disciplined organization.

Chick Ireland took over on October 1, when Stanton officially became vice-chairman—a supernumerary for the first time in his life. Ireland quickly established himself as a tough taskmaster. He gathered top CBS executives around an oval table in a Black Rock conference room and invited them to criticize each other's divisions. This kind of confrontation was anathema at CBS, an organization ruled by mutual respect if not collegiality. "Dick Salant would have died before he would question whether Janis Joplin was a suitable role model," said Jack Schneider, "and I certainly didn't want Clive Davis [then head of CBS Records] to tell me how to handle Lucille Ball. We would have these meetings and nobody would talk."

A tireless worker—he often sat in his office until midnight poring over computer printouts—Ireland never got on top of CBS. "I can't understand these people at CBS Records," he said to Stanton one day. "They can't tell me when they will have a hit." After a few months, the chemistry between Paley and Ireland began to deteriorate.

Ireland's first proposed acquisition—an $80 million deal—was Josten's, a company that made high school class rings and other educational jewelry. The new CBS chief researched the company thoroughly and persuasively argued its financial merits. It was a solid outfit that could be connected (albeit tenuously) to CBS's textbook-publishing division. In management meetings, Paley raised no objections, so Ireland put it before the CBS board.

After an enthusiastic presentation by Ireland, board members William Burden and Joe Iglehart expressed reservations—not so much about the financial prospects as the company's fit with CBS. Josten's just did not seem classy enough, so the board tabled the proposal. Unknown to Ireland, Paley had double-crossed him. He had run the Josten's deal past Walter Thayer, who had advised him against it. Rather than tell Ireland, Paley arranged with key board members to shoot down the proposal.

"Chick was crushed," recalled Schneider. "What he didn't understand was that at CBS we cared as much about style as anything, while ITT would buy anything if it made sense financially." "Chick was never the same after that," recalled a financial executive at CBS at the time. "He found out who the boss was."

That spring Ireland suffered a heart attack and stayed out of work for six weeks. As he eased back into his duties, Paley continued to second-guess him. On June 8, Ireland and Paley had lunch in the chairman's dining room. "Paley was very petulant," recalled Stanton, who dined with them that day. "He was jumping all over Ireland. Later Paley said to me, 'Maybe I was too tough on him.' I figured that Ireland had been a Marine, that he took it in stride." That night, Ireland died in his sleep of a heart attack.

When Stanton notified Paley the following morning, the CBS chairman was shocked, but within days he was orchestrating a full-fledged search for a successor. Stanton spent nearly all his time interviewing candidates, including James Robinson, then a promising executive at American Express. Paley found him appealing, but Robinson had no interest in CBS.

The leading candidate was Arthur Taylor, the thirty-seven-year-old executive vice-president of the International Paper Company and a former investment banker at prestigious First Boston. Stanton met him twice before dispatching him to Paley, who invited Taylor and his wife to Kiluna for lunch. It was, recalled Taylor, "love at first sight. We both knew I would be president of CBS." Paley asked only a couple of questions— about Taylor's views on business planning and his theories of organization

—and spoke of his own possible retirement; at that stage Paley's contract still called for his departure along with Stanton the following year.

They hashed out details in two more meetings, and shook hands on July 7, 1972. Paley was so taken with Taylor that he never bothered calling anyone at International Paper. To Paley, Taylor was a vision from Central Casting: handsome, bright, and dynamic, a financial whiz with great credentials, including degrees in Renaissance history and American economic history from Brown University. The son of a telephone worker, he had survived the bullies of Rahway, New Jersey, who took a dim view of his clarinet playing, feeble athletic ability, and studious dedication. Along the way, Taylor had picked up considerable polish; in this respect he was like Paley, able to absorb the style and manner of the well-born. Even more than Taylor's financial acumen, Paley was drawn to his youth and easy ways.

With Stanton's retirement approaching, tensions between Paley and Stanton stretched close to the breaking point. For Paley it was a fraught period anyway; at age seventy-one, he was struggling to deal with the pressures of the Nixon White House, worrying about the future of CBS, and trying to forge a relationship with Taylor. That autumn, Stanton drew up the specifications for the office he planned to use and the services he would need upon his retirement.

As stipulated in his contract, Stanton asked for office space identical to what he had at CBS. "Too much," thundered Paley to Clarence Hopper, CBS's man in charge of operations. "I won't stand for it." In a meeting in the luxurious Black Rock office that he never intended to relinquish, Paley made clear to Stanton his determination to renege.

"You don't need all that," insisted Paley.

"That is what we agreed to," replied Stanton.

"But I didn't know that was in the contract," said Paley. "Couldn't you get space in a hotel?"

Stanton burned with anger. "That would not satisfy my conditions," he said.

"But you have a lot of money," said Paley (on retirement, Stanton's CBS stock alone would be worth more than $9 million). "Why do you need this?"

"You wouldn't have any respect for me if I walked away from this," answered Stanton.

It was hopelessly petty. The money in dispute amounted to something like $20,000 a year for a company that was making nearly $200 million a year in pre-tax profits. But Paley refused to yield. Utterly dispirited, Stanton asked his friend Cyrus Vance, the prominent New York attorney, to represent him in possible legal action.

Paley instructed the board's finance committee (Joseph Iglehart, Robert Lovett, Leon Levy, William Burden, and Arthur Taylor—joined by Roswell Gilpatric, who represented CBS's law firm, Cravath Swaine & Moore) to resolve the matter. Iglehart called a special meeting with Stanton and Vance, which Paley was unable to attend; typically, he was home sick in bed. Clearly irritated by the fuss Paley had made, Lovett took the lead in pressing Stanton's case. All the committee members agreed that Stanton's position was justified. "Frank pouted until he got his perks," said David Hertz. "I'm not sure Paley really cared. But he wanted to show Stanton who was boss."

Still, when Gilpatric called Paley to convey the decision, the chairman was furious. "I don't agree with you," he said. "You should not have gone as far financially as having the company underwrite his expenses." Eventually Paley calmed down and the contract remained in effect. "The only question," recalled Gilpatric, "was how much consulting work Frank Stanton would get. The answer would be, 'Not much.' "

March 1973 had an almost surreal quality for Paley and Stanton, both still seething. Often for no apparent reason, newcomer Arthur Taylor found himself in the middle. "Stanton would call me in to say what a bad guy Paley was and Paley would do the same," recalled Taylor. "I felt like a marriage counselor." Yet amid the estrangement, Paley was calling friends outside CBS to set up investment opportunities in which he and Stanton could participate together. "Paley didn't want Stanton's animosity," explained Kidder Meade. "Paley's idea on how the future would view him was an intense motivation." But Stanton wasn't buying. "I didn't deal with it," he said. "I didn't pursue the ventures." At one point Stanton did ask Paley why he insisted on staying in his job at CBS. "I have to stay in it," Paley said. "I don't know what else I would do."

Stanton stubbornly rebuffed all of Paley's requests for parties and receptions to mark his retirement—rites Stanton found too painful to contemplate. At the CBS board meeting in mid-March, Paley gave Stanton a small sculpture called *Atom Piece* by Henry Moore, an old friend of Stanton's. The following evening, Paley hosted a reception at the Corcoran Gallery in Washington for Taylor. It also served as a farewell for Stanton on the turf he knew so well.

Several days before Stanton's departure, Paley decided to take off for Lyford Cay. Stanton caught him in the hallway after lunch as Paley was about to leave the building. Wary to the end, Paley permitted no shred of sentiment to intrude on the moment. "I won't see you again until after I'm gone," said Stanton.

"What plans do you have for your last day?" asked Paley.

"I'm going to Niles Trammell's funeral," said Stanton. (In the late forties, the courtly Trammell had been an amiable competitor as NBC's president.)

"I'm taking the company plane to the Bahamas, so it won't be available," said Paley.

"That's all right," Stanton replied. "RCA has offered me their plane."

It poured all day on March 30, Frank Stanton's final day at CBS after thirty-eight years. At 6:30 a.m. he flew to Miami for the Trammell funeral. To Stanton's surprise, Paley showed up as well. In an awkward moment, Stanton handed Paley a copy of the memo he was sending to "the organization" expressing thanks and appreciation to his "friends and colleagues." Back in New York, Black Rock showed its sadness. "There was a great loyalty a lot of people had," said Emily Greene, a veteran executive assistant. "Everyone felt very sad. Some people cried. People felt CBS would not be the same without him, which was true."

Late that afternoon, Stanton had a farewell drink with a group of executives. As the men filed out, *New Yorker* writer Lillian Ross arrived with her seven-year-old son Eric and her cocker spaniel Goldie.

While Ross watched and asked questions, her son poked through the boxes being packed by Stanton and his longtime secretary Winnie Williams. Stanton was determined to get everything organized in time to assume his new job, chairman of the American National Red Cross, two days later. His final visitor was Izzy Seigal, a staff photographer for CBS. Bashfully he presented his humble gift to Stanton: a vintage ceramic holder for kitchen matches.

Twelve hours after his day began, Stanton prepared to leave his office. He carried photographs of his wife, Ruth, as a girl with braided hair, an oversize book entitled *Homage to Henry Moore*, the *Atom Piece* sculpture, the ceramic match holder, and a brass clock.

Before turning into the elevator, Stanton paused to hug Betty, the receptionist, who was crying. His parting words were recounted by Ross in her *New Yorker* piece a month later: "I think I'll make it home in time for the seven o'clock news."

6

———

THE

Mourner

———

47

"SIGHTS JUST INCREDIBLE," Babe Paley wrote to Irene Selznick in April 1973. "Bill had no trouble finding a Chinese restaurant. Itinerary so crowded, not a moment to relax, but enjoying it all until health fails utterly." Within days of tossing off those lighthearted words, Babe was in a Shanghai hospital. Toward the end of a trip to China with her husband, she was hit with a severe respiratory illness and a fever of 104° that doctors diagnosed as pneumonia.

Paley immediately called Isadore Rosenfeld, his doctor in New York, who suggested a course of antibiotics. When Paley briefed the Chinese doctors, they already knew that Babe was allergic to penicillin. They had conferred with Babe's physician and had her medical history. Paley was impressed, but continued to call Rosenfeld daily.

In New York, Arthur Taylor sometimes went to the doctor's office, waiting for Paley to finish his conversation with Rosenfeld before he briefed his boss on CBS events. Although Paley remained apprehensive about Babe's condition, he did not overreact as he so often did when events went awry in his personal life.

Nor did Babe seem ruffled by her hospitalization. She called her children in New York and reassured them that she would be fine. She told them her room overlooked a beautiful courtyard. The Chinese doctors, she said, were "fabulous."

Two weeks later, when they returned home, Babe was examined by an army of doctors who confirmed the pneumonia diagnosis and told her to quit smoking. She did, but her cough lingered for months and she was X-rayed monthly for the rest of the year. Each time the diagnosis was pneumonia. Then, early in January 1974, a small tumor was found on one lung. On January 18—Amanda's thirtieth birthday—Dr. Paul Ebert of New York Hospital removed one third of Babe's right lung. The tumor was malignant, but Babe's doctors were hopeful that surgery had checked the cancer.

Paley grilled Babe's doctors relentlessly, acting like their chief executive officer. Some years later he said, revealingly, "I had such faith in myself and believed that, somehow, I was going to beat the rap. I tried everything, hoping to produce a miracle."

Babe managed to keep up their entertaining—less frequently than before but just as perfectly. She even gained weight and ate chocolates avidly. Then, in the spring of 1975, another tumor appeared, and the rest of her right lung was removed on May 12 at Memorial Sloan-Kettering Cancer Center. That summer, the Paleys gave up their customary European travels to stay in the Southampton villa of friends Mica and Ahmet Ertegun. The heat was blistering, and Paley bought an air conditioner for every room in the Erteguns' house. Exhausted and ill, Babe took long naps and visited quietly with friends.

Bill Paley, who had shown symptoms of the same ailment fifteen years earlier, now faced the prospect that his fifty-eight-year-old wife could die, leaving him alone in his old age. His perfectly constructed world threatened to unravel. Paley, so accustomed to controlling virtually every aspect of his existence, worked furiously to conquer Babe's illness. "He was motivated by concern for her," recalled Kidder Meade. "But he also was confronted by something he couldn't control. He had an extreme impatience for any failure."

Paley combed the globe for cures, traveling abroad to confer with doctors, and importing experts from Scandinavia and elsewhere. He read books and articles about cancer and used his position as a trustee at Columbia University to probe every conceivable contact there. "He drove the Columbia medical school crazy," recalled Meade. Once he dispatched a CBS newsman in Paris to investigate an obscure clinic in Switzerland.

After an encouraging stretch, Babe weakened again the following spring and looked especially frail at a dinner honoring her husband at the Plaza Hotel. "She took my arm," recalled one of Paley's aides. "We started walking to the staircase. She was having difficulty breathing. We stopped at the foot of the staircase and she looked up. Her jaw dropped at the prospect of walking. I suggested tactfully we take the elevator. She threw her arms around me."

In the summer of 1976, the Paleys returned to France. "All serene," Babe wrote to Irene Selznick in mid-July. "Here is perfect life for me. We will have one escapade—St. Tropez by boat overnight. Next week with Guinness [British aristocrat Loel and his wife, Gloria], destination and cast of characters unknown." Back in New York, Paley hired a new chef, Bernard Lanjuin, who tried to tempt Babe with special soups and delicacies, but she showed little appetite.

During this period, each public sighting was cause for celebration in gossip columns and the pages of *Women's Wear Daily*. "Babe's back," crowed one typical item in May 1976, noting her appearance at the fashionable Regine's restaurant to eat salmon and chat with decorator Vincent Fourcade: "She sauntered out in her black chiffon shirt and slim-legged pants, her earlobes and fingers carrying the weight of huge white pearls encircled by marquise diamond settings."

Paley became ferociously protective. A guest at one dinner party recalled that he "kept his eyes on her all night and took her home early." He constantly fretted over whether a room was too hot or too cold for her. "I would see the touch of his hand when they were sitting next to each other," recalled his friend Henryk de Kwiatkowski, "or a small glance of appreciation when she made a remark. The slightest cough from her or the slightest expression of discomfort made his face shrivel with pain."

At the outset, Babe was pleasantly surprised and genuinely grateful for her husband's newfound attentiveness. "I had no idea he cared so much," she told Slim Keith after her first operation. "He had every meal in that awful hospital with me." Recalled Slim, "The fact that he was giving her that much time Babe found extraordinary."

But after several months, Babe adopted some atypical new attitudes. To close friends, she began to question the choices she had made in her life and to contemplate a new course. Saying her artistic talent had been thwarted, she considered setting up a studio outside their apartment and spending much of her free time sculpting and drawing. "She wanted to have a separate life in the art world," said her daughter Amanda. "Several of her friends encouraged her to do it and not to worry what Bill said. But she worried that he would be too upset." She confided to one close friend that when she did broach the idea, Paley objected to the $900 monthly studio rent.

So she set up a makeshift studio in a spare room at their Fifth Avenue apartment. Using friends as models, among them socialite Louise Melhado and author Jean Stein, Babe fashioned small terra-cotta sculptures of heads. "She could have had a life that would have given more to her," said Jean Stein. "I had the feeling that she gave up so much. She told me about her father and how difficult he was. Then I realized that was all she ever knew."

As the months passed, Babe relegated her art to the sidelines again, reassuming the role of perfect hostess and helpmeet that she had played for three decades. For the first time, however, Babe dropped her propriety and openly criticized her husband. One senior CBS executive was stunned when Babe first called him to ask, "What's the old SOB doing today?" Although he thought her tone alarming, he tried to be lighthearted. "Oh, he's full of beans," he replied. "We have to jolly him up."

Jack Schneider found himself in the same awkward position when he sat next to Babe at a dinner. "How do you put up with him?" she asked quietly. "How do you stand him? We are going abroad tomorrow and I can't see how we will ever get off. He is so disorganized." Schneider was so perplexed by the encounter that he sought counsel from Stanton. "Just be careful," Stanton advised. "Don't agree with her, because she could go to Bill and say what you said. But don't openly disagree. Just acknowledge what she is saying and be as neutral as you can be."

The toll of Babe's illness on Bill Paley was evident to everyone in the upper echelons at CBS. During the first few years, Paley was away even more than usual, and on the job he often appeared preoccupied. "For the first six months I was there, Paley was spending his time with weird medicine men from all over the world," recalled one executive who came to CBS in the mid-1970s. Arthur Taylor did his best to offer support. Paley was appreciative—especially when Taylor confronted a messy scandal at CBS Records in May 1973 and fired Clive Davis, division president, amid charges that he misappropriated CBS funds for personal expenses.

For a time, Taylor and Paley seemed downright chummy. Taylor referred to the CBS chairman as his "senior partner" and entertained him at his home in Summit, New Jersey. Taylor began to feel, he later said, that Paley regarded him as "the son he never had. I really responded to that." But a sense of wariness sharpened their dealings. Even in their first meeting, Taylor had detected danger. "I am a street kid from Rahway," he once said. "I liked him but it was clear I was in the presence of an imperious man with enormous power. Street kids like that try to be cautious in such situations."

Paley's work life began to disintegrate at the time that he grappled with the horrible trauma at home. After Stanton's departure in March 1973, Paley lost the buffer he had relied on for nearly three decades. Stanton knew what was best for Paley and protected him, and he had a natural gift for managing and inspiring subordinates. "If the world only knew what Frank Stanton absorbed," said Robert Wood, president of CBS Television. "If Paley was going wild, we caught only a small percentage of it because Frank soaked so much up."

Paley's ruthlessness surfaced during Babe's illness. When Goddard Lieberson reached age sixty-four in May 1975, for example, Paley decreed that he retire early. His reasoning was mysterious. Lieberson was in top form; after languishing as a corporate vice-president, he had returned at Taylor's behest as chief of CBS Records following the Clive Davis crisis. "Goddard," recalled his wife, Brigitta, "was as happy as a lark." Lieberson's mood darkened after the announcement of his departure. Before the designated date, Brigitta called Paley. "This is such a mistake," she implored. "At the very least you should use Goddard as a kind of ambassador." "No," said Paley. "I cannot do that. We made a rule."

Lieberson's forced departure was disillusioning to Walter Yetnikoff, the new president of CBS Records, and longtime Records executive John Hammond. Over lunch at the Links Club, Lieberson poured out his unhappiness to Frank Stanton. In the end, Lieberson's closeness to Paley had meant little. "Goddard was difficult," said Stanton. "He often said he wanted to quit, although he never meant it. But Bill got tired of hearing his ploys and decided he wanted to be rid of him. Goddard couldn't believe it." By most accounts, Lieberson could have contributed several more years of first-rate performance. "His whole life was CBS," said Brigitta. "He suffered a great deal without it."

Still the front man for CBS News, Paley couldn't seem to make a decision without stirring up controversy. Against the advice of Taylor, Salant, and others, he announced in June 1973 that CBS correspondents would stop providing what Vice-President Agnew called "instant analysis" of presidential speeches. Instead, the network would present a range of viewpoints in a special broadcast offered several days after each speech. A *New York Times* report on the decision, citing unnamed CBS newsmen, portrayed it as a capitulation to political pressure. It was known within CBS that Paley had met with presidential aide H. R. Haldeman at the White House in March.

The charge that Paley yielded to direct pressure was unfair. At weekly CBS News executive committee meetings, which Paley had been attending faithfully since several months before Stanton's retirement, the CBS chairman had repeatedly objected to instant analysis, only to retreat in the face of Salant's dogged resistance. But in May 1973, shortly after the Paleys' return from China, chief CBS analyst Eric Sevareid wrote a memo contending that Nixon's statements were too ambiguous to analyze clearly on the spot. "We are not serving the public well," Sevareid said. "That shook me and persuaded Bill," said Salant. "I couldn't fight it."

Five months later, Paley announced he would restore instant analysis —an embarrassing reversal. His stated reason was that a succession of newsworthy events had shown the public ill-served by withholding the opinions of CBS correspondents. In fact, Taylor, Salant, and others had been arguing at the weekly meetings that the CBS News broadcasts suffered for "lack of spice." Paley used Sevareid's defense to defeat all arguments—until his friend Averell Harriman said he no longer watched CBS broadcasts because they didn't analyze the speeches. "That was it," said one former CBS executive. "Harriman did it for us."

Paley tried desperately to reconnect to a company that had grown too large and too complicated for him to grasp; he had neither the temperament nor the grounding to keep on top of everything as Stanton had.

His effort, however, took on new urgency beginning in 1976 when the linchpin of the network's fortunes—prime-time programming—came unstuck.

Since the beginning of the decade, CBS had managed to turn back a series of challenges to its entertainment shows. In 1970 network president Robert Wood had proposed a radical plan to "get the wrinkles out of the face of the network without eroding our popularity." He felt that CBS appealed primarily to older viewers with its rural comedies and needed to offer more sophisticated shows to draw in a younger audience. Shocked that CBS would cancel popular shows, Mike Dann heatedly objected to the plan when Wood presented it to top CBS executives. "Lower your voice, Mike," said Paley. "The room turned to ice," recalled programming executive Perry Lafferty. Several months later, Dann quit CBS.

"Gentlemen," Paley told his executives, "you finally have a network president with a vision of what is absolutely correct." Over the next two years CBS dropped such hits as "Petticoat Junction," "Red Skelton," "The Beverly Hillbillies," "Green Acres," "Hee Haw," and "Mayberry RFD." In their place, CBS found new success with shows like "All in the Family," "Maude," "The Mary Tyler Moore Show," and "M*A*S*H." The prime architect of the schedule, along with Wood, was Freddie Silverman, an energetic whiz kid who replaced Dann.

Paley went along with the choices made by Wood and Silverman, although he hated Archie Bunker, the bigoted hero of "All in the Family." Paley found the show vulgar and Bunker's insults—calling Puerto Ricans "Spics," Jews "Yids," and blacks "Spades"—offensive. Wood won Paley over by arguing that "All in the Family" would usher in a new genre of comedy in the coming decade.

Once "All in the Family" was a hit, it could do no wrong in Paley's eyes. When a number of TV critics hypothesized that the show helped diminish bigotry, CBS wanted evidence to support the theory. The network commissioned a study, which awkwardly concluded that "All in the Family" actually reinforced prejudice. Surprised and disturbed by the findings, CBS Broadcast Group president Jack Schneider brought the report to Paley. "What shall we do with it?" Schneider asked. "If we release it, we'll have to cancel the show." Replied Paley: "Destroy the study. Throw it out."

By 1974, CBS held nine out of the top ten shows, the best showing by any network in a decade. The new CBS hits, especially "The Mary Tyler Moore Show" and "M*A*S*H," were top-quality, literate comedies—conferring the "Tiffany" prestige Paley hungered for. But Paley was blind to the internal tensions that threatened to undermine CBS's success. Silverman wore down his subordinates with his constant hectoring and refusal to delegate. They called him "Frantic Freddie" and looked for excuses to avoid his calls.

Part of his panic may have been his fear that he would rise no higher at CBS, where Paley's preference for WASPs was reflected among the company's top executives. Although Silverman respected Paley's ability as an "editor," he never felt especially close to the chairman. Paley did not bother with the gestures—the occasional lunch or dinner—that would have given Silverman the pat on the back he sought. When Silverman wanted a bigger title, more money, and a limousine, Paley turned him down.

In May 1975 Silverman jumped to ABC, where he received the status and approval denied him at CBS. That fall, CBS's new programs had unusually poor showings. The most spectacular failure was "Beacon Hill," a Boston version of Britain's successful "Upstairs Downstairs" mini-series about the lives of aristocrats and their servants. Placed on the schedule at Paley's insistence, it had a fine cast headed by such Broadway actors as Nancy Marchand and George Rose. CBS commissioned top writers to turn out well-crafted scripts. No expense was spared on the show's period details.

But "Beacon Hill" failed to catch hold, and Paley canceled it after thirteen episodes. "I almost cried," he recalled. "It was one of the best shows we ever did." Arthur Taylor had a slightly different recollection: "We put it on because Bill Paley wanted a quality series. But two weeks into it, he was screaming that the circulation was too low." Afterwards, CBS conducted a study to determine what went wrong. "What the survey came up with, which couldn't have been the real cause," Paley said later, "was that the American public just didn't believe that one household could have that many servants!"

In November 1975, Paley flew to the West Coast to command a drastic rearrangement of the schedule. "Perturbed at CBS's erratic showing so far this season," *Variety* wrote that month, Paley "is actively participating in programming decisions again." A year later, in the fall of 1976, Silverman had taken a handful of incipient hits at ABC—including "Happy Days" and "Welcome Back Kotter"—to build a schedule that took a strong lead in the prime-time ratings. As CBS began its fiftieth year on the air, it fell to third for the first time in two decades.

The drop in CBS's prestige and fortunes infuriated Paley. He pointed his finger at the "complacency" of his programmers, and their failure to order enough backup shows to replace programs faltering on the air. Paley could not bring himself to acknowledge that CBS had genuine competition from ABC. Moreover, more than a half-dozen key CBS programming people left the network in the year following Silverman's departure.

CBS network president Robert Wood was the most prominent to depart—lured, he said, by the prospect of achieving fame and wealth as a producer like Norman Lear, creator of "All in the Family," and Grant Tinker, the man behind "The Mary Tyler Moore Show." But in truth Wood left because he felt beaten down by Paley.

Ironically, Wood's grievances began in the early 1970s, when CBS led the ratings from morning to night in entertainment and news. "I said to myself, 'My God, this is unbelievable. We are leading in every area,' so I merchandised it to Paley," Wood recalled. "I said, 'You should treasure this moment.' I sat back like a little kid waiting for a huge compliment. 'Robin,' he said—that was what he called me—'That is good news, but remember one thing. You can never lead by enough.' He had a smile on his face. I thought to myself, 'What the hell was that?' It wasn't the answer I was expecting."

By 1975, after nearly seven years of having Bill Paley chew on his ear, Wood had had enough. "He thought he was underpaid and underappreciated," said Jack Schneider. Shortly before Stanton's retirement, Wood came to him and said, "I can't keep delivering more money and ratings and keep taking the kind of interference I get."

During his last year, Wood became the network's invisible man. Sometimes Schneider would find him in a screening room watching old movies. When his programming people began leaving, Wood was slow to fill their positions. Finally, he called Arthur Taylor and said, "I am passing blood and I have to get out." By April 1976, they had worked out the terms of Wood's resignation.

For Wood's successor, Taylor recommended Robert Wussler, a bright and eager executive of thirty-nine who had risen from news producer to station manager to head of CBS Sports. "You've got a shot at this job," Taylor told Wussler before sending him to Paley's office. "Arrive early, wear your best suit, speak softly, and answer his questions." During the meeting, Wussler admitted he knew little about entertainment programming, but he told the Boss he could organize well and get things done. Two days later, Wussler had the job.

Taylor tried to insulate his subordinates as Stanton had done so effectively for decades, but the young president's approach alienated them. He told them to avoid talking to Paley; whenever the chairman tried to make contact, they were to alert Taylor's office. But when the phone rang, the well-schooled CBS executives knew they had to take the chairman's call. "Paley would say, 'Can you come up and talk?' " recalled James Rosenfield, a former executive at CBS. "You would stand up in your chair, hang up, and break into a cold sweat." Afterwards, "You would have to tell Arthur about it. He would always get mad and say, 'Don't do that again.' "

Taylor's pique reflected his concern about his relationship with Paley. As early as March 1975, gossip columns reported a "personality clash" between the two men. After Babe's operation in the late spring forced Paley to endure a steamy summer in New York, he was extremely irritable with his underlings. That July, *New York* magazine cited friction between chairman and president, prompting Paley to issue a strongly worded statement calling the report "absolute nonsense." Paley praised Taylor's "exceptional abilities" and "outstanding performance," and affirmed that "I would be greatly pleased to have him as my successor." Those words seemed to settle the matter for public consumption—but Arthur Taylor knew better.

48

TENSIONS BETWEEN Arthur Taylor and Paley had been growing steadily since early 1975. Unlike Stanton, who took advantage of Paley's lapses of interest in CBS to develop his own style and power base, Taylor never attained the authority that had enabled Stanton to effectively counterbalance Paley. Taylor, whose experience was exclusively in finance, was further hobbled by having to learn on the job. Other problems included his personality and management style, which did not serve him well at CBS.

Taylor was keenly aware of Stanton's role as the conscience of CBS. With his rigid integrity and strong moral streak, Taylor also wanted to do something larger—for society. "I was making $400,000 a year, and I had little respect for the programs," recalled Taylor. But it didn't take long for him to see that most CBS executives, devoted to creating entertainment and making money, took their cue from Paley. "For him it was a machine of wealth and profit," recalled Taylor.

To help assuage his conscience, Taylor came up with a concept called the Family Hour, or Family Viewing. Early in 1975 he proposed that no television station broadcast programs that were "inappropriate for general family viewing before 9:00 p.m." His words struck a chord in Washington, where, since the late 1960s, politicians had expressed concern about the harmful effects of televised sex and violence on children. A 1972 report by the U.S. Surgeon General convinced Taylor that the networks had to take a stand against sex and violence on TV.

With the assistance of the FCC, Taylor coaxed the networks to designate the hour from eight to nine each evening for shows without sex or violence. Taylor did not anticipate, however, that the new policy would bolster ABC's juvenile comedies. Meanwhile, two of CBS's most successful shows, "All in the Family" and "Kojak," had to be moved. In later time slots, they drew smaller audiences, further sharpening ABC's competitive edge.

When Hollywood writers and producers filed suit to end the policy, Taylor became messianic, appearing on evangelist Robert Schuller's "Hour of Power" TV program to urge support for this "very very important cause." He revealed that when "the world seemed darkest" and he encountered disappointment, "a great hand came down and . . . there was in fact some light coming through the clouds." Most CBS executives thought the great hand would squeeze their profits.

Paley had supported Family Viewing when it came to a vote at the network in December 1974, but he had strong reservations. Taylor's moralism made him uncomfortable, and Family Viewing hampered his freedom to make practical programming decisions. Within days of the lawsuit, recalled Taylor, "Paley's support disappeared. He was worried about getting on the wrong side of the Hollywood producers."

According to Kidder Meade, Paley "begrudgingly" let the Family Hour policy go through "because it had moved too far down the road." Had he not been spending half his time searching for medical miracles for Babe, Meade added, Paley probably would have blocked it.

Family Hour aside, Arthur Taylor proved a dedicated executive and a capable administrator. He stood behind CBS News, making room on the schedule for its programs. (Burned once again by bad publicity on his "instant analysis" decision, Paley had pulled away from the news department in the mid-1970s.) Taylor also pushed CBS into hiring and training more women and minorities. And he imposed much-needed financial controls, efficiently tracking every expenditure. Wall Street loved him. CBS profits jumped from $83 million in 1972 to $123 million in 1975. But Taylor knew his cost limits irritated the free-spending programming department, especially when he clamped down on their padded expense accounts.

Paley prodded Taylor, as he had Stanton and Ireland, to find companies for CBS to buy. Taylor favored a cautious approach, criticizing CBS's initial acquisitions in a magazine interview early in 1974. For a while Taylor seemed more interested in selling than in buying; he unloaded a variety of small interests in real estate, discount records, business schools, and technology. "It hurt Paley's feelings when I started divesting," recalled Taylor. "But he didn't really want acquisitions. He wanted the diversion he could get from a deal."

Dutifully, Taylor brought in a proposal to merge with American Express in 1975. But when Paley realized CBS would not control the new entity, he nixed the idea. He similarly balked over a merger with Insurance Company of North America. But Paley greeted other proposals with juvenile glee. Once during a corporate planning luncheon, Paley pushed a buzzer and a waiter walked in with a tray piled high with pastries. "Try these," Paley exclaimed as he grabbed a mouthful. "What do you think?" he said, turning to John Backe, president of CBS's Publishing Group. "Is CBS thinking of becoming a baker?" Backe asked. "We're interested in buying Entenmann's," replied Paley, pressing the buzzer again to summon more waiters with more trays, this time heaped with bubble gum and candies. "I'm in Disneyland," Backe muttered to himself.

Taylor tried his own unconventional techniques to win over the boss. In management meetings, Paley had been noncommittal about a plan to buy Gulbransen Industries, manufacturers of organs. For the board meeting, Taylor had an organist play "Nearer My God to Thee" and "Beautiful Dreamer." The handful of elderly board members smiled contentedly, and Gulbransen got the nod.

Few other deals won approval. Between his search for Babe's cure and his fretting over CBS shows, Paley could not bring himself to make a major decision. "I brought forward three dozen acquisitions," Taylor said, "but I couldn't get him to concentrate on one of them. He was constantly screaming, 'We have no deals.' Then I would bring him one and he wouldn't concentrate on it."

From Taylor's first day at CBS, the old guard took exception to his style. He was decent and sincere, but he could be pompous and overbearing as well. When Taylor wore a hat to work, Schneider and company mockingly passed the word that he affected a Homburg and called him "King Arthur" behind his back. They chuckled about the "No Smoking" sign he kept in his office and about his habit, when working late, of playing the Gulbransen organ he had installed outside his office, pounding out "Four Leaf Clover" and "America the Beautiful."

In 1976, Paley turned on Taylor—and by most accounts, CBS's ratings free-fall played only a small part. "Paley was constantly undoing what we had done for the previous two weeks," recalled Taylor. "It was humiliating—all the second-guessing, the coming back from a trip and redoing everything." From the beginning, Taylor had diligently kept Paley up to date with weekly summaries of company activities. When Paley was around, Taylor briefed him, frequently one-on-one.

A day or so after one of Taylor's briefings, Paley would accuse him of not keeping him fully informed. After a while, Taylor kept notes of their conversations. When Paley rebuked him, Taylor would defend himself by reading aloud from his notes. Paley would insist that it was all new to him. So Taylor simply did the briefings a second time.

Paley had a history of absentmindedness, but this kind of torment seemed calculated. "Vindictiveness was Paley's middle name," said one top CBS executive who watched Paley and Taylor closely. "He would get a fixation on someone and then he would get him. Paley would become very suspicious."

Before he left each Friday, Paley would meet with Taylor and unburden himself of his concerns about the network. "He would get in his car feeling relieved, leaving me to face a weekend with a hatful of problems, mostly manufactured," said Taylor. Sometimes Paley was abusive and demeaning; he knew how to get Taylor's goat. "Arthur was bordering on physical exhaustion," said John Backe. "He wasn't making rational judgments."

Taylor had what Schneider and Wussler regarded as an "overactive imagination." The CBS president ordered his office swept for bugs, carried a telephone with a scrambler in his briefcase, and arranged to have the CBS chauffeurs learn special driving skills to foil any attempts to kidnap top company officials. He once interrupted a meeting to complain that his phone was tapped; when the building manager conducted an inquiry, he found that Taylor had been hearing his secretary's buzzer. Years later, Taylor remained convinced that Paley eavesdropped on his phone conversations and had him tailed.

Eventually, Taylor joined the psychological warfare. When Paley yelled at him, he yelled back or just stared until Paley started to wilt, overcome by his facial tic. "He couldn't look you in the eye when he was in that kind of mood," said Taylor. But more often, after lashing out and slamming the door, Taylor would back down. Paley was like a fighter who keeps his opponent pinned to the ropes, pummeling him with body shots. "I had no power," said Taylor. "Paley had it all."

Paley never seemed to know what he expected from Taylor. He seemed to want someone to assume Stanton's duties, but Paley did not quite grasp what exactly Stanton had done all those years. At the same time, Paley sought someone in his own image as a successor. The better he got to know Taylor, the more he realized that the CBS president could not possibly become the next Bill Paley. "Bill Paley was a very impatient man," said Kidder Meade. "When the end of the road came, that was that."

The effect of Babe's declining health cannot be underestimated. The specter of her death was a constant reminder of his own mortality. When he and Taylor were still getting along, Paley asked him repeatedly what he thought about death. Taylor told him that death was the final affirmation of life, and that life would not be possible without it. Paley would have none of that; he found the blackness of death, the ultimate loss of control, anything but affirming. Taylor's youth—he turned forty in 1975 —threatened Paley all the more.

Taylor finally ran aground when he tried to raise his public profile. Paley remembered only too well what had happened years earlier when word spread that Frank Stanton was the real power at CBS. Now, he suspected, Taylor was using Family Viewing to encroach on his programming preserve. Taylor was pushing too hard, Paley felt, and getting too big for his britches.

Paley was especially vexed by Taylor's imperial style. Wherever Taylor went, he was trailed by a retinue of assistants—just like Paley. Taylor even popped up on the pages of *Women's Wear Daily,* hobnobbing with Paley's social set. "Arthur asked for trouble," said former board member Courtney Brown. "He would take people around the country on the company jet and meet with pooh-bahs."

To friends, Taylor openly spoke of aspirations for the White House. He hired consultants to advise him on leadership: *Time* magazine listed him among its two hundred rising young leaders in 1974. Some advisers counseled him on which corporate boards he should join; others wrote treatises on the economy for him. From 1973 through 1975, Taylor made some forty speeches in prestigious forums such as the Council on Foreign Relations and the White House Conference on Inflation. "It was important for Arthur to be at the center," recalled Jack Schneider. "He thought of himself as an intellectual and made historical allusions and spoke of taking the high road."

Taylor, said William Leonard, CBS's chief lobbyist at the time, "flung himself early and often upon the Washington scene." In 1976, Taylor had a new office built in the CBS Washington headquarters: a grand suite with a dining room, screening room, and bathroom. He had not yet seen it when Paley went to town unannounced in the early summer of 1976. The chairman was shocked by the grandeur of Taylor's quarters. "He hated that office," said Kidder Meade. "He thought it was part of Arthur's grandiose scheme for the future."

"Both the money spent in decorating it and the way it was decorated pissed Bill off," Leonard recalled. "He was visibly upset—especially by a very large wall hanging at the entrance, which he soon had removed." Stanton had had strong ideas about how CBS should be run, and strong tastes that were very different from Paley's. But he had asserted himself only when Paley left a vacuum. Taylor, by contrast, challenged Paley head on. He was like a man taking over an apartment and redecorating it before the previous tenant had moved out.

The final straw was Taylor's decision to bring in some experts to help alleviate tension in the executive ranks. When he asked Paley for suggestions, the CBS chairman said, "I have the best psychiatrist in the world. I will call him and get some names from him." Although Taylor knew Paley was under great stress, he was surprised by Paley's admission. It seemed a hopeful sign. Taylor went on to hire two psychiatrists who spent much of their time querying top CBS executives about the relationship between Paley and Taylor. Word reached Paley that Taylor was seeking a psychological analysis of the CBS chairman because he thought Paley was crazy.

That August, Arthur Taylor took his first vacation in four years, leaving Paley alone to fuss and stew. When the CBS president returned, the level of tension with Paley had not abated. Babe went through a bad patch in early September, prompting Paley to cancel appointments and stay at home. Then, toward the end of the month, Taylor left for a trip to Moscow to negotiate for the television rights to the 1980 Olympic Games.

Several days after Bill Paley's seventy-fifth birthday on September 28, 1976, the phone rang in the office of John Backe. "Can you come and talk to me?" said Paley. The forty-four-year-old executive had been at CBS nearly four years, recruited by Taylor from General Learning Corporation, a publishing venture run by General Electric and Time, Inc. Taylor had charged him with turning around CBS publishing, then in a state of near collapse. Drawn to the challenge, Backe had thrown himself into the reorganization, increasing sales and profits significantly.

Although Paley had little to do with publishing at CBS, he had seen Backe in meetings and had been impressed by his approach: cautious, thoughtful, well prepared. Single-handedly, Backe had just reeled in the first promising acquisition in years, Fawcett Publications, for less than $60 million, a lower price than CBS anticipated paying. Backe also had an easy way about him; he was one of the few to address the chairman as "Bill." "I find our lives are becoming increasingly entwined," Paley told Backe in his office that Friday evening. "Could you and your bride come to dinner with Babe and me on Monday night?" When Backe said yes, Paley asked him to come an hour early—alone.

In the library at 820 Fifth Avenue, Paley poured Backe a glass of wine. Characteristically blunt, Paley said, "How would you like to be president of CBS?" "What about Arthur Taylor?" asked Backe. "That is not a factor," said Paley. "It is not going to work out with Arthur." Then Paley dangled the solid gold carrot: "Furthermore, I would like you to become CEO next April at our annual meeting."

The CEO title was a gambit to defuse the criticism he would get for firing Taylor. Once he had zeroed in on Backe as the most likely replacement, Paley had gone to a prominent executive recruiter for advice on how to dump Taylor. "How am I going to have any credibility with the press?" said Paley. "Easy," said the recruiter. "Give Backe CEO. That way you can say he has better credentials for the bigger job." Replied Paley, "I don't care what the title is—as long as he knows I am in charge."

Paley was taken aback when Backe seemed blasé about the offer. "How do you feel about being CEO?" Paley asked expectantly. "I haven't the vaguest idea," said Backe. "We are two tough guys and sooner or later we will collide." Paley was incredulous. "I am offering you the most exciting job in America. How can you turn around and say no?" Backe observed that he didn't know what Paley wanted from the man who would be CBS president. "I am an operating guy," said Backe. "You seem to want someone to look good and talk well." "We want someone to run the company," said Paley—failing to note that he himself wished to remain "in charge."

At dinner that night, Backe was enchanted by Babe, who functioned well despite her illness. The tender side of Paley was impressive. Backe was touched by Paley's solicitude toward his ailing wife. Still, Backe declined the offer.

Every afternoon for the following week, Paley invited Backe to his office to discuss the job. Each time they would talk—for a half hour or hour at a time—Paley would say, "You have to take it." Whenever Backe tried to ask what had gone wrong with Taylor, Paley said, "He hasn't kept me informed." Eventually, Paley's powers of persuasion won out. On Friday, October 8, Backe accepted.

With Taylor back from Moscow the following Monday, Paley summoned key directors from outside the company to his Fifth Avenue apartment. "Arthur Taylor has to leave," he told them. They knew there had been strains between the two men but, said director Roswell Gilpatric, "it came as a real shock." Paley had no bill of particulars, but a general complaint that Taylor wanted the chairman's job and was trying to force Paley out. "Bill Paley was sensitive to anyone he thought was taking over," recalled Courtney Brown, then a director. Paley sealed his argument by claiming that Taylor had been acting unilaterally and giving the chairman incomplete or untruthful answers.

No one tried to dissuade him, but several questioned whether Backe's background was broad enough for the top job. Yet again, Paley was reaching for someone without a trace of broadcasting experience. Paley countered their doubts by praising Backe's knowledge of creative people, his good taste, his entrepreneurial spark, and his managerial ability. Paley was obviously infatuated; he thought Backe virtually perfect. "He wanted to move quickly," recalled Gilpatric. "Backe was there. He was easy to get along with, had no sharp edges."

On Tuesday night, October 12, Arthur Taylor worked late in his office, preparing for the monthly CBS board meeting the next day. Afterwards he had dinner at the nearby San Marco Restaurant with his vice-president for planning and longtime aide, Kathryn Pelgrift.

An hour before the next morning's eleven o'clock board meeting, Paley asked Taylor to his office. In some ways, Taylor was still the boyish thirty-seven-year-old who had entered Black Rock four years earlier. He had long sideburns, and his hair curled up at the edge of his shirt collar. But the strain showed on Taylor's round face; the job had aged him.

His nemesis, the tanned, white-haired CBS chairman, sat at his desk, with board members Henry Schacht and Roswell Gilpatric nearby. "We want your resignation," Paley said. Taylor was dumbstruck. "Why?" he asked. "I thought I was doing a good job." Only fifteen months earlier Paley had publicly signaled Taylor's position as his successor, calling him "outstanding" and "exceptional." Despite the ratings slump, CBS had a war chest of $400 million in cash and was about to report record sales and earnings for the first nine months of 1976.

"You've done a great . . ." Paley started to say, but Gilpatric interrupted him. "Don't answer that," said the lawyer. "It's like a marriage gone bad." With that, Taylor knew any argument was futile. He cleaned out his desk and left the building by noon. "I felt a keen sense of injustice, not anger," Taylor said later.

As in the past, Bill Paley was brutal and insensitive to his second-in-command, who for all his flaws did not deserve such callous treatment. Taylor, who had never had a contract at CBS, reached a generous financial settlement of more than $1 million: three years of base pay (more than $600,000) plus his stock, worth nearly $500,000 when he sold it on his last day.

The poor kid from Rahway could be faulted for letting CBS go to his head, but afterwards he would pursue a career consistent with the principles he preached. Assisted by Rockefeller money, he went on to head a cable television channel of wholesome family fare that would eventually meld successfully with a cultural channel owned by ABC. Later he settled in as dean of Fordham University's Graduate Business School.

A good man with a deep conscience, Taylor was too young, too eager, and too thin-skinned to cope with his relentless and unforgiving master. As he grew older, Paley magnified the failings of those beneath him. "With time and patience and without people pushing him, Arthur might have made it," said Kidder Meade. "All Arthur needed was some management and direction," said Robert Wussler. "But Paley didn't know how to give it to him."

49

ARTHUR TAYLOR'S firing created a mudslide of bad publicity. In the early going, CBS's public relations people succeeded in painting Taylor as the villain. *The Washington Post* called him a "financial martinet," who "drove out some of the most creative CBS executives." In its initial coverage, the *New York Times* correctly attributed Taylor's departure to incompatibility with Paley, noting that CBS's ratings slide was not Taylor's fault. Programming, the *Times* pointed out, was "Paley's domain." Two days later, however, the *Times* hammered Taylor for his "business efficiency mentality," and blamed him unfairly for the departure of Wood and other executives.

The following week, *TV Digest,* a widely circulated industry newsletter, hit the right nerve: neither ratings nor financial performance was the cause. Taylor was sacked because of a "personality conflict." Paley, said the piece, was a "jealous old man" who didn't want Taylor to take over.

Fortune magazine rendered the toughest and most perceptive judgment, comparing the drama at CBS to *King Lear:*

> Like the old man trying to snatch back his kingdom from his chosen heirs, William S. Paley, 75, the chairman of CBS, suddenly banished Arthur R. Taylor from the president's office. . . . Paley has anointed first one heir, then another, only to snatch back the mantle. . . . Resentment filled the old man at Taylor's blatant longing for the crown.

Several days after *Fortune* hit the newsstands, Paley summoned the author of the piece, Robert Lamb, to Black Rock. Paley gave him a wide-ranging interview—his first to the magazine in seven years—repeating points and views he had offered many times. Pressed about Taylor, Paley grew angry and defensive, insisting that his decision had not been sudden and claiming falsely that he had told the outside directors of his plan to sack Taylor five months earlier.

Then, after announcing he had to go to lunch, Paley whipped out the offending article. "You said a few things here," growled the chairman, reading sentences aloud and challenging their accuracy. "I know the people where you work," Paley said to Lamb. "I don't know who you know there—but call up Mr. Roy Larsen about Mr. Backe if you want to get the lowdown." (Larsen, along with Henry Luce, was one of the founders of Time, Inc.)

The veiled threat was an unusually confrontational display for a man noted for his cool, charming posture with reporters. But Paley felt he had been damaged by the reaction to his handling of Taylor. He was extremely agitated over this latest blot on his reputation.

Until the previous year, Paley had carefully maintained an almost spotless facade. He had endured short bursts of bad publicity when he leaned too hard on various CBS newsmen. But otherwise he had been lionized and treated with near reverence as the CBS godhead.

Paley had long relied on an efficient public relations machine that included consultants Earl Newsom and Arthur Newmyer. When Newsom died, his New York manager, Arthur Tourtellot, came to CBS to work exclusively for Paley. Along with a CBS staff headed by Kidder Meade, a West Point graduate who lost a leg in World War II, they managed to smother all evidence of Paley's peccadilloes and fan his legend. Press interviews were tape-recorded by CBS and the transcripts carefully edited before being sent out to reporters. The publicity men not only wrote Paley's speeches, statements, and letters; they even on occasion drafted people outside the company to promote the Paley cause.

For example, in July 1974, the *New York Times* op-ed page ran an excerpt from a speech Paley had given at Syracuse University calling for the elimination of the FCC's Fairness Doctrine. The speech had been Paley's first major address in six years, and when a letter highly critical of Paley's position ran in the *Times* the following week, the publicity engines at CBS went into overdrive. At first the publicity men drafted an indignant reply to be signed by Arthur Taylor. When the law department vetoed the idea, public relations aide Leonard Spinrad wrote a letter "for the signature of someone outside CBS." That letter to the *Times,* with some minor additions, was signed by David Manning White, a professor of journalism at Boston University, on July 31. The *Times* did not run the letter.

Beginning in 1975, cracks appeared in Paley's artfully constructed image, offering unsavory glimpses of both his professional and private life. The first was in the book called *CBS: Reflections in a Bloodshot Eye* by Robert Metz, a financial columnist for the *New York Times*. Published in the summer of 1975, Metz's portrait caught Paley's arrogance, coldness, and ruthlessness in some detail, prompting an incensed reaction from CBS.

At first, Meade issued a memo stating that "we intend to ignore this book." But later he reconsidered and fired off a five-page single-spaced letter to Metz's publisher, as well as book editors at newspapers and magazines around the country. The letter called the book "unseemly, scandalous trash," and sought to undermine the author's credibility by listing some forty alleged errors. Metz did make his share of mistakes, but those singled out by CBS were largely picayune and in many instances debatable. Among the quibbles: that Paley's longest vacation was six weeks, not several months; that his manservant did not accompany him on weekend visits to friends; and that he, not his chauffeur, drove his Maserati on weekends.

By August, the *Wall Street Journal* reported that CBS "has been throwing a corporate temper tantrum." Paley was said to be especially angered over Metz's accurate characterization of him as an "absentee landlord." Under apparent pressure from Paley, Carter Burden disavowed the comments he made to Metz in an interview.

Still, the book was widely reviewed and for the most part well received. It sold briskly, despite Metz's inability to obtain bookings on any network talk shows. Producers on the shows, all of whom had received CBS's letter, denied succumbing to pressure. In an interview, Metz called his blackout an "inadvertent conspiracy—people making independent judgments not to use me on their programs, but all for the same reason."

Far more damaging to Paley's reputation was a 13,000-word *Esquire* piece that hit the newsstands in mid-October 1975. Entitled "La Côte Basque, 1965," it was the first fragment of Truman Capote's long-awaited (and never finished) novel, *Answered Prayers*. In the story, a Capote-like narrator named "Jonesy" dined at La Côte Basque, the famous Manhattan restaurant, with an American friend, "Lady Ina Coolbirth," a "big breezy peppy broad" married to a wealthy British lord. Across the room, Capote wrote, were Babe Paley and her sister Betsey; the author's mingling of real names with fictitious ones underscored the story's apparent grounding in fact.

As the fascinated Jonesy listened, Ina dished the dirt on high society, much as Capote and his swans had done countless times over the years. Her most egregious tale concerned a man named "Sidney Dillon," a "conglomateur" and "adviser to Presidents" with a "twinkle-grinning tough-Jew face." He was married to "Cleo," "the most beautiful creature alive." Dillon longed for acceptance in WASP society. One manifestation of that yearning was his attraction to the wife of a former New York governor, a woman Jonesy said "looked as if she wore tweed brassieres and played a lot of golf."

The governor's wife, wrote Capote, "was the living incorporation of everything denied him, forbidden to him as a Jew, no matter how beguiling and rich he might be . . . all those places he would never sit down to a table of backgammon, all those golf courses where he would never sink a putt." Dillon, recounted Ina, had told her all about the governor's wife himself.

One night, with Cleo in Boston for a wedding, Dillon was seated next to the governor's wife at a dinner party. Afterwards he took her back to his pied-à-terre at the Pierre Hotel to get "her opinion of his new Bonnard." Their crude, unsuccessful lovemaking was capped by Dillon's discovery that the governor's wife had menstruated all over his sheets. When Dillon confronted the woman, her look revealed that "she had mocked him, punished him for his Jewish presumption."

Unable to call anyone for help ("It struck him," Capote wrote, "that he had a hundred chums but really no friends"), Sidney Dillon spent five frantic hours scrubbing away bloodstains "the size of Brazil" and then drying the sheets in his small kitchen oven before Cleo was due to arrive in the morning.

It was a scandalous piece of writing—vindictive and sickening in its details. Along with *tout* New York, Babe Paley read it immediately. The first person she called was Slim Keith. "Have you seen *Esquire*?" asked Babe. When Slim said she had not, Babe replied, "Get it, and call me." Reading it, Slim later recalled, "I didn't believe my eyes. Reading about Lady Coolbirth was like looking in a mirror. But out of the armature of me came all that terrible stuff." Slim called Babe back. "Who is that person?" Babe asked evenly. "I don't know," replied Slim. "Yes, you do," said Babe. "It reads like Bill Paley."

"I knew it was Bill, of course," said Slim years later, "because Truman had told that story to me. But I said to Babe, 'No, it isn't Bill.' I think for a while she believed me." Everyone in New York social circles recognized the lusty Bill Paley. There were simply too many clues—the pied-à-terre (substitute the St. Regis for the Pierre), the transcendently beautiful wife, even Paley's role in advising Truman and Eisenhower. The common assumption was that the governor's wife was the late Marie Harriman, who had owned an art gallery in the early days. This impression was reinforced by the hint that Dillon had asked the governor's wife for her views on a new painting.

Kidder Meade had obtained a copy of the story before publication. "I told Paley he could read it, but I didn't want to discuss it," recalled Meade. "I recommended that he ignore it, that he not react to it." Meade was right; denying that he was Sidney Dillon would only have called further attention to Paley. Capote expected a blast of anger, but Paley explained to a friend, "I have other ways of torturing the little shit."

When Capote called, Paley was quintessentially cool. After starting to read it, he told Capote, "I fell asleep. Then a terrible thing happened: the magazine was thrown away." When Capote offered to send another, Paley replied that he was preoccupied. "My wife," he said—pointedly, he didn't refer to Capote's erstwhile dear friend as Babe—"is very ill." That was the end for the Paleys and Capote.

Paley repeated his line about falling asleep all over town and got a good laugh. "Of course he didn't fall asleep," said Meade. "It was too vile, too filthy. You couldn't fall asleep reading it, especially if it was about you and your wife."

Many who knew the Paleys believed the Sidney Dillon story to be essentially true, although embroidered. "Everyone had known that story as part of the gossip," explained Charlotte Curtis. In the view of Gerald Clarke, Capote's tale was a twisted form of revenge—for Babe. "Now that she was dying," wrote Clarke, Capote "was avenging her in the one way he knew how: by holding up to ridicule the man who had caused her so much hurt."

Babe, said Charlotte Curtis, was "devastated" by Capote's treachery. She could never forgive him, explained Jean Stein, because of her ingrained loyalty to family: "Truman didn't understand the kind of woman she was, that she would have to be loyal first to her husband, and that Truman would be left out." Stein once tried to explain Capote's motivation to Babe. "She heard me," said Stein. "But she was so private and felt that whatever she had told him had been violated."

Capote wrote Babe two long letters that went unanswered. His long-time companion, Jack Dunphy, called to ask her forgiveness. "Never!" she replied, but weakened under his pressure. "Let me talk it over with Bill," she finally said. Around the same time, Truman encountered Babe and Slim at the fashionable Quo Vadis Restaurant. "Hello, Bobalink," said Truman, summoning his favorite pet name for Babe. "Hello, Truman," she replied. Slim cut him cold.

Even as Paley simmered over this embarrassment, he was girding for another negative onslaught. This time the avenging angel was David Halberstam, the celebrated reporter who had proved his adversarial mettle as a correspondent for the *New York Times* during the Vietnam War. In December, the *Atlantic Monthly* was due to publish the first of two 25,000-word excerpts from *The Powers That Be,* Halberstam's book-in-progress about CBS, Time, Inc., *The Washington Post,* and the *Los Angeles Times.*

Paley had been tracking Halberstam's project for months. Public relations aides called the author to find out who he had talked to and what they were saying. On learning that Halberstam was going to Tulsa, Oklahoma, to give a lecture, Paley had a CBS News stringer assigned to tape-record his remarks.

When Paley finally sat down with Halberstam for two interviews in mid-1975, the CBS chairman was mainly interested in damage control. In his notes following the first session, Halberstam called it "a remarkably neurotic performance: defensive, insecure . . . I have never seen such sensitivity in all the people I've interviewed in my life. . . . He seems a man so wildly defensive and so shielded as to be somewhat more pathetic than he really is." Halberstam was struck, as were so many who worked closely with Paley, by the selectivity of his memory: "the marvelous capacity of a king to hear only what he wants to hear and remember only what he wants to remember."

After the *Atlantic* began promoting the pieces in early September, CBS executives debated how to react. "We have been and are going through a period of severe criticism on several fronts," wrote Meade in a memo to Paley. "What should be our posture? High profile, low profile, business-as-usual?"

Since Halberstam was expected to focus on the network's news operations, Paley's first response, in mid-September 1975, was to hire Martin Mayer, the author of *About Television,* to write a history of CBS News. Interviewing Paley, Mayer was bemused by the CBS chairman's insistence, even in the face of contradictory documents, on sticking to his incorrect versions of various events. Mayer spent twelve weeks writing what he called a "perfectly respectable report" of 27,000 words. But Mayer's work was shelved after the first *Atlantic* article appeared; CBS needed stronger ammunition than what Mayer termed his "straightforward and neutral document."

An irate Paley went on the attack after reading Halberstam's description of the CBS chairman's relentless drive for profits, his abandonment of Murrow, his brutal treatment of various executives, his social climbing, and his sensitivity over his origins. "He really hated those *Atlantic* articles," recalled Meade. "One thing about Halberstam," recalled Meade. "He was Jewish and Paley was Jewish but Paley didn't like Jewish people. I don't understand it, but if a Jew criticized him, Paley took it more personally."

Paley's strongest reaction was to what Halberstam later termed a "neurosis about the Jewish question." The CBS chief took great exception to Halberstam's account of his refusal to back *Fiddler on the Roof,* which he had described as "too Jewish." This prompted Halberstam to reconfirm the account with Michael Burke, the man to whom Paley made the comment.

Paley mustered Meade and a small army of public relations aides to dissect Halberstam's prose for inaccuracies. At first Paley considered legal action. He consulted an attorney from Coudert Brothers to discuss possible grounds for a libel suit. The lawyer cautioned Paley that such action would involve discovery proceedings, which would only be to Halberstam's advantage. Paley ultimately bought the attorney's argument that he could not make a sufficient case.

Meade and Tourtellot then prepared a 9,000-word reply. "I spent hundreds of hours with Paley going over each of the points," recalled Meade. Paley was a man obsessed. "He kept Halberstam's articles in his pocket for several months," recalled Arthur Taylor. "He read them over and over." Paley tried initially to sell his rebuttal to the *Atlantic* as an article. Editor Robert Manning declined but offered to publish a considerably shorter letter to the editor.

Instead, Paley had his public relations men modify their piece into a point-by-point rebuttal, entitled "A Reply," by William S. Paley, and dated February 27, 1976. Paley ordered thirty thousand copies to be printed as a thirty-two-page booklet for distribution to CBS shareholders.

Most of the contentions were matters of judgment and opinion. But while Halberstam had captured the real Paley, he had slipped up on some minor facts, misstating some events that followed the 1972 Watergate broadcasts, and affixing the wrong date to Paley's scheme for luring radio stations to his network in the early days of CBS. Stanton's accompanying four-page statement—prepared at Paley's request—rebutted several more serious errors about the former president. Wisely, Paley avoided lodging specific objections to Halberstam's treatment of his personal life, saying only that "he commits one error after another."

Paley's comments were laced with bitter attacks on Halberstam as a journalist. Even after all their work on Paley's behalf, both Meade and Tourtellot counseled him not to release the pamphlet. In the end, Paley listened to his advisers. The stacks of pamphlets stayed in the warehouse.

Shifting gears yet again, Paley sent his rebuttal to Halberstam, who agreed to make some changes but dismissed the bulk of Paley's cavils as differences of interpretation. Over the next several years Paley would take his campaign behind the scenes, applying pressure on Halberstam's publishing house, Alfred Knopf, to remove offending passages from the manuscript. "I told Bill just to ignore it but he insisted on trying everything, even threatening the publisher," recalled John Backe. "He spent an enormous amount of time on it and only ended up boosting Halberstam's sales." At one point, Robert Gottlieb, Halberstam's editor, remarked to Irene Selznick, "Your friend Bill Paley has an inflated sense of his power. He should know that writers and publishers have rights, too."

Indeed, Paley's overreactions to Metz and Halberstam were all the more remarkable coming from a man who professed to uphold the First Amendment. As he was bearing down on Halberstam, Paley authored a *New York Times* op-ed piece declaring that "print journalism has always been defending the most basic rights of the press to report and the people to know against one assault after another." And in his interview with *Fortune*'s Robert Lamb in November 1976, Paley said: "You know, if someone came out with a law or a rule that a guy writing a book had to avoid certain subjects, I'd fight it, you know, to the last gasp of breath I had. There's something in me that is very opposed to any limitations that are imposed on so-called creative people."

Paley could not grasp why he attracted such bad press after so many years of laudatory coverage. Others, however, could trace the decline straight to Stanton's departure. "It was widely felt that Frank Stanton should not have left at sixty-five," recalled Meade. "Most of us inside CBS thought it was a goddamn crime. He was genetically about forty. He was at his prime, and he had at least five more years of a tremendous contribution. He was a wonderful talent and Bill Paley got rid of him, and that angered many people. There was a lot of resentment which you cannot bottle up. Even the security analysts on Wall Street felt that way. So Paley reaped the harvest of that. There was no question that it had a lot to do with the bad publicity. It was a tragic error that Bill Paley made. And all because he was jealous."

Ultimately, Paley decided that the best defense was a good offense. Since the late 1960s, publishers had periodically talked to him about a memoir. But it was not until March 1975, when he knew Halberstam was on the case, that Paley signed on with Doubleday & Company. His theory, he explained to several CBS executives, was to neutralize the Halberstam book with his own account, to be published at the same time. CBS hired an experienced researcher who supervised a staff of ten that over the next four years would amass a mountain of research at a cost to the company of more than $200,000.

For his amanuensis, Paley chose John McDonald, a veteran writer who had retired from *Fortune* several years earlier and had ghosted Alfred Sloan's memoir, *My Years with General Motors*. Both McDonald and an assistant came aboard as members of Paley's personal staff. McDonald taped more than thirty hours of interviews with Paley; no one else was interviewed except to check certain factual points.

"The problem from the beginning was that Paley wasn't willing to reveal much about himself," recalled one person who worked on the project. "McDonald would interview him for hours on end. He would ask the right questions. But Paley would more often than not respond with something unrevealing. It was extraordinarily difficult to get him to admit he failed at anything. McDonald would say, 'People won't believe you had one brilliant success after another.' So Paley would say, 'I remember once in the early thirties I heard a singer in a club and I signed him up, but on the radio he was awful. That was one of my failures.' "

Working from transcripts and other documents, McDonald and his assistant turned out chapters, trying to use as many of Paley's words as possible. Paley read the drafts and dictated comments for revisions. Invariably his changes tended to flatten the book, muting strong opinions and tamping down adjectives, as when McDonald characterized Paley's dinner parties as "glittering." "I don't want my dinner parties called glittering," Paley said.

As the book progressed, McDonald's disillusion grew. Alfred Sloan had been a man of penetrating ideas, often expressed eloquently in his writing. But Paley's letters and memoranda were mostly perfunctory; he didn't commit his deeper thoughts to writing. Through his comments and corrections on the manuscript, Paley inadvertently revealed how his desire for attention and recognition clashed with his instinctive fear of being exposed. He tried to perpetuate his myth by recounting innocuous stories that he told at so many dinner parties. In sanitizing his life story, Paley did something even his worst critics couldn't have done: he stripped his life of its richness and texture, and undermined both his power and his accomplishments.

50

IN DECEMBER 1971, Paley's old rival David Sarnoff died at age eighty after a protracted illness. Several months before the end, when Sarnoff was nearly blind and could barely speak, he invited Paley for a farewell visit. As the CBS chief reminisced with the RCA founder, Sarnoff reached out, found Paley's hand, and clasped it. Later, Paley marveled at the strength in the grip of the dying man. He knew that with Sarnoff's passing, he was the last pioneer. The responsibility for preserving the heritage of broadcasting would be his alone.

Early that year, Paley's aide-de-camp, Arthur Tourtellot, had proposed that Paley set up a broadcasting archive. Tourtellot had convened a two-day conference of museum curators, historians, librarians, and other experts at the St. Regis Hotel to discuss the proposal. Paley did not attend, but Tourtellot reported back that the group overwhelmingly favored a museum open to the public instead of a library for scholars. Paley warmed to the idea of a carefully culled collection of television and radio programs as one more way to perpetuate his legacy. A museum would assure that the man who symbolized television would be linked in the public mind only with the best of a medium that pandered far more than it enriched.

Three years later, Robert Saudek, a veteran TV producer and instructor at Harvard who had participated in the 1971 meeting, got a call from Tourtellot. Saudek had strongly endorsed the idea of a museum, and now Paley wanted to discuss his ideas over lunch.

"We talked at length," Saudek recalled of the October 1974 meeting. "He wanted to put a great deal of money in it—in the magnitude of $30 million. But he seemed to be anxious about whether it could work. He was ambivalent. Tourtellot was pushing him to be optimistic. I told him I was convinced it could work. Paley said he would put up $250,000 to start with. Then he got cold feet and thought it wasn't enough money. He was very ambivalent. He ran hot and cold."

But Paley was impressed enough with Saudek's conviction to hire him in mid-1975 to organize the museum. Paley picked out the site, a building next to Paley Park on East 53rd Street that was owned by the William S. Paley Foundation. To cover the cost of rent, he deducted $45,000 from his first yearly commitment of $250,000.

No decision was too small for Paley's attention. He approved the museum's cataloguing system and oversaw negotiations with the networks to obtain tapes of programs. He was determined to amass a hefty collection—it would start with 718 broadcasts—by the time the museum opened.

Paley was equally immersed in the museum's interior design. When the architect proposed using glass partitions inside, Paley wanted to know how much the annual window-washing bill would be. He asked astute questions about elevator capacity and crowd control. "He used his experience," recalled Saudek. "He was always skeptical, very cautious and deliberate. He penetrated to the heart of the matter and didn't take anything for granted. He was never embarrassed to ask how much something cost."

Paley insisted on bringing ABC and NBC into the museum's operations as well. They resisted at first, fearing the museum would emphasize CBS, but eventually they came around and contributed $50,000 apiece. Tourtellot favored placing historians, film curators, and librarians on the museum's board, while Paley suggested naming the other network chiefs. Later, bypassing Tourtellot's recommendations, he also included Babe, his family attorney Donald Osborn, and several friends.

One conspicuous absence from the board was Stanton, who had already contributed $1,000 to become the museum's first lifetime member. At a meeting of museum staff members to discuss board candidates, someone said, "What about Frank Stanton?" A member of Paley's secretariat replied, "That would be poison."

The board was kept intentionally small—at least in part to minimize the possibility of any leak about the museum's plans. "We kept it quiet for eighteen months," recalled Saudek. "It was amazing. Paley had said it had to be an absolute secret. He was afraid, I guess, if it got out, that people might have expectations he could not meet. He was always nervous about it, and about committing his money to it. I think he considered this museum as a personal thing, his monument. And he didn't want a failure." By keeping a lid on the project, Paley reserved the right to cancel even up to the last moment if it looked as if the museum would not work.

On November 9, 1976, the Museum of Broadcasting opened its doors for the first time. Paley announced the museum on his own, without his board—further affirmation of his role as guiding force. At a press conference he pledged a minimum of $2 million to underwrite costs for the first five years. In its style, the museum reflected CBS's spare design, even down to the identical typeface. It was an admittedly modest facility—a complex of rooms on three floors for viewing and listening, storage, and administration—and was greeted in the press with respect if not wild enthusiasm. Still, there was nothing that Paley could be ashamed of.

Why, after leaving so strong an imprint on the place, did he not name it the Paley Museum? Arthur Taylor, who watched the museum's tortuous progress until he was fired (a month before its opening), said, "He had a certain desire for anonymity, but it was not a matter of modesty. If it were modesty, he would have let someone unrelated to him develop it. What he did was to create a monument to broadcasting, knowing he was Mr. Broadcasting. He pushed ahead and took an aggressive approach to cementing his position in history." By not affixing his name, Paley could get others to help defray the costs; yet as the prime mover and biggest contributor, he could control the museum's direction. Paley's strategy was practical—and characteristically cunning.

In the autumn of 1976, with the museum on track and his book in the works, Paley threw himself into CBS, determined to restore the network's programming to its former preeminence. Babe's fragile condition curtailed his social life, so Paley really had nowhere else to turn.

"He was embarrassed that he had to fire Arthur," recalled Jack Schneider. "His whole life was coming apart. He wasn't a social lion anymore because he couldn't play the game. And there was the additional public humiliation of losing number one. He couldn't do anything else, so he thought he would plunge in and he would be the savior. But his touch didn't turn it around. It made it worse."

CBS's ratings dropped further between 1976 and 1977, and the pressure intensified to emulate ABC's formula for success: frothy comedies and what became known as "jiggle" or "T and A" (for "tits and ass") television—a plethora of curvaceous women wearing as little as possible. At first Jack Schneider and Robert Wussler resisted, contending that such shows were at odds with the network's "Tiffany" reputation. But despite Paley's periodic exhortations for quality, he wanted results. "Where are the pretty girls?" he kept asking. "I want pretty girls." "It was ironic that Paley's image was as an advocate of quality television," recalled John Backe. "He would say that for public consumption. But in program meetings the guy who would slip in the sleaze was Paley. He would want more T and A if it would get him the numbers."

The CBS chairman was on the phone every day with neophyte network president Wussler—tracking him down in bars and restaurants. Even when he was in Europe or Nassau, Paley rang twice daily, usually before ten in the morning and in the evening at around six. "Let's talk about the ratings," Paley would say, followed by, "Have you read Liz Smith [the *New York Daily News* gossip columnist] today? What did she say? What do you hear from the boys on the West Coast?"

When he felt especially anxious, Paley pestered mid- and low-echelon programming executives as well. One Saturday he reached Harvey Shephard at home when the CBS programmer was baby-sitting his four small children. "Paley was talking about something big ABC was doing and asked what we had to challenge ABC," recalled Shephard. "The boys were screaming and punching each other. I finally said, 'Mr. Paley, I cannot concentrate. Can I call you on Monday?' "

During the increasingly frequent periods when Babe's confinement prevented them from traveling, Paley followed a more rigorous schedule than he had in years, putting in a full day with several meetings devoted to programming, and lunches devoted to business, not pleasure. "I would find him in my conference room working the old-fashioned metallic programming board," recalled Wussler. "He would come in there a couple of times a week and spend a half hour to an hour there, moving around the pieces like a checkerboard. I would go in there and he would be playing with the board and I would say, 'How are you doing, sir?' 'Oh, Roberto,' he would say, 'I am trying to figure out what to do with Tuesday at eight.' "

Part of Paley's problem was that instead of making decisions based on solid information, he was winging it more than ever. And the old magic was gone. Paley was too removed from his audience. For decades, he had led a rarefied life. He did not carry cash, never stood in line, and each morning his faithful valet Dean knotted his tie. Early in 1977, after CBS acquired *Woman's Day* magazine as part of its Fawcett Publications purchase, Paley asked Jack Purcell, president of CBS Publishing, "Who would buy this? It's nothing but recipes." Purcell told him that 8 million women bought the magazine every three weeks. Paley was amazed. "Where do they go to buy it?" he said. "Supermarkets," said Purcell, who could tell by Paley's quizzical look that the CBS chairman had never been in that sort of store. Purcell subsequently took Paley to a supermarket on the West Side. After walking all around the store to inspect the displays, Paley stood transfixed as women moved through the check-out lines buying *Woman's Day* or *Family Circle*.

John Backe, by contrast, was decidedly a man of the people. Dark-eyed and heavy-browed, his earnest mien was softened by a sweet, almost shy smile. Midwestern-born, he had earned his MBA at night school in Ohio and served in the Strategic Air Command during the 1950s as a bomber pilot. He had an unassuming manner and lived a quiet suburban life; his favorite weekend diversion was flying a twin-engine Cessna.

At CBS he steered away from acquisitions, allayed the anxieties of executives rocked by the Taylor upheaval, and focused on rebuilding the program schedule. To direct more resources into TV programming—an estimated $32 million in development money—he ordered CBS's other businesses to cut back, a painful but essential move. With Paley, Backe trod carefully, watching and listening. After Backe's first month on the job, Arthur Tourtellot invited him to lunch.

"How's it going?" asked Tourtellot, whom Backe knew was Paley's closest confidant. "Let me try something on you," said Backe. "Bill Paley is very insecure." Replied Tourtellot, "You are very perceptive. One thing you should know is that the better you are in your job, the more he will try to tear you down." "Watching him operate," continued Backe, "the things he worries about amaze me. How could he be so hung up, after all he has achieved and all his money?" Replied Tourtellot, "It is so deep-seated. That is why Babe is his front."

In February 1977, Goldie Paley died at age ninety-five, and her son took the news with noticeable calm. Top CBS executives agreed they would refrain from commenting on the event, but Wussler went his own way. "I'm sorry about your mother," he said to Paley late in the afternoon of her death. "Oh Roberto," Paley replied. "That's very nice of you. Goldie had a full life. She was a helluva woman. From her deathbed, she was telling me she was ninety-five. I know she was ninety-six." (Goldie may have shaved several more years off her age; her secretary suspected as much, pointing out that Goldie had no birth certificate.)

Paley relinquished his chief executive title to John Backe in the spring of 1977 as promised. Throughout that April and May, Backe was the model of deferential respect. In interviews he emphasized that he would keep the chairman informed and seek his advice. For his part, Paley said, "This is not a charade we are going to play. I expect Mr. Backe to make the final decisions." Yet after a brief pause, the chairman added, "Of course I'd be surprised and maybe even a little disappointed if I'm not asked about problems as they arise."

Indeed, Paley was quick to stress that he would continue to come to the office virtually every day. Some observers remained appropriately skeptical. The areas in which Paley said he would keep an interest—"policy questions, acquisitions, planning and creative activities"—noted *Time,* seemed "a pretty fair definition of a chief executive's interests." Said one former CBS executive to the *Wall Street Journal,* "Bill Paley isn't going to give up control of CBS until he's carried out in an elegant, hand-carved rosewood box."

That October Backe announced a reorganization of the TV network patterned after that of top-rated ABC. He kicked Jack Schneider upstairs, replacing him with an eager financial executive, Gene Jankowski, and abolished the job of network president, thereby removing Robert Wussler from his job. Backe broke the network into thirds, creating new presidents for entertainment, sports (where Wussler landed), and administration.

Backe had conceived the realignment to break down the bureaucracy of CBS's television business. He argued that programming had to be split off from advertising sales and other chores. Moreover, said Backe, the programming chief and his staff had to move to Hollywood.

Paley resisted the reorganization at first; he perceived correctly that it would help pull programming away from his control. Schneider also tried to block the move—on the grounds that it would create another layer of management. But Backe persuaded Paley by arguing that the only way CBS could improve its relations with Hollywood producers was to move its programming executives out of New York. Backe and Paley agreed that the best man to be the new entertainment division president was Robert Daly, a forty-year-old accountant with shrewd programming instincts.

"My first order of business," Daly announced on taking over, "will be to dispel the notion that certain programs are not the CBS type." Not only did CBS parade the pretty girls, it promised in its promotions on the air, "Turn us on: We'll turn you on."

The biggest loser that October was former crown prince Jack Schneider. "My rubber band had lost its snap," Schneider said years later. "I wasn't doing a good job at putting up with Paley's nonsense, his harebrained ideas." Six months after the reorganization, Backe nudged Schneider out of the company. Not only did Paley hold Schneider responsible for CBS's programming troubles, the CBS chairman had grown weary of his irritating presence. "Jack would make a crack in the newspaper anonymously and Paley would know who made it," recalled Kidder Meade. "It would burn Paley up. Jack had his bellyful of Paley. It showed all over the place. Finally, Paley had Backe administer the coup de grâce."

Paley seemed relieved that Backe willingly stepped up to the unpalatable decisions necessary to get the network back on track. By autumn 1977, he was finding it difficult to concentrate on much of anything at work. Besides Babe's illness, he was preoccupied by his autobiography. Paley, who had squeezed all the juice from the story, predictably found John McDonald's manuscript wanting. "When it was almost finished, he worried that it wasn't snappy enough," recalled one man close to the project. "He got an idea that it wasn't a best seller. But what he wanted was impossible. He wanted zippy fast reading, but he wasn't willing to provide the raw material." Said Margaret Kennedy, who headed the book's research team, "The book was frustrating because we had to suppress so much."

Paley secretly brought in a CBS News producer named Perry Wolff to assess the manuscript. After Wolff submitted each revision, Paley would sit for hours at a Louis XV desk in his apartment, reaching for expensive soft black pencils arranged by Dean in a flower basket, and laboriously copying Wolff's corrections in his own hand so McDonald would not know about the existence of a "ghost's ghost."

Wolff's principal criticism was Paley's glaring omission of Stanton; in the original manuscript, the former CBS president only rated a couple of passing references. When Wolff wrote a chapter praising Stanton's taste and business judgment, Paley demanded a rewrite incorporating comments about Stanton's lack of programming ability and miscalculations over Hytron. The second version pleased Paley no better; he tore up both of them.

Paley continued to complain that the manuscript was "too wooden" and too much a corporate history. Finally in the spring of 1978, Doubleday called in a new writer, Alvin Moscow, who had worked with Richard Nixon on *Six Crises*. Paley rented Moscow a furnished apartment, paid all his expenses, and installed him in an office on the thirty-fifth floor of Black Rock. Moscow worked at a furious pace to put a new gloss on the manuscript. Three times a week he met Paley at the end of the day to discuss proposed changes. Each Saturday they spent several hours in Paley's apartment reviewing the week's work and planning the next chapter. Moscow probed his subject for explanations and clarifications, and Paley scrutinized every new word written by Moscow, a seasoned pro who established only one rule: he would argue a point twice. If Paley still disagreed, Moscow would drop it.

Selecting the book's 159 photographs was nearly as difficult for Paley as pulling together the prose. He pored over hundreds of pictures, intent on including all of his friends, even those he never mentioned in the text. "It was nuts," said one participant in the process. As in the book itself, Paley stubbornly diminished Stanton's presence in the pictures. The long-time CBS president appeared in only six—all either with Paley or in a group. A CBS executive who helped Paley assemble the photographs tried three times to insert a head shot of Stanton. Three times Paley threw it out. Finally, the executive said, "You have pictures of Elmer Davis and Hubbell Robinson, and their accomplishments were minuscule compared to Frank Stanton." Paley wouldn't budge.

Paley's animus toward Stanton was painfully apparent at CBS. Throughout the 1970s, Paley declined to use Stanton's services as a consultant and the two men kept a chilly distance. Both CBS executives and board members were discomfited by what they termed Paley's effort to "de-Stantonize" CBS. "You couldn't even mention his name," recalled Peter Derow, a former president of CBS Publishing. Early in his tenure, Backe had Stanton in for lunch. Afterwards, Paley summoned Backe to his office. "Don't you ever have him here again," said Paley. "He is trying to work against me." Recalled Roswell Gilpatric, "Here we were paying this huge fee to Stanton and not using him. But Bill felt Frank had served his purpose. He felt it was the end of their relationship." For his part, Stanton kept abreast of developments at CBS through his extensive network of contacts.

Stanton continued to sit on the CBS board, but he said little as a board member after his retirement. "It was deliberate," said Stanton. "I didn't think it was fair to my successors. But my silence was embarrassing to older members. They were confused because I did not comment." There was one ironically memorable moment when Stanton broke his silence. Paley had announced at the CBS annual meeting in 1977 that Backe would shortly take over as chief executive; at the board meeting afterwards, Paley neglected to make the motion putting Backe's elevation to a vote. "Bill, I think you forgot something," said Stanton, who made the motion himself.

When Stanton turned seventy early in 1978, Paley forced him off the board. (Contractually, Stanton would remain a CBS consultant until December 1987.) CBS had a policy stipulating that directors retire at that age, although members sitting on the board before the policy went into effect were exempted from the rule. Stanton, along with fellow directors Paley,

Iglehart, Gilpatric, and William Burden (Carter's uncle), fell into that category. But Paley insisted Stanton had to comply because he came from management—conveniently ignoring that the chairman did as well. "It didn't sit well with Frank, but he yielded," said Gilpatric. Backe recalled Stanton's disquieting final board meeting: "We were going into an executive session, and it was time for Frank to leave. He got up and started to walk out. I stood up and shook his hand, and I couldn't believe it: Bill Paley didn't shake his hand or anything."

51

FOR A TIME in 1976 and 1977 it seemed that Babe's cancer had stabilized after Paley pulled strings to have her treated with Interferon, then in the experimental stage. In the summer of 1977, Babe wrote Irene Selznick from the Guinness yacht off St. Tropez to say, "so far, so good—never slept so much in my life. Bill in very good humor. Paris just gay enough. . . . The boat is perfect life for me gaining a little strength if not weight."

That autumn Babe went into a decline. The cancer had invaded her central nervous system, and Paley, determined to supervise her tests and treatments, cut his schedule at CBS, coming in only three to four days a week. Even then he was on the phone with doctors or checking in at home, where he had nurses on round-the-clock shifts. "He is not as jolly as he used to be," remarked one friend at the time. "They entertain less— it's a great effort for Babe now." When they tried to have a dinner party for close friends or family, Paley often presided alone, while Babe ate on a tray in her room. Afterwards, the guests would file to her bedside for a visit.

The daughter of a doctor, Babe took a stoic, almost clinical attitude toward her condition. She spoke authoritatively about her treatment and prognosis, all without complaint. Periodically, she would be taken by ambulance to Memorial Sloan-Kettering Cancer Center for treatments, or X-ray equipment would be brought to the house.

Alarmingly thin, she wore knits by Valentino to hide her skeletal appearance. The drugs and radiation made her hair fall out, an awful reminder of what had happened to her youngest daughter. "Oh God, now I know what Kate went through," she said one day while studying her reflection in the mirror held by her maid, Winnie Dooney. When she wasn't wearing a wig, Babe would knot a chiffon scarf around her head like an exquisite turban.

A stream of friends came to see her. In the morning, her secretary typed up a list of the day's visitors and placed it inside a picture frame at her bedside. Jean Stein brought Joan Didion for tea and Robert Rauschenberg for drinks. All who knew Babe were moved by her dignity and graciousness even when she was in dreadful pain. "She would make the most terrific effort to get done up and never say a word about her illness," recalled Horace Kelland, a frequent visitor.

Babe stayed in touch with her two sisters, mostly by telephone. Widowed by her second husband, the painter James Fosburgh, Minnie was stricken with cancer too, and Betsey ended up spending more time with her than with Babe. When Minnie felt able, she would come by. Babe's son Tony visited every morning and evening, and for the first time, Babe and Amanda drew close.

Amanda's dazzling marriage to Carter Burden had broken up in 1972 when she sued him for divorce on their eighth anniversary, charging "cruel and inhuman treatment." She had been dismayed to find her marriage on the same track as her mother's. "Carter wasn't considerate of Amanda—one of those machismo things," a friend of hers said at the time. "CB is highly influenced by Bill Paley. Paley can get away with that sort of thing, but Carter just came on as sort of a bully." So Amanda did what her mother had found impossible. She left—with her mother's blessing. When the divorce lawyers reached an impasse, Paley brought in Roswell Gilpatric from Cravath Swaine & Moore to devise an agreement.

Still, in the following years when Amanda was on her own with two school-age children, Babe kept her distance, even after she fell ill. "For a long time she didn't have the desire to see me," recalled Amanda. "It is a very weird thing to have your mother not want to see you. But that changed in the last three months of her life. She waited for my visits. She would walk with me. Those moments were terrific for me."

Babe's stepchildren, Hilary and Jeffrey, also came by, as did Billie, after he realized the gravity of his mother's illness. Only Kate stayed away, resisting written entreaties from both her mother and her father.

Aware that her time was limited, Babe had all her jewelry brought to her from the bank vaults. For several days, she sat on her bed amid heaps of necklaces, rings, pins, and bracelets sparkling with diamonds, rubies, pearls, sapphires, and emeralds, examining each piece and making notes about who would get what. She kept a stack of file cards on which she wrote all her bequests—to friends as well as relatives. Sometimes she shyly asked friends what they would like, or she would ask one friend for an opinion about her proposed gift to another. "She cared so much about who got left what," said Irene Selznick. "I don't know of anyone who talked as much as Babe did about that."

During this period Babe became close to a writer named Patrick O'Higgins, who had been a personal assistant and companion to Helena Rubenstein for many years. He essentially took the place of Truman Capote, and in many respects he was more of a kindred spirit. An aristocratic Irishman, he comforted and entertained her. "Patrick was enchanting," said Jean Stein. "He made her feel safe, and he was outrageous. He had this wonderful Irish leaping laughter."

O'Higgins was also a cancer victim. He and Babe talked every day on the phone, and he was a frequent visitor. "With him she could let her hair down," recalled the art critic John Richardson, a friend of both of them. "She could say things like 'God, doesn't it hurt?' or, 'Have you had this treatment?' " Explained Horace Kelland, "She didn't like talking about herself, so when she found in Patrick someone she could safely talk to, she became very attached."

Babe went to Lyford Cay for the last time at Christmas in 1977. By then she was extremely weak. She had to lie down—covered with her new $15,000 full-length blond Russian sable coat—for the entire trip aboard the gleaming white CBS plane. Patrick O'Higgins and Jean Stein came along to keep her company. Her son Billie flew in from Washington where he had settled down as a novice restaurateur. She was overjoyed to see him, although his brooding intensity—not to mention his beard, long hair, and gold hoop earring—clearly irritated his father.

Babe had difficulty keeping up with the routine of luncheon and dinner parties at Lyford Cay. One day she handed a seating chart to Jean Stein and directed her friend to take charge of the luncheon. On another evening, Babe's frustration was evident. "She was sitting on a sofa looking absolutely marvelous," recalled Jeanne Thayer, "but she was having trouble breathing. She was talking over the top of her breath. She said, 'Oh, if my father were living, I know I would not be going through this.' I think she meant he would have protected her somehow."

At the end of their vacation, the Paleys were hit with a horrible shock. Jeff Byers, who had married Hilary sixteen years before, leaped to his death from their Manhattan duplex apartment early in the morning on New Year's Eve. With the children still asleep upstairs, Hilary had come down to make breakfast when she felt a blast of cold air from her husband's open office window.

His suicide note mentioned "business problems." The handsome and ambitious Byers was deeply in debt, the result of some bad investments and extravagant spending habits that led him to amass an impressive collection of contemporary art. Many of their friends felt that Byers strove too hard to emulate Bill Paley's way of life. "Jeff desperately wanted to be like him," said Dorothy Paley Hirshon. Several times when Byers had come up short, his father-in-law bailed him out.

The Byers had visited Nassau over Christmas, and Jeff had asked Bill Paley for money once again. "Jeff had margin calls several times," recalled Paley's friend, Henryk de Kwiatkowski. "Each time a margin call was satisfied by Paley or whomever. And Jeff went in a little deeper to try to make up what was already lost. That Christmas, Jeff did come down and ask for more; the amount is not important. Bill refused to see him. Somebody else said no for him, and that is what turned Jeff off."

Neither Paley nor anyone else realized how unbalanced Jeff Byers had become. "Bill was fond of Jeff," said Dorothy. "The suicide was Jeff's own doing." When Paley heard the news, he rushed back to New York and took charge of the arrangements. "He stepped in nicely," said one Paley family intimate. "I respected him for that. There were deep feelings involved, and he had a hard time revealing them except in a formal way."

As Babe's illness worsened in the early months of 1978, her mood toward her husband became overtly hostile. She took to referring to him as "Paley." "They are trying to bake this out of me," she said of the radiation to one friend. "They are baking me in ovens. Paley won't tell me what they are doing. I don't have a say in anything about my life."

In Paley's presence, she unleashed a flood of recriminations. Those who witnessed her anger were shocked by its bitterness. "She complained that she had knuckled under, that she had done too many things that he wanted her to do," recalled one man close to the Paley family. "Everything that she harbored against him came out. She knew she was dying. She didn't have anything to lose."

For the first time in her life, Babe Paley had the upper hand in their marriage. She was the focal point and he receded to the sidelines. Instead of fleeing or fighting back, Bill Paley took the abuse. He remained patient and attentive. The more she abused him, the more devoted he became. "He was devastated," recalled Amanda. "He was in tears many times from March to July. He was desperate, frantic, and teary."

Yet his agony could not override his old habits. "He found another girl during that time," said Charlotte Curtis. "He wasn't visible or unkind, and he did spend the rest of the time with Babe." The other girl was half Babe's age, thirty-year-old Jan Cushing, a blond woman-about-town with intense social ambitions.

They met in February in Manhattan at the fashionable Hewitt School for girls, where his granddaughter and her goddaughter were in a play. When he introduced himself, she replied, "We have two things in common." "What are they?" asked Paley. "We are both Jewish and both married to Cushings." Paley roared with laughter and asked for her phone number—as his daughter Hilary stood nearby. "I got the feeling he was a ship about to sink by the way he was acting," said Jan Cushing.

He called the next morning. "I was surprised," she recalled. "One gets the feeling he has succeeded with women his whole life—girlfriend after girlfriend. I was an attractive young girl. My youth attracted him." His overture, she said later, "was a very cozy Jewish thing to do. A WASP would have said, 'I'll call you,' and not done it."

Jan Cushing was in the midst of getting a divorce from her husband, Frederick, who came from a socially prominent Long Island family. One day when Frederick was away, Jan asked Paley over for a drink at her Upper East Side apartment. Paley started talking about Babe's illness, and to Jan Cushing's amazement, he began to cry. "He couldn't believe Babe was dying," she recalled. "He didn't want to face it. He felt in a selfish way, 'How could she leave me when I need her so much, when I have not yet even retired?' "

Over the next few months, Paley visited Jan Cushing periodically at her apartment—for tea or drinks or lunch. "We did not go around town," she later said. "He couldn't be seen out with anyone. His wife was dying." Still, he did invite Jan once for lunch in his dining room at Black Rock, and he was seen leaving her apartment. Before long, they were the talk of the town.

"It was definitely not the affair people made it out to be," she claimed years later. "It was a friendship. I was a doctor more than a girlfriend. He would rather talk to me about his feelings than talk to a man. We talked and talked." And what did he talk about? Never business, to her disappointment. The day they had lunch in his office, he got more than two dozen phone calls and chattered on non-stop about his friend, the socialite Annette Reed. Sometimes he talked about wanting to buy a home in Southampton. But mostly he talked about Babe's sickness. "He was obsessed," said Jan Cushing.

Convinced that he wasn't thinking properly, she told him in the late spring that they should stop seeing each other. " No matter what happens, if we have dinner out at a restaurant you will feel guilty," she told him. "I don't think you can continue our friendship when your wife is that sick." He agreed, and the relationship ended.

Babe took to her bed that Easter, and in the following months spent much of her time sleeping. Bothered by the noise of construction on East 63rd Street, she moved into her dressing room, an elegant chamber filled with Japanese lacquered boxes and chests, ivory candlesticks, Chinese porcelain, Fabergé picture frames, terra-cotta portrait plaques, and antique needlepoint. There she would rest on a small bed with a tufted chintz headboard as Softly, her King Charles spaniel, lay at her feet.

She used oxygen to assist her breathing, but refused to be hooked up to a lot of tubes. To ease the pain, she was given frequent shots of morphine. In early June, Babe entered the terminal stage of her illness. At her request, her doctors began gradually withdrawing nutrition so that her life would not be prolonged artificially.

Still unwilling to give up his quest, Paley located a doctor in Philadelphia offering an experimental treatment. The new doctor ordered Babe's nutrition boosted, and dispatched his nurses by train to New York. They brought glass vials filled with the medication that they would inject daily. Once Dean mistakenly tossed one of the vials out of the refrigerator, only to learn that each cost more than $5,000.

"It was a painful period for everyone," recalled Amanda. "Before that, my mother had been mellow, but when they started the medication, she had to walk to get her lung working again. She was very brave, but after three weeks we knew it wouldn't work."

In mid-June, Babe made her final visit to Kiluna, accompanied by her husband, Tony, and Amanda. They drove her in a golf cart all over the grounds. Gardening had been a lifelong passion; she had spent years, under the guidance of English landscape designer Russell Page, creating a sunken "dell" of flowering trees, shrubs, and wildflowers sloping toward an oval pond. Babe had been characteristically meticulous, mapping every planting with a small marker on a Plasticine map. Before her illness she spent hours in the dell, a straw hat on her head and white cloth gloves on her hands, digging, planting, and pruning.

Only a year earlier, when she still had strength to follow the wide paths encircling the dell, she had encountered a local real estate developer named Ed Klar who had bought some land near the Paley property. "You know Kiluna will never be sold," she said. "My husband is going to make it into a park."

Now having savored her artfully planted woodland glen for the last time, she retreated in exhaustion to a sofa in the library. Her sister Betsey came by for a visit. "How did it go?" Amanda asked later. "All she did was complain about her servants," said Babe. "That was my first indication that they didn't get along too well," said Amanda.

During her periods of consciousness, Babe took care to say goodbye to her friends. After a hiatus of seven years, she called her former hairdresser, Kenneth, and asked to be remembered to each of his employees. She invited others to tea or lunch at her bedside. "She knew she was dying but she didn't talk about it," said Aline de Romanones. "She gave me pointers about makeup."

In early July she moved back into her bedroom at 820 Fifth Avenue, surrounded by enough fine French furniture to fill a Parisian salon: intricately carved Louis XV and Louis XVI chairs, commodes, consoles, banquettes, stools, and tables, interspersed with the sort of pieces that captured Babe's flair: the small trestle table of ivory inlaid with tortoise-shell, the Chinese painted paper screen, the Chinese Export vermilion lacquer tea table, the carved and painted bidet in the shape of an elephant, the silver owl-head bellpull.

Lying on her floral Porthault sheets, she looked as beautiful as ever. "Her face never changed. It didn't get all drawn in," said one Paley family intimate. "It was odd," recalled another friend, "but when she was dying, she had no faith, no religion. She didn't believe in another world or a higher plane. She was the doctor's daughter—down to earth in her lack of belief. Her death was painful for that reason. She had not a glimmer of having a soul. Still, she was very courageous."

On July 5, Babe's sixty-third birthday, she hovered close enough to death for her family to summon Kate, who had agreed to come only at the final moment. Babe was semi-conscious, but she talked a bit, and she recognized her long-estranged daughter. Babe had wrapped her head in a chiffon turban, and she wore a beautiful lace bedjacket. She uttered no complaint. Even at the very end, with a shaky hand, Babe Paley put on her makeup.

Paley and the children sat on her bed, paralyzed with sadness. Their vigil lasted until early the next morning, when she died with Amanda holding her hand. Moments later, Bill Paley picked up the phone to call Steve Ross, then chairman of Warner Communications, who was dating Amanda at the time and would marry her a year later. In the early days of his career, Ross had been an undertaker. "Call me when it is over and I'll be there," he had said to Amanda. Arriving within minutes, Ross said, "If you go out of the bedroom, I will take care of it all." So the family filed out, leaving a silver-haired movie mogul to tend to arrangements for Babe Paley's lifeless body.

Several days later, four hundred mourners, including three Rockefellers, a Harriman, and a Vanderbilt, came at noon to pay their respects at Christ Episcopal Church in Manhasset. They were escorted down the aisle by ushers including Oscar de la Renta and Horace Kelland. The family walked in, led by Paley in his dark Huntsman suit. "I don't think I ever saw such a sad face as Bill's," recalled Leonora Hornblow. "He was very controlled—no tears—and he walked straight." The Rev. Frank N. Johnston read the eulogy, a collaborative effort by Paley, Slim Keith, and Irene Selznick that praised Babe as "a beacon of perfection in this era of casual convenience."

After the forty-minute service of scripture readings and sturdy hymns, several hundred of Babe's friends assembled at Kiluna for an al fresco luncheon. Like the service, the gathering had been meticulously planned by Babe in the last year of her life; its cost would come to $17,600. Waiters stood underneath the columned portico holding silver trays of champagne and Babe's favorite wine, Pouilly-Fumé de Ladoucette. The rooms overflowed with more than $1,500 worth of flowers, all selected by Babe.

Behind the house, on the brick terrace shaded by the two huge linden trees bought by Bill and Dorothy forty years earlier, tables held center-pieces of Chinese porcelain bowls filled with black cherries. In the dining room, its deep red walls lacquered to a high gloss, the guests circled the buffet and selected silver cutlery from napkins folded like flowers inside wicker baskets. The main course was chicken l'estragon.

Bill Paley, barely three months from his seventy-seventh birthday, stood for the entire afternoon and greeted guests. He spoke to everyone, listened intently to what they said, and graciously thanked them for their condolences. He appeared dignified, composed, and strong, the complete American gentleman.

"At the end I looked around to thank Babe for the wonderful after-noon. It was as if she was there," said Slim Keith. But some guests had more than Babe's memory on their minds that day. Sitting at one of the tables was Horst, whose images of Babe in *Vogue* had immortalized her elegant style. As the afternoon wore on, Horst was stunned to hear, not from one but from a succession of women who wandered over and whis-pered as they glanced in Paley's direction, "I'm going to marry him."

52

"POOR BILL," said Irene Selznick as she reached the front door of Kiluna after the memorial luncheon for Babe. "He's going to have to walk up that staircase all alone." Paley, however, had no intention of living with Babe's ghost for even one night. Along with his servants and all the flowers from the luncheon, he headed to Keewaydin, the Southampton home of Henry Mortimer, Babe's former brother-in-law. The Paleys had rented the house for the month of July.

Paley spent several weeks there, tended by Kate. It was as if her mother's death had broken a spell; from that day Kate became intensely attached to her father. Also in tow was Paley's ghostwriter, Alvin Moscow. Despite his mourning, Paley was determined to beat David Halberstam to the bookstores the following spring. Each day, after spending his mornings on the telephone, Paley would meet with Moscow for several hours. There was a dinner party every night, either at Keewaydin or the home of a friend, and Paley always included Moscow in the plans. Even grief was a group activity.

Friends did their best to boost Paley's spirits. The Michael Trees and the Loel Guinnesses came over from England. Louise Melhado picked up Paley's mail every day at the Southampton post office and brought it to him. At the end of the month, Paley flew to the South of France to stay at the homes of Helen Rochas and Guy de Rothschild. He wound up his trip at the Ritz in Paris, where he dined with two of Babe's old friends, Marietta Tree and Grace Dudley, widow of Eric Ward, the Third Earl of Dudley.

When Paley turned seventy-seven that September, Oscar de la Renta had a geisha flown over from Japan. At a party in Paley's honor, she presented him with a single flower. Throughout these months, said Slim Keith, "Bill didn't sit in a corner crying. His behavior was a man in a state of shock. A lot of time was spent in quiet visiting with friends."

Although their marriage may have been hollow at the core, Paley was overwhelmed by the loss of Babe. Her death shattered him in a way that surprised even those closest to him. He had assumed that his wife, thirteen years his junior, would always be there to care for him. He never dreamed she would go first; his friends knew that she had been as much a support to him as an ornament. "He was dependent on her much more than he cared to admit," said Irene Selznick.

Paley showed clear signs of depression. He started carrying a silver-framed photograph of Babe in his briefcase. "The pain," he explained some months after her death, "strikes at odd moments, particularly in the early mornings." Visiting the CBS chairman in his apartment one day, John Backe found him in his pajamas, seated on his bed. "I don't know what to do with my life," said Paley.

"He began questioning things," said one visitor who stayed with Paley. Henryk de Kwiatkowski, who saw Paley both in New York and Nassau, noticed that he was "more pensive, more brooding. There was perhaps a tinge of guilt complex not for when Babe was sick but for the years before she was sick. When you are dissatisfied, you begin to discuss your past. Before Babe's death, it was only 'What am I going to do next?' After she died, he only wanted to discuss what was in the past. It was a very sharp change."

Babe's presence remained strong in Paley's surroundings. Their home in Lyford Cay stayed just as she had left it, as did most of the decor at 820 Fifth Avenue. However, Paley felt compelled to transform Babe's bedroom into a guest room; Sister Parish guided the redecoration. After considerable agonizing, Paley also hired Renzo Mongiardino, the Italian interior designer, to paint the living room a burnt orange. The new color scheme required more than a dozen coats of paint—and tens of thousands of dollars—to achieve the lacquered effect. For many months Paley supervised as a fetching young woman marbelized the moldings and medallions and painted minute stenciled designs that created a shimmering patina.

Unable to return to Kiluna, Paley put it up for sale. "It was filled with memories that I guess depressed me," he later explained. Kiluna would be sold for $6 million in 1985 to Ed Klar, the very man Babe encountered on the property before her death. Klar planned a development of ninety homes on eighty-two acres to be called "Stone Hill." Contrary to Babe's expectations, the sale agreement contained no stipulation to preserve the dell-garden. In February 1990 the hundred-year-old white clapboard house and children's cottage would burn to the ground in a blaze set by an arsonist.

Paley took little time finding a new country property of his own. Late in 1978 he bought an elegant home called "Four Fountains" on Southampton's exclusive Halsey Neck Lane—actually a two-bedroom home with a three-bedroom guest house. Appropriately enough, the property had belonged to Eleanor Brown, owner of the McMillen decorating firm. The drawing room—40 feet long, 20 feet wide, and 20 feet tall—had at one time been used as a theater. Assisted by Sister Parish, Paley filled the room with furniture from Kiluna covered in pink, beige, and white chintz. On the walls he hung a big Degas, a Cézanne watercolor, an Edward Hopper, and a couple of Francis Bacons for a slightly grotesque counterpoint. In the garden, behind the long reflecting pool, he placed a Renoir statue of a draped woman.

Paley had to deal as well with the practicalities of settling Babe's estate, a touchy task rendered more difficult by his controlling manner. Babe left more than $7 million. For all of Paley's fits of household parsimony, he made his wife a wealthy woman in her own right: $4.2 million was in stocks and bonds, $3.8 million of that in CBS stock alone. Her interest in the William S. Paley Company, her husband's limited partnership for investment purposes, was $659,956, and she had $1.6 million in tangible personal property—$1.1 million of that in jewelry. She had decent walking-around money at the time of her death: her three checking accounts totaled some $132,000, and she had credit balances of more than $10,000 at a half-dozen stores, including $6,379 at one of her favorite jewelry stores, Verdura.

Her bequests to friends and family far outstripped the $428,800 in personal property she willed to her husband—reflecting, no doubt, her recognition that he had plenty of his own possessions. Even so, she left him furniture, objects, rugs, silver, china, jewelry, sculptures, and paintings including *The Window* by Edouard Vuillard (valued then at $45,000) and a still-life by Berthe Morisot (valued at $35,000).

She arranged for trust funds of approximately $225,000 apiece for each of her children, and for her two stepchildren as well. Back in 1964 she had set up two additional trust funds for Amanda and Tony of some $300,000 each. She gave $50,000 to her brother in Boston and $10,000 to each of his four sons. The Westover School got $35,000 and New York Hospital $200,000. She left $35,000 to her secretary Adelaide Wallace, and $15,000 to her maid, Winifred Dooney. Her old friend Marion Osborn got $25,000.

It was only in Babe's dispersal of her jewelry and other valuable assets among her children that her relations with them became clearer (see the Appendix). Her son Tony received $182,500 worth of jewelry, including the 31-carat emerald ring, as well as a painting by Camille Corot valued at $60,000—to be held by Bill Paley for his lifetime. Tony's wife, Siri, a special favorite of Babe's, received $240,500 in jewels—bringing the total bequests to Tony and his wife to $483,000. Babe dealt generously with Amanda, giving her $275,950 worth of jewelry. Amanda's daughter Flobelle received an additional $133,350 in jewelry, including an emerald necklace valued at $125,000.

Hilary also benefited from Babe's largesse, with $68,800 in jewelry and a $3,500 Russian sable coat. Babe gave Hilary's daughter Brook $46,500 in jewelry as well. Jeffrey, who had maintained congenial if not close relations with Babe, received $38,750 worth of jewelry. The estranged Kate, however, only got $30,500 in jewelry and a $400 painting by Minnie's late husband, James Fosburgh. "She didn't leave anything to Kate at first," recalled one Paley family intimate. "But then she relented and left a little." Billie fared even worse, getting a mere $3,600 in jewelry.

Babe remembered thirty-nine friends in her will, with objects ranging in value from $100 to $10,000. Lady Anne Tree got the $10,000 prize, an Italian gold necklace with a pendant of gold and enamel. The $100 trinket, a gold and turquoise charm, went to Lady Caroline Somerset, wife of the Duke of Beaufort. Among the other recipients were Diana Vreeland (a $5,000 Fabergé gold and white enamel powderbox), Louise Melhado (a $500 gold lighter in the form of a fish with emerald eyes), Horace Kelland (a $1,200 pair of turquoise porcelain frogs mounted as candlesticks), Slim Keith (a $200 pair of Japanese ceramic crab tureens), and Françoise de la Renta (a $2,500 Bulgari gold evening bag).

As lawyers and other Paley deputies distributed Babe's gifts, friends and relatives began to suspect that her wishes were not being faithfully carried out. "The bequests got fouled up," said Irene Selznick. "Things weren't as she left them." Some friends received precisely what Babe had promised: Patrick O'Higgins got the Japanese bronze monkey holding a peach-shaped box where Babe used to stash her pearls. But Selznick objected when Paley told her she would receive a pair of Korean porcelain chickens—not at all what Babe had planned. "She was very pleased with her gift for me," recalled Selznick. "She told me that repeatedly." Irene refused the chickens.

Some weeks later, Paley invited Irene to dinner. "What's this I hear that you won't take the chickens?" Paley said. "I don't want them," said Selznick. "I told Babe I wanted something small, and she said she left me something that I could hold in my hand." "But we decided it was best you got these," Paley answered. "Then you did it and Babe didn't do it," said Selznick. "We decided what was best," replied Paley, who as an executor had discretion in disposing of Babe's possessions.

Paley led Irene Selznick up the stairs at 820 Fifth Avenue to a large storeroom lined with wooden shelves: a shadowy shop brimming with Babe's belongings. "Take your pick," he said. But Selznick would have none of it, and Paley, she recalled, was "sore as hell because he was thwarted and he felt he was being so magnanimous." The chickens, she later learned, were valued at $3,500. Determined to get his way, Paley kept after Selznick on the telephone. "He wouldn't let up," she recalled. Selznick began to hear around town that she had refused Babe's bequest. Finally, Paley sent over a heavy gold link chain from Bulgari valued at $1,250. Irene Selznick stuffed it into a drawer and never wore it.

The children likewise heard rumblings that they had not received everything to which they were entitled. They never got to examine the file cards meticulously compiled by Babe—only typed lists from the attorneys. Tony Mortimer, also an executor, raised questions that prompted a dispute with his stepfather. Paley accused Tony of wanting more, and Tony contended that Paley acted unfairly.

As 1979 began, Paley was hard at work reconstructing his social life. "He realized with a terrible clap of thunder what it was that Babe did, down to casting a dinner with non-predatory pretty girls so the room would look nice and he would be amused," said Slim Keith. He gathered around him a nucleus of friends, most of them many years younger than he. Among them were John Jay Mortimer (younger brother of Stanley and Henry) and his wife, Senga; man-about-town Jamie Niven and his wife, Fernanda; gallery owner Bill Acquavella and his wife, Donna; Ahmet Ertegun, chief of Atlantic Records, and his wife, Mica, a prominent decorator; Oscar and Françoise de la Renta; Annette and Sam Reed; former Paley son-in-law Carter Burden and Burden's new wife Susan; and old standby Slim Keith, who could be counted on for tart and witty observations about everything.

At the outset Paley invited the same people all the time, taxing his chef Bernard Lanjuin, who was fearful about serving the same food to the same guests. Paley insisted that Lanjuin use Babe's recipe books and menu plans. It was easier to continue Babe's established approach, where pea soup would invariably be followed by beef, and a dessert of crème brûlée. When a dish failed the Paley taste test, he would upbraid Lanjuin, pressing him to reread the recipe to get it right.

Françoise de la Renta, arguably Babe's equal when it came to organizing social life, gave Paley guidance. Gradually, he grew more confident. He varied his guest lists. Many friends remarked that he was now inviting people who would never have passed muster with Babe, such as Barbara Walters, "60 Minutes" executive producer Don Hewitt, and Frank Sinatra. Dinner at Bill Paley's was suddenly more merry and more democratic than it had been in the Babe days.

Under Babe's influence, Paley had been selective, exclusive. Now he was turning up everywhere—a maiden visit to Elaine's restaurant, parties at the Metropolitan Museum and the Museum of Modern Art, White House galas, openings of the New York City Ballet and Metropolitan Opera, and private dinners all over town. In avid pursuit were the women who craved to be the next Mrs. Paley. They made such a stampede that the columnist Taki wrote about it in the January 1979 *Esquire*—only seven months after Babe's death. He called their chase "the greatest struggle of succession since the Wars of the Roses."

The cognoscenti, wrote Taki, had given these "plutocracy-mad ladies" an assortment of aquatic nicknames. Lee Radziwill and her sister Jacqueline Kennedy Onassis were "the barnacle sisters." The "barracuda" was Françoise de la Renta, and Helen Rochas was "the shark." Marjorie Downey, a jewelry-store owner, was "the stingray." Evangeline Bruce ("the goldfish"), widow of former ambassador to Britain David Bruce, led the pack. "Her patrician background is strikingly similar to Babe's," wrote Taki—"an aspect that the somewhat plebeian Paley admires." Recalled Leonora Hornblow, "I had the feeling Evangeline had already picked out the silver."

Paley hunted as eagerly as he was pursued; one needed a scorecard to track his changing taste. After Louise Melhado and her husband separated early in 1979, she seemed like the frontrunner. Another moment Grace Dudley was poised to give up her title. "She married Eric Dudley late in life," said Slim Keith. "She took very good care of him and he left her a lot of money. She was way up in the sweepstakes for Bill. She was a logical choice because she understood the good life and had the same friends."

By March 1979, Paley was fixated on sometime model Barbara Allen —some fifty years his junior and characterized by Liz Smith as "sweeter, prettier, younger and less pretentious" than the society women in his life. Paley took his new girlfriend to the Caribbean, and several months later gave her a gold necklace from Cartier. After she accompanied Paley to Paris, his manservant Dean clucked quietly to one of Paley's friends about having to clean up smashed champagne bottles in their room following one late night celebration. "The poor old gentleman didn't know what he was getting into," whispered Dean. Known for her fickleness, Allen was also seeing British rock star Bryan Ferry. She confided to Ahmet Ertegun that she was in love with both men and could not decide between them. "That is quite a spread—Bryan Ferry and Bill Paley," said Ertegun.

Paley professed embarrassment over the speculation about his love life, but privately he admitted being flattered. He gloried in his Don Juan bachelorhood—doing in the open what he had been doing on the sly for years. He knew he could never find another gem like Babe; by comparison, all his women were semi-precious stones. When Leonora Hornblow asked him about his plans, he said with a laugh, "Why should I get married? I have a wonderful cook." Yet his behavior dismayed some of his friends, who felt that marriage to a mature woman was more appropriate for a man his age. "All this business of chasing all these girls is so infra dig," said a close friend of Paley's. "You don't do that if you like women. You get another wife."

While his actions denigrated Babe's memory, Paley seemed intent on idealizing their relationship. His portrait of their life together was one of many false notes in *As It Happened,* the Paley memoir that Doubleday published in March 1979—only weeks before Halberstam's book was to appear. Despite abundant evidence to the contrary, Paley claimed that he and Babe were apart no more than five nights during their entire marriage.

The book received a barrage of publicity. One heavily promoted aspect was Paley's proposal that all three networks devote, on a rotating basis, two hours each week to programs aimed at "people who have knowledge and a higher than average degree of intelligence." Passed off as an innovative idea, it merely reprised a proposal made by FCC chairman John Doerfer back in 1960. But coming from Paley, the suggestion had a contradictory resonance. On the surface it underscored his reputation as a man of quality. But the underlying message was that network programming appealed to a bunch of ignorant boobs—despite numerous examples of large audiences when ABC, CBS, or NBC presented superior programs over the years. In trying to clear his conscience, Paley unintentionally showed contempt for his viewers.

Doubleday ran full-page advertisements for *As It Happened* in the *New York Times* and *Variety*, followed by numerous ads in the *Times* for several months. Paley submitted to an appearance on the "Today" show with Tom Brokaw (who once remarked on the air that Paley had been known as "William Paleontological before he changed his name"), and talked to reporters from national magazines and top newspapers, including *Newsweek, Newsday, People,* and *The Washington Post.* Those publications ran glowing interviews laced with praise for the book. All the reporters received gracious thank-you notes from Paley.

Reviewers without benefit of an imperial audience were respectful at best. *Variety* called the book a "useful memoir" that was "well organized" and "readable." Aside from observing that Paley described Babe with "lyrical elegance," the *Los Angeles Times* tepidly noted that the CBS chief remained a "distant figure in this valuable study."

Other critics were considerably more severe. The *Wall Street Journal* called it a "history of his consuming ambition," and dismissed Paley's version of events such as Stanton's forced retirement as "an exercise in self-justification" that "lacks conviction." Noted the *Journal,* "Subordinates are never so evident as when something goes wrong." The most scathing critique was Nicholas Von Hoffman's in *New York* magazine: "Paley depicts himself as a purse-proud, egotistical, vulgar, grudge-bearing man who is as greedy for praise as he is for pelf."

Paley's unwillingness to give adequate credit to Stanton was all too evident. At the urging of his public relations men, Paley had at the last minute added some lukewarm praise for his former president. *Business Week* called his words about Stanton "spare and unfeeling." The *Boston Globe*'s William A. Henry 3rd wrote that the book might have been titled "Settling Scores." Paley, noted Henry, was "meanest toward the unemployed and the dead."

As memoirs go, *As It Happened* was more self-serving than most. Any insights into Paley's character were inadvertent glimpses of his undemonstrative, mistrustful, and secretive nature. Perhaps the most profound revelation was Paley's inability to grasp the meaning of his life. He spun tales of events, people, and possessions without ever attempting to explore his motivations or assess his accomplishments.

The mixed reviews and respectable sales—a second printing brought the book up to 47,500 copies—fell far short of Paley's expectations. Anything less than best-sellerdom and unanimous praise was complete failure in Paley's eyes. After his dutiful promotional appearances he could not disavow the book fast enough. He spread the word in his crowd that he hated the memoir; he called it "boring" and rationalized the book (four years and three ghostwriters in the making) as a work rushed out under pressure when, as he said later, "my wife was dying and I was in a bad mood."

Those in the know caught the real nature of his failure. "He was so busy whitewashing the truth, so controlling, that even his best friends couldn't get through it," one friend remarked. But Paley himself lacked that insight. "I wish to hell I could do it over again," he grumbled to *The Washington Post*'s Tom Shales. "I think I could've been a little livelier."

53

IF ANYONE could find encouragement in *As It Happened,* it should have been John Backe, who was two years into his tenure as the network's CEO. Concluding the book's awkward description of his struggle with heirs apparent, Paley called Backe a "wise choice" and noted his feeling of "pleasure and comfort because my successor is in place."

But reading the galleys of the book, the forty-six-year-old Backe took little pleasure or comfort. For the first time, he felt the full impact of Paley's ego and personality flaws. "Nothing hit me harder than that book," recalled Backe. "It read as if Paley did everything. He took credit for anything that was good." Even worse, after completing the memoir in late 1978, Paley once again began to reassert himself at CBS. He spent five days in Hollywood going over proposals for the network's "second season" of prime-time shows to be launched in January. Recalled Backe, "Babe was dead, his book was written, he wanted to be in charge, and there I was."

With Paley preoccupied by his memoir, Backe had grown accustomed to a measure of independence. He and CBS Entertainment president Robert Daly had been making good progress toward regaining first place in the ratings. In the spring of 1977, CBS had placed just two shows in the top ten; by April 1978, CBS had five out of ten. ABC, which still held the lead, had only four. One building block was, ironically, the legacy of Jack Schneider, who in December 1975 had moved the CBS news magazine "60 Minutes" to Sunday at 7:00 p.m. Within a year it had entered the top twenty, and by spring 1978 it was ranked fourth.

For their first two years together, Paley and Backe were cordial and warm toward each other. But Backe needed a confidant, and Arthur Tourtellot proved invaluable as an interpreter of Paley's character. Over monthly lunches, the two would dissect Paley's intricate personality. When Tourtellot died in 1977, Backe lost his roadmap to Paley's psyche.

As with Taylor, Paley hinted at a filial fondness for Backe. They talked frequently, and every Tuesday they ate lunch together. At one of those lunches after Babe's death, Paley said, "I want to thank you for being here this past year; you really held the company together."

Sensing Paley's loneliness, Backe and his wife, Kate, invited him several times times to dinner and the theater. Each time the chairman practically clapped with childlike enthusiasm. Before Christmas in 1978, Backe gave a party for his executives and their secretaries. To everyone's astonishment, Paley showed up. "Bill just stood in the corner, looking frightened, until he caught the eye of Kate and me," recalled Backe. Once Paley managed to relax, said Jack Purcell, "He laughed and joked, and the old-time secretaries were amazed."

While Backe had always been cordial to the chairman, he didn't go overboard tending to his needs—despite a strong signal from CBS board member Franklin A. Thomas, president of the Ford Foundation. Only six months into Backe's presidency, Thomas cautioned him, "Just remember, fifty percent of your job is holding Bill Paley's hand and fifty percent is running the company." Backe was incredulous: "How can you say that? I can't sit with that old man half the time and do my job well."

Now, in the early months of 1979, it became clear that Backe had little choice. Paley was demanding an inordinate amount of attention. He was under heavy medication for his back ailment, and he sometimes had to come to the office in a wheelchair, arriving through the basement entrance. He often fell asleep in meetings, especially in the afternoon. When the chairman awoke, Backe would dutifully summarize what he had missed. Executives began joking that if they wanted Paley to approve something, they should catch him before lunch; otherwise, they should try sneaking it by him as he nodded off.

Whenever Paley professed not to remember that a topic had been covered, Backe would follow Taylor's odd precedent, repeating the meeting in its entirety. During these reruns Paley often asked the same questions he had the first time. "At least he was consistent," said Jack Purcell. But just when Paley seemed hopelessly disconnected, recalled Backe, "he would fake you out. You never knew whether he would understand and retain something and then the next minute he would be sharp as hell."

These developments were especially confusing to CBS veterans who knew that Paley had often used repetition as a technique to delay decisions, smoke out new information, or torment an adversary. "We couldn't figure out whether it was style or senility," said one CBS executive at the time.

The chairman had always loved playing devil's advocate to test the strength of an employee's argument. But now, recalled Jack Purcell, "he began to believe his positions." Before a meeting with Paley, his executives were like presidential candidates prepping for a debate. "We would practice for hours and hours and we would take turns playing Paley," said Purcell. "Then in a meeting one of us would counter him and he would lose the purpose of his question. He would decide that he would win regardless and he would take his argument to illogical extremes."

Backe felt suffocated by Paley's intrusive and mercurial ways. "Paley was always around," recalled Purcell. "That meant there was a guy called president and chief executive, and there was a guy called the boss." Like Taylor before him, Backe grew impatient with Paley's obstructions—both inadvertent and intentional. "I don't think anyone minded Paley's questions," recalled one executive from those days. "What drove John Backe nuts was when management would gear up to do something and Paley would shoot it down."

Backe was incapable of adopting Stanton's practice of avoiding public disagreements with the chief. "By the end of the second year you could see that if Backe believed in something different from Mr. Paley, he was most willing to voice it," said programmer Harvey Shephard. Backe's assertiveness raised eyebrows toward the end of 1978 when he declared in front of a CBS management seminar that the company needed a more independent board and could no longer afford to be a "fiefdom controlled by the chairman."

As CBS's programmers moved the network farther up in the ratings, Backe urged them to follow their instincts, not to cater to Paley's whims. "I will handle Paley," he told them. It was a risky tactic. "When Backe would say to us, 'Don't let this guy get into your hair,' " recalled Bob Daly, "he knew there was a chance it would get back to Paley."

Backe felt his relationship with Paley turn midway through 1979. "It became negative," recalled Backe. "He would find things wrong just to find things wrong. We would go into a board meeting after he and I had agreed on something. He would change his mind in the middle of the meeting and argue against me."

As a defensive measure, Backe started to stonewall Paley by refusing to take his phone calls. Jack Purcell soon found himself carrying messages between the two men. When Paley complained, "Can't you get John to call me?" Purcell went to Backe. "You don't have to agree with the old coot," said Purcell, "but he does deserve a call." Still, Backe dug in his heels.

It was Backe's discourtesy that rankled Paley more than anything, Purcell believed. For all his ruthlessness, Paley clung to courtesy in awkward or difficult situations. For years CBS executives would recall the time in 1978 when CBS Records president Walter Yetnikoff brought Meat Loaf, a 300-pound CBS rock star with long stringy hair, to meet Paley in his office. "Yo, Bill," said Meat Loaf. "Good afternoon, Mr. Loaf," said Paley, who then called his steward to set out fine china and cutlery so Meat Loaf could eat his brown bag lunch of cheese, beer, and a banana while they discussed song writing and life on the road.

The predictable rumors hinting Paley's unhappiness with Backe had popped up in the press periodically since January 1979. But a report in *Media Industry Newsletter* in October had a new specificity. Paley, said the report, "regards the CBS president as basically a numbers-oriented man with no feeling for the creative side."

Loyal subordinates tipped Backe on Paley's back-channel activities. Whenever Backe left town, Paley would suspiciously quiz subordinates about the nature of the trip—even after Backe had briefed him. The CBS chairman began inviting executive vice-president Jack Purcell to breakfast at 820 Fifth Avenue. "He would pump me about what Backe was doing," recalled Purcell. "It was his way of making me feel important, inviting me to the inner sanctum, thinking maybe I would open up and say something." On the advice of his lawyer, Backe began keeping a journal, he said, "to document the inconsistencies in direction and understandings that exist between the CEO and the chairman."

By the time Paley moved in to recapture his company, Backe had developed strong ideas on the course it should take—most of which Paley disagreed with or didn't comprehend. As early as 1978, Backe proposed reentering the feature film business on a small scale by financing four to six movies a year. He told Paley that they had to find new ways to make money because CBS was prevented by government regulation from entering the lucrative syndication business—selling shows to TV stations after they had appeared on the network. Backe argued that between the expanding number of independent stations and the emerging home video market, there would be a greater demand for films than when CBS had tried its hand at Cinema Center Films a decade earlier.

Paley understood that the marketplace had changed, but he felt burned by the $30 million loss CBS had taken on Cinema Center. From mid-1978 to the autumn of 1979, Paley changed his mind on the movie business no less than ten times. "He would leave for a vacation in Europe, call the CEO from Paris and stress the need to move rapidly into the movie business," Backe noted in his journal. "After being gone for three to four weeks, Paley would return and state that CBS is moving too quickly and should reevaluate. This was common procedure." In August 1979, Paley offered Bob Daly the job of heading the movie venture, but changed his mind a month later. Finally, late in 1979, Paley approved a movie division with an annual budget of $20 to $30 million.

Paley's vacillation also held up Backe's planned joint venture with MGM studios to develop software for home video. MGM would provide the films and CBS, through its Records Division, would distribute video-cassettes. When Backe briefed Paley in the summer of 1979, the chairman gave his assent. At the August 9 board meeting, however, Paley "reversed direction and tried to shoot the project down," wrote Backe. The following day another briefing by Backe turned Paley around. Still, it would take nearly a year for Backe to establish the new video group at CBS.

Paley's turnabouts not only delayed Backe's expansion plans, they demoralized CBS executives. In September 1979, Jack Purcell and publishing executive John Suhler proposed that CBS pay $50 million for *Family Weekly,* a general-interest magazine inserted in Sunday newspapers. Both men, Backe noted in his journal, were "taken apart" by Paley, who told them the publication was "poor quality, too small." The next morning, Paley called Backe and asked, "What are we doing about *Family Weekly*? If we don't move quickly, won't it slip away?" Noted Backe, "It turns out that the Chairman had dinner with Walter Thayer the night before and Thayer was enthusiastic about *Family Weekly*." Four months later, *Family Weekly* joined CBS's publishing group.

The sharpest disagreement between Paley and Backe over CBS's future concerned a proposed new channel for cable television. In 1979, Ted Turner, the brazen cable entrepreneur from Atlanta, began developing a twenty-four-hour video news service. Backe figured that CBS, with its vast news organization, could establish its own news channel and "blow Turner out of the water." Paley, however, favored a channel of cultural programs. "He was embarrassed by a lot of network television," said Backe. "He had to make up for it, which preempted the logic of a news service."

Nevertheless, Backe asked CBS Broadcast Group president Gene Jankowski to prepare an analysis of a news channel. Jankowski's report was overwhelmingly negative, predicting battles with unions and CBS-affiliated stations, as well as a $100 million loss and no profits in sight. Backe was skeptical; CBS broadcasters were averse to any entrepreneurial venture that threatened their turf. Backe pressed his idea, and Paley dug in his heels for a culture channel.

Pondering possible acquisitions remained a source of diversion and stimulation for Paley—much to Backe's dismay. The Thursday luncheon briefings had expanded into wide-ranging, full-dress performances by the acquisitions department for the chairman. "I felt like a court jester," said one participant in the weekly show. The acquisitions chief would present the latest array of possibilities, supplemented by charts and samples of merchandise. "Sometimes the boardroom looked like FAO Schwarz," recalled one executive. Apart from the proposals, Paley was briefed on the acquisition activities of other big companies. "Paley felt this information was valid for his business and his social life," explained a CBS acquisitions man.

Paley stubbornly steered clear of any major purchase or merger. In 1978 he agreed to buy Gabriel Industries, a toy manufacturer, for $27 million. CBS's toy venture, Creative Playthings, held a small sliver of the market with only $14 million in sales. At that level, Backe and his acquisition team told Paley that CBS should either shut down toys or expand its position through an acquisition. Gabriel, said one former CBS executive, was "a low-risk toy company with sales of around $40 million." Paley saw the merit in expansion.

The one time Backe proposed a substantial investment, Paley berated him coming—and took credit going. "Too big," said Paley, when Backe described a potential $1 billion merger with Crum & Forster. Backe had targeted the insurance holding company as a source of cash to help finance expansion into new video technologies as the revenue from network television began to shrink in the coming decades. But when word of CBS's interest leaked to the press in early September 1979, Crum & Forster quickly retreated. Afterwards, Backe noted in his journal, "the Chairman now concerned that we mishandled the deal. He thinks we should have done more stroking—now considers it a brilliant idea and his idea."

One of Paley's initial objections to the deal was that it had not been presented by Felix Rohatyn, a social friend who was senior partner of Lazard Frères & Company, the investment bankers. Although Rohatyn had advised rival RCA on acquisitions throughout the sixties and seventies, Paley frequently called on him for advice about possible CBS investments. Apparently unfazed by the potential conflict of interest, Rohatyn would eagerly answer each summons from Paley.

Every few months Paley would get what Jack Purcell called the "urge to merge" and call Rohatyn in the late morning to ask him for lunch. Rohatyn would immediately phone Purcell to ask what Paley had in mind. "Just bring over some annual reports," Purcell would say. On arriving at Paley's dining room, Rohatyn would hand him the first report. Paley invariably skimmed it from back to front, starting with the financial statements. Paley would grunt or comment, and Rohatyn would pass him the next one. "Felix had a superficial knowledge of these companies," said one frequent participant. "Superficial for Felix can be pretty profound."

Although these exchanges never led to a deal, they provided some memorable moments. At a luncheon late in 1979, Rohatyn tossed out the annual report for Bausch & Lomb, makers of contact lenses. Paley was captivated by the look of the report; handsomely produced, it exuded quality. "It may not make sense, but it's a good company, the right size and range," said Rohatyn.

Leaning back in his chair, Paley mused, "I think it could fit."

"Why?" asked Rohatyn.

"We are in the TV business and people need good eyesight to watch TV," said Paley. "Maybe we should do this."

When Paley excitedly called Backe into the meeting to be briefed, the chief executive was astonished. Only the day before, Paley had attended a board of directors meeting where a far-reaching corporate plan had been approved after a four-hour presentation. Several years in the making, the plan had codified Backe's vision for CBS: shedding peripheral subsidiaries like musical instruments and confining investments to the communications and entertainment business. At the end, the board had risen to applaud the new plan.

Nothing in the plan remotely could have embraced the contact lens business. When reminded of the previous day's meeting, Paley said he could not remember it, but he did recall "some discussion of a new direction some weeks ago," Backe noted in his journal. Backe listened to Paley and Rohatyn's effusions about Bausch & Lomb, and "spent the next few weeks killing the deal."

Paley and Backe squabbled about petty matters as well. When Paley wanted CBS to buy a helicopter that he could use to travel to Southampton on weekends, Backe suggested that the chairman, who was worth at least $500 million, could buy one and lease it to CBS when the need arose for executives to use it on business. Backe gave Paley a toy helicopter for Christmas in 1979, but the chairman was not amused. "I was always in the position of saying no," recalled Backe. "I had to because it was in the company's best interests."

Entertainment chief Bob Daly also felt the force of Paley's whims, but he handled the erratic chairman more deftly than Backe. A Brooklyn-born Irishman, Daly projected a savvy confidence. Paley responded to Daly's combination of sincere conviction, logical argument, sense of humor, and straightforward manner. "Paley saw him as a buccaneer, a tough street fighter and a damn good executive," recalled programmer Alan Wagner.

Daly was the first CBS executive since Stanton who could predict where Paley was going and maneuver a preemptive attack. He made certain, for example, to watch every pilot before it was shown to Paley. Daly would then send Paley the best of the batch so the chairman wouldn't panic and think everything was awful. When Daly delivered a bad show, he warned Paley in advance. By always leveling with the boss, Daly earned Paley's respect and trust. "If you don't like the way I'm programming, I will leave," Daly said on more than one occasion. Paley knew he meant it.

Like Stanton at the peak of his powers, Daly knew when to stop in dealing with Paley publicly. Even if he felt strongly about a show, Daly would postpone a decision if Paley was unalterably opposed. More often than not, Paley would back down the next day. "Bob was tough," recalled former CBS program executive Kim LeMasters. "He was every bit as smart as Mr. Paley. Bob always came in with a point of view and he didn't share everything he knew. That was a strength."

Daly was shrewd enough to throw Paley the occasional bone that would enhance the CBS image. For the 1978–79 season, Paley maneuvered "The Paper Chase," starring John Houseman as a crusty law school professor, onto the schedule. Paley not only identified with the character, he admired the show's superior writing and casting. Even after "The Paper Chase" failed to achieve success in the ratings, Daly kept it on for a while to please the chief.

But when Paley objected to an idiotic adventure show called "The Dukes of Hazzard," Daly shut him off. "It will fail," Paley grumbled. The show became a crucial hit for CBS, enabling the network to rebuild its Friday night schedule. Paley would rationalize its success by blaming the desire of juvenile viewers "for messy shows. They don't want a good beginning, a middle, and end. They want the damn thing to sort of float around, and they read something into it that the older generation can't or they feel comfortable in not having things too carefully spelled out."

Several years of badgering by Paley nearly depleted Daly's store of patience. With Daly on the West Coast, Paley was prevented from buzzing him every five minutes, but he managed to phone most days a half-dozen times. The first call would come early in the morning, Pacific time, after the previous evening's ratings had arrived. By the day's end, Daly once said, "You would be ready to throw the phone out the window."

Daly kept his equilibrium in Paley's presence, but vented his anger to Backe. In September 1979, according to Backe's journal, Daly asked for a bigger contract "if he has to continue putting up with the chairman." Less than a month later, Daly "spent an hour and one-half complaining about needless discussions with the Chairman and meddling in programming judgments. Daly admits that in spite of his better judgment, he gives in to the Chairman to get him off his back. Daly's programming people are confused by the Chairman—used to be enthusiastic about meeting with the Chairman. Now feel that the Chairman spends needless hours asking

irrelevant questions and that 75 percent of the meetings are destructive."
Still, Daly managed to keep his eye focused on the goal, and as the new
decade began, CBS Entertainment was within reach of first place.

54

TOWARD THE END of 1979, Paley began plotting to unseat
Backe. In September, he talked to his chief executive about bringing in Michael Eisner, then president of Paramount Pictures, to
replace Gene Jankowski as head of the CBS Broadcast Group. When Backe
made the approach, Eisner said he would not consider anything less than
the corporation's chief operating officer, which would place him just
below the CEO.

In November, Paley invited Eisner to see him privately in New York.
Eisner, who began his career as a programming executive for ABC, met
with Paley every day for a week. "We talked about shows, scheduling,
and weaknesses," recalled an admiring Eisner. "It was like talking to
someone about what the third act should be. I got very interested in
coming to CBS."

But Eisner was discouraged by Paley's vagueness about the job. Paley
would later tell him he had wanted him for Backe's position, but at the
time, "he kept saying, 'heir apparent.' I kept saying, 'heir. You have had
too many apparents,' " recalled Eisner. "It was jovial but I was confused
over who I would be reporting to. Because it was not clear, I decided not
to do it." Eisner would later become the highly successful chairman of
Walt Disney Co.—and would linger in Paley's mind as the prize catch
who got away.

Within CBS, Paley's resentment of Backe had grown more obvious.
Now that CBS Entertainment was on track, Backe started to broaden his
activities. He made courtesy calls in Washington, did some lobbying, and
took public positions on broadcasting issues. "Going into the job, Paley
and I agreed that because of the experience with Arthur [Taylor], I was to
concentrate on running the company and eventually do the other things,"
recalled Backe. "For the first few years I had not been a statesman, but I
was respected and had a good relationship with the affiliates."

Purely out of necessity, Backe also found himself involved with CBS
News. Backe had stayed aloof from news, where he lacked both ground-

ing and interest. He had occasionally weighed in with criticisms of news reports that he felt were sloppily done, but otherwise left the day-to-day decisions up to Broadcast Group chief Jankowski and news division president Salant. "Backe was a blank to me," said Salant, who retired from CBS in 1979.

When ABC tried to steal CBS News star Dan Rather to become its evening news anchorman for more than $2 million a year (an enormous jump beyond Rather's $300,000 salary as a correspondent for "60 Minutes"), Paley, Backe, Jankowski, and newly promoted president of CBS News William Leonard were forced to act. Walter Cronkite had told Leonard back in 1978 that he wanted to leave the anchor chair when he reached sixty-five in 1981. Since mid-1979, Leonard had been talking to Rather as well as Roger Mudd about replacing Cronkite. But after the ABC offer in January 1980, all attention focused on Rather.

The Texas-born newsman had earned his stripes as the network's aggressive White House reporter during the Watergate years. Handsome and intense, Rather had a penchant for setting off sparks. At a convention of broadcasters in 1974, he caused a stir when he tried to get President Nixon's attention. "Are you running for something?" the beleaguered president asked. Rather shot back, "No sir, Mr. President, are you?" On "60 Minutes," Rather had proved a major drawing card.

Clearly, CBS could ill afford to lose someone with Rather's star presence to a competitor (NBC had chipped in a big offer as well), so in early February, Leonard agreed to pay him $2.2 million a year for ten years. Jankowski scheduled a meeting in his conference room on the thirty-fourth floor of Black Rock to break the news to Paley and Backe. In the previous months, Jankowski had told Paley that to keep Rather aboard, CBS might have to pay him around $1 million a year, a figure ABC anchorwoman Barbara Walters had reached in 1976. When Leonard revealed the real number, Backe and Paley were flabbergasted. Backe called the amount "obscene, indecent and irresponsible," and announced his opposition. He worried—correctly—that it would upset the entire news salary structure, and expressed some misgivings about Rather: "He's too eager to please, trying to be too much to too many people, all at the same time. Not his own man."

Paley recalled how exorbitant the $4 million Jack Benny deal had seemed in 1948. "I never thought I'd live to see anything approaching that for one man," Paley said. "It's too much money for any one man. Particularly a newsman." For more than an hour Paley and Backe quizzed Jankowski and Leonard. At one point Jankowski scratched on a small piece of paper "1 point = $5 million," which meant that a drop of one point in the evening news ratings could result in a $5 million drop in profits. He slipped the paper to Paley who said, "Is that really true, Gene?" "Absolutely, Mr. Chairman," said Jankowski.

Both Jankowski and Leonard affirmed their support for the offer to Rather. But as was his custom, Paley declined to cast an overt vote. "It's your decision," he said to Backe, who knew Paley was maneuvering him toward approving the deal. "It seems we don't have a choice," Backe said. "It's been my experience in life," responded Paley in his best oracular fashion, "that some of the cheapest things turn out to be the most expensive and some of the most expensive things turn out, in the long run, to be the cheapest." With that, Paley left the room.

As part of an effort to raise Backe's profile, Kidder Meade mapped out a plan to put him in charge of the April annual meeting in New Orleans instead of Paley. The night before the meeting, Paley would have his moment in the spotlight as the speaker at a dinner for the mayor and other prominent citizens. For the annual report, Meade crafted a bullish statement on Backe as the architect of the new technologies. Paley objected, worrying that CBS might seem inattentive to broadcasting. Paley told Meade, as Backe recounted in his journal in mid-February, "that he understands the technologies very well and isn't sure they will amount to anything." Despite Paley's objection, the report noted that CBS planned to participate in the new technologies on a "major scale."

Some weeks later, Backe was going over the annual meeting script with Meade in the CBS boardroom. Paley burst in, looking flushed and glowering with anger. "I guess you want to do everything," he said to Backe, slamming the briefing book on the table.

During the dinner before the annual meeting, Paley either drank too much or the alcohol reacted badly with medication he was taking for his back. When he had to go to the men's room, he could barely rise from the chair. As he made his way toward a fountain in the lobby to relieve himself, he was intercepted by an aide who escorted him in the right direction. Board member Marietta Tree begged Backe to give the speech in Paley's stead. Just as Backe had collected his thoughts, Paley reemerged and took his place. Reading the prepared speech was beyond him, but he stood up and spoke brilliantly off the cuff. "I don't know where it came from," recalled Backe. "But it was touching and warm." For all their differences, Backe could not help admiring Paley at that moment. He saw a glimmer of Paley's peculiar genius: the ability to graft his own charm and class onto the network, so that in the end they were indistinguishable.

On April 24, 1980, Paley held a victory party at the luxurious Four Seasons Restaurant in New York. CBS had recaptured first place in prime time, and Paley lauded Backe and Daly. "I don't think anyone tasted [a victory] as sweet as the one we had the benefit to come by," he said.

Less than a week later the balloon popped when Jack Purcell confided to Backe that Paley had quietly begun a search for a new chief executive through a prominent executive-search firm. Among those Paley was slated to see was Tom Wyman, the fifty-year-old-vice-chairman of the Pillsbury Company in Minneapolis, an old friend of CBS director Henry Schacht, the chairman of Cummins Engine Company. Schacht was an important man in Paley's eyes through a crucial chain of friendship. He was friendly with CBS director Franklin Thomas, who was close to Jock Whitney. Whitney and his longtime financial adviser Benno Schmidt, also a CBS board member, had convinced Paley in the 1960s to join them as investors in Thomas's urban development group, the Bedford-Stuyvesant Restoration Corporation. The connection to Thomas thus legitimized Schacht in Paley's eyes. When Schacht had recommended Wyman as a possible board member earlier in the year, his words carried weight, and Paley was receptive.

Although his roots were in St. Louis, Wyman had the solid Eastern establishment credentials and gloss that Backe lacked. Educated at Andover and Amherst, Wyman wrote his senior thesis on William Butler Yeats and was a Phi Beta Kappa, as well as captain of the golf team—a first-rate credential for the business world. He lived in Lausanne, Switzerland, and London for five years, rising to vice-president of the Switzerland-based Nestlé Company, and put in ten years as a senior vice-president of Polaroid Corporation in Boston under its iron-willed founder, Dr. Edwin Land.

Wyman showed promise as a Stanton-style corporate image-maker, serving on numerous corporate boards and participating in community activities such as arts councils and civil rights groups. Wyman walked with a self-conscious slouch that slightly diminished his six-foot-three stature, and had a manner so understated it bordered on lethargic. He spoke deliberately, with a slight drawl.

In response to Paley's initial overture in January 1980, Wyman flew from Minneapolis to New York for a two-and-a-half-hour dinner in the library at 820 Fifth Avenue. Wyman was struck by Paley's mixture of patrician airs and gritty toughness. "He wanted to be sure that as a director I wasn't going to embarrass the elegance of the enterprise," recalled Wyman. "He was clearly interested in the time I spent in Europe. He liked that, and he liked that I was involved with Andover and Amherst. He wanted to find out how often I came east. He was looking for someone acceptable."

When Paley asked him if he would serve as a CBS director, Wyman said yes, but he could not join until the summer, after he had extricated himself from one or two other boards. Only one comment that evening puzzled Wyman. When he asked about arranging a meeting with Backe, Paley abruptly said, "He doesn't have anything to do with the board." (Backe had, in fact, talked to Schacht about Wyman as well.) When Wyman recounted Paley's comment later, Schacht replied, "I wouldn't be surprised by anything." That winter Paley contacted Wyman once more to ask about his progress. "Paley," recalled Wyman, "was brooding about his future."

Backe knew that Paley had put out feelers to other businessmen besides Wyman as possible board members, so he initially dismissed Purcell's tip about the chief executive search. But on checking back with his source, Purcell reconfirmed the report. Over the next few days, Backe contacted several board members who assured him there was nothing to the story. But Purcell came up with even more specific information. Paley, it turned out, had been operating independently of the board. Said Roswell Gilpatric years later, "If Paley thought of getting rid of Backe, he never made it known."

Paley had indeed been on the phone to Wyman several days earlier. "Are you going to be in New York next week?" he asked. Wyman told him he was heading for California. "What if I told you it was really important?" said Paley. Wyman hesitated, but Paley remained cryptic. "Henry Kissinger is coming out for the weekend and I think it would be great to get together," said Paley. Wyman declined to pick up the bone Paley tossed his way. "You don't have to worry," said Wyman. "I am excited about the board. Everything is okay. But I can't come for the weekend."

Finally Paley played a card. "You are making this very hard for me," he said. "I suppose I have to tell you I am really concerned about the management of the company. I may even have to think about replacing the president, and I would love to talk to you about being president." Wyman agreed to meet him in New York the following week.

On Friday, May 2, Backe confronted Paley in his office. "I have times, and I have names," said Backe. At first Paley denied it all, but his violent tic betrayed the anxiety of deception.

"It's coming through Heidrick and Struggles," said Backe, naming the executive-recruiting firm Paley had enlisted.

"I'm the chairman and I can do anything I want," said Paley.

"I'm notifying the board," said Backe.

"We can talk this out," insisted Paley, as Backe left, slamming the door. When Backe reached his office, his secretary announced that Paley was on the phone, summoning him back. "I tried everything I could to get him back on the track," Paley would later insist.

For all the harshness, Backe did not see that moment as the end. "I thought it could be fixed," he recalled, "although I wasn't overly optimistic." Backe told the outside directors on the board's executive committee about the breach, complaining, "He interferes too much. You have to get him out of my hair." When they asked what they should do, Backe said he only needed their vote of confidence and pledge that they would not allow Paley to continue disrupting the company's management.

Paley moved swiftly to take control by tapping executive committee members Schacht and Thomas, along with attorney Roswell Gilpatric, to represent him in dealing with Backe. They were only too happy to go along with the big boss. Backe had erred by declining to cultivate the CBS directors. During seven years in the upper echelons of CBS, Backe had watched Paley repeatedly manipulate his cronies on the board. The one time the CBS president attempted to connect with the directors had backfired. Late in 1979 he had invited several board members out for one-on-one lunches. Each time, Backe described Paley's apparent forgetfulness and explained how it was impeding progress at CBS. "I'm not trying to get Bill out of a job," Backe said. "But if you sense a problem, don't hesitate to call me."

One member reported to Paley that Backe was going to the board behind his back. Paley called Backe into his office. "He was twitching like crazy," Backe recalled. "Are you trying to get me out of here?" Paley said. Backe calmed Paley down but vowed not to bother with the directors if he could not speak candidly to them.

For their part, the directors read Backe's inattentiveness as a sign of immaturity and insecurity. "He didn't have the self-confidence that exudes from a person who is sure of himself," said Roswell Gilpatric. "I am not a politician," Backe later conceded. "I didn't romance the board. But the way Paley wanted to come back and seize the company, I don't know if it would have changed a lot."

Following the blowup, Backe went about business as usual. He even briefed Paley in his office the following Monday as if nothing had happened. On Tuesday, May 6, he flew to Los Angeles as planned to attend the annual meeting of managers of CBS's affiliated stations. Once again, he was applauded for helping steer CBS back into first place. In Backe's absence, Paley conducted a series of meetings in New York with Schacht, Gilpatric, and Thomas about firing Backe and possibly hiring Wyman. The chairman alerted the other outside directors, but kept CBS executives on the board in the dark.

Backe left Los Angeles two days later aboard CBS's Gulfstream II.

He chatted amiably with Bill Leonard for much of the trip. When they touched down in New York at 3:35 p.m., Backe's limousine was waiting. Shortly after he arrived at his thirty-fifth-floor office an hour later, Schacht, Thomas, and Gilpatric walked in. Looking "all hangdog," recalled Backe, they asked him if he would change his mind about the vote of confidence he had requested. He said no. "Then we have to ask for your resignation." They had all the details at hand: a severance package amounting to more than $2 million. Paley never even made an appearance, and Backe cleared out his office by sunset.

CBS's late evening announcement set off another wave of bad press for Paley. Wall Street analysts called him erratic and unpredictable, and CBS stock fell to a five-year low. For the first time, the board took some hits in the press for permitting Paley, who after all held only 7 percent of CBS stock, such sweeping powers. "The CBS board, it appears, frequently abandons its public responsibilities," one broadcasting industry executive told *New York* magazine.

The official line from CBS was transparently false: that Backe had resigned after discovering Paley, in concert with the board, to be conducting an official "assessment" of his tenure. "Paley gave me the impression that the board was unanimous in wanting to get rid of Backe," recalled Wyman. "It is fair to say that I had some doubts about whether that was really the case." Paley's stated reasons for Backe's inadequacy were his lack of vision and narrow focus on the business at hand. Not only was Paley vague in his justification, he was inconsistent. Having derided Backe's plans for the company, Paley emphasized that he contemplated no change in direction.

Could Backe have avoided his brutal termination? At best, he might have forestalled it by taking a conciliatory approach. Paley would have backed off temporarily, but he had made up his mind to fire Backe. It was, as always, a matter of Paley's unwillingness to accept anyone taking his place. What irritated Paley most was that Backe had forced his hand by demanding a confidence vote. "If Wyman hadn't sort of appeared, I don't know what would have been the denouement," said Roswell Gilpatric.

Backe had followed Paley's script for turning the company around. He never lost his concern for the core of entertainment programming, and his instincts about CBS's future were far better than Paley's. CBS, not Ted Turner, should have pioneered a cable news network. With a worldwide news-gathering operation in place, CBS would have been in the black far faster than Turner—instead of ultimately being forced to cut back its news division in the face of declining audiences and revenues. Backe was also right to take some small steps toward making movies and developing other new technologies. And he was on target in forging an alliance with a Hollywood studio to distribute films on videocassettes. His plan for CBS was both prudent and farsighted.

Yet Paley dumped him, he said, for not being enough of a Renaissance man; Taylor, of course, had been too much of one. But as a broadcast executive, Backe had the kind of practical approach that Paley had as a younger man. The difference was that Paley had a Darwinian instinct for survival while Backe was lost in the corporate jungle.

Three days after Backe's dismissal, Paley and Wyman had another dinner at Paley's apartment. They hit it off better than ever; Wyman listened sympathetically as Paley bemoaned his bad luck with successors. Three and a half years earlier, Paley had told Backe that Taylor had not kept him informed; now he told Wyman that Backe hadn't kept him informed. Paley was already prepared to talk specifics with Wyman about the job. "In the normal scheme the search should have taken a few months," said Wyman. "But to be honest, anxiety was high on Paley's list. He was taking heat and feeling embarrassment."

Wyman met the next day—Monday, May 12—with Paley and five key directors: Benno Schmidt, Henry Schacht, Franklin Thomas, Ros Gilpatric, and Jamie Houghton. Besides Thomas and Schacht, Wyman was friendly with Houghton from Polaroid days, as well as several summers spent together in a small seashore town in Massachusetts. "The meeting was an odd piece of geometry," recalled Wyman. "It was the first time Paley and the board had interviewed anyone together." The board members had been bashed in the press as "yes-men," and it was clear to Wyman that they were determined not to be patsies this time.

When Paley started talking about wanting a new president, one director said, "CEO, Bill." "They wanted a say in the selection," said Wyman. "They were elegant but firm." Figuring he had nothing to lose, Wyman asked, "When would Paley be willing to step down as chairman?" "You could almost hear them all saying, 'Yes, yes, that is the key question,' " recalled Wyman.

With Benno Schmidt presiding, the meeting lasted more than two hours. The upshot was an understanding that Wyman would be president and chief executive at the outset. Roughly a year later, Paley would step down as chairman. "He agreed to it, although with some visible reluctance, said Wyman. "Whether he liked it was another matter." At the end of the meeting, Benno Schmidt said to Wyman, "If you get this job offer, it is because we decided that this time it is going to work."

Three days later, Paley made the offer official, and Wyman accepted. The deal reflected the strength of Wyman's position and Paley's eagerness to bring on the new man quickly. Wyman got a $1 million signing bonus and a salary of $800,000 a year.

John Backe had learned the hard way that being chief executive was next to impossible as long as the Boss was roaming Black Rock. Tom Wyman felt that the unprecedented backing of the board would make him secure once he became chairman. After all, with Bill Paley nearing eighty, a man thirty years his junior had time on his side.

7

THE
Legend

55

ONE OF PALEY'S biggest mistakes was failing to recognize that he had the best possible CBS chief executive close at hand. Bob Daly, the architect of CBS's climb back to first place, was widely admired within the company, and Paley himself had called him "the five-star general on the Pacific Coast." Like Paley, Daly had great programming instincts, and he knew broadcasting inside and out. Daly's down-to-earth personality went a long way with advertisers, station managers, and even Hollywood stars; but more important than anything, few at CBS had ever made Paley feel more at ease than Bob Daly. Unfortunately, Paley was blinded by his fixation with style. Daly lacked the WASP cultivation that Paley so admired in Wyman.

Daly felt the disappointment keenly. He was also disillusioned by Paley's treatment of Backe, who had supported Daly all the way to prime-time victory. "John Backe finally understood what I did," recalled Daly. "He got it. . . . I contribute his support to my turnaround." Daly called Backe's firing "the finishing straw."

Three months after Backe's dismissal Daly had an offer to become chairman of Warner Brothers. Paley's reaction was, not surprisingly, at odds with his public statements on the subject of executive defections. "I have never in my life tried to coax any person working at CBS to stay if he had ideas about doing something that he thought would be better for himself or for his career. It has been a rule of mine," Paley told an interviewer in 1976. With Paley, of course, all rules were meant to be rewritten. When Daly came to him in the fall of 1980, after twenty-five years of service to CBS, Paley refused to break his contract.

Daly asked him one favor: ten minutes without interruption. "This is a job you yourself always wanted," pleaded Daly during his audience with the chairman, "running a motion picture business." Paley, however, was obdurate, focused only on finding ways to keep Daly—excluding, of course, the CBS presidency. "This is not negotiable," said Daly. Paley raised his voice: "How can you leave after all I have done for you?" Daly's temper flared: "Look at all I have done for you."

Over the next thirty days, Daly and Paley had four meetings totaling fifteen hours. Paley asked to meet with Daly's wife; Daly refused. "Whatever job you want you can have eventually," Paley promised. During the second meeting in Paley's office, Daly glanced across the room. Amid photos of Babe and the children was a new addition—a picture of Paley with his arm encircling Daly. Chuckling to himself, Daly thought, "There I was, like a prop."

The final meeting, in Paley's apartment, lasted from 7:00 p.m. to 1:00 a.m. and ended with Paley agreeing to let Daly go. As Daly turned to leave, Paley put his arm around him and showed him his paintings. "I'm no longer an employee," Daly thought to himself as he eyed the collection. But the next morning, Paley changed his mind again. Daly had to serve out his contract. After twenty more days of negotiating, Daly finally got his way.

Incapable of holding himself responsible for losing Daly, Paley blamed Warner Communications chairman Steve Ross, who had married Babe's daughter Amanda in December 1979. Daly had met with Ross in the spring of 1980 over a lunch arranged by Ted Ashley, then chairman of Warner Brothers. No job had been offered, and Daly had dutifully told Paley about meeting his son-in-law. At the time of Daly's departure, Ross was recuperating from a heart attack that had kept him hospitalized for three weeks. "Steve attested to my stepfather that he knew nothing about Bob being stolen," recalled Amanda. "My stepfather never believed it. Steve was extremely upset by my stepfather's allegations against him."

Tom Wyman sensibly kept his distance from the contretemps. He and Paley were gliding through their honeymoon. "Tom Wyman accepted as one of the principal elements in his job description that he had to get along with the chairman and keep him fully informed," said board member Roswell Gilpatric. "That was the beginning of wisdom." With barely a blink, Wyman soothed Paley on several of his sorest points with Backe. Wyman agreed to buy a corporate helicopter that Paley could use for his Southampton jaunts. Wyman likewise embraced Paley's cultural cable channel and scheduled its introduction for the fall of 1981. "Cable is a must," Wyman announced within days of his appointment. The same CBS analysts who scotched Backe's news channel as too expensive predicted that Paley's project would suffer $70 million in losses before turning the first profit of $8.6 million in 1985.

Paley seemed more conspicuously enchanted by his new Renaissance man than he had been by Wyman's predecessors. The CBS chairman escorted Wyman to Washington to introduce him around Capitol Hill, and the two men traveled to Detroit for the Republican National Convention.

To ensure that Wyman was socially well placed, Paley arranged a membership in the exclusive River Club. He also took Wyman to the "21" Club and introduced him to the management so CBS's chief executive could always get the best table. The Wymans attended a number of dinner parties at 820 Fifth Avenue with Brooke Astor, John Richardson, and other luminaries from Paley's social set. When Tom and Betsy Wyman visited the Dominican Republic, Paley asked Oscar and Françoise de la Renta to throw a party for them. The Wymans eventually built a home next to the famous designer.

Wyman was patient, self-effacing, and wily in Paley's presence. In addition to their weekly lunches, Wyman frequently trotted down the hall to give the chairman a news flash or solicit his views. He listened intently, always acknowledging Paley's wisdom and plotting the same low-key course that had proved successful with other hard-driving bosses he had served. When Paley told Wyman to ignore Backe's strategic plan, the new CBS chief ordered a new version—with a wink. Jack Purcell couldn't resist phoning Backe to exclaim, "They are turning our bar charts to pie charts!"

Wyman kept in close touch with the board of directors, with whom he had a special back-door relationship never enjoyed by Taylor and Backe. "We have rapport and interchange," said Gilpatric at the time. "He is a man of down-to-earth reality, a quick study. He gives one confidence."

Sometimes Wyman's eagerness to please his boss proved embarrassing. At the end of 1980, Paley and Wyman hosted a Christmas party for top CBS executives and their wives at a midtown restaurant. Before the appetizers were finished, Paley and Wyman disappeared. Paley had been invited to a party by one of his society friends and insisted that Wyman accompany him. "It sat very badly among the executives," recalled William Leonard. "It burned up everyone in that room."

Paley was keen to show everyone that he was back in charge. In June 1980 he gave a speech on freedom of the press to the Associated Press Broadcasters. Several months later he broke precedent and told CBS News president William Leonard that he wouldn't have to retire when he turned sixty-five in April 1981—a concession pointedly withheld from Stanton. Paley's reason was purely practical. Walter Cronkite was stepping down in the spring and Dan Rather was taking over the evening news. CBS needed Leonard for continuity. "I was under no illusion concerning the company's motivation," said Leonard. "It was simply convenient."

At work, Paley seemed less forgetful and more energetic and alert. He attended all the major program meetings, playing his role more forcefully if not necessarily more effectively. "Everybody felt they were going through the exercise for Mr. Paley," said one CBS executive. "It was a Potemkin process, but we were winning the ratings."

Around that time Paley was seated next to Sidney Urquhart, a reporter from *Time* magazine, at a dinner party. Perhaps intoxicated by Mrs. Urquhart's good looks, Paley boasted that he was as sharp as ever. When he realized his IQ now outstripped his memory, Paley confided, he had gone to a prominent neurologist at New York Hospital who had given him what Paley called "memory pills."

Memory pills or no, Wall Street wasn't completely enthusiastic about Paley's comeback at CBS. In June 1980, Joseph Fuchs, a broadcast analyst at Kidder Peabody, issued a report critical of Paley and the CBS directors for creating uncertainty about the company's stability. Wrote Fuchs: "The departure of Mr. Paley, for whatever reason, would undoubtedly be greeted in the financial community with a solid increase in the price of the stock."

When Paley read those words, he exploded. "Fuchs has a death wish for me," he sputtered to one of his public relations men. Fuchs, Paley said, would henceforth be banned from the CBS Building. After reportedly receiving a tongue-lashing from Paley, Al Gordon, chairman of Kidder, rebuked Fuchs and forced him not only to write a personal apology to Paley but to recant in a subsequent analysts' report.

In truth, Paley had become an albatross for the network. Subordinates noted with disdain his unfamiliarity with the nuts and bolts of the business. He lacked a vision for the future of broadcasting, and he didn't seem to care. "A corrosion took place," said ABC chairman Leonard Goldenson. "Bill Paley could not maintain the spirit and drive and morale to keep CBS on top."

As for Wyman, he was still keeping a low profile a year after his arrival. At the 1981 shareholder meeting in Phoenix that April—their first together—Wyman and Paley displayed an unusually casual informality. Wyman publicly referred to the chairman as "Bill" instead of the customary "Mr. Paley." "The bottom line is we feel very lucky to have him," Paley said of his chief executive.

Wyman got Paley's blessing in June 1981 to announce an ambitious plan to reenter the movie business. For all his earlier vacillations with Backe, Paley had become a true believer; if anything, he was more enthusiastic about getting into films than Wyman. He ignored Daly's warning (conveyed to Paley several months before Daly left the network) that CBS would fail without its own distribution system. Paley, characteristically, was all bravado. "I will produce as many movies as Warner Brothers," he said.

At Paley's suggestion, Wyman hired an aggressive Hollywood agent named Mike Levy to run the new CBS movie operation. CBS, said Levy, would be "synonymous" with the major studios "sooner rather than later." Wyman and Paley even took a ten-day trip to Japan to watch the shooting of a CBS film called *The Equals,* directed by John Frankenheimer. Paley brandished a samurai sword for photographers and shouted, "Critics beware."

By this time Wyman had begun to confide his frustrations with Paley to colleagues and key board members. The chairman demanded to be invited to Wyman's four-hour management committee meetings every other Monday afternoon. Yet Paley was uninterested in the basic questions about earnings and sales. He routinely raised items that were not on the agenda and generally kept the proceedings off balance. He would bring along financial analysts' reports laboriously marked by his loyal factotum John Minary to show all references to Paley. "Paley would want to know who this analyst talked to, how he got his information," said William Lilley III, Wyman's top public relations aide. "It was always a distraction, and what was so off-putting was not that he was concerned about what was said about CBS but that he was concerned about being criticized himself."

Mindful of their deal a year earlier, the most influential members of the board, known as the "inner five"—Benno Schmidt, Roswell Gilpatric, Henry Schacht, Franklin Thomas, and James Houghton—came to Wyman in May 1981. "The time has come to cross the bridge on Bill Paley," they said. But Wyman hung back. "The consequences would be potentially traumatic if we do it now," Wyman told them. "He would not like it, and there's no possibility of having a graceful transition." They agreed to wait another year.

CBS launched Paley's cable channel in October 1981 amid great fanfare. The man who brought America "The Beverly Hillbillies" now reveled in turning out highbrow fare. He immersed himself in the details of the channel's programming for months before the debut. Remembering a program called "Face to Face" on the BBC three decades earlier, Paley had it recast as "Signature." The show's interviewer sat with his face in shadow while the interview subject was presented in closeup. "Signature" made compelling television and was hailed as one of the most successful shows on CBS Cable.

Everything about CBS Cable—from Patrick Watson, the tuxedo-clad "host," to the elegant graphics—epitomized Paley's sense of style. To better control the quality, CBS produced more than half of the programs itself. There were ballets and concerts as well as plays such as *Early Days* starring Sir Ralph Richardson, a mini-series about the life of Giuseppe

Verdi, and even a revival of "Quiz Kids" hosted by TV producer Norman Lear. It was, said one reviewer, "a feast for the eye and ear."

"It's got the feel," said a beaming Paley to Patrick Watson during a party at the New York Public Library marking the channel's debut. But as he surveyed the opulent send-off that included a full orchestra, Paley seemed apprehensive. He told a former colleague that night that he was worried about whether CBS could afford the expenditure.

CBS News also drew Paley's attention that fall as ratings for "The CBS Evening News with Dan Rather" took a nosedive. Paley had never been much of an evening news viewer; he was usually en route to a party when the news appeared on WCBS in New York. But when CBS News president William Leonard changed the show's graphics to inject some pizzazz, he discovered that Paley had become attentive. "What I had done bothered the hell out of him," recalled Leonard. "He got on me, called me on the phone. He said, 'That is our masthead. You wouldn't change the masthead of the *New York Times* without telling Mr. Sulzberger, would you?'"

Paley knew that it would take more than tinkering with the masthead to correct Rather's declining popularity. Leonard had to go, so Paley terminated his benevolent post-retirement extension and asked his men to come up with a replacement. Wyman's choice was Van Gordon Sauter, a former newspaperman who had effectively run CBS stations in Los Angeles and Chicago, served as network censor, and more recently had given CBS Sports a respectable new gloss. Bearded, pipe-smoking, and portly, Sauter had a glib charm that appealed to Wyman. To others, Sauter seemed too cynical and opportunistic to be trusted with Murrow's legacy at CBS News. The straight-arrow Broadcast Group chief Gene Jankowski understood Sauter's strengths but also mistrusted him. He preferred Edward M. Joyce, who had followed Sauter's footsteps in Chicago and Los Angeles. A reserved man with a reputation for holding down costs, Joyce was both loyal and predictable. But Paley was too impatient to choose between Sauter and Joyce. "Use both of them," he commanded. "Just get it done."

The tensions between Wyman and Paley finally surfaced toward the end of 1981 after Wyman made a surprising gaffe. In an interview with the *New York Times,* Wyman said, "I don't think there's any question in anyone's mind that I'm running the company." Sounding more than faintly patronizing, Wyman acknowledged that Paley had been "helpful . . . particularly in long-range planning, and he is wonderfully toughminded and asks spectacular questions. But the initiatives have been mine."

Paley bitterly complained about the remark to friends. One who heard his lament most clearly was Frank Stanton, Bill Paley's new best friend. As his troubles with successors deepened, Paley had come to appreciate Stanton's abilities in much the way that his appreciation of Babe grew after her death. "Maybe Bill Paley was a shit to Stanton, but he decided to reach out," said Robert Wussler. "Stanton is smart and was always pretty straight with Paley. Before, Paley didn't have a basis for comparison. But the failure with various successors magnetically drew him to Stanton, who looked so much better by comparison."

Stanton was enjoying an enviably productive—and apparently lucrative—retirement, working fourteen-hour days and traveling on business more than one hundred days a year as a member of corporate and non-profit boards and an investor in an assortment of communications companies. During nearly a decade of exile from CBS during Paley's "de-Stantonization," he had remained quietly loyal to the company. When *As It Happened* was published, Stanton had bitten his tongue in the face of the book's obvious slights.

Paley had first extended the olive branch in 1980 after firing John Backe. "Frank was terrific," Paley told *Broadcasting* magazine. "He was a very good man, and particularly in certain respects there was no one better than he. He was a top guy for that office of president." Paley never let on that there had been a rift of any sort. His relationship with Stanton, Paley told *Broadcasting,* was "very healthy and very productive and very successful."

When Paley began inviting him to breakfast and lunch that year, Stanton graciously resumed their friendship. Paley needed Stanton's counsel, and Stanton was just as eager to serve. He had hated being on the outside looking in. By linking up with Paley, he could be a player again with access to the inside track at the company that was still his first love.

Paley tried in various ways to make it all up to Stanton. In 1981 he coaxed the CBS board of directors into approving a $500,000 corporate donation to create the Frank Stanton professorship of the First Amendment at the John F. Kennedy School of Government at Harvard. Two years later, CBS named Stanton "President Emeritus." The idea had actually come from Wyman during a discussion with Paley about improving CBS's battered image. Paley's only misgiving, recalled Wyman, was "Can it be graceful for me? Will it be dramatized as a rapprochement? Will I be criticized again for not making him chief executive?" Paley decided the gesture would be a plus for CBS, and the board gave its unanimous approval.

Paley invited Stanton to join him as an investor in Genetics Institute, Inc., and Thinking Machines Corporation, two new companies at the forefront of genetic engineering and computers. But the most significant symbol of their entente was a seat for Stanton on the Museum of Broadcasting board of directors in 1985.

In fact, Stanton had been advising Paley on museum business since 1981, when he recommended his friend Robert M. Batscha as a replacement for outgoing president Robert Saudek. In his mid-thirties, Batscha was gregarious and handsome. Like Stanton, the former associate professor at Queens College had a Ph.D. and used "Dr." before his name. "He's too good," said Paley. "Everything that everyone says about him is so good. He can't be that good." Paley hired him anyway and for a time was pleased with his leadership. Inevitably, however, Paley would grow dissatisfied, accusing Batscha of trying to take credit from the chairman for the museum's success.

Like their relationship of old, the new bond between Paley and Stanton was more convenient than affectionate. But they did become confidants, closer than they had ever been at CBS. At regular intervals they would sit across from each other at a small table in Paley's exquisite library. As the sun slanted through the windows overlooking Central Park, they would talk about CBS past and present, and they would find common ground.

Stanton had been Paley's subordinate, but now they were both independent and on a more equal footing. If anything, Paley was now dependent on Stanton, who was more vigorous and more widely informed about broadcasting and business in general. "Whenever I have a problem and need to get some advice, I call him," said Paley several years into their rapprochement. "They are like a husband and wife who fought like hell when they were beautiful people," said William Leonard. "Now they sit together drinking tea and eating toast. They have each other."

But Paley hadn't completely mellowed. He seemed more determined than ever to call the shots at CBS. In January 1982 he had lunch with Marvin Davis, then chairman of Twentieth Century Fox, and hatched a deal to distribute videocassettes of feature films. Over three helpings of corned beef in Paley's dining room, Davis got what he wanted: half ownership of CBS's Studio Center film and TV production facility in the San Fernando Valley, worth some $50 million. At the time, it seemed like Paley had given away the store, but Paley had shrewdly secured half the video profits from all Fox movies—an income source that would grow beyond all expectations in the following years. The Fox deal supplied significantly more movies than Backe's earlier arrangement with MGM that Paley's maneuver scuttled. (Paley thought he had also coaxed Davis into a CBS-Fox cable partnership to help absorb some of CBS Cable's mounting losses. But Davis managed to wriggle out of that portion of the agreement several months later.)

Despite another big win in the prime-time ratings, there were signs in the spring of 1982 that CBS was faltering. The company had lost more than $20 million on CBS Cable the previous year, about what had been expected. But losses were accelerating instead of declining in the new year. With $3 million in cable advertising revenues for the first quarter, CBS was taking in only half of what had been projected. Sales at CBS Records were off, and CBS's first feature film, *Back Roads,* had been a box-office failure. Overall, CBS profits had declined in 1981 and *Business Week* reported in March that questions were being raised about Tom Wyman's future. "There has not yet been serious friction between Bill Paley and Tom Wyman," said *Business Week,* "but Paley is reported to be disgruntled."

Within days of the *Business Week* report, Wyman fired Michael Levy, president of CBS Theatrical Films, and substantially scaled back its output from the $400 million investment in forty films that Levy had announced only two months earlier. Instead, CBS would make roughly four films a year at $10 million apiece. Once again the company found itself in the same Hollywood limbo it had fallen into with Cinema Center Films: as a film boutique with no means of distribution.

Ignoring Paley's grumbling about Wyman, the CBS board stood behind their hand-picked chief executive more firmly than ever. Paley further undercut his position by misbehaving in board meetings, baiting the directors, and acting petulant when he did not get his own way. He had been especially obstreperous over compensation for Wyman and his executives. "Paley couldn't stand to have anyone making any more than he did," said one board member. "We would have studies done, and we would waste hours talking about things that were not real issues. One month it would be stock options, another month it would be salaries. It wasn't a question of money. It was pure prestige. To him it was important, and it created tension with the board."

When Jock Whitney died in February 1982, the board saw an opportunity to dislodge Paley. Whitney had been ailing with heart disease for six years, and no brother-in-law could have been more devoted than Paley. Until Whitney lost his voice, Paley called him every morning to fill him in on the latest news. Many Sunday evenings on the way home from Southampton, Paley had his helicopter land at Whitney's home in Manhasset. For several hours, Paley would sit with Whitney and watch television, neither of them speaking. "Bill would come to see Jock and adore him," said Irene Selznick.

With Whitney's death, Paley and his friend Walter Thayer concocted a plan for Paley to pay $14 million for Whitney's one-third interest in the *International Herald Tribune,* the daily newspaper published jointly in Paris by the New York Times Company and the Washington Post Company. Paley wanted to become chairman of the newspaper, buy an apartment in Paris, and live there part-time while he oversaw the business. He even made a trip to Paris to reconnoiter the *Tribune* offices.

Seizing on what Roswell Gilpatric called this "fortuitous pretext," the inner five directors began orchestrating Paley's exit from the CBS chairmanship. "We felt that after two years, the future should be clarified, and we should make Mr. Wyman's authority crystal clear," said Gilpatric. "We had to break the syndrome."

But even with the *Herald Tribune* possibility, Paley resisted giving up his position. "When I step down," Paley asked Wyman, "will I be invited out to dinner? I dread the sense that I might be seen as no longer contributing to CBS's success." The board and Wyman held firm. "Paley was one tough SOB," said one source close to the negotiations. "At the core was a man with an enormous ego and need for recognition and adulation."

Benno Schmidt and Henry Schacht took the lead in pushing Paley along. As chairman of the compensation committee, Schacht had the difficult task of negotiating Paley's new contract. Paley's initial demands included an office and dining room at CBS for his lifetime, and personal use of the CBS aircraft, as well as a provision requiring his election to the board indefinitely. Schacht, who was Tom Wyman's closest ally on the board, wanted Paley to take office space outside the CBS Building. Throughout several months of wrangling, Franklin Thomas served as the peacemaker. The board finally gave in on the office and aircraft but stopped short of the lifetime board membership. "All we could do was express our intention," said Gilpatric. After signing the contract, Paley turned against Schmidt, who had been outspoken and tough in the negotiations. Eighteen months later, Schmidt would resign from the board.

Once it became clear that Paley would have to step down as CBS chairman, he launched his campaign for the chairman's job at the *Herald Tribune.* Both Katharine Graham, chairman of the Washington Post Company, and Arthur Sulzberger, chairman of the New York Times Company, had veto power over the Whitney third. But they discovered that even a simple veto could get complicated when dealing with Bill Paley.

In mid-July, Paley and Sydney Gruson, Sulzberger's deputy at the *Times,* had a four-hour lunch at Paley's home in Southampton. Gruson had to tell Paley that the *Times* and the *Post* would not permit the Paley purchase. With Paley nearing his eighty-first birthday, Graham and Sulzberger felt it would be folly for him to take on the *Herald Tribune* job.

They also resented his presumption that he could simply move in with no prior newspaper experience. "The paper," said one partner, "was not a toy."

Undaunted, Paley argued his case: "I am a wonderful businessman, I get on well with people, I have the talent and ability to contribute." When Gruson held his ground, Paley asked to see Sulzberger and Graham. They met two days later in Walter Thayer's office. "Why are you doing this to me," Paley said to Graham, "after all I have done for you?"—meaning, presumably, the Post Company's record of success as the owner of TV and radio stations affiliated with the CBS network. When that line— evidently Paley's favorite yet least effective—didn't work, he tried another approach. His involvement in the *Herald Tribune,* he said, was "Jock's great wish." "I don't understand," he finally said, "why would you object to me?" "He was terribly upset and hurt," recalled one participant in the meeting. "He was used to getting his way on everything," said another.

Knowing that their plan would be thwarted, Thayer arranged to have Paley buy into the Whitney partnership that controlled the *Herald Tribune* stake. Paley asked Thayer and Stanton to sit with him on the *Herald Tribune* board, and Paley settled for being a co-chairman along with Graham and Sulzberger. In early September 1982, CBS announced that Paley would relinquish the chairman's job to Wyman in April 1983 so he could pursue his exciting new venture with the *International Herald Tribune*. Paley would remain chairman of CBS's executive committee, and he would be paid $250,000 a year in retirement benefits plus $200,000 a year as a consultant through 1992, the year of his ninety-first birthday.

Less than a week later, CBS announced that Paley's cherished cultural cable service would shut down in December. CBS Cable had posted losses that would amount to more than $60 million since its inception—$12 million more than had been expected. For all its acclaim, the service had been poorly conceived. Advertising revenues fell far short of projections, and producing so many original programs proved too costly. When ABC began a similar service in March 1981, it bought programs from inexpensive sources overseas. It was ABC's ARTS Channel, in fact, that absorbed Arthur Taylor's Entertainment Channel and transformed itself into an enterprise that would prove profitable as well as laudable. The decision to fold CBS Cable was Wyman's. Paley had no choice but to agree. "To me it was one of our most hurtful failures," Paley said later.

For public consumption, Paley professed to support Wyman completely. "I have a successor in place," he told *Fortune* magazine. "Someone might say those are famous last words, but this time it's for real." Yet when CBS-TV president James Rosenfield commented to the *New York Times* on Paley's planned departure by saying, "Tom Wyman will be free to run the company as he sees fit. That is what is needed at this time," Paley bristled and picked up the phone. "How could you say that?" he asked angrily. As Rosenfield observed years later, "Paley has a very short memory about most things but he doesn't forget some things—like that quote."

Tom Wyman walked on eggs until April 20, 1983, when Bill Paley called the CBS annual meeting to order. Wearing a dark suit and white shirt, Paley stood at a podium in the studios of KMOX-TV, CBS's station in St. Louis, where fifty-six years earlier a tiny radio station had joined the nascent network that would become CBS. "It's difficult to tell you what a jumble of emotions I feel at this time," Paley said, his voice cracking slightly. "The memories crowd in: the battles, the victories, the disappointments, the triumphs." He cleared his throat. Those standing close to him could detect tears in his eyes. "Wherever CBS goes, my heart will go with it." CBS directors, executives, and shareholders stood and gave him a rousing ovation. It was a seemingly graceful exit, simple and heartfelt, befitting the style and elegance that Bill Paley symbolized.

56

WITHIN DAYS of Paley's farewell, he was the odd man out at CBS. He no longer received management reports and memoranda, he was excluded from Tom Wyman's strategy meetings on alternate Mondays, and his name was even removed from the CBS telephone book—technically because he was no longer an employee. Wyman explained to colleagues that he had to establish himself as the undisputed boss; otherwise Paley would be like a jack-in-the-box, popping up at unexpected moments and interfering with the operations of the company. Besides, said Wyman, Paley had not been reading the reports anyway, and his contributions to meetings had been counterproductive. Wyman still had lunch with Paley although less frequently, and he stopped making courtesy trips down the hall.

Other moves by Wyman struck at the heart of Paley's entitlements. For years Paley had treated his luncheon guests with small gifts from Tiffany—courtesy of CBS, naturally. Wyman put a stop to the gift purchases, and the pile of pale blue Tiffany boxes in the office of a public relations aide disappeared.

The hardest blow came when Wyman told Paley that he could not attend the round of meetings in May to set the prime-time schedule. "The programming department," Wyman recalled, "welcomed the decision." Paley was frantic. He made at least a dozen fruitless calls to CBS executives asking them to dissuade Wyman. With Paley as leader, the scheduling meetings had usually taken four or five days; that year they ended in two.

For the next two years, Paley went to his office every day, but it didn't much matter. "The accoutrements of power were there," recalled former program executive Alan Wagner after one visit, "but the telephone wasn't ringing the way it used to." "Nobody knew if he came to work or not," said public relations aide William Lilley, whose office was around the corner. In board meetings, Paley fell asleep more often, and he struggled to follow the discussions. When he disagreed with one of Wyman's initiatives, his questioning seemed halfhearted. "Directors and management would figuratively stare him down and he would not respond," said one CBS executive. "He would then move on."

With each new indignity, Paley seethed. Part of his boardroom ritual had been a cocktail gathering in his office before the directors' lunches. Not only did Wyman attempt to end the practice, but he rearranged the seating at the board meetings—a pecking order that mandated the youngest director to Paley's left, the eldest to his right, and the CEO across the table. "He rotated Paley out of the seat he had occupied more than fifty years," recalled director Michel Bergerac, former chairman of Revlon, Inc. "Paley found it most upsetting, and it got in the way of doing business." Paley's protests were so bitter that Wyman grudgingly restored the cocktail hour and seating order—attenuated but important symbols of the ancien régime.

Occasionally, Wyman opened the door a crack for Paley and was surprised at the result. In 1983 CBS joined Time, Inc., and Columbia Pictures to form Tri-Star Pictures, Inc. It was designed as an "instant major" film studio to create a new source of programming for the CBS network, and for Time's HBO and Cinemax pay television services. Columbia Pictures needed more movies for its distribution business, and all three companies sought a bigger piece of the growing home video market.

After Wyman negotiated the deal, he proudly brought Paley into the room. Paley expressed his pleasure but wondered, "Couldn't CBS have a piece of Time's pay television business?" "It's not for sale," said an amused Richard Munro, chairman of Time, Inc. "What about Cinemax?" asked Paley, startling everyone in the room with his laser perception. "It was a wonderful question," recalled Frank Biondi, then president of HBO, "Cinemax was the one vulnerable area."

Some CBS executives with longer memories than Tom Wyman sensed that the phoenix was only sleeping. The ever-obliging Gene Jankowski, who began each workday by praying in St. Patrick's Cathedral, routinely supplied Paley with lists of programs in development and video-tapes of new shows. Paley checked in monthly, and Jankowski dutifully briefed the man he continued to call "the Chairman." When Paley traveled to Hollywood in the spring of 1984 to receive an award, he spent an entire afternoon with Bud Grant, president of CBS Entertainment, and his dep-uty Harvey Shephard. But he rarely called them except when he had an occasional idea for a show.

As in the past, Paley sought distraction outside of CBS. "He has more charm and clout than Rhett Butler and James Bond rolled into one," gushed the *New York Daily News*. Although he was in his eighties, Paley continued to chase women with the gusto of a post-pubescent. "I go to a lot of parties where you see Bill Paley, who must be older than God, with girls in their twenties," the writer Dotson Rader said in *W,* "and people say, 'Look at that old goat, he can still get it up.' "

Paley continued to put his women into various categories according to their suitability, age, and complaisance. Evangeline Bruce or Brooke Astor or Marietta Tree would take his arm for gala benefit concerts and parties. Jeanne Murray Vanderbilt would keep him company during week-ends in Southampton. But young models and starlets would accompany him to restaurants and shows. There were also more mysterious women who only dined with him alone at his apartment.

Paley fleetingly considered marrying fortyish heiress Annette Reed, stepdaughter of Charles Engelhard, the "Platinum King" who left an esti-mated $250 million when he died in 1971. Paley even took her, along with her mother, Jane Engelhard, an old friend of Babe's, on a trip to Germany and Austria in 1984. The happy threesome ate their way through Baden-Baden and attended the Salzburg music festival. But Annette was separat-ing from her husband, Sam, and beginning a relationship with Oscar de la Renta, whose wife, Françoise, had died of cancer late in 1983. "Annette had a father thing with Bill," said one of her close friends.

Many of Paley's friends applauded when he took up with the popular Jacqueline Brynner, former wife of Yul Brynner, especially when Paley invited her to a New Year's holiday at Guy and Marie-Helene de Roth-schild's home in Marrakesh. But that romance was also short-lived. "If there was a new girl in town, Paley could hardly wait to meet her," said Charlotte Curtis.

As Paley got older, his girls got younger—many were in their thirties, some in their twenties—and his infatuations became shorter. Friends called the young girls his harem, and looked askance as he sat surrounded by four or five of them, saying nothing and listening to their giggling ac-counts of parties and people. "You're wasting your time," his friend Hen-

ryk de Kwiatkowski complained. "This is my period when I don't need
to think," replied Paley. But just as he was using them, so they were using
him. "Most of the girls were looking for something in his name and
connections," said de Kwiatkowski.

Paley's most intriguing crush was Diane Sawyer, co-anchor of the
"CBS Morning News" since the spring of 1982. By May of that year
Sawyer and Paley had made the gossip columns, and they were spotted
walking hand-in-hand. Sawyer attended his dinner parties, met him for
lunch in the library at 820, and was his house guest (along with Oscar de
la Renta and the Kissingers) in Southampton. During one large dinner,
Paley repeatedly tried to grope Sawyer, who seemed uncharacteristically
nonplussed. She later told friends that he had been taking medication that
had a "semi-intoxicating effect," and that he never again behaved that
way. She said her involvement was not romantic, but others thought Paley
was hopelessly smitten. "I don't know of anyone who caught Bill's eye
like Diane Sawyer," said Irene Selznick. So confident was Sawyer of Paley's affection that she once declined to take his telephone call in front of a
group of CBS executives.

Paley had what some of his friends called "WHT," wandering hand
trouble. His small brown eyes twinkling, he would grab the arms of his
women and rub their backs, his hands in perpetual motion. "He never
takes his hand off your leg when you are having dinner with him," said
one former girlfriend. He thought nothing of pinching Annette Reed on
the bottom in front of a group of guests at a dinner party—at Henry
Kissinger's, no less. Paley made even more of a public display in 1984
when he began a romance with Veronica Uribe, the young widow of a
wealthy Colombian businessman, by necking with her at a party in the
twenty-four-room Acapulco home of "Baron" Enrico di Portanova, an
heir to the Texas oil fortune of Hugh Roy Cullen.

Such flagrant indiscretions were rare. The private Paley usually came
out only behind the doors of 820 Fifth Avenue or in suggestively erotic
phone conversations. "He is not your Norman Rockwell kind of guy,"
said one woman he invited to his apartment in the mid-1980s in hopes of
sexual adventure. Over dinner Paley asked the woman to describe her
sexual fantasies; he especially wanted to know whether she had participated in a sexual threesome including another woman.

"He is very provocative," she recalled. "He tries to stimulate you, to
see if you are the type of girl who is going to be imaginative and creative.
He tries to psyche you into getting you into a scene. In that way Mr. Paley
is not very American. It is more European for lords and ladies to pretend
they are dogs and butlers and chauffeurs. To him, straight sex is for two
people in love who care about each other. He has more of a decadent

mentality." Throughout their conversation, the young woman was discomfited by the constant presence of Dean. "No matter what Mr. Paley said, the butler was neutral," she recalled. "It was like a scene from a movie."

Another girlfriend who went out with Paley during that period was shocked when they were sitting in a restaurant one evening and Paley said with a glance across the room, "Do you think she is pretty?" When the girlfriend said yes, Paley asked, "Would you like to be with a woman like that?" Recalled the girlfriend, "His big interest in sex was fantasy, especially a woman with another woman. That made me think he didn't like women, that he liked only to control, to say, 'Come here, do this.' "

When Paley fell for a woman, even fleetingly, he could become almost pathologically possessive. He demanded an exact accounting of her whereabouts, and rebuked her if she neglected to call. "When I wouldn't go to bed with him, he accused me of being selfish," said one woman who dated him for five months when he was in his mid-eighties. "He put on so much pressure and was so argumentative, it wasn't worth it. He was so controlling. I felt like an object. He is used to pawing women to death. He is relentless and he is not used to being turned down."

Those in his social circle, even women friends, had a different window on Paley. To them, he was the gracious host and ever enthusiastic guest. He continued to import large crowds to Lyford Cay at regular intervals throughout the winter and spring. On weekends he ferried friends to Southampton on CBS's Sikorsky S-76 helicopter. Marilyn Berger and her husband, Don Hewitt, the executive producer of "60 Minutes," were Southampton neighbors and ingratiated themselves with Paley. Whenever Paley gave them a lift on the helicopter, Berger always made certain to bring Paley's favorite Pepperidge Farm cookies, which she fed to him like a child.

Paley's social life assumed a manic, almost desperate quality. "He says he is so lonely," said his friend Marietta Tree. "He is so restless. He wants to fill up every minute with lots of people." At one Museum of Modern Art party he clowned in a vintage pink Cadillac that was part of the 1950s be-bop decor. At another he stood on a chair clapping gleefully for a twelve-year-old break dancer. Perhaps the most poignant glimpse came during a dinner party at Henry and Nancy Kissinger's. Toward the end of the evening, Paley stood at the foot of the stairs gripping the banister to hold himself up, determined to project vigor and virility. He remained standing, and was among the last to leave.

Paley fought the infirmities of aging as hard as anyone could. In the early 1980s while visiting the foreign minister of Oman with Kissinger, Paley fell and seriously gashed his head. "No man can survive a fall like that," Kissinger exclaimed. After being stitched up at a local hospital, Paley gamely attended a dinner party wearing a hat. Several years later he tumbled backwards down a steep staircase at the Coe Kerr Gallery on the Upper East Side. Amazingly, he was treated and released by the emergency room at New York Hospital.

His first brush with a life-threatening illness came in January 1985, at age eighty-three. While on vacation at the Guinness home in Acapulco, Paley collapsed from a bleeding ulcer. The CBS jet whisked him to the lavish Stavros Niarchos suite on the sixteenth floor of New York Hospital. To cheer up his friend, Atlantic Records chief Ahmet Ertegun sent around a pretty young Korean woman to entertain him one day at lunchtime. While she was visiting, one of Paley's friends, the writer and socialite Lally Weymouth, had to wait outside with Dean. Paley meanwhile suffered an attack of stomach pain, prompting nurses to rush to his room. Paley's friends assumed he and the Korean woman had been in flagrante delicto. "It was a lapse of propriety that Babe never would have permitted," commented one friend. Ertegun insisted that the encounter was innocent. "She was a friend of both of us," said Ertegun. "He was not doing anything to her."

During Paley's six-week convalescence, he lost 17 pounds, and his new doctor, Harvey Klein, ordered him to give up liquor. Paley stopped eating his enormous breakfasts of steak or broiled fish and shifted to a cup of strong tea—a special blend discovered by Babe—and toast. After his hospitalization he always had a nurse nearby, even when traveling.

Paley's health restored, he turned his attention to a task that would prove more rejuvenating than any medicine: getting even with his tormentor Tom Wyman, who was riding high as 1985 began. The CBS Cable losses were a fading memory, and Wyman had successfully unloaded such money losers as musical instruments and Fawcett paperbacks. CBS Records had bounced back after a slump in sales. Enterprises such as CBS-Fox and Tri-Star looked promising. In 1984, CBS profits were $212.4 million, up smartly from $110.8 million two years earlier.

The man who opened the breach for Paley's attack was North Carolina senator Jesse Helms, a most unlikely ally. In January, Helms and a group of like-minded conservatives launched a campaign urging citizens to buy CBS stock to "become Dan Rather's boss" and end the "liberal bias" of CBS News. Helms had taken the standard right-wing tirade and twisted it into an ominous new form. This was the era of Ronald Reagan; a serious proxy fight led by conservatives did not seem farfetched.

While that threat eventually lost steam, the Helms effort caught the eye of Wall Street, then in the middle of a takeover frenzy that was fueled in mid-March when Capital Cities Communications, owner of TV and radio stations, announced it would buy ABC for $3.5 billion. Ivan Boesky, the powerful arbitrageur, quickly gathered 8.7 percent of CBS stock, hoping that a buyer would emerge to drive up the price; by the time his stake was revealed, on April 1, CBS stock had already jumped to nearly $110 a share from $73 before the Helms scheme came to light.

As soon as it became clear in early March that CBS was "in play," Paley saw his opportunity to recapture the chairmanship by leading a leveraged buyout to take CBS private. He enlisted James Wolfensohn, the only investment banker on the CBS board, to study the possibility. Wolfensohn came up with what seemed an ideal bid of $162 a share, and Paley pressed the directors to approve the proposal. Instead of leaping at the idea, they asked the CBS investment bankers, Morgan Stanley, to conduct an evaluation of Wolfensohn's proposal.

Wyman said flatly he would not participate in a leveraged buyout. The board tried to explain to Paley that his bid would hardly be the last. "Paley couldn't understand that Saul Steinberg would come in the next week at $172 and say he would sell various CBS divisions to finance it," said William Lilley. "He simply wouldn't hear it." An item planted in Liz Smith's syndicated column in late March announcing Paley's effort to buy the company annoyed the board even more.

The much-awaited move on CBS came in mid-April from cable television maverick Ted Turner, creator of the successful and acclaimed Cable News Network. Turner offered $5.4 billion, financed by "junk" bonds— risky securities that offered high interest rates. At a price of $175 a share, Turner's bid was $67 higher than CBS's close that day.

Ted Turner had been obsessed by Paley and his network for some years. Back in 1981, Gene Jankowski and William Leonard had flown to Atlanta to ask if Turner would sell his CNN, then barely a year old, to CBS. Turner, who wore an open-neck shirt and bluejeans to their meeting in an Atlanta motel room, greeted the buttoned-up CBS men by saying, "How's old Paley?" He expressed a willingness to sell 49 percent or less of his network. Leonard and Jankowski said 51 percent or nothing. "You CBS guys are something," said Turner as he chewed tobacco and spat into a water tumbler. "Someday I'm going to own you. You bet I am."

Ten days before Turner made his bid public, when each day's newspaper produced a new crop of rumors, Paley was honored at a luncheon given by the Center for Communications at the Plaza Hotel. Appearing somewhat shaky—he stumbled and fell during the cocktail party preceding the luncheon—Paley tried to make light of his company's financial vulnerability. "It's wonderful to come into a roomful of people," he cracked, "and know that not more than five hundred of them are trying to buy CBS." Underneath, however, Paley was in a state of high anxiety.

With Dean and his nurse in tow, Paley flew on CBS's Gulfstream II to Chicago in mid-April for the CBS annual meeting. Wyman was aboard, along with several directors and top CBS executives. Paley spent the entire flight fretting about the Turner crisis. "He was a wreck," Lilley said afterwards. "He couldn't understand why this was happening—why people like Turner and Boesky and Helms were suddenly in his life. He was perplexed and frustrated." What galled Paley most, Lilley reported, was the participation of E. F. Hutton in Turner's bid. "He couldn't understand why his Southampton neighbor Robert Fomon [E. F. Hutton's chief] could do this to him."

Paley was even more annoyed that his own efforts to pull together a leveraged buyout were going nowhere. Morgan Stanley shot it down, saying that the offering price would need to climb so high that CBS would have to be dismembered in the process. Still, Paley hammered at the directors throughout April and May, trying to turn them around. He complained bitterly to Stanton that Morgan Stanley only wanted a bigger fee by bringing in a "white knight"—a merger partner more to CBS's liking than Turner—and that the board knew Paley would dump them all if he took the company private. Paley's unsuccessful gambit to seize control cost CBS $200,000 in consulting fees paid to Wolfensohn.

Even if CBS initially regarded Turner as a gnat trying to subdue an elephant, Wyman and his men were forced to defend themselves since Wall Street was taking the bid seriously. In May and June, Wyman discussed merger possibilities with both Time, Inc., and the Gannett Company, the country's largest newspaper publisher. But despite Wyman's close friendship with Time's Richard Munro, the two men could not find their way around the regulatory problems posed by Time, Inc.'s, ownership of cable television franchises in cities where CBS had TV stations. Gannett, however, seemed a possible fit.

Al Neuharth, Gannett's flamboyant sixty-one-year-old chairman, assiduously wooed Wyman to mastermind a merger that would have put Neuharth in charge and changed the company name to the faintly ridiculous Universal Media, Inc. After they had agreed on general principles, Wyman brought in Paley, who expressed a mild interest in being chairman of the executive committee in the combined company. Mistakenly taking Paley at face value, Neuharth assumed he had "blessed the deal." Toward the end of June, Wyman called Neuharth to say the deal was off. The following week, CBS announced that it would borrow nearly $1 billion to buy back 21 percent of the company's stock for $150 a share. Since CBS would pay shareholders in cash and high-grade CBS securities instead of risky junk bonds, the offer swamped Turner.

To pay off the $1 billion debt, Wyman had to sell small pieces of the company and cut staff. He unloaded KMOX-TV, the St. Louis station where Paley had delivered his farewell address, for $140 million. Even worse, from Paley's standpoint, Wyman planned to sell the company's helicopter and corporate jets, which were costing the company $10 million a year.

Paley was enraged. His retirement contract stipulated that he be provided private aircraft. He argued that he needed them because his wealth and status made him a potential kidnap victim. "It is right there in the contract," Paley complained to Stanton, who could only smile inwardly, remembering those dark months before his own retirement, and say to himself, "That's what I thought, too." Not only were the private aircraft convenient, they were a good financial deal for Paley. He reimbursed CBS at the rate of a first-class ticket, a fraction of what it cost to use a private plane. Mostly, however, giving up the aircraft represented a personal affront and a visible decline in prestige.

Memos flew back and forth between CBS directors and John Minary. At a time when CBS was grappling with extensive layoffs, Paley bogged down board meetings with his arguments against the sale. "Do you mean to take away the plane that goes to Southampton, too?" grumbled Paley. "Bill, we call that a helicopter," Wyman replied acidly. "You can lease one just as effectively." Wyman was appalled that Paley could be more concerned about his own perks than the future of the company.

After months of wrangling, Paley's new lawyer, Arthur Liman, struck a compromise. Paley bought one CBS airplane for $5.4 million, and CBS sold the helicopter. Instead of paying each time Paley took a helicopter to Southampton, CBS agreed to contribute roughly $150,000 a year to his transportation expenses. The aircraft crisis left scars in the CBS boardroom. "The airplanes became a horror," said Michel Bergerac. "They were really only a symbol for reducing costs. It was not wise of Tom to go out of his way to irritate Paley."

Wyman, the man *Forbes* magazine once said "makes an art of self-effacement the better to soothe others' egos," had turned vindictive, partly out of exasperation but also out of weakness. "All Tom wanted to do after a while was neutralize Paley," said program executive Kim LeMasters. "Tom was very insecure. His mistake was he overcaged the beast and created resentment." Paley, as Wyman would find out, was not a man who took insult lightly.

57

TAKEOVER TOM-TOMS began to beat again in July, when Laurence Tisch, chairman of Loews Corporation, a $17.5 billion holding company with interests ranging from insurance to cigarettes, bought 5 percent of CBS stock. Wyman had called on Tisch in the middle of the Helms-Turner crisis to get names of possible supporters for CBS's campaign against Turner at federal regulatory agencies. Now Tisch assured Wyman that he was only interested in CBS as an investor. Wyman was skeptical, but he played along.

Tisch continued to accumulate stock. Within weeks, he had brought his stake to 10 percent, eclipsing Paley's 8 percent to become the largest shareholder. James Wolfensohn, a tennis partner and close friend of Tisch, arranged a luncheon to bring together the oldest and the newest CBS power brokers. Paley could not recall having met Tisch before, although they had sat across the table in Paley's dining room fifteen years earlier. Typically, Paley had Tisch confused with a New York builder named Tishman.

Whether Tisch or Tishman, the interloping CBS investor came from a lower social order in Paley's eyes, despite his estimated $1 billion net worth—about twice that of Paley. Short, bald, and unprepossessing, the sixty-one-year-old Tisch was the antithesis of Paley in virtually every way. Tisch drove himself to parties in a Pontiac station wagon, inhabited a bland office fit for one of his CNA Insurance salesmen, and spent his weekends playing tennis with suburban pals at a country club north of Manhattan. Known for his philanthropy, Tisch was also a pillar of the New York Jewish community that Paley had kept at arm's length for nearly sixty years. Each week he and two of his sons gathered with a Hasidic rabbi to study the Bible and the Talmud.

Sitting in Paley's elegant library on an August afternoon, Paley and Tisch regarded each other warily. Both were strong-willed men, and neither revealed much. "Neither of us said anything that could not be published," Paley told a friend afterwards, "but I feel uneasy." Some weeks later, Paley offered a guarded but perceptive assessment of Tisch: "I found him to be straightforward, seemingly decent and with integrity. He said he has no intention of buying CBS, but I know that intentions can change.

He has invested $200 million and I wonder if he can do it just for the investment." In his biweekly lunches with Wyman early that fall, Paley asked repeatedly, "What do you know about him?"

Paley's sense of foreboding was evident one night in September when he sat down to watch the much-publicized revival of Arthur Miller's *Death of a Salesman,* starring Dustin Hoffman. The show was a proud symbol of CBS quality, and Paley looked forward to seeing it.

Along with most of the critics, Paley thought the production was magnificent. The old showman immediately zeroed in on what made it so compelling. "Dustin Hoffman was perfect," he said. "He was a small man, an average man—just as Willy Loman should have been. Before they always cast it with a big man. That was wrong."

Impressed as he was, Paley clicked off the television halfway through the program. "I was feeling down that day anyway, and it really got to me," Paley said. "It was the first time I ever turned off anything for that reason. I have turned off plenty of programs because they were bad. But this one got me by the throat." With its themes of failure and disillusionment, *Death of a Salesman* mirrored Paley's own situation. His life's work —the creation of America's greatest broadcasting company—was slipping away from him.

By October, Tisch had raised his stake to 12 percent. He told Wyman that he intended to buy no more than 25 percent—still, he insisted, acting as a passive investor. After a discussion with the directors, Wyman invited him on the board. "The assumption," recalled Wyman, "was that he would be less threatening inside the company than outside. But he was never invited to help protect the CBS family from the rest of the world— as a white knight or white squire or anything like that." Paley welcomed the move; by then he had concluded that Tisch could prove useful in ousting Wyman. "He is the only way I can get anything done," Paley told a friend. At a dinner party the same month, Paley was even more outspoken. "That son of a bitch Tom Wyman," he told one of Tisch's friends. "He stole my company, and I want to get it back."

A few days after Tisch joined the board, he and Paley drank tea and ate sponge cake in the library at 820 Fifth Avenue—the second of numerous private meetings between television's new odd couple. The caginess had disappeared. Paley relaxed and reminisced about the old days of broadcasting. Several weeks later Paley said confidently, "I was very impressed. He is a sound businessman, very direct. He says what he thinks."

When Tisch slipped into his director's chair for the first time in November, CBS was in trouble and Paley was emboldened. Paley criticized Wyman's purchase the previous February of twelve magazines owned by Ziff-Davis Publishing for $362.5 million. After the deal was announced, the losing bidders revealed that their offers had been some $40 million less, making Wyman seem like a patsy. "Paley was positive when we bought Ziff-Davis," recalled Wyman. "He has quite a capacity to move history around."

Losses at CBS Toys, meanwhile, had spiraled out of control by the autumn of 1985. In 1982, Wyman had opted to expand that business by buying Ideal Toy Corporation for $57.5 million. Unlike the previously acquired Gabriel Toys, which produced staples like Tinkertoys, Ideal specialized in fad items and was prone to wide swings in profitability. Its latest phenomenon, Rubik's Cube, accounted for nearly 40 percent of the company's sales in 1981. But even as CBS handed over the money, the cube was fading fast.

Not only did CBS fail to find the next hot toy, its efforts to bring Ideal into video game production went nowhere. In 1985, CBS Toys posted losses of $135 million before Wyman shut it down in September. He also bailed out of feature films and dumped CBS's one-third interest in Tri-Star, resulting in further losses of $20.5 million. CBS profits for 1985 plunged to $27.4 million—a staggering $185 million less than the previous year.

Beyond the financial implications, the toy debacle and other ill-fated ventures distracted Wyman from CBS's main business. The network dropped once again to second place in prime time in the fall of 1985, prompting Paley's complaints about mismanagement to grow louder.

To make matters worse, Wyman was engulfed that fall by turmoil at CBS News. For more than a year, the news division had lurched from one crisis to another under the leadership of Van Gordon Sauter, ensconced at Black Rock as an executive vice-president, and Ed Joyce, the president of CBS News, working out of the journalists' headquarters on West 57th Street. The previous spring a widely publicized lawsuit against CBS by General William C. Westmoreland had been dropped after months of testimony embarrassing to CBS News. The producer of a 1982 CBS documentary about the Vietnam War had violated numerous CBS News guidelines on ethics, and his program had been put together sloppily, with very little oversight. Paley felt that Wyman and Sauter had mishandled the controversy. Three years earlier, Paley had backed a proposal from Frank Stanton that the network should meet Westmoreland's objections by giving him time on the air. Had Wyman gone along, the case would doubtless have rested there.

Sauter also stumbled on CBS's morning news program, for years the least popular behind NBC's "Today" show and ABC's "Good Morning America." A more traditional hard-news broadcast than its counterparts, the "CBS Morning News" had long held a special place for Paley. "He watched the morning news in a way no one else did," Richard Salant once explained. "Everyone else was up and doing something else, but he would be in bed, with the valet bringing him his breakfast. He would call me afterwards and ask if the screen graphics should be to the right instead of to the left of the anchor's shoulders. He loved the little details like whether the camera should move closer. The complaints were reasonably good and had nothing to do with the substance of the broadcasts."

In the summer of 1984, Paley's friend, Diane Sawyer, had fled to "60 Minutes" when she felt the "Morning News" sinking further. That fall, Jankowski and Sauter selected Phyllis George, a former Miss America turned sportscaster, as her replacement. TV critics howled that the organization built by Murrow and Paley was being defiled—little knowing that Paley himself had been one of George's original boosters.

In March 1982—shortly after Sawyer came to the "Morning News" —Paley had met with George's agent, Ed Hookstratten. Following the meeting, Hookstratten reported, "Paley really likes her. He's pleased that she has lost weight and gotten into shape and looks great. We are talking about getting her on the morning news, but right now they have in their heads they should have a newswoman."

Two years later that notion changed, but Paley characteristically kept himself aloof from the decision. Phyllis George proved to be ill-suited for the job. In September 1985, after she had been on the air seven months, Joyce prodded Sauter to sack her. CBS continued to pay her full salary through the end of her contract—some $2 million.

At virtually the same moment, Wyman ordered layoffs at CBS News as part of his cost-cutting campaign. These were widely viewed as the dismemberment of a great news organization. Barely a month later, Don Hewitt led a group of CBS News bigwigs, including Dan Rather, Diane Sawyer, and Mike Wallace, in a proposed leveraged buyout of CBS News. Wyman called it "terribly bush," and the financial community snickered, but the proposal proved damaging to Wyman anyway. The news division seemed out of control, a hotbed of troublemakers, a source of bad publicity, and a reminder that the Tiffany shine had tarnished.

Hewitt was an agent provocateur working several angles. In the first place, he wanted Joyce fired. As executive producer of the only CBS News show that produced $75 million a year in revenues, Hewitt operated his own fiefdom at "60 Minutes." In Hewitt's view, Joyce had never given him sufficient respect. Hewitt had Paley's ear on those Southampton weekends, and he was whispering to Larry Tisch as well. Paley professed annoyance at Hewitt's LBO gambit, telling Wyman it was a "crazy idea." For his part, Hewitt insisted "there was no collusion" with Paley. But anything that weakened Wyman strengthened Paley. "A group of people in the company were publicly trying to assassinate the management," said Michel Bergerac.

The stealthiest assassin was, of course, Bill Paley, who always kept a silencer on his weapon. He played a key role in shaping one of the most negative among a flood of newspaper and magazine articles about CBS. The November 4 issue of *New York* magazine pummeled Wyman for mishandling the business and creative sides of CBS and invoked Paley as a symbol of better days. Wyman and his staff had declined to cooperate with the story. So, apparently, had Paley, who was not quoted. But Paley's fingerprints were everywhere. "Paley spent one and a half hours with me," said the writer, Tony Schwartz. "The deal was, I had to disguise his quotes. Even if I quoted his friends as saying he said something, I had to check back with him. He is always that careful."

Larry Tisch used the turbulence as his springboard for criticizing Wyman. At the November board meeting, he pointedly said that the news division could be controlled if there were fewer layers of management at CBS. Paley eagerly backed him up. The next month Wyman stripped out one layer of bureaucracy, fired Ed Joyce, and threw Sauter back to CBS News as president.

Throughout winter and spring, Tisch burrowed into CBS far more deeply than the classic "passive investor." He visited Hollywood for wall-to-wall meetings with producers and studio executives. "He spent more time asking questions since he bought CBS stock than Tom Wyman did in six years," noted Robert Daly. At directors' meetings, Tisch questioned every decision with Paley's happy concurrence. "Tisch was in effect running the meetings from the other end of the table," said Lilley.

Tisch controlled his relationship with Paley as well. He was deferential to Paley—but only up to a point. When Paley got stubbornly argumentative, Tisch would say, "Oh Bill, that's silly," and move to the next item. "If anyone else did that it would be insubordination," said Lilley.

Wyman seemed secure despite Tisch, who made the CBS directors apprehensive. They worried that his purchases of CBS stock amounted to a gradual takeover without paying a premium price. But the directors were also annoyed at Paley for causing trouble and trying to obstruct their meetings in his effort to wear Wyman down. His main preoccupation in the early months of 1986 was blocking Wyman's plans to install a company cafeteria on the ground floor of Black Rock.

New predators started circling CBS after the December 1985 announcement that General Electric would buy RCA, and with it NBC, for $6.4 billion. In February and March, Marvin Davis met several times with Wyman to propose buying CBS for $160 a share. After consulting closely with Tisch and informing Paley as a courtesy, Wyman deflected the bid. Several days later, Larry Tisch's brother Robert declared his family's intention "to control CBS and operate it as a first-class broadcasting company," and a week later the Tisch stake climbed to nearly 17 percent.

Tisch's audacious move depressed Paley. In one conversation with Carter Burden that spring, he insisted that Tisch only owned 9 percent of CBS. "Bill didn't want to come to grips with his diminished stature," said Burden. Paley's most public expression of discontent was boycotting the CBS annual meeting in April—the first one he had missed since 1946. He claimed that back pain kept him away, but that had always been his excuse for avoiding situations he found unpleasant.

As he approached his eighty-fifth birthday, Paley's thoughts turned to posterity. He began work on a new autobiography and launched a campaign to build a new Museum of Broadcasting. The original museum and memoir, he felt, were smaller than life. He wanted something grander, something that would do justice to his reputation—or at least his estimate of it.

The new and improved memoir was ordered up after Paley learned that two writers were preparing biographies about him. "I have my own stories to tell," he explained at the time. "I don't want people to use what I have, my memories." Besides trying to blunt the other books, which were bound to take chinks out of the Paley myth, he wanted to erase *As It Happened*. "I wish I could take it all back," he once said. The reprise of his life story caused considerable merriment around CBS. "Do you think he'll call it 'As It Really Happened,' or, 'As It Might Have Happened'?" cracked one former CBS executive.

"How I Believed It Happened" was probably closer to the mark. In his own mind, Paley had become the man extolled in hundreds of press releases. When he asked his public relations aides to prepare a packet of biographical material to send to one prospective collaborator, the respected writer Linda Bird Francke, they compiled a cross section of articles and books, including David Halberstam's *The Powers That Be,* which captured many of Paley's defining qualities. Paley insisted on reviewing the selections and tossed out all the books except his own and all the articles except a flattering profile from *Esquire* magazine.

Paley signed up a high-powered literary agent, Kathy Robbins, who brought several writer candidates around to his apartment. Bill Abrams, a *Wall Street Journal* reporter, found his interview fascinating but frustrating. "I have a lot of things to get off my chest," said Paley. When Abrams pressed him, Paley acknowledged that he had not been much of a letter writer and had kept no diaries, "but I have a million anecdotes when I get started." Abrams was put off by Paley's notion of autobiography as dinner-table chatter. "I decided that between his age and towering ego, I couldn't get an accurate representation," said Abrams.

By early 1986, Paley had chosen David Harris as his Boswell, and a few months later they signed a contract with Bantam Books. Harris was a San Francisco–based writer who had been a prominent sixties activist when he was married to the singer Joan Baez. He was now remotely connected to Paley by marriage. The uncle of Harris's second wife, Lacey Fosburgh, had been married to Babe's sister, Minnie. Harris rented an apartment on the Upper East Side, and Paley spun his stories yet again in a series of taped interviews. In addition, Paley gave Harris a short list of people to talk to—the six children plus friends like Slim Keith, Jeanne Murray Vanderbilt, Don Hewitt, Irene Selznick, and Carter Burden. At one point Harris contacted Paley's first wife Dorothy, who declined to see him. "He told me he is free to say what he wants about Bill, even negative things," she recalled. "I thought to myself, 'You don't know Bill Paley.' "

Paley had begun thinking about a larger and more imposing building for the Museum of Broadcasting since 1983 when he left the chairmanship of CBS. By 1986 he had found a site next door to "21" and down the block from Black Rock. He paid $12 million for the land, but wanted to tap other sources for the $40 million to finance the building—starting with $2.5 million from each of the networks. For months, Paley had tried to persuade Wyman to authorize CBS's contribution, arguing that its commitment was crucial to prying funds from ABC and NBC. In May, Wyman finally agreed—a gesture that board members saw as a significant peace overture.

At a Museum of Broadcasting testimonial dinner for Bob Hope soon afterwards, Paley was almost giddy with excitement. He flirted with museum president Bob Batscha's wife, and he pounded the table and roared with laughter as if he had been cooped up for months. In roasting Hope, Paley recalled a speech the comedian had made years earlier honoring Cardinal Spellman. "It thrills me to be at a dinner with someone so powerful, so august, whose robe I've always wanted to touch," Hope had said. "Please stand up your eminence . . . Bill Paley." All night Paley seemed intent on showing that he was more vigorous than Hope, who was a year younger at eighty-three.

That same month, Wyman invited Paley to the prime-time schedule meetings. "Tom carried Bill around on a pillow for three days and was very deferential," said one friend of Paley's. But Paley had little to contribute. "He just didn't know the game," said Kim LeMasters. "He had watched our shows but hadn't watched the competition. He wasn't as aware of the outside world. The three-year period he was on ice was damaging."

Even when tensions ran high, Paley had his customary lunch every ten days or so with Wyman, just as he had done with Backe, Taylor, and Stanton. At one, Paley choked on a veal chop. Wyman instinctively sprang to his feet, applied the Heimlich Maneuver, and dislodged the obstruction. But if Wyman felt momentarily heroic for saving the life of his nemesis, his feelings dissipated when Paley failed to thank him. "He just resumed talking about the ratings," Wyman marveled. "When we walked to his office he said, 'Thanks for having lunch.' "

Paley paused for a moment that June to take the Concorde to Paris for the *International Herald Tribune* annual meeting. By then his enthusiasm for the enterprise had waned after his partners vetoed his proposal for a television show using *Tribune* reporters. His back was bothering him, and he attended all the meetings in a wheelchair. His zest for life was undiminished, however. One evening at a *Tribune* board dinner, Ruth Stanton raved about the new gossamer illumination on the Eiffel Tower. "Let's go see it," said Paley, heading for the door midway through the meal. He and the Stantons were driven to the Tower, and Paley insisted that they go right up underneath. "He was like a boy," recalled Stanton, "so enthusiastic about how beautiful it was."

The troubles at CBS made newspaper headlines throughout the summer, with further companywide layoffs and the news division in an uproar over Van Sauter's decision to kill its morning newscast entirely. "CBS, which used to stand for the Columbia Broadcasting System, no longer stands for anything," "60 Minutes" commentator Andy Rooney wrote in his syndicated newspaper column. "They're just corporate initials now."

When Larry Tisch had pushed his stake toward 20 percent, Wyman and directors Gilpatric, Wolfensohn, and Thomas confronted him before the June board meeting to ask him to sign a "standstill" agreement. Tisch dismissed them, saying he had told them he intended to buy up to 25 percent and he would not break his word. "It was a short meeting," said Wyman.

From that moment, Tisch turned on Wyman. "He knew he had an enemy, and could never have a relationship of trust or confidence," said one of Tisch's closest friends. "Taking on Larry Tisch was like closing an umbrella in the rain. It was the beginning of the end."

Tisch criticized Wyman openly for the first time during a dinner at the Links Club before the July board meeting. On a recent trip to Hollywood he had heard an earful from Twentieth Century Fox chairman Barry Diller and other executives about Wyman's softness at the bargaining table. (Diller had renegotiated the CBS-Fox video deal on terms that some within CBS believed were far more advantageous to Fox than they had been.) "He's a nice man," said Tisch, "but he's not a good businessman."

Paley seconded Tisch in even harsher terms, deriding not only Wyman's skills as a negotiator but his lack of talent in programming and poor management of the news division.

Most of the directors defended Wyman and dismissed Paley's tirade. "It was a rehash," said one director. "It would have been the same whether it was Tom Wyman or anyone else." The directors expressed their dissatisfaction privately over the way Wyman was running the company, but they were even more vexed at Tisch for buying CBS cheap through a "creeping tender offer." At the board meeting the next day, they raised the prospect of a "poison pill" to stave off a hostile takeover. "If you do that, it's a declaration of war," said Tisch. Shortly thereafter, Tisch raised his stake to 24.9 percent.

In early August, Gene Jankowski effectively cut off Tom Wyman's legs when he admitted that 1986 broadcasting revenues would amount to only $235 million—$150 million less than he had earlier projected. The CBS network, which had finished the season in second place the previous spring, saw its lowest prime-time ratings to date on the night of August 2. The "CBS Evening News with Dan Rather" was losing viewers as well.

"Paley cared about the ratings and news, and Tisch cared about the financial shortfall," said Lilley. "It was a fatal linkage for Tom Wyman, joining the driving concerns of the two most powerful people on the board." Now that Paley and Tisch together controlled more than one third of CBS stock, Paley initiated an alliance to oust Wyman. "There was an inevitable point," said a close friend of Tisch, "when they got together and said, 'If we act together, we can change management.' " Over a series of lunches at Paley's apartment and in discussions through their tough-minded intermediary, Arthur Liman, they sketched out scenarios.

Despite their common interest in dislodging Wyman, they were unable to forge a close relationship. "I don't think either is capable of communicating with the other," said a close friend of Tisch. "They could sit and talk for hours and you would get two different versions immediately afterward." Each man had a specific goal, Paley to be chairman and Tisch to be chief executive. Not surprisingly, Paley tried to talk Tisch out of being chief executive, but Liman eventually got Paley to acquiesce.

Paley called various board members to present his scheme. "There was lots of mending fences, and reviewing what went wrong," said one man close to Paley. "He took the blame for choosing Wyman." Paley got his most sympathetic hearing from Marietta Tree, Walter Cronkite, and Newton Minow, the former FCC chief who coined the term "vast wasteland" to describe American television. The other board members—Henry Schacht, Michel Bergerac, James Houghton, Franklin Thomas, and Edson

Spencer—were in Wyman's camp, with James Wolfensohn sitting on the fence next to Roswell Gilpatric of the original "inner five."

The prospect of ousting Wyman revitalized Paley. No longer did he climb into his limousine at noon or not go to the office at all. He was out of the house by nine-thirty. "In the past six weeks Bill Paley seemed reborn," said one friend that August. As the September board meeting approached, Paley confided to another friend, "I am not going out anywhere Monday or Tuesday night. I have to be strong. I have to save my company."

Tom Wyman had not been idle during those days either. On September 2 he had lunch with his friend Francis T. Vincent, Jr., chairman and chief executive of Columbia Pictures, to discuss possibly joining forces with Coca-Cola, owner of Columbia. That very afternoon Wyman asked two of Wolfensohn's financial men to provide some background on Coca-Cola. They did a quick analysis of how a combination would work, and Vincent told Wyman that if CBS were interested, Coca-Cola would consider a merger. Despite numerous press reports of talks with such companies as Westinghouse, Philip Morris, and Gulf & Western, the only other overture during those weeks was from Michael Eisner, chairman of Disney, on September 8. Eisner called to ask Wyman about a possible CBS-Disney merger, and Wyman said he was not in a position to discuss such a proposal.

Having been given a yellow light by Coke, Wyman was busy briefing CBS directors Bergerac, Gilpatric, Thomas, Brown, Houghton, Schacht, Spencer, and Wolfensohn—conspicuously omitting Tisch, Paley, and their allies. Not only did Wyman tell eight men on the board of Coca-Cola's interest, he mentioned that he expected to raise the idea at the September board meeting.

On Sunday, September 7, Don Hewitt got an early copy of *Newsweek*'s cover story due out the next day. Titled "Civil War at CBS," it described in detail the unfolding executive suite drama and included a scorching assessment of the news division by Bill Moyers, the network's most prominent correspondent. Hewitt took the story along to the U.S. Tennis Open, where he handed it to Wyman in the CBS box. "I'll never forget the expression on Don Hewitt's face," recalled Wyman. "He enjoyed that moment enormously." Paley got an early copy as well. "He didn't seem upset at all," recalled Stanton.

The board met for dinner at the Ritz Carlton Hotel two nights later, on the eve of their September meeting. Neither Tom Wyman nor Larry Tisch was invited. In a private dining room on the second floor they ate sandwiches from a buffet and talked for five hours about the mess at CBS. Paley, who was accompanied by Liman, passionately made his case. "We have to have a change in management," he said. "Tom Wyman is not right. I have met with Larry Tisch and discussed it and he feels the same. The two of us have decided we will act together. We are asking you directors to join us."

Ever so politely, the directors asked Paley to leave the room so they could talk among themselves. "What was not expected was Paley's announcement of an alliance with Larry Tisch," said one board member. "The way he said it was not clever. It made people mad." Several Wyman loyalists complained that Paley and Tisch could prevent the board from even considering another offer. They debated alternatives to Tisch as chief executive if they did have to push Wyman out. Ironically, they briefly considered bringing back Frank Stanton.

On his return to the meeting room, Paley pressed even harder against Wyman. In his waning years, he still had the capacity to flare briefly with the brightness of the old Paley. As the hours passed, said Newton Minow, Paley "was forceful and up to his full powers, firm and in control." By the end of the evening, added Minow, "Tom Wyman's support was shakier than it had been."

When the directors met the next morning, the *Newsweek* cover story was like a hand grenade rolling down the boardroom's highly polished walnut table. Given the determination of Paley and Tisch, the board knew that Wyman would probably have to leave after a search committee had found a successor. But Wyman opened a trapdoor allowing them to push him out that very day.

Confident that he had the backing of eight directors, Wyman presented the Coca-Cola idea and recommended that a special board committee analyze any offer that might emerge. The only people who spoke up were Paley and Tisch. "We are not going to sell our stock under any circumstances," they said. "Even the good guys were bad guys because Tom Wyman's friends didn't back him," said a friend of Tisch. "None of them said a word."

Having watched his proposal slide off the table, Wyman left the boardroom. The directors quizzed Tisch on his intentions and invited Paley to speak. Typically, Paley pulled away from his earlier understanding with Tisch. Instead of making Tisch chief executive, Paley proposed naming him acting chairman of a four-man executive committee of which Paley would be a member. The chairman of CBS, of course, would be Paley.

Paley, Liman, and Tisch left the room, and the directors hashed over their options. There was no way they could oppose Paley and Tisch to support Wyman's proposal, whatever its merits. They likewise threw out Paley's cockeyed executive committee plan and sensibly decided that one person had to be in charge: Larry Tisch. At first, most of the directors strongly resisted reinstating Paley as chairman, fearing they would never get him out again. But when board emissaries Franklin Thomas and Samuel Butler, a partner at Cravath Swaine & Moore, passed the word to Paley, he got tearful and petulant.

In the end, the board named Paley and Tisch "acting" chairman and chief executive, an effort to create the illusion that the titles were subject to change. It suited Tisch perfectly to have Paley as chairman; he knew Paley's continued presence would confer legitimacy on the Tisch regime.

At 4:00 p.m. Henry Schacht and Franklin Thomas—the perennial bad news boys—walked to Wyman's office where he had been waiting alone for five hours. They told him the board had officially vetoed any proposal to sell the company. Like John Backe before him, they forced Wyman to resign.

The directors gave him a staggering settlement of $3.8 million plus $400,000 a year for life—a sum scratched out by Schacht and Thomas on a scrap of paper. Tisch was not happy with the magnitude, but he went along. The directors had betrayed Wyman, and their guilt was expressed in dollar signs. Wyman was shaken by his dismissal. Other than sitting on the boards of several companies, he would not soon run another company.

After the meeting adjourned at six-fifteen, Paley sat with Liman as the champagne corks popped. Weary but alert, Paley's well-tanned face crinkled in a grin. Only weeks before his eighty-fifth birthday he had used cunning and determination to seize the one job that could sustain him. In another office, Larry Tisch talked on the telephone, his mind whirring with the tasks he faced in his glamorous and highly visible new post. "They were two people," said a close associate of Tisch, "each with an objective, each moving down parallel paths, coming together rather fortuitously at that particular moment."

They were by no means equals. Tisch was destined to dominate by virtue of his holdings in CBS—at that moment, $780 million to Paley's $257 million—as well as his physical and mental vigor. Paley would never have selected Tisch, who hardly fit his ideal of the cool, tall WASP. Equally important, said management consultant David Hertz, who met with Paley shortly after the coup, "Tisch is too strong, and he is not someone who would listen to Paley whenever Paley wanted." Paley had made a classic pact with the devil. He had willingly ceded control of his company in exchange for an honorific and the chance to dive back into programming. But even if Paley was only a figurehead, he clung to the belief that no one would ever again shut the door in his face as Tom Wyman had done.

58

WITH AN EYE to history, Bill Paley sat down after the climactic CBS board meeting and wrote his recollections in longhand on a yellow legal pad. He was hailed as a conquering hero by the press and public. "Bill Paley takes charge again at CBS and Lee Iacocca takes Chrysler forward," blared a radio ad for a Long Island Chrysler dealer. "The capacity to lead, the ability to win, makin' all the scores."

Paley's friends celebrated his triumph, and so did his children—at a party to mark his eighty-fifth birthday, an elegant family dinner at 820 Fifth Avenue. In the Paley family, emotions and opinions had always been repressed; everything was between the lines. But on this poignant evening everyone rose to give a toast, and each child, now an adult, spoke openly and warmly. Their words evoked laughter and tears. Paley was genuinely touched.

It had taken great effort for the sons to reconcile with their tyrannical father. Tony Mortimer had barely spoken to him since Babe's death. Their antagonism over her will had been aggravated by conflicts over a perfume business that Tony and Babe had formed in 1977, using a $2 million investment from Paley. "She had a romantic idea that she could go into business with her son, but she put Bill in financial control," recalled Amanda. When Babe died, Paley became Tony's partner, and for several years Tony ran the business, which produced a fragrance using the name of Mary McFadden, the fashion designer who was the daughter of one of Babe's oldest friends, Josie Blair. Three years later Paley balked at investing $10 million for promotion, and pulled the plug. McFadden accused Paley of "grossly mismanaging" the company, and Tony was embittered. By the mid-eighties he and his stepfather reached an accommodation, helped along by Tony's wife, Siri, whom Paley adored.

Billie had an even more tortuous path to his father's good graces. Paley had opened the door during Babe's illness by inviting him to attend CBS's West Coast programming meetings in 1977. "He was a well-dressed kid, but scared and gangly," recalled Robert Wussler, who was assigned to take him around. "He was very shy and awkward. He said, 'My father and I haven't been too close and we are trying to be good friends. I don't want to do this but he wants me to.' " In meetings, Paley introduced "My son Bill," but they seemed uneasy during their four days together.

When Babe died, Billie was operating two restaurants in Washington, D.C.—a touching bid for his father's approval. "The only thing we could ever relate to together was food," he explained at the time. But Billie could not shake his old addictions, and in January 1979 he was arrested for heroin and marijuana possession. After pleading guilty, he received a suspended three-month prison sentence.

He knocked around from job to job—communications consultant, media columnist for a small magazine in Washington, partner in an art transport business—and in 1980 married Alison Van Metre, the daughter of a yachtsman and real estate developer. She was pretty, so Paley naturally took a shine to her. She and Billie had two sons, Sam and Max. Billie finally kicked his habit and became a drug counselor. Paley's feelings about him were painfully ambivalent. In one breath he would call his son "completely irresponsible"; in the next he'd say, "We're very close. He loves me and I love him." "Bill never had any particular expectations for him," said Dorothy Paley Hirshon. "The fact that Billie is sweet and nice may be enough."

Even Jeffrey returned to the fold—helped, like his brothers, by the presence of a lovely young wife, the former Valerie Ritter, who caught Paley's admiring eye. Jeffrey had retreated from the family after Dorothy and Paley divorced. But when Paley was in his eighties, Jeffrey made an effort to get to know his father. Paley responded for the first time by expressing an interest in his eldest son. Jeffrey began showing up at family gatherings, and periodically having quiet dinners at 820 with Paley.

Both Amanda and Hilary had maintained relatively harmonious relations with Paley. Amanda's marriage to Steve Ross came unglued in 1981 after less than two years, and she embarked on a career as the vice-president for planning and design for one of Manhattan's most prestigious developments, Battery Park City. Taking classes part-time, she studied for a master's degree in urban planning from Columbia University. She had succeeded on her own, not as an appendage to a famous husband, something that eluded—and finally haunted—her mother. Hilary bounced back from the suicide of her husband to marry Joseph Califano, former secretary of Health, Education and Welfare, and found her niche as a Washington hostess.

Paley's relationship with Kate was, as Carter Burden's wife Susan put it, "in and out," but always intense. She was, he often said, his favorite child. Some months after Babe's death, Kate suddenly fled to South Africa to visit Walter Thayer's daughter Susan. "She went to South Africa feeling pressured and desperate," said Susan's mother, Jeanne. "Fortunately, when she got there she met up with the right people."

During Kate's year in South Africa, Susan brought her into the fundamentalist Baptist Church, where Kate became a born-again Christian. Back in New York, she hovered over her father, occasionally serving as his escort to social events and tending to his needs much as her mother had. Paley tried to marry her off to a British friend, John Bowes-Lion, a distant cousin of the Queen, but the relationship fizzled.

Kate remained aloof from her siblings; during family gatherings, she could usually be found sitting silently in a corner. She was far more at home with her church congregation. Friends remarked on her kindness when she befriended a young South African woman disfigured by Elephant Man's disease and brought her to New York for consultation with doctors. "She has an unrecognizable trait to some people which is thorough goodness," said Jeanne Thayer.

However, "she could be very spoiled, and behave like an incapacitated old lady, insisting on a lot of fuss," said one friend of Paley's. When her needs interfered with his own, Paley grew exasperated. "She shouldn't be thinking of herself," he complained to one friend in 1987. "She should be thinking of me." Through their ups and downs, Kate remained utterly loyal to her father. She even abandoned her SoHo loft to move to an Upper East Side apartment closer to his home.

It was more than faintly ironic that most of the children of such a secular man were drawn to the spiritual life. Jeffrey became a deacon in a Presbyterian church in lower Manhattan, where he met his wife. Amanda converted to Roman Catholicism when she married and remained in the Church. Billie became interested in Judaism. Only Kate made an effort to convert Paley to her faith. Not surprisingly, she failed to snare him. The closest she came was getting him to have lunch with the minister of her Baptist church.

Paley was a man of the world—and of the flesh. His illness in 1985 had not dampened his ardor in the least. The following summer he was watching the filming of *Sweet Liberty* on Long Island when he spotted the actress Lois Chiles. Within days she was on his arm at lunch and dinner. Their relationship lasted through the autumn, and she spent a great deal of time with him at his apartment, although she stopped short of moving in. "He was very good to her," said her aunt, Virginia Innis. "It went on for longer than usual," recalled Leonora Hornblow. "They had an easy way with each other. She was very pretty and very nice. He took her to dinner parties, and she went to Nassau a good bit." His devotion, of course, was transitory; several years later he and Slim Keith watched the film *Broadcast News* together, and Paley failed to recognize Chiles on the screen.

But Paley's life was not just idle pleasure. His first task following his restoration in the autumn of 1986 was "saving" the CBS prime-time schedule. The day after his eighty-fifth birthday he flew to Hollywood for three days of meetings with the programming department. The CBS executives recognized immediately that Paley's short-term memory had degenerated. He forgot having seen shows, and story lines eluded him. Occasionally, though, he would startle his subordinates by clarifying a fuzzy program idea with sharp questions. "We were seeing the remnants of his greatness," said Kim LeMasters.

On weekends he popped cassettes into the video player at his home in Southampton and scribbled on yellow legal pads. He showed up in Hollywood that December with copious notes. He demanded that the programmers sit with him for as long as eight hours a day as he probed them about the new programs planned for January. "He left us exhausted," said LeMasters afterwards. "He had us going over the same ground again and again. It was disruptive and kept us from our jobs. He desperately wanted to be involved and up to speed." Sensing that his suggestions were not being taken seriously, Paley once kept LeMasters on the phone for forty-five minutes with the familiar refrain that he had failed to keep the chairman informed. "How could you be this rude to me after all I have done," said Paley. "You moved without my consultation and awareness."

Jankowski stood at Paley's side in February 1987 for the next round of meetings. Twenty-eight pilots had already been chosen as candidates for the fall schedule, so the programmers were holding a "show and tell" just for Paley's benefit. But that didn't stop Paley from pinning everyone down for an entire day with his queries. He argued strenuously against "Tour of Duty," a show about Vietnam, which he said was "a war people didn't want to look at. It's not a subject for entertainment." (He was half right; while Vietnam films did well in movie theaters, "Tour of Duty" flopped in the living room.) When Paley requested another session the following day, Gene Jankowski stood behind him waving his arms and mouthing: "NO, NO."

Paley's most visible involvement in programming was CBS's newest morning show, which premiered in January 1987. After Tisch hired the show's producer, Bob Shanks, Paley thrust himself into the planning—even down to offering hints on co-host Mariette Hartley's makeup—to prove he still had the touch. Paley, said the *New York Times,* "has taken a direct hand in leading the new program to the starting gate." The show was roundly panned, its ratings sank below those of its low-rated predecessors, and Paley was tarred with its failure. "He is doing himself a disservice," said Leonard Goldenson at the time.

Tisch kept abreast of Paley's programming activities through daily conversations with Jankowski. All the while, Tisch was busy learning the ropes and making contacts in Hollywood—activities that visibly disquieted Paley. During one lunch in the fall of 1986, Tisch "was bubbling over with everything he was doing," recalled a participant in the meeting. "As Paley realized Tisch was talking to talent and producers, his face fell. It was like someone took away his ice-cream cone." When CBS struck a deal late in 1986 for Grant Tinker, former head of NBC, to produce shows for CBS, the initiative came from Tisch, not Paley. But Tinker made certain to meet Paley over breakfast in his suite at the Beverly Hills Hotel when Paley came to Hollywood the following February. The deal was essentially closed, but Tinker and Tisch had agreed that Paley's approval had to be sought, if only as a ceremonial gesture.

Tisch also took charge of the beleaguered news division. The day after assuming power, he fired Van Sauter as news president. Paley made suggestions about several possible successors, including Bill Moyers and Bud Benjamin, a respected producer who had recently retired. Tisch and Paley had a lunch with Benjamin to discuss the job. "Larry was dominant," recalled Benjamin. "Three times in the meeting Larry said, 'Bill and I don't agree on that.' People don't say that to Bill Paley." Tisch eventually prevailed with his choice, Howard Stringer, a veteran CBS producer and news executive. When it came time to sign a new contract with Diane Sawyer, Tisch oversaw the negotiations that raised her annual salary by $400,000, to $1.2 million.

When he chose to enlist support from the directors who felt nervous about Tisch, Paley could still make his rival's life difficult. At the November 1986 meeting, Tisch stunned the board by presenting proposals to sell the record and publishing divisions of the company. Publishing, he said, could fetch $600 million, and among several offers for the records division, Sony was willing to pay $1.25 million in cash.

Several old Wyman allies objected immediately, pointing out that the same maneuver got Wyman fired. At first Paley seemed tempted by the scent of cash. "My head tells me we should do it but my heart says no," he said. But then he argued forcefully that CBS Records was integral to CBS, not only to its character as a company, but to its economic health. Had Paley favored the plan, it would have gone forward, but his opposition rallied a majority of the board, and Tisch retreated. "It showed that Paley was still able to make a point," said a Tisch ally, "and the board, after having gotten rid of their buddy Tom Wyman, couldn't resist the chance to show Tisch the tough guy that they were in control. Paley made it easy by creating an opportunity."

Two months later, in January 1987, the board removed "acting" from the titles of Paley and Tisch. After the September coup, the directors had formed a special committee to find a permanent chief executive. Headed by director Harold Brown, and including Frank Stanton (still a consultant to CBS) and Walter Cronkite, the committee had not met even once. The "search" had been a sham.

There had been no doubt that Tisch was firmly entrenched. He slashed costs by selling CBS's technology center, disbanded Paley's beloved acquisitions department, fired top executives, shut down the CBS Foundation, and even eliminated the on-site medical department and company-paid subscriptions to *Variety*. "Larry doesn't do things the way you and I would have done them," Paley said to Stanton over breakfast one day that winter. "If he would say that much, he is thinking a lot more," observed Stanton at the time.

Although he would never admit it, Paley had a boss for the first time since he worked for his father sixty years earlier. And the boss treated him very much as an employee. Tisch's flattery often seemed patronizing, and he thought nothing of correcting and even interrupting Paley in meetings. Yet Paley, in his instinctively imperious way, "still doesn't recognize that Larry is running it," said one close friend of Tisch four months after the September coup. "Paley views Larry as a convenience who brought him back to power and in some way will depart to leave Paley in complete control of his empire."

59

BILL PALEY wanted every last minute from life. When he made his customary trip to Lyford Cay in February 1987, he recalled, "My British friends all told me how wonderful I looked, how vigorous. It made me feel great." In fact, Paley was worn down, his energy sapped by his exertions at the office and his travels to the West Coast. After a few days of non-stop entertaining he came down with a cold that rapidly worsened until one evening he collapsed on the floor of his bedroom. He had pneumonia, complicated by emphysema.

Short of breath and taking oxygen continuously, he was flown in the CBS jet to New York Hospital, where he spent three touch-and-go days in intensive care. His daughter Kate, frantic, moved in with him for a round-the-clock vigil of scripture reading. At one point she tried to block her siblings from entering his room.

When Amanda arrived at the hospital, she found Diane Sawyer, wearing a pink angora sweater, sitting opposite Paley at a small table as Dean served them an elegant dinner. The sparkle had returned to Paley's eye, and after six more days he was back in his bedroom at 820 Fifth Avenue. To ease his breathing, he had to sleep sitting up, and he needed a portable supply of oxygen.

Although his staff had been withholding press clippings they thought might jolt his recovery, Paley was soon working the phones. "Tell me what is going on," he asked one longtime friend, who later recalled, "He said it in a strange way, as if he were grasping for bits." In Paley's absence, Tisch had demanded that $50 million be cut from CBS's $295 million news budget, setting off another wave of firings and screams of protest. The day before Tisch was due to visit him, Paley called one well-connected woman friend to ask, "What do you hear on the street about the layoffs at CBS News?" By the end of March, Paley was back in his office at Black Rock, in the words of one observer, "asking lots of questions for which there were no answers, thrashing about because he was unhappy about programming at CBS."

On May 11 and 12, Tisch sat with Paley for the first time during the annual prime-time scheduling marathon. Paley showed admirable stamina through the long days of meetings. He refused to break for lunch, snacking instead on chicken and ham sandwiches. Tisch had seen all the pilots and —in contrast to Paley—required no notes to shape his strong opinions and numerous questions. When Paley repeatedly pressed his favorite show, a Sid Caesar comedy that everyone else had rejected, Tisch firmly steered the discussion elsewhere. "Larry," said Kim LeMasters, "was a stabilizing influence."

When Paley awoke the morning of the 13th, he could barely see. A blood vessel had burst in the retina of one eye. Yet he went ahead and sat on the dais at the annual shareholders meeting, determined to read his introductory remarks. Wearing black-framed glasses, he grasped the sides of the podium and bowed his head toward the speech. To his horror, he could barely see the printed page in front of him. Wheezing slightly, he fumbled, paused, and stumbled over names, including Tisch, whom he called "Larry Kitsch." Paley's face twitched furiously as he nervously rushed through the remarks. Tisch looked discomfited and tense. "It was the worst day of my life," a deeply embarrassed Paley later told a friend.

Paley rebounded to wow the crowd yet again at the Museum of Broadcasting's "60 Minutes" tribute the following month. But overall, his mood began to darken as his ailing back worsened, despite daily workouts with a physiotherapist. Jock Whitney's court jester, Shipwreck Kelly, died that summer, and to the amazement of Kelly's Long Island pals, Paley showed up midway through the funeral. "He came up the middle aisle, hunched and limping, but you could see the flashing eyes and a ripple went through the crowd," recalled William O'Shaughnessy. "He slipped into pew number two, gave Jinx Falkenburg a nuzzle, caught his breath, held onto the pew, turned around, and started reading the room."

By September, Paley had lost sensation in his legs and could only move around by wheelchair. His vision was so bad that he needed a magnifying glass to read, and he was weakened by severe anemia.

Nevertheless, he endured a four-hour board meeting where Tisch presented a new proposal to sell CBS Records to Sony for $2 billion. At that price, said Roswell Gilpatric, "Paley could make no argument." Although his opposition to the sale a year earlier had been an emotional reaction, not a calculated negotiating ploy, Paley indulged in revisionism by remarking that he had made $750 million for CBS. The following month, Tisch sold CBS Publishing for $650 million. His health failing and his empire shrinking, Paley hit bottom. "This is the most unhappy time of Bill's life," said one friend.

With CBS dead last in the ratings, Tisch fired entertainment chief Bud Grant in November and replaced him with Grant's deputy, Kim Le-Masters. At the last minute, Paley approached Hollywood's hottest TV producer, Steven Bochco, creator of "Hill Street Blues" and "L.A. Law," about taking the job. Bochco wrote Paley a letter asking for a $10 million signing bonus. After that, LeMasters looked better to Paley.

Tisch had lost patience with Paley's freelancing, and the strains between the two men began to show. They had never been collegial, but now the "Mr. Tisch" and "Mr. Paley" formality took on a new edge. "Like other CBS chief executives, Larry doesn't have much respect for Bill Paley's business ability," said one top CBS executive. "He continues to be respectful, but he rolls his eyes at some of the things Paley says." In November, *New York* magazine wrote that Tisch had told his top people that he was "fed up" with Paley. He apparently believed that Paley was "useless baggage" and should resign. At the same time Paley told one board member that Tisch had poor judgment about programming. Resurrecting his old lament, Paley said Tisch was "crowding" him and neglecting to keep him informed.

Paley's only bright spot was the prospect of better health. Toward the end of the year, a nurse started accompanying Paley to Black Rock. She would sit outside his office, and every half hour Paley would summon her by pressing a buzzer. She would enter the room, saying, "Excuse me, it's time," and pop a pill into his mouth.

It was an experimental drug called erythropoietin, or EPO, a genetically engineered protein that stimulates production of red blood cells— thereby avoiding the transfusions traditionally used to treat anemia. The

Federal Drug Administration had not approved the drug in the United States, so Paley used his connection at Genetics Institute, the Cambridge, Massachusetts, biotechnology company where he was a big investor, to secure government approval to import it from Germany. After several months of treatment, Paley was having lunch with Stanton in his office. "Surprise," he said with a twinkling smile as he stood up from his wheelchair and walked across the room.

Once again Paley had the stamina to ply the social circuit. Laser surgery on his left eye arrested his visual trouble, a condition called macular degeneration that results from problems with the blood vessels in the retina. His back still hurt, but by using a cane he could get around with some dignity. He entertained his friends in Lyford Cay over the Christmas and New Year holidays. "The look on his face was less nervous, less anxious," said Henryk de Kwiatkowski. Later that month, Paley had a dinner party for Jeanne Murray Vanderbilt, Mike and Mary Wallace, and Don and Marilyn Hewitt. "He was in terrific shape," said one of the guests. "He was teasing Marilyn and having a great time."

Paley was also busy trying to rub out blots on his legend. In 1987 Paley obtained a manuscript of *Old Money,* a book by Nelson Aldrich, Jr., and took exception to the author's characterization of his "pathetic" effort to assume an understated style. To illustrate, Aldrich included some half-dozen quotations from *As It Happened.* After lawyer Arthur Liman claimed Aldrich had made more than "fair use" of Paley's book, Knopf held up publication for three weeks while the author paraphrased most of the quotes.

Early in 1988, Liman secured a manuscript of Gerald Clarke's biography of Truman Capote. (Paley was unusually successful in obtaining confidential manuscripts prior to publication.) It contained a number of unflattering passages about Paley that he was determined to suppress. Liman sent a list of objections to Clarke's publisher, Simon & Schuster. The publisher and author agreed to cut an assertion that Paley had once pulled down his trousers to mock Capote's homosexuality, and a quote from Capote that Paley preferred whores to Babe.

Paley's protests revealed again how preoccupied he was with his image. Above all else, Paley wanted respectability and class. Since he was unwilling—or unable—to control his racy behavior, he inevitably had to resort to intimidation to wipe the slate clean. In the end, he could only fool some of the people part of the time. In the 1989 play *Tru,* starring Robert Morse as Capote, the rift between the Paleys and the Tiny Terror would be portrayed in unsparing detail. Night after night, on a Broadway stage, theatergoers would hear Capote call Paley a "rich shit" and a "disloyal" husband to Babe.

One weekend in early February 1988, Paley took Kate to Southampton. He was intrigued when she talked eagerly about the healthful properties of cucumbers, and at her urging, his chef served the vegetable raw at several meals. Always suggestible when it came to a nostrum, Paley gorged on the cucumbers, eating more than a half dozen. His overindulgence provoked a severe gallbladder attack. With his doctor Harvey Klein and an anguished Kate at his side, he was flown to New York Hospital for emergency treatment.

Surgery was too risky, so the doctors drained his gallbladder and waited. As Paley lay in critical condition, a group of friends sat in his flower-bedecked dining room at 820 Fifth, having a dinner party that he had planned in honor of his old friends Watson and Josie Blair. "It was a little odd," one of the guests, Slim Keith, would later say. "There he was having his gallbladder drained and here we were at his house eating his food. But he had ordered cassoulet because he knew I would like it. Everything was well thought through, and the placement had all been done by Dean."

After a few days in intensive care, Paley's kidneys and already weakened lungs failed. He was hooked up to respirators, his lips were sealed with adhesive, and dialysis kept his kidneys working. Hospital personnel discreetly moved the other patients out of the ICU so Paley could have complete privacy. Four nurses tended him around the clock, and Kate was once again the vigilant watchdog. As Paley clung to life, he occasionally wrote cryptic notes.

Paley's family and aides kept his illness secret for more than a week. When word finally leaked out, the hospital acknowledged that he had been admitted for gallbladder treatment and was "recovering." Four days later, another bulletin pronounced Paley in "critical condition" from respiratory and renal failure, and obituary writers started working overtime. Yet at that very moment, Paley was off the respirator, sitting in a chair for the first time, and taking food. He still needed dialysis, but at longer intervals. Paley's situation brought to mind the old joke about the Spanish dictator Generalissimo Franco: when he was lying on his deathbed with crowds roaring outside, Franco said to an aide: "Who is out there?" "It's the people, Generalissimo," replied the aide. "They have come to say goodbye." Replied Franco, "Where are they going?"

In a remarkable turnabout, Paley settled into his luxurious suite in the New York Hospital tower several days later, surrounded by flowers and several TV sets. (Kate would later tell Jeanne Thayer that her two weeks of prayer in the ICU had saved her father's life.) The first friend to visit was Slim Keith. She found him in his chair, dozing in the sunlight. "How are you, Willie?" she said, and he reached to kiss her, forgetting about his oxygen mask. "You'll never believe it," he said. "There have been more girls in here to see me." "I know," Slim joked. "They're lining up around the block. It's worse than getting tickets to *Phantom of the Opera.*" "Really, oh really?" he replied with a grin. "That many!"

Paley signaled his recovery by growling complaints and commands to everyone. He asked to see Gene Jankowski, who spent fifteen minutes briefing him on CBS programming. Frank Stanton came by as well. John Minary kept Paley abreast of goings on at CBS, one of which threw the old man into a tizzy: Larry Tisch wanted to nominate his brother Preston to the board of directors. Using Minary and Arthur Liman as his messengers, Paley told the directors they should not support the nomination. "My sense is that Bill is concerned about the perception of two Tisches being there," said one director. "That it would look as if they were outweighing him." Under the circumstances, the directors deferred the question until the autumn. "Paley was like one of those drug kingpins on Rikers Island," said one friend afterwards. "He got the nomination blocked from afar."

After nearly a month in the hospital, Paley was released in early March. On entering his apartment, he asked to be wheeled through all the rooms four times. In each room he stopped to declare how beautiful it looked and how glad he was to be home. That evening, he had a dinner party for his house guests, Michael and Lady Anne Tree, just arrived from the Yucatan. Ever the gracious host, he instructed his nurse to wheel him in to greet the guests. "He was in extremely good spirits, full of fight, courage, and fun," recalled Lady Anne. "Even if he went to bed a couple of hours earlier than usual, we had a lot of laughs."

Soon he was asking friends such as Henry Kissinger and Sister Parish over for lunch. His friend Senga Mortimer tried to cheer him up by bringing around some pretty women he had never met, including Anna Wintour, then editor of *House and Garden,* later to be editor-in-chief of *Vogue.* She came to lunch at 820 a half dozen times over the next year. "He just wanted someone to talk to," she recalled. "He talked a lot about his past and about his family. He knew I was with HG, and he liked to talk about houses."

Paley would greet guests in a wheelchair, sometimes wearing a bright blue dressing gown of heavy silk with a simple monogram. His handshake was strong and sure, but conversation had become more disorienting than ever. "It is like listening to a short-wave station when the tuning isn't quite right," said one visitor. "It comes in sharply, then you get another language momentarily, then it comes back clearly."

When business associates came by, Paley talked even more urgently about CBS's prime-time decline. Unlike the previous year, no one was shielding him from the bad news. For the first time in history, CBS ended the season at the bottom of the ratings. Its image of quality was in tatters as well. In 1987, NBC had received more than twice as many Emmy Award nominations as CBS. Paley was well aware that on one night that spring a CBS show was seen by only 8 percent of the nation's viewers—an unthinkably paltry number for a network program. He desperately wanted a new chief of programming, and he was casting about.

At the April board meeting, the directors gave him a warm but restrained reception. "A year before, Larry said Bill was going to save us," said one director, "so we ended up in third place. This time when Bill said he would be involved in the new season, there were no cheers."

Still, Paley made one last effort to reclaim his hegemony in programming. Tisch moved the scheduling meetings that May from New York to Los Angeles, and no one expected Paley to participate. For the first time, Tisch controlled the meetings. But Paley took everyone aback by flying out on his jet for the second day. When he appeared at the meeting with his nurse, he held two manila folders, one marked YES in large block letters, the other marked NO. Inside one envelope was a list, written in black Magic Marker, of the pilots he liked, with brief comments, and inside the other, the pilots he disliked.

"Everyone's expectation was 'Oh shit, we'll have to go through everything we did yesterday,'" said one program executive. But surprisingly, Paley made no such demand. For all the fanfare of his arrival, he lacked the strength to launch a sustained challenge. Tisch remained in charge, and Paley had little to say. Tisch didn't even solicit Paley's views as he had the previous year. Even when Paley stayed on after Tisch left the next day, he had little to offer beyond his suggestion that CBS present two movie nights in the fall. LeMasters and his crew gave Paley that one. But, said LeMasters later, "He was preaching to the converted."

Tisch knew he no longer needed to worry about battling with Paley, and Paley, said Don Hewitt, "had finally concluded that he couldn't beat Tisch." Tisch was now calling every shot, informing Paley after the fact. Later that summer he kicked Gene Jankowski upstairs, elevated Howard Stringer to Broadcast Group president, and brought in ABC executive David Burke as president of CBS News.

Paley felt much more comfortable in the precincts of the Museum of Broadcasting, where he was still the supreme—and often autocratic—commander. His reception by the museum's board of directors in April had been more enthusiastic than at CBS. Paley made a dramatic entry in his wheelchair, perfectly attired in one of his $1,000 bespoke suits, holding on his lap the black cane that he called Arnold after the silver dog's head on top. Frank Stanton led the directors in a standing ovation. Afterwards, one director did remark to another, sotto voce, "His will is the only one that reads, 'If I die.' "

Stanton was Paley's chief consultant on the new broadcasting museum to be built on West 52nd Street. As with Black Rock, Paley had been plagued by indecision over the architect and the design. Stanton wanted Philip Johnson, but Paley hesitated. To prod a decision, Stanton engaged the deans of Cooper Union and the Harvard School of Design to discuss the pros and cons of a half-dozen candidates with Paley. After finally selecting Johnson, Paley complained that his design "looked too much like a cathedral." Four versions later, the dignified design—seventeen stories of beige limestone with mullioned windows and neoclassic touches such as pillars, arches, and pediments—still resembled a cathedral. That was the point, said Johnson, who believed that "museums have taken the place of the church in lay culture." Although Paley yielded to Stanton once again on the architecture, he got the last word on the facade, which he wanted to look exactly like Bergdorf Goodman's on Fifth Avenue.

The board had decided to call the new building the Museum of Radio and Television, and there was talk of adding Paley's name posthumously. He was now eager to be publicly identified with an elegant symbol of a well-respected cultural institution. Paley's former son-in-law, Warner Communications chairman Steve Ross, stepped in to raise the remaining $14 million needed to complete the building, now budgeted at $45 million. In the process Ross mended his relationship with Paley, which had been ruptured when Warner Brothers wooed Bob Daly from CBS back in 1980. Outside the museum boardroom would hang a grand new portrait, six feet by four, that Paley had commissioned at the end of 1986. Paley said it would be inappropriate to hang the picture in the lobby during his lifetime.

He had been painted a decade earlier by the distinguished British portrait artist Graham Sutherland. The picture captured the essence of the man—in this case, a glint of ruthlessness. As one friend said, "It had bite." Angry at the result, Paley stashed it in a back room in his apartment. In search of a more flattering portrayal, he enlisted Aaron Shikler, who was popular with presidents (the Kennedys, the Reagans) as well as socialites. The result was a relaxed view of Paley seated with one leg crossed. It took more than a year to complete, partly because of illness, but mostly because of Paley's demands for changes, such as smoothing out the puffiness in his face. For a while, the artist even had two separate paintings in the works. "You don't finish with Bill Paley," said Shikler at one point. "You only hope."

With the improvement in Paley's health came an upswing in his mood. No longer did he lash out at subordinates as he had immediately after his illness. "There is an overtone about Bill," said Irene Selznick, following an evening with him in June 1988, "a gentleness that I never felt before. It is a modified Bill. After his illness he seems to have found a reprieve—without pressure, pain, passion, and problems, none of the usual 'p's' for Paley. But he is not slow-paced. He is still lively and interesting, and he still has a sense of humor."

In the view of Slim Keith, Paley once again seemed focused on the future. He had his entire apartment repainted white, obliterating the meticulously lacquered burnt orange that his friends had criticized. (Michael Tree once joked that Paley had meant to match the color of Dean's hair.)

Hearing about spiraling prices and feverish activity in the art market brought Paley back in the game briefly. He craved one Van Gogh to fill out his collection, which he eventually planned to give to the Museum of Modern Art. When Stavros Niarchos offered to trade a painting by the Dutch artist for the exquisite *Pink Lady* by Picasso, Paley agreed. But Annette Reed and several other friends told him he would be crazy to give up the Picasso, so he canceled the swap that had been arranged by his friend, the dealer Bill Acquavella.

The most touching expression of his determination to go on living was his new garden in Southampton. The previous summer he had hired landscape designer Nancy McCabe to create an instant garden that looked as if it had been there forever. He paid a king's ransom to cart in forty-year-old boxwood hedges and delphinium six feet high. He went over every plan, leaving nothing to chance or error.

Paley was immensely proud of the result. He gave guided tours in his golf cart to anyone who hadn't yet seen it all. One day when the daughter of an old friend came unannounced for a visit, she found Paley swimming naked in his pool. "He seemed completely oblivious that he was starkers," she recalled. "All he could talk about was his garden. He gestured to the various plantings, saying, 'Isn't this a wonderful tree? Isn't this a beautiful perennial?' "

Sadly, Paley himself could no longer fully appreciate what he pointed out to others. His big disappointment was the failure of his eyes to improve, even after further laser surgery. His desk was littered with magnifying glasses, but when they proved inadequate, he bought an electronic reader that scanned pages and blew them up on a monitor. He could still identify his beloved paintings, make out the images on a television set at medium range, and recognize a beautiful face next to him at a dinner party. But it was clear that he had lost the one thing that had touched him with genius: the ability to *see* what others could not.

After a few small setbacks, Paley's health was otherwise improving. He had to return home early by Concorde from the June meeting of the *International Herald Tribune* board when the drain from his gallbladder got infected. Two months later he flew to Duke University to have eighteen gallstones dissolved without surgery by a doctor he called the "miracle-worker."

Endless money and a squad of attendants made all the difference, of course. His three Irish nurses rotated twenty-four-hour shifts and took turns accompanying him on trips. Wherever he went, a nurse brought along a portable supply of oxygen, because he often panicked when he felt breathless. He kept the oxygen connected the entire time during flights on his chartered helicopter. Paley insisted that a nurse stay nearby all the time. In his library at 820 was a big buzzer with the word NURSE written in huge letters.

In the evenings, his nurse would give him his medication, bathe him, and put on his socks before he went to bed. Overnight, she would sleep in an adjoining room. If he buzzed her, she would sit on a chaise in his room as he slept. The nurses kept lengthy record books, tracking Paley's feelings and logging his medications by the hour, and they phoned the results to Paley's doctor, Harvey Klein, each day. Just as his own father had done, Paley spoke to his doctor at least once a day, and saw him on weekly visits. To facilitate the billing, Paley finally put him on a retainer.

For his business affairs, Paley hired a handsome young man, Pat Gallagher, to replace John Minary, who retired in 1987. Minary continued to come to the office each day anyway, a sad reminder of Paley's own inability to let go. Liman handled any legal matter that came along.

The faithful Dean headed Paley's expanding domestic retinue. He had moved out of Paley's apartment some years earlier, but he came in each morning at six. Paley had brought his Southampton chef, François, to the city after Bernard quit several years earlier. Two secretaries fielded phone calls and wrote Paley's correspondence. Each morning a young woman would read newspapers, magazines, and mail to him. "Sometimes I say to her, 'Listen, if he is in a bad mood, don't read these things to him,' " said one business associate of Paley's. She often stayed all day, accompanying him to the office and sometimes traveling with him as well.

A light sleeper, Paley usually awoke at 5:00 a.m. when his nurse gave him a bowl of hot cereal. He would doze until seven, then have his proper breakfast. Paley suffered from incontinence, so his nurse had to help Dean get him ready for the day, a process that usually took several hours. Paley went to the office several days a week, arriving in late morning. On those days when he stayed home, he spent a good deal of time on the telephone.

There was real pathos in the decline of the aging dynamo. But unlike others who yield to their infirmity and slip from public view, Paley clung to center stage. He loved the visibility and the awe that he still inspired. If it meant risking making a fool of himself, it was a chance worth taking.

"You know a party isn't a success out there unless I go," Paley said to one old friend, explaining his frequent presence on the Southampton social circuit the summer after his illness. He went to a dance in the autumn given by socialite Anne Bass, and the seventieth birthday party for choreographer Jerome Robbins. At the Robbins fete he seemed distinctly put out that he was seated next to the well-preserved Claudette Colbert rather than a pretty young thing. There was something joyless in Paley's social activity, however. "He had an underlying fear," said one man close to him, "so he was always hanging on, proving something, and living hard to do it."

Paley's lusty ways had become the target of jokes that he himself shared. His friends told him he was becoming so forgetful that he needed to post a tally of all his girls and call it the "Dean's List." At his eighty-seventh birthday party in September 1988, Carter and Susan Burden performed a skit with Burden portraying "Paley" demanding sexual favors from his nurse, played by Susan. After many protests, the nurse agreed to his demands, but only for a considerable sum of money. At this point, Dean entered, and "Paley" said, "How much money do I have, Dean?" Replied Dean, "Are you referring to all your money, sir, or just the allowance you get from Mr. Tisch?" Everyone, especially Paley, howled.

The objects of Paley's octogenarian libido, however, always had to be on guard. Paley frequently invited Southampton neighbors Michael and Mary Meehan over to dinner, mainly because he loved to sit next to Mary, a pretty interior designer with long blond hair. That all ended after one dinner party in the summer of 1988. As the couple got into their car, Mary had a look of revulsion on her face. "Never again," she said. "Why not?" replied her husband. "When we were saying goodbye," she said, "he gave me a French kiss, right in my mouth."

In December of that year, a more proper Paley was honored by Jacqueline Onassis and all his social friends at a dinner given by the Municipal Arts Society. It was held in a candlelit CBS studio decorated with color-slide projections of Paley Park. Trees with bare branches were interspersed throughout the room to enhance the illusion of being in the park itself. Flanked by Amanda, Hilary, and Kate, Paley, said one guest, was "surrounded by more women than you could imagine."

That same month, undaunted by past humiliations at the podium, he stood up at a Museum of Broadcasting tribute to Walter Cronkite. He used a bright light, and each page of his speech contained only five lines, with letters one-inch high and words underlined and accented. But he couldn't focus, and for several excruciating minutes he stumbled incoherently, reading sentence fragments, breathing hard. "I'm sorry, I can't read this," he finally said, and then spoke ad-lib for several minutes extolling CBS News and its tradition of integrity. His delivery was fluid, strong, and passionate. He was obviously using every ounce of his strength. The audience shot to its feet and applauded him for thirty-five seconds. "Everyone was dying at the thought that he would humiliate himself," said one of the guests that evening. "They wanted him to be *Paley*. When he saved himself, there was a thrill." On returning to his table, Paley grumbled, "I bombed out," but he knew otherwise.

Paley and Tisch continued to operate at arm's length with lingering resentment on both sides. At a cocktail party in the autumn of 1988, Tisch stunned a group that included "60 Minutes" correspondent Harry Reasoner by saying, "Sometimes people live too long. Everybody's forgotten Bill Paley. They don't realize he is still around. I went to an industry luncheon this afternoon and nobody came up to me and asked, 'How's Bill?' "

When Larry's brother Preston Tisch was elected to the board in the fall of 1988, Paley lodged no further protest. Privately, he complained that Larry Tisch didn't seem to understand broadcasting. Programming was going nowhere, and the CBS network was losing roughly $20 million a year. Most of CBS's earnings were from interest on the $3 billion in cash resulting from the publishing and record company sales, prompting some financial analysts to wonder whether CBS was a broadcasting company or a huge money market fund.

For a time Paley schemed to find a buyer for CBS to get rid of Tisch. He was particularly distressed when Tisch announced a deal with the K Mart discount chain in which CBS shows would be promoted by games and banners at K Mart stores—as ignominious a counterpoint to the Tiffany image as one could find. "I made a mistake," Paley said to one business associate at the time. "I wanted to get rid of Tom Wyman so badly I would have done anything."

As irony would have it, Paley even managed a pleasant reconciliation with Wyman in early 1989 during a visit to Oscar and Annette de la Renta's. "I did it on impulse," said Wyman, who was staying at his home next to the de la Rentas. "I saw that jet land, and I knew who it was, so I called Oscar." They got together the next morning at the de la Rentas, and later Paley told a friend, "He was a mistake, but he's not a bad guy."

From time to time, Paley would get a cameo role in one of Tisch's decisions. When Diane Sawyer was about to bolt CBS for ABC in January 1989, Tisch suggested that Paley have lunch with her. Paley and Sawyer spent several hours together in his office dining room. Paley chided her for not coming to him earlier. He tried all manner of persuasion. "We are your friends," he said. "You grew up here." When she held her ground, Paley was gracious, although in recounting the conversation to a friend afterwards, he sounded angry and resentful.

Whenever Paley achieved a small victory, it was at Tisch's sufferance. During the 1988 presidential election, Paley asked David Burke to use Mike Wallace in CBS's coverage of the candidates. Tisch suggested that Burke do it "to please Paley," recalled Wallace. "Larry knows where to pick his concessions, in areas important to Bill but incidental to Larry."

Paley did manage one bona fide sneak attack that caught Tisch and everyone else off guard. In the spring of 1989, Paley decided, quite on his own, to invite his friend Henry Kissinger onto the CBS board to represent his interests when Paley could not attend meetings. After Paley made the nomination at the July meeting, several board members objected that it had not come through channels. With Tisch's concurrence, the board took it under advisement—a mild rebuke to Paley. "Ultimately we could not object," said Roswell Gilpatric. "But we did object to Paley's making it a point of personal privilege. He was upset that the board didn't go along with him." The situation might have been even more awkward had Tisch not agreed with the wisdom of Paley's unilateral move. In September, the former secretary of state was elected to the board—with the caveat that he not act as Paley's representative.

Frustrated by his diminished role at CBS, Paley asked friends and businessmen where he might find an interesting business to run. In truth, he was physically and mentally incapable of any such thing. "He so wants to be in the center," said one business associate. "He remembers when the world revolved around him."

In his social realm, everything still did. Invitations to his home were the most coveted in town. His 1989 Fourth of July party in Southampton was bigger than ever, with a guest list approaching one hundred, including Hilary and Kate, the Watson Blairs, Felix Rohatyns, Jamie Nivens, and other Southampton regulars, with the likes of the actor Michael Caine thrown in for glamour. Wearing a blue blazer, light blue shirt, and white flannels, Paley sat in a chair and greeted his friends. The guests dined on paella at round tables in his huge drawing room. Afterwards, they walked outside and Paley raised his glass to say, "I want to toast our great country," as Grucci fireworks organized by the writer George Plimpton filled the sky.

He went to dinners and dances, always with his nurse in the background. Later in the summer he made a trip to Baden-Baden with his old friend Grace Dudley. Paley even had a luncheon in his Black Rock dining room with Greta Garbo, lured out of seclusion by her neighbor and friend Walter Thayer. They laughed and reminisced, and Paley teased her about old times.

For a time in 1989 he was linked to Ghislaine Lejeune, an editor at French *Vogue* whom he met at a dinner party at the home of Nan Kempner. He spirited her to Lyford Cay for several weeks before she returned to Europe. He was even temporarily besotted with his landscape designer, Nancy McCabe, to the consternation of such friends as Slim Keith and Jeanne Murray Vanderbilt. When Paley gave McCabe an exquisite clock that had belonged to Babe, his friends said, "Enough flowers!" "Slim was wild," said Jeanne Vanderbilt. Everyone was relieved when he returned to Lois Chiles at the end of the summer. "All that is left is his wit and the gleam in his eye," said Slim Keith as she watched Paley at a dinner party, quietly clutching Chiles's hand.

The fall of 1989 was a turning point for Bill Paley, signaled by his decision to cease work on his second memoir. Earlier in the year, Paley had occasionally titillated Slim Keith by recounting spicy tales about women he said would be in the book. But when the manuscript was read to him, Paley had second thoughts about David Harris's rendition of his randy social life. The author had written honestly about Paley, believing that to be his wish. But now Liman shared Paley's misgivings and advised him to kill the book. In exchange for relinquishing all his material, Harris received a financial settlement in the low six figures.

A further deterioration in Paley's mental condition also played a role in the decision. With increasing frequency, he would call meetings and forget their purpose. He often lost track of where he was; he could be sitting in the sunshine and ask if the sun was out, or he would fail to recognize a close friend. It was an especially cruel form of senility, rather like a flickering light bulb. One moment Paley would be bright, witty, and perceptive. Then the light would go out, and when it flipped on again, he would have lost the thread. His moments of clarity were usually focused on a dollar sign. When his partners in the *International Herald Tribune* offered to buy out his stake for roughly $25 million, he demanded twice that amount and refused to budge. He might confuse the details, but the fundamental instincts remained.

With the fog thickening, his friends closed ranks. "He has withdrawn into a private world," said one friend after spending a weekend with him. "He is in and out and mostly out, but he is valiant. He wants to live so much." One unlikely source of pleasure was a black cocker spaniel named Michael (as in Tree), a gift from Kate several years earlier. At first Paley resisted getting attached. He explained to friends that he had a dog when he was six, but when it was killed in an accident, he announced melodramatically, "I never thought I would love a dog again." But as Paley grew more lonely, Michael gave him solace. The dog sat next to him in the limousine, and rode in the helicopter. He even allowed Michael into his bed, where he would stretch out behind Paley's back and fall asleep.

Although Paley still ventured out periodically—to a restaurant or to a movie where he was whisked in at a side door—he spent most of his time at one of his homes in the company of friends. When he stayed in town, he thought nothing of capturing a friend for Friday dinner, Saturday lunch, Saturday dinner, Sunday lunch, and Sunday dinner. "By the end of it," said one, "you are exhausted. He is consumed with himself and his health."

He took Slim Keith with him to Lyford Cay over Christmas at the end of 1989. She was ailing from chronic heart disease, and despite his own infirmity he went out of his way to make her comfortable. "We had a wonderful time," she said afterwards. "He is slower and so am I. We were two old farts limping around, two old friends who don't need to explain anything. We know what happened and when because we were there." Four months later, Slim died.

By 1990, most of his old friends were gone. Next to losing Slim, the deaths of Loel Guinness and Walter Thayer in 1989 had been particularly tough. By contrast, Paley barely blinked when his sister Blanche died early in 1990. On his doctor's orders, he did not attend the funeral. When Jeanne Vanderbilt said, "I'm sorry, Will," he launched into his old harangue about how his mother had hated him after "my sister"—he had never called her Blanche—was born. "It always goes back to his mother," said Jeanne Vanderbilt. "Imagine, after all these years."

Still, each death understandably rattled Paley. "Why do I have to die?" he kept asking Jeanne Vanderbilt. It was a question to which she could give no answer except to reassure him that his mother had lived into her nineties. "Whenever he talks about mortality," said one associate, "it is with a sense of disbelief." Paley began pointing to his ninetieth birthday and, some months shy of that, to the opening of the new Museum of Radio and Television in January 1991. From time to time he had his chauffeur drive him by the new building as it rose above 52nd Street. He would squint out the window and measure its progress.

As Paley's life shrank, CBS assumed greater meaning once again, Larry Tisch notwithstanding. In his senescence, Paley's role changed at Black Rock. Jay Kriegel, senior vice-president of CBS, was charged with keeping Paley abreast of corporate business and inviting him to company events. "He will come to anything," said Howard Stringer. Paley had even grown closer to Tisch. The lines were clearly drawn. Paley knew now that he could not cross them, and he knew that Tisch, not Paley, made the rules.

Since Paley really only cared about programming, Howard Stringer dropped by at least once a week with the latest reports on shows and ratings. Paley warmed to Stringer's bluff Welsh charm and quick wit. In program meetings, Stringer sat at his side, guiding Paley through his notes whenever he tried to make a point. "There is a sweetness about him," said Stringer. "I get treated with enormous affection." Yet Paley confided to a friend that he knew Stringer wasn't really listening when he made suggestions, but he was resigned to his fate.

Dismembered and stripped to bottom-line efficiency, bereft of its old style, CBS seemed to be someone else's creation. One day in August 1988, without alerting either listeners or staff, Tisch even shut down WCAU, the Philadelphia radio station where CBS began in 1927. "I feel so sorry for Bill Paley and Frank Stanton," Sony chairman Akio Morita remarked to a visitor in Tokyo in late 1988. "Larry Tisch is breaking up the company and eating it himself." Frank Stanton took a simpler view. "CBS is just another company with dirty carpets," he said to a friend some months after Tisch's takeover. Perhaps Tisch finally made CBS what it had been all along—a machine of lowbrow mass market entertainment, now shorn of its pretensions. Yet there had been something uplifting about the Tiffany image. Even if CBS had aimed high only intermittently, its news and entertainment programs had been the best in the business.

Despite the changes, CBS was the place where Bill Paley could live his legend as he approached his tenth decade. In the halls of Black Rock he would always be great, and he would get respect and admiration. It was here that his myth had grown, nurtured by repetition and embellishment. Here, in his own mind at least, he remained the wise founder, the television visionary, the seducer of women, the master of style, the toast of high society. In reality, of course, the only thing remaining beneath the myth was Bill Paley's incredible force. As Barry Diller, the chairman of Twentieth Century Fox, had said when he first met Paley: "I have seen pure willpower."

In May 1990 the CBS annual shareholders meeting was held in the auditorium at the Museum of Modern Art. As in previous years, no one knew until the last minute whether Paley would appear. But he did arrive, by a back door, assisted to the dais by Stringer. Paley wore his trademark dark blue suit and white shirt, his white pocket handkerchief crisply folded in his left breast pocket. His only duty was to read seven lines introducing Tisch. He couldn't see the text, and his ability to improvise failed him.

"You sound good," he told the audience. "All in all this is a good day for me," and turned over the meeting to Tisch.

During the meeting itself, Paley sat through two and a half hours of questions and harangues by an odd assortment of gadflies and eccentrics. Tisch fielded everything, while the old man sat impassively, his face free of the vexing twitch. Occasionally, Paley rested his head on his right hand, or blew his nose with a big white handkerchief. He put on two different pairs of glasses, one with red-tinted lenses. When an outrageous remark broke up the audience, Paley sometimes chuckled along, leaning over to ask Stringer what had just been said. "I hope you hear this, Mr. Paley," said one questioner. "He hears you," said Tisch, patting Paley patronizingly on the shoulder. But Paley registered no reaction as the speaker continued, "When you have to go to K Mart to get viewers, that's the bottom of the barrel."

It didn't much matter what Paley heard or understood. What counted was showing up, going the distance, tapping the amazing reserve of stamina yet again. Those who knew him—especially those who cared about him—told each other that Paley had put on a hell of a show.

He left as quietly as he had come, through the back door into a waiting wheelchair, and up the elevator to the ground floor. His pretty brunette nurse wheeled him to the black Cadillac Brougham at the curb. Anybody else would have headed for home and a long nap. Bill Paley rode the half block to CBS headquarters, where he climbed out into the bright spring sunshine. His body listing to the right toward the cane he called Arnold, he walked slowly across the sidewalk with his nurse guiding his steps. The door to Black Rock opened, and Bill Paley walked in, proudly.

William S. Paley's
CBS Fortune

September 1928
WSP invests $417,000—for 41%
Sam, Ben, Jay, and Lillian Paley invest
$86,000 for 9.3%
Total Paley family interest: a controlling
50.3%
Ike Levy owns 20%, Jerome Louchheim
owns 7%

December 1928
WSP invests $200,000 for 1,000 more
shares, bringing his control to 61%

March 1932
After Paramount buyback, CBS is
valued at $10.4 million
WSP owns 40% or $4 million

May 1932
WSP owns 35,694 shares: 31.7% or $3.2
million
He has sold off 8% or $800,000

February 1934
CBS 5 to 1 stock split
WSP owns 287,705 shares: 33.7% or
$3.4 million

1935
CBS shares begin public trading
WSP owns 287,705 shares: 33.7%,
which ranges from high of $13.8
million to low of $6.3 million (based
on bid prices of $48 to $22/share)

1936
WSP owns 287,705 shares: 33.7%,
which ranges from high of $17.3
million to low of $12.9 million (based
on bid prices of $60 to $45/share)

March 1937
CBS 2 to 1 stock split
WSP owns 575,410 shares: 33.6% or
$18.4 million (based on high bid price
of $32/share)

June 1937
CBS is listed on New York Stock
Exchange
WSP owns 449,235 shares: 26.3% or
$7.6 million (based on price of $17/
share)
Prior to the listing, he sold off 7.3% or
$1.3 million (based on high bid price
of $32/share)

1938
WSP owns 449,235 shares: 26.3% or
$7.4 million (year end price of $16.50/
share)

1939
WSP owns 449,235 shares: 26.3% or
$10.8 million (year end price of $24/
share)

1940
WSP owns 348,636 shares: 20.3% or
$6.8 million (year end price of $19.60/
share)
WSP has sold 100,000 shares or $2.4
million

1941

WSP owns 342,866 shares: 19.9% or
$4.4 million (year end price of $12.80/
share)
WSP has sold 5,770 shares or $150,000
(based on 1940 high price of $26/share)

1942

WSP owns 324,866 shares: 18.9% or
$4.9 million (year end price of $15.20/
share)
WSP has sold 18,000 shares or $378,000
(based on 1941 high price of $21/share)

1943

WSP owns 324,866 shares: 18.9% or
$8.5 million (year end price of $26.30/
share)

1944

WSP owns 324,866 shares: 18.9% or
$11.4 million (year end price of $35/
share)

1945

WSP owns 324,866 shares: 18.9% or
$14.6 million (year end price of $45/
share)

1946

WSP owns 322,010 shares: 18.7% or
$9.8 million (year end price of $30.30/
share)
WSP has sold 2,856 shares or $142,800
(based on 1945 high price of $50/share)

1947

WSP owns 322,010 shares: 18.7% or
$7.7 million (year end price of $24/
share)

1948

WSP owns 312,010 shares: 18.1% or
$7.2 million (year end price of $23/
share)
WSP has transferred 10,000 shares to a
trust fund

1949

WSP owns 312,010 shares: 18.1% or
$9 million (year end price of $28.80/
share)

1950

WSP owns 312,010 shares: 18.17% or
$8,833,003 (year end price of $28.31/
share)
WSP "Associates" own 38,400 shares:
1.23% or $1,087,104
WSP and "Associates" together own
350,410 shares: 20.4% or $9,920,107

"Associates" are
Shelter Rock Development Corp. (of
which WSP owns most of the shares)
Babe Paley
2 trusts established: 12/10/38 and
6/24/40 (for Jeffrey and Hilary)
3 trusts established: two on 12/30/41
(Jeffrey and Hilary) and one on
6/27/49 (Billie Paley)

1951

WSP and "Associates" own 353,710
shares: 15.1% or $11,993,344
(year end price of $34.19/share)

Additional "Associate":
1 trust established 9/7/51
(for Kate Paley)

1952

WSP and "Associates" own 302,610
shares: 12.92% or $11,819,946
(year end price of $39.06/share)

1953

WSP and "Associates" own 302,610
shares: 12.92% or $14,525,280
(year end price of $48/share)

1954

WSP and "Associates" own 308,663
shares: 12.65% or $26,430,983
(year end price of $85.63/share)

1955

WSP and "Associates" own 944,502
shares (after 3 for 1 stock split in

April): 12.6% or $25,444,883
(year end price of $26.95/share)

1956

WSP and "Associates" own 963,394
shares: 12.6% or $31,435,545
(year end price of $32.63/share)

1957

WSP and "Associates" own 952,650
shares: 12.1% or $23,282,765
(year end price of $24.44/share)

1958

WSP and "Associates" own 1,000,088
shares: 12.3% or $37,637,074
(year end price of $37.63/share)

1959

WSP and "Associates" own 1,054,474
shares: 12.57% or $46,270,318
(year end price of $43.88/share)

1960

WSP and "Associates" own 1,061,044
shares: 12.29% or $39,091,671
(year end price of $36.88/share)

1961

WSP and "Associates" own 1,079,643
shares: 12.25% or $43,045,366
(year end price of $39.87/share)

1962

WSP and "Associates" own 1,118,592
shares: 12.2% or $49,497,695
(year end price of $44.25/share)

1963

WSP and "Associates" own 2,139,478
shares (after 2 for 1 split on 1/17/64):
11.1% or $80,893,662 (year end price
of $37.81/share)

WSP "Associates" includes Sam Paley
trusts after his death on 3/31/63

1964

WSP and "Associates" own 2,110,393
shares: 10.6% or $85,998,514
(year end price of $40.75/share)

On advice of WSP counsel, "Associates"
holdings were excluded from WSP
holdings

1965

WSP owns 1,748,878 shares: 8.6% or
$87,472,155 (year end price of $44.87/
share)

1966

WSP owns 1,765,716 shares: 8.79% or
$108,591,534 (year end price of
$61.50/share)

1967

WSP owns 1,794,197 shares: 7.66% or
$97,783,736 (year end price of $54.50/
share)

total once again includes holdings of
Babe ($3,679,077) and other trusts
($1,200,635)

1968

WSP owns 1,736,148 shares: 6.9% or
$93,317,955 (year end price of $53.75/
share)

1969

WSP owns 1,725,433 shares: 6.56% or
$84,321,910 (year end price of $48.87/
share)

1970

WSP owns 1,759,694 shares: 6.49% or
$53,881,830 (year end price of $30.62/
share)

1971

WSP owns 1,687,740 shares: 6.1% or
$78,682,438 (year end price of $46.62/
share)

1972

WSP owns 1,682,292 shares: 5.9% or
$84,316,475 (year end price of $50.12/
share)

1973

WSP owns 1,683,377 shares: 6% or

$43,128,118 (year end price of $25.62/share)

1974
WSP owns 1,683,337 shares: 5.9% or $51,543,778 (year end price of $30.62/share)

1975
WSP owns 1,683,312 shares: 5.9% or $79,115,664 (year end price of $47/share)

1976
WSP owns 1,684,888 shares: 5.9% or $100,031,800 (year end price of $59.37/share)

1977
WSP owns 1,684,525 shares: 6.1% or $83,805,118 (year end price of $49.75/share)

Goldie Paley died 2/24/77 and WSP took over as trustee

1978
WSP owns 2,000,084 shares (increase of 315,559 over 1977): 7.209% or $101,504,260 (year end price of $50.75/share)

Babe died July 1978

1979
WSP owns 1,971,286 shares: 7.079% or $103,246,100 (year end price of $52.375/share)

1980
WSP owns 1,953,291 shares: 7% or $93,015,717 (year end price of $47.62/share)

1981
WSP owns 1,930,792 shares: 6.9% or

$92,436,667 (year end price of $47.875/share)

1982
WSP owns 1,930,767 shares: 6.51% or $115,363,328 (year end price of $59.75/share)

1983
WSP owns 1,944,775 shares: 6.55% or $128,841,343 (year end price of $66.25/share)

1984
WSP owns 1,944,750 shares: 6.54% or $140,751,281 (year end price of $72.375/share)

1985
WSP owns 1,909,525: 8.14% or $221,266,209 (year end price of $115.875/share)

1986
WSP owns 1,914,525: 8.11% or $243,144,675 (year end price of $127/share)

1987
WSP owns 1,914,525: 8.13% or $300,580,425 (year end price of $157/share)

1988
WSP owns 1,914,525: 8.10% or $326,426,512 (year end price of $170.50/share)

1989
WSP owns 1,894,525 shares: 8.01% or $356,170,700 (year end price of $188/share)

Bequests of
Barbara Cushing Paley

Dollar Values as of July 1978
If sold today at fair market prices, jewelry and other
items would likely be worth substantially more than
appraised value.

Monetary Bequests

Westover School *$35,000*
Winifred Dooney *(maid)* *$15,000*
Adelaide T. Wallace *(secretary)* *$35,000*
Marion Osborn *(childhood friend)* *$25,000*
Michael Cushing *(nephew)* *$10,000*
Kirke Cushing *(nephew)* *$10,000*
Reid Cushing *(nephew)* *$10,000*
William Cushing *(nephew)* *$10,000*
Henry Kirke Cushing *(brother)* *$50,000*
New York Hospital *$200,000*

Trust Funds

Amanda Mortimer Burden
(daughter) *$225,000*
Tony Mortimer *(son)* *$225,000*
Billie Paley *(son)* *$225,000*
Kate Paley *(daughter)* *$225,000*
Hilary Paley Byers
(stepdaughter) *$225,000*
Jeffrey Paley *(stepson)* *$225,000*

William S. Paley

tangible personal property, including
furniture, objects, rugs, silver, china,
jewelry, paintings, and
sculptures *$428,000*

The most valuable items (worth $8,000 or
more):

set of four Louis XVI gilded
fauteuils *$16,000*

set of four Louis XVI chairs, signed
C. Chefvigny *$8,500*

pair of Louis XV gilt-bronze
candelabra *$12,000*

oil painting, *The Window,* by Edouard
Vuillard *$45,000*

pen-and-ink and biste drawing of a
dromedary and monkey, by Giovanni
Domenico Tiepolo *$10,000*

natural blond Russian sable coat (50
inches long) *$15,000*

pearl necklace containing thirty-nine
strands with approximately 190–200
pearls on each strand, thirteen round
diamond rondels each containing eight
diamonds weighing approximately 12
cts., and six diamond balls, each
containing thirty diamonds weighing
approximately 9 cts. *$12,500*

18-ct. yellow gold, diamond, and onyx
panther brooch, set with forty yellow
diamonds, weighing approximately
10 cts. *$8,500*

pair of Meissen porcelain figural groups
on gilt-bronze bases *$16,000*

Louis XIV ebony and gilt-bronze
bureau plat *$20,000*

still-life oil painting of grapes in a basket, flowers, and a glass by Berthe Morisot *$35,000*

Jeffrey Paley

pre-Columbian gold pin in design of a man and pre-Columbian gold frog *$2,000*

pre-Columbian crocodile *$3,000*

flower bracelet—fifteen marquise, multiple round, and forty-three baguette diamonds in lily design—total weight, 34 cts. (Flato) *$15,000*

necklace—twenty-one large pre-Columbian gold balls (circa 1300–1450 B.C.) *$3,250*

necklace—seventy-one baroque graduated pearls *$5,000*

18-ct. gold pendant with cultured pearl and twenty-four diamonds, weighing approximately 1 ct. *$2,500*

ring—18-ct. yellow gold with two heart-shaped diamonds, weighing approximately 4 cts. *$8,000*

Total Jewelry *$38,750*

Hilary Byers

platinum "kitten" clip, set with 1 cultured pearl, 23 emeralds weighing approximately .58 ct., and 257 diamonds weighing approximately 9.79 cts. (Verdura) *$4,500*

ram's-head bracelet—spiral coral and pearl set with fifty-eight baguette diamonds weighing approximately 6 cts., fifty-three round diamonds weighing approximately 3 cts., fifty-eight baguette emeralds weighing

approximately 5 cts., and fifty-three round emeralds weighing approximately 2.25 cts. (Cartier) *$8,000*

18-ct. gold "star" earrings with red coral and twelve diamonds, weighing approximately ⅝ ct. (Schlumberger) *$300*

coral, black enamel, and diamond-wing "bee" pin, set with four pear-shaped rose-cut diamond wings weighing approximately 7 cts. (Verdura) *$4,000*

necklace—18-ct. gold, 27 baroque pearls, and 157 diamonds (Van Cleef & Arpels) *$20,000*

necklace—black pearls, ruby bead rondels *$7,250*

necklace—5,850 ruby beads, weighing approximately 692 cts., with six 18-ct. gold ornaments and seventy-two diamonds, weighing approximately 1.72 cts. *$19,500*

ruby and diamond earclips set with twenty-eight diamonds, weighing approximately 4 cts. *$2,500*

three-strand necklace of water pearls *$500*

18-ct. gold and coral bead necklace, with double circle pendant of coral beads and gold ornaments (Van Cleef & Arpels) *$2,500*

amethyst bead necklace, with amethyst and diamond cluster clasp *$750*

Total Jewelry *$68,800*

miscellaneous clothing previously selected and delivered to Hilary Paley Byers

natural blond Russian sable coat (34 inches long) *$3,500*

pair of small marble bowls

Brook Byers
(granddaughter)

clip—18-ct. gold and platinum with
seven reversible diamond leaves, set with
approximately 175 round diamonds,
weighing approximately 10 cts. *$5,000*

18-ct. gold, platinum, and diamond
"twin flower" ring set with
approximately one hundred round
diamonds weighing approximately 1.50
cts. (Schlumberger) *$1,250*

emerald bead bracelet
(Pietro Capuano) *$2,250*

sapphire bead bracelet
(Pietro Capuano) *$2,250*

antique gold, pearl, and enamel necklace
with four emeralds, gold and enamel
ornaments *$750*

18-ct. gold and platinum "starfish" clip
with one pear-shaped emerald weighing
approximately 3.33 cts., 118 oval
sapphires weighing approximately 41.20
cts., 97 round diamonds weighing
approximately 3.24 cts., 20 pear-shaped
diamonds weighing approximately 2.30
cts. (Schlumberger)
(held by Hilary Byers until age of
majority) *$35,000*

Total Jewelry $46,500

Tony Mortimer

earclips—two cultured pearls—14-ct.
white gold, and two hundred diamonds
weighing approximately 5 cts.
(Schlumberger) *$10,000*

earclips set with two pear-shaped
polished emeralds weighing
approximately 44.48 cts., and thirty-four

round diamonds
(Verdura) *$22,500*

ring—cabochon emerald weighing
approximately 30.92 cts., set with
thirty-four round diamonds weighing
approximately 7 cts.
(Van Cleef & Arpels) *$150,000*

Total Jewelry $182,500

Camille Corot painting, *L'atelier de Corot*
(WSP holds for lifetime) *$60,000*

Siri Larsen Mortimer
(wife of Tony Mortimer)

two pearl bracelets—one black natural
pearl with platinum, diamond, and
black and white pearl clasp; one white
cultured pearl with platinum, diamond,
and black and white pearl clasp; each
bracelet containing sixty-two rough
diamonds, weighing approximately
5 cts. (Verdura) *$7,500*

platinum and diamond earclips
containing 132 diamonds
(Schlumberger) *$3,000*

cultured button pearl ring, platinum
with ninety-six diamonds, weighing
approximately 2.33 cts.
(Verdura) *$3,500*

jeweled "blackamoor" clip
(Verdura) *$2,000*

18-ct. gold, platinum, and white enamel
clip—ribbon medallion with 141
diamonds *$22,500*

diamond "sheaf of wheat" clip—oval
blue diamond weighing approximately
7.58 cts., thirty marquise diamonds
weighing approximately 9.78 cts.,
eight pear-shaped diamonds weighing
approximately 1.09 cts., eighty-one

round canary diamonds weighing
approximately 5.01 cts., and twenty-one
round white diamonds weighing
approximately .24 cts.   *$150,000*

18-ct. gold, platinum, yellow enamel,
and diamond "leaves" earclips, set with
thirty-four round diamonds, weighing
approximately .94 cts.
(Schlumberger)   *$500*

18-ct. gold and platinum necklace of
tulip design, with diamond leaves and
butterflies, set with approximately 126
round diamonds, two pear-shaped
diamonds, all weighing approximately
10 cts. (Schlumberger)   *$6,500*

Australian cultured pearl necklace—
twenty-eight pearls with pear-shaped,
marquise, and round diamonds (twenty-
seven diamond rondels); clasp set with
fifty round diamonds (Cartier)   *45,000*

Total Jewelry $240,500

black wool cape with narrow mink
border   *$50*

Amanda Burden

bracelet—18-ct. gold set with two
hundred round diamonds, weighing
approximately 15 cts.—fruit design
(Schlumberger)   *$10,000*

jewel "swan" clip containing one
Briollet diamond, weighing
approximately 2.64 cts.
(Verdura)   *$3,000*

diamond and gold necklace set with
eighteen old mine-cut diamonds
weighing approximately 25.57 cts. and
twenty old mine-cut diamonds weighing
approximately 128.13 cts. (Harry
Winston, Inc.)   *$125,000*

earclips—72 sapphires and 322 canary
diamonds, weighing approximately
22 cts. (Danaos)   *$11,500*

diamond necklace—three circles of old-
mine diamonds strung on a satin ribbon;
each circle containing twelve old-mine
cut diamonds, weighing approximately
14 cts. (Boivin)   *$25,000*

platinum and diamond necklace
containing ninety-nine diamonds,
weighing approximately 5 cts.   *$1,750*

ring—21.25-ct. canary diamond in
special gold and diamond crown setting
(Verdura)   *$65,000*

twelve gold rings (usually worn with
canary diamond ring)   *$200*

two Indian bracelets—2 ins. wide—
diamond clips (Van Cleef &
Arpels)   *$2,000*

six diamond bracelets—three of white
diamonds (containing 396 diamonds
weighing approximately 17.32 cts.), two
of canary diamonds (containing 264
diamonds weighing approximately 11.94
cts.), one of brown diamonds
(containing 132 diamonds weighing
approximately 6.40 cts.)   *$20,000*

Total Jewelry $275,950

two Alexander Brooks portraits of
"Tony" and "Ba"

Louis Valtat painting (19th century),
Lady with a Hat   *$1,000*

Japanese painted paper small twelve-fold
tablescreen—painted with a
landscape   *$120*

miscellaneous clothing

Flobelle Fairbanks Burden
(granddaughter)

emerald bead necklace with emerald bead
and diamond clasp—thirty-one emeralds
weighing approximately 700 cts.
(Verdura) *$125,000*

gold and platinum ring with brilliants
and center of turquoise—set with
approximately one hundred diamonds,
weighing approximately 5 cts.
(Schlumberger) *$2,500*

jeweled enamel "frog" pin
(Verdura) *$350*

18-ct. gold and platinum earclips with
cabochon turquoise, set with fifty-four
round diamonds, weighing
approximately 2.75 cts.
(Schlumberger) *$1,500*

gold, turquoise, diamond, and sapphire
clip, set with seventy-four round
diamonds, weighing approximately
7 cts. (Van Cleef & Arpels) *$3,500*

18-ct. gold evening watch, inscribed on
back: "Lord, I shall be very busy today. I
may forget thee. Do not Thou forget
me" (Van Cleef & Arpels) *$500*

Total Jewelry $133,350

Billie Paley

diamond "dragon" bangle
bracelet *$1,000*

gold and enamel bracelet *$1,000*

"cherub" ring—gold and cultured half
pearl set with thirty-two diamonds,
weighing approximately 1 ct.
(Verdura) *$750*

three serpentine rings—gold with
diamonds (Bulgari) *$300 $200 $250*

Total Jewelry $3,600

Kate Cushing Paley

necklace—turquoise, gold, and
diamonds, set with 660 diamonds,
weighing approximately 1.72 cts.
(Schlumberger) *$22,500*

antique suite of gold Indian jewelry—
necklace and matching earrings *$3,000*

gold basket-weave evening bag
(minaudière) BCP diamond initials
(Schlumberger) *$2,500*

choker of gold and coral
(Panaos) *$2,500*

Total Jewelry $30,500

Mittens, oil painting by James
Fosburgh *$400*

Jayne Wrightsman

oval turquoise enamel pillbox (19th
century) *$350*

Kate Roosevelt Whitney

platinum ball bracelet with a twisted
fringe of lapis lazuli and clasp of one
engraved emerald weighing
approximately 15 cts.; forty-two
diamonds weighing approximately 2
cts.; and twenty pear-shaped sapphires
weighing approximately 6 cts. *$2,000*

family papers

bronze brass and enamel elephant cart
(small bronze elephant ridden by a
mahout, pulling a high-wheeled cart
bearing an oblong box; its sides set with
enameled panels painted with
butterflies) *$850*

small decorative watercolor of an
anemone *$100*

carved and painted wood camel *$850*

Total $3,800

Adelaide T. Wallace

Van Cleef & Arpels gold compact   *$500*

miscellaneous clothing

Total   *$500*

Diana Vreeland

Fabergé gold circular powder box—
white enamel with a ciselé laurel
border   *$5,000*

Louise Melhado

gold lighter in the form of a fish with
cabochon emerald eyes   *$500*

Eugenia McCrary
(Jinx Falkenburg)

pair of Cartier 14-ct. gold two-fold
picture frames   *$350*

Leta McBean

pair of Dresden porcelain magpies   *$350*

Horace Kelland

pair of turquoise porcelain frogs
mounted as candlesticks   *$1,200*

Nancy (Slim) Keith

pair of Japanese ceramic crab
tureens   *$200*

Gloria Guinness

ivory and tortoiseshell jewel
casket   *$3,500*

Lucy (C.Z.) Guest

Chinese porcelain box decorated with
trailing vines in red, green, and yellow
(Yung Cheng)   *$1,000*

Priscilla Grosjean

gold cigarette case with a leather
cover   *$500*

Peter Glenville

pair of silver and amethyst
candlesticks   *$2,500*

Jane Engelhard

gold "Little Prince" perfume holder with
caliber emeralds and sapphires   *$1,000*

Lady Grace Dudley

pair of Chantilly porcelain bowls   *$300*

Winifred M. Dooney

antique cabochon emerald   *$50*

rose and diamond caliber emerald
brooch   *$350*

miscellaneous clothing

Total   *$400*

Françoise de la Renta

gold evening bag (Bulgari)   *$2,500*

Natalie Davenport

pair of carved and painted wood
busts   *$800*

Jean Stein Vanden Heuvel

Bulgari gold snake chain with a gold
Oriental coin   *$500*

Marietta Tree

gold and white enamel earclips   *$200*

baroque triple-strand necklace set with
coral and lapis beads   *$1,200*

Total   *$1,450*

Lady Anne Evelyn Beatrice Tree

Italian gold mounted enamel and green
horse pendant and gold chain   *$10,000*

Jean Tailer

amethyst and Indian bead
necklace   *$1,200*

gold and agate pillbox   *$350*

Total   *$1,550*

Lady Caroline Somerset

gold turquoise charm   *$100*

Irene Selznick

white and yellow gold chain   *$1,250*

Josephine L. Schiff

turquoise-studded ivory egg with 18-ct.
gold mounts (Tiffany)   *$500*

Charles Ryskamp

Meissen ornamental "Four Seasons"
urns   *$1,600*

Gloria Romanoff

gold and enamel compact   *$1,500*

Helen Rochas

pearl-woven necklace with pearl tassels
and carved amethysts   *$2,250*

agate box   *$225*

Total   *$4,475*

Dorothy M. (Sister) Parish

pair of Regency small carved and gilt-
wood consoles   *$1,000*

pair of Meissen porcelain lions on gilt-
bronze bases   *$2,500*

Total   *$3,500*

Lady Anne Orr-Lewis

bronze and gilt-bronze sunflower
clock   *$850*

Patrick O'Higgins

ivory box   *$50*

Japanese bronze monkey holding a peach
from box above head   *$850*

Total   *$900*

Henry K. Cushing

George III silver teapot   *$300*

George III silver cream jug   *$100*

Total   *$400*

Lorraine Cooper

18-ct. yellow gold necklace with a
ca. 1795 Liberty coin   *$2,500*

Jane Choate

pair of blue and white porcelain duck
tureens   *$850*

Josephine Blair

pair of bow white porcelain busts of a
Chinoiserie man and woman wearing
fanciful hats   *$6,000*

Elizabeth Catroux

white and black pearl necklace with a
black perfume bottle pendant   *$750*

Katherine Auchincloss

antique multicolored stone Indian
bracelet   *$1,250*

Brooke Astor

Chinese Export porcelain figural
group   *$3,500*

Susan Mary Alsop

necklace of carnelian and black onyx
beads, pearls, gold, and enamel   *$1,750*

two Fabergé snapshot frames   *$850*

Total $2,600

Marella Agnelli

pair of Venetian porcelain palm
trees   *$500*

Virginia Chambers

group of fourteen terra-cotta portrait
plaques by Jean Baptist Nini—of
Benjamin Franklin and others   *$3,500*

George Butler

English silver-plated lazy Susan   *$450*

Sara Wilford

jade bead bracelet with a diamond
clasp   *$2,000*

plaster female figure by Eli
Nadelman   *$2,000*

miscellaneous clothing

Total $4,000

Museum of the City of New York

Dior—black embroidered silk dress with
chiffon scarf

Mme Gres—black velvet evening gown
with satin trim

black silk gown with pleated organdy
cuffs and ruffle at hem

Castillo—lamé gown

Thea Porter—black caftan with silver
sequins

Galitzine—shaded green silk gown

Halston—gray sequined pants suit

heavy ivory satin gown with beaded
sleeves

Sanchez—black velvet robe with black
marabou trim

Metropolitan Museum

Mme Gres—dark green taffeta evening
gown

Mme Gres—black taffeta evening gown

Mme Gres—white taffeta and chiffon
evening gown

Mme Gres—amber and yellow evening gown

Mme Gres—scarlet two-piece evening gown

Mila Schoen—orange silk pants suit, long jacket with brass buttons

Mila Schoen—pale pink wool pants suit, long jacket with brass buttons

Mila Schoen—off-white wool pants suit, long jacket

Valentino—long white satin gown and long scarf with ostrich feathers at each end

Yves St. Laurent—full long red taffeta skirt (black velvet underskirt), soutache braid

Dior—large red taffeta top, gathered at neck and waist

Dior—four-piece white chiffon ensemble with faggoting—pants, camisole, jacket, and scarf

velvet print evening gown with red flowers

René Mancini—three pairs evening shoes, black, red, wine satin

one pair evening boots

Society of New York Hospital

miscellaneous clothing

Memorial Sloan-Kettering

miscellaneous clothing

Northshore Hospital

miscellaneous clothing

Notes

ALTHOUGH THE AUTHOR tried as often as possible to encourage sources to speak on the record, a number of those interviewed requested anonymity. Salted throughout the book are impressions, conclusions, and accounts of events based on these anonymous interviews with current and former CBS executives, as well as with friends and others close to Paley.

Whenever possible, the author sought information from at least two sources in evaluating individuals and events. In some cases, it was only possible to obtain one recollection, and the knowledgeability and overall veracity of the source was weighed before including such an account. There were a number of occasions in which the participants were only Bill Paley and one other person. When accounts of those events conflicted, that conflict is indicated either in the text of the book or in the notes. As extensive as these source notes are, they are not as complete as they could have been were it not for the publisher's space limitations.

To smooth the narrative flow of historical events, some direct quotes appear in reconstructing scenes. These quotes were used only if a source's memory proved reliable across the board, and if the recollection was particularly emphatic. Obviously even the most vivid memories become distorted with time; but they are the best a researcher has to go on in the absence of contemporaneous accounts.

William Paley's 1979 memoir, *As It Happened,* was a helpful resource. In the case of biographical facts that have been published elsewhere or are otherwise well known, specific citations are omitted. The memoir, henceforth referred to as *AIH,* is cited in source notes primarily for expressions of Paley's feelings or opinions, direct quotations, or in cases of contradictory evidence.

A number of journalists were good enough to allow me access to transcripts of their interviews with WSP. These are cited as transcripts as only a small portion of the material has appeared in print.

Because certain people are mentioned so frequently in the source notes, they are referred to by their initials according to the key listed on the opposite page:

Harry Ackerman (HA)
David Adams (DA)
Susan Mary Alsop (SMA)
Charlotte Curtis (CC)
John D. Backe (JDB)
Amanda Burden (AB)
Carter Burden (CB)
Michael Burke (MB)
Blair Clark (BC)
Michael Dann (MD)
Natalie Davenport (NaD)
Lady Mary Dunn (LMD)
Fred W. Friendly (FWF)
David Hertz (DH)
Dorothy Paley Hirshon (DPH)
Leonora Hornblow (LH)
Oscar Katz (OK)
Lady Nancy ("Slim") Keith (SK)
Horace Kelland (HoK)
Perry Lafferty (PL)
William Leonard (WL)
Tex McCrary (TMc)
E. Kidder Meade (EKM)
Sig Mickelson (SM)

Alice-Leone Moats (ALM)
Edward R. Murrow (ERM)
Janet Murrow (JM)
Barbara Cushing Paley (BCP)
Goldie Paley (GP)
William S. Paley (WSP)
John Pringle (JPr)
Joseph Ream (JR)
Richard Salant (RS)
John Schneider (JS)
Irene Selznick (IS)
Eric Sevareid (ES)
Howard K. Smith (HKS)
Sally Bedell Smith (SBS)
Frank Stanton (FS)
Arthur Taylor (AT)
Walter Thayer (WT)
Marietta Tree (MaT)
Diana Vreeland (DV)
Betsey Cushing Whitney (BCW)
Kate Whitney (KRW)
Robert Wood (RW)
Robert Wussler (RoW)
Thomas Wyman (TW)

PROLOGUE

*The Scene at the St. Regis and
Bill Paley's Day*

The St. Regis dinner: author's
observations; SBS interviews with
Eric Sevareid, CBS News
correspondent; Diane Sawyer,
former CBS News correspondent;
Lettie Aronson, vice-president of
the Museum of Broadcasting; Ray
Price, columnist and speechwriter;
and Gina Henry, public relations for
the St. Regis Hotel.
Bill Paley's day: SBS int. with William
S. Paley; confidential sources

Description of Bill Paley

(Truman Capote, a one-time: transcript
of David Halberstam interview with
Truman Capote, 1974
"Purely a trick of transposition": *Time,*
September 19, 1938
The air carried: SBS int. with WSP

The Paley legend

"He is to American": *New York Times,*
October 24, 1976
"an electronic Citizen Kane": *New York
Daily News,* May 18, 1980
"brilliant brinksmanship": *The
Washington Post,* March 11, 1979
Once while he was touring: SBS int.
with Karl Fleming, former
managing editor, KCBS-TV

Paley's legend outside broadcasting

"Do cozy up": *Women's Wear Daily,*
September 28, 1987
One rarefied group: *New York* Magazine,
"Club Lit," July 20, 1987
"sex symbols for a Corporate Age":
People magazine, "Power

Romance," Fred Bernstein,
February 2, 1987
"Find out about the crushed": SBS int.
with Benjamin Bradlee, executive
editor, *The Washington Post*
"Monkey glands": SBS int. with Arthur
Taylor, former president of CBS
"All he and the person": SBS int. with
David Adams, former vice-
chairman of NBC
"He kept a cocoon": SBS int. with
Robert Wood, former president of
CBS-TV
"a certain standard of taste": *The
Washington Post,* March 11, 1979

Paley charm

"He always had a roving eye": SBS int.
with Irene Selznick, longtime friend
of the Paleys
"He listens": SBS int. with Marietta
Tree, longtime friend of the Paleys
"He is someone that": SBS int. with
Horace Kelland, friend of the Paleys
"You almost had the feeling": SBS int.
with Charlotte Curtis, former
society columnist, *New York Times*

Energy in Paley's personal life

"threw a temper tantrum": SBS int.
with WSP
To capture his first wife: SBS int. with
Dorothy Paley Hirshon, first wife of
WSP

Paley energy

"made of sets": SBS int. with IS
"Bill never just sat": SBS int. with John
Pringle, friend of the Paleys
At home Paley's six children: *Esquire,*
"What Hath William Paley
Wrought?", David McClintick
(December 1983)

"He would charge": SBS int. with
William O'Shaughnessy, radio
station owner and friend.

Paley and CBS executives

One of his top programmers:
confidential source
Paley would call: SBS int. with Robert
Daly, former president of CBS
Entertainment; SBS int. with
E. Kidder Meade, former vice-
president for corporate affairs
at CBS
"a lovable bear way": SBS int. with RW

The tic

An outward sign of Paley's internal:
observations by author; confidential
sources; SBS int. with Richard
Salant, former president of CBS
News

Pressures of CBS

"The nervous strain is terrible":
Providence Sunday Journal,
November 26, 1961
"He was the son of a": SBS int. with RS
To smother his insecurities: *AIH,*
pp. 213–214; confidential sources

Contradictions

"I don't think": *AIH,* p. 2
"Bill Paley is so contradictory": SBS int.
with IS
"he could be so logical": SBS int. with
Kim LeMasters, former president of
CBS Entertainment
When CBS owned: SBS int. with
M. Donald Grant, former chairman
of the New York Mets
never used the Yiddish: confidential
sources

"I don't think he could": SBS int.
with DPH
"that lovely impeccable taste": SBS int.
with JPr
most conspicuous in his relationships
with women: SBS int. with Alice-
Leone Moats, friend of the Paleys
from the 1930s and 1940s; SBS ints.
with several girlfriends who
requested anonymity
"There is nothing wrong": SBS int. with
WSP

St. Regis and memories of war and postwar

"Make him laugh": SBS int. with Diane
Sawyer

Bill and Babe

"perfect bones": *Vogue,* March 15, 1962
snip off the edges of stamps: SBS int.
with Kay Wight, former secretary
to WSP
He once sent food consultants: SBS int.
with Mimi Sheraton, restaurant
reviewer

St. Regis dinner

"I'd like to get you back": SBS int. with
ES
"Together and working": SBS int. with
David Hertz, management
consultant who frequently worked
with CBS
The line had been written: SBS int.
with Ray Price

Paley in the hospital

VIP suite, at New York Hospital: SBS
int. with Dr. Thomas Nash,
attending physician, New York
Hospital
It was an amazing scene: SBS int. with
DPH; confidential sources

CHAPTER 1

Paley's birth

a dark, cramped apartment: WSP birth
  certificate: place of birth listed as 258
  Ogden; SBS int. with Dorothy
  Rothe, first cousin of WSP
Glass cases: SBS int. with Dorothy
  Rothe; photo archives of the
  Chicago Historical Society;
  AIH, p. 6

Ogden Avenue

Ogden Avenue was a parade: SBS int.
  with Professor Henry Binford,
  Northwestern University; *Pilsen and
  the West Side, a Tour Guide,* William
  J. Adelman (Chicago, 1983)

Isaac Paley

Sam had been born in: Sam Paley official
  biography issued by CBS
pronounced "Paylay": "Live from New
  York: This Is TV's Bill Paley," by
  Bob Considine, *New York Journal-
  American,* May 20, 1965 (cited
  hereafter as Considine); SBS int.
  with Dorothy Rothe
had really been Palinski: SBS int. with
  Edward Bernays, public relations
  consultant to CBS in 1920s;
  confidential sources

Life in Russia

Life was hard for Jews: "Aspects of
  Chicago Russian-Jewish Life," by
  Seymour Jacob Pomrenze, in *The
  Chicago Pinkas,* edit. Simon
  Rawidowicz, College of Jewish
  Studies (Chicago, 1952), pp. 11–14;
  World of Our Fathers, Irving Howe
  (New York, 1983), p. 10
that would bring nearly 2 million:
  Howe, p. 58

Isaac Paley in Russia

In later years he never told: *AIH,* p. 5
Isaac Paley used his official: SBS int.
  with Dorothy Rothe

Voyage

Passage cost around: *"The Rest of Us":
  The Rise of America's Eastern
  European Jews,* Stephen Birmingham
  (New York, 1984), p. 41; Howe,
  pp. 25, 59
though not so prosperous as the father:
  Birmingham, p. 155
"the 'dissenters' ": Howe, p. 61

Chicago

The immigrants who journeyed:
  Pomrenze, p. 117
In the last two decades: "The Jews of
  Illinois," *The Reform Advocate,* May
  4, 1901, p. 285

Isaac in America

Isaac Paley dreamed of: SBS int. with
  WSP
"A Jew who was a communal figure":
  Pomrenze, p. 131
(He did, however, take the time): SBS
  int. with Dorothy Rothe
"next to a samovar": *AIH,* p. 4
"whether something of my
  grandfather's": Ibid.

Zelda

"The dispossession and shame": Howe,
  p. 173
"Zelda was impossible": SBS int. with
  Dorothy Rothe
In Russia Zelda had been: Ibid.

Cigar making

"The accurate judgment": "The
  Economic Development of the
  Cigar Industry in the United
  States," Willis N. Baer, Lancaster,

Pa., 1933, doctoral dissertation for
Columbia University, p. 81
Sam's tools: Ibid., p. 80; transcript of Ira
Berkow int. with Mayer Patur,
cigarmaker who worked for Sam
Paley, 1975
By smoking and feeling: Baer, p. 78
finally settling on leaf from Java:
Maxwell Street: Survival in a Bazaar,
Ira Berkow (Garden City, N.Y.,
1977), p. 362

Sam's earnings

A cigarmaker was paid: Berkow, p. 362;
Berkow int. with Mayer Patur
two hundred cigars a day: Baer, p. 82
selling cigars from baskets: SBS int. with
Louis Bein, cousin of Goldie Paley
He and eight other members: Berkow,
p. 20

Maxwell Street

By the 1890s the Maxwell Street:
"Chicago Housing Conditions IV,
The West Side Revisited," by
Sophonisba P. Breckinridge and
Edith Abbott, *American Journal of
Sociology* (July 1911)
"The streets were mud": Berkow, p. 6
"It was the most densely": Breckinridge
and Abbott
Seventy thousand shoppers: Berkow,
p. 19
One survey in 1901: Breckinridge and
Abbott
a haven of sorts: Pomrenze, p. 119
"Jews were treated": *History of the Jews of
Chicago,* edit. Hyman L. Meites,
Jewish Historical Society of Illinois
(Chicago, 1924), p. 150

Samuel Paley & Company

"a few hundred dollars": 1926
application from Congress Cigar
Company to New York Stock
Exchange

"a very tall and handsome": transcript of
Ira Berkow int. with Goldie Paley,
1975
eked out a living by: SBS int. with Louis
Bein

Goldie

Goldie always figured: Ira Berkow int.
with GP
Shortly before he emigrated: SBS int.
with Louis Bein
Unlike Isaac Paley, Morris: Ira Berkow
int. with GP
had to bring his wife: SBS int. with
Louis Bein

Goldie and Sam meet

One day Sam Paley arrived: Ira Berkow
int. with GP
"a pretty juicy girl": SBS int. with Louis
Bein
a "handsome, even beautiful": *AIH,* p. 7
"intense" and "looked out": Ibid.

Goldie and Sam team

Goldie was the driving force: SBS ints.
with Dorothy Rothe and Rochelle
Levy, wife of Robert Levy
At the shop on Ogden Avenue: Ira
Berkow int. with GP
"I wasn't ashamed of it": Ibid.

Middle-class comfort

"probably a millionaire": SBS int. with
WSP; *AIH,* p. 6
In 1904, Sam took in his brother:
Congress 1926 application to New
York Stock Exchange

Wholesale

He established his factory: SBS int. with
Louis Bein; Berkow, p. 360
La Palina, a name that: Ira Berkow int.
with GP; *AIH,* pp. 7–8; SBS int.
with Robert Paley, cousin to WSP

"They wanted to pass it off": SBS int.
    with Robert Paley
her hair piled high: SBS int. with
    Dorothy Rothe
altered to resemble a Spanish princess:
    SBS int. with Louis Bein
"He thought I was": Ira Berkow int.
    with GP

Detroit

Shortly after they began: 1926
    application to New York Stock
    Exchange says the move took place
    in 1905
when $3,500 could obtain: Baer, p. 99
One of Bill Paley's earliest memories:
    confidential source

Return to Chicago

In 1909, Sam and Jacob returned: 1926
    application to New York Stock
    Exchange
Sam moved to a different house:
    Marquette Elementary School
    records, listing at 808 Marshfield
    Avenue
The house measured about: *AIH*, p. 354;
    SBS int. with Dorothy Rothe
Years later, in the 1970s: *AIH*, pp. 7,
    354. Paley's official recollection for
    his memoir was that his father
    advocated buying the adjacent
    property; but privately recounting
    the visit several times to Newton
    Minow, each time Paley mentioned
    his parents' squabbles. The
    discrepancy is an interesting measure
    of the way Paley sanitized even
    trivial memories for public
    consumption. SBS int. with
    Newton Minow, member of CBS
    board of directors and Chicago
    lawyer

The next year the brothers: Berkow, pp.
    360, 362
"The conditions were not good": Ira
    Berkow int. with Mayer Patur

WSP's childhood

"modest middle-class life": *AIH*, p. 10
He professed to have had: *Washington
    Star*, April 8, 1979
But he also spoke: Considine; SBS int.
    with Fred Friendly, former
    president of CBS News
Willie was a quiet: SBS ints. with
    Dorothy Rothe and Evelyn August,
    friend of the Paley family in
    Chicago
To avoid going to school: SBS int. with
    WSP; *AIH*, p. 13

Blanche

He also deeply resented: *AIH*, p. 12
But when Blanche was two: SBS int.
    with DPH
Even after Blanche recovered: SBS ints.
    with DPH and Dorothy Rothe
Meanwhile, Willie sat in the corner: SBS
    int. with WSP
He felt rejected and unloved: *Newsweek*,
    March 5, 1979

Goldie and WSP

She was the sort who stubbornly: *AIH*,
    p. 10
She described herself as: Ira Berkow int.
    with GP
In one particularly stinging: SBS int.
    with WSP
"many unhappy moments": Ibid.
"verged on the neurotic": confidential
    source
In later years: SBS int. with WSP
"to show her": *Newsweek*, March 5,
    1979

"Each time, with each new one": SBS
    int. with DPH
"With Bill's appetites": SBS int. with IS

Sam and WSP

One of Bill Paley's favorite stories:
    confidential source
Willie thought of his father (and rest of
    paragraph): SBS int. with WSP

Growing up

but one incident: Ibid.
A little bit of luck: Ibid.
As a symbol of his new status: Ibid.
reinforced by the nickname "Chink":
    SBS int. with DPH
When he attended: *AIH*, p. 13
On Marshfield Avenue (and rest of
    paragraph): SBS int. with WSP
but his friends: SBS ints. with John
    Reagan ("Tex") McCrary, friend of
    the Paleys, and DPH

Military school

At Western Military Academy:
    confidential source; 1918 Western
    Military Academy Catalogue
after an initial bout: confidential source
"a turning point": SBS int. with WSP
Twice a week: confidential source

University of Chicago

"a good time Charlie": SBS int. with
    Edmund Eichengreen, fraternity
    brother at Chicago
"One quickly warmed up to him": letter
    to Edmund Eichengreen from a
    classmate nicknamed "Tech"
By this time: confidential sources
"the most exciting": confidential source
He visited the woman: AIH, p. 16
They spent much of the night:
    confidential source

"He wasn't abrasive": SBS int. with
    Edmund Eichengreen
"He was a tall, slender": "Tech"
    reminiscence

Religion

"cultural distance": *AIH*, p. 9
"I couldn't get": *Empire: William S. Paley
    and the Making of CBS*, Lewis J.
    Paper (New York, 1987), p. 5
Goldie loaded her supper table: SBS ints.
    with Robert Levy and Mimi
    Sheraton

WSP in the business

"a culture utterly devoted": Howe,
    pp. 251, 253
"I used to dream": Paper, p. 358
To mask its inferiority: SBS int. with
    Louis Bein

Changes in the cigar business

Along with other cigar manufacturers:
    Baer, pp. 86–88, 94; Howe, p. 297
The final strike: Berkow, p. 362
There were numerous advantages: Baer,
    p. 104

CHAPTER 2

New York

"thinking about sin": confidential source
But Sam eventually settled: *AIH*, p. 19
Cigarmakers there had: Baer, p. 104

WSP in Philadelphia

Just as young Bill had finished: *TV/
    Radio Age*, March 12, 1979
With the help of the plant: confidential
    source
"I knew where": *TV/Radio Age*, March
    12, 1979

University of Pennsylvania

"What a farce": *Time,* January 31, 1964

He immediately hooked up: '20–'21 and '21–'22 University of Pennsylvania catalogues; SBS int. with Professor E. Digby Baltzell, University of Pennsylvania

Sam Paley, however, kept: confidential source

"half student": *AIH,* p. 20

"quite bright": confidential source

"Absolutely not": confidential source

Paley was well enough liked: University of Pennsylvania yearbook, 1922; SBS int. with Harold Hecht, fraternity brother

After his sophomore year: SBS int. with Frederick Levy, fraternity brother

Of all the schools: SBS int. with Professor Digby Baltzell; "The Jewish Communities of Philadelphia and Boston: A Tale of Two Cities," by E. Digby Baltzell, Allen Glicksman, and Jacquelyn Litt, in *Jewish Life in Philadelphia 1830–1940* edit., Murray Friedman (Philadelphia, 1983), pp. 30–39

"Penn took Jews": SBS int. with Professor Digby Baltzell

After his graduation in 1922: computer records at University of Pennsylvania Annual Giving Development Office

"He hasn't given Penn": SBS int. with Robert Levy

"It is not significant": SBS int. with Fran Sheeley, former New York development director for Penn

In Philadelphia, anti-Semitism evolved: "German Jews Versus Russian Jews in Philadelphia Philanthropy," by Philip Rosen, in Friedman, ed., p. 203

"Philadelphia's Protestant establishment": Introduction, Friedman, ed., pp. 6, 11, 12

In selecting campus activities: University of Pennsylvania yearbook, 1922; SBS int. with WSP

"There was no particular spark": SBS int. with Frederick Levy

"I would never have expected": SBS int. with Henry Gerstley, Philadelphia friend

"lived nicely but not extravagantly": SBS int. with Harold Hecht

Philadelphia life

One of the "nice people": SBS ints. with Rose Stecker, sister of Ben Gimbel, and William Fineshriber, son of the Paleys' rabbi

In 1921 the Paleys bought: University of Pennsylvania yearbook, 1922, Keneseth Israel yearbooks, 1921–23. The house was at 5204 Overbrook

a plain stone dwelling: SBS int. with Bertiya Pope, owner of 5204 Overbrook

"They don't really count": letter from Barbara S. Wright, daughter of a golfing partner of Samuel Paley to SBS, 10/15/85

A more profound snub: confidential source

"They didn't want": SBS int. with Lester Degenstein, Philadelphia friend

"I wouldn't give a red dime": SBS int. with Henry Gerstley

"While they didn't snub him": SBS int. with William Fineshriber

At Congress Cigar

Jacob—everyone called him: *AIH,* p. 22; SBS ints. with Robert Paley and Dorothy Rothe; confidential source

"the million-dollar cigar salesman": confidential source

"If you get the details": *AIH*, p. 30

Congress Cigar was thriving: 1926
Congress application to the New
York Stock Exchange

In January of that year: Goldman Sachs
handled the public offering for
Congress Cigar. The offering price
for the 70,000 shares was $40

Later in 1926 the family: *AIH*, p. 35;
Moody's Manual of Investments, 1927.
Most sources have erroneously
reported the selling price at $30
million. *Moody's Manual* reports that
in 1926 Congress sold 200,000
shares to Porto Rican–American for
$63.75 a share, or $13,750,000. The
Paley family still held 80,000 shares
of Congress Cigar, from which they
received $320,000 a year in
dividends. Over the years, various
family members, including William
Paley, sold off these holdings for
additional profits.

Afterwards, he concentrated: *Only
Yesterday: An Informal History of the
1920s*, Frederick Lewis Allen (New
York, 1931), pp. 140–142; *AIH*,
p. 22

Bachelor life

"I lived in the south": SBS int. with
Henry Gerstley

Paley preferred: confidential source

quite the Stage Door: confidential source

During one crossing: *Goldwyn: A
Biography*, A. Scott Berg (New
York, 1989), p. 249

"She was so crisp": SBS int. with IS

"I was mad": SBS int. with IS

Paley continued: SBS int. with WSP

the legendary nightclub: *Incredible New
York: High Life and Low Life of the
Last Hundred Years, 1850–1950*,
Lloyd Morris (New York, 1951),
p. 333

"Everyone went": SBS int. with WSP

Years later: confidential source

"I wanted": *AIH*, p. 31; SBS int. with
WSP

Goldie and Sam

From Overbrook they had moved:
Keneseth Israel yearbook 1924 lists
614 East Sedgwick

Several years later: The house was at 101
West Hampton Road

To help maintain: SBS int. with DPH

"Jewish girls don't know": SBS int. with
Phyllis Maxwell, secretary to Goldie
Paley

She loved to shop: SBS int. with
Dorothy Hurt Meacham Price,
girlfriend of Paley's in the twenties

"Never do anything": *CBS: Reflections in
a Bloodshot Eye*, Robert Metz (New
York, 1976), p. 22

Once she had the means: SBS int. with
Phyllis Maxwell

"The old person": Ira Berkow int. with
GP

"Never take your diamonds" (and rest of
paragraph): SBS ints. with Phyllis
Maxwell and Robert Levy

She took up golf: Ira Berkow int. with
GP

went to lectures: SBS int. with Dorothy
Rothe

"I haven't allowed": Ira Berkow int.
with GP

"She could see well enough": SBS int.
with Phyllis Maxwell

"My husband was afraid": Ira Berkow
int. with GP

Late in life: Ibid.

Goldie "catered to": *AIH*, p. 7

"The patterns of the family": Howe,
p. 172

when he took rests: confidential source

He planned every moment; SBS int.
with WSP

"it was almost a mania": confidential source

With his guttural voice: SBS ints. with Richard Levy, cousin of Robert Levy, and William Fineshriber

But he was unassuming: SBS int. with RS

called him "The Rock": SBS int. with Robert Paley

Sam was frugal: Ibid.

He always carried: transcript of David Halberstam int. with Ralph Colin, former CBS counsel and personal attorney to WSP

"strange habits": SBS int. with WSP

Every day he took: SBS int. with DPH

He always ate lunch: SBS int. with WSP

"Sometimes when men get older": SBS int. with Phyllis Maxwell

He was fixated on the number: SBS int. with WSP

Blanche

both parents spoiled her: SBS int. with Dorothy Rothe

"No one ever said": SBS int. with DPH

Blanche was quiet: SBS ints. with Frederick and Richard Levy

After attending: SBS int. with DPH

When a local dentist: SBS int. with Henry Gerstley

Bill Paley

"She knew him better": SBS int. with DPH

Paley came to believe: SBS int. with WSP

"My son believes": Ira Berkow int. with GP

"She would never": SBS int. with WSP

"What's the matter?": SBS int. with Stuart Scheftel, Paley friend from the thirties and forties

"Sam was very much like": SBS int. with DPH

"He was always more ambitious": SBS int. with Henry Gerstley

He used to leaf through: SBS int. with WSP

"I don't think he ever": SBS int. with Henry Gerstley

"He made it clear": Ibid.

CHAPTER 3

Paley and the dawn of radio

"I was very dubious": WSP int. with National Public Radio, November 1979

Paley immediately had a set: "At CBS: Bill Paley Keeps It Up," Glenn Plaskin, *M* magazine (July 1985)

Night after night: WSP int. with Joan Burke, CBS Radio, August 9, 1977

In fact, the experience: *Only Yesterday*, Allen, p. 65

2.5 million radios: *The Powers That Be*, David Halberstam (New York, 1979), p. 15

"There is radio music": *Only Yesterday*, Allen, p. 65

Early radio

The first commercial radio: *A History of Broadcasting in the United States*, Vol. I, Erik Barnouw (New York, 1966), p. 69; "NBC: The Once and Future Company," report by David C. Adams, vice-chairman of NBC, February 21, 1979, p. 3

By 1924: David Adams report, p. 3

which was charged: Barnouw, Vol. I, p. 200

Stations popped up: Ibid., pp. 97, 99

KDKA, whose first programs: David Adams report, p. 3

When a makeshift studio: Barnouw, Vol. I, p. 71

But the American Telephone &
Telegraph Company: Ibid., pp. 81,
108

Wind, Earth, Air and Fire: *Connections:
Reflections on Sixty Years of
Broadcasting,* Mary C. O'Connell,
Oral Historian (New York, 1986),
"Oral History of Hugh M. Beville,"
p. 74

AT&T meanwhile: Barnouw, Vol. I,
pp. 113, 143–145, 185

The novelty was wearing off: David
Adams report, p. 3

Although plenty of performers:
Barnouw, Vol. I, p. 134

The birth of NBC

As the year continued (and remainder of
paragraph): Barnouw, Vol. I,
pp. 160, 186, 187

The NBC founders: *Fortune* (June 1935);
Barnouw, Vol. I, p. 204

"An investment": *Big Business and Radio,*
Gleason L. Archer (New York,
1939), p. 305

"better programs": Barnouw, Vol. I,
p. 187

David Sarnoff

But unlike: *The General: David Sarnoff
and the Rise of the Communications
Industry,* Kenneth Bilby (New York,
1986), pp. 11–12, 17

By 1906: Ibid., pp. 19, 30, 32

It was the beginning: Ibid., p. 32;
Barnouw, Vol. I, p. 77

His coolness: Bilby, p. 35

"A 'household utility' ": Barnouw,
Vol. I, p. 78

Junior executive Sarnoff: Barnouw,
Vol. I, pp. 61, 79

The inaugural program: Bilby, p. 87

The origins of WCAU

Located in one room: Broadcast Pioneers
int. with Isaac and Leon Levy (June
1964), p. 3; Isaac D. Levy,
unpublished autobiography, p. 8

Leon was a dentist: Levys' oral history
(June 1964), p. 32

The station was making: Isaac Levy
autobiography, p. 9

So when a fast-talking: Barnouw, Vol. I,
p. 194

The origins of CBS

Judson, a cultivated but: Metz, p. 11

Coats and Judson had hooked up:
Archer, p. 301

"You can't do it": Barnouw, Vol. I,
p. 194

They brought in Major White:
Broadcasting, September 22, 1952

White joined them: *Fortune* (June 1935)

AT&T told Coats: Archer, p. 302

Levy had nothing to lose: Ibid.

Leon was so taken: Barnouw, Vol. I,
p. 194; Isaac Levy autobiography,
p. 10

A guaranteed weekly income: Archer,
p. 302

In April 1927: Ibid., p. 305

"bought the operating": *Fortune* (June
1935)

Fortified by its new backer: Archer,
p. 308

Of the ten weekly hours: Barnouw,
Vol. I, pp. 222–223

Enter the Levys and Paleys

Columbia Phonograph lost: Archer,
p. 310

But Judson prevailed: SBS int. with
William Louchheim, son of Jerome
Louchheim

He knew, however: Isaac Levy
autobiography, p. 11

"Jerry, I'm worried": Ibid.

Why had Sam Paley: SBS ints. with William Louchheim and Richard Levy; *Fortune* (June 1935)

The hour-long program: Archer, p. 319; *Sponsor,* September 13, 1965

After a few weeks: SBS int. with William Louchheim; *Fortune* (June 1935); WSP entry in *Current Biography,* 1940, 1951

Congress Cigar quickly: *Sponsor,* September 13, 1965

he agreed to spend: Archer, p. 319

He was also receptive: SBS int. with William Louchheim

Louchheim was only fifty-five: *Time* magazine interview with Ralph Colin, longtime CBS counsel, April 10, 1935

"I don't want anything": SBS int. with William Louchheim

At his father's insistence: transcript of Morris Gelman int. with WSP, September 30, 1970

"a kind of parlor car": *Pageant* (November 1948)

"It was one of radio's": *Fortune* (June 1935)

Bill Paley's version

By his account: *AIH,* p. 32

In a 1958 speech: WSP speech to Broadcast Pioneers, 11/20/58

"Their first knowledge": Ibid.

Bill, his father: Ibid.; Morris Gelman int. with WSP

"You know": Morris Gelman int. with WSP

"vindication rose": *AIH,* p. 33

"What really caught": *Fortune* (June 1935)

"It is a lie": SBS int. with William Louchheim. It is worth noting that writers chronicling the Paley story

have picked one or the other version of this episode, although none has explained the choice. Those who selected Paley's version included Gleason Archer, Erik Barnouw, and David Halberstam. The version crediting the elder Paleys can be found in books by Robert Metz and Laurence Bergreen, and editions of *Current Biography* until 1951, when the story was changed to Bill Paley's version.

The Levy-Louchheim era at CBS

Louchheim and the Levys had paid: Archer, p. 316; Isaac Levy autobiography, p. 11. Their initial payment included a $100,000 surety bond to AT&T

At the time: Archer, p. 315

Colin's prophecy: Ibid., pp. 316–318

Throughout that year: Isaac Levy autobiography, p. 12; Levys' oral history, p. 9

Congress Cigar led the way; Levys' oral history, p. 11; Barnouw, Vol. I, p. 223

The new owners: *AIH,* p. 42; Metz, p. 20; Barnouw, Vol. I, p. 206

On the strength of: *Fortune* (June 1935); Barnouw, Vol. I, p. 206

"How far do you think": Isaac Levy autobiography, p. 12

To the Warners, radio seemed: Considine

"Vitaphone signed: Isaac Levy autobiography, p. 13. Ike was so proud of his role in this turnaround that he kept the telegram framed on his office wall for many years

Bill Paley buys CBS

Shortly after the Columbia: Levys' oral history, p. 10

Once again, Ike Levy: Isaac Levy autobiography, p. 13; SBS int. with

William Louchheim; Morris Gelman
int. with WSP

"You at least have": *AIH*, p. 34

While Sam could not agree: WSP speech,
November 20, 1958; Barnouw,
Vol. I, p. 224

Paley immediately hopped: WSP speech,
November 20, 1958

"Ours was an old-fashioned": *AIH*,
p. 37

At the same time: Isaac Levy
autobiography, p. 13

But while Paley was eager: Archer,
p. 320; Gelman int. with WSP

Although Sam did not tell: *Broadcasting*,
May 31, 1976

"I just bought the Columbia": Barnouw,
Vol. II (1968), pp. 5–7

Thanks to the persistence: Levys' oral
history (Ike: "We lost money until
the end of 1928"); SBS int. with
William Louchheim ("When CBS
bought into it, it was making
money")

He loved to describe: transcript of int. by
Broadcasting editors with WSP, April
12, 1976

"Louchheim had failed": *AIH*, p. 34

"William Paley had an inordinate": SBS
int. with Richard Levy

CHAPTER 4

Bill Paley's arrival at United Independent

The headquarters of United Independent:
"Recalling the Heyday of the Great
White Way," by Allen Churchill,
New York Times, January 24, 1982;
AIH, p. 63

The Paramount Building: *New York
1930*, Robert A. M. Stern, (New
York, 1987)

"Reminiscent of a grandiose": Stern,
p. 534

"I shot the wrong": *New York Times*,
January 24, 1982

Paley's office: *Fortune* (June 1935)

By one estimate: Metz, p. 26

"to impress advertisers": *AIH*, p. 38

He came to cherish: Ibid., p. 63

United Independent's dozen employees:
H. V. Kaltenborn Reminiscences,
Columbia University Oral History
Collection (1950), pp. 16–19;
Howard Barlow Reminiscences,
Columbia University Oral History
Collection (1951), p. 112; *New York
Telegram*, December 24, 1930

"Bill Paley was like": SBS int. with
Edward Bernays

"There was a very dramatic": transcript
of Chris Andersen int. with WSP,
March 19, 1979

David Sarnoff called him: confidential
source

He ordered a custom-made: Metz, p. 22;
Washington Star, April 8, 1979

"just a rich man's": *Time*
correspondent's file, 3/11/32

He was so poorly regarded: SBS int.
with RS

"There was nothing remarkable": *Time*
magazine int. with Ralph Colin,
February 10, 1935

"My imagination": SBS int. with WSP

He directed one executive: Barlow oral
history

In fact, when Paley arrived: *Fortune* (June
1935)

The new affiliation contract

He conceived it: SBS int. with WSP

Only one fifth of Columbia's: WSP
testimony, Committee on Interstate
Commerce, United States Senate, 1/
18/30, p. 1798

Paley claimed to be: In *AIH*, pp. 42–43,
Paley said that the new affiliation
contract devised by Major White

when Louchheim bought the
network obligated the stations to
pay for sustaining programs.
However, *Fortune,* in its June 1935
profile of Paley, said that White
changed the arrangement to ensure
that the stations were only paid for
the sponsored programs they
carried; there was no mention of
Columbia affiliates being compelled
to pay for sustaining programs. On
its face such a requirement seems
unlikely. Columbia affiliates were
struggling, and the Columbia
network hardly had the leverage to
make such a demand.
NBC forced its stations: Barnouw,
      Vol. II, p. 57
For the first time: Ibid., Vol. I, p. 250
"The Major closed deals": *Fortune* (June
      1935)
Paley took enormous pride: *AIH,* p. 51

Expanding Columbia's facilities

"Mr. Paley: Ibid.
On the advice of a real estate: Metz,
      p. 26
"If Paley had not done this": *Time* int.
      with Ralph Colin, February 10,
      1935
"That was one of": Morris Gelman int.
      with WSP
A document signed: agreement 6/13/29
      between WSP and Paramount
      Famous Lasky Corporation

Advertising revenues

To advertise their candidates: WSP
      testimony, Committee on Interstate
      Commerce, 1/18/30, p. 1791
Paley hardly had to lift: WSP int. with
      National Public Radio, November
      1979
Paley made one key change: *Broadcasting*
      editors' int. with WSP, April 12,
      1976

Building an organization

"In those days of course": Ibid.
"There's no question": transcript of
      Robert Lamb int. with WSP,
      November 5, 1976
"It was literally true": *AIH,* p. 46
"I thought, my God": Paper, p. 24
Bernays gave Paley ideas: *Biography of an
      Idea: Memoirs of Public Relations
      Counsel Edward L. Bernays,* Edward
      L. Bernays (New York, 1965),
      pp. 430–431
"The first period": Ibid., p. 431
"I urged him to ferret": Ibid., p. 428
"wasn't satisfied with": Ibid., p. 429
"Paley was right": Ibid., p. 430
"If Major White's knowledge": *Fortune*
      (June 1935)
It was Pickard who: Barnouw, Vol. I,
      p. 251
"hire smart people": Metz, p. 22
"proceeded to refute": Barlow oral
      history
For whatever reason: Ibid.
When Paley merged: Archer, p. 320
"The business of radio": *AIH,* p. 391
White did not object: Archer, p. 335
But by mid-1930: *Broadcasting,*
      September 22, 1952; letter from
      Ralph Colin of Goldmark, Bennitt
      & Colin to Ralph Kohn, counsel for
      Paramount
"It is perhaps": Archer, p. 335
A more lofty: Bilby, p. 233
The most important was: Barnouw,
      Vol. I, p. 224
Soon 40 million listeners: Ibid., p. 225
Advertisers clamored: Bilby, p. 233
At the end of 1928: *AIH,* p. 47
After coaxing him: Barlow oral history
"He would never have had": *New York
      Post,* March 2, 1984

Paley's shift to mass programming

His first big coup: *AIH*, pp. 66–67
"both lurid and respectable": Barnouw,
    Vol. I, p. 224

CHAPTER 5

480 Park Avenue

"He was like a little": SBS int. with
    Edward Bernays
The apartment occupied: *New York
    World*, January 24, 1930
"It seemed a Croesus-like": Bernays,
    p. 428
The master bedroom: *New York World*,
    January 24, 1930; SBS int. with
    DPH
The high-ceilinged third-floor: *New York
    World*, January 24, 1930
A guest bedroom: SBS int. with DPH
In the meantime: SBS int. with Sy Pinto,
    manager, Elysée Hotel
Two days later: SBS int. with DPH

Paley's social life

A year after arriving: *Time* file, 3/11/32
His inexperience: *New York World*,
    January 24, 1930
As it turned out: SBS int. with Edward
    Bernays
"The self-indulgent son": Bernays,
    p. 427
"asked me if he": transcript of Lynn
    Rosellini int. with WSP, March 3,
    1979

Café Society

In the late 1800s: L. Morris, p. 246
The most exclusive: Ibid., p. 326
His favorite was: Ibid.; *AIH*, p. 85
Even more important: L. Morris, p. 296;
    AIH, p. 86

"theatre, Hollywood": *Lulu in
    Hollywood*, Louise Brooks (New
    York, 1983), p. 14

Our crowd and the WASPs

These families were not impressed:
    Birmingham, p. 189
Paley would have liked: Halberstam,
    p. 32
"He was always socially": SBS int. with
    Henry Gerstley
Lowman occupied the office: SBS int.
    with Joseph Ream, former chief
    counsel for CBS
One of Lowman's first: *Maverick
    Inventor: My Turbulent Years at CBS*,
    Peter C. Goldmark with Lee Edson
    (New York, 1973), p. 42
Not only was Lowman: SBS int. with
    John Hammond, former executive
    at CBS Records
Lowman instructed Paley: SBS int. with
    FS
It was Lowman who arranged:
    confidential source
Significantly, at the time: SBS ints. with
    John Hammond and Henry Gerstley

Paley and women

"I used to wet nurse him": David
    Halberstam int. with Ralph Colin
She came from Dallas: SBS int. with
    Dorothy Hurt Meacham Price
"the woman of": *AIH*, p. 90
Her husband, Malcolm Meacham: SBS
    int. with Dorothy Hurt Meacham
    Price
"died in a fall": *AIH*, p. 90
"He always had": SBS int. with
    Dorothy Hurt Meacham Price
Toward the end of 1929: L. Brooks,
    p. 48
"shameless urchin tomboy": *The Life of
    Kenneth Tynan*, Kathleen Tynan
    (New York, 1987), p. 485

"screwy sense of humor": Ibid.,
p. 492
Almost at once: L. Brooks, p. 48;
Tynan, p. 486
"Next time bring your little": SBS int.
with DPH
"He had given up": L. Brooks, p. 48
Paley was exceedingly proud: SBS int.
with Carter Burden, former son-in-
law of WSP
Not only did he boast: Tynan, p. 486
Twenty-five years later: Louise Brooks
told Kenneth Tynan about Paley's
stipend when he tried to convince
her to be interviewed for a profile in
the late 1970s. According to
Kathleen Tynan's book, Brooks told
Kenneth Tynan that she was afraid
if she gave an interview she might
offend the Paley Foundation and
Paley himself. However, nowhere in
the Paley Foundation records is
there any mention of this stipend,
which would seem to violate the
foundation's requirement not to
make contributions "to the benefit
of any private shareholder or
individual."

Paley matures as an executive

"He was very energetic": Howard
Barlow oral history
"He was always glad": SBS int. with
Helen Sioussat, former public affairs
executive at CBS
"He was accessible": SBS int. with John
("Jap") Gude, former CBS
executive
"A poker face": Bernays, p. 427
"They gave me more day by day":
transcript of Rufus Crater int. with
WSP, May 18, 1976
"Sleep didn't mean anything": National
Public Radio int. with WSP,
November 1979

"There was a drive": transcript of Tom
Shales int. with WSP, 3/6/79
"I developed a high sense": *AIH*, p. 61

Paramount deal

From July 1928 to December: WSP
testimony, Committee on Interstate
Commerce, 1/18/30, pp. 1792, 1796
Initially he drew: Archer, p. 334
Six months later: Ibid., p. 335
Strapped for cash: *AIH*, p. 54
For several years: Barnouw, Vol. I,
p. 232
Zukor and other studio: Ibid.
Paley's account of his negotiations: *AIH*,
pp. 5–7; *TV/Radio Age*, March 12,
1979
"Spread like a monster blanket": WSP
speech in St. Louis, 1929
Zukor prevailed: Archer, p. 389;
Considine
There was one additional condition:
Agreement 6/13/29 between WSP
and Paramount Famous Lasky
Corporation; *AIH*, p. 59; Archer,
p. 389
Paramount would still control:
Columbia shareholders resolution,
10/15/29
other features of the agreement:
Agreement 6/13/29 between WSP
and Paramount; WSP and Columbia
employment contract, 8/21/29
"not the least bit self-conscious": *AIH*,
p. 57
"in a master combination": WSP speech
in St. Louis, 1929
"all our eggs": Considine

CHAPTER 6

Paley's salesmanship

He pandered to listeners: Barnouw,
Vol. I, pp. 239, 268; Bilby, p. 237
These were desperate times: *Since
Yesterday: The 1930s in America,*
Frederick Lewis Allen (New York,
1939), p. 58
By 1932 there were 12,546: Barnouw,
Vol. I, p. 239
Leading this eager exploitation:
Barnouw, Vol. I, p. 237, Vol. II,
p. 12
American Tobacco was NBC's: Bilby,
p. 241
But Paley's decorous rival: Barnouw,
Vol. I, p. 237; Bilby, p. 237
Seeing an opening: Bernays, p. 428
The thought of facing: confidential
source
"an ill-clothed scarecrow": *AIH*, p. 77
It took Paley several days: transcript of
David Halberstam int. with WSP
Whatever Hill wanted: Barnouw, Vol. I,
p. 237
NBC initially opposed: memo from Roy
C. Witmer, NBC executive, to
M. H. Aylesworth, 9/13/31

Crossley war

Back in 1930: Barnouw, Vol. I, p. 270
The results devastated CBS: *Look Now,
Pay Later: The Rise of Network
Broadcasting,* Laurence Bergreen
(New York, 1980), p. 60; *AIH,*
p. 104
"When it had been impossible":
confidential source
It was actually the invention: Considine;
Fortune (June 1935)
NBC executives cried foul: McClelland
memo to David Sarnoff, 9/19/31
The CBS survey was in fact: NBC
memo, 2/6/33

The Paramount buyback

The Price Waterhouse results: Bergreen,
p. 62
CBS profits from August 1929: letter
from Ralph Kohn, treasurer of
Paramount Publix Corporation, to
WSP, 1/6/32
At first Paramount: transcript of David
Halberstam int. with Ike Levy
Then Zukor made an offer: confidential
source
Enter Paley's well-connected friend:
Reminiscences of Prescott Bush,
Columbia University Oral History
Collection (July 1, 1966)
the ornate wood-paneled offices: *The
Wise Men: Six Friends and the World
They Made,* Walter Isaacson and
Evan Thomas (New York, 1986),
p. 111
Swope, who brokered the deal: E. J.
Kahn letter to SBS, 9/26/86
Paley's version of these events: *TV/Radio
Age,* March 12, 1979; *AIH,* p. 106

CBS Affiliate raids

In 1935 he plucked off: memo of
conversation between WSP and
Richard G. Patterson, Jr., of NBC,
4/15/35; NBC memo from Frank E.
Mason to Richard G. Patterson,
6/6/35
"a dapper fellow": confidential source
As a former Federal Radio
commissioner: Metz, p. 70;
Barnouw, Vol. I, p. 273
He also engaged in: Metz, p. 70;
confidential source
Paley did permit: Metz, p. 71
When Pickard's part ownership of
WOKO: Barnouw, Vol. I, p. 273n
In April 1935, Paley summoned: Metz,
p. 72
Richards was an unsavory character:
Barnouw, Vol. II, pp. 221–222

Ackerberg was to offer Richards: NBC
    memo, Frank E. Mason to Richard
    G. Patterson, 6/16/35
Richards agreed to the affiliation: Ibid.
In a conversation with Richard
    Patterson: Patterson memo of
    conversation, 4/15/35
He approached Powel Crosley, Jr:
    Barnouw, Vol. II, p. 130–131; NBC
    memo, Frank E. Mason to Richard
    G. Patterson, 6/6/35
Other key NBC stations: NBC memo,
    6/6/35
NBC ultimately headed off: Bergreen,
    p. 63
"Mr. Sarnoff, radio": NBC memo,
    6/6/35

Talent scout

His programming sense may well: *AIH*,
    p. 10
"I am not a highbrow": confidential
    source
"must appeal to either": John K.
    Hutchens, *Theater Arts* (November
    1943), p. 659
And at a party at the home: McClintick,
    Esquire (December 1983)
Often over the objections: Barnouw,
    Vol. I, p. 273

Paley and Bing Crosby

He sent a wire to CBS: WSP speech,
    January 20, 1958
Edward Klauber, Paley's second-in-
    command, wired back: confidential
    source
Crosby had a drinking problem: SBS int.
    with WSP
Paley overrode them all: WSP speech,
    January 20, 1958
"Crosby was awful": SBS int. with
    WSP; WSP speech, January 20,
    1958. Paley's account of this
    incident in his memoir reveals his

instinctive avoidance of any public
airing of messy personal
misconduct. He would only say that
"Crosby got off to a rather rocky
start at CBS, missing his own
opening show" (*AIH*, p. 74). But in
the privacy of luncheon and dinner
parties, Paley's account was much
more vivid, judgmental, and
detailed.

The first talent raids

The most popular programs: Barnouw,
    Vol. II, pp. 98–99
He captured Al Jolson: NBC memo,
    outstanding name talent switches,
    NBC to CBS, mid-1930s
While it was considered: NBC memo,
    Alfred Morton to Mark Woods,
    12/6/35
Although Paley thought the program
    "cruel": SBS int. with WSP
To cultivate the Major: Ibid.
"It was very important": confidential
    source
He always insisted: Barnouw, Vol. II,
    p. 95
"I think he liked": confidential source

CHAPTER 7

Dorothy and Bill meet

When he first saw Dorothy: *AIH*,
    p. 91
It was a suitably romantic: SBS int. with
    DPH

Dorothy Hart

Dorothy was born on: Biographical
    information about Dorothy Hart is
    drawn principally from a series of
    interviews between SBS and DPH

"Nothing took": SBS int. with DPH

"Dorothy's parents knew": SBS int. with IS

"One didn't think": SBS int. with DPH

"She was one of the most": SBS int. with IS

Dorothy and Jack Hearst

He captivated her: The story of Dorothy and Jack is based largely on interviews between SBS and DPH, as well as observations of those who knew them at the time

At a time when: *Citizen Hearst: A Biography of William Randolph Hearst,* W. A. Swanberg (New York, 1961), p. 386

While he didn't sweep her: In interviews with SBS, DPH provided the details of WSP's pursuit of her that were corroborated by others.

"I thought he dressed like": SBS int. with DPH

(a New York beauty): *Vogue* (April 1929)

"He got on that boat": SBS int. with IS

Ronald Tree, a friend: SBS int. with MaT

"a perfectly good lover": SBS int. with DPH

Bill and Dorothy marry

"I don't think my father": SBS int. with DPH

"It was not terribly easy": Ibid.

Part of the attraction: SBS int. with TMc

(Indeed, in his memoir): *AIH,* p. 91

Democratic politics

Both Dorothy and Bill had been: SBS ints. with DPH and WSP

"I can't imagine he would": SBS int. with DPH

"She would say": SBS int. with IS

She brought to Paley's attention: SBS ints. with DPH and Janet Murrow, widow of Edward R. Murrow

In those circles: *Only Yesterday,* Allen, pp. 81–82

Dorothy was drawn: SBS int. with DPH

Although he did the standard: SBS int. with DPH; *A Private View,* Irene Mayer Selznick (New York, 1983), p. 185

Art collecting

"He had no idea": SBS int. with DPH

"They were both eager": SBS int. with IS

Dorothy recalled taking him: The account of Paley's art acquisitions and dealings with artists that follows is based on SBS interviews with DPH, as well as WSP's recollections

In his memoir, Paley vividly: *AIH,* p. 96

"Everybody in the world has": Ibid., p. 100

"he fell ill": Ibid., p. 99

although he was never: SBS int. with DPH; confidential source

Bill's lifestyle

As a bachelor, he only managed: *Time* correspondent's file, 3/11/32

He smoked four packs: SBS int. with WSP

He was always running out: *Time* correspondent's file, 3/11/32

"There were lots of things": SBS int. with DPH

"It is not necessary": *New York Mirror,* March 30, 1941

Irene Selznick noted: Selznick, p. 185

29 Beekman Place

She got him out of his triplex: SBS int. with DPH

Paley supervised the architecture: SBS ints. with WSP and DPH "that crazy narrow": SBS int. with IS

One side of: The account of the interior of 29 Beekman Place is based on interviews with DPH, as well as the article by E. J. Kahn in *The New Yorker* called "At Home with the Paleys," January 7, 1939.

"it had no charm": SBS int. with WSP

485 Madison Avenue

She gave the boardroom: SBS int. with FS

"She has great roughnecks": ALM letter, 1/36

Dorothy's importance to Bill

"She was always ahead": SBS int. with IS

Bill Paley doted on: SBS ints. with IS and Helen Sioussat

"He was always very sweet": Metz, p. 33

He did, however, give her: SBS int. with DPH

Dorothy and her friends

Dorothy became a mentor: SBS int. with MaT

"She lavished knowledge": Selznick, p. 185

Warning signs

"There were warning signs": SBS int. with IS

"a very cute": SBS int. with Diana Vreeland, former editor-in-chief of *Vogue*

CHAPTER 8

Bill and Dorothy together

"There is no question": SBS int. with DPH

"At the first blush": DPH to Walter Wanger, 5/18/43

"he couldn't stop": SBS int. with MaT

"You could see them floating": SBS int. with IS

"He was eager": Ibid.

"For a kid who loved": *Esquire* (December 1983)

Paley and Selznick

Paley established a friendship: Berg, p. 247

"They had a lot in common": SBS int. with IS

"BILL As Seen by David O.": by David O. Selznick

The Paleys abroad

The Paleys widened: SBS int. with DPH

In England their friends: Ibid.; *Jock: The Life and Times of John Hay Whitney*, E. J. Kahn (Garden City, N.Y., 1981), p. 225

One day they were joined: SBS int. with Lord Norwich, son of Diana and Duff Cooper

The Paleys met a number: SBS int. with DPH

It was through Kommer: Ibid.; *Trumpets from the Steep*, Diana Cooper (London, 1960), p. 96

The north shore social set

Herbert Bayard Swope, an acknowledged: Kahn, p. 81

His thirty-room duplex: *Anything Goes: The Jazz Age Adventures of Neysa McMein and Her Extravagant Circle of*

Friends, Brian Gallagher (New York, 1987), p. 86

It began about a half-dozen miles: Ibid., p. 150

"all gall": *The Best in the World,* introduction by John K. Hutchens (New York, 1973), p. xix

"Age or social standing": Gallagher, p. 137

"I learned quickly": SBS int. with DPH

After his guests insisted: Gallagher, p. 171

His favorite partner: SBS int. with WSP

There was always a dizzying: Gallagher, p. 174

"could be counted on": ALM letter, 7/35

During a Swope New Year's Eve: ALM letter, 1/26/38

"I was just happy": *AIH,* p. 92

Sometimes the Swopes brought: ALM letter, 1/9/39

On Saturday nights, the crowd: SBS int. with DPH

"Swope had a curiously humanizing": SBS int. with DPH

Paley and Harriman

They had first become acquainted: WSP letter to FCC, 1932

Still, their friendship: SBS int. with DPH

It was held at Arden: Isaacson and Thomas, p. 44

"The house was so immense": ALM letter, 12/16/37

Averell employed: SBS int. with DPH

Dorothy Paley always brought: Ibid.

Heywood Broun, large and disheveled: ALM letter, 12/27/39; L. Morris, p. 166

And Robert Sherwood: Gallagher, pp. 60, 78; ALM letter, 12/27/39

One year the playwright: *Diana Cooper: The Biography of Lady Diana Cooper,* Philip Ziegler (London, 1981), p. 223

"nightmare weekend": Ibid., p. 223

Marie Harriman took an equally: ALM letter, 12/17/39

The Paleys at Kiluna

In 1938 the Paleys paid: SBS visit to Kiluna with DPH, 8/12/86

"like ten shingle farmhouses": *Time,* January 31, 1964

Although Paley always said: *AIH,* p. 90

He and Dorothy added: SBS visit to Kiluna with DPH

Kiluna, said Horace Kelland: SBS int. with HoK

At Paley's insistence: SBS int. with DPH

"My eyes were in my cheeks": SBS int. with MaT

After dinner on Saturday: SBS int. with DPH; *Time,* January 31, 1964

Twenty-two servants: SBS int. with DPH

In the afternoon there would: SBS int. with MaT

"The food wasn't very good": ALM letter, 1/9/39

"aspirin, witch-hazel": Cooper, p. 97

"This luxury taste": Ibid., p. 15

Years later Dorothy ascribed: SBS int. with DPH

"There was a lot of talk": Ibid.

Anti-Semitism

Otto Kahn, the investment banker: Gallagher, p. 135

"physically a little": Cooper, p. 16; Cooper, Ziegler, p. 222

Madeline Sherwood once recounted: ALM letter, 4/8/38

Jock Whitney

Whitney had invested: Kahn, p. 110

While Paley and Selznick had: SBS ints. with IS and DPH

Primarily through Selznick: SBS int. with IS

When the Selznicks came east: SBS int.
    with IS
"They were poles apart": Selznick,
    p. 185
"They were apples": SBS int. with IS

CHAPTER 9

Paley's thirty-fifth birthday

"one of the most dreadful": *Broadcasting*,
    March 12, 1979
As he later recounted: *Esquire* (December
    1983)
From 1929—: NBC internal memo on
    NBC-CBS income comparison,
    Lenox Lohr to Mark Woods,
    Broadcasting Yearbook, 1929–1946,
    12/28/36
From 1929 to 1936, NBC advertising:
    Archer, p. 335; *Time*, September 19,
    1938
"I thought he had": SBS int. with WSP
"When he made that decision": SBS int.
    with DPH
"Life was not meant to be devoted:
    Broadcasting, March 12, 1979
"I don't remember when": SBS int. with
    DPH

Edward Klauber

Bill Paley's first reaction: Bernays, p. 432
Klauber had drifted into: SBS ints. with
    JR and Jap Gude
"a perfectionist who took infinite": *New
    York Times*, September 24, 1954
Newsroom legend had it: Bernays,
    p. 434
The late hours of: Ibid., pp. 431–432
Only after Bernays praised: Ibid., p. 432;
    Metz, p. 38
Ralph Colin turned against him: David
    Halberstam int. with Ralph Colin

By 1936, he was being: *New York Times*,
    July 7, 1937
Klauber was proud of the salary: SBS
    int. with JR
Executives dreaded the summons: SBS
    int. with FS
Whenever the ringing began: SBS int.
    with Helen Sioussat
Although every executive: SBS int. with
    William Fineshriber
Klauber's few defenders: SBS int. with
    JR
"He was a just man": Lyman Bryson
    Reminiscences, Columbia
    University Oral History Collection
    (1951)
He insisted that Paley: SBS ints. with
    Helen Sioussat and Jap Gude
hired Frank Kizis: *Fortune* (June 1935)
Klauber streamlined CBS: Bernays,
    p. 432
An extra door connected: SBS int. with
    FS
Thus late in 1930: Bernays, p. 434
But soon afterwards: Metz, p. 40
"Ed was Paley's first": SBS int. with
    Doris Klauber Wechsler, widow of
    Ed Klauber
He checked Paley's recklessness: *Fortune*
    (June 1935)
"He was a stickler": Tom Shales int.
    with WSP, 3/6/79
"He had a Rock of Gibraltar": SBS int.
    with DPH

Paul Kesten

It was Klauber, not Paley: SBS int. with
    Jap Gude; Considine
His most famous display: SBS int. with
    FS
His apartment: Ibid.
Born in Milwaukee: "The Immaculate
    Mr. Kesten," Jack Gould, *New York
    Times*, November 4, 1945
"Elsie, set the head": SBS int. with FS

"His big asset": *Fortune* (June 1935)

Paley loved Kesten's cleverness: SBS int. with DPH

"Kesten had a feeling": *AIH,* p. 64

"He may just as readily": *New York Times,* November 4, 1945

"He was a strange man": SBS int. with DPH

Kesten had a proclivity: *New York Times,* November 4, 1945; SBS ints. with FS and Jap Gude

And he was known to drive: SBS int. with FS

He was sensitive and solicitous: Metz, pp. 50–56

"I am turning this": SBS int. with Helen Sioussat

With Paley, he was often: transcript of David Halberstam int. with DPH

Paley's executive persona

He was always nervous and tense: *Time* correspondent's file, 4/10/35

"Momentarily he can become": *Time* correspondent's file, 3/11/32

He still smoked four packs: SBS int. with WSP

He invariably had at least two: *Time* correspondent's file, 4/10/35

Yet in a crucial negotiation: Metz, p. 29; Lyman Bryson oral history

His days were so crowded: *Time* correspondent's file, 4/10/35

He wrote few memos: SBS int. with JR

He kept a radio going: *Time* correspondent's file, 3/11/32

He rarely left the office: SBS int. with DPH

Most nights Klauber performed: confidential source

Once Paley pressed Colin: *Time* correspondent's file, 4/10/35

"He has a peculiar manner": *New York Telegram,* December 24, 1930

Paley could show great patience: *Time* correspondent's file, 4/10/35

"He listened": Lyman Bryson oral history

"He never raised his voice": SBS int. with JR

And even when Paley finally: *Time* correspondent's file, 3/11/32

"In that way": *Time* correspondent's file, 4/10/35

Once when a CBS executive: Quincy Howe Reminiscences, Columbia University Oral History Collection (1962)

"When someone has prepared": *Time* correspondent's file, 4/10/35

If Paley was given: SBS int. with FS

He spent hours figuring: *Time* correspondent's file, 3/11/32

One month he would take up: *Time,* September 19, 1938

He became so enamored of: SBS int. with Helen Sioussat

"He has tremendous faith": *Time* correspondent's file, 3/11/32

He acquired imperial trappings: Lyman Bryson oral history

When Paley wanted to change: *Time* correspondent's file, 3/11/32

"He would never walk": Kaltenborn Reminiscences, p. 169

"He was away quite frequently": Ibid., p. 168

"There was never business": SBS int. with DPH

CHAPTER 10

Stanton arrives in New York

Frank Nicholas Stanton turned: Biographical material on Frank and Ruth Stanton is drawn primarily from a series of interviews with FS.

The Stantons had left: SBS int. with FS

Stanton's youth

He was born: *The New Yorker*, January 25, 1947; *Dayton Daily News*, May 23, 1966

"It was all I knew": SBS int. with FS

"banging his head": *Dayton Daily News*, May 23, 1966

"remarkably like Mickey Rooney": *The New Yorker*, January 25, 1947

While still in the primary: *New York Herald Tribune*, April 29, 1968

He drew posters: SBS int. with FS

He maintained an A — average: *The New Yorker*, January 25, 1947

"Frank always had to be": *Dayton Daily News*, May 23, 1966

"It is surprising": SBS int. with James Reston, *New York Times* columnist

As a neophyte member: *The New Yorker*, January 25, 1947

Once years later: *Time*, December 4, 1950

His industriousness took him: SBS int. with FS

His shaping experience: Ibid.

"A few people are born": *The New Yorker*, January 25, 1947

For all practical purposes: SBS int. with FS

Helen Stanton once remembered: *Dayton Daily News*, May 23, 1966

"My mother and father": SBS int. with FS

"My father was so busy": Ibid.

Stanton's independent spirit: Ibid.

He was also active: *The New Yorker*, January 25, 1947; SBS int. with FS

As a boy, Stanton was fascinated: SBS int. with FS

"It was a fork": Ibid.

In college

As editor of *Le Bijou: Variety*, April 4, 1973

enlisted his friend: *Time*, December 4, 1950

He produced dances: SBS int. with FS

He pioneered the use of: *Variety*, April 4, 1973; *New York Times*, June 25, 1971

"a pretty dull guy": SBS int. with FS

Stanton took up smoking (and rest of paragraph): Ibid.

Stanton had begun his studies: Ibid.

During the summer of 1929: Ibid.

In his junior year: Ibid.

He spent months cataloguing: *Broadcasting*, October 18, 1971

"gaudy paper": SBS int. with FS

Although he became known as: *Broadcasting*, October 18, 1971

After graduation

To pay bills: SBS int. with FS; *The New Yorker*, January 25, 1947

Shortly before their wedding: *Park East* (July 1951); SBS int. with FS

Frank Stanton would always regret: SBS int. with FS

Afterwards he could be seen dining: confidential source

Stanton grew more intrigued: *Printer's Ink*, November 28, 1958; *The New Yorker*, January 25, 1947

For his master's thesis: *The New Yorker*, January 25, 1947; FS talk, Gannett Center for Media Studies, 12/16/85

He wrote to NBC and CBS: *Broadcasting*, October 18, 1971

NBC sent a polite, perfunctory: FS talk, Gannett Center, 12/16/85

He tried to steer Stanton: *Printer's Ink*, November 28, 1958

"like a puppy": SBS int. with FS

Stanton focused on: *Broadcasting*, October 18, 1971

Inside the box: SBS int. with FS; *Park
East* (July 1951); *The New Yorker,*
January 25, 1947
After two years: SBS int. with FS
Stanton took his black box: Ibid.
The chief engineer: Goldmark, p. 38
The two men kept in close: SBS int.
with FS
CBS sent Stanton $100: *Printer's Ink,*
November 28, 1958; *The New
Yorker,* January 25, 1947
Kesten found this study: *Broadcasting,*
December 21, 1942; SBS int. with
FS
"The Sales Department used": FS talk,
Gannett Center, 12/16/85

CHAPTER 11

The regulators crack down

even broadcasters at the time:
Broadcasting, September 22, 1952
A new group called the National
Committee: Barnouw, Vol. II, p. 23

Paley faces Congress

On Friday, January 17, 1930: Hearings
Before the Committee on Interstate
Commerce, United States Senate,
on S6, A Bill to Provide for the
Regulation of the Transmission of
Intelligence by Wire or Wireless,
pp. 1783–1808
Paley's presentation was entirely:
Bernays, p. 432
In later years he would make: SBS int.
with AT
He made no revisions: SBS int. with
Edward Bernays; Bernays, p. 432
"I do not wish": Hearings transcript,
p. 1783
CBS had been able to: Ibid., p. 1784
programs like "Street and Smith":

Federal Radio Commission letter,
11/30
Instead, Paley kept repeating: Hearings
transcript, p. 1796
"it was the cheapest": Joan Burke int.
with WSP on CBS Radio, 8/19/77
Paley also catered to: Hearings transcript,
pp. 1784–1786
"very interested and": *Moguls: Inside the
Business of Show Business,* Michael
Pye (New York, 1980), pp. 98–99.

News programs and the CBS image

But on Inauguration Day: *AIH,* p. 119
"I recognized the importance": SBS int.
with Edward Bernays
"would depend to a considerable": *AIH,*
p. 118
They believed his assurances: Barnouw,
Vol. II, p. 23
"The public interest": Bernays, p. 433

The quality image

While NBC spent far more money: WSP
memo, 2/27/33
"Radio had so little appeal": Bernays, p. 434
Paley worked hard: *Time*
correspondent's file, 3/11/32
The enterprise also: Considine
"Out of this liaison": *Fortune* (June 1935)
Paley countered with "Piano Pointers":
Barnouw, Vol. I, p. 245; Abram
Chasins Reminiscences, Columbia
University Oral History Collection
(1950)
"It was a bitter blow": WSP speech,
11/20/58, Broadcast Pioneers
Luncheon, New York City
He could console himself: letter from Ed
Klauber to M. H. Aylesworth,
2/14/33; David Sarnoff
memorandum to RCA board, 2/33
"There was a twofold impetus": SBS
int. with William Fineshriber
By the mid-thirties they comprised:
AIH, pp. 113–114

New surge for reform

By the mid-thirties, a handful: Barnouw, Vol. II, pp. 16–17
As network commercialism: Barnouw, Vol. I, p. 243
As the political climate shifted: Ibid., p. 263; "And Now a Word from Our Sponsors: Commercialization of American Broadcast Radio, 1920–1934," Susan Smulyan, doctoral dissertation, Yale University, 1985, p. 238
James Rorty, a socialist: Barnouw, Vol. I, pp. 264–265
In 1933 the advocates: Ibid., Vol. II, pp. 22–24
This time he pleaded: Jack Gould, *New York Times,* November 4, 1945; *Broadcasting,* April 12, 1976
Working from speeches: SBS int. with Jap Gude

The CBS image takes shape

He enlisted his friend: SBS int. with FS
"smooth surfaces": "William Lescaze and CBS: A Case Study in Corporate Modernism," Dennis P. Doordan, Syracuse University, *Library Associates Courier* 19, no. 1 (Spring 1984)
"I realized that it was": "Conversation with the Chairman," *Columbine* magazine, CBS in-house publication (April 1983)
Kesten produced a stream: *Fortune* (June 1935); Metz, pp. 5–6; Victor Ratner report to CBS on radio and radio promotion, 11/46

Defeat of Wagner-Hatfield

In 1933, Paley hired: *Fortune* (June 1935)
"exactly what this amendment": CBS memorandum, 5/1/34
The Roosevelt White House: Barnouw, Vol. II, pp. 25–26; Smulyan, p. 230

The commission could strip stations: Smulyan, p. 232
"The FCC's licensing power": Barnouw, Vol. II, p. 29
The commission held pro forma: Digest of hearings, U.S. Federal Communications Commission Broadcast Division, October 1–20, November 7–12, 1934

CHAPTER 12

Paley makes good on his promises

"What I would like to know": Barnouw, Vol. I, p. 248; further details in the three paragraphs that follow from Ibid., Vols. I and II

CBS's clever publicity campaigns

Initially the competition: NBC memo, C. W. Horn to John Royal, 1/31/34
"In the past, Columbia": NBC memo, E. P. H. James to Richard C. Patterson, Jr., 11/34

The May 15, 1935, announcement

As late as May 13: letter from Fred Willis to M. H. Aylesworth, 5/13/35
There would be new time limits: CBS press release, 5/15/35
"No one in NBC should become": NBC memo, M. C. Witmer to Richard C. Patterson, Jr., 5/16/35
"Some ten-word commercials": NBC memo, Edgar Kobak to Richard C. Patterson, Jr., 5/17/35
"Let's not go 'sissy' ": Ibid.
As a result of the new: SBS int. with FS
NBC had decided to ban: NBC memo, M. H. Aylesworth to Henry K. Norton of RCA, 6/6/35; NBC

memo, Edgar Kobak to Henry K.
Norton, 6/6/35
NBC asked CBS to institute: NBC
memo, Edgar Kobak to Henry K.
Norton
"They got so many": Ibid.
"Columbia told the world": Ibid.
In fact, CBS's policy was even:
Barnouw, Vol. II, p. 61
Meanwhile, Senator Burton Wheeler:
NBC memo, A. L. Ashby to
Richard C. Patterson, Jr., 5/17/35
"it is apparent": NBC memo, M. H.
Aylesworth to Henry K. Norton,
6/6/35

NBC's frustration

By 1938, John Royal: Barnouw, Vol. II,
p. 70
"I cannot impress upon you": NBC
memo, John Royal to Fred Bate,
9/30/38
"I am certain that": letter from Niles
Trammell to Dr. James Angell,
5/29/39
"We simply cannot ignore": memo from
David Sarnoff to Lenox Lohr,
9/21/39

Culture war

In 1937, NBC launched a campaign:
Bilby, p. 236
CBS announced a series: Barnouw,
Vol. II, p. 70
"We didn't put it on": Bergreen,
pp. 91–92.

Paley-Sarnoff rivalry

In Paley's early years: AIH, p. 42
"He couldn't understand why women":
SBS int. with FS
In 1937, for example: NBC memo—
comparison between NBC and CBS
operations for 1937

Sarnoff was making $100,000: Bilby,
p. 129
Sarnoff's, paneled in white oak: Ibid.,
p. 111
He had bought a thirty-room: Ibid.,
p. 129
Although Sarnoff had the superior: SBS
ints. with DA and Edward Bernays
"He could not understand": SBS int.
with FS
Once, in the 1930s: Bilby, p. 176
A starched shirt: SBS int. with FS;
Barnouw, Vol. II, p. 70; Bilby,
p. 113
Many of those evenings he spent: Bilby,
p. 65
Sarnoff was harshly despotic: Ibid.,
p. 207
"There was no mistaking": SBS int.
with David Adams
His idea of relaxation: Bilby, pp. 236–
238
"If comedy is the center": SBS int. with
DA
"His outlook on life": Bilby, p. 238
When the actress Alice Faye: transcript of
David Halberstam int. with Jack
Gould
"He liked me very much": Pye, p. 108
Unlike Paley, Sarnoff talked: Bilby,
pp. 224–225
"To Sarnoff, Paley wanted to operate":
SBS int. with DA
When *Time* magazine: *Time*, September
19, 1938
"He thought Paley": SBS int. with DA

CBS goes public

A limited number of CBS shares:
Moody's Manual, 1936
By 1935 his share: AIH, p. 44; *Moody's
Manual*, 1936; letter from Edward
Klauber to FCC, 5/9/32
In 1936, investors drove: *Moody's
Manual*, 1937; CBS Proxy
Statement, 1940

In 1937, Paley held a meeting: SBS int. with JR
"The stock had already gotten": Ibid.
"You're out of step": Ibid.
But his views came clear: CBS Inc. Common Shares Outstanding Chart
Before that date, Paley sold off: *Moody's Manual,* 1938 (for information on stock split); CBS Proxy Statement, 1940
During the Depression years he took: memo from Mark Woods to Lenox Lohr, 2/26/40
He would say to friends: SBS ints. with Newton Minow, CBS Board member and former chairman of the FCC, and CB
"His desire for more profits": SBS int. with John A. Schneider, former president of CBS Broadcast Group
"He had a rapacious": confidential source

Purchase of CBS records

One day in December 1938: SBS int. with John Hammond; *John Hammond on Record,* John Hammond (New York, 1977), pp. 212–213
Since bailing out: Hammond, p. 214–216
In 1934, American Record bought: Ibid., p. 216
Yates had moved into: SBS int. with John Hammond
Levy got wind that: Isaac Levy autobiography, p. 15
He first approached: Ibid.; Metz, p. 152
Although he knew little: Isaac Levy autobiography, p. 15; *Wall Street Journal,* January 14, 1939
"I did the whole thing": Robert Lamb int. with WSP, 11/5/76
"I wanted to expand": Pye, p. 106
a criticism Paley even acknowledged: *AIH,* p. 330
"I devoted my life to keeping": SBS int. with FS

At Levy's suggestion: SBS int. with John Hammond
"He felt that Paley didn't really": Ibid.
"In August 1939": Hammond, pp. 217–218
"I asked him to do it": *AIH,* p. 331
"The price cut was Wallerstein": SBS int. with John Hammond

CHAPTER 13

Stanton's early days at CBS

"I was a bore": SBS int. with FS
There were 24 million radios: NBC report on FS talk, 1/31/36
"Dr. Stanton has developed": Ibid.
He felt underused: SBS int. with FS
"There was a period of nine months": Ibid.
MIT offered Stanton: *The New Yorker,* January 5, 1947

Stanton gets noticed

The FCC had done a survey: SBS int. with FS
Stanton appeared as CBS's star: *The New Yorker,* January 5, 1947
"By that time": SBS int. with FS
"brought respect to the flashy": Goldmark, p. 40
Everyone called Stanton "Doc": *Park East* (July 1951); *Broadcasting,* December 21, 1942
advertisers were bemused: FS talk, Gannett Center, 12/16/85
but Stanton showed them: *Printer's Ink,* November 28, 1958

Stanton becomes indispensable

"Most researchers": *Park East* (July 1951)
"Are you sure?": SBS int. with FS
"Every time management would ask": FS talk, Gannett Center, 12/16/85

"The question might have arisen": *The New Yorker,* January 5, 1947

When Stanton needed something: FS talk, Gannett Center, 12/16/85

The program analyzer

Stanton also developed: SBS int. with FS; *The New Yorker,* January 5, 1947

But when the mechanism was perfected: *The New Yorker,* January 5, 1947

"We used it and made a lot": SBS int. with FS

They could, for example, screen out: *The New Yorker,* January 5, 1947

Indeed, CBS found that: SBS int. with FS; *Printer's Ink,* January 28, 1958

"I guess I could have been": SBS int. with FS

Stanton's executive persona

"Swiss hotel clerk": Metz, p. 59

"a very neurotic": transcript of David Halberstam int. with Victor Ratner, former CBS promotion executive

"He had a real, good": SBS int. with Helen Sioussat

"No living man has ever": *Business Week,* July 4, 1970

Block programming

The station in that city: SBS int. with FS; FS talk, Gannett Center, 12/16/85

"He thought I was an idiot": SBS int. with FS

Stanton service to advertisers

"NBC was a sleepy organization": Ibid.

"I was enjoying myself": Ibid.

Stanton and Paley in early days

"He was very skeptical": FS talk, Gannett Center, 12/16/85

CHAPTER 14

Early days of CBS News

Instead, a half-dozen public: SBS ints. with Jap Gude and Blair Clark, former CBS News executive

An attentive listener could detect: Barnouw, Vol. I, p. 250

"Ed Klauber was an intolerant": Edward R. Murrow eulogy for Ed Klauber, 1954

Fairness and balance

By Paley's account: SBS int. with WSP; *Columbine* interview, 1983; *Christian Science Monitor,* May 11, 1977

"These guidelines were not": Morris Gelman int. with WSP

As early as the mid-1920s: "Fairness, The First Amendment and the Public Interest," by Diane S. Killory and Richard J. Bozzelli, *Gannett Center Journal* (Winter 1988), p. 67

Coughlin had been broadcasting: Barnouw, Vol. II, pp. 44–45

But the radio priest: *AIH,* p. 115; Barnouw, Vol. II, pp. 45–46

In April 1931, Paley had no choice: WSP speech to Broadcast Pioneers, 11/20/58; Barnouw, Vol. II, p. 46

"so long as we view": *New York Times* August 9, 1931

NBC had since its earliest days: David Sarnoff report to RCA Board, 1933

Editorializing by sponsors

"The gentlemen sitting": *Since Yesterday,* Allen, p. 233

"Voice of the Crusaders": Barnouw, Vol. II, pp. 14–15

In 1935 the "Ford Sunday Evening Hour": Ibid., pp. 34–35

Henry Ford, who had been fomenting:

Only Yesterday, Allen, p. 53;
    Barnouw, Vol. II, p. 34–35
"Send that Jew": Metz, p. 265
"Most sponsors did not want":
    Barnouw, Vol. II, p. 17
NBC's policy was even worse: SBS int.
    with MD
"a practice Murrow strongly objected
    to": SBS int. with BC

The Roosevelt administration

"I urge that the president": Stephen
    Early memo to Marvin Macintyre,
    secretary to FDR, 1/28/35
In January 1936, Roosevelt unveiled:
    New York Times, January 13 and 14,
    1936
Later that year: *New York Times,*
    October 19, 1936
"Now the public can see": Ibid.
"We had a big election party": Harry
    Butcher, CBS lobbyist, to Marvin
    Macintyre, 11/4/36

Early history of commentary

Boake Carter, for example, broadcast:
    Murrow: His Life and Times, A. M.
    Sperber (New York, 1986), p. 86
In 1936, at the age of fifty-eight:
    Barnouw, Vol. II, p. 74
Kaltenborn called the government: Ibid.,
    p. 76
Paley's initial tolerance: SBS int. with
    DPH
Paley had been burned: Barnouw, Vol.
    II, pp. 132–134
"wholly, honestly and militantly": "The
    American System of Broadcasting,"
    WSP, address to the Second
    National Conference on Educational
    Broadcasting, November 29, 1937

CBS versus the newspapers

The first was a fire: Considine; Metz,
    p. 42
"Paley feared that": Bernays, p. 429
Yet it wasn't until General Mills: Metz,
    p. 45

The CBS News Service

Klauber assigned the task: Considine;
    SBS int. with Jap Gude
White was a prototypical newspaperman:
    SBS int. with FS
"rather a quiet person": confidential
    source
"sensed radio's great opportunity":
    H. V. Kaltenborn reminiscence
Klauber trusted White: SBS int. with FS
Within a few months: *Fortune* (June 1935)
NBC, on the other hand: Barnouw,
    Vol. II, pp. 18–19, 101
Far more ominous was: *Fortune* (June
    1935)
That threat struck: Barnouw, Vol. II,
    p. 20

The Biltmore Agreement

In December 1933, after: Ibid., p. 21
"the man who had made": *Newsweek,*
    December 23, 1933
"virtually sabotaged": Barnouw, Vol. II,
    p. 20
Paley later rationalized: *AIH,* p. 129
"We held out": Morris Gelman int. with
    WSP; WSP speech, 11/20/58
The Biltmore Agreement fell: Barnouw,
    Vol. II, pp. 21–22

CHAPTER 15

Edward R. Murrow

"Even when Ed was telling": transcript
    of David Halberstam int. with ES
The women in his life: Sperber, p. 26
Murrow was an ambitious: Ibid., p. 20

"Neighbors remember when": transcript of David Halberstam int. with JM

After graduating from (and on): Sperber, pp. 29, 33, 36

He embraced Duggan's liberal: Ibid., p. 46

"intuitive poise": transcript of David Halberstam int. with Robert Landry, former writer for *Variety*

Willis was a foppish: SBS int. with FS

His estranged wife, Helen: Associated Press dispatch, August 1936; Alice Keith papers

Around CBS, Willis was known: SBS int. with FS

Murrow's sophistication: Sperber, p. 75

Since the infant CBS News Service: Ibid., p. 86

Paley admired CBS's new: *AIH*, p. 131; Sperber, p. 88

"She was very influential with": SBS int. with IS

"very observant": Ibid.

During the 1936 presidential: SBS int. with JR

"What are you trying": "William S. Paley—Mr. CBS," by Lewis W. Gillenson, *Look,* December 20, 1949

Indeed, when Frank Stanton went: SBS int. with FS

Murrow in London

Demand for radio news: *Since Yesterday,* Allen, p. 257

Observing the coming crisis: David Halberstam int. with JM

CBS's man in Europe: Sperber, p. 99

A former newspaper reporter: Barnouw, Vol. I, p. 247

Every Sunday at noon: SBS int. with Jap Gude

"Saerchinger was a dear": Ibid.

The head of programming: Barnouw, Vol. II, p. 76

In late February 1937: David Halberstam int. with JM

Paley did not at the time: *20th Century Journey: A Memoir of a Life and Times,* Vol II: *The Nightmare Years: 1930–1940,* William Shirer (New York, 1984), p. 284

Shirer was dismayed: Ibid., p. 286

"Dear to Paley's heart": Ibid., p. 286

The Anschluss

"for us to do the reporting": Ibid., pp. 284, 287

"the opposing team": Barnouw, Vol. II, p. 77

In the following hours: SBS int. with Robert Trout, longtime CBS correspondent

NBC's Jordan meanwhile had rushed: Sperber, p. 116

"Everything was upside down": Max Jordan memo to John F. Royal, 3/18/38

The World News Roundup

In bed with a fever: WSP speech, 11/20/58

"not only get the news": Ibid.

"out of necessity": SBS int. with WSP

"Paul said to me": SBS int. with Robert Trout

"Goddammit": Gelman int. with WSP

"With fine careless rapture": ES speech, Museum of Broadcasting tribute to Eric Sevareid, 2/22/88

Paley was elated: Shirer, p. 308

But he was unwilling: Sperber, p. 124; Shirer, p. 320

"Explain to Winston that": Shirer, p. 311

CBS's profits for the year: *Broadcasting,* September 22, 1952; NBC internal financial analysis

From CBS's Studio Nine: Sperber, p. 131; *Since Yesterday,* Allen, p. 315

"It is very obvious": NBC memo, John F. Royal to Lenox Lohr, 12/2/38

CBS builds a news organization

In mid-1939, Paley authorized: Barnouw, Vol. II, p. 139

"original, more reflective": Halberstam, p. 132

Most of them emulated: Barnouw, Vol. II, p. 150

"We've got a young fellow": SBS int. with ES

"From now on we will be sponsored": ES speech, 2/22/88

"It is completely separated": letter from H. V. Kaltenborn to William Shirer, 11/24/39

"My sponsor's sales": letter from H. V. Kaltenborn to Edward R. Murrow, 10/14/39

During the invasion: *AIH,* p. 134

Journalist Quincy Howe: Quincy Howe oral history, p. 91

Paley permitted newscasts: NBC memo, A. A. Schecter to Niles Trammell, 10/30/39

"He had a real instinct": SBS int. with DPH

His refurbished newsroom: Sperber, pp. 82, 86

Now that CBS News had a staff: *Report on Blacklisting,* Vol. II, *Radio–Television,* John Cogley (Washington, D.C.: The Fund for the Republic, 1956)

The CBS ban on recordings

The rule was designed: SBS ints. with WSP and BC

"In order to broadcast": Shirer, p. 322

In so doing, they followed: Barnouw, Vol. II, pp. 74–75

Murrow's talent

"He was a natural": *Broadcasting,* April 12, 1976

"The strongest impression": Murrow broadcast, 8/25/40

"There were no nerves": Murrow broadcast, 6/2/40

Murrow was known for: Sperber, p. 163; Murrow broadcast, 8/24/40

"There is still a sense of humor": Murrow broadcast, 3/9/41

Night after night he elegantly: Barnouw, Vol. II, pp. 140–141

"His job would have made him": David Halberstam int. with Robert Landry

Murrow and Paley

He had a history of ingratiating: David Halberstam int. with JM; David Halberstam int. with Robert Landry

"You could talk with Ed": David Halberstam int. with Robert Landry

"Even at the peak": David Halberstam int. with ES

"a kind of biting": David Halberstam int. with BC

CHAPTER 16

Paley and Lady Mary

On the balmy evening of July 13, 1937: The description of this evening and the events that follow is based on several interviews between SBS and Lady Mary Dunn, drawn from her diary entries for 1937

Mrs. Corrigan, a wealthy American: *"In Society": The Brideshead Years,* Nicholas Courtney (London, 1986), pp. 105–109

"kin to everybody fine": confidential source

Dorothy, uninterested in gambling: SBS int. with DPH

Cracks in the marriage

"just another distinguished": Zsa Zsa
    Gabor interview, *USA Today,*
    February 6, 1987
When Dorothy corrected him: transcript
    of David Halberstam int. with IS
"She has developed the most": ALM
    letter, summer 1937
"Dorothy may have been": SBS int.
    with MaT
"Dorothy has become": ALM letter,
    7/38
All decisions about (and details in the
    next three paragraphs): SBS int.
    with DPH

Children and other problems

"Dorothy Paley and": ALM letter,
    summer 1937
Paley was an indifferent father: SBS int.
    with DPH
She tended to be severe: Cooper,
    Ziegler, p. 208
Yet she felt strongly: SBS int. with MaT
In 1940, Paley selected: SBS int. with
    DPH
"I never behaved as if": Ibid.
"wore her brains": SBS int. with
    Leonora Hornblow, friend of the
    Paleys
"If Dorothy were there": SBS int. with
    DPH
Once at a party: Ibid.
"She spoke her mind": confidential
    source
"She would say no, no": SBS int. with
    IS
"Dorothy went on and on": SBS int.
    with Helen Sioussat
"It goes beyond her": confidential source
"She understood him better":
    confidential source

Paley's jealousy

Even as he was philandering: SBS int.
    with DPH
"He was always a hundred percent
    wrong": Ibid.

The 1940 Suicide

On March 8, 1940, a woman: Associated
    Press, 3/8/40
She wore a gray dress: United Press,
    3/8/40
"Dearest Bill . . .": Associated Press,
    3/8/40
First, he went home: SBS int. with DPH
"He was dreadfully upset": Ibid.
"Darling," she wrote: United Press,
    3/8/40
Klauber hurried over: SBS int. with
    DPH
In a statement: *New York Times,* March
    9, 1940
"never saw so many": SBS int. with FS
"the first—she would not": letter from
    Niles Trammell to Edwin Craig,
    3/15/40

Paley's womanizing

"He was so happy": SBS int. with DPH
"I don't know how tortured": SBS int.
    with IS
Mostly he went for classic: SBS int. with
    DPH
The Paleys never had: SBS ints. with LH
    and HoK
"I did confront him": SBS int. with
    DPH

CHAPTER 17

Facing up to television

"It is hard to tell": WSP address in St.
    Louis, 1929
"Man is a social": *New York Times,*
    September 22, 1929

Sarnoff as television pioneer

"the ultimate and greatest": Bilby,
    p. 117
At his urging, in 1928: David Adams
    report to NBC, 2/21/79
Sarnoff was dissatisfied: Goldmark, p. 25
He hired an émigré: Barnouw, Vol. II,
    p. 38
Significantly, Bill Paley was not:
    confidential source

CBS early maneuvers

"Sarnoff at RCA": Goldmark, p. 41
Only later did Goldmark learn: Ibid.,
    p. 46
"bigger and better": Ibid., p. 50
"The urge to beat RCA": Ibid.

Paley and Sarnoff at odds over television

"Television is like eating": SBS int. with
    JR
With encouragement from Klauber: *New
    York Times,* June 17, 1936
The federal regulators accepted: Bilby,
    p. 125
The FCC's caution infuriated: Ibid.,
    p. 126

RCA forges ahead

In April 1939, NBC began: Barnouw,
    Vol. II, p. 125
Consumers began buying: Ibid.; Bilby,
    p. 133

CBS makes a halfhearted effort

To cut costs, CBS concentrated:
    Goldmark, p. 47
Gilbert Seldes, the prominent: Ibid.,
    p. 51
By the early 1940s, some thirty staffers:
    letter from JR to the FCC, 10/20/44
"Before the war we did": SBS int. with
    FS

Commercial television begins

Its chairman, Lawrence Fly: Bilby,
    p. 135
But after some pressure from Congress:
    Goldmark, p. 53; Bilby, p. 137
By then even Paley: Goldmark, p. 53
In mid-1942, NBC and CBS: CBS
    Report to FCC, 12/42
Paley, who was still fearful: SBS int.
    with FS

CBS ratings

"It was a great frustration": Ibid.
As the nation went to: Barnouw,
    Vol. II, p. 165
With plenty of sponsors: Victor Ratner
    report to CBS on radio promotion,
    11/46
The advertising agencies now made:
    Barnouw, Vol. I, p. 239

Battles with commentators

"subtle, guarded advocacy": Sperber,
    p. 74
"Just don't be so": Kaltenborn address to
    the public relations and news
    committee of the National
    Association of Broadcasters,
    September 15, 1943
"I find myself going off": letter from
    H. V. Kaltenborn to Edward R.
    Murrow, 10/14/39
"the inescapable fact": letter from James
    F. Bell to H. V. Kaltenborn, 3/8/39
Roosevelt dispatched: Goldmark, p. 45
In this tense atmosphere: Barnouw,
    Vol. II, p. 125; Paul White memo,
    5/1/39
The pressure on American: *New York
    Times,* September 8, 1939
"to help the listener": Cogley, p. 71
"a kind of neutrality law": Barnouw,
    Vol. II, p. 137

"Paley understood the power": SBS int.
    with ES
"furtherest limbward": Barnouw,
    Vol. II, p. 149

Kaltenborn's departure

Pure Oil's sales were: letter from H. V.
    Kaltenborn to Edward R. Murrow,
    10/14/39
Yet late in 1939: letter from H. V.
    Kaltenborn to Karl Mundt,
    Republican congressman from
    South Dakota, 6/12/40
"due to the fact that": letter from Karl
    Mundt to Lenox Lohr, president of
    NBC, 6/5/40
"We too have enjoyed": letter from WSP
    to H. V. Kaltenborn, 5/9/40

Elmer Davis difficulties

Elmer Davis grew to be: SBS int. with
    FS
"get too much viewpoint": David
    Halberstam int. with WSP
"Once every three or four": Robert
    Lamb int. with WSP, 11/5/76
But the problems with Davis: SBS int.
    with FS

Murrow's opinions

"The course of Anglo-American":
    *Edward R. Murrow Remembers: The
    War Years,* audio cassette courtesy of
    FWF; 3/9/41 ERM broadcast
"along the banks": *New York Times,*
    December 3, 1941
Top network executives: Barnouw,
    Vol. II, p. 162
CBS Radio playwright: Sperber, pp.
    213–214; SBS int. with CBS Radio
    playwright Norman Corwin
Under the supervision of: William

Fineshriber Reminiscence, Broadcast
    Pioneers Oral History Project, p. 72
Even the highly rated Hummert:
    Barnouw, Vol. II, p. 162

Open Letter on Race Hatred

In the summer of 1943: Barnouw,
    Vol. II, p. 181
"I have a report": Ibid., p. 182
Still, Paley took: Ibid., pp. 182–183

Cecil Brown Dispute

"failing to dramatize": *New York Times,*
    September 23, 1943
"that would be of immense": *PM,*
    September 23, 1943
"some very valuable contributions":
    Brown statement, 9/22/43
There the matter might; *PM,* September
    21, 1943
"making a bid for": *New York Post,*
    September 22, 1943
"News policy as enunciated": Brown
    statement, 9/22/43
Newspaper columnists at: Max Lerner,
    PM, September 22, 1943; Dorothy
    Thompson, *New York Post,*
    September 27, 1943

The network monopoly report

From the start (and on in this section):
    "The Red and the Blue,"
    unpublished manuscript by Sally Fly
    Connell
Fly, tall and lanky: SBS int. with FS;
    Barnouw, Vol. II, p. 173
A special three-man: letter from James
    Fly to WSP, 5/9/41
"tool of democracy": *Broadcasting,* April
    15, 1938
By early 1940: Stephen Early, White
    House Reminder, 1/26/40
RCA officials planted: letter from James

Fly to FDR, 6/15/40; Barnouw,
Vol. II, p. 173

"Few things have meant": letter from
WSP to FDR, 11/8/40

"are prepared to seek": letter from James
Fly to FDR, 12/23/40

The following March: letter from James
Fly to General Watson, 3/13/41

But Roosevelt balked: Stephen Early
memo to General Watson, 3/15/41

meet in mid-April: Connell, p. 7; Sally
Fly Connell interview with Joseph
Rauh, then assistant general counsel
of the FCC, 7/16/67

Word of the White House: *Variety*,
March 26, 1941

On a Saturday morning: CBS statement,
5/5/41

"I'm sorry": Connell, p. 9

Publicly, Paley charged: *New York Herald
Tribune*, May 4, 1941

Privately, he wired: WSP telegram to
FDR, 5/5/41

He said the FCC had no legal: *New York
Herald Tribune*, May 4, 1941; *New
York Journal of Commerce*, May 20,
1941

"I fought like a steer": transcript of Don
West int. with WSP (October 1976)

But Paley made two ill-conceived: WSP
Testimony Before United States
Senate Committee on Interstate and
Foreign Commerce, 6/16/41: "Why
We Need a New Radio Law"

In fact, it was Klauber: SBS int. with JR

The hearings were confrontational:
Connell, pp. 13–14

Even worse, Paley proved: SBS int. with
FS

Over the summer of 1941: SBS int. with
Telford Taylor, then general counsel
of the FCC

Instead of eliminating: Barnouw, Vol. II,
p. 171

That autumn the FCC: Fly statement,
10/11/41; Supplemental Report on

Chain Broadcasting by the FCC,
10/11/41

Two weeks later the networks: *New York
Times*, October 31, 1941

The following January: *New York Times*,
January 1, 1942

Toward the end of 1941: Barnouw, Vol.
II, pp. 173–174; *Radio Daily*,
January 29, 1942

Throughout 1942: Connell, pp. 1, 16;
WSP Testimony Before the House
Committee on Interstate and
Foreign Commerce, 5/6/42

It was an unprecedented: Barnouw, Vol.
II, pp. 173–174

Then a vigilant FCC: Ibid., pp. 175, 178

He bitterly disliked: SBS int. with FS

"we were pretty good": Pye, p. 119

"Although we had": letter from WSP to
Sally Fly Connell, 11/28/67

"it delighted Columbia": *Time*, April 18,
1938

Firing of Klauber

Much as he hated: WSP Testimony
Before the House Committee on
Interstate and Foreign Commerce,
5/6/42

Klauber had virtually no: SBS int. with
FS

Most evenings, after dropping:
confidential source

Yet Klauber and Paley dined:
confidential source

"Klauber had a facile": confidential
source

"You've got to get rid": Sperber, p. 224

"He's evil": David Halberstam int. with
Ralph Colin

Nor could Klauber abide: SBS int. with
FS

"If you wanted to walk": Ibid.

That March Paley: CBS Proxy
Statement, 1943, p. 3

The next day: *New York Times*, August
6, 1943

After Klauber left: confidential source
too "possessive": SBS int. with WSP
"I gave my life": SBS int. with FS

CHAPTER 18

Trip to South America

Since the expansion of CBS: *AIH*, p. 141
even arranging for tutors: SBS int. with
Helen Sioussat
"many of the lesser": letter from WSP to
FDR, 10/29/40
"the most beautiful contracts":
confidential source

Paley's Latin network

Network activities: William Fineshriber
oral history
The thirty-two-year-old Standard: *AIH*,
p. 141; SBS int. with DPH
"An event of no small": *AIH*, p. 141
CBS reaped a publicity: William
Fineshriber oral history
"We are far too prone": *Fortune* (April
1941)
Paley had taken an NBC idea: *Newsweek*,
June 1, 1942; NBC memo, Mark
Woods to Frank Mullen, 1/8/41;
NBC memo, John Royal to Niles
Trammell, 1/30/41
In South America itself: *PM*, article by
Ray Joseph, January 23, 1941
"Our artists don't realize": Ibid.
"We did not slant": SBS int. with
William Fineshriber

Paley's brush with government consulting

In January 1941: Paper, p. 82
Less than a year later: Lyman Bryson
oral history; confidential source
indeed, it was done entirely: SBS int.
with FS

Paley to England, August 1942

Since the beginning: Barnouw, Vol. II,
pp. 155–156
Paley says it was pure: SBS int. with
WSP
Whitney had also worked: Kahn, pp.
135, 141
"I got the feeling": confidential source
He worried that Eisenhower: confidential
source
"Bill much thrilled": *My Three Years
with Eisenhower: The Personal Diary
of Captain Harry C. Butcher, USNR,
Naval Aide to General Eisenhower,
1942–1945*, Harry C. Butcher (New
York, 1946), p. 77
"He was one of the most": confidential
source
giving the CBS chief: confidential source
Murrow put on a big: Butcher, p. 105
and brought him around: SBS int. with
Norman Corwin, CBS radio
dramatist
Duff and Diana Cooper: confidential
source
Paley's enduring memory: *AIH*,
pp. 148–149
Lady Mary Dunn: SBS int. with LMD
"Nancy Tree had the": confidential
source
"I think I learned": transcript of Marie
Brenner int. with WSP
The closest Paley came: SBS int. with
Norman Corwin

Paley gets his post

to "defeat and dispel": WSP broadcast,
9/19/42
The general took the: confidential source
"no matter how important": Butcher,
p. 115
But his visit to London: Ibid.
Even nearsighted: Selznick, p. 241
"Don't be an idiot": SBS int. with DPH
He called on his old friend: Ibid.

"is interested in working": OWI
    headquarters memo to Barnes,
    McClure, Hazeltine, and Jackson,
    9/12/43
"What are we going to do": SBS int.
    with Simon Michael Bessie,
    publishing executive
"Send Paley airborne": C. D. Jackson
    memo to Sherwood, Barnes, and
    Barnard, 9/14/43
"freewheeling radio hotshot": C. D.
    Jackson memo to Sherwood,
    Barnes, and Hamblet, 10/9/43
"understands thoroughly": Robert
    Sherwood, memo to Hazeltine and
    Jackson, 10/16/43
"Feel strong": C. D. Jackson memo to
    Sherwood, 10/17/43
For one week in November: *Time,*
    November 22, 1943
bespoke uniforms: SBS int. with W.
    Phillips Davison, wartime colleague
    of WSP

CHAPTER 19

Algiers

To reach Algiers: confidential source
"lush, strange charm": confidential
    source
They nicknamed the house: SBS int.
    with Edward Barrett, former editor
    of *Newsweek* and OWI deputy
At OWI headquarters: SBS int. with Peg
    Pollard Finn, Paley's administrative
    aide in Algiers
Jackson assigned him: letter from C. D.
    Jackson to Hamilton Smith,
    11/28/43
His new colleagues found him: SBS ints.
    with Edward Barrett and Michael
    Bessie

Paley had been in Algiers: D. H.
    Schneider memo to C. D. Jackson,
    11/27/43
"Of Bill Paley's competence": letter
    from C. D. Jackson to Hamilton
    Smith, 11/28/43
He worked with the head: D. H.
    Schneider memo, 1/24/44
Returning to Algiers: D. H. Schneider
    report from Radio Section PWB,
    Algiers, 2/14/44
"I hope you will find it possible": memo
    from C. D. Jackson to WSP,
    1/27/44
He was not only meeting with: SBS int.
    with Peg Pollard Finn
"Think might be interested": Minutes of
    CBS affiliates advisory board,
    1/24/25
She was a pretty blonde (and the three
    following paragraphs): SBS ints.
    with Peg Pollard Finn, TMc, and
    Michael Bessie

Working in London

Shortly after Paley's arrival: SBS int.
    with Guy Della Cioppa, wartime
    aide and later CBS executive
A week later: memo from WSP to
    C. D. Jackson, 2/7/44
His first appointment: Davidson Taylor
    Reminiscences, Columbia
    University Oral History Collection
    (1967); OWI history—ABSIE file
dragooned an old friend: SBS int. with
    Stuart Scheftel
"He had a sort of mystique": SBS int.
    with W. Phillips Davison
"Straighten out with Phil Hamblet":
    memo from C. D. Jackson to WSP,
    2/12/44
Paley not only complied: memo from
    WSP to C. D. Jackson, 2/14/44
"He used his power effectively": SBS
    int. with Guy Della Cioppa

Although all planning: letter from
 Brendan Bracken to WSP, 2/27/44
While he understood: memo from WSP
 to C. D. Jackson, 2/7/44
"Radio broadcasting is an arm": memo
 from WSP to Brendan Bracken,
 2/11/44
A week later Bracken: memo from
 Brendan Bracken to WSP, 2/17/44
"in the light of the small": letter from
 WSP to John G. Winant, 2/24/44
"quite a coup": *AIH*, p. 158
Paley grew impatient: memo from C. D.
 Jackson to Robert McClure, 3/6/44
He proposed that a separate: memo from
 WSP to C. D. Jackson 2/17/44
"They have all been selected": memo
 from C. D. Jackson to Gen. Robert
 A. McClure, 3/6/44
Paley was involved in both: Davidson
 Taylor Reminiscence (1967)
No stranger to the art: *AIH*, pp. 157–
 158
He worked closely with: SBS int. with
 Nathan Halpern, wartime aide
"One of the basic": confidential source
Paley oversaw a series: Barnouw,
 Vol. II, p. 198
As Paley recalled it: *AIH*, pp. 158–159

Paley and Sarnoff

He asked for the best: Bilby, p. 143
His pleasure in his new surroundings:
 Barnouw, Vol. II, p. 198; *Star
 Spangled Radio*, Edward M. Kirby
 and Jack W. Harris (Chicago, 1948),
 pp. 244–245
The next day Sarnoff met: Bilby, p. 144
Like Paley, Sarnoff proposed: Ibid.,
 pp. 145–146
"Paley objected strongly": *Sarnoff: An
 American Success*, Carl Dreher (New
 York, 1977), p. 155
"They were really going": confidential
 source; Dreher, p. 155

CHAPTER 20

Playing in London

Off duty, "Colonel" Paley: SBS int.
 with LMD; confidential source
His personal valet was: SBS int. with
 Stuart Scheftel
In later years Paley would insist: SBS int.
 with WSP; Marie Brenner int. with
 WSP
Curiously, not even his: confidential
 sources
nor could Sherwood's widow: SBS int.
 with Madeline Sherwood, widow of
 Robert Sherwood
Paley could choose: Claridge's menu,
 Dimanche, 25 Juillet 1943; Causier
 menu, 1944
"He was floating around": confidential
 source
"Everything that happened that night":
 Marie Brenner int. with WSP
Paley made it a point: SBS int. with
 Stuart Scheftel
"It was interesting to find out": SBS int.
 with WSP
Tommy Hitchcock, the famous: Kahn,
 p. 86
Whitney, who had been: Ibid., p. 152
"He was easy, warm": SBS int. with
 Michael Bessie
"Bill and Ed met frequently": SBS int.
 with JM

Wartime loves

"a romantic place": Marie Brenner int.
 with WSP
Pamela Churchill, by then all of twenty-
 four: "The Prime of Pamela
 Harriman," Marie Brenner, *Vanity
 Fair*, July 1988
"Unless you were a": SBS int. with JM
"Pamela's parties were": Marie Brenner
 int. with WSP

They had a short-lived: confidential
sources; SBS int. with Slim Keith, a
close friend of the Paleys; Pamela
Harriman declined to discuss WSP
(Pamela Harriman letter to SBS,
10/28/86)
"I never discuss": confidential source
Lady Mary Dunn had: SBS int. with
LMD
"Very few people really": SBS int. with
Richard Holbrooke, former under
secretary of state
After Paley, she flitted: Brenner, *Vanity
Fair* (July 1988)
Paley meanwhile had hooked up: SBS
int. with TMc
"Cheer up": SBS int. with Janet
Morgan, biographer of Edwina
Mountbatten
"She wasn't in love": SBS int. with
Stuart Scheftel
"Highly intelligent without being":
Mountbatten, Philip Ziegler (New
York, 1985), p. 66
Late at night they could be: SBS int.
with Sidney Bernstein, chairman of
Granada Television
Given Paley's high profile: SBS int. with
Stuart Scheftel
later, after returning: SBS int. with Janet
Morgan
In London he began: confidential sources
"I always felt": confidential source
"well educated and quite pretty":
confidential source
"because he loved": confidential source
"a sex object": confidential source

Paley returns home

"was no longer a success": *AIH,* p. 162
"had not been a success": confidential
source
"He didn't know": SBS int. with DPH

CHAPTER 21

Paley in Paris

He also had the use: WSP int with SBS
"I could live in great": Ibid.
"All the girls were": Marie Brenner int.
with WSP
He continued to supervise: Barnouw,
Vol. II, pp. 201–203; Butcher
Diary, 10/29/44
And he was put in charge: Marie
Brenner int. with WSP
Paley's unit worked: SBS ints. with Guy
Della Cioppa and Michael Bessie
"He didn't make": SBS int. with Phillips
Davison
"Bill Paley as chief": memo from
Tommy Thompson to Edward
Barrett, 2/15/45
As civilians, Paley: C. D. Jackson,
"History of Psychological Warfare,"
unpublished manuscript, p. 4
Paley said he balked: confidential source
"I need not tell": note from Edward
Barrett to WSP, 3/14/45
"Bonjour, Col-o-nel Paley": SBS int.
with Michael Bessie
Paley expressed his: transcript of David
Halberstam int. with William Shirer

Breakdown

Shortly after receiving: SBS int. with
Edward Barrett; *AIH,* p. 167
In his hypochondriacal: SBS int.
with DPH
"Were the pressures": Ibid.
"Bill Paley reports": letter from Tommy
Thompson to Ed Barrett, 2/15/45

Germany

The next day: Marie Brenner int.
with WSP
Murrow's broadcasts: Barnouw, Vol. II,
p. 205

"a terrible trauma": Marie Brenner int. with WSP

Years later Paley vividly: Ibid.; SBS int. with Kim LeMasters

"I had seven people": Marie Brenner int. with WSP

Paley had witnessed only one: Ibid.

The Psychological Warfare Division settled: SBS ints. with Billy Wilder, film director, and Guy Della Cioppa

"I was running a far bigger": *TV Guide,* January 5, 1963

Each day he would assemble: SBS ints. with Phillips Davison and Guy Della Cioppa

"I was impressed": SBS int. with Phillips Davison

He voiced surprise when: Ibid.

With Billy Wilder: SBS int. with Billy Wilder

Marian, Paley's secretary and lover: confidential source

"Oh no": confidential source

he would remain loyal: confidential source

"The woman I fell madly": confidential sources

The effects of war

"life had never been": Paper, p. 88

Two experienced psychologists: confidential sources

Those who came to know: SBS ints. with Michael Bessie and Phillips Davison

"weren't so stupid": Marie Brenner int. with WSP

CHAPTER 22

Paley's unsettling return to New York

"He was still recovering": SBS int. with DPH

The first step, he decided: *AIH,* p. 172

Selznick's zest bolstered: confidential source; *AIH,* p. 176

Back in New York: SBS int. with FS

"carrying on": SBS int. with DPH

"Do you think I was surprised?": Ibid.

"Anatole was the kindest": Ibid.

"I don't care what you do": SBS int. with IS

"The show I want": Ibid.

The night of the Paley breakup

"You'd better dress warmly" (and the next paragraph): Ibid.

"I can't remember": SBS int. with DPH

"Oh, he used it against me": Ibid.

"She was tough as hell": SBS int. with IS

Paley on the loose

Under the ownership: "The Golden Spoon," by Jack Alexander, *The New Yorker,* May 12, 1938

On a yachting trip: SBS int. with SK

"He was funny": Ibid.

Elmer Davis and Kesten

"I knew the whole thing": SBS int. with Guy Della Cioppa

When Elmer Davis decided: SBS int. with Jap Gude

"Don't bother": Ibid.

"You know, Bill Paley": Ibid.

Paley offers the presidency to Kesten

While abroad he had: *AIH,* p. 175

"I found out that the poor": *Broadcasting,* April 12, 1976

only two months after: *New York Times,* November 4, 1945

Indeed, Kesten would continue: letter from Paul Kesten to Frank Stanton, 8/14/56

Kesten had decided: SBS int. with FS

Kesten and Stanton running CBS

Kesten oversaw programming: *Time,* December 4, 1950
Fully two thirds: Barnouw, Vol. II, p. 214
The two executives: SBS int. with FS

Paley and Kesten plans for the network

Corwin, William N. Robson: Barnouw, Vol. II, p. 214
"Perhaps it will strike you": *AIH,* p. 173
"giving up the fight": Ibid.
In the summer of 1945: SBS int. with FS
"Since Paul and I shared": Ibid.

Kesten recommends Stanton for presidency

At a welcome home: The account of Paley's overture to Stanton is based primarily on interviews with FS, as well as *Printer's Ink,* November 28, 1958, and *Broadcasting,* December 5, 1958
"I got the impression": SBS int. with Stuart Scheftel
"Don't you want it?": *Broadcasting,* December 5, 1958
"Don't pin me down": SBS int. with FS
The following Monday: Ibid.
The fact was, he admitted: Ibid.
"I was all dressed up": Ibid.
"I didn't know what": FS talk, Gannett Center, December 16, 1985
Then, on Christmas Eve (and paragraphs that follow): SBS int. with FS; *Printer's Ink,* November 28, 1958
Curiously, Paley would later: *AIH,* p. 178

The 1946 CBS Annual Meeting

"Are you all set?": SBS ints. with FS and JR
He realized that Bill Paley: SBS int. with FS

CHAPTER 23

Babe

"Mrs. Mortimer Jr. heads": *New York Daily News,* January 21, 1945

The Cushing Family

It stood for "Baby": SBS int. with LH
It was Minnie who named her: SBS int. with Betsey Cushing Whitney
The youngest of ten children: *Harvey Cushing: A Biography,* John F. Fulton (Springfield, Ill., 1946), pp. vii, 12
Dr. Kirke, as Harvey's father: *Harvey Cushing: Surgeon, Author, Artist,* Elizabeth H. Thomson (New York, 1981) p. 7
But he saw a promising spark: Fulton, p. 25
A small and fiercely determined: Ibid., pp. 27, 40
He sequestered himself: Ibid., pp. 80, 59

Harvey and Kate's courtship

Still, he found time to court (and further details): Ibid., pp. 63, 144
she had been educated: Thomson, p. 37
"entered easily into all": Fulton, p. 145
With the erect carriage and mien: "Why Leave Harvard to Go to Yale? Cushing's Odyssey," by Charles Snyder, *Neuro-ophthalmology,* Vol. 10 (New York, 1980) p. 130
"The prolonged courtship": Fulton, p. 144

Harvey Cushing's career

His brief periods of spare time: Thomson, p. 178; Fulton, p. 355
Cushing seldom socialized: Snyder, p. 132
although he often invited: SBS int. with

William Cushing, grandson of Harvey Cushing

where he delivered long, hypnotic: *A Surgeon's Odyssey,* Loyal Davis (Garden City, N.Y., 1973), p. 141

Throughout his energetic career: Fulton, p. 616; Snyder, p. 133

Wearing tennis shoes for comfort: Davis, p. 136

his legs throbbing: Fulton, p. 520

When he began operating: Snyder, p. 133

"the pivot around which we all": SBS int. with BCW

yet when Harvey Cushing heard: Snyder, p. 134

Cushing's colleagues only learned: Fulton, p. 534

"Perfectionism," said Betsey, "was drummed into": SBS int. with BCW

He usually visited them only two: Thomson, p. 156

"She has gone to bed": SBS int. with BCW

Gogs Cushing

"One day you will be": Ibid.

was bright, able, and determined: Ibid.

"Just as Harvey was": Fulton, p. 373

Harvey was undemonstrative: SBS int. with Elizabeth Yew, medical historian

Formal social functions: Fulton, p. 355

Harvey was penurious: Ibid., p. 38

Kate took to smoking cigarettes: Ibid., p. 373

"That," said her grandson: SBS int. with William Cushing

"Mrs. Cushing had a strong nature": Thomson, p. 217

"you didn't seem to need us": letter from Kate Cushing to Harvey Cushing, 7/13/20

He was subject to severe: SBS int. with Elizabeth Yew

"Please don't feel that the game": letter from Harvey Cushing to Kate Cushing, undated

The Cushing household

Under Harvey and Gogs: Thomson, p. 216

Harvey earned good fees: Ibid., p. 181

One year, for example, Minnie would: SBS int. with BCW

They lived in a large yellow: Davis, p. 140

Behind the house were: Thomson, p. 176

"The combination of": Ibid., p. 216

"My girls will all marry wealth": *Ladies Home Journal,* March 1958

"She was obsessed about": SBS int. with Connie Bradlee Devins, Boston friend and onetime secretary to Babe Cushing

Barbara's girlhood

She started out in life: SBS int. with BCW

The name "Babe" didn't stick: SBS int. with Eleanor Mittendorf, childhood friend of Babe Cushing Paley

During her girlhood she had two imaginary: SBS int. with BCW

"Barbara is wildly excited": letter from Minnie Cushing to Harvey Cushing, undated

But her looks stopped short: SBS int. with Mrs. Elliot Noyes, childhood friend of Babe Cushing Paley

"Barbara was very self-contained": SBS int. with Eleanor Mittendorf

Ever eager to please: SBS int. with BCW

Her only spark: SBS int. with Reid Cushing, Babe's nephew

Barbara was Harvey Cushing's favorite: SBS int. with BCW

When Barbara was fifteen: SBS int.
with Kate Roosevelt Whitney,
Babe's niece
"Some great black clouds overtook":
letter from Barbara Cushing to
Harvey Cushing, undated
Once when the writer: SBS int. with
BCW
"We all miss you awfully Dear papa":
Thomson, p. 227

CHAPTER 24

The debutante

The hostess for the dinner dance: SBS
ints. with BCW and James
Roosevelt, first husband of BCW
attended by four hundred guests: *New
York Times,* July 7, 1978
In 1930, at age twenty-two: Kahn,
p. 139; Fulton, p. 601
"I may have to start afresh": Snyder,
p. 136
Yale promptly offered him: Fulton,
p. 636
"You might tell son Franklin":
Thomson, p. 307

Babe's auto accident

A year later: letter from Harvey Cushing
to Barbara Cushing, 2/2/34
According to legend: SBS int. with MaT
whichever way he was looking: SBS int.
with BCW
All of Babe's front teeth: SBS ints. with
MaT and KRW
Afterwards, perhaps out of envy: SBS
int. with TMc
In fact, the dentist used: SBS int. with
MaT
including one front tooth: SBS int. with
Connie Devins

When her nieces came to visit: SBS int.
with BCW
"Why don't your teeth?": SBS int. with
Connie Devins

The Fabulous Cushing Sisters

In 1935, Babe secured: SBS int. with
BCW
Babe, Betsey, and Minnie were known:
New York Post, December 22, 1946
"The three of them had": SBS int. with
DV
They were not regarded: transcript of
David Halberstam int. with Aileen
Mehle ("Suzy")
They were even nice to women: SBS int.
with Helen Sioussat
"I remember Babe leveled": SBS int.
with ALM

Betsey Cushing

"Betsey could be rough": SBS int. with
Horst, the fashion photographer
Later in life Betsey would divulge: Kahn,
p. 139
with a rollicking sense of humor: SBS
ints. with KRW and AB

Minnie Cushing

Older and plainer: SBS int. with Henry
Mortimer, former brother-in-law of
Babe Cushing Paley
"She has her happiness safe": Thomson,
p. 218
"Minnie, of course": SBS int. with
BCW
As the eldest, Minnie also: SBS ints.
with Kay Halle, friend of the
Cushing sisters, and SK
In 1935 she became the mistress: SBS int.
with DPH; ALM letter, 12/35
the forty-five-year-old heir: *The New
Yorker,* May 12, 1938
In business, some regarded him: Ibid.

He could be moody: SBS int. with
William Cushing

When he felt depressed: *The New Yorker*,
May 12, 1938

Babe at Vogue

It was Babe who was: SBS int. with IS

She also befriended Diana Vreeland: SBS
int. with BCW

"You never knew where she was": SBS
int. with Connie Devins

Babe's salary was small: Ibid.

Her ambition, like that of: SBS int. with
Susan Mary Alsop, longtime friend
of Babe

"She stood out": SBS int. with Horst

"the tight high buttocks": *The Women
We Wanted to Look Like*, Brigid
Keenan (New York, 1977), pp. 2–4

Babe's personality

Her wardrobe budget was modest: SBS
int. with SMA

"She would come in to *Vogue*": SBS int.
with Despina Messinesi, longtime
editor at *Vogue*

"She wanted to know all about": SBS
int. with Horst

When her friend Susan Mary Jay: SBS
int. with SMA; *To Marietta from
Paris: 1945–1960*, Susan Mary Alsop
(Garden City, N.Y., 1975),
pp. 1–2

"She had trouble with language": SBS
int. with Connie Devins

For all her glamour: SBS int. with MaT

Babe "was too much of a lady": SBS int.
with SMA

Her admirers

She had a certain wariness: SBS int. with
HoK

"She was savvy": SBS int. with Connie
Devins

Courtship and marriage

They caught up again at parties: *New
York Daily News*, August 3, 1944

He was a party boy: SBS ints. with SMA
and IS

who put in time working: SBS int. with
Henry Mortimer

"He was the boy next door": SBS int.
with DV

The Mortimer-Cushing wedding: *New
York Journal American*, January 17,
1941

He had suffered a fatal: Snyder, p. 138

Babe and Stanley in New York

Babe and Stanley settled into: *New York
Journal American*, January 17, 1941;
SBS int. with Despina Messinesi

Babe took on most: *New York Journal
American*, January 17, 1941

"She adored beautiful objects": SBS int.
with DV

Right on schedule, Babe "retired": *New
York Daily News*, August 3, 1944

Gogs and the girls

"Those girls had a kind": *Billy Baldwin:
An Autobiography*, with Michael
Gardine (Boston, 1985), p. 274

Hovering behind the scenes: SBS ints.
with Henry Mortimer and IS

"She was the most charming": SBS int.
with LH

It was Gogs who had put her foot down:
SBS int. with Henry Mortimer

Gogs came to the rescue: SBS int. with
KRW

One fairy tale came true: Kahn, p. 141

Divorce

He was drinking heavily and was
subject: SBS int. with SMA

"He would drink": SBS int. with
Connie Devins

"habitually intemperate": *New York Daily News,* August 3, 1948

Babe and Bill meet

He always professed: *AIH,* p. 186
"Babe and Stanley were at": SBS int. with DPH
So, for that matter, was Janet: SBS ints. with ALM, HoK, and TMc
The Stewarts had been such: SBS int. with DPH
She even loaned him: SBS int. with IS
"Bill always wanted the best": SBS int. with HoK

Paris interlude

As Paley debated: SBS ints. with Despina Messinesi, SMA, and Mary Buell, widow of Elim O'Shaughnessy
"fell head over heels": SBS int. with SMA
others who knew: SBS int. with Mary Buell

Paley presses his case

"Everyone expected him to marry": SBS int. with ALM
She sat in bed: SBS ints. with Despina Messinesi and MaT
One snowy evening: SBS int. with MaT
When Babe recovered: SBS int. with Guy Della Cioppa
Babe was flattered: David Halberstam int. with Truman Capote
But Gogs had reservations: SBS int. with HoK; David Halberstam int. with Truman Capote

Babe's view of Bill

Rather, she found him fascinating: SBS ints. with BCW, LH, and HoK
She found his complications: SBS ints. with Connie Devins and IS

"She knew all about Stanley": SBS int. with LH
"You've got to tell me": SBS int. with Connie Devins
"In he comes": SBS int. with SMA

Bill and Dorothy's divorce

word leaked out: *New York Daily News,* July 24, 1947
A month earlier: SBS int. with MaT
"He was cold as ice": SBS int. with DPH
Once when Dorothy had taken the children: Ibid.
At one point David Selznick: SBS int. with IS
"but when he causes pain": confidential source
She had a radical mastectomy: SBS int. with DPH
"He knew he had had enough": confidential source
The eventual divorce settlement: SBS int. with DPH
Dorothy was devastated: confidential source
"You don't exist": SBS int. with DPH
"Her taste didn't change": SBS int. with MaT
She married: SBS int. with DPH

Bill and Babe's wedding and honeymoon

"the first Cushing son-in-law": *New York Daily News,* August 3, 1947
Years later Ralph Colin: SBS int. with FS
The ceremony, presided over: *New York Times,* July 29, 1947; SBS ints. with Jerome Zerbe, society photographer, and JM
Four days later: *New York Daily News,* August 2, 1947; *New York Times,* August 1, 1947
The celebrities banded together: SBS int. with LH

By day Babe sat: Ibid.

After spending some time: SBS int. with Lord Norwich

"like a frosted cake": "The New Riviera," by Charles J. V. Murphy, *Life,* November 10, 1947

"In all my years at": Ibid.

The destiny of Bill and Babe

On March 30, 1948: *New York Daily News,* March 31, 1948

"a quiet, small baby": Ibid.

The arrival of the Paleys' son: SBS ints. with DPH and ALM

"the ultimate glowing Gentile": confidential source

"Oh, he will be so bored": SBS int. with DPH

CHAPTER 25

Building the CBS Programming Department

He appointed his aide-de-camp: *Time,* April 15, 1946

Experts who had helped: *Newsweek,* January 21, 1946

Each Tuesday at 10:00 a.m.: SBS ints. with FS and Guy Della Cioppa

He did most of his talking: SBS int. with FS

In 1946, Paley introduced: *Broadcasting,* April 12, 1976

Each show was: SBS ints. with FS, and Oscar Katz, CBS research and programming executive

By the end of 1947: Considine; *Broadcasting,* September 22, 1952

Paley and his programmers

Howard would bound into: SBS int. with FS

"Bill Paley gave me my head": SBS int. with Harry Ackerman, CBS programming executive

Harry Ackerman discovered: Ibid.

Stanton first heard Godfrey: SBS int. with FS; Metz, p. 175

"Godfrey was never accepted": SBS int. with FS

"The best way to get": *Variety,* April 27, 1949; *New York Post,* August 2, 1979

CBS progress against NBC

"NBC just sat there": SBS int. with FS

"I know a good comedian": *Pageant* (November 1948)

In May 1948, when Paley: confidential source

Paley's approach arose: SBS int. with FS

Since the tax rate on incomes: Bilby, p. 246

Moreover, Correll and Gosden: Barnouw, Vol. II, p. 239

To the delight of CBS: *Variety,* September 8 and November 17, 1948

"Strangely": Bilby, p. 246

Jack Benny

Benny had appeared briefly: Barnouw, Vol. I, p. 273; WSP on "Donahue," 9/26/79

"Jack is a loyal guy": SBS int. with Irving Fein, former agent to Jack Benny

The price for Benny's departure: Bilby, pp. 24–29; *Variety,* February 2, 1949

He had been careful to maintain: SBS int. with FS; *Time* correspondent's file, 1/28/49; *Moody's Manual,* 1949

Ben Duffy, BBD&O president: SBS int. with FS

He tipped NBC president: Bilby, pp. 247–249

The NBC chief was a courtly: Ibid., p. 252

He was worried about: NBC memorandum, 11/29/48

Even more worrisome: *Variety*, October 17, 1948

Paley quietly dispatched: SBS ints. with FS and Morton Mitosky, former consultant to RCA

Paley subsequently called Benny: SBS int. with Howard Meighan, CBS executive; transcript of David Halberstam int. with Hubbell Robinson; *AIH*, p. 194

"That would demean": Bilby, p. 247

"is likely to find": *Variety*, November 24, 1948

He said he risked losing: SBS int. with FS

"Riggio looks askance": *Variety*, November 24, 1948

But the old-time tobacco: SBS int. with FS

When Paley bypassed Duffy: *AIH*, p. 197

They would only agree if: SBS int. with Irving Fein

"Our neck was way out": SBS int. with FS

"Getting Benny away from": Norman Corwin unpublished manuscript

"If it had not been for": *AIH*, pp. 195–196

"We will lose major talent": *Broadcasting*, October 18, 1971

"Why did you do this to me, Bill?": David Halberstam int. with Ike Levy

Paley denied making the comment: *AIH*, p. 200

Immediately after the war: *Variety*, January 26, 1949

Benny on CBS

CBS used all its promotional: SBS int. with Irving Fein

CBS leaked the fact: *Variety*, December 8, 1948

Benny's initial ratings: SBS int. with Irving Fein

Stanton won a contest: *Time* correspondent's file, 1/28/49

"An 'I told you so' ": *Variety*, January 5, 1949

even briefly introducing: Tom Shales int. with WSP, 3/6/79

"It was so ridiculous": Ibid.

More raids

In the following months: Barnouw, Vol. II, p. 245; Bilby, p. 249; *Variety*, January 26, 1949

Contrary to the mythology: NBC memo, 1/5/49; SBS int. with FS

"Cap Gains Nipped": *Variety*, January 5, 1949

"Words were passed": *Variety*, January 18, 1949

Benny was ultimately: SBS int. with FS; Considine

By March 1949: letter from Frank Stanton to Niles Trammell, 3/2/49

and by the end of the year: Bilby, p. 248

For the first time: *Broadcasting*, September 22, 1952

"Paley's comet": *Variety*, December 29, 1948; *Time*, February 21, 1949

Sarnoff responded by earmarking: NBC memo, from Ken Dyke to John McDonald

It bombed: SBS int. with MD

NBC sensibly locked in: Halberstam, p. 128

"Truth to tell": confidential source

As one reporter noted: *Time* correspondent's file, 1/28/49

In fact, CBS in 1949 made: *Moody's Manual*, 1949

"You know," Paley said: Barnouw, Vol. II, pp. 241–242; Corwin unpublished manuscript

CHAPTER 26

Paley's fear of TV

The raids were designed: *Broadcasting,*
October 18, 1971
"I never heard Bill": SBS int. with FS
"CBS wanted to make sure": *Business
Week,* July 21, 1951
"to slow down the progress": William
Fineshriber's oral history
"Bill did not want television": SBS int.
with FS
"When TV was getting started": SBS
int. with DA
"We are talking about": SBS int. with
FS
"I had a very strong": Morris Gelman
int. with WSP

Talent raids

"more popular in black": *Broadcasting,*
April 12, 1976
Bing Crosby waited: *On the Air: Pioneers
of American Broadcasting,* Amy
Henderson (Washington, D.C.,
1988), p. 127; *AIH,* pp. 231–232
Ed Sullivan's famous television: SBS int.
with FS
Paley objected immediately: Ibid.
A second-rate musician: Ibid.
"I have a helluva piece": SBS int.
with FS
The deal was sealed: SBS int. with FS;
Variety, November 7, 1951. WSP
was full-time chairman of the
Truman Commission in
Washington, D.C., at the time.
"Have you sold": SBS int. with FS
When Gleason became the most
watched: Metz, p. 193
During negotiations: SBS int. with FS;
"60 Minutes," 8/4/85. Gleason
loved to recount the time he
negotiated with Paley for the two-
year $11 million contract.

According to Gleason, they were at
lunch in Paley's private dining room
at CBS headquarters, surrounded by
agents and lawyers. Suffering from
a terrible hangover, Gleason fell
asleep at the table. Paley was mildly
alarmed by the comedian's apparent
lack of interest in CBS. "If that's his
attitude, you'd better give him the
money," Paley supposedly told his
aides. Stanton, who was present in
the negotiations, commented: "That
statement isn't characteristic of Bill.
Also, almost every meeting I had
with Gleason and Paley, Gleason
had his head on the table before the
entrée, he was so drunk."

Lucille Ball to TV

but he nearly lost her: SBS int. with HA
Naturally, they wanted to: *The
Washington Post,* April 27, 1989; *New
York Times,* April 27, 1989
Paley was skeptical: *AIH,* p. 238
To prevent Lucy from leaving: SBS int.
with HA
"I have Lucy under": SBS ints. with FS
and HA
"Under duress": *AIH,* pp. 237–238
"Paley and his missus": *Variety,*
January 26, 1949
"As any executive in his position": SBS
int. with HA

CHAPTER 27

Origins of CBS color

son of a hatmaker father: Goldmark,
p. 25
When the disc was spun rapidly: Bilby,
p. 117
"My first televised image": Goldmark,
p. 25

"part child and part tyrant": *Time,*
    December 4, 1950
which they saw as a relatively: FS
    statement to FCC, 12/9/46
Goldmark became a true: Goldmark,
    p. 55
Goldmark started to tinker: SBS int.
    with FS
On the screen, the system delivered:
    Bilby, p. 174
Goldmark recognized that the wheels:
    Goldmark, p. 57; SBS int. with FS
In December 1940: Goldmark, p. 65
Instead of transmitting: SBS int. with JR
Clearer pictures could be: FS statement
    to FCC, 12/9/46
"I absolutely believed in": SBS int. with
    FS
By the time Paley returned: NBC
    memo, O. B. Hanson to Frank
    Mullen, 4/27/45
"with an air of mixed": Goldmark, p. 86
"It was fashionable to be": SBS int.
    with FS
CBS color would not work: *Fortune* (July
    1953)
Paley understood that: *Time,*
    December 4, 1950
For a relatively small investment: FS
    statement to FCC, 12/9/46
But by Paley's later account: *AIH,* p. 183

CBS split between radio and TV

In those days CBS advertising: SBS int.
    with JS
"Television wasn't on Bill's": SBS int.
    with FS
After careful study: Ibid.
That month Rosell Hyde: Ibid.
By the time Frank Stanton testified: FS
    statement to FCC, 12/9/46
To their utter amazement: Barnouw,
    Vol. II, p. 243

Sarnoff's plans for color vs.
black and white TV

by the end of World War II: Bilby,
    p. 172
In 1940 Sarnoff had been well aware:
    Ibid., p. 177
"Forget it": Ibid., Goldmark, p. 64
"that television would reshape": Bilby,
    p. 172
The first RCA sets appeared: Ibid.,
    pp. 172–173; 246
"You are the generation": David Adams
    report, p. 9
He complained about: Goldmark, p. 87;
    Bilby, p. 172
Allen B. Dumont, a pioneering: Metz,
    p. 158
"It was phony": SBS int. with FS
The following autumn: Goldmark, p. 93
"It smelled ": SBS int. with FS
The outcry over the apparent: Barnouw,
    Vol. II, pp. 243–244; Goldmark,
    p. 94

Explosion of black and white TV

the "terrific momentum": *Variety,*
    December 29, 1948
It trimmed its color research: *Time,*
    March 15, 1948; *Fortune* (July 1953)
Early in 1948 Stanton expanded: FS press
    conference, 2/17/48; *Time,*
    March 15, 1948
The following September: Barnouw,
    Vol. II, p. 285
Week after week: SBS int. with DA
"CBS could count on": SBS int. with FS
At first he bought: *Broadcasting,*
    September 22, 1952; SBS int.
    with FS
Late in 1950 he paid: *AIH,* p. 223

CHAPTER 28

The LP battle

He conceived of: SBS ints. with John
    Hammond and FS
By the end of 1945: Goldmark, p. 133
"The LP," said John: SBS int. with John
    Hammond
Under tight security: SBS int. with FS;
    Goldmark, p. 133
Finally, in the spring: SBS int. with FS
"I can't believe little": Ibid.
Stanton reported to Paley: Ibid.;
    Goldmark, p. 141
Sarnoff arrived at CBS: Goldmark,
    p. 141; SBS int. with FS
And Paley said that he: *AIH,* p. 198
"I caused it to be taken": SBS int.
    with FS

CBS wins color decision

During 1948 he worked: SBS int. with
    FS; Goldmark, p. 106
CBS's converter system: *Time,*
    December 4, 1950
"Paley the impatient": Goldmark, p. 109
"the monkeys were": Bilby, p. 184;
    Goldmark, p. 109
"It would be difficult to": *Fortune*
    (July 1953)
Sarnoff sued: Bilby, p. 186
"Bill, we could have avoided":
    Goldmark, p. 114
a "gala premiere": *Variety,* June 27, 1951;
    New York Times, June 26, 1951
Trouble was, only: *AIH,* p. 208

Hytron purchase

Instead of cash: letter from FCC
    secretary to Richard Salant, 5/23/51
Lloyd put people off: SBS int. with FS
"Electronics," Paley bragged: *Fortune*
    (July 1953)

Paley's "secret ambition": Goldmark,
    p. 114
"to be king of the hill": SBS int. with FS
The timing: *Broadcasting,* May 18, 1976;
    Fortune (July 1953)
"part of the environment": SBS int.
    with FS
He wanted to buy: Ibid.
A Wall Street investment house: Ibid.
They cautioned, however: Goldmark,
    p. 115; SBS int. with FS
"I went along with": SBS int. with FS
"Bill's fundamental mistake": Ibid.
"We didn't know very much":
    Broadcasting, May 31, 1976
He and Stanton traveled: Goldmark,
    p. 116; SBS int. with FS
"Paley was not programmed": transcript
    of David Halberstam int. with Peter
    Goldmark

Sarnoff perfects color system

On July 13, 1951: *Variety,* July 18, 1951
by the "tremendous improvement":
    Ibid.

Ban on color set manufacture

In the fall of 1951: Bilby, pp. 180–181
Had CBS gone forward: *Fortune*
    (July 1953)
"It was the luckiest": SBS int. with FS

CBS fails in black and white

"I thought everybody concerned": WSP
    memos in September 1951 and May
    1952; *AIH,* p. 223
The Coffin brothers were: SBS int.
    with FS
"You want it back": Ibid.

CBS drops color

At that moment, 23 million: Bilby,
    pp. 180–181
"The boat," said Stanton: SBS int.
    with FS

Stanton builds the TV network

That same year: *AIH*, p. 219

Stanton coaxed Paley: FS appointment notes for 3/17/51 and 3/18/51; SBS int. with FS

Stanton and Paley met with: FS appointment notes for 4/4/51

But the FCC hinted: SBS int. with FS

In a complicated sleight-of-hand: SBS int. with Leonard Goldenson, former chairman of ABC; Goldmark, p. 94

Shortly after the ABC-CBS deal: SBS int. with FS; FS appointment notes for 5/11/51

"Are you out of your mind?": SBS int. with Leonard Goldenson

An imperious man: SBS int. with FS

Two weeks later: FS appointment notes for 5/23/51

As a measure of CBS's lingering: SBS ints. with FS and Leonard Goldenson

According to Stanton: SBS int. with FS

Paley recalled "raising hell": confidential source

"Frank Stanton was really": SBS int. with Leonard Goldenson

Indeed, Stanton's calendar shows: FS appointment notes, 3/17/51–5/23/51

As soon as the FCC lifted: Barnouw, Vol. II, p. 285

CBS dedicated its new: *Broadcasting,* September 22, 1951

"I went through $60 million": SBS int. with FS; Bilby, p. 197

"a big crap shoot": *Broadcasting* editors' int. with WSP, April 12, 1976

Two years later, CBS finally: *Broadcasting,* March 12, 1979

The final two purchases: *AIH*, p. 223

In 1946, Ike and Leon Levy: Levys' oral history

On hearing that Stanton: SBS int. with FS

"The fault," he said: *AIH*, p. 222

Hytron's closing

the "persistent headache": Ibid., p. 225

He kept vacuum tube: Considine; *Forbes,* January 15, 1964

The total loss: Goldmark, p. 117

"The fact that he made": transcript of David Halberstam int. with Ralph Colin

"The outstanding flop": confidential source

He held Stanton accountable: *AIH*, pp. 224–226

The major villain: Ibid., p. 223; Goldmark, pp. 115–117

Paley and color

"You always know": *Time,* December 4, 1950

for his "blind devotion": *AIH*, p. 222

"It was the best": *Broadcasting* editors' int. with WSP, April 12, 1976

"We were interested": *Broadcasting,* May 18, 1976

CHAPTER 29

Murrow becomes an executive

"If you wanted to imagine": confidential source

CBS News correspondents had: SBS ints. with Sig Mickelson, former CBS News chief, and ES

Murrow wanted to build: Sperber, p. 258

Campbell's Soup was willing; SBS int. with Jap Gude; *Edward R. Murrow: An American Original,* Joseph E. Persico (New York, 1988), p. 235

Paley stressed: Sperber, p. 258; Persico,
   pp. 235–236
Although flattered by Paley's: SBS int.
   with JM
Paley told Murrow: Sperber, p. 258
in fact, White's flippant: Metz, p. 109
Over dinner: Persico, pp. 234, 235
he would take the job: SBS int. with
   Jap Gude
Paley said he feared: Metz, pp. 109–110
he told Stanton: SBS int. with FS
Both men felt diminished: SBS int. with
   MaT; Persico, p. 364
Paley's oft-stated reason: Sperber, p. 258
"sensitivity about people": National
   Public Radio interview with WSP,
   November 1979

Murrow's strategic importance

The public appetite for: Sperber, p. 263;
   "Thought Control—American
   Style," by Bruce Oliver, *The New
   Republic,* January 13, 1947
"more diverse and insistent": *New York
   Times,* December 29, 1946

The Blue Book

so he let others in the: Barnouw, Vol. II,
   pp. 231–233
"a statement of principle": Ibid., p. 234
"snobs preaching to": WSP speech,
   "Radio and Its Critics," 10/22/46
Doubtless he was unaware: Barnouw,
   Vol. II, p. 232; Sperber, p. 518

Murrow's news organization

Murrow had launched: Persico,
   pp. 245–246; Sperber, p. 272
"The type of promotion": letter from FS
   to Charles Denny, 2/24/47
The documentary series earned: *New
   York Times,* March 29 and August
   10, 1947; Sperber, p. 274

Network editorials

But the FCC had indicated: SBS int.
   with FS
Davenport . . . devised an elegant plan:
   Sperber, p. 277
Paley summoned all his top brass: SBS
   ints. with FS, JR, and Guy Della
   Cioppa
Two years later, the FCC would: *New
   York Times,* June 3, 1949
As a practical matter: SBS int. with FS
"a lost opportunity": Sperber, p. 277;
   confidential source

Murrow's misgivings

"Ed had some ideas": SBS int. with JM
"I don't think you have": SBS int. with
   Michael Bessie; Sperber, p. 272
"He had a sense of ": David Halberstam
   int. with JM

The Shirer crisis

At CBS, commentator: Sperber, p. 279;
   Persico, p. 252
"They were in fact disenchanted": SBS
   int. with FS
Murrow told Shirer that: Sperber,
   p. 227; SBS int. with FS
he said on the air that: Persico, p. 252
His most intent listener: SBS int.
   with FS
"Bill [Paley] was sore": Ibid.
Paley's position hardened: Sperber,
   pp. 282–283
He issued a statement: Persico, p. 252
"Shirer's program was a newsman's":
   SBS int. with FS
"He said he didn't think": Ibid.
Together, Murrow and Shirer: Sperber,
   p. 292
"As far as I'm concerned": Persico,
   p. 294

Murrow resigns executive post

Murrow felt sickened: Persico,
    p. 251
"Being an executive was": SBS int.
    with FS
"I have a strong feeling": SBS int.
    with WSP
"I'll do it if you": SBS int. with FS
In fact, Murrow had selected: Ibid.;
    Persico, p. 258
and he hated the dirty business: Sperber,
    pp. 276, 292

Murrow-Paley social life

"He was like a conflagration": SBS int.
    with SK
"Ed felt that it would": SBS int.
    with JM
Babe and Bill also visited: Ibid.
"He never made a move": SBS int.
    with WSP
an anecdote according to which: Metz,
    pp. 115–116; Halberstam,
    pp. 124–125
"I don't know whether": SBS int.
    with FS
"intentionally insulting": transcript of
    David Halberstam int. with Ralph
    Colin

The Paley-Murrow-Stanton triangle

"Ed wanted to go around": SBS int.
    with FS
"Stanton never talked": SBS int.
    with ES
"I think Murrow transferred": SBS int.
    with Howard K. Smith, former
    CBS correspondent
Not surprisingly, Murrow's open: Ibid.;
    Halberstam, pp. 154–155
"They could not get on": WSP int.
    with SBS
"I think Stanton did not": *AIH,*
    p. 180

"Bill and I talked about": SBS int.
    with FS
"I hold Bill Paley to blame": SBS int.
    with FWF

CHAPTER 30

Blacklist fervor

"The networks have been growing":
    Oliver, *The New Republic,* January
    13, 1947
"red scare . . . has grabbed": *Variety,*
    August 14, 1949
When CBS fired one of: *Cogley Report,*
    p. 13
"There is going to be": Norman Corwin
    unpublished manuscript
"I was under no illusions": SBS int. with
    Norman Corwin

Campbell's Soup drops Murrow

In May 1950, Campbell's told: Sperber,
    pp. 332, 338–339; SBS int. with FS

Red Channels

Political pressure on the networks:
    Barnouw, Vol. II, pp. 265, 267;
    Sperber, p. 340

The Korea clash

the alternative, he believed: Sperber,
    p. 341
On August 14, 1950: Ibid., p. 346
"He told me": SBS int. with FS
Stanton held the broadcast: Ibid. FS said
    that WSP was not there that day. "If
    he were there I would have noted it
    on my calendar. I noted all meetings
    with him." FS calendar for August
    1940 showed no meetings with WSP
    on 14th, lunch with WSP on 16th
    and 21st, appointment with Chester

on 21st, lunch with ERM on 22nd,
lunch with WSP and Chester on
28th.
When Paley returned, he was: Persico,
p. 292
"considerable speculation": *Variety,*
September 6, 1950
who had decided before the meeting:
SBS int. with FS
"It was one of the most": National
Public Radio interview with WSP,
November 1979
"felt it was a lack": David Halberstam
int. with WSP
"The hurt just stood out": Persico,
p. 292

CBS loyalty oath

a capitulation to incessant: Barnouw,
Vol. II, pp. 276–277; Sperber,
p. 362; SBS int. with FS
"through our control": Cogley Report,
p. 17
"The fact that we had": SBS int. with FS
CBS's solution: Cogley Report, pp. 68,
122–124
Ream adapted the CBS oath: SBS int.
with JR; Barnouw, Vol. II, p. 240;
*The Proud Decades: America in War
and Peace, 1941–1960,* John Patrick
Diggins (New York, 1988),
pp. 111–112
"It was obvious to me": SBS int. with
JR
After questioning the First Amendment:
Sperber, p. 363
"Murrow," said Ream: SBS int. with JR
"I went along with it": SBS int. with FS
"I told him we were": SBS int. with FS
"I was disgusted with": *In the Storm of
the Eye: A Lifetime at CBS,* Bill
Leonard (New York, 1987), p. 70
Winston Burdett: Cogley Report, p. 128
Howard K. Smith: SBS int. with HKS;
Sperber, p. 366

CBS political screening

Working from lists: Cogley Report,
p. 125; SBS int. with FS
Ream and Berry ran down leads:
Sperber, p. 366
In many instances: SBS int. with FS
"Sorry, we can't clear": Cogley Report,
p. 63; Leonard, p. 70
"CBS and blacklisting": Cogley Report,
p. 126; SBS int. with JR
But when Mickelson went: Cogley
Report, p. 124; SBS int. with JR
"took something out of me": SBS int.
with JR
Trained in the law: Cogley Report,
p. 124; SBS int. with IS
CBS's "security officer": Cogley Report,
p. 122
and made regular trips: SBS int. with
Guy Della Cioppa
Within the company he was: Barnouw,
Vol. II, p. 278; William Robson's
oral history
"You really didn't know": SBS int.
with SM
Their attacks continued: Persico, p. 392;
Sperber, pp. 469–471; Barnouw,
Vol. III (1970) p. 55
"abridge the rights and": *AIH,*
p. 281
"Yes, it was a blacklist": SBS int.
with FS
Paley's sense of patriotism: *AIH,* p. 286;
Clearing the Air, Daniel Schorr
(Boston, 1977), pp. 274–280
"NBC had a blacklist": SBS int.
with DA
"There was cross-checking": SBS int.
with FS
"We were not as courageous": Ibid.
"Nobody said": SBS int. with SM
In 1953, Murrow asked Paley: ERM note
to WSP, 1953; Sperber, p. 410
"He stayed quite remote": SBS int.
with SM

"He was aware of it all": SBS int.
  with FS
"The chairman wants": SBS int.
  with SM
"in-house questionnaire": *AIH*, p. 281
"mild questionnaire": *AIH*, p. 282
"very small step": Sperber, p. 363
"simple thing": transcript of Loren
  Ghiglione int. with WSP, 2/16/77
"We didn't have a blacklist": WSP to
  Phil Donohue, 9/26/79

CHAPTER 31

Paley as absentee landlord

"Bill Paley Won't You": *Variety*,
  November 7, 1951, and December
  16, 1959
two to three weeks in the sunshine:
  confidential source; SBS int. with
  JPr

Stanton plants the idea

"We've got to do": SBS int. with FS
Some months later Harry Truman: Ibid.
When Truman told Stanton: Ibid.
Symington also happened to be: Kahn,
  p. 241
But when Symington called Stanton:
  SBS int. with FS

Symington works on Paley

The president felt the need: *AIH*, p. 202
"Precisely why this acquaintance":
  confidential source; *AIH*, p. 202
Although reassured by: *AIH*, p. 204

Paley agrees and selects the commission

The White House announced: *New York
  Times*, January 23, 1951: *Variety*,
  January 24, 1951
He would receive no compensation:

Hearing Before the Special
  Subcommittee on Minerals,
  Materials and Fuels Economics of
  the Committee on Interior and
  Insular Affairs, U.S. Senate, April
  9, 1954, p. 6
The "intriguing question": *Variety*,
  December 27, 1950
Hodgins was "thunderstruck": Eric
  Hodgins's oral history (April 3,
  1968)
"Eric, don't be": SBS int. with FS
As usual, Paley appropriated: *AIH*,
  p. 205
"It was no accident": SBS int. with
  Professor Philip Coombs, Amherst
  College
"We're going to play this": Ibid.

At the commission

"He was pleasant and unassuming": SBS
  int. with Harry Kahn, Paley
  Commission staff member
"He made it clear": Ibid.
"Take as much time as you need":
  National Public Radio int. with
  WSP, November 1979
The only seriously divisive: SBS int.
  with Philip Coombs; Eric Hodgins's
  oral history
The reason, Paley later said: Senate
  Hearings, 4/9/54, p. 23; *Time*, June
  30, 1952
"Messrs Paley, George Brown": Eric
  Hodgins's oral history
"Bill Paley would tell us": SBS int. with
  Philip Coombs
"She loved being": SBS int. with SMA
Most weeks he would spend: *AIH*,
  p. 207; SBS int. with FS
"lecture on the subject": SBS int. with
  Philip Coombs

The Paley Report

"Bill Paley was so proud": SBS int. with HKS

"I do not believe": Senate hearings, 4/9/54; *The New Republic,* March 29, 1975

Fortune magazine featured: *Fortune* (August 1952)

Paley not only visited Arthur F. Burns: *AIH,* p. 212; Paper, p. 150

"Perhaps Eisenhower's people did not want": confidential source

Paley tried to keep the cause alive: CBS press release, 7/2/74

Paley on the griddle

For nearly four hours: Senate Hearings, 4/9/54, p. 39

Malone also happened to be: Sperber, p. 530

"I think you are improving": Senate Hearings, 4/9/54, p. 45

Before the hearing he had neglected: SBS int. with FS

"I don't know how you can": Ibid.

CHAPTER 32

Paley's pride in high society

"When he talks about": David Halberstam int. with Truman Capote

Paley was known to display: *Time,* January 31, 1964

Paley's expanding fortune

"If you have spent your": confidential source

"One of the cats": SBS int. with Fleur Cowles, second wife of Gardner Cowles

Paley continued to: *Moody's Manuals* and CBS Proxy Statements, using 1946 and 1959 figures

This exclusive social set

"They will get rid of": SBS int. with DPH

"The Paleys were social": SBS int. with CC

"If you were giving": David Halberstam int. with Aileen Mahle ("Suzy")

Since their pied-à-terre: SBS int. with Horst

The Paleys cultivated their: SBS int. with CC

"We never go to": *Women's Wear Daily,* July 10, 1963

"Her husband objected": Earl Wilson column, *New York Post,* June 30, 1980

When she went to a restaurant: SBS int. with CC

"The people he liked were": SBS int. with SMA

"In the early days": SBS int. with IS

Weekend routine at Kiluna

"If I don't keep the house": confidential source

(His guests generally): SBS ints. with DV and SK

"competed tensely and excitedly": *Time,* January 31, 1964

Weekend cronies included: SBS ints. with HoK and Walter Thayer, longtime friend of WSP; Kahn, pp. 209, 213, and 316

Bill and Jock

"My brother-in-law Jock": SBS ints. with John David Backe and Arthur Taylor, former presidents of CBS

"Bill's friendship with": SBS int. with DV

"The Whitneys never particularly": SBS int. with ALM

"Jock would naturally adore": SBS int. with CC

"a lot of people took Jock": letter from E. J. Kahn to SBS, 9/6/86

Paley was more outgoing: SBS int. with William O'Shaughnessy

Underneath, Whitney was every bit: SBS int. with KRW

"Utterly sure of himself and": Kahn, p. 72

Their membership on the Museum: Kahn, pp. 12–28; WSP int. with SBS

On the golf course: confidential sources

a favorite game of French: Kahn, p. 32

where Paley would sit: SBS int. with Blair Meyer, nephew of Jock Whitney; Kahn, p. 32

He even convinced CBS: Kahn, p. 258

"Bill," summed up: SBS int. with WT

"Where's your clicker?": Kahn, p. 70

She remained cool: SBS int. with IS

"Betsey," he said: confidential source; transcript of David Halberstam int. with Pamela Colin-Harlech

Paley and Selznick

"Betsey didn't like David": SBS int. with IS

"charmingly ruthless": Ibid.

"David didn't love Bill": Ibid.

Paley and the Brits

Prominent among Paley's friends: *New York Times,* January 3, 1989

"I don't think Loel": SBS int. with LMD

Lusty and indiscreet: SBS int. with IS

Jeremy Tree was a friend: Kahn, pp. 225, 228

Michael Tree: SBS int. with Michael Tree

"Michael is funny": SBS int. with SK

Somerset, called "the Dazzler": SBS int. with Jeanne Murray Vanderbilt, longtime friend of the Paleys

was renowned for: SBS int. with Linda Mortimer, wife of Henry Mortimer

"David and Bill were wicked": SBS int. with LMD

Judy Montagu Gendel: SBS int. with John Richardson, friend of the Paleys

"To them, he was": SBS int. with HoK

"He loved having": SBS int. with JPr

Paley and the court jesters

"had a shield around him": SBS int. with M. Donald Grant

They were court jesters: SBS int. with SK

Fourteen years Paley's senior: Gallagher, pp. 11, 123

Before the war they had seen: SBS int. with DPH

Baragwanath was often vulgar: Gallagher, p. 12

Shortly after Paley's marriage: Kahn, p. 139; SBS int. with TMc

"Jack would say two words": SBS int. with SK

Paley relished: SBS int. with WSP and DPH; Gallagher, p. 111

"bluff, hearty": Gallagher, p. 119

renowned for his "freedom week": Ibid., p. 165

Like Paley, Baragwanath was: SBS int. with ALM, Baragwanath's girlfriend for many years

a particularly irritating: SBS int. with WSP

Less well known was: SBS ints. with SK and ALM; confidential source

When Baragwanath's career: SBS ints. with WSP and DPH

For the next several years: Gallagher, p. 221

"After Neysa died": SBS int. with SK

"I thought I'd make him": SBS int. with WSP

When Baragwanath was ill: SBS int. with CB

Capote and the Paleys

A more notorious jester: *Capote: A Biography,* Gerald Clarke (New York, 1988), p. 281

Capote had a knack for: Ibid., pp. 267, 274, and 175

He belonged more: Ibid., p. 282

serving as her intellectual: SBS int. with MaT

she considered him a soulmate: SBS int. with SMA

"At first Bill was appalled": SBS int. with IS

appreciated his ability: SBS int. with Gerald Clarke, Capote biographer; SBS int. with CB

"Capote," said Michael Tree: SBS int. with Michael Tree

"he was there every weekend": SBS int. with LH

For some two decades he accompanied: Clarke, pp. 277, 282

part entertainer: SBS int. with SK

He cultivated them; they cultivated: SBS int. with IS

He thought nothing of having: Clarke, p. 284

After meals Capote often: confidential sources

Paley's mood with friends

The Whitneys, Vanderbilts: *Golden Clan,* John Corry (Boston, 1977), p. 112; Kahn, p. 71

There was always a fierce: SBS int. with SK

in the evenings a preview: SBS int. with TMc

In the company of his friends: SBS int. with DV

"I'll bet you never heard": SBS int. with Henry Mortimer

"He had a low tolerance": confidential source

Titillating stories: SBS int. with Marguerite Platt, former governess for Paley children

"He always liked talking": SBS int. with Michael Tree

Paley gave as good: SBS int. with SK

"He would tell funny stories": SBS int. with JPr

MacArthur delighted in regaling: *Time,* January 31, 1964; *Esquire* (December 1983)

although he privately solicited: Kahn, p. 313

"Only one thing": SBS int. with HoK

"It was a cardboard": confidential source

"he didn't have to use": SBS int. with MaT

Paley himself once noted: SBS int. with WSP

Paley had a temper: SBS int. with CB; confidential source

"There is a touchy": SBS int. with JPr

"Bill does not have": SBS int. with Katharine Graham, chairman of the Washington Post Company

Bill and Babe travel

The couple spent: SBS int. with WSP

One summer the Paleys: confidential source

another year they took: SBS int. with HoK

Paley often made a detour: SBS int. with Natalie Davenport, interior designer and friend of Babe

In London they stayed: SBS int. with WSP

In Paris, the Paley suite: Ibid.; SBS int. with Despina Messinesi

Occasionally Bill and Babe would stay: SBS int. with John Richardson

"Babe and I shopped": SBS int. with SK

Gifts and favors

"He does the things that": SBS int. with CB

Jack Baragwanath, for example: SBS int. with SK

When Leland Hayward's son: *Haywire,* Brooke Hayward (New York, 1977) p. 263

"You fill in the amount": SBS int. with IS; I. Selznick, p. 88

On hearing that Katharine: SBS int. with Katharine Graham

Loel Guinness built: SBS int. with WSP

John Pringle, whose family: SBS int. with JPr

Baragwanath once had: SBS int. with CB

Paley's homes

they began a series: Baldwin, pp. 82, 124; *The Genius of Charles James,* Elizabeth Ann Coleman (New York, 1982), p. 50

Paley's bedroom was redone: SBS visit to Kiluna, 8/12/86

Babe filled her bedroom: Appraisal: Estate of Barbara Cushing Paley, by Masterson & O'Connell & Albano, 12/26/78

"Bill had the strong": Baldwin, pp. 329–331

"There was Bill Paley": Ibid., p. 331

The French furniture was: Ibid., p. 330; *Women's Wear Daily,* July 10, 1963

In the early 1950s the Paleys: SBS int. with JPr

The bamboo furniture was: SBS int. with NaD

Kiluna North, suggested: SBS int. with FS

Its spacious pine-paneled: SBS ints. with HoK and Marguerite Platt

The Paleys kept the house: SBS int. with William Cushing

It was just as well for: confidential source

they could commune on matters: SBS int. with KRW

"She was always in": SBS int. with SK

When he bought from: Kahn, p. 128

Anti-Semitism in WASP circles

"Watch out for": SBS int. with M. Donald Grant

The patter on the golf: SBS int. with EKM

"Many of those men": confidential source

The most embarrassing: SBS int. with FS. This story has been recounted several times in print as an attempt by Paley to join the F Street Club in Washington. Paley has denied the account, calling it a "complete falsehood" in an interview with Lynn Rosselini of *The Washington Star,* March 3, 1979. He could issue a denial in good conscience since he knew full well that the club in question was misnamed.

Although Jock was his sponsor: SBS int. with Jeanne Thayer, wife of Walter Thayer

"One reason for Squam Lake": Ibid.

"I live across the way": SBS int. with TMc

Another summer Babe asked: SBS int. with SMA

Sam and Goldie belonged: SBS int. with Dorothy Rothe

and the Links on Long Island: SBS ints. with Henry Mortimer and TMc

CHAPTER 33

Babe's tight ship

"She had the wisdom": SBS int. with
    TMc
She ran Kiluna with: SBS ints. with CB;
    Susan Burden, wife of Carter
    Burden; and Jeanne Murray
    Vanderbilt
Supplies were kept: confidential source
No one had to unpack: SBS int. with
    Kitty Carlisle Hart, friend of the
    Paleys
and any item of soiled: SBS int. with
    Marguerite Platt
The bedrooms offered: SBS int. with
    HoK
"They lived on a level": SBS int. with
    LMD

Food

"Bill Paley lived": SBS int. with LH
He was voracious at breakfast: SBS int.
    with WSP
On an average day: SBS int. with Robert
    Wussler, former president of CBS-
    TV; David Halberstam int. with
    Truman Capote
"Mr. Paley cannot be": confidential
    source
"I was the only": confidential source
"baby vegetables, unborn vegetables":
    SBS int. with Jan Cushing Amory,
    friend of WSP
Often she went: SBS int. with SK
"Babe thought nothing": SBS int. with
    NaD
The bounty of Sunday morning: SBS
    int. with CB
But many of the menus: SBS ints. with
    SK and BCW
"Okay, now everybody": SBS int. with
    Marguerite Platt
ordering food from: confidential source

The Paleys usually: confidential source
"Mrs. Paley didn't want": confidential
    source

Catering to WSP's needs

She made time to: *Time,* January 31,
    1964
She selected imaginative: SBS int. with
    SK; National Public Radio interview
    with WSP, November 1979
She was never a minute late: confidential
    source

Babe's striving for tranquility

"Babe wasn't combative": SBS int. with
    CB
After seeing the musical: Baldwin,
    pp. 203–204
Perhaps as a consequence: confidential
    source
"Babe always built him": SBS int. with
    NaD
"When he came in from": SBS int. with
    Jeanne Murray Vanderbilt

Following Paley's lead

During the opening: SBS int. with AB
When Paley tired of: SBS int. with JP;
    Town and Country (March 1969)
Paley spent $50,000 alone: SBS int. with
    William O'Shaughnessy
"He picked the spot": SBS int. with WT
With the help of Natalie: SBS int. with
    NaD
The Paleys were proud enough: *Holiday*
    (February 1959); *Vogue* (December
    1956); *Vogue* (March 1959)
Babe was not permitted: SBS int. with
    Gerald Clarke; confidential source
"Babe was careful": SBS int. with CC
"Really C.D.": WSP to C. D. Jackson,
    9/24/47

The importance of Babe's beauty

"that was time reserved": SBS int. with NaD

to "put on her face": confidential source

"She wanted to be": confidential source

"You are the only man": SBS int. with Michael Burke, former CBS executive

"Her skin was luminous": SBS int. with LH

learned to apply makeup: SBS int. with KRW

"She knew all the tricks": SBS int. with Marguerite Platt

At one point she was: confidential source

at other times she patronized: *New York Post,* December 16, 1976

Kenneth, her hairdresser: confidential source

On her travels: SBS int. with Aline de Romanones, friend of the Paleys

She often considered: confidential source

"She was a perfectionist": confidential source

"These marvelous dinners": confidential source

"I imagine she had": SBS int. with IS

Babe's style

On her way to lunch: *New York Times,* December 9, 1978

"She was involved": SBS int. with JPr

She always looked: Keenan, pp. 23–24

There was an understatement: SBS int. with IS; *Women's Wear Daily,* July 7, 1978

neatness, "which is grooming": *Women's Wear Daily,* July 10, 1963

"She was immaculate": SBS int. with KRW

"This was not affectation": confidential source

"an amazing gray": SBS int. with

Patricia Bernie, administrative assistant, CBS News, London

"Much of her terrific": confidential source

Babe's jewels and other possessions

Beginning in 1950: CBS Proxy Statements

Babe owned more than $1 million: Barbara Cushing Paley estate appraisal, December 1978

especially after thieves: *The Richest Women in the World,* Kit Konolige (New York, 1985), p. 353

Whenever Babe wanted to: confidential source

One of her favorites: confidential source

Among her other valuable trinkets: Barbara Cushing Paley estate appraisal, December 1978

To underline his stature: SBS int. with DPH

"She knew it was important": SBS int. with NaD

"Lots of women go": *Philadelphia Bulletin,* July 9, 1978

"She let Charles James": SBS int. with TMc

Truman Capote claimed: Clarke, p. 280

Instead of going to the couturier: SBS int. with André Leon Talley, creative director of *Vogue*

Adjoining her bedroom at Kiluna: SBS visit to Kiluna, 8/12/86

Babe's impact on Bill

"With Babe he learned": SBS int. with HoK

"She made him more glamorous": SBS int. with DV

He once confided to: SBS int. with CC

Under her influence he: SBS int. with JPr

("Always write your"): SBS int. with AB

"She raised standards": SBS int. with SK

"She always had a little gold": SBS int. with CB

"You were sitting": SBS int. with LH

"It's just beautiful": SBS int. with NaD

Bill's lack of appreciation

Even after she had: SBS int. with William Cushing

"He had no consideration": SBS int. with JDB

"Which would you rather": SBS int. with HoK

which were paid through: confidential source

Babe asked Bill to hire: David Halberstam int. with Truman Capote; confidential source

"I don't know": confidential source

"Would go through periodic": SBS int. with CB

She would try to cut costs: SBS ints. with NaD and Marguerite Platt

"You know, he liked": David Halberstam int. with Truman Capote

"Mostly men of means": SBS int. with SK

"You hear again and again": confidential source

"His generosity depends": confidential source

"He took everything for granted": SBS int. with NaD

"Anybody who wishes to": confidential source

CHAPTER 34

Bill Paley's narcissism

"He needed to control": confidential source

"He could talk himself": confidential source

"He was not a self-analytical": confidential source

Paley's anger and defensiveness

"He didn't trust a lot": SBS int. with FS

"I've often wondered how": Kahn, p. 70

"He could hide his": SBS int. with IS

"He would latch onto": confidential source

Truman Capote told: Clarke, pp. 285–286

Paley's inability to love

"I think I do not like": *Business Week,* March 3, 1979

Jeffrey and Hilary lived: SBS int. with DPH

In each case, their: confidential source

He had little concern about: SBS int. with DPH

"It was the roughest": SBS int. with JDB

"The temper," said one close friend: confidential source

A separate life

Bill and Babe spent most: SBS ints. with WT and Marguerite Platt

Most of the time: SBS ints. with Marguerite Platt and AB

Paley's distance from the children

"It was a matter": confidential source

Paley treated the girls: confidential source

As with guests, conversation: confidential source

And always, in the background: confidential source

"Nobody expressed anything": SBS int. with AB

On vacation at Squam Lake: SBS int.
with Marguerite Platt
"I put much more attention":
M magazine (July 1985)

Paley and his sons

Paley stressed the need for: confidential
source
Unlike his own father: SBS int. with
DPH; confidential source
"I didn't think it was fair": SBS int. with
WSP
Paley felt uncomfortable: confidential
source

Mistrust of his children

He once told a member: confidential
source
"The children should be": SBS int. with
DPH
Paley organized trust: CBS Proxy
Statements, 1950, 1951; Estate of
Samuel Paley, 1963; confidential
source
"He was an overpowering": SBS int.
with JPr
"He would ask my opinion": Kate
Paley, *Interview* (September 1984)
Paley fancied himself: SBS int. with
DPH
His secretary would send: confidential
source
"all his children behaved": SBS int. with
DPH
"All six brought": *AIH*, p. 190

Paley's inconsistencies

"I was amused": SBS int. with JM
"You must be thrilled": SBS int. with
LH
Whenever his son Billie: SBS int. with
Emily Greene, executive assistant to
WSP

But Paley did arrange: SBS int. with
EKM; confidential source
He also advised: SBS int. with DPH
"It was hard to be": Kate Paley,
Interview (September 1984)
"It wasn't so much": SBS int. with SMA
"As a father he was": Ibid.

Jeffrey Paley

The material on Jeffrey Paley is based on
SBS int. with DPH, unless
otherwise indicated
Jeffrey, who strove for his father's
approval: confidential source
After that, Jeffrey withdrew: confidential
source

Hilary Paley

The material on Hilary Paley is based on
SBS int. with DPH, unless
otherwise indicated
The first, under a pink-and-white:
Baldwin, p. 317
Three months later: *New York Times,*
December 27, 1957
Hilary was strong: SBS int. with HoK;
confidential sources
But she had an appealing: SBS int. with
Sidney Bernstein

Hilary idolizes Babe

Hilary worshipped her father: SBS int.
with DPH and Ben Bradlee
"That's one way of getting to": SBS int.
with DPH
"Hilary was not the same": SBS int.
with MaT
"She would talk about Babe": SBS int.
with Ben Bradlee
"She was like that from": SBS int. with
DPH
As a young woman: SBS int. with
Marguerite Platt

and married a stunningly handsome:
  New York, May 27, 1985
a WASP pedigree that brought: SBS int.
  with LH

Tony Mortimer

her two children by her: SBS int. with
  SMA
was handsome, and blessed with: SBS
  int. with Marguerite Platt
He was Babe's favorite: SBS ints. with
  SMA, CB, and David Mortimer,
  cousin of Amanda and Tony
When Babe was alone: SBS int. with
  Marguerite Platt
Yet for all of Tony's: SBS ints. with CB,
  Susan Burden, and TMc

Amanda

Tony, who gave her the: *New York
  Times,* March 23, 1966
"Babe worried about": SBS int. with
  SMA
The relationship was difficult: SBS ints.
  with HoK and CB
The teachers who accompanied: SBS int.
  with DPH; *New York Times
  Magazine,* November 7, 1971
"Ba was cute as a button": SBS int. with
  IS
Amanda was raised: *Women's Wear Daily,*
  September 27, 1972
To her contemporaries: SBS int. with
  IS
Underneath, however, was an iron will:
  Truman Capote, *Women's Wear
  Daily,* September 27, 1972

Amanda and Carter

Three days after her arrival: *New York
  Times Magazine,* November 7, 1971
"They went after Amanda": SBS int.
  with Belinda Breese, friend of AB

After the engagement: SBS int. with IS
Babe adjusted her own: SBS int. with
  Belinda Breese
"Their marriage was all so perfect": SBS
  int. with IS
They burst onto the New York: *New
  York Times Magazine,* November 7,
  1971
On weekends, Carter and Amanda: SBS
  int. with Belinda Breese
"The most beautiful girl": *New York
  Times,* March 23, 1966
With her marriage to Burden: SBS ints.
  with IS and DPH
"To Bill, there wasn't anybody": SBS
  int. with IS
"her job, and that's how": *Women's Wear
  Daily,* September 27, 1972
"Carter was from": SBS int. with
  Belinda Breese
"They simply had an overabundance":
  Truman Capote, *Women's Wear
  Daily,* September 27, 1972

Amanda and Babe

"Her mother was extremely":
  confidential source
Whenever Babe came to visit: SBS int.
  with Belinda Breese
"I didn't know I was supposed": SBS
  int. with AB

Kate Paley

"She is the most wounded": confidential
  source
"She had big black eyes": SBS int.
  with IS
Still, she was lively: SBS ints. with Aline
  de Romanones, TMc, and IS
"It was horrible": SBS int. with AB
Some doctors suggested: SBS int. with
  DPH; confidential source
"The nurse was pretty mean": SBS int.
  with AB

"Babe went crazy": SBS int. with TMc

"What he put Bill through": SBS int. with IS

She hired James Masterson: SBS ints. with Susan Burden and AB

She found the best wigs: SBS int. with SK

Throughout her childhood: confidential source

"It was a strange household": SBS int. with AB

Kate became increasingly: SBS int. with William O'Shaughnessy; confidential sources

"She was eager to please": SBS int. with Marguerite Platt

One summer when Kate was ten: SBS ints. with SMA and Aline de Romanones

"Kate cast a shadow": SBS int. with Marguerite Platt

Kate growing up

She was very bright: SBS int. with Aline de Romanones

with a strong hand and a keen eye: SBS int. with Kitty Carlisle Hart

"Oh Kate," Babe would say: SBS int. with SMA

Newspaper accounts referred to: *New York Times,* June 15, 1968; *New York Post,* June 17, 1968

"There was a strong rebellion": SBS int. with CB

For seven years, Kate had: Ibid.; confidential sources

"Kate practically disappeared": SBS int. with LH

she painted portraits of herself: SBS int. with Virginia Merriman, an acquaintance of Kate Paley in the 1970s

Occasionally Kate would call: confidential source

When she turned twenty-one: SBS ints.

with AB and John Richardson; confidential source

"When she heard I worked for": SBS int. with RS

Billie Paley

"He was very good-looking": SBS int. with LH

Babe tended to indulge: SBS int. with Marguerite Platt

"I remember when Billie": confidential source

"I spent all kinds of time": Metz, p. 402

"Billie got himself kicked": confidential source

"I was a strange child": *The Washington Post,* May 24, 1977

"based on the surrealistic": *Women's Wear Daily,* December 16, 1977

(a posting secured): SBS int. with JS

"It's a symbol of freedom": *Women's Wear Daily,* December 16, 1977

Billie and his father

"I've spent a long time": Ibid.

"I love myself": *The Washington Post,* May 24, 1977

Not surprisingly, Paley appeared: SBS ints. with JS and RoW

"He has always been stiff": confidential source

Babe's distance from the children

"Bill put pressure": confidential source

"She wanted to be a good": SBS int. with MaT

"warm but not tactile": Clarke, p. 280

With more than a trace: confidential source

Babe felt guilty over: confidential source; SBS int. with TMc

"She once told me": confidential source

Babe's unhappiness

"she was extra-super-sensitive": SBS int. with LH

"She wanted Bill heart and soul": SBS int. with MaT

"After three years of the": David Halberstam int. with Truman Capote

She sensed, in effect, that she: SBS int. with HoK; confidential source

"There was a streak": SBS int. with DV

Truman Capote once told Babe: Clarke, p. 287; David Halberstam int. with Truman Capote

"Her life with Bill": SBS int. with HoK

"She wasn't a hundred percent": Ibid.

"You could see them": SBS int. with SK

to smooth out the edges: SBS int. with TMc

and she regularly saw: Clarke, p. 283; SBS int. with AB

The one person who witnessed: David Halberstam int. with Pam Colin-Harlech

Once when a floor lamp at Kiluna: confidential source

"Betsey," said Irene Selznick, "was for the straight": SBS int. with IS

"Bill was always flirting": SBS int. with Jeanne Murray Vanderbilt

During the summer after her: Ibid.

"I think he gave her joy": SBS int. with LH

"loved loved loved": Clarke, p. 287

"She loved loved loved": SBS int. with SK

CHAPTER 35

Murrow moves into TV

from 14 full-time: SM notes for talk to FCC network study staff, 1/4/56

"Television offers keener": "Furthering Education," by WSP, *New York Times,* June 13, 1988

"See It Now"

Murrow made the jump: Persico, p. 301

"See It Now" won: Sperber, pp. 356, 370

The McCarthy broadcast

Prodded by colleagues: Halberstam, 141

Since the Radulovich: Barnouw, Vol. III, pp. 47–49

"We tried to keep it a secret": transcript of David Halberstam int. with Fred W. Friendly, producer for ERM

Only two months earlier: Persico, p. 423; Halberstam, p. 147

Afterwards, Bricker cried foul: SBS int. with FS

Memories vary: Ibid.; transcript of David Halberstam int. with Louis Cowan; transcript of David Halberstam ints. with WSP and FWF

"Are you satisfied": David Halberstam int. with WSP

"I'm with you today": Halberstam, p. 144

Despite his brave: WSP to Phil Donahue, 9/26/79

He knew McCarthy was: National Public Radio int. with WSP, November 1979

"His support of Ed": SBS int. with SK

But it was Babe: SBS int. with FS

"batten down the hatches": Ibid.

"this is no time": Sperber, p. 438

As such, it was enormously: Ibid., p. 433

In the aftermath: Ibid., p. 439; Persico, p. 381

Conservative columnists: Sperber, p. 445

"The day after the broadcast": David Halberstam int. with WSP

With Murrow's assent: Sperber, p. 460;

National Public Radio int. with
   WSP, November 1979
In response to an inquiry: memo from
   WSP and FS, 3/17/54
the Murrow program "exceptional":
   Sperber, p. 435
"We were trying to make": SBS int.
   with FS
Paley felt compelled to: "The Road to
   Responsibility," WSP speech to
   NAB, 5/30/54
"turning point in broadcasting's": *New
   York Times,* May 30, 1954
"the bible for news": transcript of Don
   West int. with WSP (October 1976)
Paley suggested that when: *AIH,* p. 284
"Certainly after the broadcast": SBS int.
   with FS
"You saw him in action": WSP to Phil
   Donahue, 9/26/79
courtesy not of CBS but of ABC:
   Barnouw, Vol. III, pp. 54–55
"It wasn't Murrow who killed": David
   Halberstam int. with Jack Gould
"We covered the hearings": WSP to
   Donahue, 9/26/79; *AIH,* p. 286
Many of Murrow's colleagues felt:
   Halberstam, p. 143
and Paley would admit: National Public
   Radio int. with WSP, November
   1979
President Eisenhower's two: Barnouw,
   Vol. III, pp. 10–11
Eisenhower himself: Ibid., p. 13;
   Sperber, p. 404
"CBS—villain to those": Cogley
   Report, p. 128
Formerly forbidden writers: William
   Robson's oral history
"In spite of the genuinely": Leonard,
   p. 79
"Bill Paley was proud": David
   Halberstam int. with FWF

Oppenheimer broadcast

In January 1955: Sperber, p. 478; Persico,
   p. 406

Continuing "See It Now" Controversies

There were other: Sperber, p. 479;
   Persico, pp. 406–407
"My very private reaction": SBS int.
   with FS
"They were unhappy with ": Ibid.
Moreover, in early February: Plotkin
   memo CBS press release, 2/2/55
"When CBS squeezed": SBS int. with
   FS
He offered to expand: Sperber,
   pp. 482–483

CHAPTER 36

The Ascent of FS

"In the 1950s Paley pulled": SBS int.
   with SM
Even the annual year-end: Sperber,
   p. 528
"Toward the end": transcript of David
   Halberstam int. with Alexander
   Kendrick, former CBS news
   correspondent

FS and Khrushchev interview

"Bill was not involved": SBS int. with
   FS
"I got the idea he wasn't": Ibid.
The CBS president defended: FS speech
   to National Press Club, 7/2/57
"As the praise in print": SBS int. with
   FS

"Where We Stand"

Called "Where We Stand": Sperber,
   p. 525; SBS int. with FS
"He didn't like it but": SBS int. with FS

Paley disputes with Smith and Sevareid

Richard Salant usually: SBS int. with HKS

At Paley's direction: SBS int. with SM

"Paley wouldn't yield": Ibid.

Only one of his: letter from William Worthy to the *New York Times,* 7/17/82; Barnouw, Vol. III, p. 100

an "old friend": Sperber, p. 512

"I'm going to have": SBS int. with ES

"fair, honest and well-founded": *AIH,* p. 302

"I rode along because": SBS int. with ES

Murrow had broadcast: Sperber, pp. 511–512; Barnouw, Vol. III, p. 100

The beginning of Murrow's slide at CBS

now mockingly known: *Air Time: The Inside Story of CBS News,* Gary Paul Gates (New York, 1978), p. 25

Murrow had resigned: Persico, p. 421

In truth, Murrow felt: SBS ints. with JR and FS; Sperber, p. 502

a "place at the table": SBS int. with FS

"It was another way": SBS int. with Jap Gude

In the seven years that followed: Metz, p. 110

"Ed would sit at the end": SBS int. with JR

Continuing troubles with "See It Now"

Paley overruled him, bowing: Sperber, p. 492

Murrow was so angry: Ibid., pp. 492–493

"was cold and stubborn": SBS int. with SM

"I was short-circuited": SBS int. with FS

Murrow wrote another: Sperber, pp. 531–532

"We had a terrific": Robert Lamb int. with WSP, 11/5/76

"But I thought you and Fred": *Due to Circumstances Beyond Our Control . . . ,* Fred W. Friendly (New York, 1967), p. 92

the CBS chairman punched: Sperber, p. 532

"I don't want this constant": Persico, p. 427; Halberstam, p. 150; Friendly, p. 92

"pretty burned up": SBS int. with JM

Paley and Eisenhower

"Ike was a hero to him": SBS int. with Guy Della Cioppa; letter from WSP to Dwight D. Eisenhower, 11/9/51: "It seems to me quite fantastic that one individual, through the force of his personality, could raise the hopes and aspirations of the people of western Europe as much as you have."

When Eisenhower had been named: letter from WSP to Dwight D. Eisenhower, 7/24/47

"I feel strongly": letter from WSP to Dwight D. Eisenhower, 9/16/48

Paley eagerly accepted: SBS int. with WSP

"The vacancy is in sight": letter from Dwight D. Eisenhower to WSP, 2/25/50

That February, Eisenhower: Diggins, p. 124

"amateur in the field": letter from WSP to Dwight D. Eisenhower, 3/12/52

When Eisenhower kicked off: SBS int. with FS

He ordered: Sperber, pp. 384–385; Halberstam, pp. 231–232

"Bill would help": SBS int. with WT

Paley's private advice was: Barnouw, Vol. II, pp. 299, 302

"He was very much under": SBS int. with Walter Cronkite, former CBS anchorman

"Henry Luce wanted to change": SBS int. with FWF

"You'll be the one man": confidential source

Nearly a decade later: letter from WSP to Dwight D. Eisenhower, 3/19/60

"more than just a political": SBS int. with WSP

"I am more convinced than ever": letter from WSP to Dwight D. Eisenhower, 1/11/55

"inner needs and desires": letter from WSP to Dwight D. Eisenhower, 1/11/56

Eisenhower sent Paley: letter from Dwight D. Eisenhower to WSP, 1/15/56

"They don't surprise me": SBS int. with WT

"How overjoyed I am": letter from WSP to Dwight D. Eisenhower, 11/9/56

In December 1956, Eisenhower: Kahn, pp. 214–221

"The circuits went dead": SBS int. with FS

The men at CBS News: SBS int. with HKS

In the 1956 campaign: Sperber, p. 489

"Bill Paley disapproved of Ed": SBS int. with HKS

CHAPTER 37

"The $64,000 Question"

"It would be a much better": SBS int. with SM

Stanton's demographic research: SBS int. with FS

Lou Cowan had a worthy: SBS int. with Geoffrey Cowan, son of Louis Cowan

Quiz show imitators: Barnouw, Vol. III, p. 58

The television boom

At CBS, net revenues: *Moody's Manual,* 1957

As the television audience grew: SBS int. with DA

An inventive solution: David Adams report; Barnouw, Vol. III, pp. 59–60

The quiz show scandals break

The seeds of the trouble: *Time,* November 16, 1959

The first hints: *Time,* April 22, 1957

Five months later, Herbert Stempel: *Time,* November 16, 1959

Stanton immediately launched: SBS int. with FS

Both the Manhattan: Barnouw, Vol. III, pp. 121–126

Murrow's October 1958 speech

"decadence, escapism and insulation": Sperber, pp. 537–540; Persico, p. 435

"Do you want to hit": SBS int. with FWF

"Ed had given up": SBS int. with JM

"He was very cool": SBS ints. with SM and FS

"He is fouling his own nest": SBS int. with RS

Paley had certainly known: Sperber, p. 110

"It was a direct attack on me": SBS int. with FWF; Sperber, pp. 541–542

Not only was he hurt: SBS int. with FS

Years later Paley described: Persico, p. 435

"never had a civil": SBS int. with FWF

Coolness between Murrow and Paley

"He got an office memo": SBS int. with Robert Trout

"What is the point": "Personal Communications: The Memoirs of

Louis G. Cowan," by Louis G.
Cowan and Martin Mayer,
unpublished manuscript, chapter 4,
p. 1

Spring public relations offensive

CBS formed a "special committee":
memo from SM to FS, 2/20/59
"strong and continuing": Committee
Report, 3/3/59
Two months later: Sperber, p. 554
"salvaged . . . from the wreckage":
Leonard, p. 78
Stanton chose Fred: SBS int. with FS

Paley's surgery

It began quite innocently (and following
paragraphs): confidential source;
AIH, pp. 248–251
"Oh, for God's sake": *AIH*, p. 249
"We would not feel very comfortable":
confidential source
"Mr. Paley, in your case": Ibid.
"I would be myself": Ibid.

Stanton's New Orleans speech

In September, Congress passed: *AIH*,
p. 292
The FCC was also considering a new:
Sperber, p. 574
once again, he did it without: SBS int.
with FS
a "hard look": FS speech text, 10/16/59
When Jack Gould: Persico, pp. 447–448;
Sperber, pp. 575–577
The next day: Sperber, pp. 576–577
"We were purring": SBS int. with FS
"He didn't flat out ask": Ibid.
"Bill was uncomfortable": Ibid.
After hours of discussion: Sperber,
p. 581
Colin returned to New York: Ibid.,
p. 582
"Bill was still pretty": SBS int. with FS

Paley would have no further: Sperber,
p. 583
"He was doing what a CEO": SBS int.
with FS
"I could not stand by": *AIH*, p. 296
"I just don't think": SBS int. with FS;
Sperber, p. 578

The quiz show scandal ends

The following month: letter from Louis
Cowan to FS, 12/8/59
Stanton had borne the brunt: Sperber,
p. 587
"He grew up with quiz": SBS int. with
EKM
Others, notably Richard Salant: SBS int.
with FS
"smeared rather badly": *AIH*, p. 246
"He knew it was something": SBS int.
with FS
"Paley vanished to the Bahamas":
Cowan manuscript, chapter 4, p. 18
"Where Is Paley?": *Variety*, December
16, 1959
"In a crisis": David Halberstam int. with
Robert Landry
"We had given very little": *AIH*, p. 246

Murrow's depression at CBS

"As Ed became more of": SBS int. with
FS
Their social relationship: David
Halberstam int. with JM; Metz,
p. 291
"I don't think I can": SBS int. with Blair
Clark, former CBS News general
manager
"When Ed was on the way down":
transcript of David Halberstam int.
with Charles Collingwood, former
CBS News correspondent; SBS int.
with HKS
Wounded as he was: SBS int. with JM
"He never lost his fascination": SBS int.
with HKS

Murrow leaves

he sought out Paley: National Public
    Radio int. with WSP, November
    1979
he assured Murrow he would: Ibid.
But he quickly moved on: Persico,
    p. 466
Afterwards, Paley expressed: SBS int.
    with FS

Murrow's illness and death

The material below is based on Sperber,
    pp. 683–700, and Persico, p. 492,
    unless otherwise indicated
"Ed, I don't know": SBS int. with FWF
"We were very close": Robert Lamb int.
    with WSP, 11/5/76
Paley preferred to blame: *Broadcasting*
    editors' int. with WSP, April 12,
    1976
"It was very difficult": "Good Night and
    Good Luck," documentary on
    BBC, April 27, 1975
"My God, I gave him": David
    Halberstam int. with WSP
"With Ed, Paley got": SBS int. with
    Robert Trout
"Murrow had a cool, disabused":
    transcript of David Halberstam int.
    with BC

CHAPTER 38

Stanton and Paley compared

"The Veronica Lake": *Time,* December
    4, 1950
His jaw often clamped: *Park East* (July
    1951)
Stanton's reading list: *The Saturday
    Review,* June 26, 1948
"just a country boy": *Time,* December 4,
    1950
"Rat smart": confidential sources

Paley's routines

at the end of the year Paley's: SBS int.
    with Emily Greene
His memos tended to be brief: Ibid.; SBS
    int. with RoW
"He told me in general": SBS int. with
    RS
Paley loathed presiding: SBS int. with
    EKM
Number-one secretary: "Tex and Jinx"
    column, *New York Herald Tribune,*
    March 3, 1950
"often hands out jobs": *Time*
    correspondent's file, 1/28/49

Stanton's routine

He kept a yearly diary: SBS int. with
    FS
"I just looked up": *Forbes,* January 15,
    1964
Every time he visited: SBS int. with
    Perry Lafferty, former CBS
    Hollywood programming executive
Once a fellow broadcaster: *National
    Biographic* (June 1953)
His desk: SBS int. with FS
His idea of: SBS ints. with RW and
    EKM
"By 10 o'clock": *Park East* (July 1951)
On trips to England: SBS ints. with FS
    and MB
If one incident typifies: *National
    Biographic* (June 1953)

Paley in business meetings

"was the kind of man": SBS int. with
    HA
On his desk, Paley had: Considine
"His mind was not well trained": SBS
    int. with William Leonard, former
    president of CBS News
At one point Amos 'n' Andy: Tom
    Shales int. with WSP, 3/6/79; *New
    York Times,* October 24, 1976

"His control was never": SBS int. with JS

He would jump from point A: SBS int. with DH

Paley's intuitive leaps: SBS int. with FS

"We would show him a pilot": SBS int. with RW

After seeming to lose track: SBS int. with MD

"If you put on a flop": SBS int. with Oscar Katz, former programming executive for CBS

"Bill told me once": SBS int. with MD

"If something got in him": SBS int. with WL

Paley acted the omnipotent: SBS int. with DH

If he wanted to explain: SBS int. with James T. Aubrey, former president of CBS Television

"Many people who own": SBS int. with DH

"He was very much a realist": SBS int. with Ray Price

"If Paley wanted to fire": SBS int. with DA

Stanton in business meetings

One day Paley's aide: SBS int. with Guy Della Cioppa

"When you go in": *TV Guide*, January 12, 1963

Stanton had always made it his business: *Broadcasting*, March 26, 1973

"by staying a step": Jimmy Breslin column, *New York Daily News*, May 24, 1977

From 1939 to 1942: Don West int. with WSP (October 1976); SBS int. with FS

Paley and Stanton compared

he shied away from appointing: SBS int. with DH

"Occasionally, if a man": SBS int. with MaT

"Overstatements in both": SBS int. with FS

"I'm curious. He is reasonably": Ibid.

"I can't imagine what Frank": *National Biographic* (June 1953)

"He had such facility in his": SBS int. with FS

"My uncles used to get": confidential source

Stanton seemed to wear: SBS int. with TMc

But most of all, Paley believed: SBS int. with Michael Dann, former programming chief at CBS

Stanton's lifestyle

Sometimes when he was on business: *Park East* (July 1951)

He liked to park: SBS int. with Lou Dorfsman, former vice president for advertising and design at CBS

"She knew more about": SBS int. with FS

"tasteful and precise": *Time*, December 4, 1950

"It's easy to do": *New York Times*, October 3, 1966

"I made it a condition": SBS int. with FS

Paley's pique

Stanton's rebuffs of: Ibid.

The Stanton town house: Ibid.

once calling Stanton: confidential source

"came rather naturally": *AIH*, p. 86

Paley's exceptions

"There were certain kinds": SBS int. with Sheryl Handler, president of Thinking Machines Corp.

he was knowledgeable without: SBS int. with Walter Yetnikoff, president of CBS/Sony

He produced a groundbreaking series: SBS int. with Brigitta Lieberson, widow of Goddard Lieberson

"Bill Paley learned": SBS int. with John Hammond

"Bill had a receptive mind": SBS int. with Brigitta Lieberson

He approached business: Ibid.; SBS int. with Walter Yetnikoff

When Paley described Lieberson: *AIH*, p. 334

Paley's summary of Stanton: Ibid., pp. 178 and 347

CHAPTER 39

Paley and Stanton co-exist

"Frank seemed to handle": Leonard, p. 178

"There were pilots we saw": SBS int. with FS

With a careful eye toward: SBS int. with FS

"He knew what was going on": SBS int. with ES

"Bill's technique of asking": SBS int. with JR

At that stage, Stanton knew: SBS int. with FS

As he grew more experienced: SBS int. with RW

"Everyone always wondered": SBS int. with FWF

In fact, Stanton talked: SBS ints. with EKM and FS

When Stanton first proposed: SBS ints. with Guy Della Cioppa and FS

"It was no use arguing": SBS int. with AT

"Nothing would disrupt": SBS int. with FS

"In private, Frank Stanton": SBS int. with JS

Stanton sets traps

He positioned himself: SBS ints. with JS and FS

In 1946, Arthur Hull Hayes: SBS int. with FS

Paley's kitchen cabinet

In later years Paley would say: *Esquire* (December 1983)

But in fact Paley talked to Selznick: *Variety*, August 31, 1949

These were often strange conversations: SBS int. with FS

Stanton as buffer

"He was above everyone": SBS int. with Sal Ianucci, former CBS Hollywood executive

"Bill was never able to": SBS int. with EKM

"That's his job": SBS int. with Guy Della Cioppa

Everyone feared him and some: SBS ints. with DH, JR, and WL

"You knew at any moment": confidential source

"Paley wouldn't yell": SBS int. with MD

Once at a meeting: SBS int. with Walter Yetnikoff

"He is what he is": SBS int. with RW

"Paley didn't like the impression": SBS int. with Guy Della Cioppa

Many times Stanton tried: Ibid.

In that capacity he had: SBS int. with Mary Elizabeth Taylor, widow of Davidson Taylor

When Taylor failed to come up: SBS int. with FS

If someone did a job: *TV/Radio Age*, March 3, 1973

When CBS was crippled: SBS int. with FS

Stanton's thoughtfulness: SBS ints. with Sal Ianucci, EKM, and DH

When CBS programmer Harry: SBS int. with HA

Before a dinner: *Printer's Ink,* December 5, 1958

If something failed: SBS int. with DA

"Frank Stanton would tell you": SBS int. with Sal Ianucci

The CBS Eye

The Eye was conceived: SBS int. with FS: "My Eye," by William Golden, from Cipe Golden, et al., eds., *The Visual Craft of William Golden* (New York, 1962)

"He was not unhappy with it": SBS int. with FS

Stanton becomes too dominant

"I let Frank Stanton": SBS int. with WSP

"Paley was shrewd": transcript of David Halberstam int. with Jack Gould

"It worked out fine": SBS int. with EKM

"A lot of people I knew": SBS int. with FS; *Business Week,* July 21, 1951

"You are talking to": SBS int. with FS

"Who else had the opportunity": Ibid.

"the boy wonder": *New York Post,* November 11, 1959

Some even thought: SBS int. with JS

"While Bill Paley was away": SBS int. with RS

"I withdrew": *People,* March 19, 1979

and so did Paley's friends: confidential source

In 1956, Stanton was asked: SBS int. with FS

CHAPTER 40

Inevitable clash

"If Paley had not gone off": SBS int. with RS

"It was a difficult": SBS int. with FS

"When I finally started": confidential source

Stanton in news

He had lobbied vigorously: Barnouw, Vol. III, pp. 160–165

Although Paley understood: SBS int. with FS

"News was taking on": Ibid.

Paley and Nixon campaign

Paley contributed $25,000: transcript of Daniel Schorr int. with WSP

"Bill was involved": SBS int. with WT

After the fourth: SBS int. with Herb Klein, former Nixon aide

"I gave Nixon advice": Daniel Schorr int. with WSP, February 17, 1977

Ambassador to Rome

Stanton found himself: SBS int. with FS

"Wonderful idea": Ibid.

"It was not the kind": Ibid.

"wasn't a central": SBS int. with WSP

Paley moves into CBS News

"maximum hysteria": SBS int. with RS

"It drove Bill Paley wild": Ibid.

That August, Paley made his: SM memo to CBS files, 8/29/60

"not now convinced": Ibid.

Over the following months: SBS int. with SM

a little too sharp and fast: SBS int. with FS

"Bill was not supportive": Ibid.

"The whole process of": SBS int. with RS

Paley attended the news executive: SBS ints. with FS, RS, and BC

"Paley wasn't interested": SBS int. with BC

"he didn't really need": SBS int. with RS

"Some policies started": SBS int. with FS

Paley and Howard K. Smith

"How Bill Paley thought": SBS int. with BC

In the spring of 1961: Gates, p. 38; Halberstam, p. 411; Sperber, p. 380

Shortly before the documentary: SBS int. with HKS

When Paley heard it: Ibid.; Halberstam, p. 411

Blair Clark ordered the quote: Gates, p. 38

Paley summoned Smith: HKS on "Tomorrow" Show, 6/18/79; *AIH*, p. 294

Instead, Smith wrote: SBS int. with RS

"It wasn't a reasoned": SBS int. with BC

What irritated Paley: SBS ints. with RS and ES

"wasn't driven off the air": Don West int. with WSP, October 1976

"always liked to be": SBS int. with RS

Cronkite replaces Edwards

In early 1962, Paley turned: Gates, p. 79

For his first year: SBS ints. with RS and BC

"How about Roger Mudd?": SBS int. with BC

although, as the newsman: SBS int. with Walter Cronkite

The following year, Paley gave his: Gates, pp. 93, 144

Paley shows his jealousy of Stanton

On both Cronkite's appointment: SBS int. with FS

As early as May 1961: WSP speech to affiliates, "The Path to Leadership," 5/5/61

"I have the sense": SBS int. with Newton Minow, former chairman of the FCC

When the group told him: SBS int. with FS

"Are you sure": Ibid.

One of CBS's many acclaimed: *Documentary in American Television,* A. William Bluem (New York, 1965), p. 109

"all the nice things": SBS int. with FWF

At the end of the four: Barnouw, Vol. III, p. 235

"He was second-guessing": SBS int. with FS

"He was wistful about": Ibid.

The following month: *Gallagher Report,* December 23, 1963

Paley fires Salant

In February 1964, Paley asserted: SBS int. with RS; *Gallagher Report,* March 4, 1964; Gates, p. 105

Both men worked emotionally: SBS int. with RS

"tight and unemotional": WSP in BBC documentary, "Good Night and Good Luck"

"man of great vigour who": Ibid.

"Dick was a hair shirt": SBS int. with FS

Heartbroken, Salant looked: SBS ints. with RS and FS

"I was devastated": SBS int. with FS

1964 Republican Convention and dumping of Cronkite

Frank Stanton stayed away: *Variety,* October 7, 1964

He sat at Friendly's elbow: SBS int. with FWF; Schorr, pp. 7–9

"It never fell out of my": Daniel Schorr int. with WSP

Cronkite talked too much: SBS ints. with FWF and WL

"I could hear them": SBS int. with Walter Cronkite

"Bill was sore": SBS int. with FS

"What the hell happened": Leonard, p. 110

"What about Roger Mudd": SBS ints. with WL and FWF

"He was headstrong": SBS int. with FS

Several days later: Gates, p. 112

When they broke the news: SBS int. with FWF

In the end, Mudd: Gates, p. 116

Paley never voiced: SBS int. with FS

CHAPTER 41

Aubrey and Paley

"I was still in my recessive": confidential source

"conventionally good-looking": *Only You, Dick Daring! Or How to Write One Television Script and Make $50,000,000. A True-Life Adventure,* Merle Miller and Evan Rhodes (New York, 1964), pp. 107, 108

"the coolest of the cool": *Business Week,* April 25, 1964

Aubrey's daring streak: confidential source

In 1948 he got a job: *Life,* September 10, 1965; *Business Week,* April 25, 1964

In 1958 he sent a message: SBS int. with FS

Aubrey as an executive

"slick as silk, smooth as": *New York Times Magazine,* November 15, 1964

"on his persona": SBS int. with James Aubrey

"not by a foot": *New York Herald Tribune,* January 19, 1964

"How did Aubrey get": Miller, p. 49

While Paley could be: SBS int. with Sal Ianucci

"Bill was caught up in": SBS int. with FS

Aubrey's routine

Aubrey was a workaholic: *Business Week,* April 25, 1964

He would watch as many: Murray Kempton in *The New Republic,* April 3, 1965; *Life,* September 10, 1965

"I could picture Aubrey": Miller, p. 108

He brought his golf: SBS int. with RW

"We try to cultivate": *Business Week,* April 25, 1964

"broads, bosoms, and fun": *New York Herald Tribune,* January 19, 1964

("an extra dry martini"): *New York Herald Tribune,* March 8, 1964

"Mike Bell must be": Aubrey memo to Dan Melnick, 5/4/64

Except as a rubber stamp: SBS ints. with MD, Sal Ianucci, and FS

"What the hell *is* this?": SBS int. with FS

Paley "genuinely disliked": *Los Angeles Times,* April 27, 1986

"I thought it was beautifully": *Broadcasting,* April 12, 1976

With his prep school: CBS official biography of James Aubrey

"Bill and I used to date": *Los Angeles Times,* April 27, 1986

Aubrey's arrogance

His charm vanished: SBS int. with FS
"You're through": *Life,* September 10, 1965
As if the incident: confidential source
"colder and colder": *Life,* September 10, 1965
"Jim had no fear level": SBS int. with RW
"Aubrey received this": Miller, pp. 107–108
"The Smiling Cobra": *Los Angeles Times,* April 27, 1986
"Aubrey was two people": SBS int. with Oscar Katz

Aubrey and Jack Benny

"Jack was uncomfortable": SBS int. with Irving Fein
Aubrey had presented his decision: SBS ints. with FS and James Aubrey
"Aubrey turned out": SBS int. with Irving Fein

Aubrey's high-handedness

Aubrey's cavalier ways: *Life,* September 10, 1965; SBS int. with FS
"They don't mean anything": SBS int. with FS
"Aubrey was a very sharp": Ibid.
"Billy, you worry": confidential source
"They were snotty remarks": SBS int. with FS
"Undisputed arbiter": *Business Week,* April 25, 1964
"absolute power": *New York Herald Tribune,* January 19, 1964
"Mr. CBS": *Time,* January 31, 1964
"TV's St. Peter": *Variety,* January 22, 1964

Aubrey's personal and professional problems

One evening during: confidential source
When CBS ignored the charges: *Closeup* letter to E. William Henry, 7/7/64; chairman's office inquiry into charges, 7/23/64; Ashbrook Bryant, chief of network study, memo to Henry on Aubrey, 8/6/64; *Closeup* letter to Henry, 8/27/64; FCC call to Leon Brooks, chief counsel for CBS, 9/16/64
Stanton hired a New York City: SBS int. with FS; *Variety,* March 3, 1965
After CBS submitted: letter from Leon Brooks to FCC, 12/21/64, with a blow-by-blow account of finances of the three Richelieu shows

Paley's displeasure with CBS programs

The one exception had: SBS int. with MD
"Aubrey's making a serious": *New York Herald Tribune,* January 19, 1964
When Aubrey touted "The Munsters": SBS ints. with Oscar Katz and MD
"We can't let": SBS int. with MD
"I have to do it for": confidential source
At one point in 1964: SBS int. with MB
"It's time to kick": SBS int. with FS

Aubrey loses it

"Aren't we going to": SBS ints. with Sal Ianucci, MB, and FS
By mid-February, Stanton told: SBS int. with FS
"persistent rumors that": *Newsweek,* February 22, 1965
"Ratings," Stanton later: SBS int. with FS
"He could not handle his own": *Broadcasting,* March 12, 1979
"Things add up in one's": SBS int. with FS
After the Gleason bash: *Life,* September 10, 1965

Stanton fires Aubrey

a "serious" matter: SBS int. with FS
Paley, who was in traction: *AIH*, p. 252
"Are you sure": SBS int. with FS
"Bill had been willing": Ibid.
"This is a difficult": Ibid.
"I'm sorry you have to": Ibid.
"Search the building!": Ibid.
Aubrey made a strong pitch: Ibid.
"You know, I deserve it all": Tom
     Shales int. with WSP, 3/6/79
"magnificent in defeat": Ibid.
Aubrey settled into a life: SBS int. with
     James Aubrey
"You know I don't read": *Los Angeles
     Times,* April 27, 1986

Paley bounces back

"What does Jim think": SBS ints. with
     MD and Sal Ianucci
"Buy the Hazel show": Ibid.

CHAPTER 42

Paley and Mike Dann

"From 1965 on, Paley": SBS int. with
     MD
"We called Mike 'the Screamer' ": SBS
     int. with Emily Greene
"I kept thinking": Miller, p. 157
"Dann was answering": Ibid., p. 159
"Same old crap": Metz, p. 321

Marathon screenings

Jim Aubrey had instituted: SBS int. with
     PL
His subordinates eyed: Ibid.
he affectionately referred: SBS int. with
     RW
He was often restless: SBS ints. with PL,
     Alan Wagner, former CBS program
     executive, MD, and Sal Ianucci

On his lap he kept: SBS int. with PL
Close by, Mike Dann: SBS int. with
     MD
"If Mr. Paley didn't like": SBS int. with
     Alan Wagner
"If something was bad": SBS int. with
     MD
The worst judgment: SBS int. with PL
"If there were a show": SBS int. with
     OK

Paley's programming role in 1960s

At one point Dann was: SBS int. with
     MD
"The operative force": Ibid.
He decreed that singers: SBS ints. with
     Alan Wagner and PL
He hated Peter Falk: SBS int. with MD
"How can you have": Ibid.
He seemed to watch: SBS int. with PL
In September 1965 he turned: SBS ints.
     with MD and PL
"What's going on with 'Rawhide'?":
     Ibid.
"kicking and screaming": SBS int. with
     MD
"Build up the older star": Ibid.
"He was good at supporting": Ibid.

Paley and CBS stars

The Paleys would take: SBS ints. with
     Guy Della Cioppa and Howard
     Meighan, former CBS-TV
     executive in Hollywood
Sometimes, if Paley: SBS int. with HA
In meetings with his performers: Ibid.
"impersonal love": confidential source
They understood and respected: SBS int.
     with Guy Della Cioppa
Once when Danny Thomas: SBS int.
     with OK
Bing Crosby kept: SBS int. with Guy
     Della Cioppa
Red Skelton wouldn't even: SBS int.
     with Howard Meighan

"Is this movement": *Variety*, March 30, 1949

Paley was selective about: SBS int. with FS

"He didn't want to see": SBS int. with Guy Della Cioppa

"Bill liked Freeman": SBS int. with FS

As time went on: Ibid.

Freeman Gosden could fracture: confidential source

Truman Capote claimed: David Halberstam int. with Truman Capote

"That part of the world": SBS int. with FS

Diversification fever

All three networks felt: SBS int. with Thornton Bradshaw, former chairman of NBC

CBS also had large amounts: SBS int. with Richard McDonald, broadcasting analyst, First Boston; *AIH*, p. 337

In 1961, Paley and Stanton: SBS int. with FS; confidential source; *AIH*, p. 337

He proved a charming and capable: SBS ints. with FS and MB

"Paley called me three": SBS int. with MB

"He frequently looked": SBS int. with FS

As early as 1960: Ibid; Halberstam, pp. 364–365

"I thought it would involve": SBS int. with FS

He had discussions with: Ibid.; *Gallagher Report*, December 16, 1963; September 1, 1964

The Yankees

He wanted to buy 80 percent: *AIH*, p. 338

Unknown to Stanton: SBS int. with FS; Considine

"The first meeting I went": SBS int. with FS

"some of the owners": Ibid.

"It's a good investment": Considine

"All my life": SBS int. with FWF

"He was like a ten-": SBS int. with MB

Other purchases

Harbridge had identified: confidential source

a "compatible product": Considine

"He was a spender of money": SBS int. with DH

"One thing that I think got": SBS int. with RW

CHAPTER 43

Black Rock: The struggle for approval

Stanton had been pushing: SBS int. with FS

"Coca-Cola bottle with setbacks": Ibid.

On November 21: *AIH*, p. 345

"he froze": SBS int. with FS

"I was never sure": Ibid.

In March 1961: *AIH*, p. 342

"If I could assure you": SBS int. with FS

"I don't want to have": Ibid.

"Let's talk some more": Ibid.

He liked Saarinen's original: *AIH*, p. 342

Building Black Rock

While vacationing in Spain: *AIH*, p. 343; SBS int. with FS

"I know why Eero wanted": SBS int. with FS

Paley pressed for: Ibid.; SBS int. with Lou Dorfsman

After months searching: *AIH*, p. 344. This seems to be typical Paley exaggeration. Stanton said that he and Paley visited the mockup together once; this was, to Stanton's knowledge, Paley's only trip to New Rochelle. Stanton consulted the models periodically, and he was astonished by Paley's claim.

"With his energy": SBS int. with RW

Stanton and Knoll selected: SBS int. with FS; *Life,* April 29, 1966

"Slightly overripe": transcript of David Halberstam interview with John Hightower, former head of the Museum of Modern Art

"It was as if Bill": SBS int. with JS

"To my mind the coldness": SBS int. with RW

"It's over": confidential sources

"It was because it was": Ibid.

"Bill did what he did": Ibid.

Tensions between Paley and Stanton

"Why are you going?": SBS int. with FS

"Well," he said angrily: Ibid.

"expressed no interest": Ibid.

"It was in the atmosphere": SBS int. with RS

"Bill Paley got more and more": SBS int. with MB

"Frank would have one view": SBS int. with DH

"Frank was warm and sensitive": SBS int. with MB

"acute case of Potomac fever": *Variety,* October 7, 1964

Johnson made the expected: SBS int. with FS

Paley spurns retirement

"Would it be possible": memo from FS to EKM, 6/2/65

"My father is on the board": SBS int. with FS

"You know," Paley said: Ibid.

"It was obvious": Ibid.

Meanwhile, Stanton's ten-year: CBS Proxy Statement, 1966

The memo, to be ratified: Draft memo, WSP to the Organization, 2/9/66

"It came out of the blue": SBS int. with FS

On February 8, Paley sent: WSP memo to FS, 1/8/66

Stanton had only: Draft memo, WSP to the Organization 2/9/66

After several minutes, Winnie: SBS ints. with RS and FS

"Let's wait and talk": SBS int. with FS

"It was one of the most": SBS int. with RS

When the board meeting ended: FS memo to the Organization, 2/9/66

Stanton was "shattered": David Halberstam int. with Ralph Colin

"I knew how hard it was": SBS int. with RW

Jack Gould recalled: David Halberstam int. with Jack Gould

Gould's subsequent article: *New York Times,* February 10, 1966. At least one published account reported Paley's reneging on the CEO title as having occurred at the time of the March board meeting; but none of the principals involved recalled the matter coming up then. All recollections as well as documents from the time refer only to the February meeting.

"If I had taken": SBS int. with FS

"I have never come back": Ibid.

"tried at one point": *AIH,* p. 348

"It was a spontaneous": SBS int. with WSP

Years later Stanton: SBS int. with FS

"Paley wouldn't have been": SBS int. with RS

Friendly resignation and Salant appointment

Privately, he lodged: Barnouw, Vol. III, pp. 278–279; FWF memo, 3/3/66

When Friendly watched: Friendly, pp. 236–241

Stanton and Friendly agreed: SBS int.
with FS; Friendly, p. 241

During their meeting: SBS ints. with FS
and EKM

"Don't worry, Fred can": Ibid. In his
book, FWF gives a detailed account
(pp. 234–254) of his resignation.
However, he skirts his premature
release of the resignation letter, an
action that WSP, FS, and EKM all
vividly recalled as a decisive factor
in FWF's departure.

Paley telephoned Friendly: *AIH,* p. 300;
SBS int. with Herbert Mitgang,
New York Times reporter and former
executive at CBS News; Friendly p.
253

"You had no right": SBS int. with
Herbert Mitgang

Stanton immediately proposed: SBS int.
with FS; *New York Times,* February
17, 1966

"I want to get some notion": SBS int.
with RS

Paley subsequently came up: SBS int.
with FS

But Stanton meanwhile: Ibid.

"We have resolved": SBS int. with RS

CHAPTER 44

Changes in Babe

they had not had sexual: Clarke, p. 287;
confidential sources

"nice New England": SBS int. with
HoK

by now she was up to: SBS int. with AB

"She wouldn't have a cigarette": Ibid.

"Maybe it was the cigarette": SBS int.
with Jeanne Thayer

The pressures on Babe

"Mrs. P had only one": Clarke,
p. 280

"She makes excellence": *Vogue* (May
1967)

"He wore her down": SBS int. with
Horst

"I never heard a cross": SBS int. with
AB

"She ran establishments": SBS int. with
Jeanne Thayer

Relations with her children

She favored him financially: memo from
Sullivan & Cromwell to Mr. Harry
Zankel, Guardian ad Litem, re
Estate of Barbara C. Paley,
11/26/82

"Tony knew all": confidential source

820 Fifth Avenue

Details are based on SBS ints. with AB,
HoK, John Richardson, and Mario
Buatta, New York decorator, as
well as author's observations

Babe's routine

Most mornings she awoke: confidential
source

"She once told me": SBS int. with
Jeanne Murray Vanderbuilt

She considered exercise: *Women's Wear
Daily,* July 7, 1978

If she felt even: *Ladies Home Journal*
(March 1958)

She gave small luncheons: confidential
source

"She was always shopping": confidential
source

On Mondays and Fridays: confidential
sources

At Monsieur Marc's: confidential source

"She was a person to get on":
confidential source

"She was mired in household":
    confidential source

Babe and her friends

Those closest to her included:
    confidential sources; list of bequests,
    Barbara Cushing Paley Estate:
    Judicial Decree, 12/23/82
"I was so at ease": SBS int. with Jeanne
    Thayer
"She had very distinct": SBS int. with
    DV
"He didn't like it when": confidential
    source
"After dinner in Nassau": SBS int. with
    HoK
"I remember once": SBS int. with
    Marion Osborn, childhood friend of
    BCP
"She was always thinking": Ibid.
"She was interested in": SBS int.
    with Aline, the Countess of
    Romanones
"She had an odd sort of": SBS int. with
    SK
"How are your finances?": SBS int. with
    SMA
"She rarely complained": SBS int. with
    HoK
"would not have occurred": SBS int.
    with SK
She told him that she: Clarke, p. 287
"It was since the birth": confidential
    sources

Babe copes with sexual rejection

Capote said Babe had a romance: Clarke,
    p. 287
Other friends talked: SBS ints. with
    HoK and Jeanne Murray Vanderbilt;
    confidential sources
"With him it was more": SBS int. with
    HoK
"During the ten-day": confidential
    source

"If he had known she": confidential
    source
"I would not think she got": SBS int.
    with IS
Partly this was a residue: SBS int. with
    HoK
"had trouble with men": SBS int. with
    CB
"coolly amiable glance": *Time,* January
    31, 1964
"She wasn't a woman who": SBS int.
    with LH
"I don't believe she minded":
    confidential source
"disinterested up to a point": SBS int.
    with HoK
"It was very tough on her": confidential
    source
"She was so chic and so stylish":
    confidential source

Paley's womanizing

To Paley, Babe's friends: confidential
    source
"Bill was never faithful": SBS int. with
    ALM
His conquests were: confidential sources
"Paley was fucking": SBS int. with
    MD
"Sexy but tarty-looking": confidential
    source
There were rumors in the sixties:
    confidential sources
Babe even braced him: SBS int. with SK;
    confidential sources
He lacked the generosity: confidential
    sources
he never wished to create: SBS ints. with
    TMc and JPr
"It was the mores of": confidential
    source
Still, *Babe* knew: David Halberstam int.
    with Truman Capote
"I thought, 'Bill loves'": SBS int. with
    HoK

Twenty years after the fact: confidential
source

Sam's death

Goldie and Sam rarely visited: SBS ints.
with IS and AB
"We want independence": Ira Berkow
int. with GP
"There were times when I know":
confidential source
Sam had suffered his first: *AIH*,
p. 362
"never missed a beat": SBS int. with
Robert Levy
Sam left an estate of: Samuel Paley will
and codicils dated 10/15/59, 9/19/
60, 10/15/62; Samuel Paley Estate
distribution, 5/2/68
indeed, it was originally: William S.
Paley Foundation press release, 2/1/
66
changing hot dog brands: *Esquire*
(August 1979)
He made frequent inspections: letter
from EKM to Jack Gould, 6/17/70

Death of Selznick

He heard the news on the radio: *Esquire*
(December 1983)
Selznick, his dearest friend: SBS int.
with IS; Selznick, p. 380
"Are you all right?" (and paragraphs that
follow): SBS int. with IS

Museum of Modern Art

In May 1969, Paley convened: WSP
letter to *Fortune* (September 1974);
AIH, p. 365
Among other perceived faults: *New York
Times*, May 12, 1969
"It was typical of Bill": SBS int. with
FS
When Ralph Colin: Metz, p. 389;
Halberstam, pp. 30–31; *AIH*, p. 365

"Has MOMA gone network?": *New
York Times*, May 12, 1969
A meticulous scholar: Persico, p. 449
Colin never felt Paley was: David
Halberstam int. with Ralph Colin;
Metz, p. 390
One source of Colin's: Metz, p. 390;
confidential source
Especially annoying was: SBS int. with
EKM; Metz, p. 389
For his part, Paley began: confidential
source
"Ralph had an obnoxious": SBS int.
with EKM
He summoned his adviser: Halberstam,
p. 31; *AIH*, p. 366; Metz, p. 392
Taking his cue: SBS int. with FS
"It is conceivable to me": SBS int. with
EKM

CHAPTER 45

Paley the diversification dilettante

"Bill would go away": SBS int. with JS
"overly cautious": *Forbes*, January 15,
1965
At $280 million, CBS's purchase:
Moody's Manual, 1967
The Holt deal came: SBS int. with FS
when Stanton had urged him: Ibid.;
Metz, p. 256
The company was a leading: Metz,
p. 257
The perception lingered: *New York
Herald Tribune*, April 29, 1968
"Bill Paley enjoyed doing": SBS int.
with DH

Paley wants to be movie mogul

except for one deal: *Variety*, December
16, 1950; May 30, 1951; SBS ints.
with Fritz Berlinger, friend of the
Paleys and Levys, and Robert Levy

In part, he believed that: *Life,* September 10, 1965

Paley also resisted: SBS int. with FS

As late as 1963, when Aubrey: *Gallagher Report,* July 29, 1963

Only when Aubrey's schedule: SBS int. with Sal Ianucci

At that point he began: Barnouw, Vol. III, p. 306; SBS ints. with Gordon Stulberg, former head of CBS Cinema Center Films, and JS

"He always figured if they": SBS int. with JS

CBS and Broadway

Paley was further: Ibid.; *AIH,* p. 335

In 1955, Goddard Lieberson had convinced: Herman Levin draft deal memo, 5/23/55

In subsequent years CBS put: *AIH,* p. 336

CBS in the movie business

They told Paley: SBS int. with FS

"I want to be in": Ibid.; SBS int. with JS

On Schneider's recommendation: Ibid.; *Moody's Manual,* 1967

Paley's pride: SBS ints. with Gordon Stulberg and JS

Every six to eight weeks: SBS int. with Gordon Stulberg

"He reacted in a curious": SBS int. with FS

One dilemma was how: SBS ints. with Gordon Stulberg and JS

"What better way to get": SBS int. with JS

"Set up a distinct": SBS int. with Gordon Stulberg

"That was how he set it": Ibid.

"We have to get together": Ibid.; SBS int. with JS

"It was clear": SBS int. with JS

"We didn't distribute": Ibid.

In mid-1970, Paley shifted: *Business Week,* July 4, 1970

a total loss of some $30 million: *New York Times,* October 24, 1976

Beginning in the mid-sixties, ABC had: *Up the Tube: Prime Time TV and the Silverman Years,* Sally Bedell (New York, 1981), p. 110

"Cinema Center was disposed of": SBS int. with Courtney Brown, former member of CBS board of directors

Yankees investment falls apart

By that time, Holt, Rinehart: *Financial World,* March 6, 1974

Paley would later insist: *AIH,* p. 338

"Bill Paley was determined": SBS int. with MB

While CBS was frittering: *New York Herald Tribune* April 29, 1968; SBS int. with Richard McDonald

Rather conspicuously, Stanton: SBS int. with FS

Paley and EVR

"His tone," recalled Goldmark: Goldmark, p. 172

Despite Paley's fear: Ibid., pp. 172, 177

"Marvelous," he proclaimed: Ibid., p. 181

"EVR must be good": Ibid., p. 188

"smelling profit for the first": Ibid.

"Bill, Peter may have": Ibid.; SBS int. with FS

was "hopping mad": Goldmark, p. 201

"an ingenious invention": SBS int. with FS

"EVR was on the brink": Goldmark, p. 201

"Bill Paley didn't have the guts": SBS int. with DH

In the end, Paley blamed: *AIH,* p. 227; SBS int. with FS

"How are we going to": SBS ints. with
      FS and DH
"I was on my way out": SBS int. with
      FS

CHAPTER 46

After the board meeting

"In the evening, Frank": confidential
      source
amid repeated rumors that: *Gallagher
      Report,* November 8, 1966; *New
      York Herald Tribune,* March 8, 1966;
      New York Daily News, September 8,
      1966
Stanton signed a new contract: CBS
      Proxy Statement, 1967
At Stanton's suggestion: SBS ints. with
      FS and JS
As part of the reorganization: SBS ints.
      with JS and RS

Paley tries for Court of St. James's

his own hope, following: SBS int.
      with WSP
"It would have been the ultimate": SBS
      int. with JS
Paley felt he had been: Daniel Schorr int.
      with WSP
But he had made no: Ibid.; *AIH,* p. 313
In 1967, Paley helped found: letter from
      WSP to Lee Heubner, 7/16/79
Early in the 1968 campaign: SBS ints.
      with Ray Price and WT
Not surprisingly, at the: *AIH,* p. 313
In a penthouse suite: SBS int. with
      William O'Shaughnessy
Toward the end of 1968: SBS int. with
      Peter Flanigan, former White House
      aide; David Halberstam int. with
      Ralph Colin
Flanigan's father: SBS int. with Herb
      Klein

"He was so galled": confidential source
There was talk, toward the end: SBS int.
      with WT; Peter Flanigan's memo to
      Richard Nixon, 9/16/69: "Walter
      Thayer informed me that Bill Paley
      would much prefer London to Paris
      even with the chance that the
      London post is some substantial
      time away."
"Bill has been offered": SBS int. with FS

Nixon White House versus CBS

"Bill didn't disagree": Ibid.
"Within the White House": SBS int.
      with Herb Klein

"The Selling of the Pentagon"

"We can solve this": SBS int. with FS
On July 1: *Newsweek,* July 26, 1971
Just as suddenly, Paley entered: SBS ints.
      with FS and EKM
Ever since February: SBS int. with FS
Still, it was crucial: SBS int. with RS
"one person out front": SBS int. with
      EKM
"Jock made jokes": Ibid.
"This doesn't look good": Ibid.
"So much had gone on": SBS int.
      with FS
Just to show he: *AIH,* p. 307: memo
      dated 7/9/71
When Paley insisted on: SBS int.
      with EKM
"Fortunately, Bill didn't": SBS int.
      with FS
CBS mounted an enormous: Schorr,
      p. 47; *Time,* July 26, 1971
"I think you are going": SBS int.
      with FS
"The White House isn't": Ibid.
Mills announced: *Newsweek,* July 26,
      1971
Staggers, beginning to feel: Schorr, p. 48
He grumbled over: *AIH,* p. 308

"Frank Stanton made a mistake": SBS
 ints. with RS and FS
But the CBS president felt: SBS int.
 with FS

The Watergate newscast controversy

Stanton saw it on the: Ibid.; Schorr,
 p. 33
"He was negative": SBS int. with FS;
 AIH, p. 317
Paley had encountered Colson's: Schorr,
 pp. 44–46
"Frank would be puzzled": SBS int.
 with Herb Klein
"Colson talked to me for": Daniel
 Schorr int. with WSP, 2/17/77
Colson later claimed: Schorr, p. 55
Paley contended: *AIH*, pp. 320–321
The following Monday, Paley convened:
 SBS ints. with FS, AT, JS, and RS;
 AIH, p. 318
Paley never mentioned: Daniel Schorr
 int. with WSP; SBS int. with FS
Although Stanton remained: SBS ints.
 with FS and RS
"I didn't share Bill's": SBS int. with FS
"Bill Paley is the master": SBS int.
 with RS
"They knew I had been": Ibid.
The chairman objected: WSP memo to
 RS, 11/1/72
During a subsequent one-on-one: letter
 from RS to SBS, 2/12/86
But it was not until: Charles Colson
 speech in Kennebunkport, 11/13/72
"My antennae went off": SBS int.
 with RS
Virtually everyone: *More* magazine
 (December 1972)
"Paley put great store": SBS int. with
 RS
On one occasion: Daniel Schorr int. with
 WSP
a "complete surprise": Ibid.
To further buttress: Daniel Schorr int.
 with WSP; *AIH*, pp. 321–322

Paley urges Stanton to retire

"very unhappy, dark": SBS int. with FS
Paley's contract originally stipulated:
 CBS Proxy Statement, 1972
"Until such date as": CBS Proxy
 Statement, 1973
"So what!": *M* magazine (July 1985)

Paley and Schneider clash

Schneider had run the: SBS ints. with Sal
 Ianucci and FS
"If we go to color": SBS int. with JS
"He was a good leader": SBS int. with
 Sal Ianucci
Paley began to mistrust: SBS ints. with
 EKM and MD
"Their relationship lacked": SBS int.
 with RW
"He made it obvious": SBS int. with FS
"Have you got a minute?" Ibid.; SBS
 int. with JS
"He didn't like me anymore": SBS int.
 with JS
"Sent me back downstairs": SBS int.
 with FS

Chick Ireland

Paley had concluded: *AIH*, p. 348
They were mere broadcasters; SBS int.
 with RW; confidential source
Jerry Roche, an executive: SBS int. with
 Jerry Roche, executive recruiter at
 Heidrick & Struggles
Ireland had already: SBS int. with FS
"I blew it": Ibid.
"Who was that guy": Ibid.
persuaded that Ireland had: *AIH*, p. 350
"Dick Salant would have died": SBS int.
 with JS
"I can't understand these": SBS int. with
 FS
an $80 million deal: Ibid.; SBS ints. with
 JDB and Roswell Gilpatric, former
 member of CBS board of directors

He had run the Josten's deal: SBS ints.
with JS and WT; confidential source
"Chick was crushed": SBS int. with JS
"Chick was never the same":
confidential source
As he eased back: confidential sources
"Paley was very petulant": SBS int.
with FS
When Stanton notified Paley: Ibid.

Paley picks Arthur Taylor

"love at first sight": SBS int. with AT
They hashed out: Ibid.; *Broadcasting*, July
17, 1972
Paley was so taken with: SBS int.
with FS
Even more than Taylor's: SBS ints. with
AT and FS

Paley and Stanton relationship founders

That autumn, Stanton drew up: SBS int.
with FS
"Too much," thundered Paley: Ibid.
The money in dispute: SBS int. with
Roswell Gilpatric
Utterly dispirited: SBS int. with FS
Paley instructed the board's: Ibid.; SBS
int. with Roswell Gilpatric
"Frank pouted until he got": SBS int.
with DH
"I don't agree with you": SBS int. with
Roswell Gilpatric
"The only question": Ibid.

Stanton's sad retirement

both still seething: SBS int. with FS
"Stanton would call me in": SBS int.
with AT
"Paley didn't want": SBS int. with EKM
"I didn't deal with it": SBS int. with FS
"I have to stay in it": Ibid.
At the CBS board: *Broadcasting*, March
26, 1973
"I won't see you": SBS int. with FS

In an awkward moment: Ibid.; FS memo
to CBS Organization, 3/30/73
"There was a great loyalty": SBS int.
with Emily Greene
Stanton was determined: SBS int. with
FS; *The New Yorker*, April 21, 1973
"I think I'll make it home": *The New
Yorker*, April 21, 1973

CHAPTER 47

Babe falls ill in China

"Sights just incredible": BCP postcard to
IS, April 1973
Babe was in a Shanghai: *AIH*, p. 369
Paley immediately called: SBS ints. with
AB and AT
Although Paley remained: SBS int.
with EKM
She called her children: SBS int.
with AB
Two weeks later: *AIH*, p. 369

The cancer diagnosis

She was X-rayed: SBS int. with AB;
AIH, pp. 369–370
On January 18: SBS ints. with AB and
Dr. Edward Beattie, Babe's second
surgeon
Paley grilled Babe's: SBS int. with MaT
"I had such faith": *M* magazine
(July 1985)
Babe managed to keep up: *W* magazine,
September 16, 1977
Then, in the spring of 1975: *AIH*, p. 370;
SBS int. with Dr. Edward Beattie;
date of operation was May 12, 1975
Exhausted and ill: confidential source
"He was motivated": SBS int.
with EKM
Paley combed the globe: Ibid.
"He drove the Columbia": Ibid.
Once he dispatched: SBS int. with RS

Babe lives with cancer

"She took my arm": SBS int. with
    Morris Harth, former CBS public
    relations aide; Suzy column on
    Skowhegan benefit at Plaza,
    May 9, 1976
"All serene": BCP postcard to IS,
    7/15/76
"Babe's back": *Women's Wear Daily,*
    5/25/76

Paley's attitude toward Babe

"kept his eyes on her": confidential
    source
"I would see the touch": SBS int. with
    Henryk de Kwiatkowski, a friend of
    WSP

Babe's attitude

"I had no idea": SBS int. with SK
"She wanted to have a separate": SBS
    int. with AB
She confided to one: confidential source
So she set up: SBS int. with Jean Stein,
    author and friend; confidential
    source
"She could have had": Ibid.
"What's the old SOB doing":
    confidential source
"How do you put up": SBS int. with JS

Paley distracted on the job

"For the first six months": SBS int. with
    Jack Purcell, former president of
    CBS Publishing and later CBS
    executive vice-president
especially when Taylor confronted: SBS
    int. with AT; *AIH,* p. 337; *Los
    Angeles Times,* December 15, 1974

Paley and Taylor at the outset

his "senior partner": SBS int. with JS
"the son he never had": SBS int.
    with AT
"I am a street kid": Ibid.

Paley and Lieberson departure

When Goddard Lieberson reached: *AIH,*
    p. 337
"Goddard," recalled his wife: SBS int.
    with Brigitta Lieberson
Lieberson's forced departure: SBS ints.
    with Walter Yetnikoff and John
    Hammond
"Goddard was difficult": SBS int.
    with FS
"His whole life was CBS": SBS int. with
    Brigitta Lieberson

"Instant analysis"

Against the advice of: SBS ints. with AT
    and RS
A *New York Times* report on the
    decision: *New York Times,* June 14,
    1973
It was known within CBS: Schorr,
    pp. 59–61
At weekly CBS News executive: Ibid.,
    p. 273
"We are not serving": SBS int. with ES
"That shook me": SBS int. with RS
In fact, Taylor: SBS int. with AT
"That was it": confidential source

The 1970 turnaround

to "get the wrinkles out": Bedell, p. 188
"Lower your voice": SBS int. with PL
"Gentlemen," Paley told: SBS int.
    with RW
although he hated Archie: SBS int.
    with JS
Paley found the show vulgar: Bedell,
    pp. 44–45
"What shall we do": SBS int. with JS
Silverman wore down: Bedell, p. 91

Silverman departure and CBS decline

Paley did not bother with: Bedell,
    pp. 99–100
That fall, CBS's new programs: *AIH,*
    pp. 267–268

Placed on the schedule at Paley's: SBS int. with AT

"I almost cried": Tom Shales int. with WSP, 3/6/79

"We put it on because": SBS int. with AT

"What the survey came up with": WSP interview in *Columbine* (April 1983)

"Perturbed at CBS's": *Variety*, November 19, 1975

A year later, in the fall: Bedell, p. 139

At the "complacency": *Wall Street Journal*, April 20, 1977; *The Washington Post*, April 17, 1977

Robert Wood's departure

lured, he said: Bedell, p. 188

"I said to myself": SBS int. with RW

"He thought he was underpaid": SBS int. with JS

"I can't keep delivering": SBS int. with FS

Sometimes Schneider would: Ibid.

"I am passing blood": SBS int. with AT

Paley chooses Wussler

"You've got a shot": SBS int. with RoW

Taylor and Paley

He told them to avoid: Ibid.; SBS int. with James Rosenfield, former president of CBS Television

"Paley would say": SBS int. with James Rosenfield

As early as March 1975: *New York* magazine, March 17, 1975

After Babe's operation: SBS int. with AT

That July, *New York*: Metz, p. 405; CBS statement, 7/14/75

CHAPTER 48

Family Viewing

With his rigid integrity: Bedell, p. 99

"I was making $400,000": SBS int. with AT

Early in 1975 he proposed: *See No Evil: The Backstage Battle Over Sex and Violence on Television*, Geoffrey Cowan (New York, 1979), p. 19

His words struck: Ibid., p. 58; SBS int. with FS

With the assistance of: *Broadcasting*, April 12, 1976; Cowan, p. 93

Most CBS executives: Bedell, p. 102

"very very important": transcript, "Hour of Power," 12/28/75

Paley had supported: Cowan, p. 108; *Newsweek*, October 25, 1976

"Paley's support disappeared": SBS int. with AT

"begrudgingly" let the: SBS int. with EKM

Taylor's accomplishments

Paley had pulled away from: SBS int. with RS

Taylor also pushed CBS: SBS int. with AT

And he imposed: Ibid.; *TV/Radio Age*, April 26, 1974

But Taylor knew his: Bedell, p. 97; SBS int. with RoW

Taylor favored: *Advertising Age*, February 26, 1973

criticizing CBS's: *Financial World*, March 6, 1974

"It hurt Paley's feelings": SBS int. with AT

"Try these": SBS int. with JDB

Paley had been noncommittal: SBS int. with AT

"I brought forward three": Ibid.

CBS reaction to Taylor

When Taylor wore a hat: Ibid.; *Forbes,*
     May 1, 1975
"King Arthur": SBS int. with RS; Metz,
     p. 401
They chuckled about: *TV Digest,*
     October 27, 1972; *Forbes,* May 1,
     1975; *TV/Radio Age,* April 26, 1970

Paley turns on Taylor

"Paley was constantly": SBS int.
     with AT
From the beginning: *Broadcasting,*
     May 31, 1976
A day or so after: SBS int. with AT
"Vindictiveness was": confidential
     source
"He would get in his": SBS int. with AT
"Arthur was bordering": SBS int.
     with JDB
The CBS president ordered: SBS int.
     with RoW
and arranged to have: SBS ints. with JS
     and Emily Greene
He once interrupted: SBS int. with FS
Years later, Taylor: SBS int. with AT
"He couldn't look you": Ibid.
"I had no power": Ibid.

Paley's disenchantment

"Bill Paley was a very": SBS int.
     with EKM
The specter of her death: SBS int.
     with AT
Taylor finally ran: Ibid.; SBS int. with JS
Paley remembered only: SBS int. with
     AT
Taylor was pushing: SBS int. with
     EKM; confidential source
Wherever Taylor went: SBS int. with JS
Taylor even popped up: *Women's Wear
     Daily,* July 31, 1975
"Arthur asked for": SBS int. with
     Courtney Brown

To friends, Taylor openly: SBS ints.
     with JDB and EKM
"It was important": SBS int. with JS
"flung himself early": Leonard, p. 188
"He hated that office": SBS int.
     with EKM
"Both the money spent": SBS int.
     with WL
"I have the best": SBS int. with AT
Taylor went on to hire: SBS int. with JS;
     confidential sources
Word reached Paley: SBS int. with WL
When the CBS president: SBS int. with
     AT
Babe went through a bad patch: Don
     West int. with WSP, October 1976

Paley hires Backe

"Can you come": SBS int. with JDB
Although Paley had: Ibid.; *AIH,* p. 352;
     Advertising Age, October 18, 1976
"I find our lives": SBS int. with JDB
"How would you like": Ibid.
"How am I going to": confidential
     source
"How do you feel about": SBS int.
     with JDB
"You have to take it": Ibid.

Paley fires Taylor

"Arthur Taylor has to leave": SBS int.
     with Roswell Gilpatric
"Bill Paley was sensitive": SBS ints.
     with Courtney Brown and Roswell
     Gilpatric
No one tried to: Ibid.
"He wanted to move": SBS int. with
     Roswell Gilpatric
An hour before the: SBS ints. with AT;
     Newsweek, October 25, 1976
"We want your": SBS ints. with AT and
     Roswell Gilpatric
"You've done a great . . .": SBS int.
     with AT
"I felt a keen sense": Ibid.

Taylor, who never had: Ibid.;
  Broadcasting, October 18, 1976
"With time and patience": SBS int.
  with EKM
"All Arthur needed": SBS int.
  with RoW

CHAPTER 49

Bad publicity

a "financial martinet": *The Washington
  Post,* October 14, 1976
"Paley's domain": *New York Times,*
  October 14 and 16, 1976
The following week: *TV Digest,*
  October 18, 1976
"Like the old man": *Fortune,* "A New
  Prince Steps Up to Test the Royal
  Temper," Robert Lamb,
  (November 1976)
Several days after: SBS int. with Ann
  Morrison, Lamb's researcher
claiming falsely that: Robert Lamb int.
  with WSP, 11/5/76; SBS int. with
  Courtney Brown; confidential
  source
"You said a few things": Robert Lamb
  int. with WSP
But Paley felt he had been: SBS int.
  with EKM

Paley's public relations army

Paley had long relied: SBS ints. with
  EKM and AT
Press interviews were: EKM memos,
  4/3/75, 2/28/77
when a letter highly critical: *New York
  Times,* July 15, 1974, from the Rev.
  Everett C. Parker, director, Office
  of Communication, United Church
  of Christ
When the law department vetoed: memo
  from Leonard Spinrad to EKM,
  7/26/74

CBS: Reflections in a Bloodshot Eye

"We intend to ignore": EKM memo to
  CBS directors, officers, and
  department heads, 7/2/75
But later he reconsidered: *Newsweek,*
  August 11, 1975; letter from E.
  Kidder Meade to Edward Kuhn, Jr.,
  editor of Playboy Press, 6/25/75;
  Broadcasting, July 21, 1975; *Los
  Angeles Times,* August 10 and
  September 18, 1975
"has been throwing": *Wall Street Journal,*
  August 17, 1975
"inadvertent conspiracy": *Los Angeles
  Times,* September 15, 1975

La Côte Basque, 1965

"Have you seen *Esquire?*": SBS int.
  with SK
"I knew it was Bill": Ibid.
The common assumption was: *New York*
  magazine, February 9, 1976; SBS
  int. with John Richardson
"I told Paley he could": SBS int. with
  EKM
"I have other ways": Clarke, p. 471
"I fell asleep": *New York* magazine,
  February 9, 1976
"Of course he didn't fall": SBS int.
  with EKM
"Everyone had known": SBS int.
  with CC
"Now that she was": Clarke, p. 467
was "devastated": SBS int. with CC
"Truman didn't understand": SBS int.
  with Jean Stein
Capote wrote Babe two: Clarke, p. 472
Around the same time, Truman: SBS
  int. with SK

The Powers That Be

Public relations aides called: Halberstam
  notes on first interview with WSP,
  undated; Paper, p. 295
"a remarkably neurotic": Halberstam

notes on first interview with WSP,
pp. 2, 6
"We have been and are": EKM memo to
WSP, 9/9/75
Paley's first response: Leonard Spinrad
memo to EKM, 9/5/75; *The
Washington Post,* December 28, 1975
Interviewing Paley, Mayer was bemused:
Paper, p. 302
"perfectly respectable report": *The
Washington Post,* March 14, 1976
"He really hated those": SBS int. with
EKM
"One thing about Halberstam": SBS int.
with EKM
"neurosis about the Jewish question":
SBS int. with David Halberstam
The CBS chief took great: Paper,
pp. 298–299
He consulted an attorney: SBS int. with
EKM
"I spent hundreds of hours": Ibid.
"He kept Halberstam's articles": SBS
int. with AT
Paley tried initially: WSP preface to "A
Reply," by WSP, February 27, 1976
Most of the contentions: "A Reply," by
WSP, February 27, 1976
Even after all their work: SBS int. with
FS; confidential source
Shifting gears yet again: Paper, p. 301
"I told Bill just to": SBS int. with JDB
"Your friend Bill Paley": SBS int.
with IS

Paley's overreaction

"print journalism has always": *New York
Times,* December 19, 1976
"You know": Robert Lamb int. with
WSP, 11/5/76
"It was widely felt": SBS int. with
EKM; "Media Industry Newsletter,"
10/18/76: "CBS has begun to show
deep dark circles. Some date it back
to the departure of Frank Stanton."

Paley begins his memoir

His theory, he explained: SBS int. with
Jack Purcell
CBS hired an experienced: SBS int. with
Margaret Kennedy, head researcher
on the Paley project; proposal for
CBS history department, 8/3/77
"The problem from the": confidential
source
Working from transcripts: confidential
source
"I don't want my dinner": confidential
source
As the book progressed: confidential
source
But Paley's letters and memoranda: SBS
int. with John McDonald

CHAPTER 50

Sarnoff's death

In December 1971, Paley's old rival:
Bilby, pp. 279, 284; Broadcast
Pioneers Library interview with
Kenneth Bilby, 1989

Origins of Museum of Broadcasting

that year, Paley's aide-de-camp: SBS int.
with Robert Saudek, former
president of Museum of
Broadcasting
Tourtellot reported back: Arthur
Tourtellot memo to WSP, 10/23/74
"We talked at length": SBS int. with
Robert Saudek
Paley picked out the site: Ibid.
He was determined: Museum of
Broadcasting press release
"He used his experience": SBS int. with
Robert Saudek
They resisted at first: Ibid.

Tourtellot favored placing: Tourtellot
  memo, 10/23/74
"What about Frank Stanton?":
  confidential source
"We kept it quiet": SBS int. with Robert
  Saudek
"He had a certain desire": SBS int.
  with AT

Paley tries to save programming

"He was embarrassed": Bedell, p. 191
ABC's formula for success: Ibid., p. 199
"Where are the pretty": Ibid., p. 213;
  SBS ints. with JDB and RoW
"It was ironic that": SBS int. with JDB
"Let's talk about": SBS int. with RoW;
  Bedell, p. 189
"Paley was talking about": SBS int. with
  Harvey Shephard, former CBS
  program executive
"I would find him": SBS int. with RoW
"Who would buy this?": SBS ints. with
  Jack Purcell and JDB

John Backe's early days

At CBS he steered: SBS int. with JDB
To direct more resources: Bedell, p. 191
he ordered CBS's other: SBS int. with
  Jack Purcell
"How's it going?": SBS int. with JDB

Goldie's death

"I'm sorry about": SBS int. with RoW
Goldie may have shaved: SBS int. with
  Phyllis Maxwell

Paley gives up CEO

"This is not a charade": *Wall Street
  Journal,* April 20, 1977
"policy questions": *Time,* May 2, 1977
"Bill Paley isn't going": *Wall Street
  Journal,* April 20, 1977

Backe reorganizes CBS network

Backe had conceived: SBS int. with JDB
Paley resisted: Ibid.
"My first order of business": Bedell,
  p. 205

Schneider loses out

"My rubber band had": SBS int. with JS
"Jack would make a crack": SBS int.
  with EKM

The Paley memoir

"When it was almost": confidential
  source
"The book was frustrating": SBS int.
  with Margaret Kennedy
Paley secretly brought: confidential
  sources
Wolff's principal criticism: confidential
  source
"too wooden": confidential source; Sam
  Vaugham, Doubleday publisher,
  letter to John McDonald, 1/29/77
"It was nuts": confidential source
"You have pictures of": confidential
  source

De-Stantonizing

"You couldn't even mention": transcript
  of David Halberstam int. with Peter
  Derow, former president of CBS
  Publishing; SBS ints. with RoW and
  AT
"Don't you ever": SBS int. with JDB
"Here we were paying": SBS int. with
  Roswell Gilpatric
For his part, Stanton: SBS int. with FS
"It was deliberate": Ibid.
"Bill, I think you forgot": Ibid.; SBS
  ints. with JDB and Jack Purcell
"It didn't sit well": SBS int. with
  Roswell Gilpatric
"We were going into": SBS int. with
  JDB

CHAPTER 51

Babe's decline begins

For a time in 1976 and 1977: SBS int. with AB

In the summer of 1977: letter from BCP to IS, 7/30/77

The cancer had invaded: SBS int. with Dr. Edward Beattie

Paley, determined to: SBS int. with JDB

"He is not as jolly": *W* magazine, September 16–23, 1977

When they tried to have: confidential source

Attitude toward her illness

Periodically, she would be taken: confidential source

she wore knits by: SBS int. with Andre Leon Talley

"Oh God, now I know": SBS int. with John Richardson

When she wasn't wearing: SBS int. with AB

In the morning, her secretary; confidential source

"She would make the most": SBS int. with HoK

Babe stayed in touch: confidential source

Betsey ending up spending: SBS int. with AB

When Minnie felt able: confidential source

"Carter wasn't considerate": *Women's Wear Daily*, September 27, 1972

When the divorce lawyers: SBS int. with Roswell Gilpatric

"For a long time she": SBS int. with AB

Babe's stepchildren: confidential source

Only Kate stayed away: SBS int. with AB

Babe readies her bequests

Babe had all her jewelry: confidential source

She kept a stack: SBS int. with AB

Sometimes she shyly asked: SBS ints. with IS and HoK

"She cared so much": SBS int. with IS

Patrick O'Higgins

"Patrick was enchanting": SBS int. with Jean Stein

"With him she could let": SBS int. with John Richardson

"She didn't like talking": SBS int. with HoK

Last visit to Lyford Cay

She had to lie down: SBS int. with Jean Stein

although his brooding intensity: Ibid.

"She was sitting on a sofa": SBS int. with Jeanne Thayer

The Jeff Byers suicide

With their children still: SBS int. with DPH

"business problems": *New York Times,* January 1, 1978

"Jeff desperately wanted": SBS int. with DPH

Several times when Byers: SBS int. with Henryk de Kwiatkowski

"Jeff had margin calls": Ibid.

"Bill was fond of Jeff": SBS int. with DPH

"He stepped in nicely": confidential source

Babe turns on Paley

She took to referring: confidential source

"They are trying to bake": confidential source

In Paley's presence, she unleashed: confidential sources

"She complained that she": confidential source

He remained patient: SBS int. with AB; confidential sources

"He was devastated": SBS int. with AB

Paley and Jan Cushing

"He found another girl": SBS int. with CC

The other girl was: the account of the Paley–Jan Cushing relationship that follows comes from SBS interview with Jan Cushing Amory

Before long, they were: confidential sources

Babe's final illness

Babe took to her bed: SBS int. with AB

Bothered by the noise: confidential source

She used oxygen: SBS int. with AB

Still unwilling to give up: Ibid.; confidential sources

"It was a painful period": SBS int. with AB

Last visit to Kiluna

she had spent years, under the: *Architectural Digest* (November–December 1973); SBS int. with HoK

"You know Kiluna": SBS int. with Ed Klar, real estate developer

"How did it go?": SBS int. with AB

After a hiatus of: confidential source

"She knew she was": SBS int. with Aline de Romanones

In early July she moved: SBS int. with AB; confidential source

"Her face never changed": confidential source

"It was odd": confidential source

On July 5: SBS int. with AB

Paley and the children sat: Ibid.; *AIH,* p. 370

Moments later, Bill Paley: SBS int. with AB

Babe's memorial service

They were escorted: SBS ints. with HoK and Marion Osborn

"I don't think I ever": SBS int. with LH

"a beacon of perfection": Associated Press, July 9, 1978

Waiters stood underneath: Konolige, p. 301

"At the end I looked": SBS int. with SK

"I'm going to marry": SBS int. with Horst

CHAPTER 52

Paley's mourning

"Poor Bill": SBS int. with LH

Along with his servants: SBS int. with Henry Mortimer

It was as if: SBS int. with AB

Also in tow: confidential source

The Michael Trees: confidential source

Louise Melhado picked up: SBS int. with Henry Mortimer

"Bill didn't sit": SBS int. with SK

Her death shattered: Ibid.; SBS int. with IS

"He was dependent on her": SBS int. with IS

"The pain," he explained: *Esquire* (December 1983)

Visiting the CBS chairman: SBS int. with JDB

"He began questioning": confidential source

"more pensive, more brooding": SBS int. with Henryk de Kwiatkowski

Paley redecorates and finds new digs

Their home in Lyford: SBS int. with SK
Sister Parish guided: confidential source
After considerable agonizing: SBS ints.
   with Mario Buatta and John
   Richardson
"It was filled": *Newsday*, April 11,
   1979
Klar planned a development: SBS int.
   with Ed Klar; deed of sale dated
   3/20/85
Late in 1978: SBS int. with Jeanne
   Murray Vanderbilt; Suzy column,
   New York Daily News, February 11,
   1979
Assisted by Sister Parish: SBS int. with
   SK

Babe's estate

Babe left more than: All figures and
   descriptions pertaining to Babe's
   belongings come from BCP Estate
   documents filed in Manhasset,
   N.Y.
"She didn't leave": confidential source
"The bequests got fouled up": SBS int.
   with IS
Some friends received: SBS int. with
   John Richardson
But Selznick objected: SBS int. with IS
The children likewise: confidential
   source
Paley accused Tony: SBS int. with AB

Bill Paley, social lion

"He realized with": SBS int. with SK
He gathered around him: Ibid.; SBS int.
   with John Richardson
At the outset Paley: SBS int. with SK
Many friends remarked: SBS ints. with
   John Richardson, Henryk de
   Kwiatkowski, and SK

Paley and the women

"the greatest struggle": "Panting for
   Paley," Taki, *Esquire*, January 30,
   1979
"I had the feeling": SBS int. with LH
"She married Eric Dudley": SBS int.
   with SK
"sweeter, prettier": *New York Daily
   News*, April 26, 1979
"The poor old gentleman": confidential
   source
"That is quite a spread": SBS int. with
   Ahmet Ertegun, friend of WSP
Paley professed embarrassment: *People*,
   April 9, 1979
but privately he admitted: SBS int. with
   SK
"Why should I get": SBS int. with LH
"All this business of": confidential
   source

As It Happened

Despite abundant evidence: *AIH*,
   p. 189
One heavily promoted aspect: Suzanne
   DeVito, publicist, Doubleday, letter
   to EKM, 1/9/79
Paley submitted to an appearance:
   Broadcasting, May 7, 1979
"William Paleontological": "Today"
   show, 2/4/81
"useful memoir": *Variety*, March 21,
   1979
"lyrical elegance": *Los Angeles Times*,
   April 1, 1979
a "history of his consuming": *Wall Street
   Journal*, March 21, 1979
"Paley depicts himself": *New York*
   magazine, April 30, 1979
At the urging of his: SBS ints. with
   EKM and Morris Harth
"spare and unfeeling": *Business Week*,
   March 26, 1979
"Settling Scores": *Boston Globe*, March
   13, 1979

He spread the word: *M* magazine (July
    1985)
"my wife was dying": SBS int. with
    WSP
"He was so busy whitewashing": *M*
    magazine (July 1985)
"I wish to hell": Tom Shales int. with
    WSP, 3/6/79

CHAPTER 53

Backe and Paley honeymoon

a "wise choice": *AIH,* p. 353; *Variety,*
    May 14, 1980
"Nothing hit me harder": SBS int. with
    JDB
"Babe was dead": Ibid.
One building block was: SBS ints. with
    RS, WL, and Burton Benjamin,
    former CBS News executive
Arthur Tourtellot proved: SBS int. with
    JDB
As with Taylor, Paley hinted: Ibid.
"I want to thank you for": Ibid.
"Bill just stood": Ibid.
"He laughed and joked": SBS int. with
    Jack Purcell
"Just remember": SBS int. with JDB

Paley roars back in

He was under heavy medication: Ibid.;
    SBS int. with Jack Purcell
When the chairman awoke: SBS int.
    with JDB
"At least he was consistent": SBS int.
    with Jack Purcell
"he would fake you out": SBS int. with
    JDB
"We couldn't figure out": confidential
    source
"he began to believe": SBS int. with Jack
    Purcell
"Paley was always around": Ibid.

"I don't think anyone": confidential
    source
"By the end of the second": SBS int.
    with Harvey Shephard
Backe's assertiveness raised: SBS ints.
    with JDB and James Rosenfield
"I will handle Paley": SBS int. with JDB
"When Backe would say to us": SBS int.
    with Robert Daly, former president
    of CBS Entertainment

Relationship with Backe goes sour

"It became negative": SBS int. with JDB
"Can't you get John": SBS int. with Jack
    Purcell
"Yo, Bill": SBS int. with Walter
    Yetnikoff
"regards the CBS president": "Media
    Industry Newsletter," October 15,
    1979
Whenever Backe left town: JDB Journal
    entry, 2
"He would pump me": SBS int. with
    Jack Purcell
"to document the inconsistencies": SBS
    int. with JDB; JDB Journal entries
    from 1978 through 1980

The movie business

He told Paley that: SBS int. with JDB
Paley understood that the marketplace:
    Ibid.
"He would leave for a ": JDB Journal
    entry, 1; SBS int. with Robert Daly

WSP versus Backe on home video

Paley's vacillation also: SBS int. with
    JDB
"reversed direction and": JDB Journal
    entry, 3

WSP holds up Family Weekly

In September 1979, Jack Purcell: JDB
    Journal entries, 14, 15; *Business
    Week,* May 26, 1980; SBS int. with
    Jack Purcell

The fight over cable TV

The sharpest disagreement: SBS ints.
	with JDB and Jack Purcell
"blow Turner": SBS int. with JDB
Jankowski's report was overwhelmingly:
	Ibid.; confidential source

Acquisitions

"I felt like a court": confidential source
"Sometimes the boardroom":
	confidential source
"Paley felt this information":
	confidential source
At that level, Backe and his: SBS int.
	with JDB; *AIH,* p. 339
"a low-risk toy company": confidential
	source
"Too big": JDB Journal entry, 7
But when word of CBS's: *Variety,*
	September 9, 1979
"The Chairman now concerned": JDB
	Journal entry, 7

The Felix Rohatyn connection

One of Paley's initial objections: JDB
	Journal entry, 5
Although Rohatyn had advised: Bilby,
	p. 313
Paley frequently called: SBS ints. with
	JDB and Jack Purcell
The "urge to merge": SBS int. with Jack
	Purcell
"Felix had a superficial": confidential
	source
"It may not make sense": SBS int. with
	Jack Purcell; confidential source
When Paley excitedly called: SBS int.
	with JDB

Long-range plan

Several years in the making: Ibid.; SBS
	int. with Courtney Brown; *Business
	Week,* May 26, 1980
"some discussion": JDB Journal entry,
	20

"spent the next few weeks": SBS int.
	with JDB
Backe gave Paley a toy: SBS int. with
	JDB
"I was always in the position": Ibid.

Paley and Daly

A Brooklyn-born: SBS int. with Kim
	LeMasters
"Paley saw him as a buccaneer": SBS
	int. with Alan Wagner
He made certain, for example: SBS int.
	with Robert Daly
"If you don't like": SBS int. with Kim
	LeMasters
Even if he felt strongly: SBS int. with
	Robert Daly
"Bob was tough": SBS int. with Kim
	LeMasters
Paley not only identified: SBS int. with
	Alan Wagner
But when Paley objected: SBS ints. with
	Harvey Shephard and Robert Daly
"It will fail": SBS int. with Robert Daly
"for messy shows": *Newsweek,* March 5,
	1979
With Daly on the West: SBS int. with
	Kim LeMasters
but he managed to phone: SBS int. with
	Robert Daly
"You would be ready": Ibid.
"if he has to continue": JDB Journal
	entry, 11
"spent an hour": JDB Journal entry, 16

CHAPTER 54

WSP tries to hire Eisner

In September, he talked: SBS int. with
	JDB; JDB Journal entries, 12, 19
"We talked about shows": SBS int. with
	Michael Eisner, chairman of Walt
	Disney Co.
"he kept saying": Ibid.

Backe raises his profile

"Going into the job": SBS int. with JDB

The Rather decision

Backe had stayed aloof: SBS ints. with JDB, EKM, and RS
"Backe was a blank": SBS int. with RS
When ABC tried to steal: *Who Killed CBS? The Undoing of America's Number One News Network,* Peter J. Boyer (New York, 1988), p. 51
(an enormous jump beyond): Ibid., p. 50
Walter Cronkite had told: SBS int. with WL
so in early February: Ibid.; Boyer, p. 51
In the previous months: Leonard, p. 30
"obscene, indecent": Ibid., p. 31; SBS int. with JDB
"He's too eager": Ibid., p. 32
"I never thought": Ibid.
At one point: SBS ints. with WL and JDB
Both Jankowski and Leonard: SBS int. with JDB
"It's your decision": Ibid.; SBS int. with WL
"It seems we don't": Ibid.

1980 CBS annual meeting

As part of an effort: SBS int. with JDB
Paley objected: JDB Journal entry, 22
Despite Paley's objection: CBS Annual Report, 1979
"I guess you want": SBS int. with JDB
During the dinner before: Ibid.; confidential source
"I don't know where": SBS int. with JDB

The victory party

On April 24, 1980: *Broadcasting,* April 28, 1980
"I don't think": *Variety,* April 30, 1980

Backe gets a tip

Less than a week later: SBS ints. with JDB and Jack Purcell

Paley considers Wyman as director

He was friendly with: SBS ints. with FS and Thomas Wyman, former president of CBS
Franklin Thomas, who was close to: Kahn, p. 183
Wyman showed promise: *Business Week,* June 9, 1980; SBS int. with TW
"He wanted to be sure": SBS int. with TW
"He doesn't have": Ibid.
(Backe had in fact): SBS int. with JDB
"Paley," recalled Wyman: SBS int. with TW

Backe confirms the tip

Backe knew that Paley: SBS int. with JDB
But on checking back: Ibid.; SBS int. with Jack Purcell
"If Paley thought": SBS int. with Roswell Gilpatric
"Are you going to be": SBS int. with TW

Backe and WSP showdown

"I have times, and I have": SBS int. with JDB
"I tried everything": *Broadcasting,* May 19, 1980
"I thought it could be": SBS int. with JDB
Paley moved swiftly: Ibid.; SBS int. with Roswell Gilpatric

Backe and the board

Backe had erred: SBS int. with Roswell Gilpatric
During seven years in: SBS int. with JDB

"I'm not trying": Ibid.

"He was twitching": Ibid.

"He didn't have the self-confidence":
     SBS int. with Roswell Gilpatric;
     New York Times, December 28, 1980

"I am not a politician": SBS int. with
     JDB

After the blowup

Once again, he was applauded: *The
     Washington Post,* May 11, 1980

In Backe's absence: SBS ints. with JDB,
     Jack Purcell, and Roswell Gilpatric

He chatted amiably: Leonard, p. 192

Looking "all hangdog": SBS int. with
     JDB

Paley never even made: Ibid.; SBS int.
     with Roswell Gilpatric

The aftermath of Backe's firing

Wall Street analysts: *Business Week,* May
     26, 1980; *New York* magazine, May
     26, 1980

"The CBS board": *New York* magazine,
     May 26, 1980

"Paley gave me the impression": SBS
     int. with TW

Paley's stated reasons: *Time,* May 26,
     1980; *Business Week,* May 26, 1980

Paley would have backed off: SBS ints.
     with Courtney Brown and Roswell
     Gilpatric

"If Wyman hadn't sort of": SBS int.
     with Roswell Gilpatric

Paley hires Wyman—with some help

Three days after: SBS int. with TW

now he told Wyman that Backe: Ibid.;
     SBS int. with DH

"In the normal scheme": SBS int. with
     TW

Wyman met the next: Ibid.; SBS int.
     with Roswell Gilpatric

"The meeting was an odd": SBS int.
     with TW

"They wanted a say": Ibid.

The upshot was an understanding: Ibid.;
     SBS int. with Roswell Gilpatric

"If you get this": SBS int. with TW

The deal reflected: Ibid.; *Newsweek,* June
     2, 1980

CHAPTER 55

Daly's departure

"the five-star general": *Variety,* April 30,
     1980

"John Backe finally understood": SBS
     int. with Robert Daly

"I have never in my life": Robert Lamb
     int. with WSP, 11/5/76

"This is a job": SBS int. with Robert
     Daly

"There I was": Ibid.

Paley blamed Warner Communications:
     SBS int. with AB

Daly had met with Ross: SBS int. with
     Robert Daly; *New York* magazine,
     December 8, 1980

"Steve attested to my": SBS int. with
     AB

Paley and Wyman honeymoon

"Tom Wyman accepted": SBS int. with
     Roswell Gilpatric

Wyman agreed: SBS ints. with TW and
     Roswell Gilpatric

"Cable is a must": *Los Angeles Times,*
     May 23, 1980

The same CBS analysts who scotched:
     "CBS Cable 1980 Strategic Plan,"
     p. 59

To ensure that Wyman: SBS int. with
     TW

When Paley told Wyman: SBS int. with
     JDB

"They are turning our bar": SBS int. with Jack Purcell

"We have rapport and interchange": SBS int. with Roswell Gilpatric

"It sat very badly": SBS int. with WL

Paley rejuvenated

In June 1980 he gave: *Variety*, June 11, 1980

"I was under no illusion": Leonard, p. 224

"Everybody felt they were": confidential source

Around that time: SBS int. with Sidney Urquhart, reporter for *Time*

"The departure of Mr. Paley": Kidder Peabody report on CBS by Joseph Fuchs, 6/2/80

"Fuchs has a death wish": confidential source

After reportedly receiving: Ibid.; Kidder Peabody report on CBS by Joseph Fuchs, 8/6/81

"A corrosion took place": SBS int. with Leonard Goldenson

Wyman and Paley

"The bottom line is": CBS press release, 4/81

"I will produce as many movies": SBS int. with Robert Daly

CBS, said Levy: *New York Times*, June 28, 1981

"Critics Beware": *Time*, June 15, 1981

"Paley would want to know": SBS int. with William Lilley III

"The time has come": SBS ints. with TW and Roswell Gilpatric

CBS Cable

He immersed himself in the details: SBS int. with William Lilley

Remembering a program called: WSP int. with *Columbine*, 4/83

"a feast for the eye and ear": "Bill Paley's Big Gamble on CBS Cable," by Orde Coombs, *New York* magazine, May 24, 1982

"It's got the feel": Ibid.

He told a former colleague: SBS int. with FS

Paley meddles in news

"What I had done bothered": SBS int. with WL

"Use both of them": confidential source

Paley-Stanton rapprochement

"I don't think there's any": *New York Times*, October 18, 1981

One who heard his lament: SBS int. with FS

"Maybe Bill Paley was a shit": SBS int. with RoW

"Frank was terrific": *Broadcasting*, May 19, 1980

When Paley began inviting: SBS int. with FS

In 1981 he coaxed: Harvard University press release, 7/13/81; confidential source

"Can it be graceful for me?": SBS int. with TW

"He's too good": SBS int. with FS

"Whenever I have a problem": SBS int. with WSP

"They are like a husband": SBS int. with WL

Paley and Marvin Davis

In January 1982 he had: confidential source

Davis got what he wanted: *Variety*, February 17, 1982

New problems at CBS

The company had lost: *Business Week*,
  March 8, 1982; CBS Cable 1980
  Strategic Plan
"There has not yet been": *Business Week*,
  March 8, 1982
Paley, however, undercut his position:
  SBS int. with William Lilley;
  confidential source
"Paley couldn't stand": confidential
  source

Jock's death and the IHT

Until Whitney lost his: SBS int. with
  Michael Tree
Many Sunday evenings: SBS ints. with
  KRW and Tom Salant, WSP
  helicopter pilot
"Bill would come to see": SBS int. with
  IS
With Whitney's death: SBS ints. with
  Walter Thayer and Charles Rees,
  Whitcom partner

The inner five plan Paley's exit

"fortuitous pretext": SBS int. with
  Roswell Gilpatric
"We felt that after two": Ibid.
"When I step down": SBS int. with
  TW
Benno Schmidt and Henry Schacht: SBS
  int. with Roswell Gilpatric;
  confidential source
"All we could do was express": SBS int.
  with Roswell Gilpatric
Paley turned against Schmidt: Ibid.;
  confidential source

Paley compromises on the IHT

In mid-July, Paley and Sydney: The
  account of Paley's negotiations is
  based on interviews with several
  confidential sources

In early September 1982: *New York
  Times*, September 9, 1982
Paley would remain: CBS Proxy
  Statement, 1983

Wyman folds CBS Cable

CBS Cable had posted: SBS int. with
  William Lilley III; CBS Cable 1980
  Strategic Plan
The decision to fold: SBS int. with TW
"To me it was one": WSP int. in
  Columbine, 4/83

Public harmony

"I have a successor in place": *Fortune*,
  August 9, 1982
"Tom Wyman will be free": *New York
  Times*, September 9, 1982
"How could you say": SBS int. with
  James Rosenfield
"It's difficult to tell you": *Esquire*
  (December 1983); WSP speech,
  4/20/83

CHAPTER 56

Wyman shuts Paley out

He no longer received: SBS ints. with
  TW and William Lilley
For years Paley had treated: SBS int.
  with William Lilley
"The programming department": SBS
  int. with TW
He made at least a dozen: SBS int. with
  James Rosenfield; confidential
  source
With Paley as leader: SBS ints. with Kim
  LeMasters and Harvey Shephard
"The accoutrements of power": SBS int.
  with Alan Wagner

"Nobody knew if he came": SBS int. with William Lilley

"Directors and management": confidential source

"He rotated Paley out": SBS int. with Michel Bergerac, member of CBS board of directors; confidential sources

"Couldn't CBS have a piece": SBS int. with Frank Biondi, former president of HBO

routinely supplied Paley: SBS ints. with TW and George Schweitzer, CBS public relations aide

Jankowski dutifully briefed: SBS int. with Kim LeMasters

When Paley traveled: SBS int. with Harvey Shephard

The social whirl

"He has more charm and clout": *New York Daily News,* May 18, 1980

"I go to a lot of parties": *W* magazine, June 7, 1985

Paley continued to put: SBS ints. with CC and SK

Paley even took her, along with: *Women's Wear Daily,* July 30, 1984; confidential source

"Annette had a father": confidential source

"If there was a new girl": SBS int. with CC

"You're wasting your time": SBS int. with Henryk de Kwiatkowski

By May of that year: *Women's Wear Daily,* May 12, 1982

During one large dinner: confidential sources

"Semi-intoxicating effect": confidential source

"I don't know of anyone": SBS int. with IS

So confident was Sawyer: *Bad News at Black Rock,* Peter McCabe (New York, 1987), p. 42

what some of his friends called "WHT": SBS int. with Henry Mortimer

"He never takes his hand": confidential source

He thought nothing of: author's observation

Paley made even more of: *New York Post,* April 10, 1984

"He is not your Norman": The description of Paley's sexual proclivities is from SBS interviews with several confidential sources

Paley the genial host

"He says he is so lonely": SBS int. with MaT

"No man can survive": *Esquire* (December 1983)

Several years later: confidential source

Paley's 1985 hospitalization

"It was a lapse of": confidential sources

"She was a friend of": SBS int. with Ahmet Ertegun

During Paley's six-week: SBS int. with WSP

Paley and the LBO

He enlisted James: SBS int. with William Lilley; confidential source

Instead of leaping: confidential source

Wyman said flatly he would not: SBS int. with TW

An item planted: Liz Smith column, *New York Daily News,* March 20, 1985

The Turner bid

"How's old Paley?": Leonard, p. 221

"You CBS guys are something": Ibid., p. 222

"It's wonderful to come": WSP speech to Center for Communications luncheon, 4/9/85

"He was a wreck": SBS int. with
William Lilley

He complained bitterly: SBS int. with FS

Paley's unsuccessful gambit: CBS Proxy
Statement, 1986

The Wyman defense

Al Neuharth, Gannett's flamboyant:
Confessions of an S.O.B., Al
Neuharth (Garden City, N.Y.,
1989), p. 215

"blessed the deal": Ibid., p. 223

The aircraft dispute

Even worse from Paley's: SBS ints. with
TW and Roswell Gilpatric

His retirement contract stipulated: SBS
int. with Roswell Gilpatric

"It is right there": SBS int. with FS

He reimbursed: SBS ints. with William
Lilley and Roswell Gilpatric

Paley bogged down: SBS ints. with
Walter Cronkite, William Lilley,
and Roswell Gilpatric

"Do you mean to take away": SBS int.
with William Lilley

After months of wrangling: SBS int.
with Roswell Gilpatric; CBS Proxy
Statement, 1986

"The airplanes became": SBS int. with
Michel Bergerac

"makes an art of": *Forbes,* December 31,
1984

"All Tom wanted to do": SBS int. with
Kim LeMasters

Chapter 57

Larry Tisch buys a stake

Loews Corporation, a $17.5 billion:
Time, September 22, 1986

Now Tisch assured: *Wall Street Journal,*
November 1, 1985

Wyman was skeptical: SBS int. with TW

Within weeks he had brought:
Memorandum on Control of CBS,
Inc, George Vradenburg III, VP and
General Counsel, CBS, Inc.,
10/1/86

James Wolfensohn, a tennis: "Gambling
on CBS," Ken Auletta, *New York
Times Magazine,* June 8, 1986

Paley and Tisch meet

although they had sat: FS calendar,
6/3/70

Typically, Paley had Tisch: *New York
Times,* June 8, 1986

he and two of his sons: "Inside the $12
billion Tisch Dynasty," by Patricia
O'Toole, *Manhattan Inc.* (March
1985)

"Neither of us said": confidential source

"I found him to be": SBS int. with WSP

"What do you know": SBS int. with
TW

"Dustin Hoffman was perfect": SBS int.
with WSP

"The assumption": SBS int. with TW

"He is the only way": confidential
source

"That son of a bitch": confidential
source

"I was very impressed": SBS int. with
WSP

CBS financial problems

"Paley was positive": SBS int. with TW

In 1982, Wyman had opted: CBS annual
report, 1984

CBS News turmoil

under the leadership: *Prime Times, Bad
Times: A Personal Drama of Network
Television,* Ed Joyce (New York,
1988), p. 267

Three years earlier: SBS int. with FS

"He watched the morning news": SBS
     int. with RS
"Paley really likes her": SBS int. with
     Ed Hookstratten, Hollywood agent
Joyce prodded Sauter: Joyce, p. 496
Barely a month later, Don Hewitt:
     Newsweek, November 4, 1985; *New
     York Times,* October 23, 1985
"terribly bush": Joyce, p. 515
In the first place, he wanted: Ibid., p. 514
In Hewitt's view, Joyce had never:
     confidential source
telling Wyman it was "a crazy idea":
     SBS int. with TW
"there was no collusion": SBS int. with
     Don Hewitt, executive producer of
     "60 Minutes"
"A group of people": SBS int. with
     Michel Bergerac
"Paley spent one and a half": SBS int.
     with Tony Schwartz, magazine
     journalist

Tisch burrows in

At the November board: confidential
     source
"He spent more time asking": SBS int.
     with Robert Daly
"Tisch was in effect running": SBS int.
     with William Lilley
"Oh Bill, that's silly": Ibid.; SBS int.
     with Roswell Gilpatric
His main preoccupation in: SBS int. with
     William Lilley
Marvin Davis met several times:
     confidential source
After consulting closely: confidential
     sources
"to control CBS": *USA Today,* March
     24, 1986

Paley's petulance and posterity

"Bill didn't want to come": SBS int.
     with Carter Burden
He claimed that back pain: SBS int. with
     William Lilley

Paley learned that two writers: They
     were the author and Washington
     writer Lewis Paper
"I have my own stories": SBS int. with
     WSP
"I wish I could take it": Stephen G.
     Smith conversation with WSP
"Do you think he'll": confidential source
When he asked his public: SBS int. with
     William Lilley
"I have a lot of things": SBS int. with
     Bill Abrams, *Wall Street Journal*
     reporter
Harris rented an apartment: confidential
     sources
In addition, Paley gave Harris: SBS int.
     with CB; confidential sources
"He told me he is free": SBS int. with DPI

Paley's new museum

Paley had begun thinking: WSP int. in
     Columbine, 4/83
In May, Wyman finally agreed: SBS ints.
     with FS and Newton Minow
At a Museum of Broadcasting
     testimonial: SBS int. with Peter
     Kaplan, TV writer

Wyman attempts rapprochement

"Tom carried Bill around": confidential
     source
"He just didn't know": SBS int. with
     Kim LeMasters
At one, Paley choked: SBS int. with TW
"He just resumed talking": Ibid.

June 1986 IHT meeting

By then his enthusiasm: SBS int. with
     Benjamin Bradlee
"Let's go see it": SBS int. with FS

Tisch rift with Wyman

"CBS, which used to stand": *Time,*
     August 25, 1986
When Larry Tisch had pushed:
     confidential sources

Tisch dismissed: SBS ints. with TW and
Roswell Gilpatric; Larry Tisch letter
to TW, 6/12/86
"He knew he had an enemy":
confidential source
Tisch criticized Wyman openly: SBS
ints. with Roswell Gilpatric and
Newton Minow
Diller had renegotiated: confidential
sources
"He's a nice man": SBS ints. with
Roswell Gilpatric and Newton
Minow
"It was a rehash": confidential source
"If you do that": SBS int. with Roswell
Gilpatric
Shortly thereafter, Tisch raised:
"Control of CBS, Inc.,"
memorandum by George
Vradenburg III, vice-president and
general counsel, 10/1/86

Tisch and Paley come together

"Paley cared about": SBS int. with
William Lilley
Over a series of lunches: confidential
sources
"I don't think either": confidential
source
"There was lots of mending":
confidential source
"In the past six weeks": confidential
source
"I am not going anywhere": confidential
source

Wyman and Coca-Cola

On September 2, he had lunch: SBS int.
with TW; confidential source
They did a quick analysis: Minutes of
CBS board of directors meeting,
executive session, 9/10/86, p. 84
The only other overture: SBS int. with
TW; confidential source
Having been given a yellow: SBS int.
with TW; confidential sources

Before the board meeting

"I'll never forget": SBS int. with TW
"He didn't seem upset": SBS int. with
FS
The board met for dinner: SBS ints. with
Roswell Gilpatric and Newton
Minow
Paley, who was accompanied: Minutes,
9/10/86, p. 87
"We have to have a change": SBS int.
with Roswell Gilpatric
"What was not expected": confidential
source
Several Wyman loyalists: confidential
source
Ironically, they: SBS int. with Newton
Minow
"was forceful and up to": Ibid.
"Tom Wyman's support": Ibid.

The board meeting

Confident that he had: SBS int.
with TW; Minutes, 9/10/86,
p. 84
"We are not going": Ibid., p. 85
"Even the good guys": confidential
source
Having watched his proposal: Minutes,
9/10/86, pp. 85–88
Instead of making Tisch: Ibid., p. 87;
SBS int. with Roswell Gilpatric
At first, most of the directors: SBS ints.
with Roswell Gilpatric and Newton
Minow
But when board emissaries: Ibid.;
confidential source; Minutes,
9/10/86, p. 89
At 4:00 p.m. Henry Schacht: SBS ints.
with Roswell Gilpatric and TW;
confidential sources
The directors gave him: CBS Proxy
Statement, 1987
Tisch was not happy: SBS int. with
Roswell Gilpatric; confidential
sources

Wyman was shaken: confidential sources

After the meeting adjourned: Minutes, 9/10/86, p. 91

"They were two people": confidential source

"Tisch is too strong": SBS int. with DH

CHAPTER 58

Paley triumphant

With an eye to history: SBS int. with Don Hewitt

"Bill Paley takes charge": October 1986 Huntington Chrysler Plymouth advertisement

at a party to mark: confidential sources

Paley's reconciliation with his children

conflicts over a perfume business: *Women's Wear Daily,* June 24, 1981

"She had a romantic idea": SBS int. with AB

"grossly mismanaging": *New York Daily News,* June 25, 1981

"He was a well-dressed": SBS int. with RoW

"The only thing we could": *The Washington Post,* May 24, 1977

in January 1979 he was: Washington, D.C., Superior Court criminal records: arrested 1/4/79, pleaded guilty to one count of marijuana possession and one count of heroin possession; sentenced, 4/19/79: three months confinement suspended without probation on each count

Billie finally kicked: SBS ints. with DPH and IS

"completely irresponsible": "An Intimate Talk with William Paley," by Tony Schwartz, *New York Times Magazine,* December 28, 1980

"We're very close": Ibid.

"Bill never had any particular": SBS int. with DPH

Paley responded for the first: Ibid.

"in and out": SBS int. with Susan Burden

"She went to South Africa": SBS int. with Jeanne Thayer

During Kate's year in South Africa: SBS ints. with WT and Jeanne Thayer

during family gatherings: SBS ints. with AB and DPH

"She has an unrecognizable": SBS int. with Jeanne Thayer

"she could be very spoiled": confidential source

"She shouldn't be thinking": confidential source

Paley and Lois Chiles

"He was very good": SBS int. with Virginia Innis, aunt of Lois Chiles; confidential sources

"It went on for longer": SBS int. with LH

several years later he and Slim: SBS int. with SK

Paley tries to save CBS programming

"We were seeing the remnants": SBS int. with Kim LeMasters

On weekends he popped: SBS int. with SK

"He left us exhausted": SBS int. with Kim LeMasters

"How could you be this rude": Ibid.

Jankowski stood at Paley's side: Ibid.; confidential source

"a war people didn't want": confidential source

When Paley requested: confidential source

Paley and the Morning News

After Tisch hired: "CBS Orders Up a Morning Show, Light on the News," by Peter J. Boyer, *New York Times*, January 4, 1987
"has taken a direct hand": Ibid.
"He is doing himself": SBS int. with Leonard Goldenson
Tisch kept abreast: confidential sources
"was bubbling over with": confidential source
When CBS struck a deal: SBS int. with Grant Tinker
"Larry was dominant": SBS int. with Bud Benjamin
When it came time to sign: *Newsweek*, January 12, 1987

The board shoots down records deal

At the November 1986 meeting: *Wall Street Journal*, November 13, 1986
Several old Wyman allies; confidential sources
"My head tells me": confidential sources
Had Paley favored: confidential sources
"It showed that Paley": confidential source

The Paley-Tisch power alignment

Two months later: CBS press release, 1/14/87
"Larry doesn't do things": SBS int. with FS
"still doesn't recognize": confidential source

CHAPTER 59

Illness, February 1987

"My British friends all told": SBS int. with WSP
three touch-and-go days: Ibid.

At one point she tried: SBS int. with DPH
When Amanda arrived: SBS int. with AB

Paley bounces back

"Tell me what is going on": confidential source
"What do you hear": confidential source
"asking lots of questions": confidential source
"was a stabilizing influence": SBS int. with Kim LeMasters
When Paley awoke: confidential source
"Larry Kitsch": videotape of CBS annual meeting on 5/13/87
"It was the worst day": confidential source
"He came up the middle": SBS int. with William O'Shaughnessy
By September, Paley had lost: confidential sources

CBS divests records and publishing

"Paley could make no argument": SBS int. with Roswell Gilpatric; letter from Akio Morita to WSP and Larry Tisch, 10/13/87
Paley indulged in revisionism: SBS int. with FS
"This is the most unhappy": confidential source
Bochco wrote Paley a letter: confidential source
"Like other CBS chief": confidential source
"fed up" with Paley: *New York* magazine, November 23, 1987
At the same time Paley told: confidential source
Paley said Tisch was "crowding": confidential source

Paley's health improves

"Excuse me": confidential source

Paley used his connection: SBS int. with Sheryl Handler; confidential source

"Surprise," he said: SBS int. with FS

Laser surgery on his left: confidential source

"The look on his face": SBS int. with Henryk de Kwiatkowski

"He was in terrific shape": confidential source

Paley tends to the legend

In 1987, Paley obtained: confidential source

After lawyer Arthur Liman: SBS int. with Nelson Aldrich, Jr.

Early in 1988, Liman secured: SBS int. with Gerald Clarke

It contained a number of: confidential sources

a "rich shit": *Tru*, by Jay Presson Allen, Act II, p. 5

Illness, February 1988

Always suggestible when: confidential sources; SBS int. with SK

Surgery was too risky: confidential sources

"It was a little odd": SBS int. with SK

He was hooked up: Ibid.

Hospital personnel discreetly: confidential source

Kate was once again: SBS ints. with SK and DPH

Yet at that very moment: confidential source

(Kate would later tell): SBS int. with Jeanne Thayer

"How are you, Willie": SBS int. with SK

Paley blocks Bob Tisch nomination

Paley signaled his: confidential source

Using Minary and Arthur Liman: confidential source

"My sense is that Bill": confidential source

"Paley was like one of those": confidential source

Paley goes home

On entering his apartment: SBS int. with SK

That evening, he had a dinner: SBS ints. with SK and Lady Anne and Michael Tree

"He was in extremely good": SBS int. with Lady Anne Tree

Soon he was asking friends: SBS int. with SK

"He just wanted someone": SBS int. with Anna Wintour, editor-in-chief of *Vogue*

"It is like listening": confidential source

Paley was well aware: confidential sources

"A year before, Larry said": confidential source

Last programming hurrah

Tisch moved the scheduling: SBS int. with Kim LeMasters

"Everyone's expectation was": confidential source

"He was preaching to": SBS int. with Kim LeMasters

"had finally concluded that": SBS int. with Don Hewitt

The Museum of Broadcasting

that he called Arnold after: Stephen G. Smith conversation with WSP

Frank Stanton led the directors: SBS int. with FS

"His will is the only one": confidential
    sources
To prod a decision: SBS int. with FS
"looked too much like": Ibid.
"museums have taken the place": Philip
    Johnson at Museum of Broadcasting
    press conference, 7/7/88
he got the last word: SBS int. with FS
The board had decided: confidential
    sources

The Paley portrait

"It had bite": confidential source
"You don't finish with": SBS int. with
    Aaron Shikler, portrait artist

Paley mellows

"There is an overtone": SBS int. with
    IS
He craved one Van Gogh: SBS int. with
    John Richardson; confidential
    sources
The previous summer he had hired: SBS
    int. with SK
He gave guided tours: SBS int. with
    Howard Stringer
"He seemed completely": confidential
    source

Paley's medical coterie

His big disappointment was: confidential
    source
He had to return home early:
    confidential sources
"miracle-worker": confidential source
His three Irish nurses: SBS int. with
    Jeanne Murray Vanderbilt
In the evenings, his nurse: Ibid.;
    confidential sources
Paley spoke to his doctor at least: SBS
    int. with Jeanne Murray Vanderbilt

Paley's routine

Minary continued to come: SBS int.
    with George Schweitzer;
    confidential source
He had moved out of: confidential
    source
Paley had brought his Southampton:
    SBS int. with Jeanne Murray
    Vanderbilt
"Sometimes I say to her": confidential
    sources
Paley usually awoke: SBS ints. with
    WSP and Jeannne Murray
    Vanderbilt
"You know a party isn't": confidential
    source
At the Robbins fete he seemed: SBS int.
    with Bill Blass
"He had an underlying fear":
    confidential source
His friends told him he was: SBS int.
    with Jeanne Murray Vanderbilt
"How much money": confidential
    source
"Never again": SBS int. with Michael
    Meehan
"I'm sorry": audio tape of WSP speech,
    12/5/88
"Everyone was dying": SBS int. with
    Peter Kaplan

Bitterness over Tisch

"Sometimes people live": SBS
    conversation with Larry Tisch at
    John Diebold cocktail party, 9/22/88
Privately, he complained:
    confidential source
"I made a mistake": confidential source
"I did it on impulse": SBS int. with
    TW
"He was a mistake": confidential source
"We are your friends": confidential
    sources
"to please Paley": SBS int. with Mike
    Wallace, CBS News correspondent

The Kissinger appointment

In the spring of 1989, Paley: confidential sources
"Ultimately we could not": SBS int. with Roswell Gilpatric

Still the social lion

"He so wants to be": confidential source
"I want to toast": confidential source
"Slim was wild": SBS int. with Jeanne Murray Vanderbilt
"All that is left is": SBS int. with SK

Paley drops his memoir

Earlier in the year: Ibid.; SBS int. with IS
But when the manuscript: William Norwich column, *New York Daily News,* December 15, 1989; SBS int. with SK; confidential sources

Mental deterioration

he could be sitting: SBS int. with Ahmet Ertegun; confidential sources
When his partners in the *International:* confidential source
"He has withdrawn": confidential source
One unlikely source of pleasure: SBS int. with Jeanne Murray Vanderbilt
"I never thought": Ibid.

"By the end of it": confidential source
"We had a wonderful time": SBS int. with SK

Facing death

Next to losing Slim: SBS int. with IS
"I'm sorry, Will": SBS int. with Jeanne Murray Vanderbilt
"Why do I have to die?": Ibid.
"Whenever he talks about": confidential source
From time to time he had: SBS int. with SK

Paley clings to Black Rock

"He will come to anything": SBS int. with Howard Stringer
Howard Stringer dropped by: Ibid.
In program meetings, Stringer: SBS int. with Kim LeMasters
"There is a sweetness": SBS int. with Howard Stringer
Paley confided to: SBS int. with FS
"I feel so sorry": Stephen G. Smith interview with Akio Morita
"CBS is just another company": confidential source
"I have seen": SBS int. with Barry Diller
In May 1990 the CBS annual; SBS observations at shareholders meeting, 5/9/90

Bibliography

Adelman, William. *Pilsen and the West Side—A Tour Guide*. Chicago: Illinois Labor History Society, 1983.

Aldrich, Jr., Nelson W. *Old Money: The Mythology of America's Upper Class*. New York: Alfred A. Knopf, 1988.

Allen, Frederick Lewis. *Only Yesterday: An Informal History of the 1920s*. New York: Perennial Library, Harper & Row, 1964.

————. *Since Yesterday: The 1930s in America, September 3, 1929–September 3, 1939*. New York: Perennial Library, Harper & Row, 1986.

Alsop, Susan Mary. *To Marietta from Paris: 1945–1960*. Garden City, N.Y.: Doubleday, 1975.

Archer, Gleason L. *Big Business and Radio*. New York: American Historical Company, 1939.

Baer, Willis N. *The Economic Development of the Cigar Industry in the United States*. Lancaster, Pa.: The Art Printing Company, 1933.

Baldwin, Billy, with Michael Gardine. *Billy Baldwin: An Autobiography*. Boston: Little, Brown, 1985.

Barnouw, Erik. *A History of Broadcasting in the United States*. Vol. I, *A Tower of Babel: To 1933*. New York and London: Oxford University Press, 1966.

————. *A History of Broadcasting in the United States*. Vol. II, *The Golden Web: 1933 to 1953*. New York and London: Oxford University Press, 1968.

————. *A History of Broadcasting in the United States*. Vol. III, *The Image Empire: From 1953*. New York and London: Oxford University Press, 1970.

Bedell, Sally. *Up the Tube: Prime Time TV and the Silverman Years*. New York: Viking Press, 1981.

Berg, A. Scott. *Goldwyn: A Biography*. New York: Alfred A. Knopf, 1989.

Bergreen, Laurence. *Look Now, Pay Later: The Rise of Network Broadcasting*. Garden City, N.Y.: Doubleday, 1980.

Berkow, Ira. *Maxwell Street: Survival in a Bazaar*. Garden City, N.Y.: Doubleday, 1977.

Bernays, Edward L. *Biography of an Idea: Memoirs of Public Relations Counsel Edward L. Bernays*. New York: Simon & Schuster, 1965.

Bilby, Kenneth. *The General: David Sarnoff and the Rise of the Communications Industry*. New York: Harper & Row, 1986.

Birmingham, Stephen. *"Our Crowd":
The Great Jewish Families of New York*.
New York: Berkley Books, 1984.

———. *"The Rest of Us": The Rise of
America's Eastern European Jews*. New
York: Berkley Books, 1985.

———. *The Right People: A Portrait of the
American Social Establishment*. Boston:
Little, Brown, 1968.

Bluem, A. William. *Documentary in
American Television*. New York: Hastings
House, 1965.

Blum, John Morton. *V Was for Victory:
Politics and American Culture During World
War II*. New York: Harcourt Brace
Jovanovich, 1976.

Boyer, Peter J. *Who Killed CBS?: The
Undoing of America's Number One News
Network*. New York: Random House,
1988.

Brooks, Louise. *Lulu in Hollywood*. New
York: Alfred A. Knopf, 1982.

Brooks, Tim, and Marsh, Earle. *The
Complete Directory to Prime Time Network
TV Shows 1946–Present*. New York:
Ballantine Books, 1988.

Brown, John Mason. *The Worlds of
Robert E. Sherwood: Mirror to His Times
1896–1939*. New York: Harper & Row,
1965.

Brown, Les. *Television: The Business
Behind the Box*. New York: Harcourt
Brace Jovanovich, 1974.

———. *The New York Times
Encyclopedia of Television*. New York:
Times Books, 1977.

Burke, Michael. *Outrageous Good Fortune*.
Boston: Little, Brown, 1984.

Burns, Joan Simpson. *The Awkward
Embrace: The Creative Artist and the
Institution in America (An Inquiry Based on
Interviews with Nine Men Who Have—
Through Their Organizations—Worked to
Influence American Culture*. New York:
Alfred A. Knopf, 1975.

Butcher, Harry C. *My Three Years with
Eisenhower: The Personal Diary of Captain
Harry C. Butcher, USNR, Naval Aide to
General Eisenhower 1942–1945*. New
York: Simon & Schuster, 1946.

Clarke, Gerald. *Capote: A Biography*.
New York: Simon & Schuster, 1988.

Cogley, John. *Report on Blacklisting*. Vol.
II, *Radio–Television*. Washington, D.C.:
Fund for the Republic, 1956.

Coleman, Elizabeth Ann. *The Genius of
Charles James*. New York: Holt, Rinehart
& Winston, 1982.

Cooper, Diana. *Trumpets from the Steep:
Autobiography*. New York: Century
Publishing, 1984.

Corry, John. *Golden Clan: The Murrays,
the McDonnells, and the Irish American
Aristocracy*. Boston: Houghton Mifflin,
1977.

Courtney, Nicholas. *"In Society": The
Brideshead Years*. London: Pavilion
Books, 1986.

Cowan, Geoffrey. *See No Evil: The
Backstage Battle Over Sex and Violence on
Television*. New York: Simon &
Schuster, 1979.

Coward, Noël. *The Noël Coward Diaries*,
edited by Graham Payn and Sheridan
Morley. New York: Macmillan, 1983.

Curtis, Charlotte. *The Rich and Other
Atrocities*. New York: Harper & Row,
1976.

Davis, Loyal. *A Surgeon's Odyssey*.
Garden City, N.Y.: Doubleday, 1973.

Diggins, John Patrick. *The Proud Decades: America in War and Peace, 1941–1960*. New York: W. W. Norton, 1988.

Dreher, Carl. *Sarnoff: An American Success*. New York: Quadrangle Books, 1977.

Fonzi, Gaeton. *Annenberg: A Biography of Power*. New York: Weybright & Talley, 1970.

Friedman, Murray, ed. *Jewish Life in Philadelphia, 1830–1940*. Philadelphia: Ishi Publications, 1983.

Friedrich, Otto. *City of Nets: A Portrait of Hollywood in the 1940's*. New York: Perennial Library, Harper & Row, 1987.

Friendly, Fred W. *Due to Circumstances Beyond Our Control . . .* New York: Vintage Books, 1967.

Fulton, John F. *Harvey Cushing: A Biography*. Springfield, Ill.: Charles C. Thomas, 1946.

Gallagher, Brian. *Anything Goes: The Jazz Age Adventures of Neysa McMein and Her Extravagant Circle of Friends*. New York: Times Books, 1987.

Gates, Gary Paul. *Air Time: The Inside Story of CBS News*. New York: Harper & Row, 1978.

Glazer, Joel, ed. *Neuro-ophthalmology*, Vol. 10. New York: Mosby Publishers, 1980.

Golden, Cipe; Weihs, Kurt; and Strunsky, Robert, eds. *The Visual Craft of William Golden*. New York: George Braziller, 1962.

Goldmark, Peter C., with Lee Edson. *Maverick Inventor: My Turbulent Years at CBS*. New York: Saturday Review Press/E. P. Dutton, 1973.

Halberstam, David. *The Powers That Be*. New York: Alfred A. Knopf, 1979.

Hammond, John, with Townsend, Irving. *John Hammond on Record: An Autobiography*. New York: Ridge Press/ Summit Books, 1977.

Hayward, Brooke. *Haywire*. New York: Alfred A. Knopf, 1977.

Henderson, Amy. *On the Air: Pioneers of American Broadcasting*. Washington, D.C.: Smithsonian Institution Press, 1988.

Howe, Irving. *World of Our Fathers: The Journey of the East European Jews to America and the Life They Found and Made*. New York: Touchstone, 1983.

Hutchens, John K., and Oppenheimer, George, eds. *The Best in the World: A Selection of News and Feature Stories, Editorials, Humor, Poems, and Reviews, from 1921 to 1928*. New York: Viking Press, 1973.

Isaacson, Walter, and Thomas, Evan. *The Wise Men: Six Friends and the World They Made*. New York: Simon & Schuster, 1986.

Joyce, Ed. *Prime Times, Bad Times: A Personal Drama of Network Television*. Garden City, N.Y.: Doubleday, 1988.

Kahn, Jr., E. J. *Jock: The Life and Times of John Hay Whitney*. Garden City, N.Y.: Doubleday, 1981.

Keenan, Brigid. *The Women We Wanted to Look Like*. New York: St. Martin's Press, 1977.

Kendrick, Alexander. *Prime Time: The Life of Edward R. Murrow*. Boston: Little, Brown, 1969.

Kirby, Edward M., and Harris, Jack W.

Star Spangled Radio. Chicago: Ziff–Davis, 1948.

Kluger, Richard. *The Paper: The Life and Death of the New York Herald Tribune*. New York: Alfred A. Knopf, 1986.

Konolige, Kit. *The Richest Women in the World: An Intimate Look at Their Life-Styles . . . Their Loves . . . Their Money*. New York: Macmillan, 1985.

Lawford, Valentine. *Horst: His Work and His World*. New York: Alfred A. Knopf, 1984.

Leonard, Bill. *In the Storm of the Eye: A Lifetime at CBS*. New York: G. P. Putnam's Sons, 1987.

McCabe, Peter. *Bad News at Black Rock: The Sell-Out of CBS News*. New York: Arbor House, 1987.

Meites, Hyman L., ed. *History of the Jews of Chicago*. Chicago: Jewish Historical Society of Illinois, 1924.

Metz, Robert. *CBS: Reflections in a Bloodshot Eye*. New York: Signet, New American Library, 1976.

Miller, Merle, and Rhodes, Evan. *Only You, Dick Daring! or How to Write One Television Script and Make $50,000,000*. New York: William Sloane Associates, 1964.

Morris, Jan. *Manhattan '45*. London and New York: Oxford University Press, 1987.

Morris, Lloyd. *Incredible New York: High Life and Low Life of the Last Hundred Years, 1850–1950*. New York: Random House, 1951.

Neuharth, Al. *Confessions of an S.O.B.* Garden City, N.Y.: Doubleday, 1989.

O'Connell, Mary C., Oral Historian. *Connections: Reflections on Sixty Years of Broadcasting*. New York: National Broadcasting Company, 1986.

Paley, William S. *As It Happened: A Memoir*. Garden City, N.Y.: Doubleday, 1979.

Paper, Lewis J. *Empire: William S. Paley and the Making of CBS*. New York: St. Martin's Press, 1987.

Persico, Joseph E. *Edward R. Murrow: An American Original*. New York: McGraw-Hill, 1988.

Pye, Michael. *Moguls: Inside the Business of Show Business*. New York: Holt, Rinehart & Winston, 1980.

Rawidowicz, Simon, ed. *The Chicago Pinkas*. Chicago: College of Jewish Studies, 1952.

Saarinen, Aline B. *The Proud Possessors: The Lives, Times and Tastes of Some Adventurous American Art Collectors*. New York: Random House, 1958.

Schorr, Daniel. *Clearing the Air*. Boston: Houghton Mifflin, 1977.

Selznick, David O. *Memo from David O. Selznick,* edited by Rudy Behlmer. New York: Viking Press, 1972.

Selznick, Irene Mayer. *A Private View*. New York: Alfred A. Knopf, 1983.

Sevareid, Eric. *Not So Wild a Dream*. New York: Atheneum, 1976.

Shirer, William L. *20th Century Journey: A Memoir of a Life and the Times*. Vol. II, *The Nightmare Years: 1930–1940*. New York: Bantam Books, 1985.

Sioussat, Helen. *Mikes Don't Bite*. New York: L. B. Fischer, 1943.

Sperber, A. M. *Murrow: His Life and Times*. New York: Freundlich Books, 1986.

Stern, Robert A.M. *New York 1930.* New York: Rizzoli, 1987.

Swanberg, W. A. *Citizen Hearst: A Biography of William Randolph Hearst.* New York: Charles Scribner's Sons, 1961.

Thomson, Elizabeth H. *Harvey Cushing: Surgeon, Author, Artist.* New York: Neal Watson Academic Publications, 1981.

Tynan, Kathleen. *The Life of Kenneth Tynan.* New York: William Morrow, 1987.

Vickers, Hugo. *Cecil Beaton: A Biography.* Boston: Little, Brown, 1985.

Vreeland, Diana. *DV.* New York: Vintage Books, 1985.

Warhol, Andy. *The Andy Warhol Diaries,* edited by Pat Hackett. New York: Warner Books, 1989.

Ziegler, Philip. *Diana Cooper.* London: Hamish Hamilton, 1981.

———. *Mountbatten.* New York: Alfred A. Knopf, 1985.

Zweigenhaft, Richard L., and Domhoff, G. William. *Jews in the Protestant Establishment.* New York: Frederick Praeger, 1982.

Acknowledgments

The process of reporting, organizing, and writing this book took five years, but in a sense, the work began nearly a decade earlier. As a reporter on the broadcasting beat since the mid-1970s, I wrote often about Bill Paley and filed away details and anecdotes. Many people I came to know in my years as a newspaper and magazine reporter helped me enormously on this project. So did many of Bill Paley's friends, without whom it would have been impossible to get behind the myth that surrounded him for most of his working life. Beginning in the fall of 1985, I conducted more than 675 interviews with some 275 people. Most who spoke with me did so on the record, although some requested anonymity.

A score of those I interviewed, among them key CBS executives and board members as well as Paley intimates, gave me countless hours of their time. Their insights and memories were extraordinary. I should like to thank one individual in particular, Dorothy Paley Hirshon, who endured endless questions that opened up painful memories. She even consented to spend one muggy August afternoon in 1986 walking me through Kiluna, the Paley country estate since the mid-thirties. It was her first visit since Bill Paley left her forty-one years earlier, but her recollections were sharp and vivid.

Irene Selznick was also an essential authority on Bill Paley's personal life. Her understanding of his character and his relationships with his two wives, his family, and friends was based on an amazingly clear memory stretching back more than sixty years.

I only wish space could permit greater recognition of the dozens who shared their recollections: Bill Abrams, Harry Ackerman, David Adams, Nelson Aldrich, Jr., Susan Mary Alsop, Jay Presson Allen, Peggy Azar, Jan Cushing Amory, James Aubrey, Evelyn Baskin August, John D. Backe, Edward Barrett, Louis Bein, Burton Benjamin, Michel Bergerac, Fritz Berlinger, Edward Bernays, Patricia Bernie, Lord Sidney Bernstein, Simon Michael Bessie, Frank Biondi, Mary Boies, Benjamin Bradlee, Thornton Bradshaw, Belinda Breese, Courtney Brown, Amanda Burden, Carter Burden, Susan Burden, Mary Buell, Michael Burke, Margaret Carson, Blair Clark, Gerald Clarke, Philip Coombs, Norman Corwin, Geoffrey Cowan, Fleur Cowles, Walter Cronkite, Charlotte Curtis, Reid Cushing, William Cushing, Robert Daly, Michael Dann, Natalie Davenport, W. Phillips Davison, Lester Degenstein, Henryk de Kwiatkowski, Guy Della Cioppa, Peter Derow, Constance Bradlee Devins, Barry Diller, Dennis P. Doordan, Lady Mary Dunn, Edmund K. Eichengreen, Michael Eisner, Ahmet Ertegun, Irving Fein, William S. Fineshriber, Jr., Peg Pollard Finn, Donald Flamm, Peter Flanigan, Karl Fleming, Fred W. Friendly, Henry Gerstley, Roswell Gilpatric, Leonard Goldenson, Katharine Graham, M. Donald Grant, Emily Greene, John "Jap" Gude, David Halberstam, Kay Halle, John Hammond, Sheryl Handler, Kitty Carlisle Hart, Morris Harth, Harold Hecht, Nate Halpern, David Hertz, Don Hewitt, Richard Holbrooke, Ed Hookstratten, Leonora Hornblow, Horst, Sal Ianucci, Harry Kahn, Oscar Katz, Nancy "Slim" Keith, Horace Kelland, Margaret Kennedy, Ed Klar, Herb Klein, Perry Lafferty, Kim LeMasters, Ernie Leiser, William Leonard, Frederick Levy, Michael Levy, Richard Levy, Robert Levy, Rochelle Levy, Brigitta Lieberson, William Lilley III, William Louchheim, Richard McDonald, John McDonald, John "Tex" McCrary, Phyllis Maxwell, E. Kidder Meade, Howard Meighan, Virginia Merriman, Despina Messinesi, Sig Mickelson, Newton Minow, Morton Mitosky, Alice-Leone Moats, David Mortimer, Henry Mortimer, Linda Mortimer, Janet Murrow, Arthur Newmyer, Lord Norwich, Mrs. Elliot Noyes, Miriam Osborn, Elise O'Shaughnessy, William O'Shaughnessy, Barney Ostrow, Robert Paley, Marguerite Platt, Dorothy Meacham Price, Ray Price, John Pringle, John Purcell, Bernard Rappaport, Bronson Ray, Joe Ream, Charles Rees, James Reston, John Richardson, Aline de Romanones, James Roosevelt, James Rosenfield, Dorothy Rothe, Richard Salant, Tom Salant, Robert Saudek, Diane Sawyer, John A. Schneider, Eric Sevareid, Stuart Scheftel, Harvey Shephard, Mimi Sheraton, Madeline Sherwood, Aaron Shikler, Holly Cowan Shulman, Helen Sioussat, William Small, Howard K. Smith, Sandy Socolow, Frank Stanton, Rose Gimbel Stecker, Jean Stein, Howard Stringer, Gordon Stulberg, Arthur Taylor, Mary Elizabeth Taylor, Telford Taylor, Jeanne Thayer, Walter Thayer, Elizabeth Thomson, Grant Tinker, Laurence Tisch, Mrs. Arthur Tourtellot, Lady Anne Tree, Marietta Tree, Michael Tree, Robert Trout, Jeanne Murray Vanderbilt, Diana Vreeland, Alan Wagner, Mike Wallace, William Walton, Doris Klauber Wechsler, Betsey Cushing Whitney, Kate Roosevelt Whitney, Kay Wight, Billy Wilder, Anna Wintour, Robert Wood, Robert Wussler, Thomas H. Wyman, Walter Yetnikoff, and Jerome Zerbe.

My thanks as well to William S. Paley, who while working on his own autobiography, graciously reminisced with me over two lunches and later invited me into his home. In addition, the CBS corporate public relations department generously opened its files and gave me its transcripts of numerous press and broadcast interviews with Paley dating from the company's earliest days.

My literary agent, Amanda Urban, was a friend long before she was an agent. With her sure sense of timing, she knew when the moment was right to begin the book, and her counsel and support throughout were invaluable.

At Simon and Schuster, my editor, Alice Mayhew, was a patient and wise sounding board; when my manuscript took shape, she refined it with her insights and keen eye. Her assistant, George Hodgman, was marvelously attentive. He had both a sharp pencil and a steady manner. Ann Adelman was a meticulous copy editor, whose care was evident throughout. Natalie Goldstein searched for photographs with energy and resourcefulness; she found so many good pictures that choosing among them was a painful task. Eric Rayman perceptively probed the legal aspects of the manuscript. I am also grateful for the support of Charles Hayward, president of Simon and Schuster's Trade Division, and Jack McKeown, publisher of the Trade Division.

Another bulwark was the Gannett Center for Media Studies at Columbia University, where I spent a year conducting research. Everette E. Dennis, executive director of the Center, enthusiastically backed my work, and his capable staff were enormously helpful—especially my two diligent research assistants, Joel Bloom and David Raizman, as well as Jane Coleman, Wendy Boyd, Beverly Greenfield, Gregory Berzonsky, Craig Fisher-Lemay, Jeffrey Litvak, Kathy McCarthy, Larry Norman, and John Polich.

I also wish to thank others who assisted my research: Linda Amster, Susan Baum, Barbara Oliver, and Gary Salvucci. I am equally indebted to an assortment of archivists and librarians: Susan Alon and Frank Georgi at the Yale Medical Library's Harvey Cushing Collection; Rosemary Ashbee of the Savoy Hotel in London; Mary Ann Bamberger at the Special Collections Library of the University of Illinois at Chicago; Dennis Bilger at the Harry S. Truman Library; Michael Desmond at the John F. Kennedy Library; William R. Emerson at the Franklin D. Roosevelt Library; Howard Gotlieb of the Special Collections at the Boston University Library; Catharine Heinz of the Broadcast Pioneers Library in Washington, D.C.; Marc Hilton at the Chicago Historical Society; Bruce Laverty of the Athenaeum in Philadelphia; Janice L. O'Connell at the Mass Communications History Center of the State Historical Society of Wisconsin; Herb Pankratz and Martin Teasley at the Dwight D. Eisenhower Library; Phyllis Sichel at Keneseth Israel; and Mary Wolfskill at the Library of Congress.

Additional research centers that yielded useful documents were the

National Archives, the Oral History Research Collection at Columbia University, and the Foundation Center Library. And I owe special thanks to Paul Springer of Paramount Pictures Corporation for sharing rare documents on the stock swap between Paramount and CBS in 1929.

Many of my journalistic colleagues generously offered advice and tips as well as their own invaluable research. Chief among these were David Halberstam, who shared scores of interviews he conducted for *The Powers That Be*; Ira Berkow, who gave me a singular interview with Goldie Paley; Marie Brenner, for a conversation with Bill Paley on his wartime experiences; Jonathan Larsen, who opened the door to his uncle, Jerome Zerbe, and his superb photographs of Bill Paley's wedding to Babe; and Don West, managing editor of *Broadcasting* magazine, who provided interview transcripts and countless photographs. Thanks as well to Ken Auletta, A. Scott Berg, Patty Bosworth, Peter Boyer, Brock Brower, Graydon Carter, Richard and Shirley Clurman, John Corry, Byron Dobell, Geraldine Fabrikant, Arthur Gelb, Harry Hurt, E. J. Kahn, Peter Kaplan, Nick Lemann, Robert Lenzner, Janet Maslin, Herb Mitgang, Janet Morgan, Maureen Orth, Eric Pace, Frank Rich, Charlie Rose, Tony Schwartz, David Sendler, Anne Sperber, Alessandra Stanley, Evan Thomas, Michael Thomas, Sidney Urquhart, Shelley Wanger, and John Weisman.

Others who shared unpublished material were David Adams, the family of Sally Fly Connell, Norman Corwin, Richard Levy, and Holly Cowan Shulman.

Experts in various fields patiently guided me when I was out of my depth. These included physicians Edward Beattie, Leon Demar, and Elizabeth Yew; historians Edmund Bacon and E. Digby Baltzell of the University of Pennsylvania, and Henry Binford of Northwestern University, an expert in Chicago history whose tour of the West Side evoked Bill Paley's childhood haunts; lawyers Dinsmore Adams (for helping decipher Babe Paley's estate documents), Terry Lenzner (who obtained financial documents on CBS filed in Washington), and Roger Kirby (for general legal advice). Keith Carlson, assistant vice president of research at the Federal Reserve Bank of St. Louis, expertly computed the 1990 value of various amounts of money in earlier decades.

I am grateful to several officials at the University of Pennsylvania for helping with details of Bill Paley's college years: Steve Derby in the development office, Hamilton Elliott in university archives, Margaret Gilbert in alumni records, Virginia Scherfel in facilities development, and Fran Sheeley, former director of Penn's New York development office. Col. Ralph B. Jackson, son of the former head of Western Military Academy, was kind enough to share documents about the school.

Thanks as well to various public relations people who helped me out:

Ann Morfogen and George Schweitzer at CBS, Peggy Hubble at NBC, Letty Aronson, Richard Auletta, Gina Henry, Patricia Matson, and Bud Rukeyser.

My family provided unwavering support for the past five years. My three children were amazingly tolerant of the hours I spent plugged into my word processor. My youngest grew from a toddler scribbling on my files to a companion sprawled on the floor nearby reading his books. I am also indebted to Gladys Campbell for keeping the household running smoothly. My mother-in-law, Nora O'Leary Smith, graciously provided me with a place to do my work and kept me nourished at lunchtime when I lost track of the hours. My parents, Ruth and Jim Rowbotham, offered words of encouragement when the book seemed an endless task.

And finally my thanks to my husband Stephen Smith, who came up with the idea of a Paley biography in the first place. After spending his days as executive editor of *Newsweek,* he would spend many evenings helping me through organizational tangles and listening patiently when I needed to talk through some perplexing facet of Bill Paley's character. He also gave the manuscript a careful and insightful reading. I gave him the title Editor-for-Life—poor man.

Index

Picture Credits